CONSTITUTIONS
of the World

CONSTITUTIONS
of the World

ROBERT L. MADDEX • SECOND EDITION

CQ PRESS

A DIVISION OF C O N G R E S S I O N A L QUARTERLY INC.
WASHINGTON, D.C.

Copyright © 2001 Congressional Quarterly Inc.

1414 22nd Street, N.W., Washington, D.C. 20037

Produced by Archetype Press, Inc.

Washington, D.C.

Project Director: Diane Maddex
Assistant Editor: Gretchen Smith Mui
Art Director: Robert L. Wiser

Printed in the United States of America

Cover: Magna Carta (1215), handwritten in Latin and confirmed in 1297 with the seal of Edward I of England. Photograph courtesy Staples & Charles Ltd.

Library of Congress Cataloging-in-Publication Data

Maddex, Robert L.
    Constitutions of the world / Robert L. Maddex
       p.   cm.
    Includes bibliographical references and index.
    ISBN 1-56802-682-X
    1. Constitutions. 2. Constitutional history. I. Title.
    K3157.E5M33 1995
    342'.02—dc20   95-11374
    [342.22]   CIP

The Author

Robert L. Maddex is the author also of *The Illustrated Dictionary of Constitutional Concepts*, *State Constitutions of the United States*, and *International Encyclopedia of Human Rights*, all published by CQ Press. An attorney in the Washington, D.C., area, he specializes in international law and has served as chief counsel of the Foreign Claims Settlement Commission of the United States and as an adviser on constitutional issues to several nations.

Contents

Preface

The best form of government, Aristotle suggested in *The Politics,* is the one "in which every man, whoever he is, can act best and live happily." Those who do so, he said, are destined to attain a state of *eudaimonia*—beyond any individually enumerated pleasures. Today the nations of the world have developed varied forms of government, most of them undergirded with written or traditional constitutions. The ideals expressed so often and so unequivocally in these constitutions, as Aristotle (384–322 B.C.) would no doubt agree, represent goals, not accomplishments, and they are met to varying degrees in different countries at different times. Yet, because no world or regional governments exist to raise the level of political organization beyond individual nation-states, national constitutions remain the highest form of human organizational aspiration.

This new edition of *Constitutions of the World* presents the constitutions and constitutional histories of one hundred nations. Of the original eighty countries, eleven have significantly revised their constitutions and many have done some major or minor tinkering with their systems of government. Australia and Canada, on the other hand, have rejected major changes; an Australian referendum on whether to change the country from a monarchy to a republic failed, while one in the Canadian province of Quebec narrowly rejected secession from the nation.

Parliamentary goverment remains the predominant form, while single-party dictatorships—such as those in China, Cuba, North Korea, and Vietnam—continue to lose ground to multiparty systems that permit more citizen participation. The new or newly revised consitutions of post-communist countries such as Azerbaijan, Armenia, Bosnia and Herzegovina, Bulgaria, the Czech Republic, Georgia, Hungary, Poland, Romania, Russia, Slovakia, and Ukraine illustrate how new democracies are structuring their governments and creating institutions to protect freedom and individual rights. The unwritten constitutions of Israel, New Zealand, and the United Kingdom, all democratic nations, provide strong contrasts with the written constitutions of theocratic Iran and the dictatorships of Iraq and Libya. Saudi Arabia, which has no constitution, is included as an example of a preconstitutional state, while the constitution presented for Tibet is actually a proposal for establishing a theocratic democracy in the event the country regains its independence from China.

This book is organized alphabetically by country. Each chapter begins with a brief introduction to the country, which is followed by a historical overview emphasizing legal and constitutional development. Background information on indigenous populations and early forms of political and social organization is included to show that historically the forms of governing derived from western Europe and the United States are not, in fact, unique and can be compared with the self-organizing methods of earlier people everywhere on earth.

Next, the country's current constitution is presented, with comments on major items of interest. The constitutional profile has been arranged from a structural or functional point of view: first, the preamble or other introductory material; then the parts or articles dealing with fundamental rights; the structure of the government, generally the executive, legislative, and judicial branches; and the amending process. (Many of the documents relied on are translations into English, and some translated works and transliterations of foreign words have been standardized, such as the word *shari'a,* meaning Islamic law. Some typographical editing of translated materials was required for clarity and uniformity.) Each area is described under a separate heading to facilitate comparisons among countries.

In addition to this basic formula, entries may provide comparisons with other nations and describe the implementation of constitutional provisions in actual practice. If the operation of a country's government deviates significantly from the provisions of its constitution, such discrepancies may be noted. In the end, however, a description of a constitution is merely a snapshot in time—at any given moment formal and informal changes are taking place in constitutions and constitutional processes all over the globe, altering the picture.

One indication of the growing interest in world constitutions is the increased availability of information about them on the Internet. A relatively expedient way to research a particular national constitution is to go to http://www.google.com and request a search for the "constitution of (country)." No single authoritative site yet provides all of the constitutions of the world in English and in official English translations.

While a well-crafted constitution may provide a basis for efficient and just governance, it alone cannot ensure political stability or enforcement of human rights. For each country, the proper mix of traditional and democratic institutions, education, economic stability, internal and external security, and, perhaps most important, the ability and motivation of key political leaders is necessary for a constitution to be effective. What national political leaders do is increasingly subject to judgment by a broader audience, not least of which is world public opinion. For example, efforts have been made to hold national leaders such as the former Chilean dictator Augusto Pinochet and Slobodan Milošević of Yugoslavia accountable to international and regional standards of behavior. If constitutional democracies continue to unite to enforce norms of just governance in errant nation-states, for many the twenty-first century will be a better time in which to live.

In addition to the staffs of embassies and the departments and ministries of the countries included in *Constitutions of the World*, the following people deserve special appreciation for their assistance: Gretchen Smith Mui, editor, and Robert L. Wiser, designer, Archetype Press; Chris Anzalone, acquisitions editor, CQ Press; Lloyd N. Cutler of Wilmer, Cutler and Pickering and former legal counsel to the president of the United States; A. E. Dick Howard, White Burkett Miller Professor of Law and Public Affairs, University of Virginia School of Law; Phuong-Khanh Nguyen, senior foreign law specialist, Library of Congress; Herman Schwartz, professor of law, Washington College of Law, the American University; and, for her dedication in making yet another book out of many words, my wife, Diane Maddex, president of Archetype Press.

Introduction

Since the world's first modern, written national constitution was drafted for the United States of America in 1787, an explosion of new technology and science has almost obscured the equally astounding explosion of constitutions and constitutionalism throughout the world. In fact, in many countries more people are directly affected by the radical change in their relationship with those who govern them than they are by the trappings of technology and science so pervasive in postindustrial societies. Farming in most of the Third World, for example, continues today much as it did two thousand years ago, but farmers can go to the polls in many of these countries and vote their opinion on the success or failure of their leaders.

Of course, not all people in all the countries that have adopted modern constitutions can exercise their fundamental human rights or enforce the popular sovereignty so grandiosely declared in constitutional documents and politicians' speeches. But what is clearly evident is the evolving desire in nearly all these nations to strive for a system of constitutional government that meets these expectations. In 1787, except in the United States, Britain, and perhaps a few other countries, the mere expectation of popular sovereignty, individual rights, or checks and balances on the absolute power of rulers was an absurd pipe dream, as foolish then as planning a trip to the moon or watching a live sports event being played halfway around the world.

But having a national constitution and truly appreciating its potential are two different things. The average person may believe that constitutions—although highly desirable—are to be read and understood only by a select few: people in government, lawyers, judges, and scholars. Young people in countries with high rates of literacy and compulsory education can often recite the lyrics to all the latest popular songs or the most trivial statistics of their favorite sports heroes, yet they have almost no knowledge of their own country's constitution.

The underlying premise of *Constitutions of the World* is that constitutions are important to everyone—the constitution of our own country, to be sure, but the constitutions of other countries as well. By coming to know the differences and similarities in these supreme laws that represent the aspirations of people like us, we can better understand them and ourselves. The global village predicted by Marshall McLuhan thirty years ago has come to pass. The walls of many nations are being breached by international business, communications, and travel, and new regional configurations such as the European Union are emerging— configurations primarily for economic rather than ideological or defensive purposes. How countries set about organizing their governments is no longer a matter of idle curiosity for the citizen of the world. It is as important as knowing your next-door neighbors.

The Constitutions of Nations   "Every country has its own constitution," one Russian is alleged to have remarked in the nineteenth century; "ours is absolutism moderated by assassination" (quoted by George Vernadsky in *A History of Russia,* 1961). According to "Junius," a commentator on the British constitution (reputedly Sir Phillip Francis, letter of April 24, 1769), "The right of election is the very essence of the constitution." Whatever form the modern national constitution takes, its primary goal should be to define limitations on those who rule at the highest level in a nation-state. A nation-state is simply the basic international unit of theoretically independent and sovereign territory that may be bound by external restrictions under international law but that otherwise is generally free to manage its own internal affairs. Unfortunately, too many national constitutions today are extremely ineffectual documents or outright shams that try to mask unbridled dictatorships.

A constitution, by itself, cannot ensure a democratic government or guarantee fundamental liberties for all those under its jurisdiction. Most countries, however, at least find it necessary to have some written constitution or constitutional laws and traditions in order to promote the idea that those holding political power are limited by some rules. Many countries take these rules seriously enough to rework them frequently. For example, just since 1990 more than thirty of the one hundred countries featured in *Constitutions of the World* have written new constitutions, and half again as many have revised or significantly amended their constitutions.

Defining a national constitution is not a simple exercise. A constitution may be viewed both as a process—a description of what actually takes place in the running of a national government—and as a stated or assumed expectancy that may vary to a greater or lesser degree from the actual practices of governing authorities. For example, in a country dominated by the Communist Party, the party's rules, whether written or merely tacitly understood, more closely resemble the "constitution-as-process" of the country—that is, how the power to run the country is maintained, directed, channeled, and transferred—than the formally expressed constitution. Any officially acknowledged constitutional documents and traditions that purport to define the roles of national government institutions and officials and set forth the rights of individuals and societal goals may be characterized as a "constitution-as-expectancy." The frequency with which such expectancies are lived up to varies widely from country to country.

Constitutions of the World, while often noting the disparity between written or customary rules governing a country and the actual process observed or reported, presents a structural summary of the more important formal rules of the constitution-as-expectancy of one hundred nations. Each chapter provides a snapshot of the ideals and goals declared by the originators of the current constitutional documents and traditions in each country. The text gives a frame of reference not only for comparing a de jure (legal or formal) constitution with a de facto (actually observed) process, but also for comparing formal constitutions with each other.

De jure constitutions may be "written," in the sense of being encompassed basically in a single document like the U.S. constitution, or "unwritten" in the sense of being expressed in more than one document as well as in laws of constitutional stature and rigidly adhered to traditional practices, such as the United Kingdom's constitution. Even so-called written constitutions, however, are never totally encompassed in written documents alone; they all draw on a multitude of assumptions and nongovernment institutions for their substance. In the United States, for example, the role of political parties in organizing elections and the executive and legislative branches of the government after elections is not dealt with in the written constitution, nor was it contemplated by its framers. It is, therefore, only in the social, political, and historical context of each country that a national constitution truly comes to life.

The History of Constitutions

Constitutions and compilations of constitutions are not new. Plato (427?–347 B.C.) concerns himself with constitutions in both *The Republic* and his last work, *The Laws;* Aristotle compiled some 158 constitutions of Greek city-states. At Benjamin Franklin's request, the French ministry of foreign affairs authorized the publication of *Constitutions des Treize Etats de l'Amerique* in 1783, which, together with the U.S. constitution, became a source of reference for the constitution makers of Europe.

The framers of the U.S. constitution reviewed many systems of contemporaneous governments and also looked to the early Greek and Roman constitutions for guidance. Whether drafting a modern constitution or simply analyzing one, the historical setting is crucial to the process. To a large extent, constitutions of nations are unique plants that need the proper historical soil and sociological climate to grow and flower.

Any attempt to understand or compare constitutions today thus would not be possible without some historical background and political and social context in which to frame the fundamental principles contained in the documents themselves. And while it is possible to analyze and compare the constitutions of countries in the abstract, the importance of the context in which the principles developed and in which they are consulted internally on a daily basis cannot be overstated.

Like most human creations, constitutions are a response to a problem presented by nature—human nature in this instance. We need to organize ourselves politically, dividing into rulers and the ruled. The specific problem that a constitution tries to address is how to create a stable and secure human community within a prescribed territory under a political organization flexible enough to adapt to external and internal changes that may threaten the community's stability and security. The problem has grown more acute as population has increased and the world, in terms of communications and travel, has shrunk. For the past two hundred years nation-states appear to have been searching for the perfect balance of authoritarian stability and individual freedom to survive as legally recognized sovereign entities. From the first limitations on absolute monarchs to the constitutional limitations on the rulers or governors of the nation-state, constitutions have developed to provide some of this stability and predictability.

Constitutions of the World offers an overview of one hundred constitutional solutions being tried by some of the world's major countries. The differences and the similarities can be startling.

Common Elements of Constitutions

With a few exceptions, all constitutions contain some common elements. From Magna Carta of 1215 to today, constitutional documents and traditions take the general form of a contract or an agreement between the ruled and the rulers. Limitations on the rulers are exacted by the ruled in exchange for allowing the rulers to preserve some elements of their right to govern and for preserving the stability of the governing system itself. Whether a constitution develops from the initial state of a strong central authority into a more decentralized one with checks and balances wrested by the subjects or citizens from their rulers, or whether it develops from a loosely knit decentralized confederation into a grant of sovereignty to a more centralized authority, it has the general elements of an agreement between those who govern and those who are governed.

Other key conceptual features commonly found in constitutions include a purposeful division or separation of the three basic powers or functions of government—the executive, legislative, and judicial—identified early on by Aristotle and rediscovered by the French lawyer and philosopher Montesquieu (1689–1755); an emphasis on the "rule of law," meaning that all citizens, including those chosen to govern, are equally subject to the laws of the land; and the supremacy of the constitution or constitutional documents over ordinary law. This latter feature has many variations, from the traditional constraints on the theoretical supremacy of the United Kingdom's parliament to the new voluntary subordination of nation-state sovereignty to regional or international authorities.

Common structural features can also be found. Almost all constitutions contain a preamble or introductory clauses or articles; recite a set of fundamental rights and guarantees, and sometimes duties, for those under a nation's jurisdiction; describe executive, legislative, and judicial officials and bodies and their powers and duties; and provide a procedure for amending the constitution. Some revised or new constitutions contain transitional provisions. Many written documents contain extensive additional material, especially the *dirigiste* types of constitutions, like those of Brazil and Portugal, that describe details of social and political goals in addition to rules for governing the country and a list of individual rights. The formats of the constitutions of the major countries of the world nonetheless seem remarkably alike.

Constitutions can be categorized on the basis of the type or structure of a nation's system of government. For example, the basic, if no longer prevalent, form is that of a traditional unlimited, or "unconstitutional," monarchy, also called an autocracy and similar to a dictatorship. Sovereignty, or the source of political power in such a system, is focused in one person such as a king or an emperor. Theoretical underpinnings for these governments are often religious ("the divine right of kings") or legitimist (the hereditary right to rule). Military dictatorships, on the other hand, rely more on raw fire-power than philosophical contortions for their political authority. Other general forms of modern government include the parliamentary constitutional (limited) monarchy, the presidential system, and the presidential-style parliamentary system. Nation-states may also be categorized as unitary or as variations of federal systems that divide power vertically between the national government and semisovereign subunits, such as states or provinces. The term *republic* used in the names of many countries simply denotes the fact that they are not monarchies. (See the glossary for definitions of other constitutional terms.)

Preamble. Preambles are not found in all constitutions, but when they are they tend to contain hyperbolic language that does little to shed light on the system of government or the practicality of the constitution itself. However, in the case of some constitutions of communist countries, the preamble may reveal the motives for the document, which otherwise bears little resemblance to how the national political power structure actually operates. A preamble may also provide a clue as to the inspiration and sources of principles that informed the document's drafters.

Fundamental Rights. Most written constitutions recite a list of fundamental rights of the country's citizens or inhabitants, analogous to the U.S. bill of rights, and many also include a list of duties of their citizens. Key fundamental rights include freedom of the press, religion, association, assembly, and petition of grievances against government authorities, as well as protections for private property and persons accused of crimes. But the fact that a right is not expressly provided for in a constitutional document does not always mean that it is not recognized in other law or by judicial rulings or tradition.

Some constitutions expressly limit guaranteed fundamental rights. Regardless of whether such limitations are expressed, how well any guaranteed rights are implemented varies from country to country. In some extreme cases, violations of human rights in countries with express constitutional guarantees of fundamental rights are noted in the text. The absence of such notation, however, is not intended to imply that violations do not occur in a particular country.

A number of nations have incorporated regional, multinational, and international standards of human, civil, and political rights into their constitutions or laws. This trend toward international and verifiable standards of human rights provides hope for real progress in this area, but many countries still have abysmal records with respect to human and civil rights.

Structure of Government. Although most constitutional documents deal with them separately, it is often difficult to draw clear lines of distinction among the powers and duties of the three traditional branches of government—executive, legislative, and judicial—plus other branches defined in a few constitutions. Typically, parliamentary systems tend to blur the lines more between the legislative and executive branches than do presidential systems. Historically, model parliamentary systems, such as the British and French governments, have evolved from a clash between monarchs or absolutists and the less powerful members of society. Therefore, the division of powers in these countries today is more the result of pragmatic compromises than of a carefully thought-out theory of the separation of powers. Many presidential-style parliamentary systems have evolved by way of amendments and revisions that have created a president who is both head of state and head of government as in a pure presidential system, but with a prime minister continuing in a role with less than his or her traditional executive powers. Presidential systems, on the other hand, tend to start out with the concept of a fairly strict separation of powers.

Executive: With few exceptions, all constitutions place the executive power of national government—the power to execute or implement laws and policy—either in the hands of a monarch or monarchlike president and a prime minister and cabinet or in the hands of a president and cabinet. Almost all European monarchies, with the possible exception of Monaco, provide the monarch with a basically ceremonial role in both the executive and legislative functions. In presidential-style parliamentary systems the powers of the president vis-a-vis the prime minister run the gamut. The trend, however, with Bangladesh and Greece as exceptions, has been toward granting more power to the president at the expense of the prime minister and the legislature. This is particularly true in many African countries.

Key powers of the executive generally include appointment of government officials, supreme command of the armed forces, some veto power over legislation, and relatively exclusive control of foreign policy. In some countries, however, powerful political or military figures without any formal position in the government in fact exercise great influence extraconstitutionally on the government's executive functions.

Legislature: Legislatures come in two basic forms: parliaments and congresses. The term *parliament* is derived from the French word *parlement*, which evolved into a sort of court in France; in England the word took on the meaning first of a council of state and then a legislative body. The term *congress* is more directly related to the notion of a formal meeting of delegates. Both, however, have come to mean a supreme legislative body or a legislature with the power to make laws.

The main difference between a congressional legislature and a parliamentary legislature is that a congress is theoretically a separate branch of government, not fused with the executive branch in the person of a monarch or granted constitutional control over a prime minister as head of government and cabinet as in the case of a parliamentary system. "The principles of a free constitution are irrevocably lost when the legislative power is nominated by the executive," wrote the English historian Edward Gibbon (*The Decline and Fall of the Roman Empire*, 1776–88).

There are other general distinctions between a congress and a parliament. A congress or its divisions, called houses or chambers, has a set term of years between elections; a parliament, at least the more politically powerful lower house, may be dissolved for elections before its constitutional term has expired. A parliament is either supreme in its power to change the constitution or its supremacy has been limited by a written constitution; a congress, like other branches, is bound by the constitution and has only a partial role to play in the amendment process. In a parliamentary system the head of government (the prime minister, premier, or chancellor) and the cabinet members are subject to questioning (interpellation) by the elected representatives in the legislature and even to being censured and expelled from power; a congress generally can only confirm key appointments, investigate executive branch activities, and remove the head of government by an impeachment process.

Judiciary and Constitutional Review: Courts in many nations, to the extent that they choose to undertake the task, are often the ultimate guarantors of how well a constitution does its job. This is true also in many parliamentary systems that started out with no form of judicial or constitutional review.

A clear distinction can be made between the ability of regular judicial courts to interpret the constitution and declare laws unconstitutional and the ability of some extrajudicial or special judicial body to function in a similar manner, that is, to have some constitutional responsibility to ensure that laws conform to the constitution. The term *judicial review* is used when the constitutionality of laws is determined by ordinary judicial courts, and *constitutional review* is used when either a separate judicial body in the court system or an extrajudicial body determines the constitutionality of laws.

In the United States the role of the federal courts in maintaining the integrity of the constitution was understood, if not expressly mentioned, by the framers. It took a specific declaration of the policy by the supreme court, however, to bring to life the principle of judicial review. Other countries—Germany, for example—have created a special court for the purpose of constitutional review; in France a constitutional council can implement constitutional review only when called on by other branches of the government.

Under the historic model of the parliamentary constitutional system, the supremacy of the legislature over the other branches of government theoretically precludes any form of judicial review of legislation for constitutionality, because the same parliament that can pass a law with a simple majority could also change the constitution just as easily. But in most countries with a parliamentary system of government, some form of judicial or constitutional review has developed. The parliamentary form of government in Norway, for example, did not impede the growth of judicial review, although the power is used sparingly.

In presidential systems of government, the constitution typically assigns the judicial branch the role of interpreting the law, while the legislature makes the laws and the executive enforces them. All three branches must join together to make the system work. In some countries, however, whether the national government is a presidential or parliamentary type, the courts' role has been reduced to determining the prevailing winds from the executive branch and making their decisions accordingly; examples of fearless and inspiring decisions by courts faced with outright executive branch intimidation nonetheless can be found.

The extrajudicial forms of constitutional review run the gamut from the power to strike down laws for not conforming to the constitution to merely a consultative role on proposed legislation if asked by other government authorities. It is difficult for the executive and legislative branches of any national governments to allow another independent branch to look over their shoulders and point out their mistakes. And just as certainly, excessive zeal by courts in the process of reviewing the actions of the executive and legislative branches can hamstring a government. But when judicial or constitutional review is engaged in conscientiously, it can result in fewer mistakes by government officials, a closer approximation of legislative and executive branch action to the standards set by the rule of law, and more effective enforcement of constitutional rights.

Other Constitutional Bodies: A few constitutions contain unique provisions to deal with their special situations, such as those establishing water authority boards in the Netherlands and institutions to accommodate the role of traditional or tribal leaders in a few African countries. The Philippines and Iran divide power among more than the three traditional branches of government. Unique provisions like these are generally noted in the text.

Amending Constitutions

That constitutions are not intended to be perfect is evidenced by expressly stated processes for revising or amending them. Constitutional change by means of an orderly procedure is far preferable to overthrowing a government by force whenever a country's constitution has fallen out of favor with a majority of its people. As President Abraham Lincoln said in his first inaugural address on March 4, 1861: "Whenever they [the American people] shall grow weary of the existing government, they can exercise their constitutional right of amending it, or their revolutionary right to dismember or overthrow it."

In fact, constitutions can be categorized on the basis of the ease with which they may be changed. "Flexible" constitutions, such as those of the United Kingdom and New Zealand, may be altered by a simple majority vote in the legislature. "Rigid" constitutions, as in the United States and Russia, have amendment procedures that require more than a simple majority vote of the legislature; how rigid they are depends on the degree of difficulty of the amending process, such as requiring supermajorities of the legislature and ratification by referendum or political subdivisions of the nation-state.

The Future of Constitutions and Constitutionalism

The most promising aspect of this age of constitutionalism is that the importance of structuring a national system of government to minimize the arbitrary and capricious use of power is at least generally recognized, if not always perfectly implemented. The elements of human nature that thwart efforts to create a predictable process for exercising political power in a nation-state are best minimized when citizens, in addition to having an adequate constitution, are educated and allowed free access to information inside and outside the country and when there is a broad-based entrepreneurial segment of society that demands stability, reasonableness, and predictability from the government.

Stability and predictability under a national constitution are only the first goals. The next step is for all citizens to acknowledge that the right to rule and make rules—sovereignty—has to be shared by everyone in the nation. The fact that some citizens are chosen to actually wield executive, legislative, judicial, and other power is an expedience, because not everyone can spend the time on or develop the necessary expertise required for such jobs. It is much harder to maintain a political system reliant on coercion than one based on the consent of the governed; the blame for bad decision making can be shared in a democracy because leaders and lawmakers are chosen by the people. There must also be a willingness to allow the system to grow to include all adult citizens in the democratic process and to expand the access of the people to government decision making. The revolution wrought by the concept of constitutionalism must be an ongoing one, because if it stagnates the only alternative is to return to the clearly inadequate undemocratic institutions of the past.

The similarities and differences in the constitutions of the major countries of the world provide a fertile field for analyzing and comparing the structures of national governments. The temptation to conclude, however, that one constitution or structure is necessarily better than another should be avoided. Just as the work of the structural anthropologist Claude Lévi-Strauss (1908–90) shows that there is no hierarchy of human cultures, there appears to be no basis for believing in a hierarchy of constitutions. Some constitutions seem to work better than others, but too many variables—economic, social, political, geographical, and even human factors—must be considered when trying to determine why a constitution in a particular country seems to work well and one in another does not.

Similarly, morality as such should not be a significant factor in analyzing constitutions, because morality finds its sources in aspects of human activity outside the law—in the family, religion, and philosophy, for example. A constitution is not just law; it is supreme law, as many constitutions declare on their face. Thus it is best that a constitution be as neutral as possible to the individual systems of morality at play within a nation. Constitutionalism, the ideal of governing on the basis of abstract principles of constitutional government, attempts to elevate the rule of law to such a high status that morality can be taught and appreciated and applied within the nation-state, leaving laws to deal solely with legally proscribed behavior.

Listing every possible fundamental right in a constitutional document has far less impact on the morality of a nation than the ability of its citizens to call on the courts for protection of traditional liberties and uncompromising redress of violations by whatever culprit, public or private. The fact that there are now a number of international touchstones of civil and human rights—such as article 45 on human rights of the United Nations Charter (1945), the Universal Declaration of Human Rights (1948), the European Convention for the Protection of Human Rights and Fundamental Freedoms (1950), the International Covenant on Civil and Political Rights (1966), the American Convention on Human Rights (1969), the Helsinki Final Act (Helsinki Accords) (1975), and the African Charter on Human and Peoples' Rights (1981)—can only help further the development of more humane nation-state governments. Another potential safeguard against abuse by government officials is the position of ombudsman, which has been established in a growing number of countries. The ombudsman may investigate and act on citizens' complaints that their constitutional rights have been infringed by government authorities.

Constitutions of the World was undertaken to make important national constitutions understandable in terms of their history, organization, and operation as well as their stated goals for efficient and humane systems of government. An additional goal is that the book simply encourage wider interest in constitutions and the constitutional process.

Constitutions at a Glance

Country	Type of Government[1]	Type of State	Most Recent Constitution[2]	Type of Legislature[3]	Judicial or Constitutional Review[4]	Ombudsman
Albania	Presidential-style republic	Unitary state	1998	Unicameral parliament	Constitutional review	No
Algeria	Presidential-style republic	Unitary state	1996	Bicameral parliament	Limited constitutional review	No
Argentina	Presidential-style republic	Federal state	1853	Bicameral congress	Judicial review	Yes
Armenia	Presidential-style republic	Unitary state	1995	Unicameral parliament	Limited constitutional review	No
Australia	Commonwealth	Federal state	1901	Bicameral parliament	Judicial review	No
Austria	Presidential-style republic	Federal state	1945 (restoration)	Bicameral parliament	Constitutional review	Yes
Azerbaijan	Presidential-style republic	Unitary state	1995	Unicameral parliament	Constitutional review	No
Bangladesh	Presidential-style republic	Unitary state	1972	Unicameral parliament	Judicial review	Yes
Belarus	Presidential-style republic	Unitary state	1994 (revised)	Bicameral parliament	Limited constitutional review	No
Belgium	Constitutional monarchy	Federal state	1831 (revised)	Bicameral parliament	Limited constitutional review	No
Bolivia	Presidential republic	Unitary state	1967 (revised)	Bicameral congress	Constitutional review	No
Bosnia and Herzegovina	Presidential-style republic	Unitary state	1995	Bicameral parliament	Limited constitutional review	No
Brazil	Presidential republic	Federal state	1988	Bicameral congress	Judicial review	No

Country	Type of Government[1]	Type of State	Most Recent Constitution[2]	Type of Legislature[3]	Judicial or Constitutional Review[4]	Ombudsman
Bulgaria	Presidential-style republic	Unitary state	1991	Unicameral parliament	Judicial and constitutional review	No
Cambodia	Constitutional monarchy	Unitary state	1993	Bicameral parliament	Limited constitutional review	No
Canada	Constitutional monarchy	Quasi-federal state	1867 (revised)	Bicameral parliament	Limited judicial review	No
Chad	Presidential-style republic	Unitary state	1996	Bicameral parliament	Constitutional review	No
Chile	Presidential republic	Unitary state	1981	Bicameral congress	Limited judicial and constitutional review	No
China	Dictatorship (presidential-style)	Unitary state	1982	Unicameral parliament	No review	No
Colombia	Presidential republic	Unitary state	1991	Bicameral congress	Constitutional review	Yes
Costa Rica	Presidential republic	Unitary state	1949	Unicameral congress	Constitutional review	No
Croatia	Presidential-style republic	Unitary state	1990	Bicameral parliament	Constitutional review	Yes
Cuba	Dictatorship (presidential-style)	Unitary state	1976	Unicameral parliament	No review	No
Czech Republic	Presidential-style republic	Unitary state	1993	Bicameral parliament	Constitutional review	No
Denmark	Constitutional monarchy	Unitary state	1953	Unicameral parliament	Judicial review	Yes
Ecuador	Presidential Republic	Unitary state	1998	Unicameral congress	Constitutional review	No

Country	Type of Government[1]	Type of State	Most Recent Constitution[2]	Type of Legislature[3]	Judicial or Constitutional Review[4]	Ombudsman
Egypt	Presidential-style republic	Unitary state	1971 (revised)	Unicameral parliament	Constitutional review	No
Ethiopia	Presidential-style republic	Federal state	1996	Bicameral parliament	Limited constitutional review	No
Finland	Presidential-style republic	Unitary state	2000	Unicameral parliament	No review	Yes
France	Presidential-style republic	Unitary state	1958	Bicameral parliament	Limited constitutional review	No
Georgia	Presidential-style republic	Unitary state	1995	Unicameral parliament	Constitutional review	No
Germany	Presidential-style republic	Federal state	1949	Bicameral parliament	Constitutional review	No
Ghana	Presidential republic	Unitary state	1993	Unicameral parliament	Judicial review	Yes
Greece	Presidential-style republic	Unitary state	1975	Unicameral parliament	Constitutional review	No
Haiti	Presidential-style republic	Unitary state	1987	Bicameral parliament	Limited judicial review	Yes
Honduras	Presidential republic	Unitary state	1982	Unicameral congress	Limited judicial review	No
Hungary	Presidential-style republic	Unitary state	1949 (revised)	Unicameral parliament	Constitutional review	Yes
Iceland	Presidential-style republic	Unitary state	1944	Unicameral parliament	Judicial review	No
India	Presidential-style republic	Federal state	1950	Bicameral parliament	Judicial review	No
Indonesia	Presidential-style republic	Unitary state	1959 (restoration)	Unicameral parliament	No review	No
Iran	Theocratic republic	Unitary state	1979	Unicameral parliament	No review	No
Iraq	Dictatorship (presidential-style)	Unitary state	1970	Unicameral parliament	No review	No

Country	Type of Government[1]	Type of State	Most Recent Constitution[2]	Type of Legislature[3]	Judicial or Constitutional Review[4]	Ombudsman
Ireland	Presidential-style republic	Unitary state	1937	Bicameral parliament	Judicial review	No
Israel	Presidential-style republic	Unitary state	Unwritten	Unicameral parliament	Technically no review	No
Italy	Presidential-style republic	Unitary state	1948	Bicameral parliament	Constitutional review	No
Japan	Constitutional monarchy	Unitary state	1889 (rewritten in 1947)	Bicameral parliament	Judicial review	No
Jordan	Constitutional monarchy	Unitary state	1952	Bicameral parliament	Limited constitutional review	No
Kenya	Presidential-style republic	Unitary state	1964 (revised)	Unicameral parliament	Judicial review	No
Kuwait	Constitutional monarchy	Unitary state	1962	Unicameral parliament	Limited judicial review	No
Laos	Dictatorship (presidential-style)	Unitary state	1991	Unicameral parliament	No review	No
Lebanon	Presidential-style republic	Unitary state	1926	Unicameral parliament	No review	No
Liberia	Presidential republic	Unitary state	1986	Bicameral congress	Judicial review	No
Libya	Dictatorship	Unitary state	1969 (revised)	Unicameral congress	No review	No
Malaysia	Constitutional monarchy	Federal state	1957 (revised)	Bicameral parliament	Limited judicial review	No
Mexico	Presidential republic	Federal state	1917	Bicameral congress	Judicial review	No
Monaco	Constitutional monarchy	Unitary state	1962	Unicameral council	Limited judicial review	No
Mongolia	Presidential-style republic	Unitary state	1992	Unicameral parliament	Constitutional review	No
Morocco	Constitutional monarchy	Unitary state	1972 (revised)	Bicameral parliament	Limited constitutional review	No

Country	Type of Government[1]	Type of State	Most Recent Constitution[2]	Type of Legislature[3]	Judicial or Constitutional Review[4]	Ombudsman
Mozambique	Presidential-style republic	Unitary state	1990	Unicameral parliament	Judicial and constitutional review	No
Nepal	Constitutional monarchy	Unitary state	1990	Bicameral parliament	Judicial review	Yes
The Netherlands	Constitutional monarchy	Unitary state	1814 (revised)	Bicameral parliament	No review	No
New Zealand	Constitutional monarchy	Unitary state	Unwritten	Unicameral parliament	Technically no review	Yes
Nicaragua	Presidential republic	Unitary state	1987	Unicameral congress	Judicial review	No
Nigeria	Presidential republic	Federal state	1999	Bicameral congress	Judicial review	No
North Korea	Dictatorship (parliamentary-style)	Unitary state	1972 (revised)	Unicameral parliament	No review	No
Norway	Constitutional monarchy	Unitary state	1814	Semibicameral parliament	Judicial review	Yes
Pakistan	Military government	Federal state	1973 (suspended 1999)	Bicameral parliament	Limited judicial review	No
Panama	Presidential republic	Unitary state	1972	Unicameral congress	Judicial review	Yes
Paraguay	Presidential republic	Unitary state	1992	Bicameral congress	Constitutional review	No
Peru	Presidential republic	Unitary state	1993	Unicameral congress	Judicial and constitutional review	No
The Philippines	Presidential republic	Unitary state	1987	Bicameral congress	Judicial review	Yes
Poland	Presidential-style republic	Unitary state	1997	Bicameral parliament	Constitutional review	Yes
Portugal	Presidential-style republic	Unitary state	1976	Unicameral parliament	Judicial and constitutional review	Yes
Romania	Presidential-style republic	Unitary state	1991	Bicameral parliament	Limited constitutional review	Yes

Country	Type of Government[1]	Type of State	Most Recent Constitution[2]	Type of Legislature[3]	Judicial or Constitutional Review[4]	Ombudsman
Russia	Presidential-style republic	Federal state	1993	Bicameral parliament	Limited constitutional review	Yes
Saudi Arabia	Monarchy	Unitary state	None	None	No review	No
Singapore	Presidential-style republic	Unitary state	1963	Unicameral parliament	Judicial review	No
Slovakia	Presidential-style republic	Unitary state	1993	Unicameral parliament	Constitutional review	No
South Africa	Presidential republic	Unitary state	1997	Bicameral parliament	Constitutional review	Yes
South Korea	Presidential-style republic	Unitary state	1948 (revised)	Unicameral parliament	Constitutional review	No
Spain	Constitutional monarchy	Unitary state	1978	Bicameral parliament	Limited constitutional review	No
Sri Lanka	Presidential-style republic	Unitary state	1978	Unicameral parliament	Judicial review	No
Sudan	Presidential republic	Federal state	1998	Unicameral congress	Constitutional review	No
Sweden	Constitutional monarchy	Unitary state	1975	Unicameral parliament	Limited judicial review	Yes
Switzerland	Confederation	Federal state	2000	Bicameral parliament	Judicial review	No
Syria	Presidential-style republic	Unitary state	1973	Unicameral parliament	Limited constitutional review	No
Taiwan	Presidential-style republic	Unitary state	1947	Bicameral parliament	Constitutional review	No
Tanzania	Presidential-style republic	Unitary state	1985	Unicameral parliament	Limited constitutional review	Yes
Thailand	Constitutional monarchy	Unitary state	1997	Bicameral parliament	Limited constitutional review	Yes
Tibet	Theocratic republic	Federal state	1991 (proposed)	Unicameral parliament	Judicial review	No

Country	Type of Government[1]	Type of State	Most Recent Constitution[2]	Type of Legislature[3]	Judicial or Constitutional Review[4]	Ombudsman
Turkey	Presidential-style republic	Unitary state	1982	Unicameral parliament	Limited constitutional review	No
Uganda	Presidential republic	Unitary state	1995	Unicameral parliament	Constitutional review	Yes
Ukraine	Presidential-style republic	Unitary state	1996	Unicameral parliament	Constitutional review	No
United Kingdom	Constitutional monarchy	Unitary state	Unwritten	Bicameral parliament	Technically no review	No
United States	Presidential republic	Federal state	1789	Bicameral congress	Judicial review	No
Venezuela	Presidential republic	Federal state	1999	Unicameral congress	Constitutional review	No
Vietnam	Dictatorship (presidential-style)	Unitary state	1992	Unicameral parliament	No review	No
Yugoslavia	Presidential-style republic	Federal state	1992	Bicameral parliament	Constitutional review	No
Zambia	Presidential republic	Unitary state	1991	Unicameral parliament	Limited judicial and constitutional review	Yes
Zimbabwe	Presidential republic	Unitary state	1980	Unicameral parliament	Limited judicial review	Yes

Notes

1. Descriptions in parentheses are constitutional provisions, as opposed to actual types of governments in existence today.

2. "Revised" means that the document has been significantly changed since the date of the constitution's adoption. "Restoration" means that the constitution that went into effect on the date shown was a constitution previously in effect.

3. Classification as to congress or parliament is based on government structure—for example, whether there are a prime minister and cabinet and/or whether there is a requirement for a no-confidence vote—not on the actual powers or responsibilities associated with the parliamentary form of government. "Unicameral" indicates that a legislature has one house or chamber, "bicameral" that it has an upper and a lower house or chamber, and "semibicameral" that it divides itself into two houses or chambers after elections.

4. "Judicial review" means that the judicial branch of government reviews the consitutionality of laws and actions in the regular course of the adjudication process, as in the United States. "Constitutional review" means that either a separate body within the judicial system or a body outside the judicial system is charged with reviewing the constitutionality of laws and actions. "Limited" means that review is available only to certain persons or entities or is restricted to certain aspects of a constitution.

Once an isolated and little-understood country, Albania emerged from its communist system of government and adopted a progressive democratic constitution in 1998 after encouraging input from experts and the public.

General Information

The Republic of Albania on Europe's Balkan Peninsula occupies 28,749 square kilometers and is bounded on the north by Yugoslavia, on the east by Macedonia, on the southeast by Greece, and on the west by the Adriatic Sea. Tiranë is the capital of this country of approximately 3.5 million persons.

Albania's major industries include cement, textiles, and refined petroleum; among its chief agricultural products are grains, sunflower seeds, and tobacco. With one of the lowest per capita gross national products in Europe, Albania relies heavily on foreign assistance while struggling to convert to a private, competitive market economy.

Type of Government: Presidential-style parliamentary republic, with a president, a prime minister and council of ministers (cabinet), a unicameral legislature, a judiciary, and a constitutional court

Dates of Constitutions: 1914, 1929, 1946, 1976, 1991, and 1998

Constitutional History

Beginning in at least 1,000 B.C. Illyrian ancestors of the Albanians inhabited the western Balkan Peninsula. The ancient Greeks established colonies there, and the Roman Empire administered it as the province of Illyricum in 168 B.C. Successive invasions by Goths, Huns, Avars, Serbs, Croats, and Bulgars occurred between the fourth and seventh centuries. In the eleventh century Albanians became divided in the north between allegiance to the Catholic Church and in the south to the Orthodox Church. From the twelfth to the fifteenth centuries Albania was dominated by the Serbs, Venice, Naples, and, finally, after the defeat of the Albanian national hero Skanderberg at Nis, by the Ottoman Turks.

Two-thirds of the Albanian population had become adherents of Islam by the eighteenth century. After the Russians defeated the Ottomans, the Congress of Berlin in 1878 gave the Serbs and Montenegrins control over much of the region. The Ottomans returned in 1881 and remained until independence was declared 1912. After the Second Balkan War in 1913, the Great Powers (Britain, Germany, Russia, Austria-Hungary, France, and Italy) confirmed Albania's independence as a monarchy under a constitution drafted by an international commission in 1914.

After World War I Albania was admitted to the League of Nations as an independent state in 1920. A tribal chieftain, Ahmed Zogu, with the backing of the Yugoslav army, seized power in 1928, becoming King Zog I of Albania. A constitution promulgated in 1929 gave him virtually absolute power. In 1939, however, after Mussolini's troops occupied the country, the Albanian parliament voted to unite with Italy.

Yugoslavia's Marshall Tito organized the Albanian communists under the leadership of Enver Hoxha during World War II. In 1945 Yugoslavia and the Soviet Union officially recognized the communist government in Albania, and Hoxha began to wield dictatorial power in Albania until his death in 1985. Communist Albania adopted a Soviet- and Yugoslav-inspired constitution in 1946 and another Soviet-style constitution in 1976. The latter, adopted a year after the Helsinki Final Act promoting human rights in Europe, appeared to grant citizens certain rights such as freedom of speech and association, but in fact it subordinated individual rights to citizens' duties to the state.

With the collapse of communist governments in Europe, Albania held open elections in March 1991; the communists retained power, only to be defeated in elections the following year. An interim constitution was adopted on May 21, 1991, and a year later the country adopted the European Convention for the Protection of Human Rights and Fundamental Freedoms (1950). Unsuccessful attempts to develop a new constitution followed, including one emphasizing a strong presidency that was defeated by referendum in 1994. A new draft, which took into consideration the suggestions of international experts and the public, was finally approved by referendum on November 22, 1998, and promulgated six days later.

Influences

The rejected 1994 constitution, which attempted to solidify the president's powers, and subsequent public comment influenced the framers of the 1998 constitution, as did the language in international human rights documents such as the United Nations's Universal Declaration of Human Rights (1948).

The Constitution

"We, the people of Albania, proud and aware of our history, with responsibility for the future, and with faith in God and/or other universal values," begins the constitution's preamble. After noting the nation's "determination to build a social and democratic state based on the rule of law," it recognizes "religious coexistence and tolerance," "human dignity and personhood," "prosperity," and "the centuries-old aspiration of the Albanian people for national identity and unity." Finally, the preamble notes "a deep conviction that justice, peace, harmony and cooperation between nations are among the highest values of humanity."

Article 1 proclaims that "Albania is a parliamentary republic . . . a unitary and indivisible state," adding that "[g]overnance is based on a system of elections that are free, equal, general and periodic." According to article 2, "Sovereignty . . . belongs to the people" and is exercised "through their representatives or directly." Article 4 declares in part: "The Constitution is the highest law in the Republic of Albania."

Fundamental Rights

"The fundamental human rights and freedoms are indivisible, inalienable, and inviolable and stand at the base of the entire juridical order," proclaims article 15, while article 16 extends constitutional rights to "foreigners and stateless persons in [its] territory." Article 17 mandates that limitations on these rights must be necessary to protect "the public interest or . . . the rights of others."

Rights guaranteed include equality before the law, minority rights, the right to life, freedom of expression, freedom of the press and other media, the right to information, freedom of conscience and religion, and protection from torture, cruel, inhuman, or degrading punishment or treatment; forced labor is prohibited except, for example, after a judicial decision, during military service, or in a national emergency. Articles 27 and 28 are devoted to the right to liberty, and articles 29 through 34 address the rights of persons accused of crimes. Other rights relate to personal data, correspondence and other forms of communication, and place of residence. Article 42 prohibits infringement of the rights to life, liberty, property, and other constitutional and legal rights without due process of law.

Political rights, including the rights to organize collectively and to bring public complaints, are extended in articles 45 through 48. Articles 49 through 58 focus on economic, social, and cultural rights, encompassing work, education, marriage and family, national health care and social security, artistic and scientific pursuits, and information "about the status of the environment and its protection."

Division of Powers

"The system of government in the Republic of Albania," states article 7, "is based on the separation and balancing of legislative, executive and judicial powers."

The Executive

President. Article 86 declares: "The President of the Republic is the Head of State and represents the unity of the people." The chief executive must be "an Albanian citizen by birth who has resided in Albania for not less than the past 10 years and who has reached the age of 40."

According to article 87, a presidential candidate must be "proposed to the Assembly [parliament] by a group of not less than 20 of its members." The president "is elected by the Assembly by secret ballot and without debate by a majority of three-fifths of all its members" or, if such a majority is not reached, two more elections may take place at seven-day intervals; a fourth balloting, if necessary, is limited to the two candidates with the highest number of votes. If a fifth ballot fails, the legislature is dissolved, new elections are held, and a majority of the new members elect a president for a five-year term; he or she may be reelected only once.

The president's powers under article 92 include addressing messages to the assembly; granting pardons, citizenship, decorations and titles of honor, and the highest military ranks, all "according to law"; appointing and withdrawing diplomats "on the proposal of the Prime Minister"; and entering into "international agreements according to law." Article 93 authorizes the president to issue "decrees in the exercise of his powers."

The president is given immunity for official actions but "may be dismissed for serious violations of the Constitution and for the commission of a serious crime." Dismissal must be proposed by one-fourth of all legislators, and a two-thirds vote is necessary to send the matter to the constitutional court, "which, when it verifies the guilt ... declares his dismissal from duty."

Article 91 directs that the assembly speaker exercise the president's functions if he or she is unable to do so for a period of less than sixty days. For more than sixty days, parliament may, by a two-thirds vote, ask the constitutional court to determine "conclusively the fact of his incapacity"; an election for a new president follows an affirmative finding.

Prime Minister and Cabinet. The prime minister is appointed by the president "on the proposal of the party or coalition of parties that has the majority of seats in the Assembly" and must be approved by the assembly. Pursuant to article 102, the prime minister "represents the Council of Ministers and chairs its meetings," is responsible for principal national policies, "assures the implementation of legislation and policies" approved by the council of ministers, and "coordinates and supervises the work" of the ministers and other government institutions. If a majority of legislators express a lack of confidence in the prime minister, another prime minister is selected within fifteen days.

Under article 95, the prime minister, deputy prime minister, and other ministers constitute the council of ministers, which "exercises every state function that is not given to the organs of other state powers or of local government."

Parliament. The Albanian parliament, called the assembly, numbers 140 deputies elected for four-year terms. According to article 64, "One hundred deputies are elected directly in single member electoral zones with an approximately equal number of voters. Forty deputies are elected from multiname lists of parties or party coalitions according to their ranking." Candidates "may be presented only by political parties, coalitions of parties, and by voters ... [and] rules for the designation of candidates ... [and] for the ... conduct of elections ... are regulated by the electoral law." Disqualified candidates include judges and prosecutors, active military personnel, police and national security staff, mayors, and the president and other "high officials."

Parliament "elects and discharges its Speaker" and "operates according to regulations approved by a majority of all its members." "The Speaker," states article 76, "chairs debates, directs the work, assures respect for the rights of the Assembly and its members, and represents the Assembly in relations with others." Deputies are granted certain immunities for opinions expressed in the assembly and from criminal prosecution, unless they are "apprehended during or immediately after the commission of a serious crime."

Article 81 provides that the "Council of Ministers, every deputy and 20,000 electors each have the right to propose laws." Certain laws—for example, those on the organization and operation of constitutional institutions, citizenship, general and local elections, referendums, codes, and states of emergency—require the approval of a three-fifths majority of all legislators. "A draft law is voted on three times: in principle, article by article, and in its entirety," according to article 83, although passage may be expedited in some cases. "The President . . . promulgates an approved law within 20 days from its submission" but "has the right to return a law for re-consideration only once." This veto power, however, may be overridden by "a majority of all the members of the Assembly."

The Judiciary

High Court. Article 135 decrees that Albania's judicial power "is exercised by the High Court, as well as by the courts of appeal and courts of first instance, which are established by law." The court's original jurisdiction extends to adjudicating criminal charges against a number of officials, including the president, the prime minister, and judges of the high court and the constitutional court.

According to article 136, the members of the high court and its president are appointed by the president with the consent of the assembly for terms of nine years, but they may not be reappointed. "Only citizens with higher legal education may be judges." Article 137 extends certain immunities, but under article 139 a high court judge may be removed by the court itself if he or she is convicted of a crime, fails to appear without reason for more than six months, reaches the age of sixty-five, resigns, or is declared "incapable of acting by a final court decision." A judge may also be removed by a two-thirds vote of the assembly for various reasons, including for a violation of the constitution.

Constitutional Court

Article 124 provides that the constitutional court "guarantees respect for the Constitution and interprets it conclusively" and "is subject only to the Constitution." The court "is composed of nine members . . . appointed by the President . . . with the consent of the Assembly . . . for nine years [one-third every three years] without the right to be reelected . . . [from] among lawyers with high qualifications and with professional work experience of not less than fifteen years." The court's president is also appointed by the Albanian president with the consent of the assembly for a three-year term from among the members of the court. Members are granted certain immunities and may serve until seventy unless removed for various reasons.

At the request of the president, the prime minister, one-fifth of the assembly members, or any court, political party, or religious community, among others, the constitutional court decides on the compatibility "of a law with the Constitution or with international agreements . . . , of international agreements with the Constitution, prior to their ratification . . . [and] of normative acts of the central and local organs with the Constitution and international agreements." The court also adjudicates "conflicts of competencies among the powers [of government] as well as between central government and local government [and] the constitutionality of parties and other political organizations"; plays a role in the "removal from office of the President of the Republic"; and has final authority in the "adjudication of the complaints of individuals for the violation of their constitutional rights to due process of law, after all [other] legal remedies . . . have been exhausted."

Amending the Constitution

Article 177 requires a vote of "not less than one-fifth of the members of the Assembly" to initiate the amending process. Proposed amendments must be approved "by not less than two-thirds of all members of the Assembly." By the same majority, the assembly may call for a referendum on an amendment. An amendment approved by the assembly cannot be returned by the president as in the case of ordinary legislation. An amendment approved by referendum is promulgated by the president and becomes effective on the date provided for.

Both the military and the Muslim religion are extremely influential in Algeria, a former French colony. Its 1996 constitution, however, mandates control of the military by an elected head of state and prohibits religion as the basis for political parties.

The Democratic and Popular Republic of Algeria, located in northwestern Africa, is approximately 2.4 million square kilometers and is bounded on the north by the Mediterranean Sea; on the east by Tunisia and Libya; on the south by Niger, Mali, and Mauritania; and on the west by Western Sahara and Morocco. Algiers is the capital of this country of more than thirty-one million persons.

Algeria produces oil and natural gas, but the country's political and religious unrest, relatively fast-growing population, and large external debt have tended to destabilize its economy.

Type of Government: Presidential-style parliamentary republic, with a president, a prime minister and council of ministers (cabinet), a council of state, a bicameral legislature, a judiciary, and a constitutional council

Dates of Constitutions: 1963, 1976 (revised in 1989), and 1996

Around 1200 B.C., when Phoenician traders began settling in what is today Algeria, they found the Berbers living there. The famous and powerful Phoenician city of Carthage was destroyed by Rome in 146 B.C. after the third Punic War, but the Romans also established the northern provinces of Mauritania and Numidia. After the decline of Rome, Vandals conquered the northern territory in A.D. 440 but then were supplanted by Byzantine forces a century later, while the lands to the south remained in the hands of the Berber tribes.

Conquered by the Arabs in the seventh century, the inhabitants of the area converted to Islam and adopted the Arabic language, becoming part of the Arab Maghreb (Arab West). The Arabs and Berbers, together called Moors, conquered the Iberian Peninsula, where their culture lasted until the end of the fifteenth century. In 1518 the Ottoman Turks took control of northern Algeria, governing it as the Algerian Regency. While most Algerians opposed the Turks, Algiers remained firmly in their grasp. For nearly three centuries piracy was rampant along the coast of the Barbary States, the territories along the southern Mediterranean Sea.

At the beginning of the nineteenth century the rulers in Algeria, called *deys,* were chosen by the janissaries, the elite Turkish troops, and invested with authority from Istanbul. They governed absolutely with the assistance of a *diwan* (council) of five high Turkish officials. Algiers was the main province, with three others ruled by *beys* assisted by lieutenants. The tribes, however, recognized only traditional Arab *shaykhs* as leaders and holy men as the arbiters of disputes.

France seized Algiers in 1830 and for twenty-seven years tried to annex the rest of Algeria despite fierce resistance. The 1848 constitution of France's Second Republic included Algeria; however, when the Second Empire was established in 1852, the policy of acquiring land for French settlers at the expense of the indigenous Algerians was expanded. The "Arab bureaus," set up by the French to act as intermediaries with the Muslims but which in fact governed the tribes, instead wanted to develop a class of landed native peasantry dependent on the French for their land ownership. The French emperor, however, sought to replace the Muslim power structures by introducing mixed-member administrative and judicial systems.

With the end of the French empire in 1871, civilian administration replaced military rule. Algeria became autonomous in 1898. Nationalist aspirations developed after World War I, but French settlers opposed reforms. Even though some political reforms were introduced after World War II, a widespread revolt was mounted by the indigenous population in 1954, and a national liberation front began conducting guerrilla warfare. In the wake of bitter and protracted fighting, felt heavily France, Algeria proclaimed its independence in 1962.

Algerians had approved the new French constitution of the Fifth Republic, but after independence the prime minister, Ahmed ben Bella, increased his personal power and was elected president under a constitution promulgated in 1963. After a coup in 1965 the constitution was suspended, and Col. Houari Boumedienne ruled through a mostly military revolutionary council. In 1976 Boumedienne ran unopposed for the six-year-term presidency under a constitution approved by a national referendum that created a single-party state and gave sweeping powers to the president. His successor some two years later, however, began liberalizing the regime and instituting progressive reforms. After handily winning a multiparty election in 1995, Gen. Lamine Zeroual, the former president designated by the military, reorganized the government, and a new constitution was approved by referendum on November 28, 1996. The country's legislature was changed from a unicameral to a bicameral parliament.

Influences

Algeria's 1996 constitution was influenced by the 1958 French constitution, which similarly makes reference to the "Rights of Man and of the Citizen," as well as by the country's Arab and Islamic heritage.

The Constitution

The preamble states in part:

Algeria, land of Islam, integral part of the Great Maghreb Arab country, Mediterranean and African, is honored by the radiance of its [1954] Revolution . . . and the respect which the country has sought to achieve and preserve and by reason of its commitment to all the just causes of the world.

Articles 1 and 2 declare: "Algeria is a Democratic and People's Republic. . . . Islam is the religion of the State." According to article 6, "The people [are] the source of all power. National sovereignty belongs exclusively to the people." Article 7 adds that they exercise power "by means of the referendum and by the intermediary of elected representatives."

Article 11 proclaims: "The State derives its legitimacy and its raison d'etre from the will of the people. Its motto is: 'By the People and for the People.'" Article 14 adds that Algeria "is founded on the principles of democratic organization and social justice." This is reinforced in article 27, which states: "Algeria declares its solidarity with all the peoples who are fighting for political and economic liberation, for the right of self-determination and against all racial discrimination."

Fundamental Rights

Rights and liberties are set forth in articles 29 through 59. Among them are equality "before the law without . . . discrimination on the basis of birth, race, gender (sex), opinion or all other conditions or personal or social circumstances"; personal inviolability; freedom of conscience and opinion and of commerce and industry; rights of authorship; "private life and the honor of the citizen"; secrecy of correspondence and private communications; inviolability of the home; and freedom of expression, association, and assembly.

Article 42 extends the "right to establish political parties," but "political parties cannot be founded on a religious, linguistic, racial, sexual, corporatist or regional basis." Political and civil rights are guaranteed, as are rights of the accused, such as the presumption of innocence and "the right to get in touch with [one's] family immediately." Recalling the French constitution, article 32 notes: "The fundamental liberties and the Rights of Man and of the Citizen are guaranteed." Duties of citizens include respecting the constitution, loyally discharging "obligations toward the national collectivity," and protecting "public property and the interests of the national collectivity."

Division of Powers

The constitution is divided on the basis of executive, legislative, and judicial powers.

President. The president is head of state and "personifies the unity of the Nation," states article 70. "He is the guarantor of the Constitution.... He appeals directly to the Nation." According to article 7, the chief executive "may have direct recourse to the expression of the will of the people." The president is directly elected for five years and may be reelected one time. Qualifications for the office include having "solely native Algerian citizenship," being "of Moslem faith," being at least forty years old on election day, having an Algerian spouse, and documenting "participation in the Revolution of November 1, 1954 for candidates born before July 1942." Candidates born after that date are required to give proof that their parents were not involved "in hostile acts against the Revolution of November 1, 1954."

Pursuant to article 77, the president is the supreme commander of the armed forces and is responsible for national defense, conducts foreign policy, presides over the council of ministers, appoints the prime minister, may dismiss the government, and signs presidential decrees. Other powers and duties include granting pardons and commuting sentences, referring any "question of national importance to the people by way of referendum," and concluding and ratifying treaties. Powers of appointment extend also to civilian and military employees, the president of the state council, the secretary-general of the government, the governor of the Bank of Algeria, magistrates, ambassadors, and special envoys.

According to article 95, the president may declare a state of war after consulting with, among others, the presidents of the two chambers of parliament. In this case, "the Constitution is suspended and the President . . . assumes all the powers." He or she continues in office "until the end of the war."

If the president is incapacitated and the constitutional council verifies "a serious and enduring illness," two-thirds of the members of parliament may vote to empower the upper chamber's president to act as interim president for up to forty-five days. He or she also becomes president in the event of the president's death or resignation.

Prime Minister and Cabinet. The prime minister is appointed by the president and "presents the members of the government which he has chosen to the President . . . for appointment." As the head of government, he or she "implements and coordinates the program adopted" by parliament's lower house. If the prime minister's programs are not approved by that house, the incumbent and his government have to resign, and the lower house may also be dissolved.

Parliament. Article 98 declares: "The legislative power is exercised by a Parliament composed of two chambers, the National People's Assembly [lower house] and the Council of the Nation [upper house]." According to article 99, parliament "controls the action of the government under conditions specified [in] the Constitution." As stated in article 10: "The people choose their representatives freely. The representation of the people has no other limits than those specified in the Constitution and the electoral law."

Upper House. Article 101 limits the number of members of the council of the nation to "half, at the most, of the members of the [lower house]." Two-thirds of the members are elected from and by "the members of the Communal People's Assemblies and by the People's Assemblies of the Wilaya"; the other one-third are designated by the president "among the personalities and [experts] in the scientific, cultural, professional, economic and social fields." They serve six years, half of them elected every three years, as is the council president.

Lower House. Members of the assembly, called deputies, are elected by universal, direct, and secret suffrage for a term of five years, and their president is elected for the legislature's term. The assembly holds the exclusive power to vote on motions to censure the government, which, if approved "by a majority of two-thirds," require the prime minister and the cabinet to resign.

Under article 115, the organization of both houses "as well as the functional relations between [them] and the Government are determined by an organic law."

Bills may be introduced by the prime minister or at least twenty members of the lower house and must first be presented in the cabinet after the advice of the council of state is obtained; they are then filed by the prime minister with the assembly. Article 120 provides that the upper house "deliberates on the text" as voted by the assembly and adopts legislation by a majority of three-fourths of its members. Under article 123, however, an organic law is adopted by an absolute majority of deputies and three-quarters of the members of the council of the nation and is submitted for review by the constitutional council. Laws are promulgated by the president, whose veto may be overridden by a two-thirds vote of the lower house. When the assembly is not in session, the president may "legislate by ordinance."

Legislative subjects authorized by the constitution include "fundamental rights and duties of persons"; "general rules pertaining to personal status and family law [such as] marriage, divorce, ... and inheritance"; "nationality"; "judicial organization"; general "rules of criminal law and ... procedure ... and civil procedure ..."; "territorial division of the country"; and "the budget of the State."

The Judiciary

Articles 138 and 139 declare that the "judicial power is independent" and "protects the society ... [and] guarantees ... everyone the protection of their fundamental rights." Article 143 adds that "[j]ustice recognizes remedies against illegal acts of the administrative authorities." All authorities must assure "the execution of judicial decisions," states article 145.

Supreme Court. "The Supreme Court constitutes the regulatory organ of all activity by the courts and tribunals," article 152 declares. "A Council of State is instituted [as a] regulatory organ of the activity of administrative jurisdiction. [Together they] assure the unification of jurisprudence throughout the country and watch over the respect for the law." A tribunal is also created to settle conflicts between the court and the council. The organization and functions of these three bodies are established by organic law.

Constitutional Council

"A Constitutional Council is established," states article 163, "to watch over the respect for the Constitution." It consists of nine members, three of whom are appointed by the president; two each are elected by the lower and upper houses of parliament, while two are named by the supreme court and the council of state. They hold six-year terms, except that half of those not appointed by the president "are renewed" every three years.

Among other responsibilities, the council "watches ... over" referendums and presidential and legislative elections; "rules on the constitutionality of treaties, laws and negotiations"; and, when requested by the president, gives its opinion on "the constitutionality of organic laws ... [and] the internal regulation of each of the two chambers of Parliament." The presidents of those two houses may also request the council's opinion.

Amending the Constitution

According to article 174, the president may propose a constitutional amendment, which "is voted on equal terms by the [two houses of parliament] under the same conditions as a legislative text." If approved, it is then submitted for a popular vote by referendum and, if again approved, is promulgated by the president. Article 176 authorizes the president, if first approved by the constitutional council, to "directly promulgate [a] law containing [a] constitutional revision ... if it has received the approval of three-quarters ... of the members of the two chambers of Parliament." Article 177 additionally permits three-fourths of the members of both houses of parliament, in joint session, to propose an amendment that the president can submit to a referendum. Certain matters—including the republic itself, the declaration that Islam is the state religion, and fundamental liberties—may not be changed.

After the "liberator" José de San Martín wrested his native Argentina from the Spanish in 1816, a constitution proposed in 1819, which would have centralized the government, fueled a conflict between the port city of Buenos Aires and Argentina's other provinces. The 1853 constitution, in force today, provides for a federal system of government.

General Information

The Argentine Republic's 2.8 million square kilometers make it the second largest nation in South America and the eighth largest in the world. Located in the southeastern part of the continent, the country is bounded on the west by Chile, on the north by Bolivia and Paraguay, on the northeast by Brazil and Uruguay, and on the east by the Atlantic Ocean. One-third of Argentina's more than thirty-seven million citizens live in Buenos Aires, the capital.

Before the Great Depression in the 1930s, the export of beef and wheat made Argentina the seventh richest country in the world. Having survived a period of government corruption and abuse, the country may be on the way to economic stability.

Type of Government: Presidential-style federal republic, with a president, a prime minister and cabinet, a bicameral legislature, and a judiciary

Date of Constitution: 1853 (major 1949 amendments were repealed in 1956; significantly amended in 1994)

Constitutional History

The Spaniard Juan Diaz de Solis was the first European to reach the estuary of the Rio de la Plata (Silver River), in 1516, but when he landed he was killed by the inhabitants. Continuing the Spanish exploration, the Italian John Cabot (born Giovanni Caboto) followed in 1526 and established the first settlement, a fort called Sancti Spiriti. The territory's name was derived from *argentium,* the Latin word for silver.

Buenos Aires, after first being abandoned because of the extreme hostility of the natives, became a prosperous seaport by the eighteenth century as well as the political, commercial, and cultural center of the country. The city's early development suffered as a result of Spain's emphasis on exploiting silver in what is now Peru, and a historic antagonism developed between the "inlanders" of the fertile Argentine plains, which are excellent for raising cattle and wheat, and the *portenos* (the inhabitants of Buenos Aires).

The Spanish ruled their dominions in America under appointed representatives called viceroys, who governed along with *audiencias* (councils that combined executive, legislative, and judicial functions). The inhabitants, called *crillos,* handled local administrative affairs through political bodies named *cabildos.* After the defeat of the Spanish fleet by the British at the Battle of Trafalgar in 1806–7, Britain invaded Buenos Aires, giving Argentina's *crillos* society a chance to organize its own military defense and provisional government, which fostered the idea of independence.

After Napoleon's brother Joseph ascended the Spanish throne in 1808, the *cabildo* of Buenos Aires established the first local government on May 25, 1810, and appointed Gen. José de San Martín as the leader of its armed forces. He defeated the Spanish on July 9, 1816, winning independence for the United Provinces of Rio de la Plata. After a constitution was proposed in 1819 two major factions emerged: the Unitarians, represented by the *portenos,* who favored the centralized government of Buenos Aires; and the Federalists, represented by the provincial governors, who wanted a federal form of government. Another constitution was drafted in 1826, but relations between Buenos Aires and the provinces between 1820 and 1859 were governed instead by agreements. After several civil wars, the Federalist-turned-centralist dictator Juan Manuel de Rosas was overthrown in 1852, and the governors of twelve of the provinces met at the town of San Nicholas de los Arroyos and authorized a constitutional convention. The convention was held in August 1852, with delegates elected in the same manner as members of the provincial legislatures; each province was entitled to two delegates. On May 1, 1853, a general constituent congress adopted a new constitution, which was greatly influenced by the constitutionalist Juan Bautista Alberdi. Buenos Aires refused to accept the new document until 1861, when some of its proposed amendments were incorporated.

The 1853 constitution has been amended six times. Although major amendments that greatly increased the powers of the president were made in 1949 during the presidency of Juan Domingo Peron, after his overthrow in 1955 the military government that followed reestablished the 1853 constitution by decree dated May 1, 1956. In August 1994 a constitutional convention approved a number of constitutional reforms that had been agreed on by President Carlos Saúl Menam and former President Raúl Ricardo Alfonsín, which allowed Menam to run for an additional four-year presidential term. Another important amendment incorporated ten international human rights agreements, including the Universal Declaration of Human Rights (1948), Convention on the Elimination of All Forms of Discrimination Against Women (1979), and Convention on the Rights of the Child (1989).

Influences

The Argentine constitution creates a representative republican federal democracy modeled after the U.S. constitution, but it was also influenced by the constitutions of Chile, Switzerland, Germany, and France.

The Constitution

The preamble of the constitution of the Argentine Republic contains language that echoes the aspirations of the framers of the U.S. constitution: ". . . in order to form a national union, ensure justice, preserve domestic peace, provide for the common defense, promote the general welfare and secure the blessings of liberty to ourselves and our posterity. . . ."

The federal government is given control of national expenditures and authority to intervene in the territory of a province to guarantee the republican form of government and to repel foreign invasions. Each province is required to adopt its own constitution in accordance with the national constitution, ensuring the administration of justice, municipal government, and elementary education.

Article 2 of the constitution adds, "The federal government supports the Roman Catholic Apostolic faith."

Fundamental Rights

Article 14 states that all inhabitants of the nation have certain rights, in accordance with the laws that regulate their exercise, including working in and practicing any lawful industry; navigating and trading; petitioning authorities; travel; publication without prior censorship; use and disposal of property; association for useful purposes; freedom of religion and of teaching and learning; and legal protection for labor to ensure dignified and equitable working conditions, including a limited working day, paid leave, fair remuneration, a flexible minimum wage, equal pay for equal work, a share in profits, control, and management of enterprises, and the free and democratic organization of labor unions. Trade unions are guaranteed the right to strike, collective agreements, and conciliation and arbitration. Benefits guaranteed include social security, flexible retirement pay and pensions, full family protection, including family welfare and economic compensation, and access to decent housing.

"The private actions of men that in no way offend public order or morality, nor injure a third party," article 19 states, in part, "are reserved only to God, and are exempt from the authority of the magistrates." Rights not enumerated in the constitution but that arise from the sovereignty of the people and a republican form of government are not to be construed as thereby denied.

Argentina is a federal state. Power at the national level is divided among the president, as head of state; the legislature; and the courts, which exercise judicial review. Each of Argentina's provinces has its own government and constitution that must conform to the principles of the national document.

President. According to article 87 of the second section of the second part of the Argentine constitution, "The executive power of the nation shall be vested in a citizen with the title of 'President of the Argentine nation.'" To be eligible for election as president or vice president, a person must have been born in Argentine territory or, alternatively, born of a native citizen, and possess the qualifications necessary to be elected to the upper chamber of the national legislature.

As a result of a constitutional amendment approved in October 1994, the terms of the president and vice president have been reduced from six to four years, with the potential for reelection for only one consecutive term. "If they have been reelected or succeeded each other," adds article 90, "they may not be elected to either office, except after the interval of a term." The president and vice president are elected directly by the people but must receive a certain percentage of the vote, otherwise a runoff election may be held between the two slates receiving the most votes.

Twenty express powers and responsibilities of the president are listed in article 99. The president is the supreme head of the nation and has charge of its general administration and must faithfully execute the country's laws. He or she is commander in chief of the armed forces; participates in enacting and promulgating the laws; appoints judges to the supreme court and lower federal courts with the consent of the upper house of the legislature; grants pardons and commutes punishments, except in cases of impeachment; and grants government benefits such as pensions and death benefits. Other duties include appointing and removing diplomats with the consent of the upper house, appointing and removing cabinet ministers and other officials of government departments, presiding over the annual opening session of the legislature, overseeing the collection of revenues, concluding and signing treaties, receiving foreign diplomats, and declaring war with the approval of the legislature.

Prime Minister and Cabinet. Article 100 states: "The Chief of the Cabinet Ministers [prime minister] and other Secretary-Ministers . . . shall have under their responsibility the handling of the Nation's business, and shall endorse and legalize the acts of the President through their signatures, without which [the president's] acts have no effect." The prime minister, who has political responsibility to the national congress, among other duties, exercises "the general administration of the country," makes "appointments of employees of the administration, except for those which fall to the President," performs duties delegated by the president, submits bills to the legislature, and attends sessions of the legislature, participating in debates but not voting.

Congress. According to article 44, "A Congress consisting of two Chambers, one of Deputies of the Nation and the other of Senators of the provinces and of the City of Buenos Aires, will be vested with the Legislative Power of the Nation."

Upper House. The senate is composed of three senators from each province and three from Buenos Aires, "elected directly and jointly, with two seats corresponding to the political party obtaining the greatest number of votes, and the remaining one to the political party receiving the next largest number of votes." They are elected for six-year terms, with one-third elected every two years. Each senator has one vote. Senators must be at least thirty years old, citizens for at least six years, have a minimum annual income or salary, and be natives of their provinces or residents for at least two years.

Lower House. The chamber of deputies is composed of "representatives elected directly, by a simple majority of votes, by the people of the Provinces, the City of Buenos Aires, and the Capital in case of transfer [of the capital]. . . ." Deputies are elected for four-year terms, one-half every two years. Members must be twenty-five years of age, citizens for four years, and natives of their province or residents for the two previous years.

Each chamber determines its own rules of procedure and may discipline its members by a two-thirds vote. Members of both chambers are free to express their opinions and may not be arrested during office except "when surprised *in flagrante* in the commission of a capital or other infamous or grave crime." Either chamber may summon cabinet ministers for explanations or reports. The clergy and governors of the provinces are prohibited from membership in congress.

The legislature is empowered to pass laws regarding import and export duties and direct taxes; borrowing money on the nation's credit; the use and disposition of national lands; national banks; the national debt; the national budget; subsidies to the provinces; regulation of the free navigation of internal rivers; coinage of money and adoption of a uniform system of weights and measures; regulation of foreign trade and trade between provinces; the post office and mail service; settlement of permanent boundaries; establishment of courts inferior to the supreme court; authorization of the president to declare war and make peace; administration of the territory of the capital; and general development of the prosperity of the country and the progress and welfare of the provinces.

With certain exceptions, bills may be initiated in both houses either by members or by the executive branch. Bills approved by both houses are sent to the president; if not returned within ten days, they are considered approved. A two-thirds vote in each chamber is required to override the president's veto.

Ombudsman. Article 86 creates a Defender of the People office "within the ambit of the . . . Congress" for the "defense and protection of human rights and other rights."

The Judiciary

"The judicial power of the nation," states article 108, "shall be vested in a supreme court of justice and in such lower courts as the congress may establish in the territory of the nation." The president is expressly prohibited from exercising judicial functions.

Supreme Court. The supreme court consists of five members appointed by the president with the consent of the upper house of the legislature. Members must be lawyers with at least eight years of practice and otherwise possess the qualifications to be a member of the upper house. They hold office contingent on their good behavior. The supreme court is authorized to adopt its own rules and appoint all subordinate employees.

The constitution gives the supreme court appellate jurisdiction over all cases dealing with the constitution and laws of the nation, except some cases involving civil, commercial, penal, mining, labor, and social security codes (which may be enforced by the provinces), treaties with foreign nations, admiralty and maritime cases, and suits between citizens of different provinces. The supreme court has original and exclusive jurisdiction in cases involving ambassadors, foreign ministers, and consuls and in which a province is a party.

Argentina permits both federal and provincial jurisdiction. Since 1865 the federal supreme court has exercised the power of judicial review over the constitutionality of acts and laws along lines similar to those followed by the U.S. supreme court, although the principle of the supremacy of the constitution, enunciated in article 31, has been less forcefully applied during periods of de facto governments.

The Argentine constitution has been characterized as rigid because it can be amended only by a constitutional convention. According to article 30: "The constitution may be amended entirely or in any of its parts. The necessity of amendment must be declared by the legislature by a vote of at least two-thirds of the members; but it shall not be effected except by a convention called for the purpose."

The constitution was amended, but not significantly, in 1860, 1866, 1898, 1957, and 1976. Then in 1994 a package of reforms made significant changes and nearly doubled the length of the document.

Amending the Constitution

ARMENIA

The smallest of the former republics of the Soviet Union, Armenia asserted its independence by referendum in 1991 and adopted a constitution in 1995 guaranteeing human rights and freedoms "in accordance with the principles and norms of international law."

General Information

The Republic of Armenia has an area of approximately 29,800 square kilometers and is bounded on the north by Georgia, on the east by Azerbaijan, on the south by Iran and the Nakhichevan region (a separate part of Azerbaijan), and on the west by Turkey. A country of some 3.3 million persons, it is located in the Transcaucasian region of southeastern Europe between the Black Sea and the Caspian Sea; its capital is Yerevan.

Armenia's major industries include chemicals, machinery, and textiles; among its chief agricultural products are grapes for wine, potatoes, and cotton. Poor economic conditions contributed to the emigration of some 100,000 Armenians in 1998 and 1999.

Type of Government: Presidential-style parliamentary republic, with a president, a prime minister and government (cabinet), a unicameral legislature, a judiciary, and a constitutional court

Dates of Constitutions: 1863, 1922, 1936, 1978, and 1995

Constitutional History

Ancestors of the Indo-European Hayq or Hayk, as Armenians call themselves, conquered the Urartu civilization occupying present-day Armenia in the seventh century B.C. The name *Armenians* is derived from the Greek word for members of a legendary Armen tribe. The territory became part of the Persian empire around 550 B.C. and was conquered by Alexander the Great in 331 B.C. and by the Romans 140 years later. Under King Tigranes II ("the Great"), Armenia extended its power under the Romans in the first century B.C., becoming an area of contention between the Roman and Parthian-Persian empires for the next several centuries.

The Kingdom of Armenia lasted nearly five hundred years but was finally split into two parts—one under the domination of the Byzantine empire and the other under Persia. Armenians had adopted the Christian religion around 300 A.D., so when the Persians attempted to convert them to Zoroastrianism, they rebelled in 451. Armenia was ceded to the Arabs in 653, and then, beginning in 806, the Bagratid family was installed to rule over the Armenians. Armenian cultural development and relative independence continued during the Middle Ages until invasions by the Byzantine Greeks and Seljuk Turks in the eleventh century.

From the sixteenth to the twentieth centuries Transcaucasian Armenia was generally ruled by the Ottoman Empire as an autonomous community under religious leaders of the Armenian Apostolic Church accountable to the central government. Russia's influence in the region began in the eighteenth century, and by 1863 reform in the Ottoman government allowed Armenia to have its own constitution. The question of which camp Armenia was to be in after the Russo-Turkish War, which ended in 1878, led to a number of massacres of Armenians by both sides. During World War I the Ottoman government's mass deportation of some 1.75 million Armenians to the Middle East is conservatively estimated to have resulted in 600,000 deaths.

Armenia, Azerbaijan, and Georgia forged a Transcausian alliance after being conquered by the Russians. In May 1918 Armenia declared itself an independent republic, which the Allied forces and Turkey recognized in 1920. A constitution was promulgated on February 2, 1922, but that same year the three nations were merged into the Transcausian Soviet Federated Socialist Republic within the Soviet Union. In 1936 a new Soviet constitution approved by Stalin allowed the three Transcaucasian countries to separate and become individual Soviet republics. Then in 1978 Armenia adopted a constitution based on the 1977 "Brezhnev" constitution for the Soviet Union. On September 23, 1991, Armenia again declared its independence, which became official on December 26, when the Soviet Union was dissolved.

Fighting between Christians and Muslims intensified in 1992 and 1993, in particular over claims to the Armenian enclave of Nagorno-Karabakh in neighboring Azerbaijan. A cease-fire occurred in 1994, and on July 5, 1995, a new constitution strengthening the powers of the president was adopted by referendum. A constitutional commission, however, was created by the Armenian parliament in 1998 to study possible changes. Violence reemerged on October 27, 1999, when the prime minister, speaker of parliament, and eight others were gunned down in parliament and forty people were taken hostage.

Influences

The 1995 constitution of Armenia is similar to a number of other constitutions of former republics of the Soviet Union, with a strong executive president and a parliamentary-style legislature.

The Constitution

The preamble to the 1995 constitution of Armenia declares the Armenian people's "faithfulness to universal values," noting in part that the document was adopted "to ensure the freedom, general well-being and civic harmony of future generations...."

Articles 1 proclaims: "The Republic of Armenia is a sovereign, democratic state, based on social justice and the rule of law." According to article 2, "[P]ower lies with the people [who] exercise their power through free elections and referenda, as well as through state and local self-governing bodies and public officials as provided by the Constitution."

Fundamental Rights

"The state," proclaims article 4, "guarantees the protection of human rights and freedoms based on the Constitution and the laws, in accordance with the principles and norms of international law." Rights protected by the constitution include the multiparty system, private ownership of property, the environment and natural resources, equality before the law, nondiscrimination of citizens on the basis of "national origin, race, sex, language, creed, political or other persuasion, social origin, wealth or other status," the rights of those accused of crimes, and the right to life, except that the death penalty is permitted "[u]ntil such time as it is abolished ... for particular capital crimes, as an exceptional punishment."

Other human and civil rights enumerated in the constitution are security of the person; prohibition against torture or treatment of a cruel or degrading nature; privacy and family life; freedom of movement, thought, conscience, religion, opinion, speech, and association, including the right to form and join political parties; assembly; and the right "to participate in the government of the state directly or through ... freely elected representatives," among others. Social and economic rights such as social security, health and medical care, and education are also guaranteed.

Division of Powers

"State power," mandates article 5, "shall be exercised in accordance with the Constitution and the laws based on the principle of the separation of the legislative, executive and judicial powers."

The Executive

President. As specified in article 49, "The President of the Republic of Armenia shall uphold the Constitution, and ensure the normal functioning of the legislative, executive and judicial authorities [as well as] be the guarantor of the independence, territorial integrity and security of the Republic." To become president, which carries a five-year term of office, a candidate must be thirty-five years of age, be a citizen of Armenia, have resided there for the preceding ten years, have the right to vote, and be elected by more than half the votes cast. In the event that no candidate receives the required majority, a runoff election is held in fourteen days between the two candidates with the most votes.

Powers and duties of the president enumerated in article 55 include addressing the people and parliament, signing and promulgating laws passed by parliament, dissolving parliament after consultation with that body's president and the prime minister, appointing and removing the prime minister, making appointments to civilian positions, representing Armenia in international relations, appointing and recalling diplomatic representatives, and receiving the credentials of foreign representatives. The president also appoints members and the president of the constitutional court and other judges, serves as the commander in chief of the armed forces, and grants citizenship, political asylum, orders and medals, and pardons to convicted individuals.

"The president may be removed from office," pursuant to article 57, "for state treason or other high crimes." Removal requires an appeal to the constitutional court by a majority of the members of parliament, followed by a two-thirds vote of all parliamentary members on the basis of the court's finding. The president's resignation may be accepted by a majority vote of all the members of parliament. A president's incapacity may, on the recommendation of the government and a determination of the constitutional court, lead to his or her removal by a two-thirds vote of all the members of parliament. Until a new president is elected, the duties of the office devolve first on the president of parliament and then on the prime minister.

Prime Minister and Cabinet. Article 85 declares: "Executive power ... shall be vested in the Government of the Republic of Armenia," adding that it "shall be composed of the Prime Minister and the Ministers." The president is to chair government meetings unless he or she recommends that the prime minister perform this function or in the event that the prime minister is requested to do so by a majority of the members of the government, for example, if the president is incapacitated. Under article 87 the prime minister is responsible for overseeing "the Government's regular activities and shall coordinate the work of the Ministers." Decisions of the government must "be signed by the Prime Minister and approved by the president."

The Legislature

Parliament. Article 62 vests legislative power "in the National Assembly." It is required "for purposes of organizing its own activities ... [to] adopt resolutions which shall be signed and published by its President." The assembly has 131 deputies (members), who must be citizens and have resided in Armenia for the preceding five years, be eligible to vote, and be at least twenty-five years of age. A deputy may not hold any other public office or "engage in any other paid occupation except for scientific, educational and creative work."

According to article 68, "Procedures for elections ... shall be prescribed by law" and the date of elections "shall be fixed by Presidential decree." Unless dissolved earlier in accordance with the constitution, each assembly's authority expires "in June of the fourth year following its election." Each deputy, pursuant to article 66, is to "be guided by his or her conscience and convictions" rather than "by any compulsory mandate." The constitution also notes that a deputy "may not be arrested and subjected to administrative or criminal prosecution ... without the consent of the National Assembly."

The assembly elects its president "for the duration of its full term by a majority vote of the total number of Deputies" and also elects two vice presidents. Article 74 mandates that "within twenty days of the formation of a newly elected National Assembly or of its own formation, the Government shall present its program" for approval, triggering a vote of confidence. A vote of no confidence must be proposed by "not less than one-third of the total number of Deputies" and also "must be passed by a majority vote of the total number of Deputies."

The deputies and the government both have the right to propose legislation. Laws and resolutions generally must be "passed by the majority vote of the Deputies present at a given sitting, if more than half of the total number … participate in the voting. …" Exceptions, such as in the case of the removal of the president or a presidential veto, are set forth in article 71. The president signs and promulgates laws passed by parliament but "may remand a law to the National Assembly with objections and recommendations … ," although he or she "shall sign and publish the law within five days of the second passing of such law." Article 112 permits laws to be submitted for a popular referendum on the request of the assembly or the government.

Besides passing laws and overseeing the government, the assembly makes certain appointments on the recommendation of the president and names "members and the President of the Constitutional Court from among the members of the Court." It may also "upon the determination of the Constitutional Court, terminate the powers of a member of the … Court."

Article 91 provides that "justice shall be administered solely by the courts in accordance with the Constitution and the laws." Courts expressly authorized in article 92 include "courts of first instance, the review courts and the court of appeals," as well as "economic, military and other courts as may be provided by law." It prohibits the "establishment of extraordinary courts."

The Judiciary

Article 94 creates a judicial council, presided over by the president of the republic, with the minister of justice and the prosecutor-general serving as vice presidents. Other council members are chosen from among legal scholars, judges, and prosecutors. The council aids the president in judicial selections and plays a role in training and disciplining judges.

As set forth in article 99, a constitutional court is composed of nine members, five of whom are appointed by the assembly and four by the president of the republic. Article 96 mandates that judges and members of the constitutional court are appointed for life, although there are mandatory retirement ages of sixty-five and seventy. They are to be "independent and may only be subject to the law."

Constitutional Court

Cases may be submitted to the court by the president, at least one-third of the deputies, presidential and parliamentary candidates, and the government. The court's jurisdiction includes deciding "on whether the laws [and] resolutions of the National Assembly, the orders and decrees of the President … and the resolutions of Government are in conformity with the Constitution, … whether the obligations [to be] assumed [in an international treaty] are in conformity with the Constitution," and "disputes concerning referenda and the results of presidential and parliamentary elections." The court also has jurisdiction in cases involving "obstacles facing a presidential candidate," "grounds for removal of the President," certain presidential actions such as declaring martial law, the president's incapacity, "removal of a member of the Constitutional Court," and "suspension or prohibition of a political party in cases prescribed by law."

Decisions of the court are "final, may not be subject to review and shall enter into legal force upon their publication," according to article 102.

According to article 111, "The Constitution shall be adopted or amended by referendum, which may be initiated by the President of the Republic or the National Assembly." The president is authorized to call for a referendum if requested to do so by a majority of the assembly deputies and "may remand the Draft Constitution or the draft of constitutional amendments" to the assembly "with his or her objections and suggestions." The president is directed to submit to a referendum when the draft constitution or amendments "are reintroduced by at least two-thirds of the total number of Deputies of the National Assembly." Article 114 prohibits amending articles 1 and 2, which, respectively, create Armenia's sovereign state and protect the power of the people; article 114 itself also may not be amended.

Amending the Constitution

AUSTRALIA

Since its first national constitutional law went into effect in 1901, Australia has been gradually severing its umbilical cord to Britain. However, a proposal to change from a constitutional monarchy to a republic was defeated in a referendum on November 6, 1999.

General Information

The Commonwealth of Australia, an island continent in the Southern Hemisphere, comprises approximately 7.7 million square kilometers, including the island of Tasmania on its southeastern coast. It is bounded on the west and south by the Indian Ocean; on the north by the Timor, Arafura, and Coral Seas; and on the southeast by the Tasman Sea. The country has a population of approximately nineteen million persons, and its capital city, Canberra, is located in a federal district called the Australian Capital Territory.

Australia produces thirty percent of the world's wool products, and seventy-five percent of its export revenues are derived from farm and ranch products and minerals. The country is virtually self-sufficient in its fuel needs and has major offshore oil and natural gas deposits for exploitation. A stable political tradition and a basically sound economy make Australia's future, barring cataclysmic events, a bright one.

Type of Government: Parliamentary federal commonwealth, with the "queen of Australia" (the British monarch), a governor-general and executive council, a prime minister and cabinet, a bicameral legislature, and a judiciary. (Technically, the British monarch is still head of state, but unlike in Canada, she has no power, even formally.)

Date of Constitution: 1901 (significantly amended in 1986)

Constitutional History

For thousands of years a stable population of approximately three hundred thousand aboriginal people resembling certain people of southern Africa lived a nomadic life here without an elaborate system of government. Shortly after the voyages of Ferdinand Magellan, the Portuguese sailor Pedro Fernandez de Quiros reached the shores of the New Hebrides islands in 1606 while searching for *tierra austral* (the "south land") for Phillip III, a Hapsburg king of Austrian blood. Thinking that he had reached his goal, he named the land Australia del Spirito Santo. Landings by Asians on the continent itself probably occurred earlier; Dutch sailors reached its shores in the early 1600s. The discovery of the continent, however, is credited to Capt. James Cook, who sighted Botany Bay on April 20, 1770.

In 1787 the British, to relieve prison overcrowding, sent 730 convicts and a contingent of marines to Australia under the command of Arthur Phillip. On January 25, 1788, the British flag flew over his encampment at Sydney Cove. Phillip was governor of the settlement— actually, an open-air prison—in the territory called New South Wales. Soon free settlers, as well as more convicts, arrived. The government of the territory was authoritarian, and the governors, including the notorious Capt. William Bligh of the mutinied H.M.S. *Bounty*, were given extensive powers, legislating virtually by fiat.

As the colonies created out of New South Wales began to develop permanent settlements, the desire for local representative government increased. In 1850 the Australian Colonies Act effectively transferred power from London to Australia; it established elective legislative councils as well as local legislatures that had the authority, with the assent of the governor or, in some cases, the monarch, to make laws for the "peace, welfare, and good government" of the respective colonies and to vary their individual constitutions. New South Wales, Victoria, South Australia, and Tasmania set up bicameral legislatures at the outset. Queensland became a colony in 1859, but Western Australia, which continued to receive convicts, did not acquire self-government until 1889.

Of the early acts affecting Australia passed by the British parliament, the most important was the Colonial Laws Validity Act of 1865, which ensured the legality of Australian laws that deviated somewhat from "English law" norms. This law, together with the 1850 act, propelled the various legislatures in the colonies to expand into sovereign bodies in their own right, while the gold rush of the 1850s spurred economic and demographic expansion.

By the turn of the century the colonies each had a parliamentary and cabinet form of government modeled on England's. All had adopted the secret ballot, sometimes called the "Australian ballot," with suffrage for males at least twenty-one years old; South Australia also granted suffrage to women. Some colonies, however, still permitted plural voting for property owners. A constitutional convention, with representatives also from New Zealand and Fiji, was held in 1883 in Sydney, but it succeeded only in creating a federal Australasian council with representatives from both self-governing and non-self-governing colonies. Although the council was legally sanctioned in 1885 by Britain, it did not receive the full support of the colonies; however, it provided a forum for colonial leaders.

On October 24, 1889, Henry Parkes from New South Wales called for the Australasian governments to consider the need for a true federation. Constitutional conventions held at the end of the century saw a consensus develop for the "states' rights" federalism of the United States, rather than the centralist federalism of Canada, to preserve substantial autonomy for the Australian colonies.

Australia's preeminent constitutional document is the Commonwealth of Australia Constitution Act, approved by the British parliament in 1900 and made effective January 1, 1901; it contains the nation's basic organic constitutional document, called the commonwealth constitution. Other constitutional documents include the individual constitutions of the six states, which also have their origins in British legislation; the British Statute of Westminster of 1931; and the Australia Act of 1986, enacted in both the United Kingdom and Australia, which severed intergovernmental ties between the two countries (except for the "queen of Australia"). Some constitutional principles regarding the structure and processes of government may also be found in ordinary legislation, prerogative instruments of the United Kingdom, custom and tradition, and judicial decisions.

Australia's constitution draws on the parliamentary system of government in the United Kingdom as well as the U.S. constitution, particularly the doctrine of enumerated powers in the allocation of authority between the federal and state governments.

Influences

The Constitution

Australia's basic constitutional document is contained in the ninth clause of the Commonwealth of Australia Constitution Act of 1900, a statute of the British parliament. Eight "covering clauses" present prefatory material. The first "whereas" clause of the act contains language similar to a preamble: "Whereas the people of New South Wales, Victoria, South Australia, Queensland and Tasmania, humbly relying on the blessings of almighty God, have agreed to unite in one indissoluble federal commonwealth. . . ." The sixth state, Western Australia, was added before the act became effective on January 1, 1901.

Fundamental Rights

Written guarantees of fundamental rights in the Australian constitution are scant: section 116 of article 9 of the 1900 act, which applies to the federal government, guarantees freedom of religion; section 117 prohibits discrimination but limits the extent of protection; and section 51 requires just compensation for federal property acquisitions. The system of fundamental rights protection in Australia works, however, because any interference with civil liberties has to be justified to a court's satisfaction by showing that the action in question had some statutory or judicial authority. No presumption of authority is given to the federal government. States, on the other hand, are not so tightly restrained.

For many reasons a tradition of guaranteeing individual rights and liberties woven into the unwritten fabric of national life may afford more protection than words simply embossed on parchment. Australia has seen several unsuccessful attempts to legislate a bill of rights; a "mini," or abbreviated, bill of rights proposal was defeated in a 1988 national referendum.

Division of Powers

In Australia, a federal state, power at the national level is divided between the prime minister and the legislature, without a strict separation of the executive and legislative authority, and the judiciary, which exercises judicial review, although judicial matters may be framed as administrative matters by the government and the parliament. The federal government is given specifically enumerated powers by the constitution, but with certain exceptions, such as defense, they may be exercised concurrently with the states; federal law prevails in the case of any inconsistency.

The Executive

Monarch. Technically, the British monarch and his or her representative, the governor-general, who is the titular commander in chief of the armed forces, still acts as head of state, assisted by an executive council. To a greater extent than in the Canadian constitution, however, this relationship is fictitious.

Prime Minister and Cabinet. The prime minister, as in Canada, is not mentioned in the original constitutional document yet is the real head of government as the leader of the majority party in the lower house of parliament. Any actions by the governor-general are taken solely on the advice of the elected government leaders.

The ministers who make up the cabinet are responsible for their acts and the acts of the government departments they oversee to the lower house of parliament, which can vote to force a minister's resignation. In practice, a minister is simply dropped or moved to another position if the majority party so desires. Major actions taken by the ministers are formalized in an executive council presided over by the governor-general. The executive branch today dominates the legislature because of the strength of the political party system in Australia, the fact that the cabinet controls the legislative proposals introduced in the parliament, and the fact that much legislation delegates powers to the executive branch. Lobbying, for example, focuses on ministers and other executive branch officials rather than on legislators, as in the United States.

The Legislature

Parliament. The upper house of the bicameral Australian federal parliament is called the senate, and the lower house is called the house of representatives.

Upper House. Senators sit for six-year maximum terms; half are elected from the states and territories every three years. A 1973 law fixed the number of senators from the two territories, the Australian Capital Territory and the Northern Territory, at two each, and a 1983 law increased the number of senators from each state from ten to twelve. Originally, the senate was to be a house of review for legislative proposals; however, the strong party system forces the senate to act generally along party lines.

Lower House. Members of the house of representatives are elected for terms of three years, but the body may be dissolved earlier. Article 9, section 24, of the 1900 act requires that the number of seats be set by law, based on population, and "as nearly as practicable, twice the number" of the members of the upper house.

Section 51 of part 5, article 9, of the 1900 Commonwealth of Australia Act lists the subject areas for which the federal parliament may legislate. These are areas in which federal legislation preempts state legislation.

A uniquely Australian procedure to end stalemates in which the senate twice rejects house-passed proposals is created by section 57. The two houses may be dissolved, and after new elections, if the same stalemate occurs, a joint sitting of the houses may be convened to vote on the proposal. This double dissolution occurred in 1974 and 1975, nearly triggering a constitutional crisis.

Most bills are introduced in the lower house by the government. The first reading is a formality, but at the second reading the government explains the proposal and major debate can occur. If passed on second reading, the bill goes to committee, where the opposition's views are considered. After the committee reports out the bill in final form, there is a formal third reading. If a majority of the senate is of the same party as the majority in the house, the bill will routinely be approved by that body. As a formality, assent by the governor-general or, in special cases, the monarch is also required.

In addition to ordinary legislation, parliament must approve treaties, rules issued by the governor-general in council implementing legislation, tax proposals, and government budget requests, as well as scrutinize the activities of the ministers and provide a forum for the opposition, which serves as a "ministry in waiting" should the government in power lose the confidence of the lower house.

The Judiciary

While the court system in Australia is similar in some respects to that of the United States, its high court is the ultimate court of appeal even from state courts, which provides more uniformity in the nation's laws. The acknowledged supremacy of the Australian constitution and the requirement of a referendum for amendments support the power of judicial review exercised by the Australian courts. Unlike in Canada, where court cases are styled *Regina v. _____*, in Australia they are styled *Commonwealth v. _____*.

High Court. Article 9, section 71 of the 1900 act describes Australia's highest court:

The judicial power of the commonwealth shall be vested in a federal supreme court to be called the high court of Australia, and in such other courts as it invests with federal jurisdiction. The high court shall consist of a chief justice, and so many other justices, not less than two, as the parliament prescribes.

The constitution requires that the justices be appointed by the governor-general in council, that they be removed only on request by both houses of parliament "for proved misbehavior or incapacity," and that their remuneration set by parliament not be diminished while they are in office. The mandatory retirement age is seventy years. Judicial appointments at the national level are made from the ranks of senior barristers by the chief government legal officer and the cabinet, with input from the bar association.

Federal Court. In 1977 a twenty-five-member federal court assumed some of the high court's jurisdiction and replaced the national industrial and bankruptcy courts.

Amending the Constitution

Chapter 8 of the 1900 act, Alteration of the Constitution, provides that a proposed amendment must be initiated in parliament by an absolute majority vote in each house and that after passage a referendum is to be held. If only one house passes a proposed amendment, the governor-general may also submit it to a referendum. Since the first referendum on November 8, 1906, forty-four such votes were taken as of September 3, 1988, and only eight amendments were approved. The double majority of votes necessary for approval—that is, a national majority as well as a majority in a majority of four of the six states—has the potential to make constitutional changes difficult.

With the centennial of the 1900 act approaching, there has been some debate about whether the constitution should be changed to create a republic with an Australian head of state (instead of the British monarch) and to add a bill of rights.

AUSTRIA

On April 27, 1945, Austria declared Germany's involuntary annexation of the country in 1938 null and void and proclaimed the restoration of its democratic republic in the spirit of its constitution of 1920.

General Information

The Republic of Austria in central Europe is 83,860 kilometers in area and borders on the Czech and Slovak Republics to the north and northeast; Hungary to the east; Italy and Slovenia to the south; and Switzerland, Liechtenstein, and Germany to the west. Vienna is the capital of this country of approximately eight million inhabitants.

The mixed economy of Austria, in which the government holds major interests in large enterprises and there is close cooperation among labor, management, and government, has led to stable development. An abundance of natural resources, a strong democratic government, and a key position in post–U.S.S.R. Europe should assure Austria of a bright future.

Type of Government: Presidential-style parliamentary federal republic, with a president, a chancellor (prime minister) and cabinet, a bicameral legislature, and judicial, administrative, and constitutional courts

Dates of Constitutions: 1867, 1920 (significantly amended in 1929 and restored in 1945), and 1934

Constitutional History

The Danube River area was settled between 80,000 and 10,000 B.C. Indo-Europeans called Illyrians moved into what is now Austria between 800 and 400 B.C. With an economy based on salt and iron ore, the people established tightly organized principalities. Later, the Romans incorporated much of the region into their empire as Rhaetia, Noricum, and Pannonia.

Germanic tribes succeeded the Romans, and after the sixth century A.D. Bavarians coming from the west met Slavs and Avars from the east. The Franks, under Charlemagne, created a system of border protectorates that lasted until an invasion by the Magyars, who were in turn ousted in the latter part of the tenth century. The Alpine foothills became known as Osterreich (Austria) during the rule of the Babenbergs, who persuaded Frederick I ("Barbarossa"), the Holy Roman Emperor from 1152 to 1190, to turn the margraviate of Austria into a duchy. In 1282 Rudolf of Hapsburg gave his two sons the duchies of Austria and Styria, laying the foundation for six hundred years of Hapsburg rule.

In 1526 Bohemia, Hungary, and Austria were united under the Hapsburgs, who built a vast worldwide empire. Out of the Congress of Vienna in 1815 emerged a "Holy Alliance" of Austria, Prussia, and Russia, which was enthusiastically supported by the hierarchically organized Austrian conservative elite, who owned most of the land. After the revolution of 1848 a neoabsolute government was put in place. In 1867, however, a constitutional law established a parliamentary monarchy with constitutional review and judicially protected civil liberties. Another basic constitutional law was adopted in 1920, after the Hapsburgs were driven out and Austria became a democratic republic.

The constitutional law enacted on October 1, 1920, created a parliamentary form of government with the basic power residing in the legislative branch. In 1925 the constitution was completed by defining the relationship between the united federation of the provinces, called the Bund, and the individual provincial states, the *Länder* (sing. *Land*). Amendments in 1929 provided for an elected federal president along the lines of the U.S. constitution rather than one appointed by the parliament. In actual practice, the Austrian presidency has not evolved into a highly political office.

A 1934 constitution created a "Christian-Corporate Federal State." After Austria was annexed by Nazi Germany in 1938, the country was administered under the Nazi constitutional structure called a *Gaue*. The 1920 constitution was restored on April 27, 1945. In February

2000 European Union nations and other democracies reacted negatively to the planned participation of the Freedom Party in a new coalition government and condemned the xenophobic and racially intolerant policies of its leader, Joerg Haider. To reinforce the country's commitment to tolerance for minority rights, a constitutional amendment, effective August 1, 2000, noted that the republic "recognizes its traditional linguistic and cultural plurality, which is represented in its [indigenous] national minorities. Language and culture, existence and preservation of these national minorities must be respected, secured and promoted."

Largely the product of one man, Hans Kelsen—who defined democracy as the closest approximation to the idea of freedom within the framework of social realities—the 1920 constitution was modeled on the basic parliamentary democratic form, but an amendment in 1929 created an elected president. The constitutional court established in 1921 became the model for other European countries.

The Constitution

Austria's basic constitutional document is the 1920 constitutional act, as revised in 1929. This act is supplemented, however, by the Basic Law of December 21, 1867; the European Convention for the Protection of Human Rights and Fundamental Freedoms (1950), which was incorporated into Austrian constitutional law in 1964; and a law defining procedures before the constitutional court. Changes in the constitution have also resulted from other legislation, such as a 1955 constitutional law on neutrality, a 1974 law concerning free and independent radio and television, a 1975 law on political parties, and a 1977 law regarding the office of the people's attorney (ombudsman).

The fundamental rights of Austrian citizens likewise are not set forth in one document, although many of them are detailed in the Basic Law of 1867. Article 7 of the constitutional act of 1929 states that federal nationals are equal before the law and may not be discriminated against on the basis of birth, sex, estate, class, or religion; a 1997 amendment guarantees "equal treatment to the impaired," while one passed in 2000 amends article 8 to guarantee that "language and culture . . . shall be respected, secured and fostered." Article 144 gives jurisdiction to the constitutional court to hear cases of alleged infringement of a constitutionally guaranteed right or personal right by an illegal ordinance, unconstitutional law, or unlawful treaty. Other rights include personal liberty; privacy in the home and in communication; and freedom of movement, immigration, property, association, expression, conscience, and religion, although churches must be recognized by law and are subject to the general laws of the land.

The division of powers between Austria's federal government and individual states is somewhat complicated. Basically, legislative and executive powers with respect to major policy areas are vested in the federal government. Among them are matters relating to the Austrian constitution, foreign policy, immigration, civil and criminal law, the judiciary, the military, and organization and command of the police. In the areas of nationality, certain professional organizations, housing, roads, and traffic regulation, legislative power rests with the federal government, but executive power resides in the states.

In matters such as social welfare, population policy, land reform, protection of plants against disease and pests, and certain aspects of electrical power, the federal government is charged with passing basic laws, but the states are responsible for enacting implementing legislation and executing the laws. Under article 15 of the constitutional act, the states may legislate and execute laws relating to other matters, such as zoning, regional planning, hunting, land transfers, conservation, and the local police.

The Austrian constitution divides the federal government into three branches: the executive branch (Verwaltung), including the president, as head of state, the chancellor (prime minister), as head of government, and the cabinet; the legislative branch (Gesetzgebung); and the judicial branch (Gerichtsbarkeit). Provision is also made for constitutional review. The actual separation of powers, however, is not as strict as under the U.S. constitution.

The Executive

President. The largely ceremonial head of the Austrian state is the federal president, who is elected for six years by direct, popular vote (the voting age is nineteen) and may be elected for only one succeeding term; a majority of the votes cast is required, otherwise a runoff election must be held between the two candidates who received the most votes. The president represents the republic in international matters, opens and discontinues parliamentary sessions, and can dissolve the parliament. The president appoints the federal chancellor, who is usually the leader of the majority party, and at the chancellor's suggestion appoints the other members of the federal government.

The duties of the president include signing treaties, administering the oath of office to governors of the provinces, verifying laws passed by the legislature, and commanding the army. The president is held responsible for violations of constitutional law and may be deposed by referendum pursuant to action by the legislature.

Prime Minister and Cabinet. Similar to a prime minister, the chancellor is head of the federal government. Together with the vice chancellor and the cabinet ministers, who may be aided by state secretaries, the chancellor conducts government affairs not otherwise entrusted to the president. Only ministers may vote on actions to be taken by the federal government, and such votes must be unanimous. The government approves draft bills to be introduced in the legislature.

The Legislature

Parliament. The bicameral Austrian parliament is called the Bundesversammlung (federal assembly). It consists of an upper house called the Bundesrat (federal council) and a lower house called the Nationalrat (national council).

Upper House. Based on their relative populations, the parliaments of the states send to the federal council a total of sixty delegates, who serve for periods corresponding to the term of their respective parliaments. In matters of legislation, if the federal council rejects a bill, its action may be overridden by what is called a "persisting vote" by the national council, which requires a majority vote in the presence of at least half the members. Ordinary laws are enacted in the two houses by a simple majority vote.

Lower House. The members of the national council must be at least twenty-one years old. Its 183 members are elected for four years by proportional representation and direct vote. This legislative body acts on bills, generally submitted by the federal government. Bills may also be introduced by a member of the national council if they are supported by at least eight other members, by the government on behalf of the federal council, or by referendum. A committee of the national council may propose amendments to a bill.

A bill may be subject to a first reading in which the sponsor explains the measure, after which it is either accepted and sent to a committee or rejected. The committee prepares a final version of the bill that is debated at a second reading, at which time the main debate on the measure occurs. Changes in the bill may be proposed if at least eight members agree. If no action is taken to return the bill to committee or suspend debate, a final vote, called the third reading, is taken, and the bill, if passed, then generally goes to the federal council for rejection, approval, or suspension of action for up to eight weeks. If the measure is approved or no action is taken during the eight-week period, the president confirms that the bill has constitutionally passed, and it is then promulgated by the chancellor as law.

Ombudsman. Following the Scandinavian constitutional practice of having an ombudsman, in 1977 Austria instituted the Office of the People's Attorney, which is accountable only to the national council. The office investigates complaints by persons who believe that they have been treated unjustly by any administrative authority.

"Judicial and administrative powers shall be separate at all levels of proceedings," states article 94 of the federal constitutional act. This has been interpreted to mean that laws that authorize appeals from an administrative authority to a court and vice versa, unless expressly provided for in the constitution, are unconstitutional.

The constitution provides for three types of courts: judicial, administrative, and constitutional.

Judicial Courts. Judicial courts are established by law, and judges are appointed by the president, although this authority may be delegated to a minister. A list of candidates is recommended by competent tribunals and submitted by the government.

Administrative Court. Under chapter 6 of a federal constitution act adopted in 1929, an administrative court is established in Vienna to adjudicate complaints based on illegal substantive or procedural rulings by administrative authorities. The justices are appointed by the federal president from candidates proposed by the government.

Constitutional Court. According to article 147, as amended in 1999, "The Constitutional Court consists of a President, Vice President, twelve additional members and six alternate members. The President, Vice President, six additional members and three alternates are appointed by the Federal President on the recommendation of the Federal Government. . . ." Qualifications for these members include being a judge, an administrative official, or a professor of jurisprudence. The president names the remaining members and alternates based on nominations by the legislature's upper and lower houses.

This court, in addition to determining the constitutionality of federal and state statutes under article 140 of the 1929 constitution act, hears cases involving certain monetary claims against government authorities and conflicts between the courts and administrative authorities; between the administrative court and all other courts, including conflicts between the administrative court and the constitutional court itself; between different courts; between the federal government and the state governments; and between state governments. The constitutional court arbitrates jurisdictional disputes between the federal and state governments and questions involving audits of public funds. Other cases the court may hear are those involving treaties, administrative regulations, statutes, elections, and the removal of persons from certain political offices, as well as impeachment cases and disputes involving violations of fundamental rights, which make up the bulk of its workload.

Constitutional amendments or constitutional laws require a two-thirds majority in the lower house with at least one-half the members present, whereas a referendum must be held for a total revision of the constitution, which is otherwise handled as ordinary legislation. Even a partial revision of the constitution may require a referendum if one-third of the members of either house request it.

AZERBAIJAN

Azerbaijan is an oil-rich nation that includes the Nakhichevan Autonomous Republic, which is separated from it by Armenian territory. Azerbaijan has maintained a protracted conflict with neighboring Armenia over the Armenian enclave of Nagorno-Karabakh, which lies wholly within its territory.

General Information

Some 86,600 kilometers in area, the Republic of Azerbaijan and the Nakhichevan Autonomous Republic in southern Europe's Transcaucasia are bounded on the north by Georgia and Russia, on the east by the Caspian Sea, on the south by Iran, and on the west by Armenia. Baku, on the Caspian Sea, is the capital of this country of approximately 7.7 million inhabitants.

In 1901 Azerbaijan provided half of the world's oil supply, and oil refining, chemicals, and textiles remain among its major industries. The country's chief agricultural products include grain, cotton, and rice. Although Azerbaijan's economy has suffered from its long recent conflict with Armenia, foreign interests in its petroleum potential make future prospects optimistic.

Type of Government: Presidential-style parliamentary republic, with a president, a prime minister and cabinet, a unicameral legislature, and a judiciary, including a constitutional court

Dates of Constitutions: 1924, 1936, 1978, 1991 (constitutional act), and 1995

Constitutional History

Settled in the ninth century B.C. by the Scythians, parts of Azerbaijan (a name perhaps derived from the Persian "land of fire," a reference to burning surface oil) fell to the Medes in the eighth century B.C. and then to the Persians two centuries later. Azerbaijan was conquered by Alexander the Great in 330 B.C. and annexed by the Romans several hundred years afterward. In the seventh century Arabs dominated the area and were succeeded by Turkish peoples several centuries later. Mongols, including Tamerlane, invaded the area, but in the sixteenth century the Azerbaijani Safavid dynasty seized power in Persia and held off the threat of the Ottoman Turks.

The Russians, however, began moving into northern Azerbaijani territory at the beginning of the 1700s. The Treaty of Turkmanchay in 1828 gave Russia the Nakhichevan khanates, and Azerbaijan was divided into three Russian administrative districts. Russia exploited the region, but the discovery of oil at the end of the nineteenth century resulted in an influx of Russians particularly in and around the port city of Baku. Riots erupted in 1905 as resentment over Russian domination and Armenian influence increased in the region. When the communists came to power in Russia, a short-lived Transcaucasian Federal Republic was formed by Azerbaijan, Armenia, and Georgia on April 22, 1918. After this collapsed, the Azerbaijanian Democratic Republic was created on May 28, 1918.

On April 28, 1920, the Russians used force to establish the Azerbaijan Soviet Socialist Republic. The country remained relatively independent until it was merged on December 30, 1922, with the other Transcaucasian nations of Armenia and Georgia to become the Transcaucasian Soviet Federated Socialist Republic, an integral part of the Soviet Union subject to the U.S.S.R.'s 1924 constitution. The Transcaucasian federation was dissolved under the Soviet Union's 1936 "Stalin" constitution, after which the separate Azerbaijan Soviet Socialist Republic took its place as a member of the union.

A 1978 constitution for Azerbaijan was installed based on the 1977 "Brezhnev" constitution of the Soviet Union. Like all constitutions of communist countries, it was more for show than for substance, with real power concentrated in the leadership of the Communist Party. The problem of dealing with Armenians who had taken jobs in Azerbaijan and with the Armenian population of Azerbaijan's enclave of Nagorno-Karabakh, however, led to a confrontation with the Communist Party leader Mikhail Gorbachev in May 1988. In August 1989 a national organization to protect Azerbaijani interests—including its territorial integrity—organized demonstrations and strikes to protest the Communist Party leadership.

A state of emergency was declared in January 1990, and on August 30 of that year the former Communist Party leader in Azerbajain declared the country's independence. He then orchestrated amendments to the constitution to provide for the election by the people of a national president. When the Soviet Union disbanded on December 26, 1991, Azerbaijan formally became an independent state under a constitutional act dated October 18, 1991. Work on a new constitution began in 1992, and the document was adopted on November 12, 1995.

Like the 1993 Russian constitution, the constitution of Azerbaijan follows the basic structure of the 1958 French constitution of the Fifth Republic.

Influences

The Constitution

Article 1 declares: "The sole source of state power in the Azerbaijan Republic [is] the people of Azerbaijan." According to article 2, the "[s]overeign right of the Azerbaijanian people is the right of free and independent determination of their destiny and establishment of their own form of governance. The people of Azerbaijan exercise their sovereign right directly—by way of nation-wide voting-referendum, and through their representatives elected based on universal, equal and direct suffrage by way of free, secret and personal ballot." Article 3 provides that the "following questions may be solved only by way of referendum: 1. acceptance of the Constitution of the Azerbaijan Republic and introduction of amendments thereto; [and] 2. change of state borders. . . ."

Azerbaijan "is a democratic, legal, secular, unitary republic," proclaims article 7, while article 8 provides that the "President of the Azerbaijan Republic is the Head of the Azerbaijanian state. . . ." The nation, relates article 10, "develops its relations with other countries based on principles recognized in international legal standards."

Articles 12 and 18, respectively, declare that the "highest priority objective of the state is to provide rights and liberties of a person and citizen" and that "[r]eligion . . . is separated from the state. All religions are equal before the law." Under chapter III, Basic Rights and Liberties of a Person and Citizen, rights and freedoms are guaranteed to "[e]veryone, from the moment when they are born. . . ." Such rights and freedoms include equal rights before the law and between men and women, as well as equality "irrespective of race, nationality, religion, language, sex, origin, financial position, occupation, political convictions, membership in political parties, trade unions and other public organizations."

Specific rights set forth in articles 27 through 39 are the right to life; limitations on the death penalty; freedom, including the freedom to travel; the right to own property, including intellectual property; the right to safety; personal immunity; sanctity of the home; and rights to marriage, work, strikes, rest, social security, and a healthy environment. Other rights guaranteed in articles 40 through 45, respectively, include the rights to a cultural life, protection of one's health, education, a home, a nationality, and the use of one's "mother tongue." Freedom of thought, speech, conscience, meetings (assembly), information, creative activity, citizenship, and participation in political life and government, including "the right to elect and be elected to state bodies and also to take part in referendum[s]," are expressly set forth in articles 54 through 56.

Chapter IV, Main Responsibilities of Citizens, notes that obligations include paying taxes, maintaining loyalty to and defending the "motherland," respecting state symbols, protecting historical and cultural memorials, and protecting the environment. But, according to article 79, "No one may be forced to carry out obligations contradicting the Constitution and laws of the Azerbaijan Republic."

Fundamental Rights

The constitution divides power among the legislative, executive, and judicial branches of government in the Azerbaijan Republic and the Nakhichevan Autonomous Republic.

Division of Powers

President. Article 99 declares: "Executive power in the Azerbaijan Republic belongs to the President of the Azerbaijan Republic." The president must be a citizen, not younger than thirty-five years old, a permanent resident for longer than ten years, be eligible to vote, not have been previously convicted, possess "no liabilities in other states," have a "university degree," and not maintain "double citizenship." According to article 101, the president is elected for a five-year term "by way of general, direct and equal elections, with free, personal and secret ballot" by a "majority of two-thirds of votes." If no candidate obtains the required majority, a runoff election decides by a "simple majority of votes." Under article 106, the president "enjoys the right of personal immunity," while article 108 states that the president and his family "are provided for by the state," including security by "special security teams."

Among the thirty-two powers and duties of the president set forth in article 109 are announcing elections to parliament; submitting the state budget to parliament for approval; approving state economic and social programs; appointing the prime minister with the consent of parliament; and dismissing the prime minister, appointing and dismissing cabinet ministers, and accepting ministers' resignations. Other major responsibilities include receiving the credentials of foreign representatives, concluding interstate and government agreements and submitting them to parliament for ratification, announcing referendums, signing and issuing laws, settling questions of citizenship, granting pardons, and announcing a state of emergency and martial law.

If the president resigns, the "Chairman of the Parliament . . . will carry out powers of the President" until a new president is elected. Article 107 authorizes parliament, by a majority of ninety-five votes, to dismiss the president "[i]n case of grave crime . . . on initiative of [the] Constitutional Court . . . based on conclusions of [the] Supreme Court."

Prime Minister and Cabinet. "For implementation of executive powers," states article 114, "the President . . . establishes [a] Cabinet of Ministers, [which] is the highest body of executive power of the President." The cabinet includes the prime minister, his or her deputies, ministers, and heads of other central executive bodies. The prime minister is appointed by the president with the consent of parliament. According to article 117, "As a rule, the Prime Minister . . . [chairs] meetings of the Cabinet of Ministers." The cabinet prepares a draft of the state budget for the president and implements it, along with economic and social programs. The cabinet also oversees "the ministries and other central bodies of executive power" and "solves other questions delegated to it by the president."

Parliament. Article 81 declares: "Legislative power . . . is implemented by the Parliament (Milli Majlis) of the Azerbaijan Republic." The Milli Majlis consists of 125 deputies "elected based on majority and proportional voting systems and general, equal and direct elections by way of free, individual and secret voting" for five-year terms. Any citizen of Azerbaijan who is at least twenty-five years of age is eligible, but persons with dual citizenship, who work for either of the other two branches of government, who are "involved in other payable activity except scientific, pedagogical and creative activity," and "religious men," among others, are disqualified under article 85. Deputies are granted certain immunities, including for their activity in parliament and from responsibility for criminal activity, except in cases "when the deputy may be caught in the act of crime." Deputies may lose their mandate by relinquishing Azerbaijani citizenship, being convicted of a crime, or resigning voluntarily, as well as on the abolition of a deputy's political party.

Two sessions of parliament must be held every year. The constitution gives it authority under article 94 to make rules regarding, among other concerns, the "use of rights and liberties of a person and citizen," presidential and parliamentary elections, referendums, the judicial system, legal proceedings, martial law and states of emergency, the status of "physical persons" and legal entities, family relationships, defense and military service, territorial borders, ratification "and denunciation" of international treaties, statistics and standards, commerce, and banking. Parliament also has authority to organize its own work, establish diplomatic representations based on presidential recommendations, approve the national budget and its execution, appoint judges based on the president's recommendation, and announce "war and conclusion of [a] peace treaty."

Deputies, the president, the supreme court, and the parliament of the Nakhichevan Autonomous Republic are authorized to initiate legislation in the Milli Majlis. Special rules apply with respect to bills not submitted by a deputy: they cannot be amended without approval of the initiator and must be voted on within two months. If passed, regular proposed laws are submitted to the president for signature within fourteen days, and urgent ones are submitted within twenty-four hours. Unless otherwise specified, a law becomes effective from the date of its publication.

Article 125 states that judicial power "is implemented by law courts ... through the Constitutional Court ..., Supreme Court ..., Economic Court ..., [and] ordinary and specialized law courts." Article 127 declares that "[j]udges are independent, they are subordinate only to the Constitution and laws of the Azerbaijan Republic, [and] they cannot be replaced during the term of their authority." Judges are also granted immunity, but their authority may be annulled or they may be dismissed by a vote in the Milli Majlis—an eighty-three-vote majority is required for judges of the three major courts and sixty-three votes for other judges. To be a judge, a person must be a citizen, be at least thirty years old, be eligible to vote, and have a "higher juridical education," as well as at least a five-year "working experience in the sphere of law."

The Judiciary

Supreme Court. Pursuant to article 131, the "Supreme Court ... is the highest judicial body on civil, criminal, administrative and other cases ... ; it exercises control over [the] activity of general and specialized law courts; [and] gives explanations as per practices in activity of law courts in an order envisaged by legislation." Judges are appointed by the Milli Majlis on the recommendation of the president.

Constitutional Court. Composed of nine judges, the constitutional court is appointed in the same manner as the supreme court. The president, parliament, cabinet ministers, supreme court, procurator's office, and the parliament of the Nakhichevan Autonomous Republic may pose questions to the court regarding, among other matters, the constitutionality of laws, decrees, orders, and legal actions of the president, parliament, and cabinet ministers, as well as decisions of the supreme court. The court also reviews "interstate agreements . . . that have not yet become valid," intergovernmental agreements, any "prohibition of political parties or other public unions," and the "settlement of disputes [over] authority between legislative, executive and judicial powers."

Constitutional amendments, according to article 157, may be proposed by the president or at least sixty-three parliamentary deputies, except that, according to article 158, neither "may propose amendments ... as per provisions contained respectively in Chapters VI [executive power] and V [legislative power] of the present Constitution." The document notes that changes "in the text of the Constitution ... may be made only by way of referendum," adding that the "Constitutional Court ... shall not take decisions concerning changes ... made by way of referendum." However, according to article 155, changes to certain articles, including 1 and 2, "are not subject to referendum." A proposal for an amendment must twice pass parliament at an interval of six months by a majority of ninety-five votes and be signed by the president after each vote.

Amending the Constitution

BANGLADESH

Sometimes defined as a Fourth World country because of its economic plight, Bangladesh is facing its problems under a democratic constitution adopted a year after it acquired independence from Pakistan on December 16, 1971.

General Information

The People's Republic of Bangladesh is approximately 144,000 square kilometers and is bounded by Burma and India on the east, India on the north and west, and the Bay of Bengal on the south. Dhaka (formerly Dacca) is the capital of this country, which has an estimated population of more than 129 million persons.

Industrial development in Bangladesh has been slow. The agricultural economy is based primarily on rice, jute, and tea. A country with one of the world's highest population densities, Bangladesh is prone to natural disasters such as severe, extensive flooding and cyclones.

Type of Government: Presidential-style parliamentary republic, with a president, a prime minister and cabinet, a unicameral legislature, and a judiciary

Date of Constitution: 1972 (significantly amended in 1991)

Constitutional History

Bengal, which is today the Indian state of West Bengal and the nation of Bangladesh, is believed to have been settled around 1000 B.C. by Dravidan-speaking people later called the Bang. Unlike India and Pakistan to the west, however, this area did not develop a large-scale civilization until about A.D. 700. A number of empires, including the Mauryan, Gupta, and Harsha, had influenced the territory earlier, but the Pala dynasty maintained a stable government that lasted until the twelfth century while spreading Buddhism. By the thirteenth century Islamic Turks had overrun Bengal, which then became loosely associated with the Delhi sultanate. Later, under the Moghuls, the province became the richest in the empire, only to be sapped of its resources by the military.

Moghul power was declining when the first Europeans arrived. After the Moghuls were defeated by Robert Clive of the British East India Company in a battle at Plassy in 1757, Britain expanded its hegemony over India, Pakistan, and Bangladesh. British rule ended in 1947 with the formation of an independent India and a bifurcated, Muslim-dominated eastern and western Pakistan. Eastern Pakistan was equally subject to the Pakistan constitution, but when national elections returned a majority of eastern Pakistanis to the parliament, the president, who was from western Pakistan, prevented the newly elected legislature from meeting and selecting a prime minister.

After suffering under the domination of the western portion of the country for almost twenty-five years, Bangladesh proclaimed its independence in 1971. India immediately attacked the mostly western Pakistani forces in the country, defeating them in two weeks. When the Bangladesh leader Sheik Mujibur Rahman, known as Mujib, was released from prison in western Pakistan and returned to his country, he was acclaimed president and then prime minister under a constitution adopted on November 4, 1972, which became effective on December 16. In three years, however, the government had become corrupt, and Mujib, by then a virtual dictator, was ousted in a military coup and assassinated. New elections in 1978 were followed by another coup in 1981, and in 1985 martial law was imposed. Following demonstrations and riots in 1990, free elections were held in 1991, after which Begum Khaleda Zia was sworn in as the first female prime minister. That same year, the constitution was amended to reduce the powers of the president and to restore a parliamentary system of government.

Influences

Bangladesh's constitution has alternated between providing for a strong president and a strong prime minister. In its present form, with its strong prime minister, it is similar to the British model, with a mostly ceremonial president.

The second paragraph of the preamble to the 1972 constitution of the People's Republic of Bangladesh, which was substituted in 1977, establishes the basis of the current document:

Pledging that the high ideals of absolute trust and faith in the almighty Allah, nationalism, democracy, and socialism, meaning economic and social justice, which inspired our heroic people to dedicate themselves to, and our brave martyrs to sacrifice their lives in, the war for national independence shall be the fundamental principles of the constitution.

Article 7 notes the underpinning of the republic: "All powers in the republic belong to the people, and their exercise on behalf of the people shall be effected only under, and by the authority of, this constitution."

Fundamental Rights

Article 26, part 3, Fundamental Rights, repeats an earlier reference to the principle that laws inconsistent with the constitution are void.

Rights guaranteed include equality before the law and equal protection of the laws; no state discrimination solely on the basis of religion, race, caste, sex, or place of birth; and equal rights for women, except for provisions favoring women or children and for the advancement of "any backward section of citizens." In spite of this language, reports of atrocities against women have increased in recent years. Other guarantees include no deprivation of life or liberty, except by law; no ex post facto criminal laws; and other protection for those accused of crimes. Freedom of movement, assembly, association, thought and conscience, the press, and speech and expression are guaranteed with some restrictions, as are the practice and propagation of religion, security in the home, and privacy of communication.

In 1988 the eighth amendment to the constitution made Islam the state religion but did not prohibit other religions.

Division of Powers

In Bangladesh, a unitary state, power is divided among the president, the prime minister, the legislature, and the courts, which exercise judicial review and advisory functions.

The Executive

Since September 1991 the Bangladesh government has returned to a parliamentary-style system with a ceremonial president as head of state and a prime minister as head of government. Article 48(3) provides that, with the exception of appointing the prime minister and the chief justice, the president "shall act in accordance with the advice of the prime minister," and article 55 provides that the executive power shall "be exercised by or on the authority of the prime minister."

President. The president is elected by the legislature for a five-year term and is limited to two terms. To be president, a person must be at least thirty-five years old, qualified for election to the legislature, and not have been removed from the office by impeachment. Once elected he or she is granted immunity for all official acts; however, the constitution provides for impeachment by a majority of the members of the legislature. According to article 61, the president has supreme command of the country's defense, as regulated by law. A 1996 amendment gives the president authority to administer such law during "a Non-Party Care-Taker Government" between parliaments.

Prime Minister and Cabinet. The president appoints as prime minister a member of the legislature "who appears to him to command the support of the majority of the members." He or she also appoints the ministers of state to serve as the other members of the cabinet, as well as the deputy ministers, nine-tenths of whom must be members of the legislature and one-tenth of whom may be chosen from persons eligible for election to the legislature. All executive acts are taken in the name of the president, but the cabinet is collectively responsible to the legislature.

| The Legislature | **Parliament.** Legislative power in Bangladesh is vested in a unicameral parliament, the Jatiya Sangsad ("house of the nation"). It consists of 300 members elected for five-year terms, unless dissolved earlier, directly from single territorial constituencies. By amendment in 1990 a minimum of thirty seats are reserved for women. |

Parliament. Legislative power in Bangladesh is vested in a unicameral parliament, the Jatiya Sangsad ("house of the nation"). It consists of 300 members elected for five-year terms, unless dissolved earlier, directly from single territorial constituencies. By amendment in 1990 a minimum of thirty seats are reserved for women.

To be elected, a person must be a citizen and at least twenty-five years old; he or she may not have been legally declared of unsound mind, "an undischarged insolvent," a citizen of a foreign state, convicted of certain crimes, or otherwise disqualified. No person may be a member of parliament from two constituencies at the same time but may run in more than one constituency. Once elected, members are granted certain privileges and immunities.

The president summons parliament to session and may address the body or send it messages. At the first sitting a speaker and deputy speaker are elected from among the members; they hold office until a successor is chosen. Parliament makes its own rules of procedure and is required at the least to appoint a public accounts committee and a committee of privileges.

Sixty members constitute a quorum, and, unless otherwise specified in the constitution, decisions are made by a majority vote of those present and voting, with the presiding member voting only in the case of a tie. All laws begin as bills in parliament and after passage require the assent of the president; except that if the president returns any bill other than a money bill, and the bill is passed again by a majority vote of the total membership, it becomes law even without the president's assent. Money bills may be introduced only on the recommendation of the president.

Ombudsman. Article 77 authorizes an office of ombudsman.

The Judiciary

Supreme Court. Article 94(1) provides that "there shall be a supreme court for Bangladesh (to be known as the supreme court of Bangladesh) comprising the appellate division and the high court division." Under article 100, the permanent seat of the supreme court is the capital. An amendment in 1988 to establish six new permanent benches of the high court outside the capital was struck down as unconstitutional because it was beyond the authority conferred by the constitution. This was the first instance in which an amendment was rejected by the court.

The chief justice and other judges are appointed by the president, and article 94(4) provides that they "shall be independent in the exercise of their judicial functions." A judge may not be removed except by the president on the recommendation of a judicial council consisting of the chief justice and the two next most senior judges. The council is also required to establish a code of conduct for judges.

The appellate division has jurisdiction to hear appeals from the high court division, and an appeal lies as a matter of right in cases involving the interpretation of the constitution, sentences of death or life imprisonment, or contempt of court. The high court has original, appellate, and other jurisdiction and may fashion remedies in cases involving enforcement of the fundamental rights in part 3 of the constitution. The president is authorized to request advisory opinions of the supreme court.

Amending the Constitution

According to article 142, a bill for an amendment must be passed by at least two-thirds of the members of parliament and becomes effective with or without the president's assent. However, amending the preamble or articles 8 (fundamental principles), 48 (the president), 56 (prime minister and ministers), or 142 (amendments) requires a referendum on whether the president should assent to it. The president will be deemed to have assented if the majority of the total votes cast are for him or her to assent.

Formerly the Byelorussian Soviet Socialist Republic in the Union of Soviet Socialist Republics, Belarus declared its independence in 1991. A democratic constitution approved in 1994 was revised in 1996 to give the president extensive powers.

General Information

The Republic of Belarus is some 207,600 kilometers in area and is bounded on the north by Lithuania and Latvia, on the north and east by Russia, on the south by Ukraine, and on the west by Poland. Minsk is the capital of this country of approximately 10.4 million inhabitants.

The major industries of Belarus include manufacturing, textiles, and machinery; among its chief agricultural products are grain and vegetables. Although the country's overall economic potential is good, its heavy reliance on imported raw materials and its Soviet-style collective-farm agriculture are obstacles to improvement.

Type of Government: Presidential-style parliamentary republic, with a president, a prime minister and council of ministers (cabinet), a bicameral legislature, and a judiciary, including a constitutional court

Dates of Constitutions: 1919, 1937, 1978, and 1994 (revised in 1996)

Constitutional History

Possibly the region from which the eastern Slavic peoples originated, the territory now known as Belarus was much fought over and partitioned throughout history. Belarus's capital, Minsk, was included in the early Kievan Rus' state in the early Middle Ages and became the capital of a principality in 1101. The Mongols invaded in the thirteenth century, and later the territory became part of the Grand Principality of Lithuania. At the beginning of the sixteenth century, the region became the spoils of Poland and Russia.

The Polish-Russian domination influenced the area's class structure, with the upper classes generally embracing Roman Catholicism and the lower classes (serfs) adhering to the Moscow-based Orthodox Church. The Russian empire under Catherine the Great incorporated the eastern part of the Belarus region in 1772, while the central portion, including Minsk, was acquired in the second partition of Poland in 1793. The remaining territory was merged into the empire during the third partition of Poland in 1795 and remained a part of Russia until 1918.

After the Russian Revolution in 1917 and the collapse of the Russian empire, the Soviet government in Russia gave part of Belarus and other lands to Germany under the terms of the Treaty of Brest-Litovsk of March 3, 1918. On March 25 of that year, however, anticommunists proclaimed the creation of an independent state called the Belorussian Democratic Republic. The Red Army occupied the area, and a new communist Belorussian Soviet Socialist Republic was installed with a constitution adopted on February 4, 1919. From then until 1991, when the U.S.S.R. fell, Belarus's constitutional history was closely linked to that of the Soviet Union, with nominal Soviet-style constitutions adopted in 1937 and 1978.

Belarus declared its independence on August 25, 1991, but true independence came about only after the breakup of the Soviet Union on December 26. The Belorussian Soviet Socialist Republic changed its name to the Republic of Belarus, although the country's ruling body continued to be the supreme soviet under its 1978 constitution. A new constitution, adopted on March 15, 1994, was revised by referendum on November 24, 1996, to incorporate additional presidential powers, such as issuing decrees and appointing members of the legislature's upper house as well as half of the constitutional court's membership.

Influences

Belarus's 1994 constitution creates a multiparty democracy with an executive president in place of the former collegial supreme soviet ruling body of the communists; the 1996 revisions reflected President Aleksandr Luskashenko's desire for greater executive powers, continuing the policy of concentrating power in a single person.

The Constitution

"The Republic of Belarus," declares article 1, "is a unitary, democratic, social state based on the rule of law," while article 2 proclaims:

The individual, his rights, freedoms and guarantees for their attainment manifest the supreme goal and value of society and the State. The State shall bear responsibility towards the citizen to create the conditions for the free and dignified development of his identity. The citizen bears the responsibility towards the State to discharge unwaveringly the duties imposed upon him by the Constitution.

"The people shall be the sole source of state power and the repository of sovereignty," notes article 3, which adds that they "shall exercise their power directly through representative and other bodies in the forms and within the bounds specified by the Constitution." According to article 4, "Democracy . . . shall be exercised on the basis of diversity of political institutions, ideologies and views. The ideology of political parties, religious or other public associations, [and] social groups may not be made mandatory for citizens." Later, in article 137, the constitution declares that it alone "shall have the supreme legal force. Laws, decrees, ordinances and other instruments of state bodies shall be promulgated on the basis of, and in accordance with, the Constitution of the Republic of Belarus."

Fundamental Rights

"Safeguarding the rights and liberties of the citizens . . . shall be the supreme goal of the State," proclaims article 21. "Every individual shall exercise the right to a dignified standard of living, including appropriate food, clothing, housing and . . . a continuous improvement of necessary living conditions." Other rights guaranteed in articles 22 through 62 include equality before the law; the right to life; personal liberty, inviolability, and dignity; the presumption of innocence; privacy, including "one's correspondence and telephone and other communications"; the right to be secure in one's home; freedom of movement; and choice of residence. Torture and "cruel, inhuman, or undignified treatment or punishment" and subjection to medical or other experiments without one's consent are prohibited. The constitution also guarantees freedom of thought, belief, and expression; the right to information; freedom of assembly and association; and the rights to participate in the governing of the state, to vote, and to acquire and own property.

"Religions and faiths shall be equal before the law," states article 16, adding that "[r]elations between the State and religious organizations shall be regulated by the law with regard to their influence on the formation of the spiritual, cultural and state traditions. . . ." Article 31 provides for freedom of religion "or to profess none at all. . . ."

Social rights include the right to work, to health care, to housing, to education, to social security, to preservation of one's cultural heritage and language, and to a "conducive environment." According to article 41,

The State shall create conditions necessary for full employment of the population. Where a person is unemployed for reasons which are beyond one's control, he shall be guaranteed training in new specializations and an upgrading of his qualifications having regard to social needs. . . .

Citizens are called on to abide by the constitution and public laws, respect national traditions and the rights of others, preserve the nation's historical and cultural heritage, protect the environment, pay taxes, and defend the republic.

Division of Powers

"State power in the Republic of Belarus," explains article 6, "is exercised on the principle of division of powers between the legislature, executive, and judiciary."

The Executive

President. As article 79 describes, the president is "the Head of State, the guarantor of the Constitution of the Republic, [and] the rights and liberties of man and citizen." It adds that the office holder "shall personify the unity of the nation, [be responsible for the] implementation of the main guidelines of the domestic and foreign policy, [and] shall represent the State in the relations with other states and international organizations." The president is also authorized to protect Belarus's sovereignty and "its national security and territorial integrity, [and] shall ensure its political and economic stability, continuity and interaction of bodies of state power. . . ." The president "shall enjoy immunity, and his honor and dignity shall be protected by the law."

To be president, a person must be a citizen by birth, thirty-five years old, eligible to vote, a resident for at least ten years, and, according to article 81, nominated by no fewer than 100,000 voters and "elected directly . . . for a term . . . of five years by universal, free, equal, direct and secret ballot" but "for no more than two terms." If a candidate fails to receive a majority of the votes, a runoff election is held between the two candidates with the most votes.

Among the president's responsibilities delineated in article 84 are calling national referendums and "regular and extraordinary" elections for parliament and local representative bodies; dissolving parliament; appointing the prime minister, with the consent of the lower house of parliament; determining the government's structure; forming, dissolving, and reorganizing the presidential administration; appointing the chairpersons of the constitutional, supreme, and economic courts "from among the judges of these courts" and dismissing them; appointing six members of the constitutional court and other judges; appointing six members of the national elections and referendums commission; and dismissing numerous officials. The president is also authorized to "deliver annual messages" to parliament; "chair meetings of the Government"; "appoint leading officials of bodies of state administration"; "resolve issues regarding the granting of citizenship"; grant pardons; conduct negotiations; receive credentials of diplomatic representatives; sign bills; and "have the right to abolish acts of the Government." The president is the commander in chief of the armed forces, is authorized to issue decrees and orders, and is empowered to form and head the nation's security council.

The president may be removed by a two-thirds majority vote of all the members of each house of parliament if "persistently incapable" of discharging official duties "on account of the state of his health"; the vote is based on the findings of an ad hoc parliamentary commission. The president may also be removed "for acts of treason and other grave crimes," again by a two-thirds vote of each house of parliament after charges supported by "a majority of the whole [lower house of parliament] on behalf of no less than one-third of the number of deputies" and an investigation by the upper house. If removal is based on a crime, the supreme court examines the merits of the charge. The prime minister, according to article 89, acts as president until a new president is sworn in.

Prime Minister and Cabinet. Under article 106, the executive power of Belarus is "exercised by the Government—the Council of Ministers. . . ." Consisting of the prime minister along with his or her deputies and ministers, the council is "accountable to the President . . . and . . . the Parliament."

Parliament. Article 90 declares that the national assembly, Belarus's parliament, "is a representative and legislative body" and includes two chambers: a lower house of representatives and an upper council of the republic.

The Legislature

Upper House. The council of the republic "consists of eight deputies from every region (*oblast*) and the city of Minsk, elected at the meetings of deputies of local Councils of Deputies . . . from among their ranks." The president appoints another eight members. All members must be citizens, thirty years old, and residents of the jurisdiction represented for at least five years. Parliamentary terms for both chambers are four years.

Responsibilities of the upper house include approving or rejecting draft laws, consenting to appointments by the president, and electing six judges of the constitutional court and six members of the national elections commission. Among other duties are adopting resolutions calling for the dissolution of local councils of deputies, participating in the removal of the president for treason or other grave crimes, and considering presidential decrees "on the introduction of a state of emergency, martial laws," or mobilization of troops.

Lower House. The house of representatives has 110 members, called deputies, who are elected "on the basis of universal, equal, free, direct electoral suffrage and by secret ballot." A deputy must be a citizen at least twenty-one years old and, according to article 92, "may simultaneously be a member of the Government."

Among the lower house's responsibilities are considering draft laws regarding changes in the constitution and other bills, calling presidential elections, consenting to the president's appointment of the prime minister, approving or rejecting "the report of the Prime Minister on the policy of the Government," and considering the prime minister's call for a vote of confidence. One-third of the members may bring up a no-confidence vote. It accepts the president's resignation and plays a role in removing the president for grave crimes.

"The first session of Parliament after the elections," mandates article 93, "shall be called by the Central Commission on Elections and National Referenda and shall be convened no later than 30 days after the elections." Each house elects a chairperson and a deputy who "conduct proceedings and [are] in charge of the regulations of the operations of the chambers."

Bills may be introduced in the lower house by the president, members of the legislature, the government, and at least 50,000 citizens eligible to vote. In general, a bill becomes law after approval by a majority of all the members of each house and signature by the president. The president may veto a bill by returning it to the lower house, "together with his objections," but a two-thirds majority of each house may override the veto.

The Judiciary

"The courts shall exercise judicial power in the Republic of Belarus," proclaims article 109. "The judicial system . . . shall be determined by the law." Article 110 adds that "[i]n administering justice judges shall be independent and subordinate to law alone." According to article 112, "The Courts shall administer justice on the basis of the Constitution, the laws and other enforceable enactments adopted in accordance therewith." Although the supreme court is referred to in the constitution, neither its makeup nor its jurisdiction is spelled out.

Constitutional Court. Article 116 explains that "[s]upervision of the constitutionality of enforceable enactments of the state shall be exercised by the Constitutional Court. . . ." The court is to consist of twelve judges ("specialists in . . . law"), six appointed by the president and six elected by the council of the republic for eleven-year terms, ending at age seventy.

The president, houses of parliament, supreme court, supreme economic court, and cabinet ministers may request rulings on matter such as "the conformity of laws, decrees and edicts of the President, international agreements and other obligations . . . to the Constitution and other instruments of international law. . . ." The president may also request a ruling on parliamentary "instances of systematic or flagrant violation of the Constitution."

Amending the Constitution

Articles 138 and 139 provide that the president or "no fewer than 150,000 citizens" may initiate an amendment in parliament, which may be adopted after it has been debated and approved twice by both houses with at least a three-month interval. Two-thirds of the elected deputies of both houses must vote in favor. Another provision allows for adoption of constitutional amendments by majority vote in a referendum. Certain sections of the constitution—those regarding the principles of the constitutional system, individual rights, the presidency, and amendments to the constitution—may be changed only by referendum.

Since 1830, when it became an independent country composed of two major linguistic cultures, Belgium has been evolving from a unitary into a federal nation. Major constitutional amendments in 1993 reflect this trend.

General Information

The Kingdom of Belgium in western Europe is approximately 30,500 square kilometers and is bounded by the North Sea and the Netherlands on the north, Germany and Luxembourg on the east, and France on the south and west. The capital of this country of approximately ten million inhabitants is Brussels, which is also the home of the North Atlantic Treaty Organization (NATO) and, as the headquarters of the European Economic Community, the de facto capital of Europe.

One of the first countries to undergo heavy industrialization, Belgium has the second largest port in Europe, Antwerp. Belgium is working to solve its recent economic problems, although it is a wealthy country by any standard. Constitutional changes in 1993 to decentralize power and consolidate the nation's evolving federal system of government should ease historic tensions over language and cultural differences between the Flemish- and French-speaking regions.

Type of Government: Federal parliamentary constitutional monarchy, with a monarch, a prime minister and cabinet, a bicameral legislature, and a judiciary

Date of Constitution: 1831 (significantly amended 1970–93)

Constitutional History

In 1795 the southern provinces of what is now Belgium were annexed to France. After the defeat of Napoleon and the Congress of Vienna in 1815, they were merged with Holland to form the United Kingdom of the Netherlands to serve as a buffer against a resurgence of French imperialism. Following an armed uprising against the Dutch army, this unity collapsed, and on October 4, 1830 a provisional government, including both Flemish and French provinces, declared the region to be an independent political state called Belgium. A national congress drafted a modern liberal constitution in two weeks, and it was officially proclaimed on February 7, 1831. Leopold I of Saxe-Coburg, who derived his authority from the constitution, became king on July 21, now a national holiday.

Belgium rapidly embarked on industrialization, but at the outset of World War I, despite the country's guaranteed neutrality, German troops occupied it in the process of invading France. When the war was over, Belgium became a member of the League of Nations and acquired small German-speaking regions on its eastern border and a mandate over two former German colonies in Africa, Rwanda and Burundi. Leopold II began developing the Congo Free State for his own gain and at the cost of an estimated eight million African lives.

Although Belgium had proclaimed its neutrality in 1936, Germany violated its territory again during World War II. Leopold III remained in the country during the war, and some claimed he collaborated with the Germans; however, voters approved his return in 1950 from exile after the war, albeit with diminished powers.

In the postwar years Belgium had to confront decolonization of its African territories and increasing friction between the Flemish- and French-speaking regions. Through a series of constitutional revisions in 1970, 1980, and 1988–89, culminating in extensive changes in 1993, the unitary state of Belgium has evolved into a federal nation-state with the decentralization of some powers of government.

Influences

The 1831 constitution was derived from the principles of the French Revolution and influenced by the fundamental rights included in the British constitution. More recently, linguistic and ethnic diversity has reshaped its structure.

The Constitution

Title 1, revised by a 1993 amendment, declares in part that Belgium is a federal state composed of French, Flemish, and German communities in three geographic regions, including the city of Brussels, as well as four linguistic regions: "the French ..., the Dutch ..., the bilingual ... Brussels-Capital, and the German language Region."

"All powers emanate from the nation," states article 33, which adds: "They are exercised in the manner established by the Constitution." It restricts federal authority to those matters "which the Constitution and the laws based on the Constitution formally confer upon it." Although the regions "are competent for other matters," according to article 4, any such laws must be "passed on a majority vote in each linguistic group of each of the Chambers [of the legislature], on condition that the majority of the members of each group are present and that the total votes in favor within the two linguistic groups attain two-thirds of the votes cast."

Fundamental Rights

Articles 8 through 32, Belgians and Their Rights, address nationality and political rights. They provide that all Belgians are equal before the law, guarantee individual liberty, mandate that penalties for crimes must be applied in accordance with the law, allow compensation for the taking of private property, and declare that the "civilian death penalty is abolished and may not be reestablished." Other individual rights include freedom of opinion and religion, private and family life, human dignity, freedom of the press, peaceful assembly, association, and the right to petition public authorities.

Among cited social and economic rights are the right to work, social security, decent housing, a sound environment, and education. Article 30 addresses the issue of language: "The use of the languages spoken in Belgium is optional; it may only be regulated by law and only pertaining to acts of public authorities and judicial matters."

Division of Powers

In Belgium, a federal state, power is divided at the national level among the monarch, as head of state; the prime minister, as head of government; the legislature; and the courts, one of which exercises limited judicial review.

The Executive

Monarch. Article 37 describes the role of the monarch: "To the King belongs the federal executive power, as it is regulated in the Constitution." The constitutional powers of the monarch are heridiary in the direct line of natural and legitimate heirs of Leopold Georges Chrétien Frédéric of Saxe-Coburg "in order of primogenture." The person of the monarch is inviolable; his ministers, however, are accountable for official acts, which they must countersign. "The King has no other powers," states article 105, "than those formally attributed to him and the particular laws passsed on the basis of the Constitution itself."

The king appoints and dismisses his ministers, federal secretaries of state, judges of the courts, and other officials; confers ranks in the army; issues decrees and orders necessary for the execution of the laws; "sanctions and promulgates the laws"; grants reprieves except in the case of a minister or a member of the communal or regional governments; and confers titles of nobility and military orders.

As in other constitutional monarchies, the Belgian king is a ceremonial head of state and is vested with executive authority by the constitution. Although he has no real political power, he has, in the words of one commentator, the right to be consulted, to encourage, and to warn.

Prime Minister and Cabinet. The prime minister is appointed by the king after elections held every four years; alternatively, after the lower house has adopted a motion of no confidence with "the absolute majority of its members," it then "proposes to the King the appointment of a successor to the Prime Minister."

The council of ministers (cabinet) is limited to fifteen members and, "[w]ith the possible exception of the Prime Minister, . . . consists of as many French-speaking as Dutch-speaking Ministers." It is responsible to the lower house of parliament, which can request the ministers' presence. The upper house may also request the presence of cabinet members with respect to certain matters, including the revision of the constitution or laws concerning the council of state. Article 100 provides that the ministers "have access to each Chamber [of the legislature] and they must be heard when they demand it."

According to article 103, the lower house "has the right to impeach Ministers and to bring them before the Court of Cassation. . . ." It also states that the "law determines the cases of responsibility, the penalties to be imposed on Ministers, and the manner of proceeding against them, either on the basis of an accusation accepted by the [lower house] or on the legal action brought by the injured parties."

Parliament. Article 36 provides that federal legislative power "is exercised collectively by the King, the Chamber of Representatives and the Senate." Members of both houses "represent the Nation, and not only those who elect them." In each, "the elected members . . . are divided into a French language group and a Dutch language group. . . ." The king convenes and closes both houses.

Upper House. The senate is composed of seventy-one members. Twenty-five are elected by the Dutch electoral college and fifteen by the French electoral college, while ten are designated by the council of the Flemish community, ten by the French council, one by the German community, six by the Dutch and Flemish senators, and four by the French senators. On election day six or seven senators must be domiciled in the bilingual Brussels region.

Lower House. The 150 members of the chamber of representatives are elected directly on the basis of proportional representation by citizens who are at least eighteen years old, resident for at least six months in the same commune, and not otherwise excluded from voting, which "is compulsory and secret."

The king and the lower house are authorized to act in cases of naturalization, "laws relative to civil and criminal responsibility of the Ministers," state budgets and accounts, and "determination of the army contingent."

Together the two houses are responsible, among others activities, for constitutional revision, laws adopted by the majority as required under the constitution's article 4, consenting to treaties and guaranteeing "international and supranational obligations," and the organization of courts and tribunals. Legislative bodies as well as the king may introduce bills, none of which "can be adopted, if it has not been voted on article by article." Bills adopted by the lower house are submitted to the senate, which has at most sixty days to adopt or amend them. If no action is taken within sixty days on a passed bill, it is considered passed and transmitted to the king for promulgation. If the senate amends a bill, the lower house "decides definitively, either to adopt or reject . . . [the] amendments."

"The judicial power," states article 40, "is exercised by the courts and tribunals. The decisions and judgments are executed in the name of the King."

Court of Cassation. "There is one Court of Cassation for the whole of Belgium," declares article 147. "This court does not deal with the content of the [cases] submitted to it, save [in regard to] the judgments of Ministers and the members of the government of a Community and a Region." Members are appointed by the king from lists presented by the court, as well as by the chamber of representatives and the senate. Judges are appointed for life and may not be removed or suspended "except by specific judgment."

Special Court of Arbitration

Traditionally, the Belgian courts have not had the power of judicial review, leaving to the legislature the task of ensuring the compliance of laws with the constitution. The courts, in fact, apply a "principle of reasonableness," which permits laws to be construed as much as possible in accordance with the constitution. Since the 1988 constitutional revision, however, a special court of arbitration has been given some judicial review functions in the areas of constitutional rights of equality, nondiscrimination, and freedom of education. The court exercises its powers by annulling laws and providing preliminary rulings.

Amending the Constitution

Amendment of the constitution begins with a uniform declaration of the need to revise the document, after which the legislature is automatically dissolved, and a new one elected and convened. Although intended to give the electorate an input into the amendment process, constitutional changes are generally not a major election issue. The revisions agreed to by the newly convened houses of the legislature then must be adopted by at least two-thirds of the total votes cast in each house with at least two-thirds of the members present.

Bolivia is named for Simón Bolívar Palacios, the South American hero of independence from Spain, but it has had a tortured constitutional history. The country has seen more military coups—nearly two hundred—than it has enjoyed years of independence.

General Information

The Republic of Bolivia, the fifth largest nation in South America, occupies a little over one million square kilometers and is bounded on the north and east by Brazil, on the south by Paraguay and Argentina, and on the west by Chile and Peru. La Paz is the capital of this landlocked country of some eight million inhabitants.

Bolivia's major industries include mining (tin, lead, and zinc, among other metals), smelting, and handicrafts; among its chief agricultural products are coffee, sugar cane, cotton, and coca (a source of cocaine). One of the poorest nations in the Western Hemisphere, Bolivia has an economy that has been growing modestly in recent years, partly as a result of the illicit drug trade.

Type of Government: Presidential republic, with a president and cabinet, a bicameral legislature, and a judiciary, including a constitutional tribunal

Dates of Key Constitutions: 1825, 1826, 1831, 1880, 1938, 1944, 1947, 1961, and 1967 (revised in 1994)

Constitutional History

As early 21,000 years ago, human settlements were made in the territory now occupied by Bolivia; cultivation began around 3,000 B.C. and copper production a millennium and a half later. The collapse of the Tiwanakan empire established in the Andes in the sixth century B.C. was followed by the rise of the Aymara people. They, in turn, were conquered in the first half of the first millennium A.D. by Quecha-speaking peoples, the Incas, from Peru (known as Biru), the "land of gold." The Inca empire quickly fell in 1532 to Spanish explorers seeking gold.

The discovery in 1545 of the world's largest concentration of silver at Potosí began the history of mineral exploitation in the Bolivian region. Spain ruled its colonial territory under the vice royalty system, which included regional governing councils *(audiencias)* that combined administrative, executive, and judicial powers. Rebellion against Spanish rule led by Simón Bolívar Palacios and Antonio José de Sucre resulted in a declaration of independence on August 6, 1825, and Bolivia's first constitution. As the first president of Upper Peru, as Bolivia was then called, Bolívar granted equality to all citizens and halved taxes, called for a redistribution of land to the native peoples, and sought to reduce the influence of the Catholic Church. Although he was in office only five months, his reforms were adopted in Bolivia's second constitution in 1826, which Bolívar wrote after leaving the country.

A new constitution in 1831 introduced a bicameral legislature of senators and deputies, while a confederation with Peru begun in 1836 ended three years later. The constitution of 1880 retained the bicameral legislature and fostered active political parties but only for the upper class. The 1938 constitution elevated the general welfare above private property, and its successor in 1944 allowed women to vote—only in municipal elections—and gave the president a six-year term with the possibility of immediate reelection. In the 1947 constitution the president's term was reduced to four years and the powers of the senate increased.

A revolution in 1952 aimed at joining workers, peasants, and the middle class against the ruling upper class led to a debate on Bolivia's political structure, which was reflected in a new constitution in 1961 authorizing universal suffrage, nationalization of the mining industry, and agrarian reforms. A military coup in 1964, however, brought a temporary return of the 1947 constitution, although the coup's leader, General René Barrientos Ortuño, was forced to accept a new, more liberal democratic constitution in 1967. Extensive revisions in 1994 detailed the composition of the legislature's lower house and created a new constitutional tribunal.

The Constitution

The 1967 constitution was influenced by Bolivia's liberal democratic constitution of 1880 and the socially progressive movements of Latin American countries such as Chile and Peru.

Article 1 of the constitution (as amended in 1994 and codified in 1995) states that Bolivia is "free, independent, sovereign, multi-ethnic and culturally pluralistic, constituted as a unitary Republic," adding that it "adopts for its government the democratic representative form, founded in the unity and solidarity of all Bolivians." According to article 2, "Sovereignty resides in the people; it is inalienable and imprescriptible...." Article 4 supports representative government and declares: "All Armed Forces or groups of persons who attribute to themselves the sovereignty of the people commit the crime of sedition."

"The Constitution of the State," proclaims article 228, "is the supreme law of the national juridical system. The courts, judges, and authorities shall apply it with preference over the laws...." Article 229 adds that the "principles, guarantees, and rights affirmed by this Constitution may not be altered by laws which regulate their exercise and they need no previous regulations for their enforcement."

Fundamental Rights

Article 6 guarantees the right to a "legal personality ... in accordance with the laws" and constitutional rights regardless of "race, sex, language, religion, political or other opinion, origin, economic or social condition, or any other. The dignity and freedom of the person are inviolable," it adds. "To respect them and protect them is a primary duty of the State."

Specific rights guaranteed include the rights to "life, health, and safety"; to free expression of "ideas and opinions, by any means of dissemination"; to "assemble and to associate for lawful purposes"; to work and obtain "fair remuneration for ... labor"; to receive an education and acquire culture; to teach, travel, and petition "individually or collectively"; and to receive social security. Rights related to privacy and individual property ownership are also provided, as are rights such as the presumption of innocence for persons accused of crimes. Torture, coercion, and extortion are prohibited, along with trials by special commissions. Article 15 adds that

Public officials who, without a state of siege having been declared, take measures for the molestation, confinement, or exile of citizens, and have these measures carried out, as well as those who close printing establishments or any other means of free expression ... shall be subject to payment of compensation for damage....

In article 3, the constitution acknowledges that the "State recognizes and upholds the Roman Catholic Apostolic Religion" but adds that "the public exercise of any other worship" is protected. "Relations with the Catholic Church shall be governed by concordats and agreements between the Bolivian State and the Holy See," it declares.

Duties of citizens catalogued in article 8 include complying "with the Constitution and the laws of the Republic," working "in some socially useful activity," acquiring "at least an elementary education," caring for and educating minor children, performing "civic and military services," cooperating "with the organs of the State and the community in social service and security," and safeguarding "the property and interests of the community."

Part three of the constitution sets out a number of "special regimes," which serve as directive principles to ensure basic rights as well as the orderly operation of government. Topics that affect rights include economic organization, national property, social relationships, agrarian and rural labor, education, cultural preservation, families, the armed forces, the national police, elections, and political parties; other areas addressed are state economic policy, revenues and budget, and administration of municipalities.

Division of Powers

"The independence and coordination of [legislative, executive, and judicial] powers is the basis of the government," states article 2. "The functions of the public power, legislative, executive, and judicial, cannot be united in a single organ."

President. "The executive power is exercised by the President of the Republic together with the Ministers of State," proclaims article 85.

The president and vice president are elected "by direct suffrage . . . [and] at the same time and in the same manner." The president's term of office is five years, with reelection possible after an intervening term. Presidential qualifications are "the same . . . [as] those of a Senator," but there are a number of disqualifications; bars to holding office include being a relative "by blood or affinity within the second degree" of a president or vice president in office during the last year before the election, being an active member of the armed forces, or being a member of the clergy or a minister "of any religious faith." Article 90 mandates that if none of the slates for president and vice president receives an absolute majority of the votes, "Congress shall elect [one] by an absolute majority . . . through oral roll call voting."

The president's powers and duties include complying with and enforcing the laws, issuing decrees and orders, negotiating and concluding treaties (which must be ratified by congress), conducting foreign relations, appointing diplomats and receiving foreign officials, "administer[ing] the national revenues" in accordance with law and "strictly subject to the budget," submitting an annual written message to the legislature, enforcing court decisions, granting amnesty, making certain appointments, and visiting "the various centers of the country at least once during his term of office in order to study their needs." The president also commands the armed forces and the national police force and is empowered to "exercise the highest authority in the National Agrarian Reform Service."

The president may not leave the country without the consent of Congress, which may also impeach the president and vice president, among others, "by a two-thirds vote of its total members"; a trial in the supreme court follows for any crimes committed.

Cabinet. Pursuant to article 99, "The business of public administration is conducted by the Ministers of State [cabinet]," who are appointed and removed by the president. Article 102 requires that all presidential decrees and orders "be signed by the appropriate minister [or] they shall not be valid nor obeyed." Ministers may attend legislative sessions, "but they must withdraw before a vote is taken."

Congress. "The legislative power is vested in the national Congress, composed of two chambers, one of Deputies and one of Senators," states article 46. "The chambers," adds article 48, "must function with an absolute majority of their members, at the same time, in the same place, and one house may not open or close its sessions on a different day from the other."

Upper House. "The Senate," according to article 63, "is composed of three Senators for each department, elected by universal and direct suffrage: two for the majority and one for the minority, according to law." Senators serve for five years and must be Bolivian by birth and have fulfilled military duties, be thirty-five years of age, and be registered voters.

The senate plays a role in impeaching certain officials, restoring Bolivian nationality, approving municipal ordinances on licenses and patents, conferring public honors, "granting pecuniary awards, by a two-thirds vote," approving certain high-level military and national police appointments, and approving "the appointments of ambassador and ministers plenipotentiary proposed by the President of the Republic."

Lower House. The chamber of deputies is composed of 130 members, half of whom in each of the country's departments or electoral districts "are elected in single-representative circumscriptions" by a simple majority; the other half are elected as established by law in so-called pluri-representative circumscriptions from lists headed by candidates for president, vice president, and senators. Deputies must be twenty-five years old but otherwise have the same qualifications as senators; they are proposed by political parties and elected for five years.

Deputies may initiate action with respect to the budget, development plans of the executive branch, "loans which obligate the general revenues," and approval of "military forces to be maintained in time of peace." They also play a role in determining a state of siege, impeaching certain officials, and proposing selected appointments by the president.

In addition to other joint duties, the two houses "verify the credentials issued by the electoral courts," undertake investigations, "decide on a declaration of war," determine the strength of the armed forces, and "authorize the trial of the President and Vice President" and others in the supreme court "for crimes committed in exercising their functions."

Legislation may be initiated by legislators, the vice president, and the executive branch. Bills must pass both houses and once "sanctioned by the legislative power may be objected to by the President" within ten days. A presidential veto is overridden if "both chambers, by a majority of two-thirds of the members present, find the objections to be unfounded."

The Judiciary

Article 116 declares that judicial power "is exercised by the Supreme Court of Justice . . . , the Constitutional Tribunal [and other judicial bodies] established by law."

Supreme Court. "The Supreme Court is the highest tribunal of ordinary, contentious, and administrative-contentious justice of the Republic," states article 117. "It is composed of twelve Ministers who are organized into specialized chambers, subject to the Law." Congress elects these ministers "by two-thirds of the votes of its total members from nominations proposed by the Council of the Judicature." Qualifications are generally the same as those for senators, except that these nominees must "hold the title of *Abogado* [lawyer] *en Provision Nacional*, and . . . have exercised with fitness a position in the judicature, one's profession, or university professorship for at least ten years."

The court is authorized to select by a two-thirds vote "members of the Superior Courts of Districts, from nominations proposed by the Council of the Judicature"; decide appeals "in the regular administrative jurisdiction"; determine "charges . . . against the President and the Vice President [and others] for crimes committed in exercising their functions"; resolve "contentious cases resulting from contracts, negotiations, and concessions of the Executive Power . . ."; and decide internal "boundary questions."

Constitutional Tribunal. The constitutional tribunal, according to article 119, is made up of "five Magistrates who form a single chamber and are appointed by . . . Congress by a two-thirds vote of members present" for a term of "ten unextendable years," but they may be reelected after an intervening period equal to their term in office. Qualifications are the same as for members of the supreme court. The tribunal's jurisdiction includes "matters of pure right against the unconstitutionality of laws, decrees and any kind of non-judicial resolution"; conflicts among public agencies; appeals involving taxes and legislative resolutions; "revision of Constitutional appeals of *amparo* and habeas corpus"; the "constitutionality of treaties" and "[p]etitions regarding procedures in reforming the Constitution."

Amending the Constitution

Article 230 provides that the constitution may be amended by Congress "in an ordinary law approved by two-thirds of the members present in each of the chambers." The law is then sent to the president, who may not veto it. The amendment is next taken up at the first legislative meeting of a "new constitutional term" and must pass both houses by a two-thirds vote. Each house discusses and votes on the amendment based on "the declaratory law." If enacted, the change "shall be forwarded to the executive for promulgation" without any right of objection.

A former member of the Socialist Federal Republic of Yugoslavia, Bosnia and Herzegovina declared its sovereignty on October 15, 1991, and in April 1992 the European Community and the United States recognized the independence of the new nation. Subsequent fighting among Bosnian Serbs, Muslims, and Croats led to intervention by the North Atlantic Treaty Organization (NATO) and the stationing of NATO troops there under a peace agreement drafted in Dayton, Ohio, on November 21, 1995.

BOSNIA AND HERZEGOVINA

General Information

The Republic of Bosnia and Herzegovina occupies approximately 19,700 square miles in the Balkan Peninsula of Eastern Europe. It is bounded on the north and west by Croatia and on the east and south by Yugoslavia. Sarajevo is the capital of this country of approximately 3.8 million persons.

Steel, mining, and timber are the country's major industries; key agricultural products include grains, fruits, and vegetables. The ravages of war, difficulties in switching from a socialist to a market economy, and widespread corruption have crippled Bosnia and Herzegovina's economy. Economic assistance and the presence of NATO troops under the terms of the Dayton Peace Accords, however, have helped improve the nation's financial situation.

Type of Government: Presidential-style parliamentary republic, with a collective Croat, Muslim, and Serb presidency; a chair and council of ministers (cabinet); a bicameral legislature; a judiciary; and a constitutional court

Dates of Constitutions: 1910, 1921, 1931, 1946, 1952, 1963, 1974, 1992, and 1995

Constitutional History

In the sixth and seventh centuries Slavs, Serbs, and Croats migrated into the part of the Balkan Peninsula now occupied by Bosnia (named for the Bosna River) and Herzegovina (derived from the *Herceg*, or duke, of Hum, a region to Bosnia's southwest). In 1326 Bosnia, governed by Hungary, annexed the territory of Hum, which separated in 1448 and became known as Herzegovina. After the Ottoman Turks conquered Bosnia in 1463, many Bosnians converted to Islam and became members of a military caste under the Ottoman governors.

The Congress of Europe held in Berlin in 1878 placed Bosnia-Herzegovina under the administrative authority of the Austro-Hungarian Empire. The Bosnian Serbs (Christian Orthodox), Muslims, and Croats (Roman Catholics) then formed three distinct factions based on their religious and cultural differences. In 1910, two years after Austria-Hungary formally incorporated the territory, a constitution was promulgated for Bosnia and elections were held for its parliament. On June 28, 1914, Archduke Franz Ferdinand, the heir apparent to the Austro-Hungarian throne, was assassinated in Sarajevo by Serbian nationalists who suspected him of opposing further expansion of independent Serbia—triggering the beginning of World War I.

With the defeat of Austria-Hungary in that war, a Kingdom of Serbs, Croats, and Slovenes was established in the Balkans on December 4, 1918. After the Muslim party and the Serbian radicals agreed to keep Bosnia and Herzegovina a separate administrative unit in the new kingdom, a constitution called the "Vidovdan" constitution was adopted on June 28, 1921. In 1929 Bosnia-Herzegovina became an integral part of the "land of the South Slavs," Yugoslavia. On January 26, 1929, however, King Alexander annulled the constitution and declared himself the only political authority. In 1931 he promulgated a new constitution that reestablished the parliament but made ministers and municipal officials serve at his pleasure.

Josip Broz, who was of mixed Croatian and Slovenian parentage, became the head of Yugoslavia's Communist Party in 1937. After leading the partisan antifascist resistance during World War II with the Soviet Union's support, Broz (known by his code name, "Tito") and the Communist Party filled the power vacuum at the end of the war. A communist-dominated constituent assembly promulgated a new constitution on January 31, 1946. Based on the Soviet Union's 1936 constitution, the Yugoslav document recognized five nationalities—Croats, Macedonians, Montenegrins, Serbs, and Slovenes—and created six republics similar to those in the earlier kingdom, five of them based on the five nationalities as well as Bosnia-Herzegovina with its three religious groups. Other socialist Yugoslav constitutions pertaining to Bosnia-Herzegovina were adopted in 1952, 1963, and 1974. This last constitution created a federal presidency of nine persons—one from each of the six republics and two from the autonomous provinces of Vojvodina and Kosovo, with Tito as the ninth member and president for life. A new Bosnian constitution in 1974 and later amendments guaranteed equal rights to all nationalities living within its borders.

After Tito's death in 1980, the collegial presidency continued, with one member becoming president for a year. (Switzerland is the only other major country with a presidency that rotates annually.) The Yugoslav federation began disintegrating, however, and a referendum ending on March 1, 1992, overwhelmingly supported Bosnian independence, which was opposed by most Bosnian Serbs because of its threat to Serbian domination of the region.

The Serbs' dissatisfaction led to war in which Serbian sympathizers and troops from the Yugoslav army attempted to undermine Bosnian independence. The fighting was to end officially under the Dayton Peace Accords signed in Paris on December 14, 1995. A new constitution for Bosnia and Herzegovina was adopted and annexed to the agreement along with fifteen international human rights agreements that were to apply in the country, including the Convention on the Prevention and Punishment of the Crime of Genocide (1948), Geneva Conventions I–IV regarding the protection of victims of war (1949), and International Covenants on Civil and Political Rights and on Economic, Social and Cultural Rights (1966).

Influences

Structurally similar to the U.S. constitution, Bosnia and Herzegovina's constitution creates a collegial presidency reminiscent of the 1974 Yugoslav constitution, consisting of "one Bosniac [Muslim] and one Croat, each directly elected from the territory of the Federation, and one Serb directly elected from the territory of the Republika Srpska [the Serbian political entity in Bosnia and Herzegovina]."

The Constitution

The preamble to the 1995 constitution of Bosnia and Herzegovina heralds a clear break with the former socialist system, noting that the nation is

Convinced that democratic governmental institutions and fair procedures best produce peaceful relations within a pluralist society, [and]

Desiring to promote the general welfare and economic growth through the protection of private property and the promotion of a market economy. . . .

Paragraphs 1, 2, and 3, respectively, of article I declare in part: "The Republic of Bosnia and Herzegovina, the official name of which shall henceforth be 'Bosnia and Herzegovina,' shall continue its legal existence under international law as a state, with its internal structure modified as provided herein and with its present internationally recognized borders. . . . [It] shall be a democratic state, which shall operate under the rule of law and with free and democratic elections. [It] shall consist of the two Entities, the Federation of Bosnia and Herzegovina and the Republika Srpska."

Fundamental Rights

"Bosnia and Herzegovina and both Entities shall ensure the highest level of internationally recognized human and fundamental freedoms," states article II, paragraph 1. Paragraph 2 adds that the "rights and freedoms set forth in the European Convention for the Protection of Human Rights and Fundamental Freedoms [1950] and its Protocols shall apply directly in Bosnia and Herzegovina. These shall have priority over all other law."

Specific human rights are enumerated in paragraph 3. They include the right to life; the right "not to be subjected to torture or to inhuman or degrading treatment or punishment"; the right "not to be held in slavery" or required to perform forced labor; "liberty and security of person"; "a fair hearing in civil and criminal matters"; privacy; "family life, home, and correspondence"; freedom of thought, conscience, religion, and expression; and "peaceful assembly and freedom of association." Other rights guaranteed include the right "to marry and to found a family" and the rights to property, education, and "liberty of movement and residence." Paragraph 4 addresses nondiscrimination, while paragraph 5 guarantees refugees the right to return and to regain or be compensated for lost property. Paragraph 8 directs authorities to "cooperate with and provide unrestricted access to: any international human rights monitoring mechanisms" established for the nation.

Power is divided among the country's geographic and ethnic entities, as well as among the executive, legislative, and judicial branches of government at the national level.

Division of Powers

President. "The Presidency of Bosnia and Herzegovina," declares article V, "shall consist of three Members: one Bosniac and one Croat, each directly elected from the territory of the Federation, and one Serb directly elected from the territory of the Republika Srpska." Members of the presidency are elected directly in each entity for four-year terms, may succeed themselves once, and then after a period of four years are again eligible for reelection.

The Executive

Members select a chair from among themselves by rotation or otherwise, as "determined by the Parliamentary Assembly." Paragraph 2 also requires that decisions of the presidency first be by consensus, but if that fails, then by a majority of the three members. The dissenting member, however, may within three days appeal any decision believed to be "destructive of a vital interest" of the entity he or she represents, and a two-thirds vote of the local legislature of that entity can nullify the decision.

The presidency is responsible, among other duties outlined in paragraph 3, for conducting foreign policy; appointing ambassadors; "negotiating, denouncing, and with the consent of [parliament], ratifying treaties"; executing parliamentary decisions; proposing an annual budget to parliament on the recommendation of the council of ministers; and reporting to parliament on annual expenditures. Under paragraph 5, the presidency is required to select and serve on a standing committee on military matters. "Each member of the presidency shall, by virtue of the office, have civilian command authority over armed forces," the article notes, adding that

Neither Entity shall threaten or use force against the other Entity, and under no circumstances shall any armed forces of either Entity enter into or stay within the territory of the other Entity without the consent of the government of the latter and of the Presidency. . . .

Cabinet. To chair the council of ministers (cabinet), the presidency nominates a person who "shall take office upon the approval of the House of Representatives," as provided in article V, paragraph 4. The chair in turn nominates the other members of the council, including a foreign minister, who similarly require the lower house's approval and only two-thirds of whom may come from the Federation of Bosnia and Herzegovina; deputy ministers "shall not be of the same constituent people as their Ministers." The council is responsible for "carrying out the policies and decisions of Bosnia and Herzegovina" and must resign if parliament issues a vote of no confidence.

Parliament. According to article IV, a parliamentary assembly consists of two chambers: an upper house of peoples and a lower house of representatives. Each house adopts its rules by

The Legislature

majority vote and selects "from its members one Serb, one Bosniac, and one Croat to serve as its Chair and Deputy Chairs, with the position of Chair rotating among [them]."

Upper House. The house of peoples numbers fifteen delegates: five Croats, five Bosniacs, and five Serbs. Members are selected by the legislative bodies of the respective territories, nine of whom make a quorum, provided that at least three Bosniac, three Croat, and three Serb delegates are present.

Lower House. The house of representatives comprises forty-two members elected directly by the people, two-thirds from the Federation of Bosnia and Herzegovina and one-third from the Republika Srpska. A majority of all members elected to this lower chamber create a quorum.

Paragraph 4 gives parliament responsibility for enacting legislation "as necessary to implement decisions of the Presidency or to carry out the responsibilities of the Assembly under this Constitution," deciding "the sources and amounts of revenues for . . . Bosnia and Herzegovina," approving the budget, consenting to the ratification of treaties, and other matters "necessary . . . or as . . . assigned to it by mutual agreement of the Entities."

All legislation must be approved by both chambers by a majority of those present and voting, although an effort is to be made "to see that the majority includes at least one-third of the votes of Delegates or Members from the territory of each Entity." As with decisions of the presidency, a decision of parliament may be declared by a majority of the appropriate delegates "to be destructive of a vital interest of the Bosniac, Croat, or Serb people." If a majority of the representatives of another entity object to this declaration, a joint commission of parliament tries to resolve the matter or it is referred to the constitutional court.

The Judiciary

Under article XI, paragraph 3 directs: "All proceedings in courts or administrative agencies functioning within the territory of Bosnia and Herzegovina when the Constitution enters into force shall continue in or be transferred to other courts or agencies . . . in accordance with any legislation governing the competence of such courts or agencies."

Constitutional Court

Article VI mandates a constitutional court with nine members; four are selected by the federation legislature and two by the Srpska legislature; three other noncitizens are selected by the president of the European Court of Human Rights after consultation with the presidency of Bosnia and Herzegovina. Parliament is authorized to "provide by law for a different method of selection of the three judges" named by the European Court of Human Rights.

The court's authority, as stated in paragraph 3, extends to disputes that arise between the various jurisdictional entities within Bosnia and Herzegovina, including "whether any provision of an Entity's constitution or law is consistent with this Constitution." Any such disputes may be referred only by a member of the presidency, the chair of the council of ministers, the chair or deputy chair or one-fourth of the members of either chamber of parliament, or one-fourth of either chamber of a legislature of one of the entities. The court is also granted appellate jurisdiction over issues "arising out of a judgment of any other court in Bosnia and Herzegovina," as well as in disputed matters concerning documents such as the European Convention for the Protection of Human Rights and Fundamental Freedoms. Decision are final and binding, states paragraph 4.

Amending the Constitution

"This Constitution," states article X, paragraph 1, "may be amended by a decision of the Parliamentary Assembly, including a two-thirds majority of those present and voting in the House of Representatives." However, according to paragraph 2, none of the human rights and fundamental freedoms cited in article II or this paragraph itself may be eliminated or diminished.

Independence from Portugal came easily for Brazil in 1822, but today this country, which is larger than the continental United States and endowed with a wealth of natural resources, struggles under a constitution that prevents needed government reform.

The Federative Republic of Brazil is some 8.5 million kilometers in area. It is bounded by the Atlantic Ocean on the east, and it abuts every other South American country except Chile and Ecuador. A nation of approximately 174 million persons, its capital is Brasilia, a planned, modern federal district two hundred miles inland.

The resources of Brazil, whose name is derived from a valuable red dyewood found along the country's coast, include rare metals such as chromium; until the mid-1970s its primary source of foreign exchange was coffee. Brazil weathered runaway inflation in the early 1990s and a severe economic downturn at the end of the twentieth century; it may have taken sufficient fiscal and monetary measures to maintain the nation's economic stability for the near future.

Type of Government: Presidential federal republic, with a president and ministers of state (cabinet), a bicameral legislature, and a judiciary

Dates of Constitutions: 1824, 1891 (suspended in 1930), 1934, 1937, 1946, 1967, and 1988

In 1500 the king of Portugal, eager to discover a western route to India, paid scant attention to a report that land had been found on the Portuguese side of the Spanish-Portugese demarcation line in the New World established by the Treaty of Tordesillas in 1493. A few years later, however, when the western route appeared to be illusory, the king began giving large tracts of Brazilian land *(capitania-donatorios)* to Portuguese nobles to develop. But the grantees failed politically, and widespread anarchy ensued, forcing him in 1549 to limit their power and create a governor-general for the whole territory.

Brazil came under the control of Spain in 1580, after its king inherited the throne of Portugal. During the seventeenth century Brazil became more politically stable and settlement of the interior began. Although Brazilian law has its roots in Portuguese law, an early source was the Codigo Philippino promulgated in Spain in 1603; together with Roman law, it had a marked influence in Brazil, where no civil code was enacted until 1916. After the separation of the crowns in 1640, Portugal continued to ignore its South American colony, although its liberal policies helped reduce inefficiency and corruption in government, eliminate Indian slavery, and bring about equality between the Brazilians and Portuguese.

At the beginning of the eighteenth century precious metals were discovered, and mining camps sprang up under the ruthless rule of men from São Paulo, called *Paulistas.* Minerals were added to the export of sugar grown on plantations with African slave labor. At the beginning of the nineteenth century Napoleon's forces in Portugal sent the king and fifteen thousand aristocrats sailing to Brazil, which became the seat of government. In 1815 the country was proclaimed the Kingdom of Brazil. The king was able to return to Portugal in 1821, leaving his son, who declared Brazil's independence the next year and was crowned emperor. Two years later a constitution was adopted that would become more honored in the breach, and by amendment in 1834 legislative assemblies controlled by presidents appointed by the Portuguese crown were established in the provinces.

When slavery was abolished in 1871, the king lost the support of the landowners and was forced to abdicate. The Federative Republic of Brazil was proclaimed in 1889 by a military leader, and in 1891 a new constitution, based on the U.S. model, was imposed on the country. Although this government was even less democratic than the monarchy, the economy grew with increased exports of natural rubber and coffee, which amounted to three-fourths of the world's supply in 1901. The republic developed steadily until 1910 but then experienced two decades of turmoil. In 1930 the constitution was suspended after a revolution led by Getulio Vargas, who served as president and virtual dictator until 1945. New constitutions were promulgated in 1934, 1937, and 1946, after Vargas's ouster. Vargas was again elected president in 1950 but killed himself in 1954. His successors struggled with a deteriorating economy, and when the president resigned in 1961 the legislature created a parliamentary system; the military allowed the constitutional government to continue for three more years.

From 1964 to 1985 Brazil was governed by the military, even though some "elections" were held under a 1967 constitution that established a military-technocrat government. The popular Tancredo Neves was elected president in 1985, but he died suddenly and his vice president took office instead. Strikes and natural disasters ensued, exacerbated by the president's lack of initiative. In 1992, just as a new president seemed ready to take the drastic measures necessary to turn around the government and the economy, scandal led to his resignation. Subsequently, runaway inflation and a scandal-plagued congress have only made matters worse.

A new and excessively detailed constitution approved September 2, 1988, and effective October 5, has been held by the courts to preclude laying off employees in the swollen ranks of the government, and it contains other restrictions that hamper programs for privatizing state industries, essential steps in revitalizing the economy. But, when asked in 1993, the people rejected constitutional reform and a chance to change the system of government, confirming the current presidential structure.

Influences

The drafters of the 1988 Brazilian constitution realized the need not only for political reform but also for social and economic reform, so they created a document modeled on the Portuguese constitution. Such constitutions have been categorized as *dirigiste* types—ones that go beyond simply organizing powers and guaranteeing rights, in the classical, eighteenth-century sense, to include programs for reshaping society.

The Constitution

The short preamble to the constitution describes the aim of the document as instituting "a democratic state for the purpose of ensuring the exercise of social and individual rights, liberty, security, well being, development, equality, and justice...."

Article 1 states:

The Federative Republic of Brazil, formed by the indissoluble union of the states and municipalities and of the federal district, is a legal democratic state founded on: 1—sovereignty; 2—citizenship; 3—the dignity of the human person; 4—the social values of labor and of free enterprise; and, 5—political pluralism.

All power emanates from the people, who exercise it by means of elected representatives or directly, as provided by this constitution.

Article 2 declares the powers of the union to be the legislative, executive, and judicial, "independent and harmonious," while article 3 sets forth the nation's fundamental objectives, which include the eradication of poverty and substandard living conditions.

Fundamental Rights

Chapter 1, entitled Individual and Collective Rights and Duties, is included under title 2, Fundamental Rights and Guarantees, and lists many detailed rights, freedoms, and guarantees, such as equal rights and duties for men and women; freedom from torture or inhuman treatment; freedom of expression of thought, although anonymity is forbidden; freedom of conscience and the exercise of religious cults; the inviolability of private life, honor, the home, and secrecy (privacy) of communication; freedom of association, except for paramilitary organizations; the right to property and inheritance; and the right to petition the government in defense of rights against illegal acts or abuse of power.

Legal rights include due process of law, the presumption of innocence, and habeas corpus proceedings. There is also a "habeas data" process to ensure accuracy of government information about a person. Social rights are spelled out in some detail in the constitution and include education, health, work, housing, leisure, security, social welfare, protection for motherhood and childhood, aid to the poor, and workers' rights, political rights, and political parties. The constitution also deals with economic and financial order and social order.

In Brazil, a federal state, power at the national level is divided among the president, as head of state and government; the legislature; and the courts, which exercise judicial review.

President. Article 76 provides that executive power is to be exercised by the president of the republic, assisted by ministers of state. The president and vice president, who must be Brazilian citizens by birth and at least thirty-five years old, run together. An absolute majority of votes is required for election; if necessary, a runoff is held between the two candidates who receive the most votes. The term of office is four years, and the president "may be reelected for only one subsequent term."

The Brazilian president has a role similar to that of the U.S. president. He or she is chief of administration and chief executive, responsible for foreign relations, and is commander in chief of the armed forces, with power to promote general officers of the military. In addition to initiating legislation and being able to veto bills, however, the president may also issue provisional measures having the force of law, without legislative authorization, and "delegated" laws, with such authorization. Thus, on exceptional occasions, the president is a legislator as well as an executive.

To some extent the president's powers under the 1988 constitution can be said to have been diminished when compared with the previous constitution: many appointments now depend on confirmation by the upper house of the legislature, and some administrative powers require approval by the legislature. But the executive has gained considerable political power as a result of being elected directly.

Article 85 lists acts of the president that are to be considered criminal, and article 86 provides for charges being brought against the president by a vote of two-thirds of the lower house of the legislature. If the president or vice president leaves the country for more than fifteen days without authorization by the legislature, the office may be forfeited.

Cabinet. The president also has the power to appoint ministers and secretaries of the cabinet, who coordinate and supervise the agencies of federal administration, implement the laws, and report annually on their ministries to the president.

Council of the Republic. Article 89 creates a council of the republic to be consulted by the president on high-level policy questions. Its members are the vice president, the top officers and the majority and minority leaders in both houses of the legislature, the minister of justice, and six Brazilian citizens over the age of thirty-five, two appointed by the president and two elected by each house of the legislature.

Congress. Legislative power in Brazil is exercised by a national congress composed of an upper house, the federal senate, and a lower house, the chamber of deputies.

Upper House. Three members of the senate are elected by majority vote from each of the states and the federal district for eight-year terms, but one-third and two-thirds are elected every four years, alternately, and each senator is elected with two substitutes. The areas of exclusive competence for the senate include conducting legal proceedings and trial of government officials; consenting, by secret ballot after a public hearing, to the appointment of certain officials and diplomatic heads of foreign missions; and establishing the debt limit of the nation, the states, the federal district, and the municipalities.

Lower House. Deputies are elected by a proportional system in each state, territory, and the federal district of Brasilia. The total number of deputies is established by law; however, according to the constitution each territory elects four deputies. The chamber's exclusive powers include instigating legal proceedings against the president, vice president, and ministers by a two-thirds vote of its members and following up should the president not render accounts for the past fiscal year within sixty days of the opening of a legislative term, as required by the constitution.

According to article 61, bills for supplementary and ordinary laws may be initiated by members or committees of congress, the president, the supreme federal court, superior courts, the attorney general, and citizens; however, the president alone can introduce bills relating to troops and certain administrative measures.

Generally, decisions in each house are by majority vote, a quorum being an absolute majority of members. If the president believes that a bill is unconstitutional or against the public interest, article 66 requires him or her to veto it. The veto may be rejected, however, by an absolute majority vote in each house by secret ballot.

Because Brazil does not have true political parties with party programs and discipline and because there are more than thirty parties, the president can generally create a majority in congress by distributing favors. The legislature's lack of power negates the ability to balance or check the power of the executive branch.

The Judiciary

Even though the Brazilian judiciary is more highly regarded than the legislature, it does not approach the prestige of the U.S. supreme court. The constitution establishes a supreme federal court, as well as federal regional courts, state and territorial courts, a labor court, electoral courts, military courts, and a court of the federal district. The supreme court is to propose a "statute of the judicature" for organizing the court system. Judges enjoy protected pay and life tenure and may be removed only when it is in the public interest.

Supreme Court. The supreme federal court is composed of eleven justices, who are nominated by the president and approved by the upper house of the legislature; they are selected from citizens between the ages of thirty-five and sixty-five with notable judicial learning and spotless reputations. The duty of the court is essentially to safeguard the constitution. For example, on extraordinary appeal it judges whether decisions are contrary to the constitution and whether a treaty or federal law is unconstitutional. On ordinary appeal, it reviews matters involving political crimes and writs of habeas corpus and mandamus. The court has first-instance jurisdiction in these and other types of cases.

Amending the Constitution

Proposals for amending the constitution may be made by at least one-third of the members of either house of the legislature; the president; and more than one-half of the legislative assemblies of the federal units. Measures are approved by a three-fifths vote in two readings in each house. The constitution may not be amended during a state of federal intervention, defense, or siege. No amendment may abolish the federal form of government; the direct, secret, universal periodic vote; the principle of separation of powers; or individual rights and guarantees.

Bulgaria's first constitution in 1879 was considered liberal for the time. After a century the country has returned to a democratic system that protects the rights of individuals against the state.

The Republic of Bulgaria is approximately 111,000 kilometers in area and is bounded by the Black Sea on the east, Turkey and Greece on the south, Macedonia and the territory of the former country of Yugoslavia on the west, and Romania on the north. Sofia is the capital of this country of some 7.8 million inhabitants.

During the communist regime between 1944 and 1990, Bulgaria's generally agrarian economy was transformed into one based largely on industry and construction. Today the country is trying to develop into a democracy with a market economy.

Type of Government: Presidential-style parliamentary republic, with a president, a prime minister and council of ministers (cabinet), a unicameral legislature, a judiciary, and a constitutional court

Dates of Constitutions: 1879, 1947, 1971 (significantly amended in 1990), and 1991

In the seventh century A.D. the Bulgars from Asia conquered the Slavic people living in what is today Bulgaria. After a few hundred years the invaders were completely assimilated, and the Bulgarians converted to Christianity. The Bulgarian kings legislated through orders called *khrissovuli*, and the law developed from the Roman and Byzantine codes. Their territory expanded until the fourteenth century, when they were conquered by the Ottoman Turks, who administered the Bulgarians through the Orthodox Church until 1878.

After Turkey's defeat by Russia in 1878, a large Bulgarian state including eastern Rumelia and Macedonia was envisaged. Under the Treaty of Berlin, however, the European powers created a smaller principality, still a vassal state of the Ottoman Empire but with a constitution quite democratic for the time. The 1879 "Tirnovo" constitution, named for the medieval capital where it was drafted, extended suffrage to all males over twenty-one, created a unicameral parliament, and provided for freedom of religion, speech, press, and assembly, as well as for local self-government and free elementary education. When the Russian czar's favorite nephew was installed as prince, he suspended the constitution, only to be forced to abdicate after approving union with eastern Rumelia without informing the czar. The second prince, also an outsider, consistently circumvented the constitution.

At the beginning of the twentieth century Bulgaria appeared to be a relatively progressive nation, but its development was at the expense of a large foreign debt. In 1912 the Balkan War broke out, and Macedonia, which was coveted by Bulgaria, fell to the Serbs and Greeks. Bulgaria lost territory to Romania and Turkey in 1913, as it did again after World War I, having sided with Germany and Austria. Between world wars, political turmoil reigned; the country's second largest political party, the Communist Party, was banned in 1923.

Bulgaria joined the Axis powers in World War II but sued for a separate peace in 1944. However, the Soviet Union declared war and occupied the country, installing a communist regime through a resistance group called the Fatherland Front. In 1947 a constitution modeled closely on the 1936 "Stalin" constitution of the Soviet Union, except for its unicameral legislature, was promulgated. It vested sovereignty in the legislature, but real authority lay with the Communist Party.

From 1958 on, attempts were made to draft a new constitution, which finally went into effect in 1971. Under it, Bulgaria remained a socialist state of working people headed by the working class, with the Communist Party—the only legal party—having the leading role in society and the state. The 1971 constitution was significantly modified in 1990 to reflect changes similar to those sweeping eastern Europe and the Soviet Union. On November 15, 1990, the country's name was changed to the Republic of Bulgaria, and on July 12, 1991, a new constitution was adopted that reflected a multiparty democracy intent on moving toward a free and open society. In 1994, however, socialists (former Communist Party members) won a majority of seats in Bulgaria's parliament.

Influences

Elements of other European parliamentary-style constitutions are evident in Bulgaria's constitution.

The Constitution

In the preamble to the 1991 constitution of the Republic of Bulgaria, the representatives of the constituent assembly, the Seventh Grand National Assembly, declare their loyalty to "elevating to the ranks of supreme principle the rights of the individual" and resolve to "create a democratic, law-governed, and social state...."

Article 1 establishes the source of sovereignty:

(2) The full power of the state originates with the people. It is exercised by the people directly and through the authorities identified in this constitution.

(3) No group of people, political party, or other organization, state institution, or individual person may usurp the right to exercise the people's sovereignty.

Fundamental Rights

"The fundamental rights of the citizen are irrevocable," states article 57(1), but the article then provides that the rights may not be abused or exercised to the detriment of others and that some rights may be limited under extreme conditions.

"The Republic of Bulgaria," notes article 4(2), "guarantees the life, dignity, and rights of the individual and provides conditions for the development of the individual and civil society." According to article 6(2), "All citizens are equal in the eyes of the law. No limitations to their rights or privileges are permitted on the basis of race, nationality, ethnic affiliation, sex, origin, religion, education, beliefs, political affiliation, personal or social position, or property status."

Chapter 1, Fundamental Principles, and chapter 2, Fundamental Rights and Obligations of the Individual, set forth rights and guarantees such as freedom of religion and, with some limitations, freedom of expression and the press; the inviolability of private property and payment in advance for taking of such property; and protections for those accused of crimes, as well as for the family, motherhood, and children. Article 46(2) provides that spouses enjoy equal rights and obligations in marriage and the family.

Division of Powers

Article 8 divides power in Bulgaria, a unitary state, among the executive, legislative, and judicial branches, including the president, as head of state; the prime minister, as head of government; the legislature; and the courts. Express provision is made for judicial and constitutional review.

The Executive

President. The president, as head of state, is elected with the vice president to a five-year term by an absolute majority in direct elections in which at least one-half of the voters participate. To be president, a person must be a citizen by birth, at least forty years old, qualified to be elected to the legislature, and a resident of the country for the previous five years.

The president is commander in chief of the armed forces and appoints and dismisses members of the high command. Other powers and duties of the president include scheduling the elections for the legislature, local governing bodies, and national referendums authorized by the legislature; issuing appeals to the people and the legislature; concluding treaties; promulgating laws; appointing and dismissing ambassadors at the request of the council of ministers; appointing and dismissing other state officials in accordance with law; awarding orders and medals; granting pardons; and, after consulting groups in the legislature, suggesting the formation of a government by the leader of the majority group.

According to article 103(1), "The president and the vice president may not be held liable for any actions committed by them in the performance of their duties, with the exception of treason or violation of the constitution."

Prime Minister and Cabinet. With the guidance of the prime minister, the council of ministers (cabinet) implements domestic and foreign policy in accordance with the constitution and the laws.

Parliament. A unicameral parliament, named the Narodno Sobranie (national assembly), legislates and supervises the government. It consists of 240 representatives elected for four-year terms. Any Bulgarian citizen who does not also hold other citizenship, is at least twenty-one years old, and is not legally disqualified may be elected; after registering to run, candidates must resign any state position.

At the first session of the assembly, members elect a chairman and deputy chairman. The chairman summons the assembly to sessions, prepares the parliamentary agenda, and opens and presides over meetings. Permanent and temporary commissions (committees) are also elected. One-half of the representatives constitute a quorum, and, unless otherwise required by the constitution, decisions are made by a simple majority vote.

The powers and duties of the assembly include adopting the state budget; determining the amount of taxes; scheduling the election of the president; calling for national referendums; appointing and dismissing the prime minister and, on his or her recommendation, the cabinet; making changes in the cabinet on the advice of the prime minister; creating, reorganizing, and dissolving ministries as proposed by the prime minister; ratifying certain types of treaties; and declaring war and making peace.

Article 117 of chapter 6, entitled the Judicial Branch, states:

(1) The judicial branch protects the rights and legitimate interests of citizens, juridical persons, and the state.
(2) The judicial branch is independent. Judges, court assessors, prosecutors, and investigators are guided strictly by the law in the exercise of their functions.
(3) The judicial branch has a separate budget.

The court system consists of a supreme court of appeals, a supreme administrative court, and other courts, including military courts. Courts are given authority by the constitution to supervise the legality of legislation and the actions of administrative bodies.

Supreme Courts. The supreme court of appeals oversees the accurate and equal application of laws by the courts. The supreme administrative court does the same in the administrative area and rules on the legality of acts by the council of ministers, individual ministers, and other acts indicated by law. The presidents of the two supreme courts and the prosecutor general are appointed for single seven-year terms and are dismissed by the president of the republic when proposed by a high judicial council, a twenty-five-member body that appoints, promotes, demotes, transfers, and dismisses judges and other judicial personnel.

The constitution also creates a constitutional court of twelve members who serve nine-year terms and may not be reelected. This court provides mandatory interpretation of the constitution, settles government jurisdictional disputes, rules on the consistency of treaties with the constitution, issues opinions on the constitutionality of political parties

The Legislature

The Judiciary

Constitutional Court

and associations, and, among other things, rules on charges brought against the president and vice president by the legislature.

Amending the Constitution   Amendments may be introduced by one-fourth of the members of the legislature and the president. They must be approved by a majority vote of three-fourths of the members after three rounds of balloting on separate days. If the vote for an amendment is at least two-thirds but not three-fourths, however, it may be reconsidered between two and five months later; if it repasses by the same two-thirds margin, it will be approved. The constitution also provides for a "grand" national assembly of 400 members "elected in accordance with common procedures," which, among other duties, may adopt a new constitution.

The 1991 signing of the Agreements on a Comprehensive Political Settlement of the Cambodian Conflict was the first step in the transition to a new Cambodian government, which culminated in the adoption of a new constitution in 1993.

The Kingdom of Cambodia on the southeast Asian peninsula formerly known as Indochina encompasses slightly more than 181,000 square kilometers and is bounded by Thailand on the northwest, Laos on the north, Vietnam on the east and southeast, and the Gulf of Thailand on the southwest. Phnom Penh is the capital of this nation of roughly twelve million persons.

Cambodia's economy was devastated by war and brutally repressive internal policies in the 1980s, and the history of conflict between political factions makes prospects for a stable government problematic.

Type of Government: Parliamentary constitutional monarchy, with a monarch and royal council, a prime minister and cabinet, a bicameral legislature, a "national congress," a judiciary, and a constitutional council

Dates of Constitutions: 1947, 1970, 1976, 1981, and 1993 (significantly amended in 1999)

Approximately four thousand years ago a Neolithic culture inhabited the region of Cambodia. Later people of Malayo-Polynesian origin merged with Khmer people from southeast China. Chinese accounts mention a powerful Hindu state, influenced by the Indian culture, called Funan, which was founded around A.D. 100. In the sixth century, after Funan's decline, the Khmer state of Chenla came to prominence. It was followed by the Hindu-Buddhist Kingdom of Angkor, in Kampuchea (Cambodia) at the beginning of the ninth century. Angkor became an empire under the Khmer rulers, who owned the land as well as the subjects and derived their power from their divinity, a concept known as *devaraja*. Below the royal family were the Brahmin priests, commoners, and a large slave class.

Near the end of the twelfth century, Cham, a Muslim neighbor, invaded Angkor. The Chams (or Champas) were later driven out, but in 1353 the Thais captured Angkor. In 1431 the Khmers recaptured their capital, only to abandon it, after which a period referred to as the "dark ages" set in. In 1863 the French, who had been excluded from India by the British, established a protectorate in Cambodia, thus saving it from being partitioned between Thailand and Vietnam, which often fought over control of Cambodian territory.

The French had other protectorates in Indochina, but the Cambodians paid the highest taxes per capita. This inequity led to a nonviolent tax revolt in 1916, and in 1925 villagers killed a French official who threatened to arrest tax delinquents. Before and during the French colonial period, Chinese and Vietnamese immigrants often played key roles in the commerce and government in Cambodia.

Nationalism was developing among a small urban elite before World War II, but in 1941 the French selected as the new king Prince Norodom Sihanouk, the nineteen-year-old great-grandson of the recently deceased king, who they thought was more manageable than the rightful heir. After the war Cambodia became an autonomous state in the French Union, and in 1947 a constitution was promulgated that left the powers of the king ambiguous. In 1953 Sihanouk dissolved the legislature and declared a state of martial law, and the French acceded to the country's request for full independence. When Sihanouk later failed in his attempt to amend the constitution to acquire more power, he abdicated, formed a new political party, and became prime minister when his party received eighty-three percent of the vote.

In 1970 the legislature gave Sihanouk a vote of no confidence, abolished the monarchy, and created the Khmer Republic. Sihanouk, in exile in Beijing, supported Cambodian communists, called the Khmer Rouge, who were aided by North Vietnam. The republic fell and was replaced by Democratic Kampuchea under a 1976 constitution that defined the postrevolutionary communist society as "workers, peasants, and all other Kampuchean working people." A blood bath ensued as the communist leader Pol Pot tried to restructure Cambodian society, killing between eleven and thirty-two percent of the population in three years.

Vietnamese forces took Phnom Penh and created a People's Republic of Kampuchea; its constitution, promulgated in 1981, defined Cambodia as a democratic state advancing toward socialism. Released from Khmer Rouge house arrest, Sihanouk sought help from the United Nations. In 1982, in Kuala Lumpur, Malaysia, a coalition of three anti-Vietnamese factions formed the Coalition Government of Democratic Kampuchea, with Sihanouk as president. Twelve years later agreement was reached among all the factions under United Nations auspices, and the constitution of the reconstituted Kingdom of Cambodia was adopted on September 21, 1993, and took effect three days later, when Prince Norodom Sihanouk was sworn in as monarch. Constitutional amendments of March 6, 1999, included the addition of an upper house to the legislature.

Influences

The 1993 constitution was influenced both positively and negatively by the 1947 constitution, particularly the problem of determining the succession to the throne.

The Constitution

"Cambodia is a kingdom whose king shall comply with the constitution and a multi-party, liberal democratic system," declares article 1. "The Kingdom of Cambodia is an independent, sovereign, peaceful, permanently neutral and non-aligned state." The country's motto—"Nation, religion, king"—is set forth in article 4.

Article 51 emphasizes that "the Kingdom of Cambodia adopts a multi-party liberal democratic regime. Cambodian citizens are the masters of the nation's fate."

Fundamental Rights

Chapter 3, Rights and Obligations of Cambodian Citizens, begins with article 31, which states, in part: "The Kingdom of Cambodia shall recognize and respect human rights stipulated in the United Nations Charter, the Universal Declaration of Human Rights, and all covenants and conventions related to human rights, and women's and children's rights."

The rights of citizens include equality before the law and entitlement to the same rights and freedoms and obligations regardless of race, color, creed, sex, language, religious belief, political tendency, ethnic origin, social wealth, or other status. The exercise of rights and freedoms, however, may not adversely affect the rights and freedoms of others and must be in accordance with law.

Division of Powers

In Cambodia, a unitary state, power is divided among the monarch, as head of state; the royal council, which elects a new monarch; the prime minister, as head of government; the legislature; the judiciary; and the constitutional council, which has limited pre- and postenactment constitutional review authority.

The Executive

Monarch. The first sentence of article 7 describes the monarch's role: "The king holds the throne but shall not hold power. The king shall be the head of state for life. The monarch cannot be violated." According to article 17, this sentence "absolutely cannot be amended." The monarch is the symbol of national unity, whose role is to guarantee independence, sovereignty, territorial integrity, the rights and freedoms of the people, and respect for international treaties.

Article 10 addresses the question of succession: "Cambodia's monarchy is of elected origin." According to amendments in 1999, seven days after the death of a king, a royal council consisting of the presidents of both houses of the legislature, the prime minister, supreme monks of both Buddhist orders, and the first and second vice presidents of the upper house elects a new king, who must be at least thirty years old and descended from prescribed royal blood lines.

The monarch formally appoints the prime minister and cabinet and signs decrees for government personnel actions, such as the appointment or dismissal of ambassadors and high civil and military officials, when presented to him by the cabinet, and actions with respect to judges when submitted by the supreme council of judges. The king is the supreme commander of the armed forces but appoints a commander in chief; receives credentials from foreign representatives; signs and ratifies treaties, with the approval of the legislature; bestows medals on the cabinet's recommendation; and grants military and civilian promotions according to law.

Article 30 provides that in the absence of the monarch the president of the upper house of the legislature becomes the interim head of state.

Prime Minister and Cabinet. According to chapter 10, on the Royal Government, the cabinet is chaired by the prime minister, assisted by deputies, along with state ministers, ministers, and state secretaries. All members of the royal government are collectively responsible to the lower house of the legislature for general policy and individually responsible to the prime minister and the lower house.

Parliament. The bicameral parliament consists of a senate (upper house) and a national assembly (lower house). Before amendments in 1999, the Cambodian parliament was unicameral.

Upper House. Article 99 specifies that the senate's membership may not exceed "half of all the members" of the lower house. Two senators are nominated by the king, two are elected by the lower house by majority vote, and the remainder are "universally elected" for terms of six years, after which they may be renominated and reelected. As article 112 provides, "The Senate has the dut[y] to coordinate the work between the lower house and the government."

Lower House. Cambodia's national assembly consists of at least 120 members who are "elected by free, universal, equal, direct and secret ballot" for five-year terms. Candidates must be Khmer citizens by birth of either sex, have the right to vote, and be at least twenty-five years of age. At its first session, the assembly chooses a chairman, vice chairmen, and members of legislative committees by a vote representing a two-thirds majority. In addition to passing legislation, the lower house is authorized to approve the national budget, grant general amnesties, and declare war.

Members of both houses are granted parliamentary immunity; any "accusation, arrest or detention . . . shall be made only with the permission [of the particular legislative body] except in cases of *flagrante delicto*. Legislation may originate in either house. "Any law approved by the Assembly and finally reviewed by the Senate and signed by the King . . . shall go into effect in Phnom Penh ten days fter signing and throughout the country twenty days after its signing."

National Congress. Article 147 creates a national congress, to be called by the prime minister once every year and chaired by the monarch. All citizens may attend the congress, whose purpose is to inform citizens on issues of national interest and to adopt proposals for consideration by authorities and the legislature.

The Judiciary

Article 128 declares that "the power of the courts is independent." The Cambodian courts' independence is to be guaranteed by the monarch, and the courts are to be impartial and protect the rights and freedoms of the people. A supreme council of judges, established by law and chaired by the monarch, the president of the supreme court, or its general prosecutor, may discipline errant prosecutors as well as errant judges, who may not be removed from office.

Historically, Cambodia has had no true judicial system, and it will be some time before the judicial system under the new constitution can be accurately assessed.

Constitutional Council

Chapter 12 creates a constitutional council to ensure respect for the constitution and interpret the constitution and laws. It may also determine contested elections of members of the legislature. The council consists of nine members having nine-year terms, although one-third of the members change every three years. Three appointments are made by the monarch, three by the lower house of the legislature, and three by the supreme council of judges.

The monarch, prime minister, or one-tenth of the members of the lower house, or one-fourth of the members of the upper house of the legislature may send draft laws to the council to be examined for constitutionality before promulgation. The monarch, the presidents of each house the legislature, the prime minister, and the same proportion of members of the houses of the legislature, or the courts may send a promulgated law to the council for such examination. The internal regulations of the legislature and other organic laws also must be sent to the council for examination before promulgation. The monarch must consult the council on all proposed amendments to the constitution. Any provisions of draft laws found unconstitutional may not be promulgated; if already promulgated, they may not be implemented. Decisions of the council are declared by the constitution to be "final."

Amending the Constitution

As article 151 states: "The initiative to review or to amend the Constitution shall be the prerogative of the King, the Prime Minister, the Chairman of the National Assembly at the suggestion of one-fourth of all the Assembly members." Amendments are adopted by a vote of at least two-thirds of the members of the lower house, except during a state of emergency or if such amendments might impinge on the multiparty liberal democratic system or the constitutional monarchy.

With the Constitution Act of 1982, including the Charter of Rights and Freedoms, constitutional emphasis in Canada has been significantly shifted from the diversity of the provinces to the diversity of the nation under "pan-Canadianism."

With an area of about ten million square kilometers, Canada, whose name is derived from the Huron-Iroquois word *Kanata* (settlement), is the second largest country in the world. Situated north of the United States's forty-eight contiguous states, it is bounded on the west by the Pacific Ocean and Alaska, on the north by the Arctic Ocean, and on the east by the Atlantic Ocean. In addition to bordering on all the Great Lakes except Lake Michigan, Canada is endowed with many large and small bodies of water. Ottawa is the capital of this country of more than thirty-one million inhabitants.

A highly industrialized country, Canada is in the top ten countries of the world in the value of its annual goods and services produced, and its citizens enjoy a standard of living nearly equal to that in the United States. Its major exports are cars, wheat, natural gas, lumber, oil, ores, pulp, and paper. The United States, Japan, and the United Kingdom are Canada's major trading partners.

Type of Government: Parliamentary constitutional monarchy, with a monarch (the queen of England), a governor-general, a prime minister and cabinet, a bicameral legislature, and a judiciary

Dates of Constitutions: 1763, 1791, and 1867 (significantly amended in 1982)

Just as social and economic conditions inform the constitutional process, so the geography of a country shapes the social and economic processes. Nowhere is this fact more evident than in the development of Canada. Unlike the other countries of the New World, Canada retains two strong links to its European history—British and French language and culture. The seeds of both took root in soil that also nurtured more than fifty aboriginal Indian nations and other native populations, who are today seeking the right of self-government. An agreement ratified in 1992 grants the Inuits in the Northwest Territory the right of self-government by 1999.

The human history of North America dates from around 12,000 B.C. The earliest inhabitants probably arrived via a land bridge between Siberia and Alaska. By the time of Columbus's first voyage, the Northeast was home to two linguistically similar tribes: the Algonquians and the Iroquois. In the Northwest were the Tlingt and Nookta, among others, and along the Arctic coast were the Inuit, or Eskimos, which derogatorily means "fish eaters." The native peoples had their own economic system, but there was little need or inclination for them to create a large, tightly controlled political organization or a theory of land ownership in the European sense.

Following Viking explorers in the early part of the eleventh century, John Cabot, an Italian exploring for England, discovered Newfoundland in 1497. Jacques Cartier followed in 1534. Although the Spanish and Russians arrived earlier, Capt. James Cook's visit to the Pacific Northwest in 1778 is the most noted by historians.

From the outset of European immigration Canada was a battleground of cultures and religions, although many settlers came to escape religious persecution and the devastation of religious wars in Europe. From 1625 to well into the twentieth century, Quebec, first permanently settled by Samuel de Champlain in 1608, remained hostile to French Protestants in part because of the influence of the Jesuits. The French settlements became known as New France. The British expanded northwest of Quebec and conquered the French territory after a battle on the Plains of Abraham on September 13, 1759, and another victory at Montreal a year later.

Immigrants were governed to a large extent by private charter companies, such as the Company of New France and the Hudson Bay Company. The Treaty of Paris in 1763 confirmed Britain's hegemony over the French territory, and a constitution was promulgated the same year; under it, four new governments were created, including one for Quebec, and governors were appointed and directed to call assemblies and make local laws, subject to approval of a council and assembly. To thwart the possibility of rebellion, the Quebec Act of 1774 granted Catholics the right to practice their religion and restored their traditional property and civil rights laws. In 1777 Britain relinquished the right to levy taxes without the consent of local representatives. The British parliament acted in 1791 to split Quebec into upper and lower Canada (today Ontario and Quebec) and give them an English form of government. Ultimate authority still rested in Britain, which had a legislative veto called the "royal disallowance" and made all the major political appointments.

In the following years grievances were voiced about the stranglehold of the governing elite, who feared rampant democracy and anyone who dared criticize the government. Reformers included William Lyon MacKenzie and Louis-Joseph Papineau, who drew on American Jacksonian democracy for their ideas. After rebellions in 1837 and 1838 challenging the politics of the elite, real reforms were instituted in the British North America Act of July 1, 1867. The act formally united upper and lower Canada with Nova Scotia and New Brunswick into "one dominion under the name of Canada." It vested executive authority in a governor-general and a council styled after the British privy counsel. The armed forces remained under the monarch, who, with the Canadian parliament, formed the legislature. The judiciary consisted of judges appointed by the governor-general from the bars of the respective provinces. The act also provided for the governments of the four provinces under their own constitutions.

Between 1867 and 1982 independence for Canada was a slow and gradual process. In 1931 Britain's Statute of Westminster retained only two controls over Canada: the power to amend certain provisions of its constitution and to keep its final court of appeals in Britain. Representatives of the dominion were included in the British war cabinet during World War I, and Canada was granted separate membership in the League of Nations after the war. The right of criminal appeal to the privy council was abolished in 1935 and in civil matters in 1949. On April 17, 1982, the Canada Act, including the Constitution Act, proclaimed by the British monarch gave Canada the right to internally amend its own constitution. Later that year Quebec's claim that the constitution could not be altered without its consent was rejected by the supreme court of Canada. From time to time political movements in the French-speaking province of Quebec support its secession from the rest of Canada; however, a referendum to declare Quebec independent failed by a narrow margin in October 1995.

Influences

Britain has had the most influence on the Canadian constitution. The Canadian concept of a federal system is somewhat unique, except that the solution to the problem of bilingualism in the provinces is similar to Finland's.

The Constitution

The April 17, 1982, proclamation of the Constitution Act by Elizabeth II, queen of England, noted its aims:

And whereas it is in accord with the status of Canada as an independent state that Canadians be able to amend their constitution in Canada in all respects;

And whereas it is desirable to provide in the constitution of Canada for the recognition of certain fundamental rights and freedoms. . . . "

Schedule A, article 2, of the 1982 act states: "No act of parliament of the United Kingdom passed after the Constitution Act, 1982, comes into force shall extend to Canada as part of its law." And article 52(1) of schedule B of that act provides that "the constitution of Canada is the supreme law of Canada, and any law that is inconsistent with the provisions of the constitution is, to the extent of the inconsistency, of no force or effect."

Schedule B, article 52(2), of the 1982 act declares that the constitution of Canada includes "(a) the Canada Act of 1982, including this act; (b) acts and orders referred to in the schedule; and (c) any amendment to any act or order referred to in paragraph (a) or (b)." The schedule referred to lists thirty acts, including the 1867 act. Article 52(3) directs that "amendments to the Constitution of Canada shall be made only in accordance with the authority contained in the Constitution of Canada."

Fundamental Rights

The Canadian bill of rights was passed in 1960, but inconsistent legislation could still be passed notwithstanding the act, and the jurisdiction of the provinces was unaffected. In 1969, however, the supreme court held that an act dealing with the Indians was discriminatory and violated the bill of rights. The Charter of Rights and Freedoms of 1982 has been held to be a part of the Canadian constitution, not merely an ordinary statute, and therefore the courts require that it be interpreted generously to give a full measure of the rights and freedoms it guarantees. The court has further ruled that a presumption of constitutional validity for laws is incompatible with the innovative and evolutionary character of the charter as a constitutional instrument.

The fundamental guarantees in the 1982 charter include the right to life, liberty, and security; freedom of conscience, religion, thought, belief, opinion, expression, the press and other media, peaceful assembly and association; the right to vote and be elected to the lower house of parliament or legislative assemblies; freedom to reside in Canada or travel, subject to reasonable restrictions; and the right to be secure from unreasonable search or seizure and arbitrary detention. Also included are equal protection of the laws, a number of safeguards in criminal procedures, and the right to use either French or English in debates or proceedings in parliament; both languages also were declared authoritative in statutes, records, and journals of parliament. Rights with regard to language and education in either language are spelled out in some detail. The charter states that it applies to the national parliament and government, the territories, and the legislatures and governments of the provinces.

Division of Powers

The 1867 act expressly divides legislative power between the federal and provincial governments, with residual powers being assigned to the federal legislature; Canada thus has been described as a quasi-federal state. There is no explicit separation of powers under the Canadian constitution; functions of the prime minister and cabinet contain both executive and legislative responsibilities, while the monarch and the monarch's representative, the governor-general, are merely symbolic of executive or legislative power. Parliament and the judiciary, however, are dealt with separately in the constitution, and the courts have some powers of judicial review.

The Executive

Monarch. The purely ceremonial monarch is the queen of England, who is represented here, as in New Zealand, by a governor-general.

Prime Minister and Cabinet. The act of 1867 did not provide for a prime minister, so tradition to a large extent defines this position. The prime minister is a link between the governor-general and the political and administrative branches of the government. As the monarch's representative, the governor-general formally summons the lower house of the parliament and dissolves it for elections. From among the members of parliament the prime minister selects ministers, some of whom will head government departments, and dismisses them at his or her pleasure. The prime minister selects a cabinet to work with him or her to make government policy, setting the agenda and presiding at cabinet meetings. Individually and collectively the ministers are responsible to parliament, may be questioned any time on their actions, and may be required to resign if they lose the confidence of that body.

In Canada the prime minister is often elected by a national constituency that supersedes local interests; his or her coattails, therefore, confer additional power in the elected house of the legislature. Unlike the president of the United States, the prime minister can be assured of either an absolute majority of seats for his or her party or at least a relative majority during the administration. The prime minister is not only the chief executive but also the chief legislator because the government introduces most of the important legislation. The prime minister's powers include appointing members of the upper house of the legislature and, as the central figure in the government, commanding access to the nation's media.

The Legislature

Parliament. The Canadian parliament is bicameral, consisting of an upper house, known as the senate (rather than the house of lords, as in Britain), and a lower house, the house of commons.

Upper House. The 1867 act requires that senators be chosen from regions. Currently there are 104 seats in the senate. To be a senator a person must be at least thirty years of age and meet certain status requirements. Technically, a senator is appointed by the governor-general on the advice of the government and holds office until the retirement age of seventy-five. The senate has the same formal powers as the house, except that it may not initiate money bills. Today, however, its role is mostly advisory, and it tends to routinely approve legislative proposals.

Lower House. Members are elected to the more important body, the house of commons, at least every five years from each of 295 constituencies, called ridings. The candidate who receives the relative majority of the votes in a riding wins the election. This manner of electing representatives is also used in New Zealand and the United States. The seats in the house are distributed among the provinces by population, except that Quebec is guaranteed at least seventy-five seats.

If a majority of candidates from one party wins seats, they form a government; or if there is only a relative majority party, it may form a minority government. The presiding officer in the house is the speaker, who is nominated by the prime minister from among the majority party members. The majority party tries to maintain strict party discipline on most issues to ensure that the government's legislation is passed.

Two basic types of bills are considered by the parliament: public bills, which affect the public at large; and private bills, which affect only one individual or a select group of individuals. Generally, public bills are submitted by the government. A bill goes through the formality of a first reading, and then on second reading debate is entertained. If it passes on the second reading, a bill goes to a committee that may approve, amend, and report it out for debate and a third and final reading. In recent times the role of committees has increased, but unlike in the United States, the committee chairmen are not so independently powerful. If a bill passes the house, it goes to the senate and then to the governor-general for assent. While debate on measures may be lively, the Canadian party system in parliament ensures that almost all government bills are passed.

The Judiciary

The 1867 act gives scant direction for the court system. It authorizes the legislature to "provide for the constitution, maintenance, and organization of a general court of appeal for Canada and for the establishment of any additional courts for the better administration of the laws of Canada." The court system still bears the imprint of the British judicial system. It is hierarchical, except that the provincial and federal courts share some judicial functions and responsibilities. There are three judicial levels: lesser provincial courts; provincial courts, including a supreme court; and federal courts, including a supreme and a federal court of Canada. The supreme court of Canada is the final court of appeal in most cases.

Canadian courts have some powers of judicial review. They can determine which of the governments—federal or provincial—has the authority to legislate in certain instances, and they can declare laws unconstitutional if they do not meet the standards of the 1982 Charter of Rights and Freedoms. In fact, since the charter came into force, many individual rights cases have been filed with the courts. In addition to cases coming before the courts in the course of litigation, a constitutional question may be brought in a taxpayer's suit, or an opinion may be requested by the federal government or a province.

Judges originally were to be appointed by the governor-general, but today the prime minister is responsible for such appointments and no legislative confirmation is required. Judges of superior courts hold office during good behavior or until reaching the retirement age of seventy-five. They are removable under the 1867 act by the governor-general "on address of the senate and the house of commons."

Schedule B, part 5, of the 1982 act sets forth procedures for amending the Canadian constitution. Generally, it requires resolutions by both the upper and lower houses of the legislature and "resolutions of the legislative assemblies of at least two thirds of the provinces that have, in the aggregate, according to the then latest general census, at least fifty percent of the population of all the provinces." An amendment that reduces legislative powers or the proprietary rights or any other rights or privileges of the legislature or government of a province requires a resolution by a majority of the members of the two houses of the legislature and the legislatures of the provinces; it will not be effective in provinces that do not support the resolution by a majority of its members.

Part 5, article 41, provides that some amendments—such as those regarding the office of the monarch or the governor-general, the use of the English and French languages, the composition of the supreme court of Canada, or article 41—can be accomplished only by resolutions in both chambers of the federal legislature and the legislative assemblies of each province.

Amending the Constitution

CHAD

Historically a crossroads for commerce between the Mediterranean and West Africa, Chad was a French colony from around 1900 until its independence in 1960. In 1996 the nation held its first multiparty presidential election under a new constitution.

General Information

The landlocked Republic of Chad is some 1,284,640 square kilometers and is bounded on the north by Libya, on the east by Sudan, on the south by the Central African Republic, and on the west by Cameroon, Nigeria, and Niger. N'Djamena is the capital of this nation of approximately 8.4 million inhabitants. The northern two-thirds of Chad lies in the hot, arid Sahara Desert.

Cotton textiles, meat packing, and beer are the major industries in Chad. Its chief agricultural products include cotton, cattle, and sorghum. Although Chad is one the world's poorest countries, its reliance on subsistence farming may be supplemented in the future by the exploitation of oil found in its southern region.

Type of Government: Presidential-style parliamentary republic, with a president, a prime minister and council of ministers (cabinet), a bicameral legislature, a judiciary, and a constitutional council

Dates of Constitutions: 1959, 1960, 1962, 1978, 1982 (interim), 1993 (transitional), and 1996

Constitutional History

The northern part of what is now Chad contains evidence of some of the earliest human settlements, with samples of art dating back more than nine thousand years. Although the Lake Chad region was settled by 500 B.C., little evidence exists to document the origins of the present-day peoples of Chad. Africans began establishing political states in central Chad more than one thousand years ago. Often influenced by Arabic-speaking immigrants, the rulers of these militaristic kingdoms were considered possessed of divinity and spiritual as well as political power.

Arabs gradually gained control of the trade—including slaves—across the Sahara, converting many Africans to Islam. A confederation of nomadic peoples in the ninth century A.D. established the Kanem empire northeast of Lake Chad, which gave rise to the ruling Sayfawa dynasty. The political state that resulted from the merger of the Kanem with the Borno peoples on the western edge of Lake Chad reached its high point during the reign of Mai Idris Aluma, between 1571 and 1603. The Ottoman Empire laid claim to the territory of Chad in the eighteenth century, and at the end of the nineteenth century France expanded from its colonial base on Africa's west coast into southern Chad.

Chad was administered as a part of French Equatorial Africa beginning in 1910 and as a separate colony in 1920. In 1940 the colonial administration in Chad sided with the Free French resistance movement led by Charles de Gaulle rather than the Nazi-condoned Vichy government in France. Limited self-governing institutions, including a territorial assembly (limited legislature), were extended to Chad and other French colonies under the French constitution of 1946. In 1958 Chad's territorial legislature voted to remain a member state of the French community created under the French constitution adopted that year but declared the country a republic, and on August 11, 1960, it gained its independence.

The territorial legislature had enacted a constitution for Chad on March 31, 1959. A second constitution of November 28, 1960, was replaced on April 16, 1962. The preamble to the 1962 document referred to both France's Declaration of the Rights of Man and of the Citizen (1789) and the United Nations's Universal Declaration of Human Rights (1948). However, constitutional amendments in 1965 resulted in single-party rule. Following a military coup in 1975, a new constitution in 1978 failed to unite warring factions in a coalition government.

In 1981 Libya proclaimed its merger with Chad, but Libya's domination was resisted with the support of France. After dissolving the government, Chadian President Hissien Habré promulgated an interim constitution, called the Fundamental Law of 1982. In 1988 Habré appointed a constitutional committee to draft a permanent document, although he was ousted in 1990. A new permanent constitution was adopted by referendum in March 1996 and promulgated on April 14, 1996, replacing the Charter of Transition of April 5, 1993. The nation's first multiparty presidential election was held several months later.

Influences

The 1958 French constitution had a significant impact on Chad's 1996 constitution that is visible, for example, in its reference to "the rights of man" and the creation of a constitutional council similar to France's.

The Constitution

The preamble to the constitution outlines Chad's "stormy institutional and political evolution," in which "[y]ears of dictatorship and single party [rule] have prevented the blossoming of any democratic culture and of political pluralism." It affirms "our total opposition to any regime whose policy would be founded on . . . arbitrariness, dictatorship, injustice, corruption, extortion, nepotism, clannishness, tribalism, confessionalism, or confiscation of power."

Article 1 proclaims: "Chad is a Republic, sovereign, independent, secular, social, one and indivisible, founded on the principles of democracy, the rule of law and justice. The separation between State and religions is affirmed." According to article 3, "Sovereignty belongs to the people, who exercise it either directly by referendum or indirectly by the intermediary of their elected representatives."

Fundamental Rights

"Liberties and fundamental rights are recognized and their exercise is guaranteed to citizens under the conditions and forms specified by the Constitution and the law," states article 12. Rights guaranteed in articles 13 through 27 include equality of the sexes and of all persons before the law; the rights to life, personal integrity, security, freedom, and "protection of [one's] private life and possessions"; the rights of "moral persons"; a prohibition against torture, slavery, and arbitrary detention or arrest; the presumption of innocence; and freedom of opinion, expression, communication, conscience, religion, the press, association, assembly, circulation, demonstration, and parade. The latter freedoms, however, may be restricted "to safeguard the public order and good morals," and the "law determines the conditions of their exercise."

Other rights include the right to belong to a union and to strike; to have access to public employment, work, culture, education, and "the protection and . . . the enjoyment of [one's] intellectual and artistic works." Article 38 extends to parents "the natural right and the duty to raise and educate their children," while article 39 adds: "The State and the Decentralized Territorial Collectives establish the conditions for the blossoming and well-being of youth." Citizens' duties include respect for the constitution, "defense of the Fatherland," and respect for and protection of the environment.

Division of Powers

"The principle of the exercise of power," declares article 7, "is the Government of the people, by the people and for the people, founded on the separation of Executive, Legislative and Judicial Powers."

The Executive

President. "The Executive Power is exercised by the President of the Republic and the Government," states article 59. The office holder "is elected for a five-year mandate by direct universal suffrage . . . [and] is re-eligible once." Any citizen "of either sex" may run who possesses only Chadian nationality and who is "at least 35 years old and at the most seventy," has "all civic and political rights," is in good physical and mental health, is "of good morals," and "deposits a surety whose amount is specified by law."

The president "is the Chief of the State" and, among other responsibilities, "sees to the respect of the Constitution," "assures . . . the regular functioning of the public powers as well as the continuity of the State," and guarantees "the independence, national sovereignty and unity, territorial integrity, and . . . the respect of treaties. . . ." Other powers and duties of the president include appointing the prime minister and, on the prime minister's recommendation, the other members of the government; promulgating laws adopted by parliament; presiding over and signing decrees and ordinances of the council of ministers; and accrediting and receiving ambassadors. The president "is the Supreme Chief of the Armies," "exercises the right of pardon," and "informs the Nation by a message" and "communicates with . . . Parliament by messages that he has read and which do not give rise to any debate."

In the case of the president's temporary absence or incapacity, the prime minister acts "within the limit of the powers . . . delegated to him." If the presidency becomes vacant, those powers—with some exceptions, including the power to appoint a prime minister—"are provisionally exercised by the President of the Senate and, in case of the incapacity of the latter, by the Vice President of the same Senate." The president and other government members may be impeached by a two-thirds majority in each house of parliament.

Prime Minister and Cabinet. "The government," pursuant to article 93, "is composed of the Prime Minister and the Ministers." It executes national policy as "determined in the Council of Ministers." According to article 94, "The Prime Minister is the Chief of the Government. He is appointed by . . . the President. . ." and "directs, coordinates and animates the governmental action," "disposes of the administration," and "is charged with the execution of the policy of National Defense." The president may delegate to the prime minister "the presidency of the Council of Ministers . . . for a specific agenda." Article 103 requires that the prime minister's acts be "countersigned, if necessary, by the Ministers charged with their execution." They are appointed by the president on the prime minister's recommendation.

The Legislature

Parliament. "The legislative power," article 106 declares, "is exercised by a Parliament composed of the National Assembly and the Senate." Both the senate and the assembly elect a president and "bureau" to administer their affairs, every two years in the senate's case; members of the bureaus may be replaced following the vote of two-thirds of their members.

Upper House. "Senators are elected [indirectly] by . . . an electoral college composed of the regional, departmental, and municipal councilors," for six-year terms, staggered one-third every two years.

Lower House. Members of the assembly, called deputies, are elected for four-year renewable terms by universal suffrage. The assembly elects its president and bureau at its first session for the duration of parliament; however, according to article 115, "the members of the Bureaus of Parliament may be replaced following the vote of two-thirds of their Assembly."

Articles 125 through 145 detail the relationship between the executive and legislative powers. For example, article 125 declares that laws are passed by parliament and that "law determines the rules concerning: civic rights and fundamental guarantees . . . , taxes . . . , nationality . . . , [and] the electoral regime." On the other hand, according to article 129, "[T]he Government may demand from the Parliament the authorization to take . . . measures which are normally of the domain of the law . . . ," and pursuant to article 130, government members "have access to the parliament and its commissions." Article 145 sets forth "[t]he means of information and control of the Parliament on the action of Government," including interpellation (questioning of government officials), written and oral questions, a commission of inquiry, censure motions, and hearings by commissions.

"The judicial power in Chad is exercised by the Supreme Court, the Courts of Appeal, the Tribunals, and the Justices of Peace," declares article 148. "It is the guardian of the liberties and of the individual property, and sees to the respect of the fundamental rights." According to article 150, the president "is the guarantor of the independence of the Magistrature."

Supreme Court. Article 157 provides that the supreme court "is the highest jurisdiction of Chad in judicial, administrative and financial matters [and it] takes cognizance of the contentions of local elections." The court is composed of judicial, administrative, and accounts chambers.

A president and sixteen members, called counsellors, make up the court. The president is appointed by Chad's president after consulting with the presidents of the assembly and the senate. Eight counsellors are selected as follows: "from among the high magistrates of the judicial order respectively: three by the President of the Republic; three by the President of the National Assembly; two by the President of the Senate." Seven are chosen "from among the specialists of Administrative Law, Budgetary Law and Law of the Public Accounts, respectively: three by the President of the Republic; two by the President of the National Assembly; two by the President of the Senate."

"The powers and the other regulations of the organization and functioning as well as the procedure to be followed before the Supreme Court," are, according to article 158, "determined by an organic law [affecting the nature of the government]." Article 159 provides that the "members of the Supreme Court are irremovable" except for crimes or incapacity.

High Court of Justice. According to articles 177 and 178, a high court of justice—consisting of six deputies, four senators, two members of the constitutional council, and three members of the supreme court—"is competent to judge the President of the Republic and members of the Government as well as their accomplices in case of high treason. Any deed affecting the republican form [of government], the unification and secularity of the State, the sovereignty, the independence, and the integrity of the national territory is considered a crime of high treason."

A constitutional council is instituted under article 164 to be "the judge of the constitutionality of laws, treaties and international agreements," as article 166 explains. "It is informed about contentions affecting presidential, legislative, and senatorial elections. It sees to the regularity of the operations of the referendum and proclaims its results. It rules obligatorily on the constitutionality of organic laws, before their promulgation, and the internal regulations of the Assemblies before they enter into effect." Article 171 notes that "[e]very citizen may raise the exception of unconstitutionality before any jurisdiction regarding a matter that concerns him. In this case, the jurisdiction suspends judgment and [transfers the matter to] the Constitutional Council, which must make a decision within a maximum of forty-five (45) days."

The council is composed of nine members ("three magistrates and six jurists of the high level") selected for terms of nine years, one-third every three years: one magistrate and two jurists named respectively by the president, the assembly president, and the senate president.

"The initiative of the revision [of the constitution] belongs concurrently to the President of the Republic upon decision taken in the Council of Ministers and to the members of Parliament," declares article 223. A draft revision or an amendment "must be voted on, in identical terms, by a two-thirds majority of the members of the National Assembly and the Senate." Article 224 requires approval by referendum, except in the case of "a technical revision," which needs the "approval of a three-fifths majority of [parliament] meeting in Congress."

Amendments may not be proposed if they interfere with territorial integrity, independence, national unity, the republican form of government, division of powers and secularity, freedoms and fundamental rights of citizens, and political pluralism.

CHILE

After a military coup in 1973, Chile, whose economy had been devastated by the policies of an elected Marxist president, underwent a politically repressive but economically successful period of military rule. An election in 1989 ushered in a popular democratic government.

General Information

The Republic of Chile is a long, narrow strip of land of some 757,000 square kilometers in the southwestern part of South America and includes Easter Island. It is bounded on the north by Peru, on the east by Bolivia and Argentina, and on the west and south by the Pacific Ocean. The Strait of Magellan bisects the southern tip of Chile. The capital of this country of more than fifteen million persons is Santiago.

Except for vastly increased wine production and export, Chile's economy has been in recession. The arrest of former President Augusto Pinochet for human rights violations has reopened antagonism between left- and right-wing factions, endangering a fragile democracy.

Type of Government: Presidential republic, with a president and ministers of state (cabinet), a bicameral legislature, a judiciary, and a constitutional court

Dates of Constitutions: 1818 (provisional), 1823, 1828, 1832, 1833, 1925, and 1981 (significantly amended in 1989)

Constitutional History

Attempts by the Incas and the Spaniards in the fifteenth century to occupy the area that is now Chile were met with fierce hostility from the indigenous Araucanian Indians. Finally, in 1541, Santiago was founded by the Spanish, although wars with the Indians continued until near the end of the nineteenth century.

As part of the Spanish viceroyalty of Peru, Chile was governed from Lima by the Spanish monarchs, who communicated their orders and decrees through a consultative body called the Consejo de Castilla. Royal laws, general laws for the Indies under Spanish rule, and the general laws of Spain were applied in Chile in that order. As in other Spanish dependencies, the local unit of government was generally the *cabildo*, which was democratic to the extent that it was open to Creoles, the locally born offspring of European immigrants and their grandchildren. During the Spanish period the land-owning aristocrats, neglected by the governments in Lima and Spain, developed their estates into little fiefdoms.

In 1812 and 1814 provisional regulations concerning the organization of the government were issued. After Chilean forces under Gen. Bernardo O'Higgins and Argentine forces led by José de San Martín defeated the Spanish and obtained independence for Chile in 1818, however, O'Higgins became Chile's first president under a near revolutionary provisional liberal democratic constitution. This document served as the basis for the practical 1833 constitution, which lasted until 1925, although other constitutions were adopted in 1823, 1828, and 1832. Nonetheless, from 1833 to 1861 Chile was republican in name only, as the presidency was practically a dictatorship. Many amendments were made to the constitution after 1871.

In 1925 Arturo Alessandri Palma, having been temporarily ousted from the presidency by the military and then reinstalled, was able to make progressive changes in the old constitution, which had favored the aristocracy, military, and the clergy over the middle class and workers. The 1925 constitution increased the powers of the president and the lower house of the legislature at the expense of the more conservative upper house.

After 1938, following more military ousters and an attempted Nazi coup, constitutional government all but disappeared. During World War II Chile prospered, but between 1946 and 1948 the economy soured and political parties proliferated. In 1970 a Marxist, Salvador Allende Gossens, was elected president. His attempts to implement socialist policies led to a general disintegration of the economy and to the nationalization of copper mines owned by U.S. companies. A military junta, headed by Maj. Gen. Augusto Pinochet Ugarte, seized power on

September 11, 1973. Using repressive measures, he set about rebuilding the economy. Human and civil rights were deemed expendable by the junta, but the economy improved.

In September 1980, by a two-to-one margin, a plebiscite extended Pinochet's term as president for eight years and approved a new constitution to take effect on March 11, 1981, which called for an extension of military rule until 1997. On December 14, 1989, by a vote of fifty-four percent, a civilian was elected president, and the constitution was extensively amended. Even some members of the junta backed the amendments against Pinochet. The former leader was later placed under house-arrest and ordered to stand trial for having covered up the deaths or "disappearances" of political prisoners during his time in office.

The Chilean constitution of 1981 was drafted to reflect other successful free-enterprise government systems such as those in Switzerland and Singapore.

Chile is a democratic republic, but unlike Argentina and Brazil, for example, which are federal or federative republics, Chile is a unitary state. "Sovereignty rests essentially with the nation," declares article 5. "It is exercised by the people through plebiscites and periodic election, as well as by the authorities established by this constitution."

The beginning of article 1 proclaims: "Men are born free and equal, in dignity and rights. The family is the basic core of society."

Article 19 of chapter 3, Constitutional Rights and Obligations, contains twenty-six enumerated rights and freedoms guaranteed to all persons. They include the right to life, physical and psychological integrity of the individual, and the life of those about to be born; equality before the law and equal protection under the law in the exercise of rights; respect for and protection of private and public life and the honor of the individual and family; the inviolability of the home and private communication; freedom of conscience and the manifestation of all creeds and cults not opposed to morals, good customs, or public order; the right to personal freedom and individual security, a contamination-free environment, protection of health, and education; the freedom to teach, express opinions, and disseminate information; the right to assemble peacefully, to petition government, and to associate, except that political parties must conform to certain rules; the right to obtain social security and acquire property; and the freedom to work and affiliate with unions.

By amendment, state agencies are now required to respect and promote the rights guaranteed by the constitution and international treaties ratified by Chile and in force. In 1991 a commission on truth and national reconciliation appointed by the president reported that during the period September 1973 to March 1990 more than two thousand individuals were killed by the state. Pinochet criticized the report and vowed that no member of the armed forces would be tried for any human rights abuses reported.

Chile is a unitary state. Power is shared by the president, as head of state and government; the legislature; the courts, which exercise limited judicial review; and the constitutional court, which exercises preenactment constitutional review.

President. According to article 24, "The government and the administration of the state are vested in the president of the republic, who is the chief of state. His authority extends to all that aims at the preservation of the internal public order and the external security of the republic, in accordance with the constitution and the law."

To be eligible for the presidency, an individual must have been born in Chilean territory, must be at least forty-five years old, and otherwise must qualify as a citizen with the right to vote. He or she is elected for a term of eight years and may not be reelected for a consecutive

Influences

The Constitution

Fundamental Rights

Division of Powers

The Executive

term, although a 1989 amendment limits the current president's term to four years. The election is by direct ballot, and an absolute majority is required to win; if necessary a runoff is held between the two candidates with the most votes. An "election qualifying court" is required immediately to proclaim the president-elect to the president of the senate.

Twenty-one special powers are vested in the president; power to dissolve the lower house of the legislature has been deleted. The president's powers include to make, sanction, and promulgate laws; to convene and close extraordinary sessions of the legislature; to issue decrees pursuant to the constitution having the force of law; to call for a plebiscite on proposed constitutional amendments; to designate certain nonelected members of the upper house; to declare "situations of constitutional exception in instances and forms prescribed" in the constitution; to appoint and remove ministers of state and certain other officials, including mayors; to appoint and dismiss diplomats and other international representatives; to grant pensions, retirement, widows' and orphans' pensions, and other pensions in accordance with law; to appoint justices of the higher courts, civil judges, and certain members of the constitutional court, as well as supervise the ministerial conduct of judges and other employees of the judiciary; to grant pardons; to conduct foreign and international relations, including signing and ratifying treaties, which must be submitted to the legislature for approval; to command the nation's armed forces and take supreme command during time of war; to declare war, subject to law and in consultation with the national security council; and to supervise the nation's revenue collection and its expenditures.

"States of constitutional exception" include foreign or internal war, internal disturbances, and emergency and public calamity, during which the president has additional powers; article 41 has been amended to restrict the courts from questioning the facts relied on to invoke the exceptional powers.

The president may not leave the national territory for more than thirty days during his last ninety days in office without permission of the upper house of the legislature. If the president is unable to take office, the president of the upper house acts as vice president, and, if necessary, a new election is held.

Cabinet. The constitution charges the ministers of state (cabinet) with assisting the president in governing and administering the nation. The president may entrust one or more ministers with coordinating the work of the secretaries of state and relations with the legislature. Article 35 requires that regulations and decrees of the president may not be enforced without being countersigned by the respective minister.

The Legislature

Congress. The bicameral legislature, the national congress, consists of an upper house, the senate, and a lower house, the chamber of deputies. Both must concur in making laws.

Upper House. Two senators are elected by direct ballot for eight years from each region or district, except that six regions are divided into two districts, for a total of thirty-six senators. They are replaced, alternately, every four years. Senators may also be appointed from among qualifying former presidents, who can be members for life; former members of the supreme court and a former comptroller general, elected by the court; and other high officials enumerated in article 45. Such appointments, other than former presidents, are made every four years, after senatorial elections; at the end of 1993 eight senators who had been appointed by Pinochet remained. To be elected a senator directly, a person must be a Chilean citizen with the right to vote, must be at least forty years old, must have been a resident in the region or district three years before the election, and must have completed secondary education.

Exclusive powers of the senate include acting as a jury on accusations by the chamber of deputies; judging judicial actions against any minister for damages stemming from the performance of duties; taking cognizance of jurisdictional conflicts between political or administrative authorities and higher courts of justice; declaring the incapacity of the president or president-elect; and giving its opinion when so requested by the president. The list of powers is followed by an express prohibition barring the senate from exercising oversight of government acts.

Lower House. The 120 members of the chamber of deputies are elected by direct ballot from electoral districts for four-year terms. Chilean citizens who are twenty-one years old, have the right to vote, have completed secondary education, and have resided in the district three years before the election are eligible to be deputies.

Among the chamber's exclusive powers is control of government administration through official communications to the president, which includes inquiries that, although they must be responded to, otherwise incur no other penalty under the constitution. It may also accuse high officials, including the president, of grave improprieties, in which no fewer than ten nor more than twenty deputies must concur. A majority vote of half of the total deputies is required to approve the motion to accuse the president.

Laws submitted by the president or members may originate in either house of the legislature, except that laws regarding taxes, budgets, and recruitment must originate in the chamber of deputies and laws of amnesty and general pardon must originate in the senate. Article 62 sets out six areas about which only the president may propose legislation. Laws, except those of a constitutional nature, require an absolute majority of both houses for approval. Once approved, a bill is sent to the president. If disapproved, a bill may become law if two-thirds of both houses approve it. In addition to passing legislation, the congress approves international treaties and declares states of siege.

The Judiciary

The judiciary consists of regular and special courts. Pursuant to article 79 the supreme court is entrusted with the executive, correctional, and economic supervision of all the courts, except the constitutional court, the election-qualifying court, the regional electoral courts, and the military courts in time of war. It also has jurisdiction over disputes about competence between political or administrative authorities and courts of justice, except where the senate is involved.

Supreme Court. The supreme court has authority to enforce compliance with the constitution. According to article 80, it may, "by means of an official letter or upon request of a party, in matters of which it takes cognizance or which have been submitted to it by an appeal filed for a cause followed before another court, declare inapplicable for such particular cases all legal precepts contrary to the constitution."

According to a 1997 amendment, the supreme court consists of twenty-one members appointed by the president from a list of five candidates drawn up by the court; they must then be confirmed by the senate by a two-thirds vote. Judges, except lower court judges, remain in office until the age of seventy-five, as long as they properly perform their duties, although the president of the supreme court may serve out his or her term.

Constitutional Court

Article 81 provides for a constitutional court of seven members, including three justices of the supreme court, a lawyer appointed by the president, two lawyers elected by the national security council, and a lawyer elected by an absolute majority of the members of the upper house of the legislature. They serve for a total of eight years and are partially replaced every four years. They may not be removed, and their decisions may not be appealed.

The constitutional court's jurisdiction includes "control of the constitutionality of constitutional organic laws before promulgation." Its jurisdiction also extends to laws that interpret a precept of the constitution; the constitutionality of decrees having the force of law; constitutional questions that arise during the processing of bills, constitutional amendments, and treaties; questions regarding the constitutionality of calling a plebiscite and complaints against the president in the promulgation of laws; determination of the unconstitutionality of organizations, movements, and political parties; and the ineligibility of ministers of state and members of the legislature.

Amending the Constitution

The 1980 constitution, as amended, provides that the president or any member of the congress may propose an amendment, in the general manner of laws. Approval requires a three-fifths vote of the total members of the upper and lower houses in office. If the reform concerns certain fundamental portions of the constitution, a two-thirds vote in each house is required. Sixty days later, the legislature meets in an open plenary session, during which approval of the amendment requires a majority vote of members present. If the president totally disapproves, the proposal may be passed again by a two-thirds vote of all members; and if the president still disapproves, he or she may submit the question to a vote of the people. If the president partially objects, the objection will be sustained by a three-fifths vote or a two-thirds vote as required to amend fundamental portions of the constitution.

The statue of the *Goddess of Democracy* in Tiananmen Square during the protests in June 1989 became a symbol of universal aspirations for freedom and democratic government. The constitution of China, however, remains as little more than a facade for the ruling Communist Party.

The People's Republic of China is nearly ten million square kilometers, making it the third largest nation in the world. It is bounded on the south by Vietnam, Laos, Burma, India, Bhutan, and Nepal; on the west by Pakistan, a sliver of Afghanistan, and several former republics of the Soviet Union; on the north by Mongolia and Russia; on the east by North Korea, the Yellow Sea, and the East China Sea; and on the southeast by the South China Sea. The capital of this country of approximately 1.3 billion persons is Beijing, which has an urban population of around eleven million inhabitants.

Hampered in its economic development by Soviet-style central planning and shortages in capital and technology, China has progressed in recent years by improving its flexibility and experimenting particularly in the areas of agriculture and high technology. The country has recently created special economic zones for more market-oriented activities, encouraged foreign investment, even by the United States, and run up export surpluses. After bouts with high inflation in 1988 and political turmoil in 1989, China appears to have stabilized, while moderating its reforms.

Type of Government: People's democratic dictatorship, with a president, a premier (prime minister) and state council (cabinet), a unicameral legislature, and a judiciary. The Chinese Communist Party, in fact, controls all facets of the government, and its activities are basically outside the law, constitutional or otherwise.

Dates of Constitutions: 1905, 1912 (provisional), 1949 (Common Program), 1954, 1975, 1978, and 1982

China's human history extends back approximately ten thousand years. Apparently, people of Mongol origins settled in the northern part, mixing with the local population between the sixth and fourth millennia B.C. The first dynasty arose about 2200 B.C., followed by the Shang dynasty, a city-state monarchy ruling over an agricultural society that lasted until nearly 1000 B.C. The succeeding Zhou dynasty fell around 800 B.C., leaving a number of independent, warring, feudal-type states.

By this time, however, legal codes had developed, but they reflected the laws of absolute rulers who governed under a "mandate of heaven." In the fifth and fourth centuries B.C., principles developed by K'ung Fu-tzu (Confucius), or Master Kung, came into vogue: that the ruler and officials must have the best interests of the people at heart, and that the people must be loyal and obedient to authority to create harmony among the classes. By the third century A.D. Taoism and Confucianism were used as legitimizing forces for centralized authoritarian rule over the uneducated masses.

The Qin (Chin) faction finally subdued its neighbors, including the Chu faction in the central Yangzi Valley, and began its dynasty in 221 B.C. In addition to unification, the Qin standardized the systems of writing and weights and had the Great Wall built for protection from raids by Mongol warriors from the north. The Qin dynasty was followed by the Han, a golden era in Chinese history; ethnic Chinese, who make up about ninety-five percent of the inhabitants of China, still refer to themselves as Han people. After the short-lived Sui, the Tang dynasty, which fell in the tenth century, developed the classical Chinese civilization that lasted until the twentieth century. Confucianism took over as the predominant social belief. A competent, merit-based civil service begun during the Han period became entrenched in the Tang dynasty. The Chinese Song, the Mongol Yuan, and the Chinese Ming dynasties followed until the Manzhous (Manchus) from the north, who called themselves Qing (Ch'ing), settled in from 1644 to 1912.

After Marco Polo traveled to Asia in the late thirteenth century, Chinese contact with Europeans—Portuguese, Spanish, French, and British—began again on a large scale in the sixteenth century. A series of "unequal" treaties with the Western powers, which actually reduced China's sovereignty, culminated in antiforeign protests and a rebellion by a secret society called the Boxers. The rebellion produced reforms by the Manzhou rulers, including copying the Japanese constitution in 1905 and pledging to institute a constitutional government by 1917.

A revolution led by Sun Yat-sen resulted in a republic under a provisional constitution in 1912, with Sun as president. He resigned shortly thereafter and founded the Kuomintang (Nationalist People's Party), which, under the subsequent leadership of Chiang Kai-shek, unified most of China by 1928. Japanese aggression postponed further democratic reforms. After World War II the communist forces of Mao Zedong (Mao Tse-tung) defeated Chiang, who fled with his followers to the island of Taiwan, formerly called Formosa.

The People's Republic of China was established in Beijing on October 1, 1949, and a document called the Common Program served as its constitution. The first five-year economic plan in 1953 emphasized industrialization, collectivization, and political centralism. A formal constitution was adopted in 1954 by the first national people's congress, which defined the country as "a people's democratic state led by the working class and based on the allegiance of workers and peasants." Power and ideological struggles within the party leadership resulted in new constitutions in 1975—clearly a Maoist document—and 1978, two years after Mao's death. The upheaval caused by the "Great Leap Forward" in 1958, the Cultural Revolution in 1966, and the rise and fall of the Gang of Four in the 1970s affected those in power and those seeking power.

With the establishment of the supremacy of Deng Xiaoping, the central committee of the Communist Party called for a constitutional revision committee in 1980. In June 1982 a follower of Deng took over the chairmanship of the party, and on December 4, 1982, the new constitution was adopted. It was amended in 1988, 1993, and 1999.

Influences

The 1954 constitution was based on the Soviet-style model constitution. Later constitutions were developed to solidify the government structure and reflect the policies of the winners of political power struggles.

The Constitution

Because real implementation of constitutional provisions by the Communist Party is lacking, the preamble is probably the most relevant section of the Chinese constitution, at least with respect to revealing the direction party leaders want to take the country.

In a break with the past, the preamble to the 1982 constitution sets forth the long history of China, including the role of Sun Yat-sen, while eliminating references to the Cultural Revolution highlighted in the previous two documents. While calling for Han chauvinism to be combated and for socialism and reunification of the "motherland" to be supported, the preamble emphasizes the importance of modernization, the need for foreign investment capital, and the abatement of the traditional communist class struggle. Everyone is directed to "uphold the dignity of the constitution and ensure its implementation." A 1999 amendment added Deng Xiaoping, the former Chinese communist leader, to Marx, Lenin, and Mao Zedong as persons providing guidance for "Chinese people of all nationalities."

Article 1 of chapter 1, General Principles, defines the state:

The People's Republic of China is a socialist state under the people's democratic dictatorship led by the working class and based on the alliance of the workers and peasants.

The socialist system is the basic system of the People's Republic of China. Sabotage of the socialist system by any organization or individual is prohibited.

The next two articles establish that all power belongs to the people and that it is to be exercised through the national people's congress and local people's congresses, which are to be instituted through democratic election.

The General Principles assert that the state undertakes to continue to support the socialist legal system; that no laws shall contravene the constitution; that the public owns the means of production and that other resources such as minerals, waters, forests, and beaches are owned by the people as a whole or by collectives; that land in cities is owned by the state; that socialist property is sacred and inviolable; and that the state works to enhance the productivity of labor, combat waste, and practices a socialist market economy. Article 18 expressly permits foreign investment in China in accordance with its laws; article 11 was amended in 1988 to sanction private-sector economic development.

Fundamental Rights

Equality of all citizens before the law—a provision in the 1954 constitution left out of the two intervening documents—was restored in the 1982 constitution, indicating some retrenchment in the policy of "class justice." Article 48 provides that women enjoy equal rights with men. Citizens are also to enjoy freedom of religious belief, so long as religion does not disturb the public order or the state education system and is not foreign dominated. Privacy of correspondence is guaranteed, except where state security or criminal offenses permit it to be censored. Work and education are both a right and a duty. The rights of Chinese citizens living abroad, their relatives, and those who return are protected—provisions most likely calculated to encourage remittances to help finance modernization efforts. The fact that in the 1982 document fundamental rights have now been placed ahead of the chapter on state structure may indicate a conscious effort to emphasize them, at least in theory.

Division of Powers

China is a unitary state. Under the official government constitution of the People's Republic of China, power is divided among the president, as head of state; the premier (prime minister); the legislature; and the courts, which do not exercise judicial review. According to the unofficial constitution of the Chinese Communist Party, there are four levels of power. At the lowest level is the organizational unit in a factory, school, commune, or other entity or activity; next are the local party congresses; then the national party congress (not the national people's congress); and, finally, at the apex is the central committee, the military committee, the politburo or political bureau, the standing committee, and the party secretariat. This structure has been developed to keep power from gravitating into the hands of one person and from giving rise to a personality cult.

The Executive

President. Article 79 provides for a president and vice president to be elected by the legislature. The position of president was restored in the 1982 constitution, although the incumbent has a mostly ceremonial role except in foreign affairs. All citizens at least forty-five years of age who have the right to vote and stand for election are eligible for these positions, which last for the term of the legislature but may not be held for more than two consecutive terms by the same person.

The duties of the president include promulgating the laws; appointing and removing the premier, vice premiers, state councilors, ministers, and other high officials; conferring medals and honors; issuing pardons; proclaiming martial law or a state of war and issuing troop mobilization orders; receiving foreign diplomats; appointing and recalling representatives abroad; and ratifying and abrogating treaties and agreements with foreign nations.

The vice president may be assigned duties by the president and becomes president if the office is vacant.

Prime Minister and Cabinet. Article 85 creates a cabinetlike body called the state council to serve as the executive arm of the highest organ of state power, the legislature. The council includes the premier, vice premiers, state councilors, ministers, and about sixty other officials who also serve for the five-year term of the legislature. The state council is charged with administering the government.

The Legislature

Parliament. The constitution declares the unicameral parliament, called the Quanguo Renmin Daibiao Dahui (national people's congress), to be the highest organ of state power and the primary source of legislative power. It has more than three thousand delegates, who are elected by the provincial people's congresses for terms of five years. According to the official comments of the drafters, the congress's power has been increased in the new constitution. It now appoints a military affairs control commission that is responsible to the congress. Formerly, the Communist Party was to be directly in control of the armed forces. The premier is responsible nominally to the congress, but in fact serves the congress's standing committee, which is composed of a chairman, vice chairmen, a secretary general, and members elected by the congress. Ministers are responsible to the premier for their departments.

At least one session a year is called by the standing committee or by one-fifth of the members of the congress. The congress is expressly responsible for, among other duties, amending the constitution; supervising the enforcement of the constitution; electing the president and vice president of the nation, sometimes referred to as the chairman and vice chairman; approving both the premier of the state council, who is nominated by the president, and the other members of the council; electing the president of the supreme court, the chairman of the central military commission, and the procurator general; approving the budget; changing or annulling decisions of the standing committee; approving the creation of new administrative subdivisions; and deciding on war and peace. Legislative measures including resolutions are passed by a majority of the deputies.

The congress also has the power, according to the constitution, to recall or remove from office anyone it has approved, including the president and vice president.

The Judiciary

According to article 123, "The people's courts in the People's Republic of China are the judicial organs of the state." Article 125 adds, "All cases handled by the people's courts, except for those involving special circumstances as specified by law, shall be heard in public. The accused has the right of defense."

Regardless of the language of the constitution, however, a defense lawyer who enters a not-guilty plea in a sensitive case will suffer at the hands of the system, which may view such action as a form of dissent or a counterrevolutionary measure calling for the suspension of the rule of law.

The organization of the courts is determined by law. There is a supreme people's court, which is responsible to the legislature and its standing committee; local courts at different levels responsible to the local bodies establishing them; military courts; and special courts.

Supreme Court. The highest judicial body, the supreme people's court, supervises the administration of the local and special courts. The terms of office for the president of the supreme court and the procurator general are the same as that of the national legislature, and they may not serve more than two consecutive terms.

Amending the Constitution

Amendments to the constitution may be proposed by the standing committee or more than one-fifth of the members of the legislature. They are approved if passed by a majority vote of more than two-thirds of all the members.

The 1991 constitution, which became a popular best seller in Colombia, draws from various sources to create a peaceful revolution that increases participatory democracy in the national government.

The Republic of Colombia is more than 1.1 million square kilometers and is bounded on the west by the Pacific Ocean and Panama, on the north by the Caribbean Sea, on the east by Venezuela and Brazil, and on the south by Peru and Ecuador. Bogota is the capital of this country of approximately forty million inhabitants.

A country with abundant natural resources, Colombia traditionally has been a leading exporter of coffee. The basis of its informal economy, however, is the export of refined cocaine, which has a profound impact on its internal politics and its external relations, particularly with the United States.

Type of Government: Presidential republic, with a president and cabinet, a bicameral legislature, and a judiciary, including a constitutional court

Dates of Key Constitutions: 1811, 1821, 1886, and 1991

The territory now known as Colombia has been inhabited for more than twenty thousand years, with much of its population drawn from Central America. By A.D. 1500 the inhabitants had developed social organizations directed by matrilineal hereditary leaders and united in large confederations, such as one created by the Muisca people around Bogota and Tunja.

Instituted after the region's conquest by Spain were the standard *encomienda* system of land holding, which allowed landowners the right to use indigenous labor, and the *hacienda* system, in which such labor was under contract. The elites in the colonial society *(peninsulares)* were those born in Spain. Two colonial oversight councils for administration and trade were under the Spanish crown. Locally, there were regional courts or governors *(audiencias)*, which had executive, legislative, and judicial power, and administrative councils *(cabildos)* in the cities. To maintain compliance with the law, colonial authorities could institute a public judicial inquiry *(residencia)* and a secret investigation *(visita)*.

In 1717 the viceroyalty of New Granada was established, encompassing Colombia, Venezuela, Panama, and Ecuador. An uprising against Spain came in 1781, and the French Revolution added fuel to the movement for independence. In 1810 the viceroy was expelled, and a junta took control. A constitution was written for the newly formed United Provinces of New Granada a year later. Troops led by Simón Bolívar Palacios and Francisco de Paula Santanda defeated the Spanish in 1819, and in 1821 the former became president and the latter vice president of the new Republic of Gran Colombia under a new constitution.

Gran Colombia became New Granada when Venezuela and Ecuador left the union, then it became the United States of New Granada, the United States of Colombia, and finally the Republic of Colombia in 1886. The 1886 constitution, which followed nine previous constitutions and attempts at both federal and unitary forms of government, set up a unitary republic, and power at the national level was divided among the executive, legislative, and judicial branches.

The conservatives held power until the beginning of the twentieth century, when civil war broke out; it lasted three years and became known as the Thousand Days' War. After Panama seceded because of the proposed construction of the Panama Canal, Colombia began an era of economic development that lasted until the Great Depression of the 1930s. A succession of dictatorships and military governments followed. In 1957 the conflict between conservatives and liberals was resolved temporarily with an agreement called the Pact of Sitges, which divided the appointed government positions equally regardless of election results. Under this Frente Nacional (national front), the presidency alternated between the Liberal and the Conservative Parties.

Guerrilla warfare and the Medellin and Cali drug cartels, which opposed extradition of drug kingpins to the United States, made effective government nearly impossible; in 1985, for example, a guerrilla assault killed eleven members of the supreme court. The present government under President Cesar Gaviria Trujillo lifted the state of emergency in force since 1984 in honor of the new constitution and has taken steps to stabilize the country. The current constitution, which went into effect on July 5, 1991, could play a significant role in this ongoing struggle; in fact, the presidential elections held in June 1994 were peaceful.

Influences

The concept of an absolute majority for election of the president derives from the French model, while the legislative vote of no confidence and other measures is based on the British parliamentary system.

The Constitution

The preamble of Colombia's 1991 constitution declares that one goal is to "strengthen the unity of the nation and ensure its members life, peaceful coexistence, work, justice, equality, knowledge, freedom, and peace within a legal, democratic, and participatory framework. . . ." Articles 3 and 4 espouse the principles of the sovereignty of the people and the supremacy of the constitution.

Fundamental Rights

Colombian citizens' fundamental rights are affirmed in article 5: "The state recognizes, without discrimination whatsoever, the primacy of the inalienable rights of the individual and protects the family as the basic institution of society." Fundamental rights under the constitution include the right to life and a guarantee against the death penalty; a prohibition against cruel, inhuman, and degrading punishment; equal protection of the laws without discrimination on the basis of gender, race, national or family origin, language, religion, political opinion, or philosophy; and the right to personal and family privacy. Freedom of conscience, religion, and expression are guaranteed, in addition to the right to dignity, to work, and to choose a profession or occupation.

Certain groups are specifically protected in article 13, which provides, in part:

The state will promote the conditions necessary in order that equality may be real and effective and will adopt measures in favor of groups which are discriminated against or marginalized.

The state will especially protect those individuals who on account of their economic, physical, or mental condition are in obviously vulnerable circumstances and will not sanction any abuse or ill-treatment perpetrated against them.

Title 4, Concerning Democratic Participation and Political Parties, authorizes, in addition to the vote, plebiscites, referendums, popular consultation, open town meetings, legislative initiative, and recall of officials.

Division of Powers

In Colombia, a unitary state, the constitution divides power among the president, the legislature, and the courts, which exercise constitutional review through a constitutional court.

The Executive

President and Cabinet. Although the 1991 constitution reduces the number of the president's powers, it allocates important new powers, thus ensuring a strong role for the president.

Article 115 delineates the president's role: "The President of the Republic is the chief of state, the head of government, and the supreme administrative authority. The national government is composed of the President of the Republic, the cabinet ministers, and the directors of administrative departments."

The president is elected to a four-year term by "one-half plus one" of the secret and direct ballots cast. To be eligible to run for president, a person must be a Colombian by birth, a citizen of good standing, and more than thirty years old. Anyone who was president or in certain high government positions one year before the election may not be elected president. A vice president is elected on the same day and in the same manner as the president and replaces him or her in the case of a temporary or permanent vacancy.

Article 189 sets forth the responsibilities of the president, who is also the supreme commander of the armed forces. These include providing for the external security of the nation; managing international relations and appointing and receiving diplomats; convening and adjourning the legislature; reporting to the legislature at the beginning of each term on the programs and activities of the government; appointing cabinet ministers and directors of departments; creating, merging, or dissolving government positions or merging national administrative organs in accordance with law; supervising the ministries and other government entities; and inspecting and supervising the public services.

The 1991 constitution took away the president's power to appoint the governors of the states, who are now popularly elected.

Congress. The Colombian congress, which has the responsibility to amend the constitution, pass laws, and exercise political control over the government and the public administration, is composed of an upper house, the senate, and a lower house, the chamber of representatives. Article 179 lists general disqualifications for membership in the congress; and article 183 lists the bases for losing membership, including excessive absenteeism.

Upper House. One hundred senators are "elected in one national electoral district," and two more are elected from Indian communities, all for four-year terms. To be a senator, a person must be a Colombian citizen by birth, in good standing, and more than thirty years old.

The senate's powers include allowing in foreign troops and authorizing the government to declare war; accepting or rejecting the resignation of the president or vice president; approving certain military promotions; granting the president temporary leave and determining the qualifications of the vice president to serve as president; and electing the national attorney general and judges of the constitutional court, as well as participating in the impeachment process.

Lower House. The number of representatives from territorial and special electoral districts is based on population, but in addition five representatives of ethnic groups and political minorities are elected, also for four-year terms. Representatives must be citizens in good standing more than twenty-five years old.

Powers of the chamber of representatives include examining and approving the general budget and treasury account; bringing impeachment charges under the constitution and receiving complaints against specific officials; requesting assistance in determining the respective jurisdictions of the houses of congress; and collecting evidence.

The congress as a whole is authorized to pass laws relating to specific areas set forth in articles 150 through 152. Laws may originate in either house and be proposed by members, the national government, certain constitutionally stipulated entities, or in certain cases by popular initiative, except that revenue bills must originate in the lower house and bills involving international relations must originate in the upper house. In general, the passage of laws requires an absolute majority vote of the congress. To become law a bill must be officially published by the congress, be approved at the first reading by the appropriate committee in each chamber and at a second reading in each chamber, and be approved by the government.

Ombudsman. The lower house of the legislature elects an ombudsman to supervise the promotion, exercise, and awareness of human rights.

The Judiciary

Article 228 provides that the administration of justice is a public function, decisions are independent, and the functioning of the judiciary will be decentralized and autonomous.

The constitution creates a supreme court of justice, a council of state, and a constitutional court. To be eligible to be a member of these bodies, a person must be Colombian by birth, a citizen in good standing, and a lawyer; must not have been sentenced to imprisonment except for political crimes or crimes of strict liability; and must have held a position in the judicial branch or the public ministry or have practiced honorably as a lawyer or professor of law for ten years. Judges are elected to eight-year terms and may not be reelected.

Supreme Court. The highest court of ordinary jurisdiction is the supreme court. It hears cases on appeal, tries the president and other government officials, and handles cases of diplomats involving international law.

Council of State. A council of state acts as an administrative review court to consider national government decrees held unconstitutional by the constitutional court and consult on matters involving government administration. It also proposes amendments to the constitution.

Constitutional Court. This court decides on citizen petitions against acts amending the constitution, the constitutionality of referendums or constituent assemblies, and petitions by citizens regarding the constitutionality of laws and decrees with the force of law, as well as other matters regarding the constitution. Judges on the constitutional court come from various legal specializations and are elected for single eight-year terms by the senate from lists presented by the president, the supreme court, and the council of state.

Amending the Constitution

Title 13 provides for three basic ways to amend the constitution: by the legislature in two ordinary and consecutive legislative periods; by a constituent assembly called for by the legislature with the approval of the electorate, if at least one-third of them vote; and by referendum approved by more than one-half of the people voting, where the number of such votes exceeds one-fourth of the electorate. Amendments approved by the legislature must be submitted for a referendum in certain cases, including amendments to the chapter on fundamental rights.

Costa Rica has enjoyed a relatively stable democracy for a half century under its 1949 constitution. Peace in Central America has been enhanced in part because of the efforts of Costa Rican President Oscar Arias Sánchez, a winner of the Nobel Peace Prize.

General Information

The Republic of Costa Rica, the second smallest country in Central America, is some 51,000 square kilometers and is bounded on the north by Nicaragua, on the east by the Caribbean Sea, on the south by Panama, and on the west by the Pacific Ocean. San José is the capital of this country of approximately 3.7 million persons.

The major industries of Costa Rica include food processing, textiles, and plastics; coffee, bananas, sugar, and rice are among its chief agricultural products. Serving as the home for thousands of retired Americans and a rapidly growing tourist industry contribute to Costa Rica's relatively prosperous economy.

Type of Government: Presidential republic, with a president and government council (cabinet), a unicameral legislature, a judiciary, and an independent electoral tribunal

Dates of Constitutions: 1821 (provisional), 1825, 1844, 1847, 1848, 1859, 1869, 1871, and 1949

Constitutional History

The land now occupied by Costa Rica ("Rich Coast") was the home of the Guaymi people when Christopher Columbus made contact on his fourth voyage to the New World in 1502. In the absence of exploitation by Spain, many colonists became small landowners and made a meager living from raising cacao and tobacco—a contrast to the large-scale *encomienda* system of farming in other Spanish colonies that may have contributed to the relative ease with which Costa Ricans assimilated democratic ideas.

Costa Rica remained isolated from the mainstream of colonial development for nearly a century and a half. On September 15, 1821, Costa Ricans declared their independence from Spain, encouraged by similar movements in other colonies such as Guatemala and Mexico. A provisional constitution was drafted in December of that year, and a formal constitution in 1825 acknowledged the country's independence within the United Provinces of Central America, which also included El Salvador, Guatemala, Honduras, and Nicaragua under an 1823 federal constitution. A lack of harmony among the members, however, led Costa Rica to reassert its complete independence in 1838.

After the overthrow of the dictator Braulio Carrillo Colina in 1842, a new constitution was adopted in 1844, followed by others in 1847 and 1848. The latter abolished the army, replacing it with the national guard. The generally unstable government of Costa Rica operated under successive constitutions in 1859, 1869, and 1871, but a series of democratic reforms finally led to the direct election of the president in 1913. A new constitution went into effect on November 7, 1949, which, with a number of amendments, has continued in force.

Influences

Costa Rica's 1949 constitution, based on its 1871 constitution, included innovations such as judicial review of legislative acts, political rights for women, and guarantees of social, economic, and educational programs.

The Constitution

"Costa Rica is a free and independent democratic Republic," declares article 1. "Sovereignty resides exclusively in the Nation," adds article 2. Articles 3 and 4 prohibit usurpation of the state's sovereignty or the rights or the people. "Public treaties, international agreements and concordats duly approved by the [legislature]," according to article 7, "shall have a higher authority than the laws...."

Fundamental Rights

Individual rights and guarantees are set forth in articles 20 through 48. They include a prohibition of slavery, the inviolability of human life and private premises, freedom of movement and private communications, and the rights to associate "for lawful purposes" and "to meet peacefully and unarmed." Other guarantees are the right "to petition any public official or State entity," freedom to express opinions, freedom to communicate thoughts, access to government "information on matters of public interest," equality before the law, a prohibition of detrimental retroactive laws, as well as protections for those accused of crimes. Imprisonment for debt and cruel or degrading treatment, life imprisonment, and the penalty of confiscation are banned; "[p]roperty is inviolable"; "[p]rivate monopolies . . . are prohibited"; the temporary and exclusive rights of creators and merchants are recognized; and the right to a habeas corpus and *amparo* proceeding (a Latin American procedure for vindicating individual rights) are guaranteed. In addition, article 31 states:

The territory of Costa Rica shall be a shelter for all those persecuted for political reasons. If their expulsion is decreed on legal grounds, they can never be sent back to the country where they were persecuted.

Articles 50 through 74 address social rights and guarantees, including the right "to a healthy and ecologically balanced environment"; protection for the family, mothers, children, the elderly, the destitute, and the infirm; equal rights of spouses in marriage; and detailed protections for workers. The constitution further promotes "cooperatives as a means to provide better living conditions for workers" as well as low-cost housing and family homesteads.

Article 75, as amended in 1975, declares that the "Roman Catholic and Apostolic Religion is the religion of the State, which contributes to its maintenance, without preventing the free exercise . . . of other forms of worship that are not opposed to morality or good customs."

Division of Powers

"The Government of the Republic," proclaims article 9, "is popular, representative, alternative and responsible. It is exercised by three distinct and independent branches: Legislative, Executive, and Judicial." However, a supreme electoral tribunal is given "the rank and independence of the Government Branches."

The Executive

President. Article 130 states that executive power "is exercised, on behalf of the people," by a president and cabinet ministers "in the capacity of subordinate collaborators." To be eligible for the presidency, a person must be a citizen by birth, a "layman or a laywoman," and more than thirty years old. There are restrictions against former presidents and vice presidents, as well as against "[a]ny ancestor or descendant by consanguinity or affinity or sibling of the person occupying the Presidency . . . at the time of the election," and several other enumerated high officials covering the year before an election.

The president and two vice presidents are elected for four-year terms "simultaneously and by a majority vote that exceeds forty percent of the total number of validly cast votes." Article 138 provides that if "two tickets obtain an equal number of sufficient votes, the oldest candidate shall be considered elected as President. . . ."

The exclusive powers and duties of the president listed in article 139, as amended in 1968, 1975, and 1997, include appointing and removing cabinet ministers, representing the nation in official acts, having supreme command of the law enforcement forces, presenting an annual message to the legislature, and informing the legislature as to the motives for trips outside the country. Among the joint powers of the president and the appropriate cabinet ministers are appointing and removing "members of the law enforcement forces, employees and officials who hold positions of trust, and others . . ."; sanctioning and enforcing the laws; exercising "the initiative in the enactment of laws and the right of veto"; providing for "the collection of and expenditure of the national revenues according to law"; and "supervising the proper operation of administrative services and agencies."

Cabinet. The president and ministers together make up the government council (cabinet). Cabinet ministers are "established by law for the management of the matters pertaining to the Executive Branch." Ministers are required to have the same qualifications as the president, except that they must be at least twenty-five years old. According to article 143, vice presidents "may hold office as Ministers."

Cabinet ministers are required by article 144 to "submit to the [legislature] every year . . . a report on matters that concern their Ministries." They may attend or may be compelled to attend legislative sessions, with the right to speak but not to vote. Article 146 mandates that "decrees, resolutions and orders of the Executive Branch require the signatures of the President of the Republic and the appropriate Minister in order to be valid. . . ."

Congress. Article 105, as amended in 1989, states: "The power to legislate resides in the people, which delegate this power, by means of suffrage, to the Legislative Assembly. Such a power may not [be limited] except in the case of treaties, in accordance with . . . International Law."

The legislative assembly is composed of fifty-seven representatives, who are "elected by provinces," "hold office for four years and may not be reelected to a succeeding term." A representative must be twenty-one years old and a Costa Rican citizen by birth or naturalization, with ten years of residency after naturalization. Those not eligible include the president or acting president, cabinet ministers, supreme court justices, members of the supreme electoral tribunal, active military personnel, provincial civil or police members, managers of autonomous institutions, and "[r]elatives of the . . . President . . . , to the second degree of consanguinity or affinity inclusive"; other incompatibilities are set forth in article 112.

The legislature is required to meet on May 1 each year and may not hold sessions "unless they are attended by two-thirds of the total membership." Among its exclusive powers set forth in article 121, as amended in 1968, are to "[e]nact, amend, repeal and give an authentic interpretation to the laws . . . ; [d]esignate the premises to be used for its sessions . . . ; [a]ppoint the regular and alternate justices of the Supreme Court . . . ; [and] [a]pprove or disapprove international conventions, public treaties and concordats." Other powers include authorizing the executive branch "to declare a state of national defense and to reach peace agreements"; it may also suspend by a vote of two-thirds of its entire membership certain civil rights found in articles 22, 23, 24, 26, 28, 29, 30, and 37 (protecting, for example, freedom of movement and communication, peaceful association, freedom of expression, and access to government information). The legislature may additionally vote by a two-thirds majority of all the members to impeach the president and other high officials.

Article 123 provides that during regular sessions "the initiative for enactment of laws can be taken by any member . . . , or by the Executive Branch through the Cabinet Ministers." To become a law, generally "every bill . . . shall be the subject matter of two debates, each on a different non-consecutive day, obtain the approval of the Assembly and the sanction of the Executive Branch, and be published in the Official Journal. . . ." There is another procedure for acts that do not have the status of law, such as appointing supreme court justices. Within ten business days the executive branch may veto a bill, except "the Regular Budget of the Republic," by returning it "with pertinent objections." A veto may be overridden "by a vote of two thirds of the total membership" of the assembly. If a bill is vetoed on the grounds of unconstitutionality, it must be submitted to a specialized chamber of the supreme court, as provided for in article 10, as amended in 1989.

"The judicial power is exercised by the Supreme Court of Justice and by other courts established by law," states article 152. According to article 154, "The Judicial Branch is subject only to the Constitution and the law, and [its] decisions . . . impose no responsibilities other than those specifically set forth in legislation." Article 153 mandates that "in addition to the functions vested in it by this Constitution, the Judicial Branch shall hear civil, criminal, commercial, labor, and administrative-litigation cases, as well as any others established by law. . . ."

Supreme Court. The supreme court, according to article 156, "is the highest court of the Judicial Branch, and all courts, officials and employees of the Judicial Branch are subordinate to it. . . ." Article 157 provides that it "shall be composed of the number of Justices . . . necessary for a good service; they shall be elected by the Legislative Assembly, which shall make up the different Court Chambers established by law." The justices are elected for eight-year terms and continue in office, "unless otherwise decided by the . . . Assembly by a vote of two-thirds of its entire membership." The legislature also appoints at least twenty-five alternate justices from which temporary court absences are filled.

A justice must be "a Costa Rican by birth, or by naturalization, with residence in the country for no less than ten years after . . . naturalization," but the chief justice must be a citizen by birth. Justices must also be able to exercise civil rights, be lay people, be more than thirty-five years of age, have a law degree, and have "practiced the profession for at least ten years, except [for] judicial officials with not less than five years of judicial experience." Candidates are disqualified if they are related to a justice "by consanguinity or affinity to the third degree inclusive." The court chooses the chief justice from among its own members.

As article 167 provides, "For discussion and passage of bills of law concerning the organization or functioning of the Judicial Branch, the . . . Assembly shall consult the Supreme Court. . . . It shall require a vote of two-thirds of the entire membership of the Assembly to depart from the views of the Court." Article 10 creates a special chamber of the court to determine the constitutionality of laws, to solve government jurisdictional disputes, and to "hear any consultations [or opinions] on constitutional amendment bills, ratification of international agreements or treaties and other bills, as provided by law."

Supreme Electoral Tribunal

"The organization, direction, and supervision of acts pertaining to suffrage," declares article 99, "are the exclusive function of the Supreme Electoral Tribunal, which does enjoy independence in the performance of its duties. All other electoral organs are subordinate to the Tribunal." The tribunal is "ordinarily" composed of three regular members and six alternates appointed by the supreme court by a vote of no less than two-thirds of its members. They must have the same qualifications as members of the supreme court and hold office for six years.

The tribunal's functions described under article 102 include convoking popular elections; appointing the members of the electoral boards; and interpreting, "with exclusive and compulsory effect, all constitutional and legal provisions on electoral matters." In addition, the tribunal conducts "the official count of the votes" for the major elective government offices and those for municipal governments and representatives to constitutional assemblies.

Amending the Constitution

Article 195, as amended in 1977, directs that amendments be "signed by at least ten representatives" and "submitted to the Assembly at regular sessions." Such proposals must "be read three times at intervals of six days" and then "be sent to a commission appointed by [an] absolute majority of the Assembly, which has to render its opinion within . . . twenty business days." Two-thirds of the assembly must next approve the amendment, which is prepared as a "bill of law through a commission," approved by "an absolute majority," and sent to the executive branch to be returned "with the Presidential Message to the Assembly . . . [and] his observations, or his recommendation." If again passed by "a vote of no less than two-thirds of the entire membership, it . . . become[s] a part of the Constitution. . . ."

Under article 196, as amended in 1968, a "general amendment" of the constitution requires that a constituent assembly be called "by a vote of no less than two-thirds of the membership of the . . . Assembly." The approval of the executive branch is not required.

The first country to recognize the independence of the United States in 1776, Croatia declared its own independence from Yugoslavia on June 25, 1991, six months after adopting a new, democratic "Christmas" constitution.

The Republic of Croatia on the Balkan Peninsula is 56,538 square kilometers in size and is bounded on the north by Slovenia and Hungary, on the east by Yugoslavia, on the south by Bosnia and Herzegovina, and on the west by the Adriatic Sea. Zagreb is the capital of this country of approximately 4.3 million persons.

Croatia's major industries include chemicals, plastics, and machine tools; olives, wheat, and corn are among its chief agricultural products. After gaining its independence, Croatia—like Bosnia and Herzegovina—suffered from conflict with Serbia, which left a toll of high unemployment and heavy debts.

Type of Government: Presidential-style parliamentary republic, with a president, a prime minister and government (cabinet), a bicameral legislature, a judiciary, and a constitutional court

Dates of Constitutions: 1921, 1946, 1947, 1953, 1963, 1974, and 1990

As early as 6,000 B.C. agriculture was practiced by peoples in the region that is now Croatia, and by 700 B.C. trade with Italy and Greece was flourishing. The Veneti people, who probably spoke an Italic language, inhabited parts of Slovenia and Croatia; the Illyrians and Celts intermixed there in the fourth century B.C. A century later Rome conquered the Illyrians. The Roman Empire's split into eastern and western domains led to a division in the Balkans between Eastern Orthodox Serbs and Roman Catholic Croats and Slovenes.

Croats, who were south Slavs, had settled on the Dalmatian coast by the beginning of the seventh century A.D., and in 877 they came under the rule of the Byzantine Empire. In a political move to thwart Venetian expansion, the Byzantine Empire acknowledged the first Croatian ruler, Tomislav, in 910. Fear of Venice's power led to close Croatian and Hungarian cooperation, and in 1102 a Hungarian was made ruler of the Croatians by mutual agreement. Split into inland and Dalmatian Croat groups, the latter fell in succession under the rule of Byzantium, Hungary, Venice, France, and Austria.

After coming under the hegemony of the Hapsburg monarchy, the Croatian Sabor (parliament) elected a king from the Hapsburg dynasty. Croatia was later conquered by the Turks but freed by the Hapsburgs in 1699, gaining some autonomy. The Hapsburgs, however, retained military control over the region and at the end of the eighteenth century tried to introduce reforms, including the German language. An attempt in the 1830s to impose the Hungarian language angered Croatians and spurred support for a separate Slavic kingdom within the Austrian empire.

In 1867 Austria gave Croatia back to Hungary, which granted the Croats more autonomy and their own parliament. Tied to Hungary until after World War I, Croatia became a part of the Kingdom of the Serbs, Croats, and Slovenes in 1918. A constitution adopted in 1921 created a central unitary government rather than a federal system in which the various historic regions could retain some control over local affairs. Because Serbs predominated, they supported the unitary government as a way of fostering their hegemony over the entire nation.

In 1929 Alexander I abolished the constitution and assumed dictatorial authority. His successor in 1934, the regent Prince Paul, was ousted in 1941, making Croatia a nominally independent state until it was merged by the communist leader Marshall Tito (Josip Broz) into the Republic of Yugoslavia in 1946. Subject to the 1946 Yugoslav constitution, Croatia adopted its own constitution in 1947. New constitutions for Yugoslavia were promulgated in 1953, 1963, and 1974.

The current constitution of Croatia (sometimes called the "Christmas" constitution) was adopted on December 22, 1990, before the country's formal declaration of independence from Yugoslavia on June 25, 1991, which led to war with Serbian-dominated Yugoslavia. Peace accords were signed in Paris in 1995, and control of Serbian-held territory was returned to Croatia in 1998. Franjo Tudjman, an authoritarian general under Tito, had been elected president by the Croats in 1990 and again in 1997 but died in 1999. An election a month later ushered in the opposition party and renewed hope for a stable multiparty constitutional democracy. On January 27, 1998, the Croatian parliament adopted a new amended text of the constitution.

Influences

Croatia's long struggle to recapture and maintain its independence significantly influenced its 1990 constitution, as evidenced by the historical recitation at the beginning of the document, and the 1997 amendment, which prohibits joining Croatia with any other nation. The limited role of and nonelective method by which some members of the upper chamber of parliament are selected are also found in the constitutions of Chile, Singapore, and the United Kingdom.

The Constitution

Introductory text in part I summarizes "Historical Foundations" for the Croatian constitution, noting in part:

At the historic turning-point marked by the rejection of the communist system and changes in the international order in Europe, the Croatian nation by its freely expressed will in the first democratic elections (1990) reaffirmed its millennial statehood.

"The Republic of Croatia is a unitary and indivisible democratic and social state," proclaims article 1. "Power ... derives from the people and belongs to the people as a community of free and equal citizens." Article 2 declares that the "Croatian Sabor [parliament] and people shall directly, independently and in accordance with the Constitution and law, decide: on the regulation of economic, legal and political relations ... ; on the preservation of natural and cultural wealth and its utilization; [and] on association in alliances with other states." Article 135 prohibits initiation of "any procedure for the association of the Republic of Croatia in alliances with other States if such association leads, or might lead, to a renewal of a Yugoslav State community or to any Balkan State alliance of any kind."

Fundamental Rights

Article 3 declares: "Freedom, equal rights, national equality, love of peace, social justice, respect for human rights, inviolability of ownership, conservation of nature and the human environment, the rule of law, and a democratic multiparty system are the highest values of the constitutional order of the Republic of Croatia." Article 6 provides that the "[f]ormation of political parties shall be free," adding that the "work of any political party which ... violently endangers the democratic constitutional order, independence, unity or territorial integrity ... shall be prohibited."

"Citizens ... shall enjoy all rights and freedoms," according to article 14, "regardless of race, color, sex, language, religion, political or other opinion, national or social origin, property, birth, education, social status or other characteristics. All shall be equal before the law." Article 15 states that "[m]embers of all nations and minorities shall be guaranteed freedom to express their nationality, freedom to use their language and script, and cultural autonomy." Articles 16 and 17 address restrictions on rights "by law to protect the freedoms and rights of other people and public order, morality and health" and in the event of "a state of war or an immediate threat to ... independence and unity"; however, "the right to life, prohibition of torture, cruel or degrading treatment or punishment ... , or ... freedom of thought, conscience and religion" may not be suspended.

Articles 21 through 47 set forth other rights, among them the right to life, personal freedom, personality, movement, peaceful assembly, public protest, and free association; freedom of thought and expression, the press, privacy, conscience, and religion; and protection for those accused of crimes, including an "autonomous and independent" legal profession and the presumption of innocence. Capital punishment, forced labor, "maltreatment," and medical experimentation without consent are prohibited. Other guarantees include the inviolability of one's home; the right "under equal conditions, to take part in the conduct of public affairs, and have access to public services"; and "freedom and secrecy of correspondence and all other forms of communication," as well as the "safety and secrecy of personal data."

Articles 48 through 69 address economic, social, and cultural rights, noting that "[e]ntrepreneurial and market freedom shall be the basis of the economic system of the Republic." The right of ownership is guaranteed, along with the rights to work, to social security, to health care, and to "assistance for weak, helpless and other unprovided-for citizens." "Receiving humanitarian help from abroad may not be forbidden," states article 57. Under article 68, "The Republic shall protect scientific, cultural and artistic goods as national spiritual values."

"In the Republic of Croatia," declares article 4, "government shall be organized on the principle of the separation of powers into the legislative, executive and judicial branches."

Division of Powers

President. As head of state, declares article 94, the president "shall represent the Republic at home and abroad, be responsible for abiding by the Constitution, and ensure the continuance and unity of the Republic and the regular functioning of the government." Croatia's president is popularly elected for a term of five years and must receive a majority of all the votes or a runoff election is required. Elections are mandated "no less than 30 and no more than 60 days before the expiry of the term [of the] incumbent President."

The Executive

The president's duties, according to article 98, include calling parliamentary elections and convening its first session; calling referendums; appointing and relieving the prime minister; granting pardons; conferring decorations and awards; and performing "other duties specified by the Constitution." Article 99 authorizes the president, "at the Government's proposal," to establish diplomatic offices, appoint and recall diplomatic representatives, and receive foreign diplomats. The office holder, under article 100, also serves as commander in chief of the armed forces, appoints and relieves of duty members of a national defense council, and, based on "the decision of the [lower house of parliament] . . . may proclaim war and conclude peace." Other presidential powers and duties include issuing decrees "with the force of law," taking "emergency measures in the event of a state of war" or other immediate threat to the nation's independence and unity, convening and presiding over meetings of the government and placing items on its agenda, making an annual report to parliament on the state of the nation, and dissolving the chamber of deputies, with the prime minister's countersignature, following a no-confidence vote or if it "has failed to approve the state budget within a month. . . ."

On the president's death, resignation, or permanent disability, the president of parliament temporarily takes over pending election of a new president within sixty days. According to article 105, the president may also be impeached "for any violation of the Constitution that he has committed in the performance of his duties." Impeachment may be instituted by the lower house of the legislature by a two-thirds majority vote of all representatives and must be "decided upon by the Constitutional Court . . . by a two-thirds majority vote of all the judges."

Prime Minister and Cabinet. Under article 108, Croatia's government consists of a prime minister, deputy prime ministers, ministers, and other members. It sets its own rules of procedure, while the "internal organization of ministries shall be regulated by Government decrees." The government is also authorized to "introduce bills, propose the state budget, and enforce laws and other regulations enacted by [parliament]."

According to article 111, the government is responsible to the president and the lower house of parliament. The prime minister is appointed and dismissed by the president, and he or she must "present the Government to the lower house not later than 15 days from his nomination and ask for a vote of confidence in the Government."

The Legislature

Parliament. Article 70 vests legislative power in the Croatian Sabor, its parliament, "a body of the elected representatives of the people." It consists of an upper house of counties and a lower house of representatives.

Upper House. Three members of the house of counties are elected from each county for four-year terms. The president automatically becomes a lifelong member of the upper house when he or she leaves office and may also "nominate up to 5 members . . . from among citizens especially deserving for the Republic."

The upper house is directed under article 81 to "propose to the [lower house] bills and the calling of referenda," as well as give opinions to the lower house, especially on "the enactment of the Constitution and laws"; it also has fifteen days in which to return a law passed by the lower house.

Lower House. The house of representatives is limited to between 100 and 160 members, "elected on the basis of direct universal and equal suffrage by secret ballot" for four-year terms. The chairman of the lower house also serves as president of parliament.

Pursuant to article 80, the house is to "decide on the enactment and amendment of the Constitution; pass laws; adopt the state budget; decide on the war and peace; [and] decide on alterations of the boundaries of the Republic." The chamber is additionally authorized to "call referenda; carry out elections, appointments and dismissal from office, . . . supervise the work of the Government . . . ; grant amnesty for penal offenses; [and] conduct other affairs as specified by the Constitution."

Parliamentary members are granted immunity for "an opinion expressed or vote cast in the Sabor." Each house, however, may withdraw immunity for criminal acts, and immunity does not extend to members "caught in the act" where the offense carries a penalty of imprisonment for more than five years.

A majority of members constitutes a quorum, and a majority of those voting is generally necessary to make decisions. However, article 83 requires that laws "which regulate national rights shall be passed by the [lower house] by a two-thirds majority vote of all representatives." Article 89 requires that laws be promulgated by the president within eight days of their passage by the lower house.

Ombudsman. Article 93 establishes the position of ombudsman, "who shall be a commissioner of the [parliament], shall protect the constitutional and legal rights of citizens in proceedings before government administration and bodies vested with public powers." The method of election and mode of work of the ombudsman, who is elected by the lower house for a term of eight years, are regulated by law.

The Judiciary

"Judicial power shall be exercised by the courts," declares article 115, which adds that they are to be "autonomous and independent . . . [and] . . . administer justice on the basis of the Constitution and law." Under article 116, the "establishment, jurisdiction, composition and organization of courts and court proceedings shall be regulated by law." Court judgments are "passed publicly," based on hearings that are open to the public except in certain cases—for example, if a minor is on trial—and lay assessors, as well as judges, may administer justice. Article 120 mandates that "[j]udicial office shall be permanent" and provides the basis for removing a judge.

Supreme Court. Croatia's highest court is the supreme court, which is dedicated to ensuring "uniform application of laws and equality of citizens."

Constitutional Court

"The Constitutional Court," declares article 122, "shall consist of 11 judges elected by the lower house of the parliament at the proposal of the upper house for a term of eight years from among outstanding jurists, especially judges, public prosecutors, lawyers and university professors of law." It elects its own president for four years. Under article 125, the court decides, among other matters, on the conformity of laws with the constitution and on the conformity of other regulations with the constitution and law. It is also empowered to "protect the constitutional freedoms and rights of man and citizen," decide jurisdictional disputes between the branches of government, determine the impeachability of the president, settle certain electoral disputes, and supervise and potentially ban political parties.

Amending the Constitution

Article 136 allows constitutional amendments to be proposed by at least one-fifth of the members of the lower house, the president, or the government. Then, according to article 137, the lower house, "upon obtaining the opinion of the [upper house], shall decide by a majority vote of all representatives whether or not to start proceedings. . . ." An amendment is finally approved by a two-thirds majority vote of all members of the lower house, "on the basis of a prior opinion" of the upper house, and the lower house promulgates it.

CUBA

Cuba's leadership refuses to recognize that its experiment as a communist state is a failure, and minor changes in the country's constitution in 1992 do little to help alleviate the economic problems of this island off the southern tip of the United States.

General Information

The Republic of Cuba, an island in the Caribbean Sea, is approximately 114,500 kilometers in area, including the Isle of Pines. Havana is the capital of this country of approximately eleven million persons.

With the end of communist rule in the Soviet Union, Cuba has lost much-needed foreign assistance, cheap oil, and trading partners. The Cuban economy, historically based on the production of sugar, has deteriorated under Fidel Castro's communist government.

Type of Government: Communist Party dictatorship, with a presidential-style parliamentary government including a president, a council of state and council of ministers (cabinet), a unicameral legislature, and a judiciary

Dates of Constitutions: 1812 (Spanish constitution abrogated in 1814 and reimposed in 1820 for three years), 1901 (superseded by provisional law in 1933), 1935 (de facto), 1940 (suspended in 1952), 1959, and 1976

Constitutional History

After failing to circumnavigate the island of Cuba on his first trip to the New World and thinking that he had reached China, Christopher Columbus declared it to be "a province of Cathay." The gentle and peaceful Arawak people who lived on the island had no concept of a nation, each village having its own chief, medicine man, and gods. The Arawak became extinct as a result of disease and forced labor imposed by the Spanish, who began growing sugar cane on the island shortly after their arrival in 1511.

In 1538 Hernando de Soto was appointed governor of Cuba, which became an administrative center under a captain-general appointed by the king of Spain. By the eighteenth century its authority extended to North America, including Louisiana and Florida. For protection against pirates, richly laden cargo ships bound for Spain linked up with escorts in Havana. In 1762 the British captured Havana, holding it for almost a year, and Thomas Jefferson explored the possibility of annexing the island in 1805.

In 1810 Cuban delegates to Cadiz, Spain, participated in drafting the first Spanish constitution of 1812. In 1811 Cubans themselves produced two constitutions in draft form only, one based on independence and a second one based on autonomy under the Spanish monarchy. With the return of absolutism in 1814, the 1812 constitution was abrogated, then reimposed by the Spanish military in 1820 for three years. In 1823 the United States announced the Monroe Doctrine, which warned against further European intervention in the New World. The resulting status quo helped keep Cuba a colony of Spain, although proslavery southern states in America tried unsuccessfully to capture Cuba. In 1878 a Cuban struggle for independence ended without victory, after which dictatorial rule by the Spanish governor continued.

The leaders of a renewed liberation effort in 1895 included José Marti, a young poet who died early in the fighting. Their cause bore fruit on May 20, 1902, when an explosion on the U.S. battleship *Maine,* sent to protect Americans in Havana, brought war with Spain and a U.S. military government. A constitution modeled after the U.S. system, but with a clause allowing the United States to intervene in Cuba's internal affairs under certain conditions, had been approved by a constitutional assembly on June 12, 1901. Between 1823 and 1901 a number of short-lived constitutions were proclaimed by rebel groups. On February 16, 1903, Cuba leased land and water areas at Guantanamo and Bahia Honda Bays to the United States, and from 1906 to 1909 the entire island was again under U.S. administration.

The 1901 constitution was superseded by a provisional government law in 1933, and a president was appointed, with the support of a strong-man military sergeant, Fulgencio Batista. During the following seven years seven presidents did Batista's bidding. Having promoted himself to colonel, he remained in power until 1958. During his rule, a constitutional law was promulgated in 1934, a de facto constitution adopted in 1935, and a de jure constitution promulgated in 1940, under which Batista was inaugurated president. That constitution was suspended in 1952, and a new constitutional law was issued.

In 1953 a young lawyer and politician arrested for attacking a barracks declared in court his intention to fight to restore the 1940 constitution; instead, after his release and the theoretical reestablishment of the constitution under a general amnesty granted by the newly "elected" Batista, Fidel Castro led a guerrilla war that forced Batista to flee the country. Under a de facto constitution, the 1959 Fundamental Law of the Revolution, all state power was vested in a council of ministers, with Castro as prime minister. After a brief period a social revolution based on Marxist-Leninist principles developed. As relations with the United States deteriorated, Castro courted the Soviet Union, which began a program of massive aid.

The position of prime minister was abolished when a new constitution went into effect on February 24, 1976, and Castro became president. This constitution, with some slightly liberalizing amendments, was published in the Cuban official gazette on August 1, 1992. More significant proposals for change were developed before a Cuban Communist Party congress met in October 1991, such as reestablishing the position of prime minister to handle the day-to-day affairs of government, with Castro retaining an overall leadership role as president, but the proposals never made it to the agenda of the congress. U.S. restrictions on contact with Cuba were reduced in 1999.

The Constitution

The original 1976 constitution was based largely on the 1936 constitution of the Soviet Union.

The preamble to the 1976 constitution of the Republic of Cuba asserts that Cuban citizens are heirs "of the creative work and the traditions of combativity, firmness, heroism, and sacrifice fostered by our ancestors; by the aboriginal natives who preferred extermination to submission; by the slaves who rebelled against their masters. . . ." It later invokes the vision of José Marti and the doctrine of Marx, Engels, and Lenin, closing with a quote from Marti expressing his desire that the fundamental law of Cuba recognize human dignity.

Article 1 provides that Cuba is an independent and sovereign socialist state, while article 5 declares the Communist Party to be "the highest leading force of the society and the state." In fact, Communist Party leaders assigned to specific government areas have far more power than the official heads of departments.

Chapter 6, Equality, provides that all citizens have equal rights and duties and that discrimination on the basis of race, color, sex, national origin, and religious belief (recently added) is prohibited. Violations are declared to be punishable by law. Article 43, formerly article 42, establishes the right of all citizens to be served at restaurants and other public establishments; however, one exclusive hotel in Havana warns tourists not to invite Cubans into the hotel or, if inviting them to the hotel bar, to have them register at the front desk by name and identification number. Chapter 7, Fundamental Rights, Duties, and Guarantees, recites the rights and duties of workers in the Cuban socialist society.

All power is in the hands of Castro as head of the Cuban Communist Party, although the constitution of the unitary state of Cuba divides power among the president, the council of state and cabinet, the legislature, and the courts.

In the 1992 official version of the constitution, chapter 8, which previously dealt with the supreme organs of people's power, was changed to provide for a state of emergency; chapter 9 now describes the principles of organization and functions of the state organs, and chapter 10 covers the supreme organs of people's power.

The Executive

President. The president is head of state and government, by virtue of being elected president of the council of state. Castro, as head of the Cuban Communist Party, has held the position since 1976; he was prime minister from 1959, when, after the revolution, all state power was concentrated in a council of ministers led by the prime minister. In addition to the president's power to control and supervise the activities of the ministries and assume the leadership of any ministry or central agency of administration, among other things, the 1992 version of the Cuban constitution gives him power to declare a state of emergency.

Council of State and Cabinet. The powers of the council of state include appointing, in consultation with its president, a council of ministers (cabinet); calling a special session of the legislature; setting dates for elections; issuing legal decrees between sessions of the legislature; initiating legislation; arranging for referendums called for by the legislature; ratifying and denouncing international treaties; supervising the local people's organs, including revoking or modifying their laws when it is in the interest of the nation; and issuing general instructions to the court and the office of the attorney general.

The Legislature

Parliament. The Cuban national assembly is declared the supreme organ of state power, expressing the sovereign will of the people and serving as the only body with constituent and legislative authority. The first direct elections for the assembly, whose term is five years, were held on February 24, 1993. While only about two-thirds of the members were sponsored by the Communist Party, they all indicated support of the single-party system.

The 589-member assembly, whose deputies are not entitled to personal privileges or economic benefits, elects the council of state from its members, including a president, a first vice president and five other vice presidents. Additional powers include enacting laws and calling for referendums; determining the constitutionality of laws and decrees; revoking, in whole or in part, decrees of the council of state; approving economic and social development plans and state budgets; approving general foreign and domestic policy guidelines; declaring war and approving peace; electing a president, vice president, and secretary of the assembly; electing a president, vice president, and other judges of the supreme court; and exercising the highest supervision over the organs of the state and government.

The Judiciary

The constitution declares that justice comes from the people and is exercised on their behalf by the people's supreme court and other courts established by law. Judges are to be independent in administering justice and to obey only the law; however, the courts are required to be subordinate to the legislature and the council of state, and judges may be recalled by these bodies. The courts are to function as a collegial body with professional judges and lay judges having equal rights and duties, but priority is to be given to lay judges because of their social importance and work.

As in other communist-dominated countries, the courts in Cuba are not able to function independently of either the party or government agencies. There are many political prisoners in Cuba— human rights agencies estimate three thousand—which indicates that appeal to the courts to protect human rights violations is futile.

Amending the Constitution

The legislature may amend the constitution by a majority vote of at least two-thirds of all the members in a roll-call vote; but a total revision or amendment affecting the authority of the legislature, the council of state, or rights and duties in the constitution must be approved by a majority of all citizens eligible to vote in a referendum and, of course, by Fidel Castro.

After more than forty years under communist rule, the western half of the former country of Czechoslovakia, now the Czech Republic, is being governed under a multiparty democratic constitution that became effective in 1993.

The Czech Republic in central Europe is approximately 78,900 square kilometers and is bounded by Germany on the west, Poland on the north, Slovakia on the east, and Austria on the south. Prague is the capital of this country of approximately ten million persons.

An industrialized nation in 1948 when the communists took over, Czechoslovakia was the world's eighth largest exporter of weapons before 1989. Broad privatization laws were passed in 1991. The Czech Republic, which is oriented toward western Europe, should continue to progress economically under a stable democratic system of government.

Type of Government: Presidential-style parliamentary republic, with a president, a premier (prime minister) and council of state (cabinet), a bicameral legislature, and a judiciary, including a constitutional court

Dates of Constitutions: 1920, 1948, 1960, 1969, and 1993

A Slavic group called the West Slavs inhabited the area of the former Czechoslovakia sometime after the first century A.D. By the seventh century the Czechs had settled in their present territory and by the ninth century had established the Great Moravian Empire. At the beginning of the tenth century the empire was conquered by the Hungarians, who then ruled the eastern Slovakian part. The Premysl dynasty, which included "good King Wenceslas," ruled until 1306 in the western region, called Bohemia or the Czech Kingdom. A succession of Luxembourgs and Holy Roman Emperors followed.

In the fifteenth century Jan Hus, a Reformation leader, was burned at the stake for heresy, igniting religious wars that culminated with the Thirty Years' War, which began in 1618. The Czechs were basically Protestant, while their rulers tended to be Catholic. The parliament elected George of Podebrady king in 1458; a little ahead of his time, he tried to found a European organization to ensure peace. After the reign of the Jagiellonians, during which the power of the parliament was strengthened, the Hapsburgs ruled the Czech kingdom from 1526 until 1918.

Czech constitutional law at this time developed out of the regional and national parliaments, and legal works in the 1400s and 1500s for the most part escaped the influence of Roman law. In 1550 the parliament enacted the constitutions of King Vladislav, codifying laws governing the nobility, and in 1627 a constitutional document, influenced by Roman law, made the monarchy hereditary rather than elective.

During World War I Czechs and Slovaks opposing the Austro-Hungarian forces were headquartered in France, and many moved to the United States. Under the leadership of Thomas Masaryk and Edward Beneš, an agreement was signed in Pittsburgh to create an independent Czechoslovakian republic of Bohemia, Moravia, part of Silesia, Slovakia, and subcarpathian Ruthenia. The document was proclaimed in Prague on October 28, 1918. A model democracy under a 1920 constitution, the country was occupied by Nazi Germany following the disastrous Munich agreement in 1938. After the war the Soviet Union and Czechoslovakian communists colluded to establish a communist regime in the country in February 1948. On May 9, 1948, a communist constitution, consolidating "the revolutionary achievements of the working class," was adopted by a national constituent assembly. The Soviet Union's evolution from outright exploitation to mutual trade relations with its Eastern Bloc countries culminated in 1960. In Czechoslovakia a new constitution was promulgated, proclaiming the country to be second only to the Soviet Union in becoming a "socialist republic."

In January 1968 Alexander Dubček became the first Slovak to serve as the top Communist Party official, but his attempt to liberalize the regime, called "Czechoslovakia's Road to Socialism" or "Socialism with a Human Face," was premature and resulted in an invasion by the Soviet Union and its eastern European allies in August. Following the brutal crushing of the "Prague Spring," the country returned to the conservative communist fold under a 1969 constitution that provided for mutual recognition of Czech and Slovak sovereignty.

Major changes were again undertaken in 1988, but this time with the support of the Soviet Union under Mikhail Gorbachev. New governments were inaugurated in both the Czech and Slovak Republics, and French President François Mitterand met with the dissident Václav Havel, although Dubček remained under house arrest. After Havel's arrest in 1989, a quarter million demonstrators marched in Prague. On December 10 the first noncommunist government in forty-one years was sworn in.

After the Slovak government rejected a strong central government for a Czechoslovakian federation proposed by the Czechs during constitutional talks in 1992, both sides drew up virtually identical separation plans. A multiparty democratic constitution went into effect for the separate Czech Republic on January 1, 1993.

Influences

European presidential-style parliaments served as models for the new republic. The new nation's first president, playwright Václav Havel, observed that the president, "rather than be an author of specific political solutions . . . should become a guarantee of their legitimacy, guardian of their scope and of the rules for their drafting; a guardian of the political culture which surrounds the drafting."

The Constitution

The preamble to the 1993 constitution begins: "We, the citizens of the Czech Republic in Bohemia, Moravia, and Silesia, at a time of the renewal of an independent Czech state. . . ."

Article 2 elaborates on the scope of the new act:

(1) All state power derives from the people; they exercise this power by means of their legislative, executive, and judicial bodies.

(2) A constitutional law may stipulate the cases when the people exercise state power directly.

(3) The state power serves all citizens and can be exercised only in cases and within the scope stipulated by law, and by means specified by law.

(4) Every citizen may do whatever is not forbidden by law, and no one may be forced to do what the law does not enjoin.

"The political system," adds article 5, "is based on the free and voluntary foundation and free competition of political parties respecting fundamental principles and rejecting force as a means for asserting their interests."

Fundamental Rights

The constitution declares that it is based on respect for the rights and freedoms of the individual and the citizen, that fundamental rights and freedoms enjoy the protection of the judiciary, and that a charter of fundamental rights and freedoms, a constitutional law that became effective on February 8, 1991, "was part of the constitutional order of the Czech Republic."

Division of Powers

In this unitary state, power is divided among the president, the premier, the legislature, and the courts, including a constitutional court that exercises constitutional review.

The Executive

President. The president, elected for a five-year term by a majority vote of both houses of the legislature at a joint session, is head of state and commander in chief of the armed forces. Any citizen eligible for the upper house of the legislature is eligible to be president but must be nominated by at least ten members of either house and may not be elected for more than two consecutive terms.

The powers and duties of the president include appointing and dismissing the premier (prime minister) and other members of the government; convening and dissolving the lower house of the legislature; appointing judges, the chairman, and deputy chairmen of the constitutional and supreme courts; granting pardons and amnesty, as well as mitigating penalties; returning other than constitutional laws to the legislature; signing laws; appointing the president and vice president of the supreme inspection office and members of the bank council of the national bank; representing the state in external affairs; negotiating and ratifying international treaties; receiving and accrediting diplomats; appointing and promoting generals; and conferring state distinctions. The president may also be authorized by law to exercise other powers not expressly specified.

Certain actions of the president require the countersignature of the premier or other designated member of government. The president is granted broad immunity for his or her actions but may be prosecuted for high treason on indictment by the upper house of the legislature. If the office becomes vacant, the functions are expressly split between the premier and the chairman of the legislature's lower house.

Prime Minister and Cabinet. According to article 67, the government is the supreme body of executive power and is composed of the premier (prime minister), deputy premiers, and ministers. The president appoints the premier, who suggests other members of the government, which the constitution makes accountable to the lower house of the legislature.

Parliament. Article 15 vests legislative power in a bicameral parliament, the Parlament Ceské Republiky, composed of an upper house, the senate, and a lower house, the chamber of deputies. Until the elections of 1994, however, the parliament operated under the 1993 constitution as a unicameral body.

According to article 34, the houses of parliament "are continually in session" but may be adjourned by resolution up to a total of 120 days a year. Members may not serve in both chambers at the same time and may not be the president or a judge. They enjoy certain immunities unless caught in a criminal act or immediately thereafter.

Upper House. The senate is to consist of eighty-one members who are elected by universal, equal, and direct suffrage for six-year terms. Citizens eligible to vote may run for the senate if they are at least forty years old.

Lower House. The 200-member chamber of deputies is similarly elected but for four-year terms based on proportional representation. Candidates must be at least twenty-one years old and eligible to vote.

The president may dissolve the chamber under certain circumstances, including where there is a no-confidence vote in a new government whose premier was appointed by the president on the suggestion of the chairman of the lower chamber. If the chamber is dissolved, the senate may pass measures that cannot be postponed, with the exception of constitutional laws, the budget and annual accounts, election laws, and international agreements involving human rights and freedoms. Members of the lower chamber also have the right of interpellation, to pose questions to members of the government; replies to matters falling under their jurisdiction must be provided in thirty days.

A bill may be submitted by deputies, the senate, the government, and representatives of "higher territorial self-governing entities." Draft laws on the budget or annual accounts are submitted by the government and handled only in the lower house, which may also investigate affairs in the public interest. Both houses set up committees and commissions in accordance with law as well as elect and dismiss a chairman and vice chairmen.

One-third of the members of each house constitute a quorum; generally, matters are passed by a vote of a majority of those present. A declaration of war and permission to allow foreign troops into the country require a vote of a majority of the members in each house, and a constitutional law or international treaty involving rights and freedoms requires a three-fifths majority vote in each chamber. The government can require action by the lower chamber in thirty days; the senate must act on a measure in thirty days or it is presumed to be passed. The president may return an adopted bill, but a veto may be overridden by an affirmative vote of a majority of all the members of the lower chamber. Adopted laws are signed by the chairman of the lower chamber, the president, and the premier.

The Judiciary

According to article 81, "Judicial power is exercised by independent courts on behalf of the republic." The constitution contains provisions for ensuring the independence of the judiciary, and the courts are charged, above all, with protecting rights in a manner determined by law. Only courts may decide guilt or impose penalties for criminal acts.

The judiciary consists of a supreme court, a supreme administrative court, and high, regional, and district courts, whose jurisdiction and organization are to be determined by law.

Constitutional Court. A constitutional court is composed of fifteen judges appointed by the president with the consent of the upper house of the legislature for ten-year terms. This court may, in addition to other actions, nullify laws, parts of laws, or regulations that contradict a constitutional law or a treaty that establishes rights and freedoms; hear constitutional complaints by self-administering bodies alleging unlawful state interference and interference by bodies of public power with constitutionally guaranteed rights and freedoms; enforce legal remedies in parliamentary elections; and hear a constitutional indictment of the president by the upper house of the legislature.

Amending the Constitution

Article 9 provides that amendments must be made by constitutional laws, and changes or interpretations that threaten the democratic and law-observing state are inadmissible. Article 39 provides that a constitutional law requires the consent of a three-fifths majority of the members of each house of the legislature.

Europe's oldest monarchy—with a lineage extending back more than a thousand years without a major revolution—Denmark began its constitutional development, like England, with a thirteenth-century document limiting the authority of the monarch.

The Kingdom of Denmark is a little more than 43,000 kilometers in area and occupies the Jutland Peninsula, north of Germany. It is bounded by the Skagerrak on the north, the Kattegat on the east, and the North Sea on the west. Denmark is responsible only for foreign affairs and defense of its North Atlantic territories, the Faeroe Islands and Greenland. More than one-fourth of this country's little more than five million inhabitants live in or near the capital city of Copenhagen.

Denmark is a highly industrialized and prosperous country that allows its citizens to enjoy a high standard of living in a social welfare state. Recently the government has taken strong measures to reduce the nation's large debt, and Denmark appears to be on the road to genuine economic reform and continued political stability, having generally approved incorporation in the European Union (Maastricht Treaty).

Type of Government: Parliamentary constitutional monarchy, with a monarch, a prime minister and council of ministers (cabinet), a unicameral legislature, and a judiciary

Dates of Constitutions: 1849, 1855, 1863, and 1953

The land of Denmark became hospitable to nomadic hunters after the last ice age around 12,000 B.C. By 4000 B.C. the people were engaged in agriculture, and later advanced Bronze and Iron Age cultures developed. The Greeks and Romans had some impact, although the Roman Empire never extended to Danish lands. As the Roman Empire declined in the West, a wealthy warrior class arose and began to control areas of the country.

A tribe called the Danes migrated from Sweden around A.D. 500 and settled in the land that would take its name. The Frankish king Charlemagne extended his dominion into northern Europe, bringing Viking raids in response and causing many people to trade their liberty for protection, a stimulus to the development of feudalism in Europe. Denmark, which historically also included the southern part of modern Sweden, was a Viking kingdom, but it fell to a Norwegian chieftain in the latter half of the tenth century; his son, Canute the Great, conquered England. The origins of the current Danish monarchy extend to Gorm the Old, Canute's ancestor. In 1282 the king was forced to issue a document requiring a national assembly to be held once a year.

Fearing Germany, Denmark formed the Union of Kalmar with Norway and Sweden in 1397. Following the Thirty Years' War Denmark's star was eclipsed by Sweden, and Denmark lost its Swedish provinces. The Danish monarch then stripped the nobility of its political influence, and an absolutist government was created in 1665. An insane king's physician took control of the government twenty years before the French Revolution, making liberal changes until he was executed for having an illicit affair with the queen.

Danish law developed from provincial laws dating from the end of the twelfth century. A law code was produced late in the seventeenth century, but, unlike in Germany, Roman law had little influence until after natural law came into vogue and legal theories in the Roman law countries came to be appreciated in the eighteenth and nineteenth centuries, respectively.

By the end of the eighteenth century a progressive landowners' government had extended civil rights to the peasants and mandated compulsory education for all children. The reforms were halted after 1814, the year in which Denmark was forced to cede Norway to Sweden; but in 1830 consultative provincial assemblies were set up, and a liberal constitution was adopted in 1849.

In 1855 a new constitution included the duchies of Slesvig and Holstein, which lay between Denmark and Germany. But Holstein and German dissatisfaction led to another constitution in 1863 incorporating only Slesvig. The following year Austria and Germany declared war, and Denmark ended up losing one-third of its territory.

Retrenchment began again with the abolition of universal suffrage. This set the stage for a constitutional struggle that ended in 1901, when the king appointed the first Liberal Party government and the idea of a cabinet responsible to the majority in the legislature became accepted. This change, however, was not formally adopted until the current constitution, which also abolished the upper house of the legislature, went into effect on June 5, 1953.

Influences

The 1849 constitution was inspired by both the Belgian and the Norwegian constitutions, and for many years Nordic countries have influenced one another's legal systems. The 1953 constitution is similar to the 1849 version.

The Constitution

In addition to the 1953 Constitution of the Kingdom of Denmark Act, the 1953 Succession to the Throne Act is a document of constitutional status. The Faeroe Islands have been self-governing within the Kingdom of Denmark since 1948, and Greenland was granted self-government as a distinct community within the kingdom in 1979.

Fundamental Rights

Article 4 of the constitution act provides that the state will support the Evangelical Lutheran Church, and article 6 requires the monarch to be a member of the state church. Part 6, however, provides for freedom of religion.

Part 7 guarantees personal liberty and due process of law, the inviolability of dwellings, the right to private property, free and equal access to trade, the right to work, public assistance, free primary education, freedom of speech, a free press without prior censorship, and freedom of assembly and association; it also abolishes feudal estates. Article 81 requires able-bodied males to contribute to the country's defense.

Division of Powers

Power in this unitary state is divided among the monarch, as head of state; the prime minister, as head of government; the legislature; and the courts, which exercise customary and restrained judicial review.

The Executive

Monarch. The monarch, currently a queen, is not answerable for her actions, which today are chiefly ceremonial. All of her official acts must be countersigned by a minister of the government.

The monarch's official duties include appointing and dismissing the prime minister and other ministers, assenting to legislation, impeaching ministers for inefficient or dishonest administration of their offices, introducing bills in the legislature, and granting clemency. Article 7 indicates that the monarch is to preside over the council of state or the ministers, but she does not, in fact, attend cabinet meetings. Viewed as politically neutral, the queen does not vote in elections, remaining above politics.

Prime Minister and Cabinet. With the growth of the Danish welfare state, the power of the prime minister and the cabinet, called the council of ministers, has expanded. In 1993 the cabinet, whose members are generally but not necessarily members of the legislature, had twenty-four members, including seven women.

The prime minister presides over the cabinet and, according to article 18 of the 1953 constitutional act, is to submit the minutes of the votes of the ministers to the monarch, who may decide to have a matter brought before her or him in a council of state. In fact, however, as in other European monarchies, the prime minister and cabinet are responsible for all acts of the government. Most of the governments formed have had to be minority coalitions, which are permitted to govern without a vote of confidence for a short time until a majority can be created. Since the 1960s prime ministers have had to dissolve the parliament and call new elections about every two years.

Parliament. The Danish unicameral parliament is called the Folketing. According to article 28, "The Folketing shall consist of one assembly of not more than one hundred and seventy-nine members, of whom two members shall be elected in the Faeroe Islands, and two members in Greenland." Technically, legislative power resides in the monarch and the parliament, but as in most parliamentary systems today the parliament itself is virtually supreme.

Any subject living in Denmark who is eighteen years old and not otherwise disenfranchised may vote in general elections by direct vote and may be elected to parliament for a maximum term of four years. There are three election zones—Copenhagen, Jutland, and the islands—and seventeen districts with 103 constituencies. The constitution requires that in determining the parliamentary seats to be allotted to each area, the number of inhabitants and electors and the density of the population must be considered. The proportional electoral system devised is complicated, however, and allows for many parties to win seats in the Folketing.

After elections the parliament elects a president and vice presidents, and at the first meeting the prime minister renders an accounting of the state of the country and presents the government's program. The parliament is authorized to make its own rules of procedure.

Any member may introduce a bill, which must pass three readings. One-third of the members may ask the president of the parliament to submit a passed bill for a referendum, except for certain types of legislation including money bills; a majority of those voting may defeat the measure, provided they constitute no less than thirty percent of the eligible voters. Referendums have rarely been called for, but the threat alone ensures that the majority takes the minority's concerns into consideration.

In addition to ordinary legislation, the parliament passes a finance act, initiates amendments to the constitution, may express its lack of confidence in the government, elects auditors to examine the annual public accounts, and may appoint committees to investigate matters, appoints one or two persons (but not members) to control the civil and military administration of the state.

Ombudsman. The parliament also appoints a traditional ombudsman and, since 1975, an ombudsman for consumer affairs.

The constitution provides that the exercise of judicial power is to be governed only by statute and that the administration of justice must always remain independent of the executive power. It also provides that in the performance of their duties judges are to be directed solely by the law, which includes legislation, executive orders issued pursuant to legislation, and custom and judicial practice.

The jurisdiction of the courts of justice, which is not spelled out in the constitution, includes deciding private conflicts and imposing punishment, deciding questions of the scope of administrative authority, and, by custom, deciding if laws are compatible with the constitution. This last function is exercised with deference to the legislators.

At the bottom of the hierarchy of the ordinary judicial courts in Denmark are the lower circuit courts. The next level consists of two high courts, one each for the eastern and western circuits. The high courts are courts of first instance, although lower courts may refer cases to a high court.

Supreme Court. The highest court, the supreme court, consists of a chief justice and fourteen other judges. It hears only cases on appeal, and generally these are cases that were adjudicated in the first instance by the high courts. The supreme court often divides into two sections with at least five judges hearing each case.

Amending the Constitution

After the parliament passes a bill to amend the constitution, a new election must be held. If the bill is again passed, without change, it must then be approved in a referendum by a majority vote, with at least forty percent of the electorate voting. It becomes effective after receiving the royal assent.

After liberation from Spanish rule in 1822, Ecuador experienced alternating periods of constitutional and military government. For more than twenty years the country has maintained a civilian democracy.

The Republic of Ecuador is approximately 280,000 square kilometers and, except for the Galapagos Islands, is situated on the continent of South America. It is bounded by Colombia on the north, Peru on the east and south, and the Pacific Ocean on the west. Quito is the capital of this country of approximately thirteen million persons.

Ecuador's economy is based on oil, minerals, and agriculture, but its confrontational politics and ailing economy do not support a prognosis of long-term stability.

Type of Government: Presidential republic, with a president and cabinet, a unicameral legislature, a judiciary, and a constitutional tribunal

Dates of Constitutions: 1812, 1821, 1830, 1835, 1843, 1845, 1851, 1861, 1897, 1906 (reinstated in 1935 and 1939), 1929, 1945 (reinstated in 1972 and 1976), 1946, 1967, 1979, and 1998

Limited archeological exploration indicates that in 3500 B.C. people lived on the coast of the territory of what is now Ecuador, and many other sites date from about two thousand years ago. In the fifteenth century invading Incas met with stiff resistance from tribes such as the Canari, Cara, and Quitu. By 1500, however, the territory had been incorporated into the Incan Empire, which was to be ruled by Atahualpa, whose father was the Incan emperor and whose mother was the daughter of a Cara king. Atahualpa had defeated a half brother for the throne, only to be conquered in 1532 by Francisco Pizarro and killed a year later.

Like other Spanish colonies in America, Ecuador was ruled in the name of the monarch through a council of the Indies and a house of trade, which governed commerce between Spain and the colonies. The instruments of government in the New World were the viceroy or provincial governor, the *audiencia* (a combination of executive, legislative, and judicial functions), and the *cabildos* (municipal councils). Although permitted its own *audiencia* in 1563, Ecuador remained a part of the viceroyalty of Peru until it was placed under the viceroyalty of New Granada in the early eighteenth century.

After Napoleon deposed the king of Spain in 1808, a group of leading citizens of Quito seized power from the French representative. In 1810, by agreement, a junta composed mostly of *criollos* (pure-blooded Spaniards born in the colonies) was permitted to govern. A constitution promulgated in February 1812, however, lasted only until November of that year, when troops from Peru put down a rebellion. The forces of the South American liberators José de San Martín and Simón Bolívar Palacios combined to bring independence to Ecuador in 1822, and the country joined with Colombia and Venezuela in the confederation of Gran Colombia under its constitution of 1821.

Ecuador seceded from Gran Colombia in 1830 and established a strong presidential system with a unicameral legislature and an independent judiciary under its own constitution. An 1835 Bolivian-style constitution emphasized the unitary and centralized nature of the state. In 1843 a new constitution extended the president's term from four to eight years and made Catholicism the state religion. Constitutions in 1845 and 1851 were attempts at liberalization after authoritarian regimes, but in 1861 the constitution resuscitated the strong presidency with a legislature that met biannually. An anticlerical trend informed the 1897 constitution, and the 1906 constitution detailed protections for civil and political rights. The presidents generally were authoritarian, from the military, and dictatorial, although from 1895 to 1925 there was a period of liberal leadership.

A semiparliamentary system was tried under the 1929 constitution, but in 1935 and then again in 1939 the 1906 constitution was reinstated. Checks on the president were incorporated in the 1945 constitution, causing it to be replaced by the incumbent José María Velasco Ibarra in 1946. After three years under the 1967 constitution, the same president, in his fifth term, assumed extraconstitutional powers, suspending the constitution and ruling by decree. Following a coup, his successor reinstated the 1945 document in 1972, but it was suspended in 1974. The next junta in 1976 again reinstated the 1945 constitution.

A new constitution patterned after the 1945 and 1967 documents was promulgated in 1979. In 1997, however, a constitutional crisis was precipitated when the legislature removed the president on the grounds of mental incapacity and installed in the presidency its chairman rather than the vice president, as required by the constitution. After a referendum voiced support for the new president and for calling a constitutional assembly in 1997, a new constitution was adopted on June 5 and went into force on August 10, 1998.

Influences

Influenced by its predecessors, Ecuador's 1998 constitution makes concessions recognizing the problems of the nation's diverse cultures, especially the rights of indigenous peoples.

The Constitution

The preamble "proclaims the will to strengthen the unity of the Ecuadoran nation by recognizing the diversity of its regions, people, ethnicities and cultures," adding that the constitution establishes "the fundamental norms that support the rights and liberties, organize the State and democratic institutions and propel the economic and social development."

Article 1 declares that "Ecuador is a social state of law, sovereignty, unitary, independent, democratic, multicultural and multiethnic. Its government is republican, presidential, elective, representative, responsible, alternating, participatory and administered through decentralization. Sovereignty resides in the people." Under article 3, the state's duties include "[t]o strengthen national unity in its diversity," "ensure the application of human rights, the fundamental liberties of men and women, and social security," "eradicate poverty . . . ," and "guarantee the functioning of the democratic system and a public administration free from corruption." Article 272 adds: "The Constitution shall prevail over any other legal norm."

Fundamental Rights

"The highest duty of the State," proclaims article 16, "consists of respecting and enforcing respect for the human rights guaranteed by this Constitution." Such rights under article 23 include the "[i]nviolability of life"; "personal integrity"; and a prohibition of "cruel penalties and tortures," "sexual violence," and "the undue application and use of genetic human material." Also guaranteed are equality before the law; liberty; the "right to the free development of one's personality"; a healthy environment; personal and family privacy; freedom of opinion, expression, conscience, and religion; the inviolability of the home and correspondence; the rights to travel, to petition the authorities, and to work without duress and make contracts; and freedom of "association and of assembly for peaceful purposes."

Article 24 addresses the rights of persons detained and accused of crimes. Under article 26, citizens are extended "the right to elect and to be elected, to present bills to the National Congress, . . . [and] to supervise the acts of the organs of public power. . . ." Articles 30 through 82 cover economic, social, and cultural rights in areas such as property, work, the family, health, vulnerable groups, social security, culture, education, science and technology, communication, and sports. Articles 83 through 92 deal with collective rights, in particular the rights of "indigenous and black or Afro-Ecuadoran peoples," the environment, and consumers. The rights of habeas corpus, habeas data (the right to information about oneself), and *amparo* are also guaranteed.

Division of Powers

Article 118 recognizes government responsibilities as those "of the Legislative, Executive and Judicial Function."

President. Article 164 provides that the president "exercises the Executive Function [and is] chief of State and of the government, and the person responsible for the public administration." The president and vice president, who serves in the president's absence, are elected on the same ballot for a four-year term by an absolute majority of votes cast in "a universal, equal, direct and secret manner." If necessary, a runoff election is held forty-five days later. Incumbents may be reelected only after the expiration of another full term.

A candidate must be Ecuadoran born, possess political rights, and be at least thirty-five years old; disqualifications include being the spouse, parents, children, or siblings of the current president, vice president, and ministers—"unless they resign before ... their candidacy"—and others set forth in article 101, such as certain civil and military officials.

The president is required to comply with and enforce "the Constitution, the laws, international treaties and agreements and other juridical norms"; present "a plan of government"; "[e]stablish general policies of the State"; "participate in the ... formation and promulgation of laws"; and "[i]ssue the regulations necessary for the application of the laws...." He or she also convokes popular referendums, directs the public administration, appoints and removes ministers of state, defines foreign policy, exercises "maximum authority over the public force," politically directs any wars, and sets the country's population policies.

Under article 130, the president and vice president may be subjected to a "political trial" (impeachment) by the legislature and may be removed from office by a vote of two-thirds of the members of the legislature.

Cabinet. According to article 176, "The ministers of State [cabinet] shall be freely appointed and removed by the President ... and shall represent him in matters corresponding to [their] ministry." The ministers' powers and duties include directing the policy of their ministry; signing, "along with the President, decrees issued on matters that concern their ministry"; informing the legislature on matters for which they are responsible; and attending legislative sessions and participating in debates.

Congress. "The Legislative Function," declares article 126, "is exercised by the National Congress, located in Quito." It is composed of "two legislators elected for each province, and one more for each three hundred thousand inhabitants ... [as] established by the last national population census." Under article 127, "To be a deputy, one must be Ecuadoran by birth, be in full enjoyment of the rights of citizenship, be at least twenty-five years old ... and be a native of the respective province, or have continuously resided in it for at least three years immediately prior to the election."

Legally recognized parties may support candidates, while unaffiliated citizens may also be candidates. Deputies are elected for four years and "may be reelected indefinitely." According to article 99, "In plural elections, citizens may select preferred candidates from one list or from several lists. The law shall reconcile this principle with that of proportional representation of minorities." Congress elects a president and vice presidents every two years.

The legislature installs the nation's president and vice president and has responsibilities related to either's resignation, impeachment, disability, or abandonment of their posts. The legislature also amends the constitution, oversees "the acts of the Executive Function and the Supreme Electoral Tribunal," approves the budget and oversees its execution, appoints certain officers including the attorney general and "members of the managing boards of the Constitutional Tribunal and Supreme Electoral Tribunal." Article 141 outlines legislative subjects, including regulation of "fundamental liberties and rights guaranteed in the Constitution," crime and punishment, taxes, the powers and duties of subordinate authorities, and reform or derogation of laws. Matters requiring organic laws—such as legislative, executive and judicial activities and the electoral system—are set out in article 142.

Bills may be introduced by a "legislative block" (ten deputies) or by the president, the supreme court, or the "Legislation and Codification Commission." Other government units may introduce bills on matters within their jurisdiction. A number of special rules govern the presentation of certain types of legislation. Once introduced, a bill must generally receive at least two debates. After approval, a bill is sent to the president, who may veto it in total or in part. A veto may be overridden by two-thirds of the legislators. Bills vetoed on constitutional grounds are sent to the constitutional tribunal.

The Judiciary

"The exercise of the judicial power corresponds to the organs of the Judicial Function," declares article 191. "There shall be justices of the peace, responsible for equitably deciding individual, community or neighbor conflicts," it states, adding that "authorities of the indigenous peoples shall exercise functions of justice, applying their own norms and procedures...."

Pursuant to article 198, judicial bodies are the supreme court of justice; courts, tribunals, and other judicial forums established by the constitution and law; and a national council of the judicature. The council is the judiciary's "governing, administrative and disciplinary organ." Judicial bodies are to be independent; "[m]agistrates and judges ... are only subject to the Constitution and the law," article 199 indicates.

Supreme Court. "The Supreme Court," according to article 200, "shall have jurisdiction in all of the national territory and its seat shall be in Quito. It shall act as a court of cassation [appeal] ... and shall additionally exercise all the powers attributed to it by the Constitution and the laws." Members must be Ecuadoran by birth; enjoy political rights; be forty-five years of age; be a doctor of jurisprudence, law, or legal sciences; and have fifteen years of experience. Jurists have no fixed term of office; vacancies are filled by "a favorable vote of two-thirds of [the court's] members."

Constitutional Tribunal

Ecuador's constitutional tribunal, according to article 275, consists of nine members designated for four-year terms by a majority of the legislature—two selected from nominees named by the president, two by the supreme court, two by the legislature, one by mayors and "provincial prefects," one by workers and indigenous and peasant organizations, and one by the "Production Chambers." The tribunal, among other responsibilities, resolves complaints regarding the constitutionality of laws, administrative acts, and denials of habeas corpus, habeas data, and *amparo* suits; reviews presidential assertions that proposed laws are unconstitutional; rules "whether international treaties or agreements conform to the Constitution"; and settles "conflicts of competence or of powers assigned by the Constitution."

Amending the Constitution

According to article 280, the constitution "may be reformed by the National Congress or through popular referendum." Proposed amendments may be presented in the legislature by "twenty percent of its members or a legislative block," as well as by the president, the supreme court, the constitutional tribunal, or one percent of the registered voters. Except in urgent cases, amendment bills follow the same procedures as laws, except that a period of one year must elapse between the first and second debate, and the vote after the second debate "requires two-thirds of the total members" of the legislature. The president's approval is also required.

An amendment may be submitted to a referendum in emergency cases or when the legislature has failed to act 120 days after the lapse of the one-year period. In both events, states article 283, the proposed amendment is to be submitted to the electorate, and if it is approved it is "immediately incorporated into the Constitution."

For nearly five millennia Egypt's destiny was in the hands of strong rulers or foreign interventionists. Significant 1980 amendments to the 1971 constitution, including provision for multiple political parties, may finally give the Egyptian people an important role in their national government.

General Information

The Arab Republic of Egypt in northern Africa is approximately one million square kilometers and is bounded on the north by the Mediterranean Sea, on the west by Libya, on the south by Sudan, and on the east by the Red Sea, Jordan, the Gaza Strip, and Israel. The capital of this country of approximately sixty-eight million inhabitants is Cairo.

Egypt's strategic location—it is the western gateway to Asia and the site of the Suez Canal, which links the Mediterranean Sea with the Red Sea and the Indian Ocean—has influenced much of its six-thousand-year history. In the late 1920s and 1930s, when the price of Egypt's main crop, cotton, plunged on the world market, the nation began to industrialize. Today oil, textiles, and tourism are among its chief industries.

Type of Government: Presidential-style parliamentary republic, with a president, a prime minister and council of ministers (cabinet), a unicameral legislature, a judiciary, and a constitutional court

Dates of Constitutions: 1923, 1956, 1958 (provisional), 1964 (provisional), and 1971 (significantly amended in 1980)

Constitutional History

Historians consider Egypt the first large-scale, organized human society. For their time the early Egyptians were an advanced people who believed in life after death and charted the heavens to predict floods for agricultural planning. Ancient Egyptians equated the unification of Upper (southern) and Lower (northern) Egypt under the first pharaoh with the beginning of the universe.

The Egyptian civilization lasted for thousands of years under the pharaohs. It was eventually conquered by the Greek Ptolemies, then by the Romans, and in A.D. 642 by the Arabs, whose influence still lingers. While under Arab rule in the ninth century, Egypt was allowed local hereditary rulers, and in 1260 the Egyptian ruler Qutuz successfully defeated the invading Mongols, keeping the Islamic religion alive. Later conquerors included the Fatimids, Mamluks, and Ottoman Turks.

Under the Ottomans, the Sunni Muslim influence in religion, education, and religious law courts continued, as did the Mamluk influence. In the late eighteenth century the Mamluk leaders *(beys)* broke free from Ottoman control, only to be conquered by Napoleon on July 1, 1789. When the French withdrew after occupying Egypt for three years, the Mamluks and Ottomans fought for control. Out of this conflict a junior commander of the Albanian contingent of the Ottoman forces, Muhammad Ali, rose to become an Ottoman viceroy, then governor, and finally the father of modern Egypt. Ali and his successors tried to modernize the country and make it competitive but were thwarted by fluctuations in the world price of cotton, the expense of improving the country's infrastructure, unfavorable Suez Canal development concessions, and British and French intervention in the country's affairs.

Just thirteen years after its creation, a powerless assembly of delegates consisting mainly of Egyptian nobles was ordered dissolved in 1879 by the Egyptian *khedive* (Turkish viceroy) after he suspended payment on European loans. The *khedive* was forced into exile, and the British occupied Egypt from 1882 until February 28, 1922, when the nation was unilaterally granted its independence.

Sultan Ahmad Faud became King Faud I of Egypt under a 1923 constitution, which provided for a parliament, and his son, Faruk, was named as his heir. In the 1924 elections the

Wafd Party, which had grown out of an Egyptian delegation that sued for independence from Britain, won 179 of 211 parliamentary seats. In 1952 Faruk was forced to abdicate after a revolution by the Free Officers' Movement, which included Lt. Col. Gamal Abdul Nasser. A revolutionary command council dictated policy to the civilian cabinet, and in 1953 the constitution was abrogated and a republic proclaimed. In 1956 a new constitution created a national assembly with limited powers, a cabinet, and a president, the position to which Nasser was elected; this constitution lasted twenty months. The union between Syria and Egypt occurred on February 21, 1958, and on March 5, 1958, a provisional constitution for the United Arab Republic was approved. This union, however, was abolished on September 27, 1961.

On September 27, 1962, President Nasser issued a constitutional declaration on collective leadership, and a presidential and executive council was formed to exercise the power of the state. The declaration included translated passages from the *Communist Manifesto* and was regarded by some as superseding the 1956 constitution. In 1964 Nasser again issued a declaration creating a provisional constitution, which lasted until 1971.

On May 20, 1971, Nasser's successor, Mohamed Anwar El Sadat, asked the national assembly to draft a permanent constitution and outlined certain basic principles to be considered. The establishment of the Federation of Arab Republics, composed of Syria, Libya, and Egypt, called for each country to make its constitution conform to the terms of the federation. This and the fact that one goal of the 1952 revolution—the establishment of a sound democratic life—had not yet been realized led to the proclamation of a new constitution on September 11, 1971.

Influences

The 1971 constitution was based on the 1956 Nasser document and retained its authoritarian style and single-party structure. Partly as a result of internal pressures and the Egyptian-Israeli Peace Treaty signed in Washington, D.C., on March 26, 1979, the constitution was amended on May 22, 1980, to create a multiparty system.

The Constitution

The 1980 amendments to the 1971 constitution were so significant that the Egyptian government now refers to the amended document as the 1980 constitution. In addition to creating the multiparty system, key changes included specifying Arabic as the official language and Islamic jurisprudence as the principal source of legislation; creating the Shoura council, which the president and cabinet must consult on major government issues; and establishing the press as a "popular, independent authority."

The Egyptian constitution recognizes Islam as the official state religion. In Islamic countries, law and the Islamic religion have been conjoined for centuries. With respect to the relationship of the Islamic religion to government and politics, the Egyptian constitution falls somewhere between the secular constitution of Turkey and the theocratic constitution of Iran.

The current constitution includes a statement by Anwar Sadat officially acknowledging the May 22, 1980, amendments and a constitutional proclamation dated September 11, 1971, which serves as a preamble. The proclamation expresses four goals: world peace, Arab unity, the constant development of life in the nation, and human freedom. This last goal undoubtedly reflects the Egyptian people's frustration with the previous failures of constitutional safeguards for the individual, particularly after the 1952 revolution.

Article 1, part 1, on the State, establishes Egypt as an Arab nation: "The Arab Republic of Egypt is a democratic, socialist state based on the alliance of the working people. The Egyptian people are part of the Arab nation and work for the realization of its comprehensive unity." However, approximately ninety percent of the Egyptian population consists of the *fellah* (Hamatic people descended from the ancient Egyptians), while only eight or nine percent are of Arabic descent.

The rights of the Egyptian people include equal opportunity; protection of motherhood and the family on the basis of religion, morality, and patriotism; equality for women within the rules of Islamic jurisprudence; the right to hold public office; and the right to social and health insurance and education, including religious education. Work is a right, a duty, and an honor.

Discrimination on the basis of race, ethnic origin, language, religion, or creed is generally prohibited; personal freedom is recognized, and individuals are protected from unlawful arrest or detention and coerced self-incrimination; people are to be protected in their homes and in their communications, except by legal warrant; freedom of religion, opinion, press, scientific research, artistic and cultural activity, residence and movement are affirmed; and the right to vote and to address public authorities in writing individually (but not as a group) are guaranteed. A 1980 amendment added a chapter on the press, defining it as "a popular, independent authority exercising its true vocation in accordance with the stipulations of the constitution and the law" and guaranteeing freedom of the press, forbidding press censorship, and incorporating other safeguards for the press.

As a unitary state, power in Egypt is divided among the president, as head of state; the prime minister, as head of government; the legislature; the courts; and the constitutional court, which has constitutional review functions.

President. Article 73 delineates the president's powerful role: "The head of state is the President of the Republic. He shall assert the sovereignty of the people, respect the constitution and the supremacy of the law, safeguard the national unity and the socialist gains, and maintain the boundaries between authorities in a manner to ensure that each shall perform its role in the national action."

The legislature nominates the president, who then must be approved for a six-year-term by an absolute majority of the votes cast in a plebiscite; he or she may be reelected without limitation. The president must be at least forty years old, an Egyptian born of Egyptian parents, and free to exercise civil and political rights. Article 81 prohibits the president from engaging in a profession, undertaking commercial, financial, or industrial activities, and dealing in property with the state.

The president may appoint, dismiss, and define the duties of vice presidents, one of whom may be designated to act for the president if he or she is unable to carry out those duties. However, if there is a vacancy or if the president becomes permanently disabled, the president of the parliament (if it is in session) or the president of the supreme constitutional court assumes the presidency.

The president appoints the prime minister, other ministers, and deputies and presides over meetings of the council of ministers when he or she attends them; commands the armed forces; declares war with the approval of the parliament; proclaims a state of emergency; appoints and dismisses diplomatic representatives and accredits foreign diplomats; issues regulations necessary to implement laws; issues other regulations, including regulations organizing the public services; issues decisions with the force of law during the recess between sessions of the parliament when such measures cannot be delayed, although such decisions must be submitted later to the parliament for ratification; appoints civil and military officials; and grants amnesty (but not a general amnesty) and commutes sentences. The president presides over the national defense council and is the supreme chief of the police authority.

The president is also authorized to conclude treaties, except peace treaties and other treaties involving territorial rights and the sovereignty of the nation, which must be approved by the parliament; to call for public referendums on important matters affecting the supreme interests of the state; and to "take urgent measures" if the national unity or the safety of the nation is endangered or if the constitutional role of state institutions is obstructed.

The president may be impeached for treason or a criminal act by a proposal made by at least one-third of the members of the parliament and an affirmative vote of two-thirds of the members. The impeachment is then tried by a special tribunal established by law.

Prime Minister and Cabinet. The prime minister is charged with supervising the work of the ministers and deputies. The appointee must be Egyptian, thirty-five years old, and able to exercise his or her political and civil rights.

The council of ministers (cabinet) consists of the prime minister and the ministers and their deputies. Among other things, it establishes general policy and, with the president, controls its implementation in accordance with presidential laws and decrees; it also oversees the work of the ministries and affiliated agencies.

The Legislature

Parliament. The Egyptian unicameral parliament, formerly the national assembly, is now the Majlis al-Sha'ab (people's assembly). At least 350 members must be elected, of which at least one-half must be workers and farmers elected by direct, secret, and public ballot. The president is authorized to appoint up to ten members. The rules concerning elections are determined by law, and elections are conducted under the supervision of the judiciary. Members serve for five-year terms.

The assembly decides on the validity of its members, and membership may be revoked on the grounds of loss of confidence or loss of status required for membership, such as being a worker or a farmer. Revocation of membership requires a two-thirds vote of the assembly. Members are exempted from criminal prosecution, except in cases where they are caught in flagrante delicto or where the assembly (if in session) or the president gives special permission.

Bills may be proposed by the president or any member of the assembly. A law passed by the assembly is promulgated by the president; if he or she objects, it must be returned within thirty days. The president's veto may be overridden by a vote of two-thirds or more of the members.

In addition to acting on legislation and the national budget, the assembly oversees government operations by directing questions, including interpellation, to the prime minister, his or her deputies, other ministers, and their deputies. The assembly may, by a majority vote, withdraw its confidence from members of the government, who then must resign. The assembly may inspect or investigate administrative departments and public agencies or projects.

The Judiciary

Part 4, Sovereignty of the Law, affirms that the law is supreme, that the state shall be subject to law, and that the independence and immunity of the judiciary are guaranteed to safeguard rights and liberties.

Chapter 4, on the Judiciary Authority, requires the judiciary and judges to be independent and to issue judgments in accordance with law. No authority may intervene in cases or judicial affairs; however, the constitution authorizes a state security court for administrative disputes and disciplinary cases, as well as a supreme council, presided over by the president of the republic, which is to supervise "the affairs of the judiciary organizations."

Constitutional Court

According to article 174, chapter 5, "The supreme constitutional court shall be an independent judiciary body, having its own moral person in the Arab Republic of Egypt, and having its seat in Cairo." It is given the sole authority to "undertake judicial control" of the constitutionality of the laws and regulations and "to undertake the explanation of the legislative texts. . . ." The court may be assigned other duties by law.

The 1980 amendments established a consulting body called the Shoura council to ensure that the principles of the 1952 and 1971 revolutions are preserved. The body consists of no fewer than 132 members. Two-thirds are elected directly, half of whom must be workers and farmers, and one-third are appointed by the president.

Shoura Council

The constitution requires that the Shoura be consulted on proposed amendments to the constitution; drafts of laws complementary to the constitution; general plans for social and economic development; peace treaties, alliances and all treaties affecting territorial integrity and sovereignty; and drafts of laws submitted by the president to the parliament and other matters of general policy also submitted by the president.

The president or at least one-third of the members of the legislature may request an amendment to the constitution. By a majority vote the legislature can agree to discuss the amendment, and by a two-thirds vote it can approve it, after which the amendment must be ratified by the people in a plebiscite.

Amending the Constitution

ETHIOPIA

Ethiopia, which has known only authoritarian rule and five years of colonial occupation during its two-thousand-year history, adopted a democratic system of government under a constitution that was officially published in 1996.

General Information

The Federal Democratic Republic of Ethiopia, formerly the People's Democratic Republic of Ethiopia, occupies approximately 1.1 million square kilometers in eastern Africa. It is bounded by Eritrea (until recently a part of Ethiopia) on the north, Djibouti and Somalia on the east, Kenya on the south, and Sudan on the west. Addis Ababa is the capital of this nation of more than sixty-four million persons.

Ethiopia is one of the world's poorest countries in gross national product per capita. More than eighty percent of the people are engaged in agriculture, including raising livestock; coffee is the major crop. The effects of the war that led to independence for Eritrea in 1993 continue to hamper economic and democratic development in Ethiopia.

Type of Government: Presidential-style parliamentary federal republic, with a president, a prime minister and council of ministers (cabinet), a bicameral legislature, and a judiciary, including a constitutional council

Dates of Constitutions: 1931, 1955, 1987, 1991 (transitional), and 1996

Constitutional History

A part of the East African cradle of our human ancestors, modern Ethiopia is the site of the discovery of the remains of "Lucy," a 3.5-million-year-old hominid. The Ethiopian kingdom is said to have been founded by Menelik I, the fabled son of King Solomon and the queen of Sheba, a city in Yemen. Early Greeks—Homer around 800 B.C. and Herodotus around 450 B.C.—referred to Ethiopians in their writings. By the fourth century A.D. the country had converted to Christianity but had to stave off later attempts to introduce the Islamic religion, which had spread throughout its northern neighbors. A branch of the Coptic Christian Church based in Alexandria, Egypt, was established there, and in the fourteenth century the Roman Catholic pope sought the country's help for the crusades.

At the beginning of the sixteenth century Ethiopia's territory extended from Egypt nearly to Lake Turkana in modern Kenya. In 1526 the Islamic state of Adal in Africa on the Gulf of Aden began a *jihad* (holy war) against Ethiopia but was expelled with the help of Portuguese sailors in 1543. Ethiopia was weakened by the struggle, however, and cattle herders to the south (the Oromo) were able to settle in its more sparsely populated southern region, some becoming Christians and others Muslims. Until the mid-nineteenth century the government was centralized in the north, where selling subjects as slaves was profitable. An emperor and his court ruled over and collected taxes from lesser kingdoms. Menelik II, who was from the south, expanded the empire and defeated an Italian invasion in 1896.

In 1930 Haile Selassie became emperor. A constitution in 1931 established a bicameral legislature while leaving the emperor with absolute power. Fascist Italy seized the country in 1935, but Selassie was restored to the throne in 1941. In 1952, through a United Nations decision, the former Italian colony of Eritrea was annexed as an autonomous region and in 1962 was integrated into the unitary state of Ethiopia. A new constitution in 1955 created a lower house of elected members and an upper house of members appointed by the emperor.

Selassie was deposed in 1974 and died a year later. A provisional military government blamed all the nation's ills on the United States. When Somalia attacked in 1977, the Soviet Union and Cuba came to Ethiopia's aid. In 1984 the country became a communist regime and promulgated a Soviet-style constitution in 1987. During widespread famine from 1984 to 1986, the government criticized U.S. aid as too meager, when in fact U.S. law prohibited aid to countries, such as Ethiopia, that had confiscated property of U.S. citizens. Military rule was ended in 1991, after which a national conference met and approved a transitional government charter, pending a new democratic constitution. On December 8, 1994, elected representatives ratified a constitution that was finally published on December 10, 1996.

The drafters looked at both presidential and parliamentary styles of governments, like those in the United States and the United Kingdom, but they followed the latter to a large extent.

The Constitution

The preamble to the Ethiopian constitution states that "the nations, nationalities, and peoples of Ethiopia" are committed to self-determination and the rule of law and notes the nation's determination "to consolidate, as a lasting legacy, the peace and the prospect of a democratic order which our struggles and sacrifices have brought about. . . ."

Article 5 makes Amharic the "working language" of the nation, and article 7 provides that in the constitution the masculine gender applies equally to the feminine gender.

Article 13 requires all organs of the state at all levels to respect and enforce the express fundamental rights and freedoms of the constitution, which are to be interpreted in conformity with the Universal Declaration of Human Rights (1948), international human rights covenants, and other relevant international agreements to which Ethiopia has acceded.

Rights encompassed in the constitution include life, liberty, and security of the person; humane treatment; equality of citizens; privacy; and freedom of religion, belief, and opinion. Other rights and freedoms include rights for persons arrested or detained and those accused of crimes; the right of assembly, petition, and association; freedom of movement; and marital, family, personal, women's, and children's rights. The right of property is set forth, but the "right of ownership of rural and urban land, as well as of all natural resources, is exclusively vested in the state and the peoples of Ethiopia."

In Ethiopia, a federal state, power is divided vertically, between the national and nine state governments, and horizontally at the national level among the president, as head of state; the prime minister, as head of government; the cabinet; the legislature; and the judiciary, which includes a council of constitutional inquiry that, together with the upper house of the legislature, exercises some constitutional review.

President. The president is nominated by the lower house of the legislature and is elected for a six-year term if approved by a two-thirds majority of both houses in a joint session. A person may be elected president only twice.

The president opens the annual sessions of the legislature; signs and proclaims laws; appoints ambassadors and special envoys based on nominations submitted by the prime minister; receives credentials of foreign representatives; awards medals, prizes, and gifts according to law; grants military titles based on nominations submitted by the prime minister; and grants pardons in accordance with law.

Prime Minister and Cabinet. Article 72, the Powers of the Executive, states: "The highest executive powers of the Federal Democratic Republic of Ethiopia are vested in the prime minister and the council of ministers." The prime minister is elected by the lower house of the legislature from among its members for a term as long as the lower house, or five years. As in the British parliamentary system, the prime minister is chosen by the majority party or a majority coalition of parties in the lower house.

The prime minister is the chief executive, chairman of the council of ministers (cabinet), and commander in chief of the armed forces. Responsibilities include the nomination of ministers, who may be from either house or outside the legislature, for approval by the lower house. Among other duties are implementing the laws; leading, coordinating, and representing the cabinet; supervising implementation of cabinet policy and foreign policy; ensuring the efficiency of the federal administration; and appointing certain officials. A deputy prime minister serves the prime minister.

The cabinet is responsible to the prime minister, except that cabinet members are collectively responsible to the lower house of the legislature for all decisions they make as a body.

The Legislature

Parliament. The parliament, Yehezeb Tewakayoch Mekere Bet, consists of an upper house, the federal council, and a lower house, the council of people's representatives, which article 50 defines as the highest authority of the federal government. Each elects a speaker and deputy speaker.

Upper House. The upper house includes members elected for five years by state councils and represents "the nations, nationalities, and peoples." It includes a minimum of one representative each; an additional representative is elected for every million persons. The federal council plays no role in legislating but instead interprets the constitution, determines the division of revenue between the federal and state governments as well as subsidies provided by the federal government to the states, and may order intervention if a state threatens the constitutional order.

Lower House. Members of the lower house are elected for five-year terms from electoral districts based on a plurality of votes. The number of seats, including twenty reserved for minority nationalities, may not exceed 550. The lower house has the power to legislate on all matters within the federal jurisdiction assigned by the constitution. In addition, it may proclaim a state of emergency or war, levy taxes, ratify international agreements, and approve, among others, members of the council of ministers and federal judges.

The Judiciary

Article 78 states, in part: "Supreme federal judicial authority is vested in the Federal Supreme Court." The lower house of the legislature has authority to establish lower courts, but courts outside the regular court system are prohibited. Religious and cultural courts recognized before ratification of the constitution may continue in accordance with the constitution.

Supreme Court. The federal supreme court is the highest court of Ethiopia and has final jurisdiction over federal matters. It also has express authority to review and correct final decisions on appeal to correct a "basic error of law"; state supreme courts have the same authority with respect to appeals involving state matters.

The chief justice and vice chief justice of the federal supreme court are nominated by the prime minister and appointed by the lower house of the legislature, as are all other federal judges; their nominations, however, must be based on recommendations made by a federal commission for judicial administration.

Council of Constitutional Inquiry. Judicial powers are granted to an eleven-member council, including the chief justice and vice chief justice. It refers questions of federal and state laws contravening the constitution to the legislature's upper house for final determination.

Amending the Constitution

Amendments involving the rights and freedoms in chapter 3 of the constitution and article 94, which deals with federal and state financial expenditures, require a majority vote of all state councils and a two-thirds majority of the two legislative houses. Other amendments need a two-thirds majority vote of both houses of the legislature in a joint meeting and approval by two-thirds of the states based on a majority vote of the citizens in each state.

At the beginning of the twentieth century Finland established its own unicameral legislature elected by universal suffrage, thus becoming the first country in Europe and the second in the world in which women could vote.

General Information

The Republic of Finland in northeastern Europe is approximately 337,000 square kilometers and is bounded by Norway on the north, Russia on the east, the Gulf of Finland and the Baltic Sea on the south, and the Gulf of Bothnia and Sweden on the west. Helsinki is the capital of this country of approximately five million inhabitants.

In this century Finland has developed from a basically agricultural country, heavily dependent on forestry exports, into a thriving modern nation with a diversified economy. From 1956 to 1981 Finland's international stature grew; it was chosen to host the Conference on Security and Cooperation in Europe that culminated in 1975 with the signing of the Helsinki Accords, a strong statement in support of universal human rights.

Type of Government: Presidential-style parliamentary republic, with a president, a prime minister and cabinet, a unicameral legislature, and a judiciary

Dates of Constitutions: 1919 (supplemented by constitutional acts in 1922 and 1928) and 2000

Constitutional History

The ancestors of the Finns can be traced to the Stone Age. For centuries before and after its eastern border was determined under the peace treaty of Pahkinasaari in 1323, the region has been influenced by its neighbors, Sweden and Russia. Free Finnish peasants were allowed to participate in the election of the Swedish king in 1362, and Swedish civil and criminal law was applied in Finland until its independence on December 6, 1917.

In addition to the seven hundred years of influence during the annexation by Sweden, the legal system of Finland can be traced to general European legal traditions and particularly the ancient Roman concept of the overriding authority of the ruler. The Finnish constitution, therefore, tends to focus on the powers of the national chief executive, as well as the rights of the people and the sanctity of the law.

As a part of the Kingdom of Sweden, Finland participated in the operations of the government, sending delegates to Stockholm to the Diet of the Four Estates, consisting of the nobility, clergy, burghers, and peasants, as well as in the election of Swedish kings. In 1772 a Swedish constitution gave the king significant powers, a concept reflected in the president's powers under the Finnish constitution.

Even after being ceded to Russia in 1809, Finland retained its own legal system, although a small body, the senate, was set up to run the country under the leadership of a Russian governor-general appointed by the czar. Toward the close of the nineteenth century Russia attempted to end Finland's relative autonomy but was thwarted when military defeat and civil unrest weakened the empire to such an extent that the Finns were able to establish their own unicameral parliament in 1906 and elect representatives by universal suffrage.

The Russian Revolution in 1917 led to Finland's independence on December 6, followed by civil war and intense debate over whether the country should become a monarchy or a republic. Social and economic development, however, proceeded quickly; a supreme court and a supreme administrative court were established in 1918, and a constitution was adopted in 1919.

The constitution of July 17, 1919, was later supplemented by the Parliament Act of January 13, 1928, which dealt with the structure of the government and citizen rights, and the Ministerial Responsibility Act and Act on the High Court of Impeachment, both of November 25, 1922, as well as other laws of constitutional significance. In response to a report by a committee of parliament recommending integration of the nation's constitutional documents, the draft of a new unified constitution was prepared by the government and presented to the legislature on February 6, 1998. After parliamentary elections in 1999, the draft was unanimously adopted by the new parliament and became effective on March 1, 2000. The new constitution, in addition to codifying the earlier constitutional documents, restores to parliament the balance of political power, which had shifted to the president during the cold war. Now the prime minister and cabinet are the leading policy makers.

Influences

Scandinavian law, particularly the Swedish legal system, has influenced Finland's constitution.

The Constitution

"Finland is a sovereign republic," declares section 1. "The constitution of Finland is established in this constitutional act." According to section 2, "The powers of the State in Finland are vested in the people, who are represented by the Parliament. Democracy entails the right of the individual to participate in and influence the development of society and his or her living conditions."

Fundamental Rights

In section 1 the constitution proclaims that it "shall guarantee the inviolability of human dignity and the freedom and rights of the individual and promote justice in society." Sections 6 through 23 set forth basic rights and liberties, including equality before the law, regardless of "sex, age, origin, language, religion, conviction, opinion, health, disability or other reason that concern his or her person"; the rights to life, personal liberty, integrity, and security; a prohibition against retroactive laws; and freedom of movement, religion, conscience, expression, assembly, and association. Other rights guaranteed are privacy; education; access to information, including "[d]ocuments and recordings in the possession of the authorities"; the right to participate in elections and government; protection of private property; the right to one's language and culture; the right to work; and social security. Section 20 notes that the "public authorities shall endeavor to guarantee the right to a healthy environment." Section 21 extends legal rights, including the right to a speedy trial and to appeal to "a court of law or other independent organ for the administration of justice," while section 22 guarantees that public authorities "shall guarantee the observance of basic rights and liberties and human rights." Emergency situations that might warrant "provisional exceptions to basic rights and liberties," may, under section 23, be provided for by law.

Division of Powers

Section 3 declares that "legislative powers are exercised by the Parliament ... [,] governmental powers are exercised by the President of the Republic and the Government [cabinet], the members of which shall have the confidence of the Parliament ... [and] judicial powers are exercised by independent courts of law...."

The Executive

President. Pursuant to section 54, the president is elected directly for six years but may not serve more than two consecutive terms. A candidate must be a native-born Finnish citizen nominated by "any registered political party from whose candidate list at least one Representative was elected to the Parliament in the most recent parliamentary elections" or "by any group of twenty thousand persons who have the right to vote." Victory requires "more than half of the votes cast," otherwise a runoff election is held "between the two candidates who have received the most votes."

The president's powers and duties include making "decisions in Government on the basis of proposals for decisions put forward by the Government," appointing the government and ministers, issuing "an order concerning extraordinary parliamentary elections" and pardons, and handling "[m]atters referred to in the Act on the Autonomy of the Åland Islands." Other functions relate to matters presented by ministers and the government as well as decisions on certain military issues, including military appointments.

Prime Minister and Cabinet. Section 60 specifies that the government consists of the prime minister and "the necessary number of Ministers [cabinet]," who "are responsible before the Parliament for their actions in office." According to section 61, "The Parliament elects the Prime Minister, who is thereafter appointed . . . by the President." The president then "appoints the other Ministers in accordance with a proposal made by the Prime Minister."

The prime minister directs government activities, "oversees the preparation and consideration of [government] matters," and "chairs the plenary meetings of the Government," where "matters within the authority of the Government are decided." After a government is appointed, it "shall without delay submit its program to the Parliament in the form of a statement." In addition to its other responsibilities, the government "implements the decisions of the President." The president dismisses it or a minister when either loses parliament's confidence.

Parliament. Section 24 mandates that the unicameral parliament consist of 200 representatives elected by direct, proportional, and secret ballot for four years. Representatives are elected from twelve to eighteen constituencies, plus the Åland Islands, which are entitled to one representative. Candidates must be nominated by registered political parties and groups of persons who have the right to vote, as provided for by law. Qualifications include having the right to vote, which, according to section 14, is extended to Finnish citizens eighteen years of age; excluded are military officers and certain government officials, including the chancellor of justice, the parliamentary ombudsman, and justices of the supreme court.

Section 30 extends to representatives certain immunities, such as protection from court action or deprivation of liberty "owing to opinions expressed . . . in the Parliament or owing to conduct in the consideration of a matter. . . ." Parliament's consent is necessary for a representative to be "arrested or detained . . . before the commencement of a trial. . . ." Section 31 grants freedom of speech to representatives, while section 29 requires a representative "to follow justice and truth in his or her office . . . [and to] abide by the Constitution. . . ." Section 32 requires disqualification for conflicts of interest.

Using a secret ballot, parliament elects its own speaker and two deputy speakers for each session. Article 35 requires the appointment of parliamentary committees such as the Grand Committee, Constitutional Law Committee, and Foreign Affairs Committee. A speaker's council, which is generally responsible for the legislature's operations, consists of the speaker, deputy speakers, and committee chairpersons.

Legislative proposals and other matters are generally initiated by the government or a parliamentary representative; the courts may suggest legislation through the government. Committees prepare proposals "before their final consideration in a plenary session of the Parliament." Two readings are required for a legislative proposal and a proposal on parliamentary rules of procedure, while other matters are considered in one reading. Measures are passed by a simple majority. Interpellations (questions) may be addressed to the government or a minister by "at least twenty Representatives," each of whom "has the right to address questions to a Minister on matters within the Minister's competence"; if a motion of no confidence in the government is put forward, parliament may take a vote of confidence following the interpellation. Article 53 authorizes parliament to "organize a consultative referendum" of the voters, a device that has taken on new significance in European countries as a means of making major decisions relating to integration into the European Union.

Ombudsman. Article 38 establishes the positions of parliamentary ombudsman and two deputy ombudsmen, "who shall have outstanding knowledge of law." The ombudsmen are appointed by parliament for four-year terms but may be dismissed "for extremely weighty reasons" by a two-thirds vote of parliament based on an opinion of its Constitutional Law Committee.

The Judiciary

"The Supreme Court, the Courts of Appeal and the District Courts are the general courts of law," states section 98. "The Supreme Administrative Court and the regional Administrative Courts are the general courts of administrative law." The supreme administrative court is the final court for administrative matters. Provisional courts are prohibited.

A chancellor of justice and a deputy chancellor, who "shall have outstanding knowledge of law," are appointed by the president and "[a]ttached to the Government," according to section 69. The president also appoints tenured judges, who under section 103 may "not be suspended from office, except by a judgment of a court of law."

Supreme Court. The supreme court, according to section 99, is the final court with respect to civil, commercial, and criminal matters and supervises the administration of justice in these areas. It is composed of a president "and the requisite number of Justices." Unless otherwise specified by law, five members constitute a quorum.

High Court of Impeachment. Under section 101, a high court of impeachment "deals with charges brought against a member of the Government" and other officials, including the chancellor of justice and the parliamentary ombudsman. Members include the president of the supreme court, who presides, and the president of the supreme administrative court, the three most senior ranking presidents of the courts of appeal, and five members elected by parliament for four-year terms. Other details are to be "laid down by an Act."

Amending the Constitution

According to section 73, a "proposal on the enactment, amendment or repeal of the Constitution" may be introduced in parliament using the same procedures as any other measure but, after a second reading, it must await further action "until the first parliamentary session following parliamentary elections." Once reported out of parliamentary committee, it must then "be adopted without material alterations in one reading in a plenary session by a decision supported by at least two-thirds of the votes cast." However, a proposed amendment "may be declared urgent by . . . five-sixths of the votes cast" in parliament and then be approved in the same parliamentary session by a vote of two-thirds.

The constitution of the Fifth Republic of France, adopted in 1958, grants its presidents such power that—like French monarchs of the past—they may consider themselves the embodiment of the state itself.

France, the largest country in western Europe, is approximately 547,000 square kilometers, not including its overseas territories. It is bounded by Belgium, Luxembourg, Germany, Switzerland, and Italy on the east; the Mediterranean Sea, Monaco, Spain, and Andorra on the south; the Bay of Biscay and the Atlantic Ocean on the west; and the English Channel on the north. Paris, a city of approximately 2.2 million inhabitants, is the capital of this country of more than fifty-nine million persons.

Heavily dependent on imported fuel, France produces a large percentage of its electricity by nuclear power. With most of its work force employed in industry, commerce, and services and only about six percent working in agriculture, the country is still self-sufficient in the production of foodstuffs. Although France must play a major role in the economic and political integration of Europe, the country continues to be plagued with internal scandals and entrenched political divisions.

Type of Government: Presidential-style parliamentary republic, with a president, a premier (prime minister) and council of ministers (cabinet), a bicameral legislature, a judiciary, and a constitutional council

Dates of Key Constitutions: 1791, 1793, 1795, 1799, 1814, 1815, 1848, 1852, 1875, 1946, and 1958

The nation-state of France rose slowly from the ashes of the Roman Empire and the Frankish kingdoms that replaced the empire. In A.D. 843 the Kingdom of Western Francia, the predecessor of France, was created by the Treaty of Verdun out of Charlemagne's empire. By the reign of Louis VI, from 1108 to 1137, the royal court had become an effective organ of government administration, and the doctrine of the superiority of the monarch—that vassals of the king owe primary allegiance to the king—had been propounded. During the mid-thirteenth century the Parlement (from which the English word *parliament* is derived) established by the French monarch Saint Louis (Louis IX) became the sovereign court of appeal for the system of royal courts throughout the country.

Centralization of power continued, culminating under Louis XIV (the "Sun King") and Louis XV, who declared in 1766:

Sovereign power resides in my person alone. To me belongs all legislative power with neither any responsibility to others nor any division of that power. Public order in all its entirety emanates from me, and the rights and interests of the nation are necessarily bound up with my own and rest only in my hands.

In May 1789, during the reign of Louis XVI, with financial and political conditions crumbling, elected deputies met at the first estates general assembly held since 1614. When the First Estate, the clergy, and the Second Estate, the nobles, rejected the request of the Third Estate, the urban bourgeoisie, to vote by head count rather than by orders (estates), the Third Estate adopted called itself a national assembly and agreed to implement constitutional reform. These acts represented a fundamental challenge to the monarchy and the nation's existing social and political order.

After the revolutionaries stormed the royal fortress and prison called the Bastille on July 14, 1789, France's Rubicon had been crossed. On August 26, the National Constituent Assembly, formed by the revolutionaries, issued the Declaration of the Rights of Man and of the Citizen, which affirmed the rule of law, equality before the law, and representative government and guaranteed private ownership of property and conditional free speech.

Since the revolution in 1789, France has had fifteen constitutions. On September 13, 1791, a constitution was promulgated by a legislative assembly, but after attempts to restore the monarchy were repelled, a convention was called and a new constitution was promulgated on August 10, 1793. Subsequently, a document was adopted in 1795, but it failed to limit acts of the legislature. Desiring stronger executive leadership, the legislature drew up a new constitution in 1799, which made Napoleon first consul with substantial executive powers for ten years, while preserving the supremacy of the civilian administration. In 1804, however, Napoleon crowned himself emperor of France.

After Napoleon's defeat, the monarchy was restored under Louis XVIII, the brother of Louis XVI. As king he wielded strong executive powers under both an 1814 constitutional charter, which required ministers to countersign royal acts and the parliament to consent to taxation, and an 1815 charter. After a revolution during the reign of Charles X, who tried to restore the divine right of kings, further unrest resulted in the Second Republic. Its 1848 constitution lasted until a plebiscite reestablished the hereditary empire in 1852 under Louis Napoleon, Napoleon's nephew, who was the popularly elected president of the Second Republic.

Defeat at the hands of Prussia and the capture of the emperor in 1870 set the stage for the creation of the Third Republic in January 1875. To avoid repeating the mistakes of the Second Republic, the constitution was amended to have the president elected by the parliament rather than by popular vote. The Third Republic lasted until October 21, 1945, when it was repudiated in a referendum by a large popular majority.

The Fourth Republic was born of the aftermath of World War II and anxiety over the burgeoning political power of the Communist and Socialist Parties. In a speech in Bayeux on June 16, 1946, Gen. Charles de Gaulle argued for a strong presidential regime having a nonpartisan head of state while preserving the parliamentary system. The voters, however, approved a bicameral assembly, with the upper house and the president having limited authority. Politically unstable governing coalitions, a costly war in Algeria, and the real possibility of a civil war, however, doomed the Fourth Republic.

On June 1, 1958, de Gaulle, now prime minister, was granted emergency powers for six months, and a new constitution was prepared by a committee of experts and ministers. The result, which included a strong president who could select the prime minister and run the government, was adopted by eighty percent of those who voted on September 28, 1958, and was promulgated on October 4, 1958.

Influences

The current French constitution under the Fifth Republic has evolved from the basic concepts spawned by the 1789 revolution. These concepts and earlier French constitutions have profoundly influenced the constitutions of many countries.

The Constitution

The preamble to the 1958 constitution of France reaffirms the 1789 Declaration of the Rights of Man and of the Citizen and the preamble to the 1946 constitution of the Fourth Republic.

"France is an indivisible, secular, democratic and social Republic," declares article 1, while article 2 proclaims: "The motto of the Republic is 'Liberty, Equality, Fraternity.' Its principle is: government of the people, by the people and for the people." According to article 3, "National sovereignty belongs to the people, who exercise it through their representatives and by means of referendum. No section of the people nor any individual may attribute its exercise to itself."

Fundamental Rights

The equality of all citizens is assured in article 1 "without distinction of origin, race or religion. [The nation] respects all beliefs." Other rights are incorporated in the preamble, among them the rule of law, representative government, private ownership of property, freedom of opinion, and the presumption of innocence. A 1999 amendment to article 3 notes: "The law promotes the equal access of women and men to the electoral mandates and elective functions." In addition, article 66 provides that "[n]o one may be arbitrarily detained. The judicial authority, guardian of individual liberty, ensures the observance of this principle under the conditions specified by law." Article 4 underscores that "[p]olitical parties and groups contribute to the exercise of suffrage."

In France, a unitary state, power is divided among the president, as head of state and, to some extent, head of government; the premier (prime minister), as head of government; the legislature; the courts; and the constitutional council, which has limited preenactment constitutional review.

Division of Powers

President. The president is head of state and must be elected by an absolute majority of votes cast by direct universal suffrage; otherwise, a runoff election is held between the two candidates with the most votes. By amendment in 2000, his or her term of office was reduced from seven to five years.

The Executive

According to article 5, "The President . . . shall see to it that the Constitution is respected, . . . ensure . . . the proper functioning of the public authorities and the continuity of the State." Presidential duties and powers include appointing a premier and terminating him or her on the resignation of the government; appointing, on the proposal of the premier, the other members of the government; presiding over the council of ministers (cabinet); promulgating or vetoing laws; submitting certain government bills, including those for ratification of selected treaties, for approval by referendum; dissolving the legislature after consulting with the premier and presidents of the houses of the legislature; signing ordinances and decrees of the council of ministers; making appointments to civil and military posts and other appointments required to be done in meetings of the council of ministers; appointing and receiving foreign representatives; taking emergency measures under conditions set forth in article 16; communicating with the legislature; and granting pardons. With certain exceptions, acts of the president must be countersigned by the prime minister and in certain cases by the appropriate minister.

In the event of a vacancy in the office of president, the president of the upper house of the legislature acts as president, except that he or she may not submit a bill for referendum or dissolve the legislature. Article 68 provides that the president may not be held accountable for official acts, except in the case of high treason, for which he or she may be indicted by a majority vote of the members of both houses of the legislature and tried by the high court of justice.

Prime Minister and Cabinet. The French premier directs the operations of the government, is responsible for the national defense, ensures the execution of the laws, and, except where preempted by the president under the constitution, exercises regulatory and appointment powers.

The council of ministers is chosen by the president, who is entitled to preside over its meetings. Collectively, the premier and the cabinet constitute the government in the parliamentary sense of the term. According to article 20, "The government shall determine and direct the policy of the nation. It shall have at its disposal the administration and the armed forces." The government is responsible to the legislature in accordance with provisions relating to the adoption of a motion of censure.

Members of the government are precluded from holding other positions, including a seat in the legislature; this restriction reflects greater separation of executive and legislative power than in some other parliamentary systems.

The Legislature

Parliament. Article 34 asserts: "All laws shall be passed by parliament." The bicameral French parliament consists of an upper house, the senate, and a lower house, the national assembly. Under article 25, the term of each house as well as the number and qualifications of members are determined by organic laws.

Upper House. The members of the senate, which included 321 members in 1999, are elected indirectly for nine-year terms; one-third are elected every three years. The great majority represent continental France, while others represent overseas territories. The senate has essentially the same power as the assembly, except as noted below.

Lower House. The national assembly consists of some 577 deputies elected directly by universal suffrage for five-year terms, although the president may call for new elections earlier. The assembly, unlike the senate, sees the budget first and can force the government to resign with a vote against an important government proposal.

The constitution of the Fifth Republic limits the parliament's legislative powers to areas specified in article 34. Other areas are considered regulatory in nature and may be modified by presidential decree. Certain measures may be implemented only by organic laws, which require special procedures and approval by a majority of all members of the assembly on final reading and may "not be promulgated until the Constitutional Council has declared their conformity with the Constitution."

Bills may be introduced by the government or members of parliament; however, "finance bills and social security finance bills shall be first presented to the National Assembly." In addition to passing laws, the parliament may authorize the government to issue ordinances having the force of law. The government is authorized by article 41 to declare a parliamentary bill or an amendment illegal or "contrary to a delegation of authority," and any dispute may be settled by the constitutional council on request by either institution. Other parliamentary powers include questioning "the responsibility of the Government by a vote on a motion of censure" and declaring war.

The Judiciary

Article 64 provides that the president "is the guarantor of the independence of the judicial authority. He is assisted by the High Council of the Judiciary. An organic law determines the regulations governing the members of the judiciary. Judges are irremovable."

High Council. According to article 65, the president presides over a high council of the judiciary. It consists of two chambers: one with jurisdiction over judges and the other with jurisdiction over public prosecutors. In addition to the president and the minister of justice, other members include judges, public prosecutors, and "three prominent citizens who are members neither of Parliament nor of the judiciary," appointed respectively by the president and the presidents of both houses of parliament. The appropriate houses each recommend judges and prosecutors for appointment and make determinations on disciplinary penalties for judges and public prosecutors.

High Court of Justice. A high court of justice created under article 67 is composed of members of the parliament elected in equal numbers by both houses after elections for these bodies. On indictment by the legislature, it tries the president for treason. Organic law further defines the composition of the court and establishes its rules and procedures.

Court of Justice

Under articles 68-1 and 68-2, "Members of the Government are penally responsible for acts in the exercise of their functions and classified as serious crimes and offenses at the time they were committed. They are judged by the Court of Justice of the Republic." The court includes fifteen members: twelve members of parliament "elected in equal number from among their ranks by the National Assembly and the Senate after every general or partial renewal by election . . . and three judges of the Court of Cassation, one of whom shall preside over the Court of Justice of the Republic." Complaints may be lodged with a petititions committee by "[a]ny person claiming to be a victim of a crime or offense committed by a member of the Government." The committee then either orders the case closed or forwards it to the chief public prosecutor at the court of cassation for referral to the court of justice. The court's work is further defined by organic law.

Constitutional Council

Title 7 creates a constitutional council of nine members with nine-year terms; one-third are replaced every three years, and three members each are appointed by the president of the republic and the presidents of the two houses of the legislature. Former presidents of the republic are ex officio members of the council for life. The council ensures the regularity of elections for president and rules on disputes in parliamentary elections and on the constitutionality of laws before they are promulgated if requested by the president, the premier, the presidents of the houses of the legislature, or, since an amendment in 1974, sixty members of either house. Unlike the courts in the United States and Germany, it has no power to nullify a law after it is enacted by the legislature.

Amending the Constitution

Under article 89, proposals for amending the constitution may be made by the president on the recommendation of the prime minister and by members of parliament. A proposal must be passed by both houses of parliament in identical terms and then be approved by referendum. Alternatively, the president may submit a proposal to parliament "convened in Congress," in which case three-fifths of the votes cast are needed for approval. No amendment may be made if the territory is threatened, and the republican form of government may not be changed.

GEORGIA

The Georgian parliament declared independence from the Soviet Union in April 1991 and four years later adopted a new democratic constitution, which expressed the desire "to solve the fundamental problems of government authority and individuals not by violence but only on the basis of Constitutional Justice."

General Information

The Republic of Georgia, one of three countries in the Transcaucasian region of southeastern Europe (along with Azerbaijan and Armenia), is bounded on the north and east by Russia, on the south by Azerbaijan and Armenia, on the west by Turkey, and on the northwest by the Black Sea. The territory includes the Abkhazian and Adjarian Autonomous Republics and the South Ossetian Autonomous Region. Tbilisi is the capital of this nation, which has an area of some 69,700 kilometers and numbers approximately five million persons.

The major industries of Georgia include hydroelectric power, mining, and metals and metal alloys; among its chief agricultural products are citrus fruit, grapes, tea, and vegetables. The nation's economic growth has suffered as a result of its continuing problems with separatist movements and Russia's economic collapse at the end of 1998.

Type of Government: Presidential-style parliamentary republic, with a president, a unicameral legislature, a judiciary, and a constitutional court

Dates of Constitutions: 1921, 1922, 1927, 1937, 1978, 1992 (1921 constitution restored), and 1995

Constitutional History

Georgia, whose name is derived from *Kurj* and *Gurj* (Arabic and Persian words for the country), has been inhabited for some seven thousand years. Early Georgian tribes included the Colchians, whose fabled wealth was the basis for the Greek legend of Jason and the golden fleece. Colchis, on the Black Sea, would become a Greek colony and later a part of the Roman Empire.

Georgians converted to Christianity in the fourth century A.D., which drew them into the ambit of the Byzantine Empire. Beginning in 813, Georgia came under the rule of an Armenian prince, whose family would continue to rule parts of the territory off and on for the next thousand years. The eastern part of Georgia fell to the Mongols in the thirteenth century, and the Turkic conqueror Tamerlane destroyed Tbilisi in 1386. The Ottoman Turks and the Persians conquered, ruled, and divided the territory until Armenia's rulers were granted substantial autonomy by the Persians in the eighteenth century.

In 1773 the Georgian King Herekle II brought portions of the country under his rule and entered into the Treaty of Georievsk with Catherine the Great of Russia, guaranteeing Georgia's independence in exchange for an acknowledgment of Russian authority. Occupied by Russian troops, Georgian territory grew to hold strategic importance in the confrontation between Russia and the Turks at the end of the eighteenth century. Unable to protect itself, Georgia, then called Kartli-Kakhetia, was gradually absorbed into Russia.

Czar Alexander III's Russification policy, however, led to a countervailing nationalistic movement and illegal Georgian nationalist organizations in the 1890s. Joseph Dzhugashvili—later known as Joseph Stalin—joined one such Marxist organization called the Third Group. A widespread peasant revolt in western Georgia in 1905 and strikes throughout the Caucasus forced the Russians to declare martial law. The Georgian Socialist Party split into the Mensheviks and the Bolsheviks, the latter under Stalin's leadership. The Russian Revolution of 1917 encouraged Georgian independence in May 1918 and its constitution of February 22, 1921, but the Red Army invaded and in 1922 Georgia was merged with Armenia and Azerbaijan into the Soviet Union's Transcaucasian Soviet Federated Socialist Republic. Communist-style constitutions were promulgated in 1922, 1927, and 1937.

Under Stalin's 1936 Soviet constitution, the Transcaucasian states were made separate republics. Increased nationalism led Georgian communists to take advantage of Moscow's decentralization policies, entrenching themselves in key political positions for personal gain. But when Eduard A. Shevardnaze, a Georgian who would become the Soviet Union's foreign minister, was made first secretary of the Georgian Communist Party in 1972, he instituted reforms that the Soviet leader Mikhail Gorbachev later adopted for the entire Soviet system. A constitution dictated by the Soviet leader Leonid Brezhnev was adopted on April 15, 1978.

After the collapse of the Soviet Union began, multiparty elections under amendments to the existing constitution were held in October 1990; independence was declared on April 9, 1991; and the 1921 constitution was restored in 1992. When a bloody separatist movement in the autonomous republic of Abkhazia was crushed, Georgia entered into agreements with Russia for economic and military cooperation. Shevardnaze, who had been confirmed as head of state by elections in 1992, was reelected president in 1995. He presided over a constitutional commission called to draft the current constitution but was injured in an assassination attempt on his way to sign the document on August 29, 1995. The constitution was finally signed and promulgated on October 17, 1995.

The main principles of Georgia's 1921 constitution were incorporated into the new constitution, which reflects a preference for the presidential managerial style of government as in the U.S. constitution. The special nature of the autonomous republics, especially the rebellious Autonomous Republic of Abkhazia, also influenced the new government structure.

"Georgia is an independent, unified and indivisible law-based state . . . ," proclaims article 1. According to article 3, "The Georgian supreme national bodies have exclusive power [regarding]: . . . citizenship, human rights and freedoms, emigration and immigration, . . . national defense, . . . issues of war and cessation of hostilities; . . . foreign policy, . . . a unified system of energy; communications, the merchant fleet, . . . and a system of environmental protection," among other concerns. "The people are the sole source of state power in Georgia," notes article 5. "State power is only exercised within the framework of the Constitution." And under article 6, "The Constitution is the supreme law of the state."

Articles 12 through 18 provide in part that no person may be deprived of citizenship nor may a citizen be expelled; "[e]veryone is born free and is equal before the law"; "life is inviolable"; only the supreme court may impose capital punishment; and honor, dignity, and freedom "are inviolable." Articles 19 through 24 guarantee "freedom of speech, thought, conscience, religion and belief"; privacy, although with some restrictions "by a court's order or without such an order by the necessity as determined by law"; inheritance; freedom of movement and residence; intellectual property rights; and the right to "freely receive and disseminate information." Article 9 "recognizes the special importance of the Georgian Orthodox Church in Georgian history" but declares "complete freedom of religious beliefs."

Other rights include freedom of assembly, except for military and police; association, including trade unions and political parties; "freedom of constituents to express their will," as well as the right to hold public office. Article 30 declares: "Labor is free. The state is obliged to foster conditions for the development of free enterprise and competition. . . . Consumer rights are protected by law." Rights to education; the equality and "the free will" of spouses, mothers, and children; health insurance; and equality in "social, economic, cultural and political life regardless of national, ethnic, religious or language origin" are also recognized, along with the rights of persons accused of crimes and the right "to know information" about oneself in the hands of the state. Article 44 imposes the duty of "[e]very individual living in Georgia . . . to obey the constitution and legislation of Georgia."

Division of Powers

The constitution divides power among the executive, legislative, and judicial branches of government.

The Executive

President. The president, proclaims article 69, "is the Head of State and exercises executive power." He or she is responsible for domestic and foreign policy, "guarantees the unity and integrity of the country . . . ," and "is the supreme representative of Georgia in foreign relations." The president, according to article 70, is elected in free, universal, equal, and direct suffrage by secret ballot for a term of five years and is limited to two consecutive terms.

Candidates must be eligible to vote, be thirty-five years old, and have lived in Georgia for at least fifteen years and live there on election day. They may be nominated by political parties or by an initiative of no fewer than fifty thousand voters. A candidate must obtain an absolute majority if at least half the eligible voters vote or a runoff election is held.

The powers and duties of the president, as set forth in article 73, include concluding international agreements and treaties, appointing and relieving ambassadors, and receiving foreign ambassadors and other diplomatic representatives; appointing government ministers with the consent of the legislature; removing ministers and receiving their resignations; and submitting the draft of the national budget to the legislature. Among the president's other powers and duties are declaring a state of emergency and seeking approval for such action from the legislature within forty-eight hours; stopping or dismissing the activities of "representative bodies of local self-government or territorial units if their activity endangers the sovereignty and territorial integrity of the country . . ."; issuing "decrees and orders, on the basis of the Constitution and the law"; and signing and issuing "laws by the procedure established by the Constitution." The president also "sets elections for the Parliament and representative bodies" and "is authorized to abrogate acts of bodies of the executive branch accountable to him." In addition, the incumbent is "authorized to address people and the Parliament, and once a year he submits a report to Parliament on the most important questions concerning the state." He also serves as the "supreme commander in chief of the armed forces of Georgia," presides over the National Security Council, and dismisses generals.

Article 75 forbids the arrest of or criminal proceedings against the president, although "Parliament has the right to relieve the President of his duties . . . for violation of the Constitution, or high treason or other capital crimes." Such violations must be "confirmed by the Constitutional Court," and high treason and other capital crimes must be "confirmed by the decision of the Supreme Court."

The Legislature

Parliament. According to article 48, "The Parliament of Georgia is the supreme representative body of the country which exercises legislative power, determines the main directions of domestic and foreign policy and exercises general control over the Cabinet of Ministers. . . ." Its 150 deputies are "elected . . . by a proportional system and eighty-five elected by a majoritarian system for a period of four years on the basis of free, universal, equal and direct suffrage by secret ballot." A member must be a "citizen having attained the age of twenty-five and with the right to vote." Only political parties that meet certain requirements and individuals "supported by 1,000 signatories" or previously elected to parliament are eligible to participate in parliamentary elections.

"The Parliament will begin its work," states article 51, "when the election of two thirds of the Members . . . has been confirmed." Certain immunities are extended to members unless waived by parliament or if a member is "caught in the commission of a crime." Article 55 directs that parliament elect its chairman and deputy chairmen "by secret ballot among them one from Abkhazian and one from Adjarian Members of Parliament by their nomination."

Legislation may be initiated by "the President, a Member of Parliament, a Parliamentary Faction, a committee of Parliament, the supreme representative bodies of Abkhazia and

Adjaria or not less than 30,000 electors," and a bill "is considered passed if it is supported by the majority of those present if those present are not less than one third of the total number of Members of Parliament...." Passage of an organic law requires a majority of all members. Bills adopted by parliament must be "submitted to the President ... within five days" and must be signed or returned within ten days. Changes proposed by the president may be adopted by parliament using the procedures required for any bill. In the case of a law or an organic law, a veto may be overridden by "three fifths of the total number of deputies," but not less than two-thirds of the membership is required to approve a constitutional amendment. If the president refuses to sign a law passed by overriding a veto, it may be signed by the parliamentary chairman. A law "enters into force only on the fifteenth day after its official publication, unless another date is provided."

The Judiciary

"Judicial power is exercised by Constitutional supervision [the constitutional court], the administration of justice and other forms determined by law," states article 82. Decisions "are binding on the whole territory of the country for all state bodies and persons," it notes, adding that the judiciary "is independent and its function is exercised only by courts." Article 84 provides that a judge "is independent in his activity and is subject only to the Constitution and law."

Supreme Court. The chairman and judges of the supreme court are nominated by the president and "elected for a period of not less than ten years by the Parliament by the majority of the total number of deputies," according to article 90. The court's "authority, organization and procedure ... and the dismissal of the Chairman and judges are determined by law." In addition to the court's functions established by law, the constitution gives it a role in the impeachment process and in selecting members of the constitutional court. Members are granted personal immunity regarding arrest, detention, and searches.

Constitutional Court

"The Constitutional Court," declares article 88, "exercises its authority in accordance with the norms of Constitutional procedure." It consists of nine judges, three of whom are appointed by the president, three elected by a three-fifths majority of parliament, and three appointed by the supreme court for a ten-year term. The court selects its own chairman for a five-year, nonsuccessive term. Members must not have served on the court before but must be thirty-five years of age and possess "a high legal education."

As set forth in article 89, the constitutional court is called to action "upon the Complaints or Submission of the President, of not less than one fifth of the Members of Parliament, of the courts, of supreme representative bodies of Abkhazia and Adjaria, of the public defenders or of a citizen and under the rules established by organic law." Among other duties, the court "decides the Constitutionality of the law, the President's normative acts and the normative acts of the supreme bodies of authority of Abkhazia and Adjaria"; "considers disputes ... between state bodies" and "the constitutionality of treaties and international agreements"; decides the constitutionality of referendums, elections, and "the creation and activity of political parties"; and hears complaints of citizens regarding citizenship and fundamental human rights and freedoms guaranteed by the constitution.

Amending the Constitution

Pursuant to article 102, the president, more than half of the total members of parliament, or no fewer than 200,000 electors are "allowed to submit a bill [to parliament] for the general or partial revision of the Constitution." Discussion of the draft begins one month after the bill is promulgated by parliament. A bill to revise the constitution requires the support of "at least two thirds of the total number of Members," after which it is then signed and published by the president.

GERMANY

The unification of East and West Germany that began on October 3, 1990, was facilitated by the constitution of 1949. Now the country as a whole can play a key political and economic role in the new European Union.

General Information

The Federal Republic of Germany is a little more than 357,000 square kilometers. Named Deutschland for the language spoken, Germany is bounded on the north by the North Sea, Denmark, and the Baltic Sea; it abuts Poland and the Czech Republic on the east, Austria and Switzerland on the south, and France, Luxembourg, Belgium, and the Netherlands on the west. Germany has an estimated population of approximately eighty-three million inhabitants. Berlin, whose population is some 3.5 million persons, is the new capital.

Germany's central European location and industrious people make it a leading economic force in Europe and the world. The recent unification of prosperous West Germany with virtually bankrupt East Germany, however, may strain its economic and political stability.

Type of Government: Presidential-style parliamentary federal republic, with a president, a chancellor (prime minister) and cabinet, a bicameral legislature, and a judiciary, including a constitutional court

Dates of Constitutions: 1848 (not implemented), 1871, 1919, and 1949

Constitutional History

In his *Germania* the Roman author Tacitus, who died in A.D. 116, describes unflatteringly the Indo-European Germanic tribes that some four centuries earlier had migrated from the north and east into the present-day territory of Germany. Some tribes settled on Roman land and converted to Christianity, forming a romanized Germanic society in the sixth and seventh centuries. United under the Frankish empire, the tribes, including the Alemanni, Saxons, and Bavarians, came under the rule of Charlemagne, who was crowned emperor on Christmas Day in A.D. 800. Scholars disagree about just when the concept of a Germany began, but the Treaty of Verdun in 843 divided the empire into western, middle, and eastern parts, setting the stage for the separation of territory into French and German.

During the Middle Ages Germany was a feudal society dominated by a military aristocracy. Although German law was influenced to some extent by Roman law, the former applied to individuals and was carried with them wherever they went, while the latter was based on where a person lived. Charlemagne is credited with revising the best known of the Germanic laws, the *Lex Salica* (Salic law). In 1037 a conflict arose between two vassal classes, and a feudal code of law, the *Constitutio de feudis,* was developed to sanction the inheritance of small fiefs. The German kings, however, were unable to control the nobles until the rise of the Hohenstaufen dynasty, with such leaders as Frederick I ("Barbarossa"), who ruled from 1152 to 1190.

The growth of towns, the colonization of the eastern Slav territories, and constitutional reforms under the succeeding Hapsburg rulers, such as regulations for the election of emperors of what was often called the Holy Roman Empire of the German Nation, did little to strengthen German unity. By the end of the fifteenth century governance of Germany took place on two levels: first, imperial assemblies or diets, called Reichstage, attended by the emperor, princes, administrators of church lands, knights, and representatives from imperial towns; and second, territorial assemblies in which the local prince and members of the privileged class came together to rule.

Not a sea power, Germany was unable to benefit as much as some other European nations from the discovery of the New World, but it became the center of a religious reformation that changed Christianity as much as Columbus's discoveries changed world maps. The Thirty Years' War left Germany devastated, and the ensuing Treaty of Westphalia in 1648 only strengthened the power of the territorial rulers and fostered a trend toward the separation of religion and politics. In the second half of the seventeenth century, however, the Prussian Hohenzollern Frederick William (the "Great Elector") impelled the development of absolutist rule, and his successor crowned himself without assistance from the church as king in Prussia.

The rise of Prussia was checked by Napoleon, and the Holy Roman Empire was abolished on August 6, 1806. But in Napoleon's wake Germany was less fragmented, and the Congress of Vienna in 1815 created the German Confederation. A German customs union in the 1830s continued the consolidation process. A European economic crisis led to widespread revolutions in 1848, and the Prussian king summoned an assembly, later called the "parliament of professors," to draft a constitution. The result was a historic document that apportioned powers between the German states and the central government and reflected a compromise between the systems in the United States and the United Kingdom. The constitution also included a list of basic rights that went beyond the U.S., Polish, and French constitutions; however, like the Polish document of 1791, it never went into effect.

In 1867, under the leadership of Chancellor Otto von Bismarck, a North German Confederation was formed with the Prussian king as president. In 1871, in a ceremony at Versailles, the German Empire was proclaimed, and a constitution was promulgated. This document created a federal empire, with a parliament (Reichstag) at the bottom that could veto legislation initiated at the next level by the federal council (Bundesrat). The real power lay in the hands of the emperor, the chancellor, and their bureaucracy.

After World War I a new, extremely democratic constitution drafted in the town of Weimar was adopted in 1919. Crippling inflation and a worldwide depression led to the Communist and Nazi Parties' winning a majority of seats in the parliament in 1932. An antidemocratic emergency provision in the Weimar constitution led to an inevitable conflict between the president and the leader of the parliament, the chancellor. By 1933 Adolf Hitler, who had become chancellor, had eliminated all opposition, paving the way for the Third Reich, World War II, and, finally, the division of Germany after the war.

Germany's current constitution, the Basic Law of May 23, 1949, was promulgated by the West German parliamentary council after the Western allies—France, the United Kingdom, and the United States—agreed to merge their three zones of postwar occupation to form the Federal Republic of Germany. The U.S.S.R. zone, or East Germany, along with East and West Berlin, remained outside the new democratic state until reunification on October 3, 1990.

Influenced by the Weimar constitution and the American occupation, the German constitution of 1949 has been the model for other countries, including Spain and Greece.

Influences

The Constitution

The preamble to the constitution of the Federal Republic of Germany, as amended on September 23, 1990, pursuant to the Unification Treaty of August 31, 1990, declares that the German people adopted it because they were "animated by the resolve to serve world peace as an equal part in a united Europe. . . ." Article 20 states:

(1) The Federal Republic of Germany shall be a democratic and social federal state.

(2) All state authority shall emanate from the people. It shall be exercised by the people through elections and voting and by specific organs of the legislature, the executive power and the judiciary.

(3) Legislation shall be subject to the constitutional order; the executive and the judiciary shall be bound by law and justice.

(4) All Germans shall have the right to resist any person seeking to abolish this constitutional order, should no other remedy be possible.

Popular sovereignty and the separation of powers are confirmed, and the supremacy of the constitution over other laws and the rule of law—*Rechtstaat* (just state), as opposed to simply *Staatsrecht* (state justice)—are established as a standard for the executive and the judiciary. The "right to resist" was added in 1968 to counterbalance legislation enacted that year that permits temporary suspension of some fundamental laws in emergencies.

Fundamental Rights

Civil rights first found expression in Germany in some state constitutions in the early nineteenth century and were incorporated into the 1848 constitution, which never went into effect. After 1871 the empire accepted the responsibility for individual rights, including the right to education and work, which even today would find little receptivity in the United States. But court review of the constitutionality of federal laws was not institutionalized in Germany until the 1920s.

The first section of the 1949 constitution is entitled Basic Rights. The rights include protection of human dignity; liberty; equality before the law; freedom of faith, conscience, and creed; freedom of expression, assembly, association, and movement; protection of marriage, the family, and illegitimate children; and the right to petition the government in writing. Also included are the right to choose an occupation; a prohibition against forced labor, except by court sentence; privacy in communications; the right to property; and the inviolability of the home.

Section 2, the Federation and the States, gives citizens the right, under article 20, to resist persons seeking to abolish the constitutional order, and, under article 21, declares unconstitutional any political party that seeks to abolish the free democratic order or endanger the existence of the federal republic.

Article 104 contains legal procedural guarantees in the event of deprivation of liberty, somewhat analogous to habeas corpus procedures in the common law countries.

Division of Powers

The German federal system is formed out of formerly sovereign states that have long, independent histories, and the country has been described as a centrist nation that grants some powers to the *Länder* (states), unlike the United States, in which all powers not granted to the federal government are reserved by the states and the people.

Germany is a federal state and the constitution prescribes a somewhat complex vertical division of power between the federal government and the *Länder* in articles 70 through 75. Article 70 states:

(1) The Länder shall have the right to legislate insofar as this Basic Law does not confer legislative power on the federation.

(2) The division of competence between the federation and the Länder shall be determined by the provisions of the Basic Law concerning exclusive and concurrent legislative powers.

According to article 71, "In matters within the exclusive legislative power of the federation, the Länder shall have power to legislate only where and to the extent that they are given such explicit authorization by a federal statute."

Areas for exclusive national legislation include foreign affairs and national citizenship. Areas for concurrent legislation, as long as federal legislation has not preempted the field, include civil and criminal law, public welfare, economic matters, labor law, land transfer and real estate transactions, ocean and coastal shipping, and highway traffic.

At the national level, power is divided among the president; the chancellor (prime minister); the legislature; and the courts, which include a constitutional court that exercises constitutional review.

The Executive

President. The federal president is head of state and moral leader of the country, a political role that constitutionally is weaker than that of the chancellor. The president, who must be at least forty years old, is elected by a federal convention consisting of the members of the upper house of the legislature and an equal number of members elected by the state legislatures. The office is limited to a five-year term with only one consecutive term permitted.

The president's duties include representing the nation in international relations; concluding treaties and accrediting and receiving envoys; appointing and dismissing federal judges, civil servants, and officers; and granting individual pardons. The president's orders and directions, however, must be countersigned by the chancellor or appropriate minister, except in the case of the appointment of the chancellor or the dissolution of the legislature's lower house. If the president is unable to perform these duties, the president of the upper house of parliament exercises the president's powers.

Prime Minister and Cabinet. According to article 62, the federal government of Germany consists of the federal chancellor (prime minister) and the federal ministers, who together make up the cabinet. The chancellor, as the parliamentary leader, is nominated by the federal president and elected without debate by the lower house of the parliament. Federal ministers are appointed and dismissed by the president on the recommendation of the chancellor, who appoints a minister as his or her deputy.

Article 65 defines the powers of the government:

The federal chancellor shall determine and be responsible for the general policy guidelines. Within the limits set by these guidelines, each federal minister shall conduct the affairs of his department independently and on his own responsibility. The federal government shall decide on differences of opinion between federal ministers. The federal chancellor shall conduct the affairs of the federal government in accordance with rules of procedure adopted by it and approved by the federal president.

Article 65a, inserted in 1956 and amended in 1968, places command of the armed forces under the minister of defense.

The term of office of the chancellor and the ministers ends when a newly elected lower house assembles. The lower house may remove the chancellor by a vote of no confidence only through election of a successor by a majority of its members; when the chancellor's term ends, the ministers' terms also end.

Parliament. The bicameral parliament consists of an upper house, the Bundesrat (federal council), and a lower house, the Bundestag (federal parliament).

Upper House. As provided for under article 50, "The Länder shall participate through the Bundesrat in the legislation and administration of the federation." The Bundesrat is composed of members appointed by the state governments, and their votes, which must be cast in blocs, are based on the population of each state (each state has a minimum of three votes and a maximum of six votes). The council's basic function is to protect the interests of the states, particularly by vetoing legislation. It elects a president every year and makes decisions by a majority vote.

Lower House. The members, or deputies, of the Bundestag are elected in general, direct, and secret ballot elections, half by direct suffrage and half on the basis of party lists in each state as regulated by law, for four-year terms. After elections the parliament elects a president, vice presidents, and secretaries and determines its own rules of procedure.

The deputies are granted immunity for their official actions, may not be arrested without permission of the Bundestag, and may not be forced to divulge confidences. Candidates are guaranteed leave to campaign and to continued employment, if elected.

Bills may be introduced by the federal government or members of either house of the legislature. By amendment in 1968, federal government bills must first be submitted to the Bundesrat, which has six weeks to state its position on the measure, unless the bill is designated as urgent. A 1969 amendment requires Bundesrat bills to be submitted to the Bundestag by the government, with the government's views, within three months.

After adoption by the lower house, a measure is submitted by the president of that body to the Bundesrat, and it becomes law if the Bundesrat consents to it. After enactment, it is countersigned by the chancellor or appropriate minister and then signed by the federal president and promulgated.

The Judiciary

Article 92, as amended in 1968, provides, "Judicial power shall be vested in the judges; it shall be exercised by the federal constitutional court, by the federal courts provided for in this basic law, and by the courts of the Länder."

Article 95 provides for a federal court of justice, an administrative court, a finance court, a labor court, and a social court. The supreme federal court of justice (the Bundesgerichshof, successor to the Reichsgericht) is the highest court for ordinary matters. Judges for these courts are selected by the appropriate federal minister and a committee of ministers from the states, and an equal number are elected by the upper house of the legislature. Under article 97 judges are to be independent and permanent and not removable except by judicial decision.

Constitutional Court. The federal constitutional court in Germany stands at the apex of the court system. Each house of the legislature elects half its judges, who include federal judges and others.

Unlike the U.S. supreme court or even the former German high court (the Reichsgericht), the court's role in constitutional review is explicit and may be "concrete," where a law's validity is questioned during litigation, or "abstract," where the federal or state governments or one-third of the members of the federal legislature question the constitutionality of a statute. Its jurisdiction includes interpreting the basic law in disputes by parties with rights vested under it; settling differences of opinion regarding the compatibility of both federal and state laws, the constitution, and the rights and duties of the federal and state governments, particularly in the area of the execution of federal law; settling public law disputes between the federation and the states and between and within states, if no other court has jurisdiction; and, by amendment in 1969, deciding complaints by individuals of unconstitutionality under specific basic law provisions and complaints by communes of constitutional infringement of the right of self-government guaranteed under article 28.

The 1949 German constitution's provision for the constitutional court was one of the most important changes over the previous constitutions. Every year thousands of constitutional complaints are filed, but only a small percentage are ruled valid.

Amending the Constitution

Article 79 requires that a statute whose purpose is the amendment of the constitution must be approved by at least two-thirds of the members of each house of the legislature. The constitution prohibits amendments to the first twenty articles and any change that would affect the division of the federation into states and the participation of the states in legislation.

A former British colony, Ghana broke with tradition in 1960 by creating an executive presidency, but the nation has not escaped intermittent periods of military rule that have plagued many African countries since their independence.

The Republic of Ghana in West Africa is 238,536 square kilometers and lies on the African Gold Coast north of the Gulf of Guinea in the Atlantic Ocean; it is bounded by Togo on the east, Burkina Faso on the north, and the Ivory Coast on the west. Accra is the capital of this country of nearly twenty million inhabitants.

Historically, Ghana's major export has been cocoa, but timber and mining, including gold and diamonds, also contribute to the economy. Poor private-sector management and a bloated government bureaucracy have impeded efforts to stabilize the nation's precarious economy.

Type of Government: Presidential republic, with a president and cabinet, a unicameral legislature, and a judiciary

Dates of Constitutions: 1925, 1946, 1950, 1954, 1957, 1960, 1969, 1979, and 1993

In the fourth century A.D. the Empire of Ghana controlled a large area of West Africa north of its modern namesake, trading in gold and slaves with nomadic peoples farther north. The Ashantis, a branch of the Akan people, settled in the central part of what is now Ghana, and the Fantis, also Akans, inhabited the coastal areas. Chiefs played a key role among the Akans, and the stool on which the chief sat was revered as a throne; a chief could be ousted, or "destooled," because of misconduct. The Ashantis, a matrilineal society of well-organized and intractable fighters, formed a confederation with a grand council of chiefs led by a paramount chief, the Asantehene. North of the Ashanti were some twenty indigenous states, each with its own form of political organization.

After the Portuguese made contact with the West African Gold Coast late in the fifteenth century, the Dutch, English, Swedes, Danes, and Germans followed. By 1664, however, the British dominated the area, and in 1872 they acquired the remaining Dutch interests there. Since the slave trade and slavery had been abolished in the first half of the nineteenth century, the territory's natural resources became the focus of colonial commerce.

The West Africa Act of 1821 marked the beginning of Britain's formal control over the Gold Coast. In 1843 a lieutenant governor was stationed there, and the establishment of courts and other institutions was authorized. The following year coastal chiefs accepted British jurisdiction and agreed to conform their customs to English law under the terms of a treaty known as the Bond of 1844. In 1874 the British laws then in effect were extended to the colony. Beginning in the twentieth century the small Gold Coast colony began acquiring territory: first the Ashanti lands, then the Northern Territories, and finally Togoland in 1957, when they joined to form the independent nation of Ghana.

In 1925 the "Guggisburg" constitution, named after the governor, provided for members of a legislative council to be elected by a provincial council of chiefs, and the 1946 "Burns" constitution allowed Ashanti representation in the legislative council. In 1947 the United Gold Coast Convention, an organization to promote self-government, was formed. As a result of political disturbances the following year, a British commission recommended constitutional reforms. To further the drive for independence, Knwame Nkrumah left the original group and established the Convention People's Party in 1949.

Under the "Coussey" constitution of 1950 the Gold Coast became the first black African colony extensively involved in its own internal administration, and under the "Nkrumah" constitution in 1954 it achieved nearly full internal self-government. In 1957, after Togoland voted to join the new nation, Ghana became an independent member of the British Commonwealth under an "independence" constitution that established a unitary government with a unicameral legislature whose members were directly elected.

Under a new constitution in 1960 Ghana became a republic with a strong executive presidency filled by Nkrumah, who had jailed or exiled any opponent. After Nkrumah's ouster in a 1966 coup, a new constitution in 1969 restored the prime minister's position as head of government, while the president remained head of state. Another military government and another coup preceded the 1979 constitution, which created an executive president to be elected by popular vote with the traditional unicameral legislature. After another coup, the constitution was formally abrogated in 1982, and a military government ruled by proclamation. In 1991 the military rulers agreed under pressure to return power to a civilian government, and a constitution for the fourth republic, approved by referendum in 1992, went into effect on January 7, 1993. Several amendments were enacted in 1996.

Influences

Ghana's constitutions have been influenced by the British parliamentary model as well as French law.

The Constitution

The preamble to the constitution of the Republic of Ghana confirms the principles of friendship and peace with all peoples of the world; freedom, justice, probity, and accountability; the sovereignty of the people; universal adult suffrage; the rule of law; and the protection and preservation of fundamental human rights and freedoms and the nation's unity and stability.

Article 1 declares the constitution's supremacy:

(1) The sovereignty of Ghana resides in the people of Ghana in whose name and for whose welfare the powers of government are to be exercised in the manner and within the limits laid down in this constitution.

(2) This constitution shall be the supreme law of Ghana and any other law found to be inconsistent with any provision of this constitution shall, to the extent of the inconsistency, be void.

Fundamental Rights

Chapter 5, Fundamental Human Rights and Freedoms, provides that the human rights and freedoms guaranteed "shall be respected and upheld by the executive, legislature, and judiciary and all other organs of government. . . ." These include the right to life; respect for human dignity; protection from slavery and forced labor; equality and freedom from discrimination on the grounds of gender, race, color, ethnic origin, religion, creed, or social or economic status; privacy of home and other property; right to a fair trial; and freedom of speech and expression, thought, conscience, belief, religion, assembly, association, information, and movement.

Article 27 provides equal rights for women and special care during maternity. Chapter 7 covers political parties, and chapter 12 deals with the freedom and independence of the media.

Division of Powers

Ghana, a unitary state, divides power among the president, the legislature, and the courts, which have the power of judicial review.

The Executive

President. Article 57 provides that the president is head of state, head of government, and commander in chief of the armed forces and that he or she "takes precedence over all other persons in Ghana." While in office, the president is not personally subject to any civil or criminal proceedings.

To be eligible for the presidency, a person must be a citizen by birth, forty years old, and otherwise qualified to be elected a member of the legislature. In addition, he or she must be nominated by a document signed by no fewer than two registered voters in each district of the legislature's jurisdiction and must designate a person to serve as vice president. The president is elected by universal adult suffrage for a four-year term and may not be elected for more than two terms.

The president appoints a council of state, in consultation with the legislature; ministers of state, with prior approval of the legislature; and ambassadors and other top officials, in consultation with the council of state. He or she receives foreign representatives; executes treaties, which must be ratified by the legislature; and, in consultation with the council of state, grants pardons and commutes sentences.

The president may be removed from office on certain specified grounds by a vote of not less than one-third of the members of the legislature, a determination by a tribunal convened by the chief justice, and a resolution approved by two-thirds of all the members of the legislature supporting the tribunal's finding or the finding of a prima facie basis for removal by a medical board convened by the chief justice.

Council of State. The council is composed of a former chief justice, a former chief of the defense staff, a former inspector general of the police, the president of the national house of chiefs, and a representative of each region in Ghana. The president may request the council of state to consider bills after they have been passed by the legislature.

Cabinet. The president, the vice president, and ten to nineteen ministers constitute the cabinet. Article 76 requires the cabinet to assist the president in determining the government's general policy.

Parliament. Article 93 provides that the legislative power of Ghana is vested in a parliament, which technically resembles a congress rather than a true parliament. It is to consist of at least 140 elected members; in 1992 the actual number of members was 200. To be qualified for election, a person must be a citizen, at least twenty-one years old, a registered voter, a resident of his or her constituency (or must have resided there five of ten years preceding the election or originally come from the constituency), and must have paid or arranged to pay all taxes due. Article 94 contains a list of disqualifications. Every citizen eighteen years old of sound mind may register and vote in public elections and referendums.

After elections the parliament elects a speaker, who has "neither an original nor casting vote," and two deputy speakers. Members are granted certain privileges and immunities, such as freedom of speech, debate, and proceedings in the parliament as well as freedom from civil or criminal process while going to, attending, or returning from the parliament.

Article 104 provides that parliamentary matters are generally determined by a majority vote of those present and that one-half of the members constitute a quorum.

Laws are enacted by bills passed by the parliament and assented to by the president. Except for financial bills, including the imposition of taxes, which must be submitted by or on behalf of the president, bills must be accompanied by an explanatory memorandum, must be published officially at least fourteen days before introduction, and must be referred to the national house of chiefs if they affect the institution of the chieftaincy. After first reading, bills are referred to a committee that reports on them and then are subject to debate and final action.

The president has seven days to inform the speaker of his or her assent or refusal to assent. In the latter case the president may either state the objections or, as provided for in article 90, refer the matter to the council of state; however, if the measure is repassed by resolution by a vote of two-thirds of the members of the parliament, then the president must assent to the measure. To be effective, the law must be published officially.

Article 125 declares that justice emanates from the people and that judicial power is vested in the judiciary, which is to be independent and subject only to the constitution. Article 127 provides that judicial and administrative functions of the judiciary, including financial administration, are subject only to the constitution, not to any person or authority. The judiciary in Ghana consists of superior courts—such as the supreme court, court of appeal, the high court, and regional tribunals—and lower courts that may be established by law.

Supreme Court. The supreme court is the final court of appeal. It has exclusive and original jurisdiction in the enforcement and interpretation of the constitution and the determination whether "an enactment was made in excess of the powers conferred on parliament or any other authority or person by law under this constitution." When such questions arise in a lower court, proceedings are stayed pending the supreme court's determination. It may also hear appeals in specific cases from determinations by the court of appeal.

The supreme court consists of a chief justice, who is responsible for the administration and supervision of the judiciary, and at least nine other members. The chief justice is appointed by the president in consultation with the council of state, and the other justices are appointed by the president in consultation with the council of state and on the advice of a judicial council made up of the chief justice as chairman and other members involved with the practice of law, such as the attorney general, judges, and others. All members of the supreme court must be confirmed by the legislature.

During military rule in the 1970s, the legislature was dissolved and the supreme court was abolished, and in 1983 three high court judges, including one woman, were abducted from their homes at night. Such a history has undoubtedly affected the independence and integrity of Ghana's judicial system.

Ombudsman

Chapter 18 creates a commission on human rights and administrative justice that acts as an ombudsman.

Amending the Constitution

Articles 289 through 292 provide that amendments are to be made by acts of the legislature solely for such purpose, that any amendment of certain specified "entrenched" provisions must be referred by the speaker to the council of state for its advice, that amendments must be officially published six months before introduction in the legislature, and that after first reading a referendum must be held and at least forty percent of the eligible voters vote and at least seventy-five percent of the votes cast must be for approval. If the amendment is approved by referendum, the legislature must pass it and the president must assent to it.

To amend a nonentrenched provision, a bill must be officially published twice. After the first reading the speaker must refer it to the council of state for its advice. If the amendment is passed by a vote of at least two-thirds of all the members of the legislature on the second and third readings, the president must then sign it.

From the Greek word *demos*, meaning "people," comes the word *democracy* itself. The cradle of Western civilization, Greece in 1975 adopted a new constitution embodying a modern parliamentary democracy.

The Hellenic Republic, or Greece, in southern Europe is bounded on the north by Albania, Macedonia, and Bulgaria; on the northeast by the European territory of Turkey; on the east by the Aegean Sea; on the west by the Ionian Sea; and on the south by the Mediterranean Sea. A country of nearly 132,000 square kilometers, approximately twenty percent of which consists of more than two thousand islands, Greece has an estimated population of nearly eleven million persons. Its capital is Athens.

A member of the European Economic Community since January 1, 1981, Greece's economy is based mainly on agriculture and industry, including small businesses and a large international shipping operation. Relations with its neighbors, including Turkey, have improved recently, and efforts were undertaken to solve the country's economic problems to justify its participation in the uniform European currency in 2001.

Type of Government: Presidential-style parliamentary republic, with a president, a prime minister and cabinet, a unicameral legislature, and a judiciary, including a constitutional court

Dates of Key Constitutions: 1822 (revised in 1823), 1827, 1864 (revised in 1911), 1927, 1952, 1968, 1973, and 1975

By 3000 B.C. the original Neolithic populations of continental Greece and the Aegean islands had been displaced by tribes from Asia, and on the island of Crete the newcomers established a culturally and technically sophisticated society. The Achaeans, forerunners of the Greeks, settled on the peninsula around the beginning of the second millennium B.C. and fell under the influence of the Minoans of Crete by 1600 B.C. By 1400 B.C. the city of Mycenae on the mainland was the region's dominant political and cultural force.

After 1100 B.C. Dorian tribes from the north overwhelmed the Mycenaeans, and in the ensuing three centuries the *polis* (city-state), such as Athens, evolved as people moved from the countryside to be near the acropolis, a defense fortification constructed on high ground. The *polis* came to symbolize the Greeks' shared set of values and led to rivalries such as that between Athens and Sparta. Athens, an open, cosmopolitan state with its form of direct democracy, and Sparta, an isolated authoritarian military state with an exclusive warrior caste, clashed in the Peloponnesian Wars (460–404 B.C.). Sparta won, but both states were greatly weakened by the conflict. The following century, in the wake of these wars, Plato and Aristotle produced their influential works of political science and philosophy.

In *The Republic,* about a utopian state ruled by philosopher-kings, Plato saw virtue as the aim of laws and as the product of *sophrosune* (self-control or temperance). In his last work, *The Laws,* he describes a sort of constitution for a new community of 5,040 colonists on Crete. In it he has Socrates state prophetically, "Well, my friends, *I* should think the real difficulty is to make political systems reflect in practice the trouble-free perfection of theory." Aristotle, a scientist and philosopher, first defined humans as political animals and identified the principle of the separation of government powers to avoid tyranny.

Between 336 and 323 B.C. Alexander the Great of Macedonia conquered most of the known world. Although his vast empire collapsed after his death, Macedonia ruled Greece for the next two centuries. The Greek culture, if not their political autonomy, continued to flourish under the Pax Romana (Peace of Rome) and had an impact particularly to the east, centering in Byzantium. But while Byzantium was Greek in language and culture, it was Roman in its law and political administration.

On May 29, 1453, Byzantium fell to the Muslim Ottoman Turks. They ruled the Greeks for nearly three hundred years thereafter but allowed the Greek Orthodox Church more powers and privileges than it had under the Byzantine emperors. The great rift between the Catholic Church of Rome and the Orthodox Church in the east was a constant source of political realignments; under the Muslims, Orthodox authorities adopted the Ottoman policy of taking money for special favors. Such exactions, in turn, fueled the fledgling nationalistic interests of the Greek intelligentsia, and the revolt that erupted in 1821 attracted volunteers from the rest of Europe, including the poet Lord Byron.

In 1822 the insurgents, having had some success, set up three regional provisional governments and created a constitution that was viewed as extremely liberal—one of thirteen the Greek nation has had in modern times. In 1823 it was revised to create a unified government, but civil war broke out the next year. In May 1827, however, after Britain and Russia agreed to intervene in the conflict between Greece and the Turks, who had been joined by Egypt, the insurgents wrote a new constitution. But the price for a Greek nation-state exacted by the powers, now joined by France, was acceptance of a hereditary monarchy, with Otto, the seventeen-year-old son of Ludwig of Bavaria, as the king.

Inspired by the glory of their ancient history, the Greeks made Athens their new capital and began to contemplate expanding the territory of their new state, which encompassed only about one-third of the Greek population previously controlled by the Ottoman Empire. Political parties began to develop, although Otto continually refused to grant a new constitution. He was overthrown in 1862, but again the three powers selected a king for Greece, George I from Denmark. A new constitution in 1864 increased democratic freedom, while maintaining a strong monarchy.

In 1911 the 1864 constitution was revised in an attempt to carry out an ambitious program of social and economic modernization and political reform. Following World War I, however, after a coup and a countercoup, a republic was proclaimed on March 25, 1924, and a new constitution promulgated in 1927. After a series of military governments and constitutional attempts at stable governments in 1952, 1968, and 1973, the current constitution of the Hellenes was adopted by a specially empowered parliament on June 7, 1975, within a year after a seven-year military dictatorship. Its supreme law became effective on June 11, 1975.

Influences

The Greek constitution, which was influenced by its 1952 and 1968 predecessors, draws on European models, and like the German constitution it expresses the principles of *Sozialstaat* (the social state).

The Constitution

The constitution of the Hellenes has no preamble but simply begins, "Constitution of Greece, In the Name of the Holy and Consubstantial and Indivisible Trinity, The Fifth Revisionary Parliament of the Hellenes Resolves: . . . ."

Article 1, section 1, sets forth the type and basis of government:

1. The form of government of Greece is that of a parliamentary republic.

2. Popular sovereignty is the foundation of government.

3. All powers derive from the people and exist for the people and the nation; they shall be exercised as specified by the constitution.

The parliamentary system of government was first introduced in Greece more than a century ago. A 1986 amendment brought the Greek constitution more in line with the classical parliamentary model by further limiting the power of the president and increasing the power of the prime minister and the government.

Article 2 declares that respect and protection of the value of people is a primary obligation of the state and that Greece adheres to generally recognized principles of international law.

Article 3, Relations of Church and State, provides that the prevailing religion is the Eastern Orthodox Church of Christ and that the text of the Holy Scripture may not be altered without prior church sanction. The language in section 2 has been interpreted by some to mean that while the constitution does not establish a state church, neither does it provide for strict separation of church and state. Although membership in the Orthodox Church is not required to hold high public office, the president must be a Christian to honestly take the oath of office required by article 33.

Fundamental Rights

Individual and social rights and protections are set forth in articles 4 through 25. These include equality; personal freedom; protection of life, honor, and liberty, regardless of nationality, race, language, and religious or political beliefs; freedom of movement; protection in the home; the right of petition, assembly, and association; freedom of religion, opinion, the press, art, science, research, and teaching; protection of property and compensation for public taking; secrecy (privacy) of communications; the right to judicial protection; protection for the family, marriage, and motherhood; and the right to work, join trade unions, and to strike. The right to establish and belong to political parties is also guaranteed.

The Greek constitution is a synthesis of individual and social rights. While not subordinated to the community, the individual is clearly viewed as a social unit in light of the following language in article 25: "The state has the right to claim of all citizens to fulfill the duty of social and national solidarity."

Division of Powers

Power in Greece, a unitary state, is divided among the president, as head of state; the prime minister, as head of government; the legislature; and the courts, including a constitutional court that has the power of constitutional review.

The Executive

President. Executive power is vested in the president, who is head of state. He or she is elected by a two-thirds vote of the legislature for a five-year term. To be eligible for the presidency, a person must be the "descendant of a Greek father," a Greek citizen for at least five years, at least forty years old, and eligible to vote.

With certain exceptions article 35 requires that "no act of the president of the republic shall be valid nor be executed unless it has been countersigned by the competent minister. . . ." Exceptions include when the cabinet has been relieved of its duties and the prime minister fails to sign, when an act appoints the prime minister, and when a referendum on a bill has been decreed (such a decree must be countersigned by the speaker of the parliament).

In appointing a prime minister, the president is limited by the language of article 37, which requires that the leader of the party with an absolute majority in the legislature be appointed prime minister. If no party has an absolute majority, the article directs the president to give an "exploratory" mandate first to the leader of the party with a relative majority and, if this mandate fails, then to the party with the second highest majority.

Other duties of the president include representing the nation internationally; concluding peace treaties; granting pardons and reducing or commuting sentences on the recommendation of the prime minister; appointing and dismissing civil servants in accordance with the law; summoning the council of the republic to meet under his or her chairmanship; convening, dissolving, and in some cases suspending a session of the legislature; promulgating and publishing the laws passed by the legislature; issuing decrees implementing the laws; and, under extraordinary circumstances and within limits, issuing acts of legislative content. The president may also proclaim a referendum on crucial national matters and bills passed by the legislature, under conditions and circumstances laid down by the constitution, and may under exceptional circumstances address messages directly to the Greek people. The president, according to article 45, is the chief of the nation's armed forces, although this command is to be exercised by the government.

Article 49 limits the president's liability while in office to acts of high treason and intentional violation of the constitution and provides for the impeachment process.

Prime Minister and Cabinet. The government consists of the prime minister and the ministers, who make up the cabinet. After the president appoints the government, pursuant to article 84, it is obliged to request a vote of confidence by the legislature. If not given a vote of confidence or if censured, the government submits its resignation to the president.

The members of the government are responsible collectively for the general policy of the state and individually for matters within their spheres of competence and for countersigning acts of the president.

The Legislature

Parliament. The Greek parliament, the Vouli, is a unicameral body. The 1927 constitution had created a second house, the senate, which had worked well under the constitution in effect until 1935. Fears that such a body would be conservative and hamper the legislative process led to its near unanimous rejection by the framers of the 1975 constitution.

The size of the parliament is limited by the constitution to between 200 and 300 members, who represent the nation. Members are elected by compulsory, direct, universal, and secret ballot for four-year terms. Most members are elected in electoral districts; however, article 54(3) states: "Part of the parliament, comprising not more than one-twentieth of the total number of its members, may be elected throughout the country at large in proportion to the total electoral strength of each party throughout the country, as specified by law."

To be eligible for election to the parliament a person must be a Greek citizen, have the legal capacity to vote, and be at least twenty-five years old on the day of the election. Many occupations, such as being a civil servant or an officer in the armed forces, disqualify candidates unless they resign before being nominated. Article 57 further limits the outside activities of members of the parliament.

The parliament convenes on the first Monday in October each year, unless the president convenes it earlier. It determines its own rules and elects a speaker and other members of the presidium. Article 73, paragraph 1, states that the right to propose laws is vested in the parliament and the government. Resolutions are passed by an absolute majority of the members present, and one-fourth of the members constitute a quorum.

Legislative powers include reviewing the nonbasic provisions of the constitution; voting on laws, regulations, and international treaty ratification; voting on the state budget; electing the president of the republic; petitioning for the deposit of a document; expressing a wish that an administrative measure be taken; petitioning for factual information; questioning an act of the government; setting up investigative committees; and expressing approval or censure of the government.

The constitution grants members unrestricted freedom of opinion and the right to vote according to their conscience, as well as freedom from arrest, unless the parliament consents or the member is caught in a felonious act.

The Judiciary

"The judicial power," declares article 26(3), "shall be vested in courts of law." According to article 87 of section 5, on the Judicial Power:

1. Justice shall be administered by courts composed of regular judges who shall enjoy functional and personal independence.
2. Judges shall in the discharge of their duties be subject only to the constitution and the laws; in no case shall they be obliged to comply with provisions enacted in violation of the constitution.

Greece's high courts are divided into administrative, civil, and criminal courts.

Supreme Court. The supreme court, Areios Pagos, is the highest court for final appeals on points of law from both civil and criminal courts.

Council of State. The council of state is the highest administrative court. It has jurisdiction over petitions to annul the executive acts of administrative authorities for abuse of power or violations of law, and it can annul presidential decrees or ministerial acts or omissions by any agent of the executive branch.

Court of Auditors. A court of auditors has jurisdiction over government expenditures.

Judges are appointed by the president and may not be removed, except for cause, until retirement. They are supervised administratively by a supreme judicial council, and there is a supreme disciplinary council for judicial functionaries with the rank of member of the supreme court and deputy prosecutor of the supreme court and above. The public prosecution authority, which according to article 87 participates in supervising regular judges, functions in both the executive and judicial branches while being independent of both.

Constitutional Court. Article 100 establishes a special highest court, or constitutional court, which has jurisdiction to hear cases involving electoral violations, referendum returns, the disqualifications of members of the parliament, conflicts between courts and administrative authorities, the constitutionality of laws and conflicting judgments, and rules of international law. The court is composed of the presidents of the council of state, the supreme court, and the court of auditors as well as four members each from the council of state and supreme court who are chosen by lot for terms of two years.

Amending the Constitution

Except for certain basic provisions relating to the form of government, the inviolability of individual liberty, basic freedoms, and separation of powers, which cannot be revised, the Greek constitution may be amended by two successive legislatures. An amendment must first be approved by an absolute majority of the members, and then, after an election, by a three-fifths majority of the members. The aim is to ensure due deliberation by the elected representatives and input from the people to protect against rash revisionism.

HAITI

Haiti was the second nation in the Western Hemisphere to achieve independence. Since then the first free black republic in the world has struggled under numerous constitutions and repressive regimes. Constitutional government returned with President Aristide in 1994.

General Information

The Republic of Haiti in the West Indies is approximately 28,000 square kilometers and shares with the Dominican Republic the largest island in the Caribbean Sea, Hispaniola. Port-au-Prince is the capital of this country of approximately seven million persons.

Most of Haiti's work force is employed in agriculture, and its cash crops include sugar, cocoa, sisal, cotton, and coffee, its leading export. In 1993, when the ruling military junta refused to allow the return of the ousted elected president, Jean-Bertrand Aristide, the United Nations imposed an oil embargo that brought the country's already depressed economy to a virtual standstill. An agreement by Haitian military leaders to allow U.S. troop intervention in 1994 has led to the restoration of Aristide and a civilian constitutional government.

Type of Government: Presidential-style parliamentary republic, with a president, a prime minister and council of ministers (cabinet), a bicameral legislature, and a judiciary

Dates of Key Constitutions: 1789, 1801, 1805, 1806, 1816, 1859, 1918, 1932, 1950, 1957, 1964, 1983, and 1987

Constitutional History

When Christopher Columbus, on his first voyage to the New World in 1492, landed on the island now called Hispaniola ("little Spain"), peoples of three linguistic groups lived in the Caribbean: the Cibony, Caribs, and Arawak, who had migrated from South America. The Arawaks, or Taino Indians, called their home on Hispaniola Ayti or Hayti, meaning "mountainous." They soon died out, leaving no written record, but apparently under the Arawaks' system of government each island was divided into provinces ruled by a paramount chief, with subchiefs and headmen under them. The Caribs' system of government seems to have been more decentralized.

In August 1500 Columbus and his brother Bartholome were sent back to Spain in chains when Hispaniola, which they administered, erupted in civil war. Order was restored, and the Spanish began developing the island, also called Santo Domingo, using the *encomienda* system of land grants, which gave settlers the right to use the natives for labor, as in other Spanish colonies in the New World.

In the seventeenth century French Huguenots began settling the island's north coast, and in 1697 the western portion, known as Saint-Domingue, was transferred to France by the Treaty of Ryswick. In the wake of the French Revolution the colonists adopted a revolutionary-style constitution in 1789. In 1791, however, slaves who had been brought in to replace the native population, which had died off, rebelled and instigated a Haitian revolution. In 1793, after French republican forces and Haitian slaves defeated the royalists, slavery was abolished for the first time anywhere in the world. In 1801 a former slave, Toussaint L'Ouverture, promulgated a constitution that made himself governor-general for life.

Haiti proclaimed its independence on January 1, 1804, and crowned its new leader emperor of Haiti. A new constitution was adopted in 1805. In 1806 the emperor was assassinated, and a new constitution creating a powerful legislature was adopted. An 1816 constitution equalized the power among the three branches and added a bicameral legislature; another constitution modeled on this document was promulgated in 1859. Of the twenty-two heads of state who served from 1843 until 1915, when U.S. marines occupied the country to keep out the Germans, only one completed a term, and many died under strange or violent circumstances.

Two additional constitutions promulgated in 1918 and 1932 during the Haiti-sanctioned U.S. occupation provided for limited rights of ownership in real property by foreigners and for a change in the election procedures for the bicameral legislature. After the U.S. withdrawal in 1934, Haiti suffered under a series of dishonest presidents and then, beginning in 1957, under François ("Papa Doc") Duvalier and his son, Jean-Claude ("Baby Doc"), who ruled as greedy tyrants. Constitutions were produced in 1950 and 1957, the latter reinstating a unicameral legislature. Papa Doc maintained his power through the use of "Volunteers for National Security," commonly called *tonton makouts* (bogey-men), who enforced his repressive measures. A constitution in 1964 made him president for life, and by amendment in 1971 he could choose his successor, who was required to be at least eighteen years old.

Baby Doc came to power in 1971, and in 1983 a new constitution legitimized certain previously de facto powers of the president and permitted him to appoint his successor. On February 7, 1986, however, after riots erupted over his lavish inauguration, Baby Doc fled to France, and military rule filled the gap. Haiti's most recent constitution, promulgated in 1987, was suspended in 1988 but restored in 1990. In the same year reasonably honest elections were held, giving Aristide the presidency by a large majority. In October 1991, after a military coup on September 29, he too went into exile but was restored in 1994 with help from the United States. In all, Haiti has had more than twenty constitutions since 1789.

Influences

Haitian law has generally been influenced by the French legal system, and to an extent the desire to avoid the evils of the Duvalier regimes influenced the drafters of the 1987 constitution.

The Constitution

The short preamble affirms basic values and defines goals reflecting the influence of the 1948 United Nations International Declaration of Human Rights. Article 1 declares that "Haiti is an indivisible, sovereign, independent, cooperatist, free, democratic and social republic." Article 4 sets forth the national motto: "Liberty, Equality and Fraternity." Article 7 "categorically" forbids the cult of the personality and the use of effigies and names of living persons on, among other things, currency, stamps, and public buildings.

Fundamental Rights

Title 3, chapter 2, Basic Rights, includes sections entitled Right to Life and Health, Individual Liberty, Freedom of Expression, Freedom of Conscience, Freedom of Assembly and Association, Education and Teaching, Freedom to Work, Property, Right to Information, and Right to Security. Chapter 3, Duties of the Citizen, states that civic duties include respecting the constitution and the laws, voting, paying taxes, defending the country in time of war, working to maintain peace, and providing assistance to people in danger. Failure to perform these duties is punishable by law, and civic service is compulsory for both sexes.

Division of Powers

In Haiti, a unitary state, the constitution divides power among the president, as head of state; the prime minister, as head of government; the legislature; and the courts, which exercise limited judicial review.

The Executive

President. Article 136 describes the president's role: "The president of the republic, who is the head of state, shall see to the respect for and enforcement of the constitution and the stability of the institutions. He shall ensure the regular operations of the public authorities and the continuity of the state." Historically, the president in Haiti has been a strongman who has seized power with the support of the military and who has merged the office with himself.

The president is elected to a five-year term by direct and universal suffrage and by an absolute majority of the votes; if no candidate receives an absolute majority, a second election is held. The president may serve for only one additional nonconsecutive term. To be eligible for the presidency, a candidate must be a native-born Haitian and thirty-five years old, enjoy civil and political rights, own real property in Haiti, and have his or her "habitual residence" in the country. The president must also have resided in the country for five consecutive years before the election and must not otherwise be disqualified by law.

The duties of the president include choosing a prime minister from the majority party in the legislature (or if there is no majority party, in consultation with the presiding officers of the two houses of the legislature); accepting the government's resignation and dismissing the prime minister; accrediting and receiving the accreditation of ambassadors; declaring war and signing peace treaties with the approval of parliament; appointing, by decree in the council of ministers (cabinet) and with the approval of the upper house, the commander in chief of the armed forces and the police and ambassadors; appointing other key officials in accordance with the constitution; promulgating the laws; and granting pardons and commuting sentences. The constitution specifically makes the president only the nominal head of the armed forces.

If the president is unable to discharge these duties, executive authority is vested in the cabinet, with the prime minister presiding. If the office is vacant, the president of the supreme court becomes the acting president of the republic.

Prime Minister and Cabinet. The government consists of the prime minister, as head of government, other ministers, and secretaries of state. The prime minister chooses the members of the council of ministers and seeks a vote of confidence from the parliament based on his or her declaration of general policy.

The Legislature

Parliament. The bicameral parliament consists of a lower chamber, the house of deputies, and an upper chamber called the senate. Article 88 vests legislative power in these two bodies.

When meeting as a single body, the parliament is known as the national assembly. The specific powers of the national assembly include ratifying declarations of war, approving international treaties, amending the constitution, and participating in the selection of the members of a permanent electoral council. The president of the senate is the president of the assembly and the president of the lower house is the vice president. Members of parliament are immune from most civil and criminal punishment while in office.

Upper House. Senators must be thirty years old, native Haitians, and residents of their department at least four years before the election; they also must enjoy political and civil rights, own real property in the district, practice a profession or trade, and must not otherwise be disqualified. Senators are elected by direct vote, three from each of nine departments, for six-year terms; one-third are replaced every two years. According to article 95-1, the senate is permanently in session.

The senate's duties include providing a list of three names for the selection of judges for the supreme court and sitting as a high court of justice to try high officials, including the president and the prime minister, that are indicted by the lower house.

Lower House. Deputies must be twenty-five years old and must have resided in the electoral district at least two consecutive years before the election, in addition to meeting qualifications similar to those for senators. The eighty-three deputies are elected by direct suffrage to four-year terms and represent municipalities, called communes.

Article 107-1 provides that any senator or deputy may introduce matters of general interest. The two houses and the executive branch may introduce any bills except money bills, such as the budget or tax laws, which may be introduced only by the executive branch in the lower house.

A majority of members in each house constitute a quorum, and acts are generally approved by a majority vote of those present. After passage by both houses, legislation goes to the president, who may return it with objections. If the objections are rejected by both houses, the law must be promulgated.

"Only the legislative branch," states article 128, "has the authority to interpret the laws, which it does by passing a law." Under article 173, the constitution states, "Judicial power shall be vested in the supreme court *(cour de cassation),* the courts of appeal, courts of first instance, courts of peace and special courts, whose number, composition, organization, operation, and jurisdiction are set by law."

The Judiciary

Supreme Court. The supreme court's explicit jurisdiction extends to conflicts of jurisdiction, matters of law and fact in all decisions of military courts, and the unconstitutionality of the laws when litigation is referred to it. Article 183-1, however, notes that "the interpretation of a law given by the houses of the legislature shall be imposed for the purpose of that law without retroactively taking away any rights acquired res adjudicata."

A judge is appointed to the supreme court for a ten-year term by the president of the republic from a list of three names submitted by the upper house of the legislature. Appeals court judges are also appointed for ten-year terms from a list submitted by the legislatures of the department involved. Article 177 affords protection to the judges in the case of removal, reassignment, and termination.

Title 6, Independent Institutions, creates an office of protector of citizens, similar to an ombudsman, to guard against abuse by the government.

Ombudsman

On the recommendation of one of the two houses, the legislature may declare that the constitution be amended. A two-thirds vote of each house in the last regular session of a legislative period is required. At the beginning of the next legislative period, the houses meet jointly as the national assembly. If two-thirds of the members are present, they may deliberate on the proposed amendment and may approve it by a two-thirds majority of the votes cast. An amendment takes effect only after a newly elected president has been installed, and in no event may a former president benefit from an amendment. No amendment may affect the democratic and republican nature of the state.

Amending the Constitution

HONDURAS

Since gaining independence in 1821, Honduras has suffered numerous rebellions and military regimes. For more than a decade now, however, the country has enjoyed a relatively stable civilian, democratic government.

General Information

The Republic of Honduras in Central America is approximately 112,000 square kilometers and is bounded on the north by the Caribbean Sea, on the south by Nicaragua, and on the west by the Pacific Ocean, El Salvador, and Guatemala. Tegucigalpa is the capital of this country of approximately 6.2 million inhabitants.

The Honduran economy depends on bananas, coffee, beef, and timber. A shortage of arable land, high unemployment, illiteracy, a landless peasantry, and disease keep the country in the grip of poverty. Hurricane Mitch in 1998 added to the country's woes.

Type of Government: Presidential republic, with a president and council of ministers (cabinet), a unicameral legislature, and a judiciary

Dates of Key Constitutions: 1825, 1839, 1865, 1880, 1894 (reinstated in 1908), 1904, 1921, 1936, 1957, 1965, and 1982

Constitutional History

Christopher Columbus set foot on the mainland of Honduras in 1502, but more than twenty years passed before a Spanish expedition crossed the country to the Pacific coast. Gold and silver deposits attracted some interest, but in 1537 the indigenous peoples used for labor revolted under the leadership of Lempira, whose name was given to the Honduran currency. Mining efforts foundered, and by the seventeenth century Honduras was an impoverished part of the Captaincy General of Guatemala in the Spanish colonial empire. Reforms under the Bourbon king of Spain in the eighteenth century revived the mining industry. British inroads along the Caribbean coast were curtailed by a 1786 Anglo-Spanish agreement acknowledging Spain's sovereignty over the area.

In 1821, with the collapse of Spanish rule, Honduras acquired independence and in 1822, along with other newly independent Central American provinces, allied itself with the Mexican Empire. Mexico became a republic the following year, and the provinces (states) then formed a federation. Honduras adopted a constitution as a member of the Federation of Central America in 1825. In 1838, when the federation disintegrated, Honduras proclaimed its complete independence and in 1839 adopted a new constitution that emphasized individual rights but retained Catholicism as the state religion.

A new constitution in 1865 held out the possibility of association with the other Central American states and established a strong presidency but did not allow immediate reelection of the president. Honduras continued to suffer harassment by the British; interference in its internal politics by its neighbors, who were constantly vying to dominate the area; the often fierce internal struggle between conservatives and liberals; and frequent military usurpation of civilian governments. In the process the nation moved from one constitution to another (sixteen in all) and then back again in an effort to find a formula for political stability.

Liberal presidents, with the support of a military strongman in Guatemala, governed from 1873 to 1882. In 1880 a new constitution intended to modernize Honduras's political institutions was adopted. It introduced the concept of municipal autonomy and separation of church and state. A more liberal constitutional document was promulgated in 1894 and was reinstated in 1908 after a 1904 constitution failed. A 1921 constitution, which included such new social provisions as an eight-hour work day and protection for working women and children, lasted less than three months.

Some economic and social progress was made in the first few decades of the twentieth century, but the worldwide depression of the 1930s severely reduced the demand for bananas, a chief staple of the economy, and a leaf blight threatened the crops. Despite hard times, the country made good on payment of its external debts, and the Communist Party was outlawed. In 1936 a new constitution, which included the civil rights enforcement process of *amparo*, extended the presidential term of office from four to six years. This constitution, although amended several times, lasted until 1957, when another constitution was adopted on the heels of a coup led by younger, reform-minded military officers. Suffrage was extended to women in 1955.

The fifteenth constitution went into effect in 1965. In 1967 and 1969 many Salvadorans tried to enter Honduras to escape conditions in their own country, resulting in border clashes and eventually war. Elections in 1971 were relatively fair by previous standards, but in 1972 the military once again took charge after a large demonstration against the government's agrarian policies. Coups occurred again in 1975 and 1978 and were followed by an influx of refugees from Nicaragua as well as other neighboring countries experiencing conflict. A constituent assembly met in 1980, however, and the sixteenth Honduran constitution became effective on January 20, 1982.

Influences

Provisions of the 1965 constitution and other Latin American constitutions that include social and economic rights relating to the family, labor, and health are evident in the 1982 document.

The Constitution

The short preamble to the constitution of the Republic of Honduras, promulgated by decree no. 131 of January 11, 1982, refers to the restoration of a Central American union and proclaims as one purpose the strengthening and perpetuation of a rule of law to ensure a politically, economically, and socially just society. Article 2 affirms the sovereignty of the people: "Sovereignty originates in the people, from whom stem all the powers of the state, which are exercised through representation."

Fundamental Rights

Title 3, Declarations, Rights, and Guarantees, provides that the dignity of the human being is inviolable and that Hondurans as well as others residing in the country have the right to life, safety, freedom, equality before the law, property, and freedom of expression (unless the right is abused), the press (with some limitations), the exercise of religions and cults (with some limitations), and association and assembly, as long as these are not contrary to public policy or morals.

Protections are also provided for those accused of crimes, and the death penalty is abolished. Social rights, children's rights, rights to labor, housing, education and culture, and social security, as well as the restriction and suspension of guarantees and the rights of habeas corpus and *amparo*, are dealt with under separate headings in the constitution.

Division of Powers

In Honduras, a unitary state, power is shared among the president, the legislature, and the judiciary, which has constitutionally defined powers of judicial review.

The Executive

President. Article 235 sets forth the president's role: "The president of the republic shall exercise the executive power on behalf and for the benefit of the people."

The president, together with three presidential designates, is elected directly by the people for a four-year term. (Under the previous constitution the term was for six years.) To be president, a person must be Honduran by birth, at least thirty years old, and a layperson, and must enjoy the rights of citizenship. The greatly expanded list of disqualifications includes being a commander or general in the armed forces. Article 239 provides that no one may be president or a presidential designate more than once and adds, "Any person who violates this provision or advocates its amendment as well as those that directly or indirectly support him shall be disqualified for ten years from holding any public office."

The powers and duties of the president include being responsible for the general administration of the state; complying with and enforcing the constitution, treaties, and laws; representing and directing the policies of the state; safeguarding independence and maintaining peace and internal security; appointing and dismissing members of the cabinet and other officials; convening the legislature in special session; restricting or suspending the exercise of rights, in agreement with the council of ministers; issuing directives and decrees; directing foreign policy; concluding treaties, with the approval of the legislature; appointing and receiving foreign representatives; declaring war or making peace when the legislature is not in session; administering the public treasury; and handling a number of other significant responsibilities.

Cabinet. The Honduran constitution provides for at least twelve departments in the council of ministers. Secretaries of the cabinet and deputies are jointly responsible with the president for their acts. Article 251 provides that the legislature may summon the secretaries and question them on matters relating to public administration.

The Legislature

Congress. The deputies of the 128-member unicameral congress, together with alternates, are elected directly for four-year terms. To be elected, a person must be Honduran by birth, twenty-one years old, and born in or a resident of the constituency for five years before the election; a candidate must also be a layperson and enjoy the rights of citizenship. As with the position of president, there is a list of disqualifying factors. Members receive certain privileges and immunities.

The deputies elect a permanent directorate, including a president, that serves for two years. Before the end of a session, the directorate appoints a permanent committee of nine deputies to function during adjournment. The committee, among other things, adopts its own regulations, completes action on pending business to be considered at the next session, recommends changes in the laws, receives complaints of violations of the constitution, and grants or denies permission to the president of the republic or the presidential designates to leave the country for more than fifteen days.

Besides enacting, interpreting, amending, and repealing laws, congressional powers include electing supreme court justices, the chief of the armed forces, the comptroller general, and the attorney general, among other officials; determining grounds for impeachment of the president; and conferring military rank from major to major general, on the recommendation of the chief of the armed forces. Historically, the legislature's role in the national government has been overshadowed by that of the president.

The Judiciary

The judicial branch in Honduras consists of a supreme court of justice, a court of appeals, and other courts created by law.

Supreme Court. The supreme court has nine justices and seven alternates, each elected by the legislature for a four-year term, as is the president of the court, and they may be reelected. The supreme court makes its own internal rules; tries impeachment cases against high officials; hears cases on appeal from the court of appeals and against authorities for abuse of rights *(amparo);* appoints justices, judges, public prosecutors, and other judicial personnel; and may declare laws to be unconstitutional in cases provided for in the constitution.

Amending the Constitution

Except for certain provisions, such as the prohibition against being elected president twice and the disqualification of certain persons from being president, the constitution may be amended by a two-thirds vote of all the members of the legislature. The amendment must then be ratified in the next annual session by the same required majority.

Seventeen years after Magna Carta in England, noble ancestors of modern Hungarians forced their king to accept the Golden Bull in 1222, limiting his power and giving them the right to resist his illegal acts. In 1989 the Hungarian people took another dramatic step by radically amending their 1949 Stalinist-style constitution to create a new democratic government.

General Information

The Republic of Hungary, in the middle of Europe, is approximately 93,000 square kilometers and is bounded by the Czech and Slovak Republics on the north, Ukraine on the northeast, Romania on the east, the territory of the former country of Yugoslavia on the south, and Austria on the west. The capital of this country of approximately ten million persons is Budapest.

Despite much adversity, Hungary's industrial and service economy is moderately well developed. Well before *perestroika* in the U.S.S.R., in 1968 Hungary initiated the "New Economic Mechanism" and is currently an associate member of the European Union.

Type of Government: Presidential-style parliamentary republic, with a president, a prime minister and cabinet, a unicameral legislature, a judiciary, and a constitutional court

Date of Constitution: 1949 (revised in 1972 and 1989)

Constitutional History

The Hungarian state began in A.D. 1000 when the pope crowned Stephen I, who was canonized after his death. During his reign as king, foreign monks introduced new agricultural methods and a Latin alphabet, and by the twelfth century Hungary was a leading power in southeastern Europe.

In the thirteenth century Andrew II dissipated his resources on foreign military adventures. The so-called lesser nobles, who were Hungarian and more numerous than the foreign nobles, who had received land grants from the king in return for their assistance, demanded that the king's taxing power be limited. They succeeded in 1222 in forcing Andrew to sign the Golden Bull, curbing his power and enhancing their own by gaining the right to resist his illegal acts and present grievances, which led to the development of a parliament.

The Golden Bull was reconfirmed in the fourteenth century. Following a series of wars with the Turks, King Matyas Corvinus reformed the legal system, expanded the power of the lesser nobles, and regularly convened the parliament while exercising absolute rule over the country through a secular bureaucracy. Influenced by Roman law, the legal system was codified in 1514. It provided that the king and the nobles were basically equal in power; the nobles acknowledged the king's right to rule, and he recognized their power to elect him. Defeat at the hands of the Turks in the sixteenth century led to the partition of the country by the Turks and the Hapsburgs. By the beginning of the eighteenth century, the Hapsburgs controlled Hungary's foreign affairs, defense, and tariffs from Vienna. In 1723 the Hungarian parliament approved the Pragmatic Sanction, by which the Hapsburg monarch agreed to the restraints of Hungary's constitution and laws. A new legal code was published in 1878 and updated in 1961.

Hungary declared its independence in 1849, following the 1848 revolution in Vienna against the absolute monarch. Hapsburg rule was restored under a dual monarchy, whereby the Hapsburg emperor also reigned as the king of Hungary until the end of World War I. As a result of the war, Hungary lost much of its territory and its population. On March 21, 1919, a coalition of Hungarian Socialist Democratic Party members and communists seized power and established the Hungarian Socialist Republic under Bela Kun, who sent the Red Army against Romania. Budapest, however, was soon occupied by Romanian forces, and a reign of terror started when an anticommunist government took control.

A right-wing dictator, Gyula Gombs, forged close ties to Germany and Italy, and in 1941 Hungary joined Hitler's invasion of the Soviet Union. Nazi Germany occupied the country in 1943, but its troops were driven out by Allied forces in 1945. Although Hungary was placed under an Allied control commission, a Soviet official was in total command. The Hungarian Workers' Party and the Communist Party then merged, and a constitution for the Hungarian People's Republic was adopted and became effective on August 20, 1949. Before then, Hungary's constitution remained basically unwritten.

Hungary quickly nationalized its banks, trade, and industrial operations and became closely linked with the Soviet Union, in 1949 joining the Council for Mutual Economic Assistance (Comecon), whose purpose was to further economic cooperation among Soviet satellite countries. After the death of Joseph Stalin in 1953, the Soviet leaders became more flexible toward eastern Europe. A student rally in Budapest supporting Polish independence efforts, however, sparked a popular revolutionary movement in October 1956, and Soviet troops surrounded Budapest, closed the country's borders, and restored the Communist Party to its position of dominance.

Technically, the Hungarian constitution of April 20, 1949, which was amended in 1972 and more significantly revised in October 1989, is still in effect. It acknowledges the possibility of a new constitution in the future.

Influences

The 1949 constitution was modeled on the 1936 constitution of the Soviet Union. The amendments effective on October 23, 1989, have transformed it, generally, into a presidential-style parliamentary republic.

The Constitution

The preamble to the constitution of the Republic of Hungary states:

In order to promote a peaceful transition to a state based on the rule of law, having a multi-party system, parliamentary democracy, and social market economy, the National Assembly, for the period until the enactment of the new constitution of the country, determines the text of the constitution of Hungary as follows. . . .

Article 2 states, in part: "(1) The Republic of Hungary shall be an independent and democratic state based on the rule of law. (2) In the Republic of Hungary all power shall belong to the people exercising its sovereignty through its elected representatives as well as directly." Previously, the constitution stated: "In the Hungarian People's Republic all power belongs to the working people."

Fundamental Rights

The constitution ensures human and civil rights for everyone in Hungary without discrimination on the basis of race, color, sex, creed, political or other opinion, national or social origin, property, birth, or other status.

Rights guaranteed include the inherent right to life and human dignity; prohibitions against torture and the deprivation of liberty, except according to law; speedy justice and compensation for unlawful arrest or detention; equality before the law; and the presumption of innocence. Other rights guaranteed include freedom of movement, with exceptions as determined by law; freedom of thought, conscience, and religion; separation of church and state; freedom of expression and the press; freedom of assembly and organization not otherwise prohibited by law; the right to petition the government; and equality of men and women in civil, political, economic, and social and cultural activities.

In the fall of 1993 one hundred thousand people marched in Budapest to demand that the government guarantee press freedom, and protests were launched against perceived censorship by the state-owned Magyar Radio.

Division of Powers

A unitary state, power in Hungary is divided among the president, as head of state; the prime minister, as head of government; the legislature; the courts; and the constitutional court, which exercises constitutional review.

President. The president, elected by the legislature for a term of four years, is head of state and commander in chief of the armed forces. Any citizen qualified to vote and at least thirty-five years of age is eligible to be elected or reelected president if nominated in writing by at least fifty members of the legislature. Election is by secret ballot; the first nominee to receive a two-thirds vote in the first or second round of voting is the winner. If a third round is required, one of the two nominees with the highest majority in the second round may win by a majority vote.

The powers and duties of the president include representing the Hungarian state; entering into international agreements in accordance with the constitution's requirements; accrediting and receiving ambassadors and envoys; setting dates for parliamentary and local government elections; attending and addressing sittings of the parliament; submitting proposals to the parliament; initiating a plebiscite; appointing and relieving, in accordance with law, undersecretaries and commissioners; appointing and relieving certain national bank officials, university professors, rectors, and generals and confirming the president of the academy of sciences; conferring medals and decorations according to law; granting individual pardons; and deciding on matters of citizenship and other matters assigned to the president by law.

The presidency becomes vacant on the expiration of the term of office; on the incumbent's death or inability to discharge the functions of the office for more than ninety days; on a declaration of incompatibility resulting from a secret, two-thirds vote of the legislature finding that the president has violated the prohibitions against holding an incompatible office or wage-earning occupation while president; on resignation; or on removal from office by impeachment. Impeachment for violating the constitution or other laws requires a proposal by one-fifth of the members of the legislature and a subsequent vote of two-thirds of the members by secret ballot, after which the constitutional court adjudicates the matter. Criminal proceedings may also be brought against the president after his term of office has expired. With certain limitations the speaker of the parliament acts in the event that the president is unable to perform his or her duties.

Prime Minister and Cabinet. The government consists of the prime minister and the cabinet ministers. The prime minister is nominated by the president and elected by the assembly at the same time that the government's proposed program is voted on. Ministers are appointed and discharged by the president on the recommendation of the prime minister. The mandate of the government is terminated in the event of a newly elected assembly, the resignation or death of the prime minister, or a vote of no confidence.

Parliament. The unicameral parliament, called the Országgyülés (national assembly), is the supreme organ of state power. The 386 seats in the assembly, including eight reserved for minorities, are filled by election every four years, and government officials, with the exception of members of the government or cabinet, may not serve in the assembly. Except during a state of emergency or martial law, the assembly may dissolve itself before the end of its term, with new elections being held within three months.

Article 19 states, in part: "(2) The National Assembly, exercising its rights deriving from popular sovereignty, shall guarantee the constitutional order of society and shall determine the structure, orientation and conditions of government." The assembly is also charged with enacting the constitution and laws of the country; entering into important international agreements; declaring war or a state of emergency and making peace; deploying the armed forces at home or abroad; electing the president, prime minister, members of the constitutional court, president of the supreme court, chief public prosecutor, and other high officials; determining the socioeconomic plan of the country and the state finances; approving the state budget and its implementation; deciding on the government's program; deciding on matters relating to local government; and granting amnesty. Article 27 grants the assembly the right of interpellation, to question the government.

Decisions declaring an emergency or war, concluding peace, and deploying the armed forces require a two-thirds majority of the members of the assembly. Enactment of a law calling for a national plebiscite requires a vote of two-thirds of the members present. Laws regarding the legal status of members of the assembly require a two-thirds vote of the members present. If the assembly is not in session and time is of the essence, the president may declare a state of war, exigency, or emergency, although the justification for the declaration will be reviewed by the assembly when it next sits.

The assembly elects its own officers, a speaker, deputy speakers, and recorders. Sessions are open to the public unless closed by a two-thirds vote. Legislation must be introduced by the president, the government, or committees or members of the assembly. More than one-half of the members of the assembly constitute a quorum; generally, measures are approved by a vote of more than one-half of the members present. Acts passed are signed by the speaker and sent to the president for promulgation. The president may return an act to the assembly, which, after a debate, may repass the measure; it must then be promulgated by the president. The president may also send a measure to the constitutional court before signing it if it is deemed unconstitutional. If the court declares the act unconstitutional, the president must return it to the assembly; otherwise, it must be signed and promulgated within five days.

Ombudsman. The constitution creates a national assembly commissioner of civil rights, or ombudsman, to investigate irregularities concerning constitutional rights and to initiate remedies. A national assembly commissioner also oversees national ethnic minority rights.

The Judiciary

Article 45, chapter 10, on the Judiciary, provides that justice in the Republic of Hungary shall be administered by a supreme court, a metropolitan court, and county and local courts. Judges are to be independent and may not be members of any political party or pursue political activity. They may not be removed from office except in accordance with law.

Article 50 directs the courts to protect and guarantee the constitutional order and the rights and lawful interests of the citizens and to punish the perpetrators of criminal acts.

Supreme Court. The supreme court is given authority to exercise control over all courts, and its rules and decisions are binding on them. The president of the supreme court is nominated by the president of the republic and elected by the legislature. The vice presidents are nominated by the president of the court and appointed by the president of the republic.

Constitutional Court

Chapter 4 creates a fifteen-member constitutional court elected by the legislature to review the constitutionality of laws and statutes and other tasks assigned by law. Proceedings in the court, which exercises its power vigorously, may be initiated by anyone; laws found to be unconstitutional are to be annulled.

Amending the Constitution

A vote of two-thirds of the members of the legislature is required to amend the constitution. An amendment in 1995 requires a vote "of four-fifths of the Members of Parliament . . . to pass . . . [a] resolution specifying detailed regulations for the preparation of the new Constitution."

The world's first parliament, the Althing, began its annual sessions in A.D. 930 and is still a venerated site in Iceland. Having preceded the English parliament, it has been characterized by constitutional observers as the "grandmother of all parliaments."

General Information

The Republic of Iceland is approximately 103,000 square kilometers and lies in the north Atlantic Ocean, southeast of Greenland and the Denmark Straits. Just south of the Arctic Circle but warmed by the Gulf Stream, it has a higher average temperature than New York City in the winter. The capital of this country of approximately 276,000 persons is Reykjavik.

Geography contributes to Iceland's isolation. Its economy relies heavily on fishing, and regular extensions of its territorial waters have led to "cod wars" with Britain. Iceland, a member of the North Atlantic Treaty Organization (NATO), is on the great circle air route and hosts an American military base at Keflavik.

Type of Government: Presidential-style parliamentary republic, with a president and state council (cabinet), a prime minister, a unicameral legislature, and a judiciary

Dates of Constitutions: 1874, 1920, and 1944

Constitutional History

Iceland was first settled in the ninth century A.D. by Norsemen and slaves taken from Ireland and Scotland. As early as 930, an upper-class parliament called the Althing, which had both legislative and judicial functions, began meeting annually, but no executive institution was created. The first code of law, called the *Gragas* (Gray Goose), was adapted from the laws of southern Norway. Under the code the island was divided into quarters, each of which was then subdivided.

The Althing endorsed a treaty in 1262 placing Iceland under the jurisdiction of the king of Norway but leaving it internally independent. The treaty was voidable if "the best men" decided that the king had failed to live up to his duties under the pact. Norwegian law codes imposed the king's authority on the Icelanders through his representative, and the Althing was reduced to an essentially judicial forum presided over by royal officials.

In 1319 Norway and Sweden were united, and the new king's sovereignty was extended to Iceland until 1371, when the two countries split up. Norway and Iceland fell under Danish rule in 1380. After the religious reformation of the sixteenth century, the Danish crown confiscated monastic properties in Iceland and imposed harsh laws and heavy taxes on the country. By the beginning of the seventeenth century Denmark totally monopolized trade with Iceland, and as Denmark's control increased, the power of the Althing waned. In 1800 it was abolished, and its judicial functions were transferred to a high court of law.

The Althing was restored in 1843 as a consultative assembly when royal absolutism came to an end in Denmark. In 1874 a separate constitution promulgated for Iceland conferred on the country limited home rule. Complete self-government was granted in 1903, and on December 1, 1918, Iceland became an independent sovereign state united with Denmark only in the person of the Danish monarch. The Icelandic constitution adopted on May 18, 1920, established a supreme court and required that laws be approved by the king, but such approval was, in fact, automatic.

The German invasion of Denmark in 1940 severed all communications between the kingdoms. Because of the island's strategic location in the north Atlantic, British troops preemptively occupied it; they were replaced in 1941 by Americans. In 1943 Iceland's union with Denmark expired, and voters in a 1944 referendum overwhelmingly approved complete independence.

On June 17, 1944, Iceland became an independent republic under a new constitution modeled on the 1920 document; changes related to its new status as a republic, such as having an elected president in place of a monarch. Compared with the U.S. constitution, the Icelandic document, although short, is more detailed with respect to the actual day-to-day working of government institutions.

Influences

If England's parliament may be termed the "mother of all parliaments," then Iceland's Althing is the "grandmother of all parliaments." Its current constitution, however, reflects some Danish, Norwegian, and U.S. influences.

The Constitution

Article 2 provides that "the legislative power is jointly vested in the Althing and the president of the Republic of Iceland. The executive power is exercised by the president and other governmental authorities in accordance with this constitution and other laws of the land. The judicial power is exercised by the judiciary."

Fundamental Rights

Chapter 6 of the constitution establishes the Evangelical Lutheran Church as the state church, but religious freedom is guaranteed. Chapter 7 provides safeguards in the case of arrest; makes homes and the right to own property inviolable; prohibits restrictions on freedom of employment, unless required for the common good; and provides for public aid, freedom of expression and thought in print, and freedom of movement, association, and unarmed assembly. Adds article 69: "A law prescribing the death penalty must never be enacted."

Although women in Iceland have had the right to vote in local elections since 1882 and in national elections since 1915, they did not participate in the national government for many years. In 1983, however, the Women's Alliance Party won three seats in the legislature, and in June 1988 the first woman president was reelected for a third term.

Division of Powers

In Iceland, a unitary state, power is divided among the president, as head of state; the prime minister, as head of government; the legislature; and the courts, which exercise judicial review.

The Executive

President. The president is head of state and is elected directly by secret ballot for a four-year term, although not at the same time that members of the legislature are elected. The role of the president, although powerful in theory, is similar to that of a constitutional monarch in other European countries. Candidates must be thirty-five years old, eligible to vote for members of the legislature, and nominated by between 1,500 and 3,000 voters.

The president exercises authority through ministers. He or she may not be a member of the legislature or receive compensation from any public or private enterprise. The president is not answerable for official acts, which must be countersigned by a cabinet minister; may not be criminally prosecuted while in office, except with the consent of the legislature; and must reside in the capital or its environs.

In addition to making appointments as provided for by law, the president concludes treaties; summons the legislature into regular and extraordinary session and dissolves it; introduces bills and resolutions; approves legislation or disapproves it, in which case it is submitted to a plebiscite to be sustained; issues provisional laws in emergencies when the legislature is not in session; suspends prosecutions and grants pardons and amnesty, except in the case of a minister; and grants exceptions from the law in accordance with traditional practice.

State Council. According to article 16, the state council is presided over by the president and is composed of his or her ministers. Laws and important government measures are to be submitted to the president at the council's meetings.

Prime Minister and Cabinet. The prime minister presides over cabinet meetings of the ministers when new legislation or important political matters are discussed. Since independence in 1944, the governments generally have been formed from coalitions of parties rather than from a single majority party.

Parliament. Article 36 specifies that the Icelandic Althing (parliament) "is inviolable. No person may disturb its peace or violate its freedom." As set out in article 32, "Sessions of the Althingi are held in one chamber." Before an amendment in 1991, the parliament was semi-bicameral, like the Norwegian parliament, because the members resolved themselves into an upper and a lower house after the elections. This system, by which the political parties created two houses with different majorities, seemed to violate the fundamental principle of majority rule and at times hampered the passage of legislation. Therefore, to strengthen the power of the government, the legislature was changed to a unicameral parliament.

The Legislature

The parliament is composed of sixty-three members "elected by the people by secret ballot on the basis of proportional representation for four years [from eight] . . . constituencies." Any citizen "of unblemished character" who has the right to vote, except supreme court judges, may stand for election. To vote, a citizen must be eighteen years old and a legal resident at the time of the election. Once elected, members may not be arrested, except if caught in flagrante delicto, and are bound only by their convictions for their actions. Each house and the parliament as a whole elect a speaker.

Bills and resolutions may be introduced by members of parliament and ministers and must be passed at three readings. A quorum for conducting business requires the presence of more than half of the members. Bills, once passed, must be submitted to the president for approval within two weeks. If the president fails to sign a bill it becomes law anyway but may later be rejected in a mandatory referendum.

According to article 59, the organization of the judiciary is determined by law. This gives the legislature extensive power over the judicial branch, although it has not greatly affected judicial independence. The supreme court is the highest national appeals court in the judicial system, which has ruled statutes unconstitutional and executive action inconsistent with statutes.

The Judiciary

Article 60 provides that "judges shall settle all disputes as to the extent of the administrative officers. But no one seeking a judicial ruling thereunto can evade obeying temporarily an order of the administrative officer by submitting the matter to judicial decision." Article 61 directs judges to be guided solely by the law and protects judges who do not also hold administrative office from arbitrary discharge or transfer. Judges may be released from office at age sixty-five without a diminution in salary.

Amendments begin as proposals introduced in a regular or extraordinary session of the legislature. If the proposal is adopted, the legislature is dissolved immediately. If the proposal is passed again without change after a general election, article 79 requires that it be ratified by the president and come into force as a constitutional act. Amendments regarding the status of the state church must be ratified in a plebiscite by secret ballot.

Amending the Constitution

INDIA

Nearly one out of every six human beings lives in India, a country of many languages and religions that is the world's largest democracy. The Indian constitution, a long and detailed document, attempts to maintain democracy while transforming a rigid, hierarchical social order into an egalitarian nation.

General Information

The Republic of India, a land of great geographic diversity on the Indian subcontinent, is approximately 3.3 million square kilometers and is bounded by the Arabian Sea on the west; Pakistan on the northwest; China, Nepal, and Bhutan on the north; Bangladesh, Burma, and the Bay of Bengal on the east; and the Indian Ocean and the Gulf of Mannar on the south. India has a population of more than one billion inhabitants, and its capital is New Delhi, a national capital territory.

A country of leaders with strong personalities such as Mahatma Gandhi, Jawaharlal Nehru, and Indira Gandhi, India has also had its share of government corruption and scandal. In the future India's burgeoning entrepreneurial spirit, which drives the economy, may not be able to weather the population increases, the faltering economic reforms, the anti-materialistic values of Hinduism, and the religious factionalism. The lives of many Indian citizens have changed little since independence from Britain in 1947 and the adoption of their own constitution in 1950.

Type of Government: Presidential-style parliamentary federal republic, with a president, a prime minister and council of ministers (cabinet), a bicameral legislature, and a judiciary

Date of Constitution: 1950

Constitutional History

The people living around the Indus River developed one of the great early civilizations. It lasted from about 2500 B.C. to 1750 B.C., when Aryans invaded the lands of the snake-worshipping Nagas in the north and the Dravidians in the south and then moved into the Ganges valley by 500 B.C. The subcontinent was united under the rule of Chandragupta Maurya, and Buddhism and the philosophy of nonviolence spread. Under the older Hindu religion, however, a caste system had developed; at the top were the Brahmins, who alone could read the ancient Sanskrit language, followed by the farmers and the traders, a large working class, and at the bottom the outcasts, the classless "untouchables."

The Gupta regime ruled during the golden age of Hindu culture in India, between the fourth and the sixth centuries A.D., under a type of constitutional monarchy in which kingdoms were divided into provinces, districts, and villages. The subcontinent suffered many incursions, particularly from the west and the Turks, who brought the Islamic religion with them. In the sixteenth century the Moghul Empire arose, lasting until the British moved in beginning in the early seventeenth century. Toward the end of the Moghul reign friction developed between the Muslims and Hindus, which the British did little to ameliorate.

The British consolidated their rule in India during the nineteenth century, but a mutiny by Indian soldiers over rumors that animal fat was used in their ammunition, which offended both Hindus and Muslims, ended the monopoly of the East India Company. It was replaced by the British government, which in 1877 proclaimed Queen Victoria empress of India. British hegemony was unifying for India, because it imposed a single administrative and court system, improved transportation and communications, and brought education to a new professional class.

Nationalism, however, continued to develop—the Indian National Congress was founded in 1885—and after World War I gained momentum under the extraordinary leadership of Mohandas (later called Mahatma) Gandhi, known as the "Great Soul." Under Gandhi the struggle for independence took the form of passive resistance, which resulted in the Indian Independence Act of 1947. The Muslim-dominated areas in the northwest and northeast formally separated and became what are today Pakistan and Bangladesh, respectively.

A new Indian constitution, drafted by a constituent assembly established in December 1946, was proclaimed on January 26, 1950. The official edition of 251 pages contained 395 articles and eight schedules. Keenly aware of the country's tradition of social inequities, the assembly deliberately set about to give preferential treatment to historically disadvantaged peoples.

In addition to being influenced by the British style of government, the drafters of the Indian constitution sent missions also to the United States, Canada, and Ireland to elicit recommendations.

The Constitution

The preamble to the Indian constitution defines the nation as "a sovereign socialist democratic republic" that intends to secure for all citizens justice, liberty, equality, and fraternity. Article 1 asserts that "India—that is, Bharat—shall be a union of states."

Part 3, Fundamental Rights, incorporates guarantees of individual rights, freedoms, and protections. The "state" is defined to encompass the government and parliament of India, as well as the government and legislature of the states of the union and all local authorities in the territory of India.

Article 13 provides that the state shall make no laws abridging rights conferred by part 3. These rights include equality before the law; prohibition against discrimination on the basis of religion, race, caste, sex, or place of birth (this is expressly extended to commercial activities and state-funded and public facilities); freedom of speech; protection of life and personal liberty; protections in the case of arrest and detention; and freedom of religion. Article 17 specifically deals with the abolition of "untouchability." Article 32 provides for the enforcement of rights in the courts.

Part 4 contains nonjusticiable general principles addressed to the legislature for securing a social order and promoting the welfare of the people. Part 4A contains fundamental duties of citizens, such as to "cherish and follow the noble ideals which inspired our national struggle for freedom" and to "safeguard public property and to abjure violence."

India is a federal union of states and centrally administered territories whose national government is divided, but not entirely separately, into three branches: executive, legislative, and judicial, the latter of which exercises judicial review. Areas of government authority are set forth in three lists defining the separate and concurrent jurisdictions of the union and the states in the seventh schedule appended to the constitution.

President. Article 53(1) describes the president's role: "The executive power of the union shall be vested in the president and shall be exercised by him either directly or through officers subordinate to him in accordance with this constitution." Article 77 requires that all executive actions of the government be made in the president's name.

The president is elected to a five-year term by an electoral college consisting of elected members of the national legislature and the legislative assemblies of the states, defined by amendment in 1992 to include the national capital territory of Delhi and the union territory of Pondicherry. Voting is based on a weighted system and is "in accordance with the system of proportional representation by means of a single transferable vote" and by secret ballot.

To be eligible for the presidency, a person must be an Indian citizen, at least thirty-five years old, and qualified for election to the lower house of the legislature and may not hold certain government offices for profit.

The president is the supreme commander of the defense forces of the union. Other responsibilities include appointing the prime minister and, on the advice of the prime minister, the other ministers; appointing the attorney general; making rules for transacting government business and allocating such business among the ministers; and granting pardons and commuting sentences.

Prime Minister and Cabinet. The prime minister communicates to the president decisions of the council of ministers (cabinet) and legislative proposals; furnishes information for which the president may ask; and at the president's request submits to the council a decision of an individual minister that had not been previously considered.

The Legislature

Parliament. Article 79 establishes a bicameral parliament: "There shall be a parliament for the union which shall consist of the president and two houses to be known respectively as the council of states and the house of the people."

To be a member of the parliament a citizen must take a prescribed oath, be at least thirty years old for the upper house and twenty-five for the lower house, and possess other qualifications established by the parliament. Members are immune from legal proceedings regarding their actions in parliament and are entitled to other privileges and immunities as defined by law.

Upper House. The Rajya Sabha (council of states) has no more than 250 members, most of whom are elected by the state legislatures; twelve members, however, are nominated by the president from among people with special knowledge or practical experience in literature, science, art, and social service. After elections the council of states chooses a deputy chairman; its chairman is the vice president of the nation (as in the United States, where the vice president is also the president of the senate). The council may not be dissolved, but one-third of its members must retire every two years.

Lower House. In the Lok Sabha (house of the people), a maximum of 530 members are chosen by direct election from territorial constituencies allotted to each state on the basis of population, and no more than twenty members are selected by law to represent the territories of the union. The lower house has a maximum term of five years, but elections may be called for sooner on the advice of the prime minister. It chooses a speaker and deputy, although the speaker, like the chairman of the upper house, may vote only in the case of a tie.

Bills may be introduced in either house, except for money bills, which are introduced only in the lower house. Article 100 provides that generally decisions of both houses are to be by majority vote, although a quorum is only one-tenth of the members of each house. In the case of a bill passed by one house and rejected by another, of disagreements on amendments to a bill, or of one house failing to act for more than six months on a measure passed by another, the president may call for a joint sitting of the two houses to deliberate and vote on the measure. There is also a special procedure for money bills, whereby the upper house returns the bill passed by the lower house with its recommendations within fourteen days of receipt. A bill passed by both houses is sent to the president for his or her assent, which may be withheld and the bill returned with recommendations. If the bill is again passed by both houses, with or without incorporating the president's recommendations, he or she must assent.

The Judiciary

Supreme Court. Article 124 creates a supreme court of India, which, as of 1986, consists of a chief justice and a maximum of twenty-five other judges. The judges, who are to hold office until retirement at age sixty-five, are appointed by the president after consultation with other judges as deemed necessary. The constitution contains protections for judges on the supreme court to help ensure its independence. In addition to being an Indian citizen, qualifications for a supreme court judge include having been a judge on a high court or courts for at least five years in succession, having been an advocate before a high court or courts for at least ten years in succession, or being, in the president's opinion, a distinguished jurist.

The supreme court has original jurisdiction in disputes between the government of India and one or more of the states, between the government and a state or states on one side and a state or states on the other side, and between states, except in certain cases of disputes arising out of treaties or agreements before the constitution was adopted. Article 32 guarantees "the right to move to the supreme court by appropriate proceedings for the enforcement of the rights conferred by this part [3]."

Appellate jurisdiction extends to criminal and civil cases certified by a high court to involve "a substantial question of law as to the interpretation of this constitution," questions of law of general importance, questions requiring decision by the supreme court, and certain particular criminal matters.

When it is expedient to have a question of law or fact of public importance answered, under article 143 the president may seek an advisory opinion of the supreme court. Article 140 authorizes the parliament to confer supplemental powers on the supreme court.

Amending the Constitution

An amendment is initiated by a bill introduced for this purpose in either house of the legislature. It must be passed by a majority of the total membership and at least two-thirds of the members present and voting. The president must then assent to the amendment. Any change in certain provisions—for example, representation of the states in the parliament, the way in which the president is elected, and the union judiciary and the high courts in the states—requires ratification by the legislatures of at least one-half of the states before the president's assent.

INDONESIA

The constitution of Indonesia, land of the Komodo dragon and Java Man, is a unique blend of national philosophy and government principles adapted from Western concepts of an integrated state.

General Information

The Republic of Indonesia is an archipelagic nation of more than 13,500 islands occupying approximately 1.9 million square kilometers. It is bounded on the north by the Strait of Malacca, on the northeast by the Celebes Sea and the Pacific Ocean, and on the south and west by the Indian Ocean. Indonesia shares territory on the island of Borneo with Malaysia and on New Guinea with Papua New Guinea. It has a population of nearly 225 million persons, and its capital is Jakarta, on the island of Java.

Indonesia (Greek for "India Islands") historically has exported spices, coffee, and tropical agricultural products. Indonesia's major industries include oil, gas, and food processing. Its political stability is threatened by economic problems and the internationally condemned treatment of the East Timorese by the Indonesian military before and after their overwhelming vote for independence in 1999.

Type of Government: Presidential-style republic, with a president and cabinet, a supreme advisory council, a unicameral legislature, a people's consultative assembly, and a judiciary

Dates of Constitutions: 1945 (reinstated in 1959), 1949, 1950 (provisional), and 1955

Constitutional History

Evidence exists that human ancestors occupied Indonesia as early as two million years ago. A species of *Homo erectus* called Pithecanthropus, or Java Man, lived there as recently as approximately five hundred thousand years ago, when the area was attached to the Asian land mass. Later, Australoids physically similar to the people of New Guinea were gradually supplanted by Mongoloid people migrating south from Asia. Around 500 B.C. Malayo-Polynesian–speaking peoples from southeastern China arrived.

After the dawn of the Christian era, the inhabitants of Indonesia found themselves on the sea routes used by traders between India and China. The lucrative spice trade led to the rise of naval and commercial powers on the islands of Sumatra and Java in the ninth century. The Hindu and Buddhist religions introduced earlier by the Indians and grafted onto the local animism were gradually supplanted by the Islamic religion, which Marco Polo encountered in northern Sumatra on his return voyage from China in 1292.

By the time the Portuguese arrived in the sixteenth century, lured by products from Java and the Moluccas (Spice Islands), a number of Islamic kingdoms were established in the area. In 1602 the Dutch, warring with Portugal and Spain, formed an East India company that combined military, political, and commercial operations and gradually supplanted the Portuguese in Indonesia, vying often with the British in the process. The French established a protectorate in the area in 1799, and the Dutch nationalized what remained of its East India company.

After France annexed the Netherlands in 1810, the British forced the French out of Java. Thomas Raffles, who was appointed lieutenant governor of Java, instituted reforms during his administration to improve the lot of the indigenous peasants. Dutch authority was restored in 1816. As economic development expanded toward the end of the nineteenth century, the country experienced a large influx of Chinese, and burgeoning Indonesian nationalism focused as much on the Chinese as the Dutch. In 1927 the Indonesian Nationalist Party was founded by a charismatic leader known simply as Sukarno, who later became the nation's first president and had a significant influence on the country's first constitution.

During World War II Indonesia was occupied for three years by the Japanese. On August 17, 1945, local leaders, including Sukarno, declared the country independent. The following day a constitution was promulgated that has been the Indonesian constitution since its rein-statement in 1959. The Dutch tried to regain their colony by military force in 1947 and 1948, and in 1949 an independent federation for Indonesia was agreed on under a constitution that unfairly weighted representation from Dutch-created states in the legislature. But on August 14, 1950, a provisional constitution making the country a unitary state was ratified by the legislature, although formal approval came in 1955. This constitution remained in effect until July 5, 1959, when President Sukarno dissolved the constituent assembly working on a new constitution and reinstated the 1945 constitution by decree.

The 1945 unitary constitution bears the input of the Indonesian leader Sukarno, while the short-lived 1949 constitution was strongly influenced by the Dutch parliamentary model, except for its federal aspects. **Influences**

The Constitution

The preamble to the constitution of the Republic of Indonesia declares that the goals of the state are to be free, united, sovereign, just, and prosperous. It also sets forth five principles, called *pancasila,* on which the state is to be based: "belief in the one and only God; just and civilized humanity; the unity of Indonesia; democracy guided by the inner wisdom of de-liberations amongst representatives; and the realization of social justice for all of the peo-ple of Indonesia."

According to article 1(2), "Sovereignty shall be vested in the people and shall be exercised by the Majelis Permusyawaratan Rakyat [people's consultative assembly]."

The constitution provides that all citizens have equal status before the law and in govern-ment but that they are to "abide by the law and the government without any exception." Every citizen is guaranteed the right to work and live in human dignity. Other rights are set forth in article 28: "Freedom of association, of verbal and written expression and the like shall be prescribed by law." The state's foundation on "belief in the one and only God" is affirmed in article 29, which also guarantees freedom of worship. Other guarantees include the right to education and care for poor and destitute children. Article 33, Social Welfare, indicates that the economy is to be based on the family system; important sectors of production and land, water, and natural riches contained therein are to be controlled by the state. **Fundamental Rights**

Indonesia's official position is that unbridled freedom is a luxury and that internal secu-rity and economic development have a higher priority.

In Indonesia, a unitary state, power is divided among the president, who is head of state and government and has a wide range of power both under the constitution and in con-cert with the military, which may be checked constitutionally only by the people's consul-tative assembly; the legislature; and the judiciary, which has no power to review laws en-acted by the legislature. **Division of Powers**

The President. The president of the Republic of Indonesia holds the power of government in accordance with the constitution, as set forth in article 4, and is to be assisted by a vice president, who becomes president on the death or incapacity of the president. Both are elected to five-year terms by the people's consultative assembly, which includes the legisla-ture and delegates from territorial regions and other groups. The constitution requires that the president be a native Indonesian citizen. **The Executive**

The duties and powers of the president include making laws together with the legislature; issuing regulations to expedite enforcement of the laws; commanding the armed forces; with the legislature declaring war, making peace, and concluding treaties; declaring a state of emergency; appointing diplomats and receiving foreign representatives; granting pardons and amnesty; and granting titles, decorations, and other honors. Unlike many parliamentary systems, the president may not dissolve the legislature, and he or she is responsible only to the almost ceremonial people's consultative assembly, not to the legislature.

Supreme Advisory Council and Cabinet. The constitution provides for a supreme advisory council to answer questions from the president and make recommendations to the government and cabinet ministers, who are appointed by the president to head the departments of the government and can be dismissed by him or her.

The Legislature

Parliament. A majority of the members of Indonesia's unicameral parliament, the Dewan Perwakilan Rakyat (people's representation council), are elected, while others are appointed for five-year terms from the military and by provisional assemblies on behalf of functional groups. The composition of this legislative body is regulated by law; it has a speaker or chairman and five vice chairmen.

The representation council must meet at least once a year, and, together with the president, it enacts the laws. The government or the legislature may introduce bills, but if a bill is not approved by either the president or the legislature, it may not be introduced again until after a general election. Bills are deliberated on at four readings and may be passed by consensus or majority vote. A quorum is two-thirds of the total membership.

Traditionally, a government-supported coalition of functional groups called Golkar, led by the military, has maintained a strong majority in the legislature, although its percentage of the contested seats in 1992 fell from seventy-five to seventy.

People's Consultative Assembly

The Majelis Permusyawaratan Rakyat, a larger body, consists of the legislature and an equal number of delegates appointed by the government and representatives from the provinces based on population. It meets only once every five years. The consultative assembly sets general guidelines, elects the president and vice president, and amends the constitution.

The Judiciary

The court system is divided into general, religious, military, and administrative areas. Although the legal system is basically derived from the Dutch, Islamic law *(shari'a)* is applied in family matters involving orthodox Muslims, and customary law *(adat)* is used in the villages.

Supreme Court. According to article 24, judicial power in Indonesia is vested in a supreme court and other courts established by law. Under article 25 "the appointment and dismissal of judges shall be regulated by law." The chief justice is elected by the legislature from a list of nominees submitted by the president, and the other members are appointed by the president on the basis of nominations by the legislature.

To increase its independence and enhance its integrity, the supreme court in 1970 was removed from the supervision of the justice department. It is the final court of appeal, generally, in both civil and criminal cases, and it may review the legality of administrative regulations but not the constitutionality of laws passed by the legislature.

Amending the Constitution

Any proposed amendment, according to article 37, must be approved by the people's consultative assembly. Two-thirds of the total members must be in attendance, and the amendment must be approved by no less than two-thirds of those in attendance.

After 2,500 years as a monarchy, Iran became an Islamic republic in 1979 under the leadership of the Ayatollah Khomeini, who was the final arbiter of the Iranian constitution until his death ten years later.

The Islamic Republic of Iran, in the Middle East, is approximately 1.6 million square kilometers and is bounded by Armenia, Azerbaijan, the Caspian Sea, and Turkmenistan on the north; Afghanistan and Pakistan on the east; the Persian Gulf and the Gulf of Oman on the south; and Iraq and Turkey on the west. Teheran is the capital of this country of approximately sixty-seven million inhabitants.

Although oil accounts for nearly all of Iran's export sales, the country has a large fishing industry. A movement to moderate the revolutionary character of government institutions inspired by the Ayatollah Khomeini is currently under way in Iran.

Type of Government: Theocratic Islamic republic, with a religious leader or leadership council, a president and council of ministers (cabinet), a unicameral legislature, and an Islamic court system, including a council of guardians

Dates of Constitutions: 1906 and 1979

Around the sixth century B.C. the empire of the Medes was supplanted by the far-flung empire of the Persians, whose provinces were administered by governors called satraps. Often beaten in battle by the Greeks, Persia succumbed to the might of Alexander the Great in the fourth century B.C. and during the following centuries fell prey to a number of other invaders.

The nation of Iran ("land of the Aryans") can trace its modern beginning to the rise of the Shi'a sect of Islam and the Safavid Empire around the sixteenth century A.D. The Safavid dynasty ended with an Afghan invasion. In the eighteenth century Nadir Shah invaded India, brought back the "Peacock Throne," and partially reunified the country. In 1906 a coalition of clergy, merchants, and intellectuals forced the reigning shah (king) to grant a limited constitution. Supplemented in 1907, it was patterned on the constitutions of Belgium and France and declared Shi'a Islam as the state religion, rather than the Sunni Islam religion practiced in most other Moslem countries. It divided the government into three branches: the executive, made up of the shah, as head of state, government officials under the shah, and the cabinet; the legislature, consisting of a bicameral parliament; and the judiciary, including a supreme court. Under this constitution, continental European legal theory and Islamic law combined to form a secular Iranian legal system.

In 1979 a popular revolution led by the Shi'a Muslim Ayatollah Khomeini ousted the reigning shah, the constitutional monarch, and established an Islamic republic on March 30 of that year. Iraq invaded Iran in September 1980, starting a war that lasted for eight years.

The constitution of October 24, 1979, can be viewed as the triumph of the Shi'a Islam religion over Iranian nationalism, which had grown under the prior constitution and the shahs. A few weeks before his death the Ayatollah Khomeini began the process for constitutional reforms such as revising the qualifications for a successor to the leader, the division of executive power, and the composition of the judiciary, as well as adding a method for reviewing and amending the constitution and changing the name of the parliament from the national consultative assembly to the Islamic consultative assembly. The constitution was amended after approval by a popular referendum held on July 28, 1989.

Islamic theology, particularly the Shi'a Islamic school of constitutional law called *imamate*, is the principal influence grafted onto the traditional form of parliamentary government.

The Constitution

The preamble expresses the revolutionary history and the general concepts that inspired the constitution. Some of the subheadings are the Dawn of the Movement, Islamic Government, the Wrath of the People, the Price the Nation Paid, Woman in the Constitution, and An Ideological Army.

Article 4 declares: "All civil, penal, economic, administrative, cultural, military, political, and other laws and regulations must be based on Islamic criteria. This principle governs absolutely and universally all the principles of the constitution, laws, and other regulations, and any determination of this matter is entrusted to the religious jurists of the council of guardians." This language indicates that Islamic law is superior not only to all other law but also to the nation-state itself and is immutable.

Article 9 asserts that "no individual, group, or authority has the right to infringe in any way on the political, cultural, economic, and military integrity of Iran under the guise of exercising freedom."

Fundamental Rights

Chapter 3, the Rights of the People, provides that all people of Iran enjoy equal rights, regardless of ethnic group, tribe, color, race, language, and the like. Equal rights are extended to both men and women, and the government undertakes to ensure the rights of women in all respects. Other rights include the right to dignity, life, property, residence, and occupation; freedom of belief; and freedom of expression, except when it is detrimental to the fundamental principles of Islam or the rights of the public. Such exceptions apply to other rights and freedoms enumerated also.

The constitution sets forth social rights, including retirement, unemployment, and old-age benefits, free education up to secondary school, and housing commensurate with an individual's or family's needs.

Division of Powers

In Iran, a unitary state, the constitution divides power among the three traditional branches of government—the executive, legislative, and judicial—under the general supervision of religious leaders. In fact, all power lies with the religious hierarchy.

The Executive

Leader or Leadership Council. In addition to declaring the primacy of Islamic law, a major element of the Iranian constitution is the creation in articles 107 through 112 of the institution of the leader or leadership council as the ultimate executive authority under the constitution.

The position of leader was created for the Ayatollah Khomeini, but the requirement that his successor be both a political and a spiritual leader "worthy of emulation" set a standard that few, if any, in Iran could meet. Khomeini died before constitutional reforms were put into effect in 1989, and his death likely made it possible for article 109 to be amended to reduce the qualifications for a successor and for article 107 to be amended as follows: "The leader is equal to the rest of the people of the country in the eyes of the law."

The responsibilities and powers of the leader or the collective leadership include establishing the general policies of Iran after consultation with a national exigency council; supervising implementation of the policies; calling for national referendums; taking supreme command of the armed forces; declaring war and peace and mobilizing the armed forces; appointing and dismissing six members, or half, of the council of guardians, the supreme judicial authority, the head of the state radio and television network, the head of the joint military staff, the head of the revolutionary guard corps, and supreme commanders of the armed forces; resolving differences among the branches of the armed forces and other problems that cannot be resolved through the nation's exigency council; approving candidates for president; dismissing the president if found guilty of violating constitutional duties by the supreme court or after a two-thirds vote of no confidence by the legislature in accordance with article 89 of the constitution; and pardoning and reducing sentences. The constitution permits delegation of these duties and powers.

Article 111 establishes procedures for selecting a successor in the event of the death of the leader and states that the leadership council will act on behalf of the leader in the event of temporary inability to perform the duties of the office.

President and Cabinet. The president, who is elected directly by the voters for a four-year term but serves at the pleasure of the leader, is responsible for implementing the constitution. The powers and duties of the president include signing legislation, treaties, protocols, contracts, and agreements concluded with other governments after approval by the legislature; over-seeing planning, budget, and state employment affairs; and approving the appointment of ambassadors on the recommendation of the foreign minister, accrediting ambassadors, and accepting the credentials of ambassadors from foreign countries.

The president appoints and dismisses ministers and is the head of the council of ministers (cabinet). The 1979 constitution provided for a prime minister, who split the executive duties with the president. This arrangement worked well when the two were in perfect harmony, but that was not always the case. The 1989 amendments strengthened the president's role by pro-viding chief executive authority after the leader but including safeguards against a possible dic-tatorship; this includes parliamentary confirmation of ministers and a procedure by which the assembly may question the president, with the ultimate sanction being the leader's dismissal of the president should the answers be unacceptable to the legislature.

Parliament. The Islamic Consultative Assembly, sometimes referred to as the *majlis,* is the national legislature of Iran. It has 270 members, five of whom represent specified religious minorities. Members are elected as representatives of the people by direct and secret ballot for terms of four years. By a two-thirds vote members may establish their own procedures for electing a speaker, organizing committees, debating issues, and maintaining discipline. Articles 84 and 86 guarantee representatives the right to express views on all matters in-volving the country and complete freedom to express their views and cast votes.

The assembly may enact laws as long as they are not contrary to the constitution or Islamic law, as determined by the council of guardians. Proposals for legislation are submitted to the legislature by either the government or a minimum of fifteen representatives. The legislature and judges are authorized to interpret the laws. In addition to passing legislation, the as-sembly is authorized to conduct investigations and approve international treaties, protocols, contracts, and agreements.

The legislature's vote of confidence is necessary to confirm the selection of the council of ministers and may be sought by the president on the council's behalf on important and con-troversial matters. The assembly may also question the president or a minister about the conduct of affairs.

Although article 156 declares the judiciary to be independent and the protector of the rights of the individual and society, the same article gives the judiciary the authority to prosecute crimes.

Head of the Judiciary. Before 1989 the highest judicial authority was a five-member supreme judicial council. Now there is a head of the judiciary branch, a person chosen by the leader, who supervises the administration of justice in Iran.

Minister of Justice. The minister of justice is chosen by the president from names presented by the head of the judiciary and coordinates the relationship between the judiciary and the legislative and executive branches of the government.

Supreme Court. The constitution provides that the courts are to be established by law, except for the supreme court, which is established by article 161 to supervise the correct and uniform application of the laws by the other courts.

Council of Guardians. The council of guardians is a body charged with reviewing all measures passed by the national legislature to ensure conformity with Islamic law. After the establishment of a supreme judicial council in 1979 under article 157, which has since been amended to replace the council with a single individual head of the judiciary, the judiciary was forbidden to enforce "secular" prerevolutionary laws that did not conform to Islamic law. Instead, they were to substitute the Islamic judgments of the Ayatollah Khomeini until acceptable laws were passed by the legislature.

In keeping with the overall intent to regard Islamic law as the nation's highest authority, the constitution requires that the head of the judiciary, the chief judge of the supreme court, and the prosecutor general must be just *mujtahids* (persons from the highest rank of religious leaders expert in Islamic law and jurisprudence).

Amending the Constitution

To amend the constitution, the leader consults with the nation's exigency council and then issues an edict to the president. This stipulates the revisions to be made by a council for revision of the constitution, whose extensive membership, including members of the council of guardians and the heads of the three branches of government, is defined in article 177. An amendment must be approved by an absolute majority vote in a referendum. Certain provisions—for example, the Islamic character of the political system and the democratic character of the government—may not be changed.

The current "interim" constitution of Iraq does little more than provide a facade of legitimacy for the totalitarian regime of Saddam Hussein and the ruling pan-Arab Ba'ath (Renaissance) Socialist Party.

The Republic of Iraq is approximately 440,000 square kilometers. It lies just north of Saudi Arabia and Kuwait and extends to the Persian Gulf on the south, Iran on the east, Turkey on the north, and Syria and Jordan on the west. The capital of this country of approximately twenty-three million persons is Baghdad.

Iraq's chief commercial products include oil, natural gas, and petrochemicals. The 1980–88 war with Iran and the 1991 Persian Gulf War created internal devastation, international debt, and economic sanctions, which have negated the benefits of the country's abundance of oil. Even if the current United Nations embargo is lifted, the future of the Iraqi people under the present dictatorial government looks bleak.

Type of Government: Single-party collegial dictatorship, under a revolutionary command council whose president is the president of the republic, with a prime minister and cabinet, a unicameral legislature, and a judiciary

Dates of Constitutions: 1968 and 1970 (both provisional)

Mesopotamia, located between the Tigris and the Euphrates Rivers, is where the world's first civilization developed and where writing is said to have been invented. The Babylonian ruler Hammurabi, who lived in the second millennium B.C., is credited with developing a sophisticated legal code that dealt with such subjects as land tenure, rent, the administration of justice, marriage, and divorce, and its extensive sections on commerce indicate a diverse economy and large-scale trade.

Around 1600 B.C. the Hittites, an Indo-European–speaking people, along with the Kassites conquered Babylon. In the twelfth century B.C. they, in turn, were conquered by the Assyrians, a Semitic-speaking people. Six centuries later the Chaldeans restored Babylon and created the Hanging Gardens, one of the seven wonders of the ancient world. Cyrus the Great brought Babylon into the Iranian Empire, replacing Assyrian savagery with firm but fair administration of justice under provincial governors later known as satraps.

As the ninth Persian Empire satrapy, Babylon and Assyria became isolated and impoverished, but the followers of Alexander the Great, who conquered the territory in 331 B.C., built many communities modeled on the Greek city-states, cross-pollinating the cultures. After periods of Roman and Iranian rule, the Muslims, under Abu Bakr, Muhammad's father-in-law, began attacking Iraqi tribes, most of whom were then Christian. The Islamic conquest was completed in A.D. 650, but a schism divided the Muslim adherents into the Shi'a Muslims, who follow Ali, Muhammad's cousin and son-in-law, and the Sunni Muslims, who reject Ali and follow Muhammad. This division is evident today: about fifty-five percent of the population are Shi'a and forty percent are Sunni.

Baghdad became a religious and political center, but in 1258 the city was sacked by the Mongols, and from 1534 until the end of World War I the territory was part of the Ottoman Empire. By the end of the war Britain and France had secretly divided up the Turkish territories, with Britain getting Mesopotamia. Faisal, the son of the sherif of Mecca and a direct descendant of Muhammad, was chosen by Winston Churchill to be king of Iraq in the hope that his religious stature would ameliorate the Muslim factional conflict.

Another perennial problem in the area was the minority Muslim but non-Arab Kurds, a fiercely independent people in the north whose population overlapped with neighboring

Turkey and Syria. Today they constitute about twenty percent of the Iraqi population and often fight against government forces.

On July 14, 1958, the Iraqi army overthrew the imposed monarchy, proclaiming Iraq democratic and part of the Arab world. In 1963 military officers supporting the Ba'ath (Renaissance) Arab Socialist Party briefly took over the country, only to be ousted in another coup. A relatively more moderate, nonparty Arab nationalist government developed and lasted until 1968, when the Ba'ath Party returned to power in a nearly bloodless coup.

Better organized than in 1963, the party formed a governing revolutionary command council, and in 1968 and 1970 it issued interim, provisional constitutions. Three of the five members of the council were Sunnis from the northwest town of Tikrit, as was Saddam Hussein al Tikriti. His ruthless political skills and his relationship to the coup leader, the Tikriti general Hasan al Bakr, who became the constitutional president of Iraq, led to his rise in power. By 1977 officials were reporting to Hussein instead of the president, and on July 16 Bakr resigned. Hussein then became president, secretary general of the Ba'ath Party regional council, chairman of the revolutionary command council, and commander in chief of the armed forces.

In 1989, following the Iran-Iraq war and several postponements, elections for the national legislature were held. President Hussein called for a new constitution creating a council of ministers responsible to a legislature, permitting the establishment of political parties, and providing for the election of the president by the people. Even if Hussein had intended the reforms to be included in the new constitution, the Persian Gulf War and its aftermath provided an excuse for again delaying true constitutional government in Iraq.

Influences

The Iraqi legal system is derived from the legal reforms of the Ottomans and is fully secularized. The 1970 interim constitution is rooted in the philosophy of the Ba'ath Socialist Party, a pan-Arab organization seeking the integration of all Arab states into a single unitary state.

The Constitution

The current provisional constitution of the Republic of Iraq was promulgated in decision number 792 on July 16, 1970, signed by the president of the revolutionary command council, Ahmed Hassan al Bakr. Regardless of such provisions of the constitution as article 2, which states that "the people are the source of authority and its [the republic's] legitimacy," Iraq is ruled by Saddam Hussein, ostensibly on behalf of the Ba'ath Socialist Party.

This constitution specifically states that it does not abrogate any previous laws or decisions by the council. The current constitution, as did the 1968 constitution, reflects the Ba'ath Party's ideals of upholding socialism but rejects collectivism. A national action charter promulgated by the council president in 1971 and the 1974 political report of the Eighth Ba'ath Party Congress contain the party's general objectives and principles to be applied in economic, political, and social areas.

Fundamental Rights

The 1970 provisional constitution provides a pro forma list entitled Fundamental Rights and Duties, but consistent violations of human rights in Iraq have been documented by a number of independent, worldwide organizations, including the United Nations Commission on Human Rights. A 1974 amendment provides an autonomous region for the Kurds, but the national rights of the Kurds and all minorities may be exercised only within the framework of Iraqi unity.

Division of Powers

Although the constitution expressly creates legislative, executive, and judicial branches of government, a revolutionary command council is the "supreme institution." In fact, all power in this unitary state rests in the hands of the president of the council.

Revolutionary Command Council. According to article 37, "The revolutionary command council is the supreme institution in the state, which on July 17, 1968, assumed the responsibility to realize the public will of the people, by removing the authority from the reactionary, individual and corruptive regime, and returning it to the people."

The Executive

Among the council's duties is electing from its members a president, who also serves as the president of the republic, and a vice president. Other council duties include selecting new members for the council, not to exceed twelve, from members of the regional leadership of the Ba'ath Party; relieving members of membership in the council; and accusing and prosecuting members. Article 40 provides that a council member enjoys full immunity unless this protection is waived by the council.

The council issues laws and decrees having the force of law and decisions "indispensable for applying" the laws; ratifies the state budget, treaties, and international agreements; declares war; and concludes peace.

President, Prime Minister, and Cabinet. The president of the republic is head of state and supreme commander of the armed forces. He appoints judges, governors, and all civil and military employees; supervises all public and quasi-official organizations; directs and controls the work of the ministries; presides over meetings with the prime minister and cabinet; and has wide-ranging additional powers.

Parliament. The first elections for the unicameral Iraqi parliament, the Majlis al-'Umma (national assembly), were held in 1980. In addition to the 250-member assembly, there is also a fifty-member Kurdish legislative council. The assembly's role is limited to considering draft legislation, because legislative power is in the hands of the revolutionary command council.

The Legislature

All Iraqi citizens over eighteen years of age are eligible to vote. To be elected to the assembly a candidate must be an Iraqi by birth and at least twenty-five years old, must have an Iraqi father, must not be married to a foreigner, must not have been subject to expropriation or nationalization, and must demonstrate satisfactorily a belief in the Ba'ath Party's principles and objectives, in addition to other qualifications. In the first two elections the Ba'ath Party won a majority of more than seventy percent, and in the second election women won thirty-three seats.

The Iraqi constitution contains only two articles concerning the judiciary. Article 60 states:

The Judiciary

(a) The judiciary is independent and is subject to no other authority except the law. (b) Access to the courts is ensured to all citizens. (c) The organization, including the levels, jurisdiction, conditions for appointment, transfer, promotion, legal action and dismissal of judges and magistrates shall be determined by law.

Article 61 provides that matters relating to public prosecution also must be determined by law.

Iraq's legal system has been set up under laws issued by the revolutionary command council and includes courts with civil, criminal, administrative, and religious jurisdiction under the supervision of the ministry of justice. All judges are appointed by the president.

Other courts operate along the French model, introduced during the Ottoman period, as modified by Islamic law; there are three main branches, one each for Sunni Arabs, Sunni Kurds, and Shi'a Arabs. Marriage, divorce, and inheritance among Jewish and Christian minorities are handled in their own religious courts.

Article 63 states that the 1970 constitution will remain in force until a permanent constitution is promulgated and that amendments may be made by a two-thirds vote of the revolutionary command council. In fact, Saddam Hussein's approval is all that is required.

Amending the Constitution

IRELAND

For eight hundred years the Irish and the English were bound together in an uneasy and often bloody coexistence. After attaining complete independence from Great Britain, Ireland adopted its second constitution in 1937.

General Information

Ireland, which shares with Northern Ireland an island in the Atlantic Ocean across the Irish Sea from the British Isles, is nearly 70,300 square kilometers. The country has a population of nearly four million inhabitants, and Dublin is its capital.

Since the 1950s Ireland's industries have grown significantly, and the number of workers employed in agriculture has shrunk to around fifteen percent. The country joined the European Economic Community in 1973, although it is still one of its poorest members. The election of the first woman as president in 1990 and a constitutional amendment in 1995 permitting divorce, however, reflect significant social change.

Type of Government: Presidential-style parliamentary republic, with a president and council of state, a prime minister and cabinet, a bicameral legislature, and a judiciary

Dates of Constitutions: 1922 and 1937

Constitutional History

Ireland was occupied as early as 7000 B.C., and by 3000 B.C. the inhabitants were farming and building complex megaliths. In 300 B.C. iron-wielding Gaelic Celts, some possibly from Galicia in northwest Spain, moved in and established five kingdoms, two of which later merged. These define the four provinces of the island today: Leinster in the southeast, Munster in the southwest, Connacht in the west, and Ulster, now Northern Ireland, in the northeast.

A high king claimed to rule the provinces, but the decentralized power structure that developed was based on the *fine* (family unit) and the *tuatha* (extended family that lived in the local government unit). The land was jointly owned and divided among the adult males. Judges, called *Brehons*, went about the island administering laws that were learned orally. When the laws were finally written down in the seventh century A.D., they were in rhythmic verse.

The Romans never made it to Ireland, but in the fifth century a captured Briton who had fled to the European continent and had become a bishop returned to Ireland and converted the people to Christianity; he was later known as St. Patrick. The Irish developed their own unique form of Catholicism, which was centered on the monasteries. Norsemen invaded around 795, and by 1014 the Vikings began settling in Ireland. In the second half of the twelfth century, a deposed Irish king asked the assistance of the Norman English, who came and brought their "common law." Thus began Ireland's eight-hundred-year involvement with the English.

Modern Ireland dates from the beginning of the seventeenth century. Henry VIII had taken the title of king of Ireland as well as king of England, and although Irish rebels were routed in battle in 1601, various forms of "Irishness" were developing. Thereafter, distinctions between old and new English immigrants and the imposition of laws made by the British parliament, as well as religious differences, fueled constant clashes; among them was the 1690 Battle of the Boyne, in which the Protestant King William defeated the Catholic James II. By the Act of Union, effective January 1, 1801, Ireland was to be represented in the British parliament, and the Roman Catholic Relief Act of 1829 allowed Catholics, who had previously been persecuted, to hold public office.

Overdependence on the potato, introduced in Ireland by Sir Walter Raleigh around 1570, led to the great famine of 1845–49; when the potato crop failed, nearly a million people died and some one and a half million people emigrated. A number of attempts to gain home rule for the island failed until 1914. Then World War I forced postponement of implementation, but a treaty was concluded on December 6, 1921, and the Irish Free State (Agreement) Act, which dissolved the union but not all ties with Britain, became law on March 31, 1922.

Support for the separation was not unanimous in Ireland, and the constitution of the Irish Free State, set in operation by a British royal proclamation on December 6, 1922, had to bridge the gap between independence and continued British influence. The constitution was tied to the 1921 treaty that limited Irish sovereignty, but after the Statute of Westminster in 1931 dominion states, such as Ireland, Canada, and Australia, were no longer subject to acts of the British parliament, thus paving the way for a new Irish constitution.

Described as rebottled wine of old and familiar vintage, the new constitution went into effect on December 29, 1937, after being approved by referendum. Criticized by some as reflecting too strongly the views of Catholic nationalism, it was amended in 1972 to confirm, if only in theory, the concept of separation of church and state. A 1995 amendment permits divorce under certain circumstances. Since 1998 the Irish state has been authorized to bind itself to the terms of the British-Irish Agrement of April 1998 regarding the future of Northern Ireland and to implement certain amendments to the constitution, particularly those relating to the sovereignty and territory of Ireland when the agreement enters into force.

The basic prototype for the 1922 constitution was the British parliamentary model. Its influence carried over to the 1937 document, which added a list of fundamental rights, as in the U.S. constitution, and provision for judicial review.

The preamble, while acknowledging the religious sentiments of the Irish people, declares: ". . . we the people . . . do hereby adopt, enact and give to ourselves this constitution."
Article 3 attempts to give extraterritorial effect to the laws of Ireland, defining the nation as the whole island rather than just the state of Ireland, which is characterized in article 5 as sovereign, independent, and democratic.
Article 6, section 1, defines the source of sovereignty: "All powers of government, legislative, executive, and judicial, derive, under God, from the people, whose right it is to designate the rulers of the state and, in final appeal, to decide all questions of national policy, according to the requirements of the common good."

The Constitution

Five areas of fundamental rights are covered in the constitution. Personal rights listed in article 40 include equality before the law for all citizens; the right of the unborn to life, with due regard for the mother's equal right to life; the right to personal liberty, which may be deprived only in accordance with law; rights similar to habeas corpus protection; and, subject to public order and morality, freedom of expression and assembly, as long as it is peaceable and without arms, and of associations, including unions. In the next four articles, family, education, private property, and religious rights are guaranteed.

In Ireland, a unitary state, power is divided among the president, as head of state; the prime minister, as head of government; the legislature; and the courts, which exercise judicial review.

President. The constitution gives the president "precedence over all other persons in the state. . . ." He or she is elected by direct vote and secret ballot, "on the system of proportional representation by means of a single transferable vote," for a term of seven years and may be reelected only once.
Any citizen thirty-five years of age is eligible to be elected president. A person who has not held the office before must be nominated by at least twenty members of the legislature or at least four county councils. If serving in the legislature, he or she will be deemed to have

vacated that seat. The president may not leave Ireland while in office without the consent of the government and may be impeached for "stated misbehavior."

The president is supreme commander of the defense forces and commissions all officers; grants pardons and commutes punishments; appoints the prime minister (the *Taoiseach*), who is nominated by the lower house of the legislature; appoints and accepts the resignations of members of the government; convenes the legislature after consultation with the council of state; summons the lower house on the advice of the prime minister and may refuse to dissolve that body even if the prime minister has lost majority support; and promulgates the laws.

The president, with the approval of the council of state and the government, may address the nation at any time and on any subject. Additional functions may be assigned to the president by law.

Council of State. The council of state consists of the prime minister, the prime minister's deputy, the chief justice, the president of the high court, the chairmen of the two houses of the legislature and the attorney general, as ex officio members; enumerated former officials including former presidents, all of whom must be able and willing to serve; and up to seven persons appointed by the president. The purpose of the body is to aid and counsel the president in the exercise and performance of his or her duties as required by the constitution.

Prime Minister and Cabinet. The prime minister is head of the government, which includes a cabinet of at least seven and no more than fifteen members. Article 28 requires that the executive power of the state be exercised by the government.

The Legislature

Parliament. The national parliament of Ireland is called the Oireachtas. It consists of the president; a senate, called the Seanad; and a house of representatives, called the Dail. Article 15, section 2, provides that "the sole and exclusive power of making laws for the state is hereby vested in the Oireachtas; no other legislative authority has power to make laws for the state."

Upper House. The senate is composed of sixty members. Eleven are named by the prime minister, six are elected by the universities, and forty-three are elected from five panels representing national language and culture, agriculture and fisheries, union and nonunion labor, industry and commerce, and public administration and social services. This occupational classification appears to be based on the Catholic Church's concern at one time about communist and fascist influences. The senate's functions are limited to delaying and attempting to amend legislation.

Lower House. As in most British-style parliaments, the lower house is the center of power because a majority of the members is necessary to support the government. The number of members is to be fixed by law but is to be at least one member per thirty thousand people and no more than one per twenty thousand people. The 166 members are elected from constituencies with three to five seats by a system of proportional representation; it uses a transferable vote that allows a voter to indicate a preference by assigning numbers—one, two, and so forth—to the candidates. The vote is then tallied by transferring votes either from a candidate who does not need them to be elected or from one who has no chance of being elected to a viable but as yet inconclusively elected candidate. Article 16 provides for the chairman of the lower house to be deemed elected in the following general election.

Citizens twenty-one years old and not under any legal disability are eligible for either house of parliament. Voting, which is by secret ballot, is open to all citizens and "such persons in the state as may be determined by law" and not otherwise disqualified by law who have reached the age of eighteen.

Bills may be introduced in either house, except money bills, which may be recommended only by the senate and must originate in the lower house. If the senate disagrees with the designation of a money bill, the president is authorized to convene a committee on privileges to decide the issue. Article 24 makes bills not acted on by the senate in the prescribed time effective for only ninety days or for such additional time as agreed to by both houses. All bills, except for proposals to amend the constitution, must be signed into law by the president.

On petition by a majority of the members of the senate and at least one-third of the members of the lower house, the president may decline to sign a bill into law if it contains a provision of national importance, unless it is approved by a referendum or by resolution of the lower house after new elections.

High Court. The Irish court system includes a high court of first instance "invested with full original jurisdiction in and power to determine all matters and questions whether of law or fact, civil or criminal." Its jurisdiction also extends to the constitutionality of laws. **The Judiciary**

Supreme Court. The highest court of appeal is the supreme court, headed by a chief justice, which hears cases on appeal from the high court and other courts. It also rules on constitutional questions; in these cases concurring or dissenting opinions are not permitted. In addition to typical judicial review functions, the supreme court has the authority to give opinions on bills before they become law when so requested by the president.

Article 37 states that the constitution does not invalidate judicial functions by other bodies, which include the land commission and the adoption board. Article 38 authorizes special courts to be set up by law where ordinary courts are inadequate to secure the effective administration of justice and the preservation of public peace and order.

The judges of the courts are appointed by the president and are to be independent and subject only to the constitution and the law in exercising their judgment. High court and supreme court judges may not be removed except by resolutions of both houses of the legislature, and their pay may not be reduced while they are in office.

Unlike the French and U.S. constitutions, which prohibit certain amendments, article 46 of the Irish constitution provides that any provisions may be amended. A proposal for an amendment is initiated in the lower house as a bill. After passage by both houses, it is submitted to the people for referendum and must be approved by a majority of the votes cast. **Amending the Constitution**

ISRAEL

For political reasons Israel, a parliamentary nation, abandoned an early attempt to create a written or single-document constitution in favor of piecemeal enactments of basic constitutional laws. A 1992 law provided for the direct election of the prime minister beginning in 1996.

General Information

Before the creation of Palestine, the State of Israel, according to the demarcation lines from 1947 to 1967, was approximately 20,700 square kilometers. It is located at the eastern end of the Mediterranean Sea, with Lebanon on the north; the Golan Heights, Central Palestine (the West Bank of the Jordan River), Syria, and Jordan on the east; the Gulf of Aqaba on the south; and Egypt and the Gaza Strip on the southwest. Jerusalem is the capital of this country of nearly six million inhabitants, although most embassies are located in Tel Aviv.

Because of the country's paucity of natural resources and its large government expenditures, Israel's basically socialist system relies heavily on deficit financing. Diamond cutting, electronics, and tourism are among Israel's major industries, and it is the world's fifth largest exporter of arms. Continuing tension between the country and its neighbors—the Palestinians in particular—and between the religious and secular elements at home hold back greater economic progress.

Type of Government: Presidential-style parliamentary republic, with a president, a prime minister and cabinet, a unicameral legislature, and a judiciary

Date of Constitution: Unwritten; 1948 (declaration of independence, earliest quasi-constitutional document)

Constitutional History

The early history of the Jewish people—the Hebrews, a Semitic tribe from Mesopotamia—began about four thousand years ago, according to biblical references, with Abraham and his covenant with God. The twelve sons of Abraham's grandson, Jacob, became the twelve tribes of Israel who migrated to Egypt to escape famine and returned under the leadership of Moses around the thirteenth century B.C. They conquered the "Land of Israel," and under a succession of kings such as Saul, David, and Solomon the nation became a power in the Middle East by the eighth century B.C.

Just before the Christian era, the Roman Empire took control of the territory, and from A.D. 70 until 1948 foreign governments ruled the land of the Israelites. After the Roman and Byzantine Empires came the Arabs, the Seljuk Turks, European crusaders, Mamluks, Ottomans, and the British. During this time the law of Palestine, as the land was called, developed from Ottoman law, which was based on both Islamic and French law. English law was engrafted during the British occupation of the area, from 1917 until May 15, 1948, the date set for termination of British jurisdiction by the British parliament.

In 1917 the British government authorized Lord Balfour to write a letter to Lord Rothschild supporting the establishment of "a national home for the Jewish people" in Palestine; it became known as the Balfour Declaration and the centerpiece of the Jewish Zionist movement. For a minority of Jews, Zionism—the ideological attempt to change the traditional Jewish acceptance of exile from a national homeland—was an organizing force advocated by the World Zionist Organization and the Jewish Agency. The council of the League of Nations approved British civil administration in the area under a mandate for Palestine. The constitution was to be a council order establishing a high commissioner with strong executive powers, an executive council, a legislative council (which never materialized because of Jewish and Arab disagreement over representation), and a judiciary composed of British and local judges.

In 1936 the Arabs in Palestine rebelled against the government under the mandate, and in 1937 martial law was imposed. The British limited immigration, but many Jews fleeing the Nazis entered illegally. After the war the United Nations approved an elaborate partitioning of Palestine into Arab and Jewish states, but conflicts continued. After the United States pledged its support, the Jewish leader David Ben-Gurion proclaimed the State of Israel on May 14, 1948. The next day the British bowed out and Arab forces began their assault on Israel. Although the country survived, its 1948–49 war for independence proved to be the most costly in its history. Arabs who remained in the Israeli state, however, were granted citizenship, with equal voting rights and guarantees of equal political and social rights in accordance with the 1948 declaration of independence.

Britain's system of government was a major influence on the form of the Israeli government, as were traditional Jewish legal and constitutional principles.

The Constitution

The Israeli constitution, like that of the United Kingdom, is based on enactments of its legislature, other documents, and traditional concepts, both legal and religious. A constituent assembly convened on February 14, 1949, to draft a constitutional document, but two days later, because of conflicts between the religious and secular factions, it transformed itself into a legislature and enacted a transition law, sometimes referred to as the "small constitution."

In reaching a decision in effect to postpone writing a single-document constitution, the members of the elected constituent assembly considered the following arguments in favor of writing such a document: The United Nations resolution supporting the State of Israel and Israel's own declaration of independence called for drafting a written constitution; assembly delegates had been elected to write a constitution; there was a need to legitimize the Israeli government and enshrine the doctrine of the separation of powers to prevent usurpation of power by one branch; unlike the United Kingdom, which also has no written constitution, Israel had no history of a democratic constitution or traditions; there was a need to guarantee fundamental rights; a single document would help students and immigrants understand how the government worked; and, finally, a written constitution would affirm the country's intentions to maintain a stable, sovereign, democratic government.

Arguments against a written constitution were that the constitution should be a bridge between the past and the future, not a set of platitudes that might have to be changed; that the population reflected only a fraction of the future immigrant population who should have a say in the type of government suitable for Israel; that the declaration of independence was not legally binding on the assembly and many in the electorate knew of some candidates' doubts about the wisdom of writing a constitution; that national unity between the political parties would be threatened over just the language in the preamble; that having fundamental laws concerning the government that could be easily amended was preferable to a rigid document; and, finally, that Jewish legal and ethical traditions could be regarded as a form of oral constitution.

The unwritten constitution of Israel today therefore consists of nine basic laws relating to these subjects: the parliament (1958); lands (1960); the president (1964); the government (1968); the state economy (1975); defense forces (1976); Jerusalem, the capital (1980); the judicature (1984); and the state comptroller (1988). These laws, together with the Law of Return (1950), the law regarding the covenant between Israel and the World Zionist Organization and Jewish Agency (1952, amended in 1971), and the declaration of independence (1948), provide the framework for the Israeli constitution. Additional individual rights are addressed in basic laws on freedom of occupation and on human dignity and liberty, as amended in 1994.

The Israeli declaration of independence, although of only quasi-constitutional stature, affirms that the State of Israel "will foster the development of the country for the benefit of its inhabitants; it will be based on freedom, justice, and peace as envisaged by the prophets of Israel; it will insure complete equality of social and political rights to all inhabitants irrespective of religion, race, or sex; it will guarantee freedom of religion, conscience, language, education, and culture; it will safeguard the holy places of all religions; and it will be faithful to the principles of the Charter of the United Nations." Other rights extended include the right to engage in any occupation, profession, or trade and a prohibition against "violation of the life, body or dignity of any person" or "the property of a person." Also guaranteed are personal liberty, freedom to travel, "privacy and intimacy," protection against searches "conducted on the private premises of a person, [or] in the body or personal effects," and "confidentiality of conversation, or of the writings or records of a person."

Like the United Kingdom, Israel relies on its courts to safeguard fundamental rights, although internal security problems have resulted in some infringements on occasions.

Division of Powers

Israel is a unitary state. Supreme power resides in the legislature, with a mostly ceremonial president, as head of state; a prime minister, as head of government; and the courts, which technically lack the power of judicial review.

The Executive

President. The president, or head of state, is elected for a five-year term in secret balloting by an absolute majority of the members of the legislature. If more than two ballots are necessary, on successive ballots the name of the candidate with the least votes is eliminated, and balloting continues. Every Israeli national who is a resident is eligible to be president, but he or she may not serve more than two consecutive terms.

The president signs treaties ratified by the legislature and laws it enacts, except statutes relating to presidential powers; takes part in forming a government, especially coalition-party governments; appoints diplomats and receives foreign diplomats; and appoints the state comptroller, judges for civil and religious courts, and the governor of the Bank of Israel.

The president's role is basically nonpolitical and ceremonial; he or she has no veto power over legislation and may not leave the country without the permission of the government. If the president is incapacitated or the office becomes vacant, the chairman of the legislature becomes acting president.

Prime Minister and Cabinet. The prime minister is head of government and the state's principal political officer. He or she is responsible for forming a government after elections or after a vote of no confidence for the predecessor government; to a large extent this means governing by a coalition of parties rather than a majority party. In 1984 a unique coalition government was formed between the Likud and Labor Parties under which a member of each party would be prime minister for half of the four-year term. As opposed to other parliamentary systems, the prime minister has been directly elected since 1996.

The Legislature

Parliament. The Israeli unicameral parliament is called the Knesset. Its 120 members, who must be at least twenty-five years old, are chosen in "general, national, direct, equal, secret, and proportional elections" for maximum terms of four years. Seats are allocated on the basis of the number of votes for slates of political party candidates. Once elected, members enjoy privileges and immunities and are exempt from military service.

The Knesset must approve the installation of a new government and may entertain a motion for a no-confidence vote at any time. It elects the president, approves the budget, and supervises the government by questioning ministers and scrutinizing government reports.

Matters for debate or legislation, including private legislation, as in the United States, may be introduced by any member of the parliament; however, as in Britain, legislation is generally introduced by the government. Any number of members constitute a quorum, and passage of all legislation, except constitutional laws and amendments, the election or removal of the president, and the removal of the state comptroller, is based on a simple majority. Much of the legislature's work is done in committees, such as the constitution, law and justice, and economic affairs committees and the house committee, which handles parliamentary rules and procedures.

In deference to its Christian, Muslim, and Jewish members, the parliament does not meet on Fridays, Saturdays, or Sundays. Although Hebrew is the official language, simultaneous translation is provided for members who wish to address the legislature in Arabic.

The basic law on judicature of 1984 vests judicial power in a supreme court, a district court, a magistrate court, and another court to be designated by law, as well as religious courts. Section 2 of the law asserts, "A person vested with judicial power shall not, in judicial matters, be subject to any authority but that of the law." **The Judiciary**

Judges are appointed by the president after being elected by a committee composed of the president of the supreme court and two other members elected by its members, the minister of justice, and another minister designated by the government, among others. Only Israeli nationals may be judges, and they are subject to a court of discipline, which hears complaints and imposes disciplinary measures as prescribed by law. Israeli courts have no authority to declare laws passed by the parliament unconstitutional.

Supreme Court. The supreme court hears appeals from decisions of the district courts. It also sits as a high court of justice to hear matters not within the jurisdiction of another court and "to grant relief for the sake of justice."

The legislature may enact or amend basic or constitutional laws by an absolute majority vote of its members—that is, one-half plus one of its total membership, or sixty-one of its 120 members. **Amending the Constitution**

ITALY

The ancient Roman republic (from *res publica,* Latin for "affairs of the people") had an unwritten constitution that limited its government. Since the conclusion of World War II, when Italy established a new republic and adopted a new constitution, numerous political parties and shifting coalitions have resulted in more than fifty national governments.

General Information

The Republic of Italy on the Mediterranean Sea is approximately 301,300 square kilometers and is bounded by the Adriatic Sea and the former territory of Yugoslavia on the east, Austria and Switzerland on the north, France and the Ligurian and Tyrrhenian Seas on the west, and the Ionian Sea and the Strait of Messina on the south. Its territory also includes the islands of Sardinia and Sicily in the Mediterranean Sea. One of the most populous countries in western Europe, Italy has more than fifty-seven million inhabitants; its capital is Rome, called the Eternal City.

Traditionally influenced by the Roman Catholic Church and more recently also by communist and socialist movements, Italy has one of the world's largest economies, and Italians enjoy a relatively high standard of living. The seemingly always unstable government, however, may require political reform to deal effectively with extensive corruption, terrorism, and organized crime, but the ability of the Italian people to solve these problems in the context of their present constitution should not be underestimated.

Type of Government: Presidential-style parliamentary republic, with a president, a prime minister and council of ministers (cabinet), a bicameral legislature, a judiciary, and a constitutional court

Dates of Constitutions: 1861, 1944 (provisional), and 1948

Constitutional History

Toward the end of the second millennium B.C., Indo-Europeans settled in what is now Italy, forming tribes such as the Etruscans, Umbrians, Samnites, and Latins; Greeks and Phoenicians colonized areas to the south. Rome is said to have been founded in 753 B.C. and later ruled by Romulus. Under the Etruscan rulers who followed, it became the center of a loose, defensive confederation called the Latin League.

The Roman Empire in western Europe lasted from just before the Christian era until near the end of the fifth century. Under Pax Romana (peace of Rome), laws replaced custom and caprice, although the public interest was still interpreted by the government to mean its own interest, with no real concern for individual rights.

After the fall of Rome the Italian peninsula saw the rise of cities such as Venice, Genoa, and Pisa and subsequently city-states. Goods from the east and north supported trading and mercantile empires, not only on the peninsula but also throughout Latin Christendom. By the thirteenth century Bologna was a center for European legal studies, and the laws of Rome, as summarized in the Corpus Juris Civilis of the emperor Justinian, were being transformed by university scholars influenced by canon or church law into a form of common law known as the *jus commune* of Europe.

During the Renaissance Roman law again was transformed, this time into "natural law" based on logic and reason. Codification of the law proceeded as governments sought underpinnings for the absolute state; the Romano-Germanic legal systems that developed during this period fostered the enlightened concept that human rights should be recognized and secured by the government, as well as the doctrine of the separation of powers, in particular limiting the judiciary to applying laws, not making them.

The 1789 French Revolution and Napoleon had a significant impact on legal systems throughout most of Europe, including the fragmented Italian states. After Napoleon's fall in 1815 Italian princes quickly moved to restore their prerevolutionary regimes, although much of the French code introduced by Napoleon could not be extricated from the local legal systems.

Unification of the Italian states resulted in a single, secular monarchy in 1861, with the pope withdrawing into the Vatican. The new country's first constitution was based on the Statuto albertino, the constitution of Sardinia, and it lasted, except for a provisional document in 1944, until January 1, 1948, when the current constitution went into effect. Benito Mussolini established his fascist regime before World War II when King Victor Emmanuel III, possibly under some misapprehension that his crown and conservative politics would be protected, appointed him prime minister. A 1946 referendum to choose between a republican form of government and a monarchy was decided by a narrow margin in favor of the former.

The 1948 constitution has been amended only eleven times—most recently in 2000, when article 48 was changed to authorize parliament to establish seats in both houses for a "Foreign Constituency" so that "Italian nationals resident abroad may exercise their right to vote in Italian elections."

The 1948 Italian constitution superficially resembles that of the Fourth Republic of France but with a greater role for the president. It has influenced other European constitutions, including Spain's.

Influences

The constitution of the Republic of Italy has no preamble, but the first twelve articles come under the heading Fundamental Principles. Article 1 sets forth two of these principles:

The Constitution

Italy is a democratic republic founded on labor.

The sovereignty belongs to the people who exercise it in accordance with the procedures and within the limits laid down by the constitution.

According to the constitution's article 2, "The republic acknowledges and warrants the inviolable rights of man—both as an individual and in social groups where man's personality unfolds—and requests the fulfillment of the unbreakable duties of political, economic, and social solidarity."

Fundamental Rights

The constitution asserts equality before the law for all citizens, without discrimination on the basis of sex, race, language, religion, political opinions, or personal and social conditions. The right to work is acknowledged, and the republic pledges to promote the implementation of this right.

The state and the Roman Catholic Church are each declared to be independent and sovereign, although the Lateran Pacts of 1929 between Mussolini and the Catholic Church, granting the latter opportunities to influence political and social affairs in Italy, are confirmed. All religious "confessions" are stated to be "equally free before the law."

Italy repudiates war as an offensive instrument and agrees to limitations on sovereignty to ensure peace and justice among nations. This agreement has been used to uphold Italy's compliance with laws of the European Economic Community.

Other rights guaranteed, although often with some limitations, include personal freedom and the freedom and secrecy (privacy) of correspondence; the inviolability of the home; and the right to move within the country, to meet and assemble peacefully, to profess a religious faith, and to express opinion. Freedom of the press is guaranteed, without prior authorization or censorship, and a person must be considered innocent until final sentence is issued. Ethical, social, economic, and political rights are also covered.

In Italy, a unitary state, power is divided among the president, as head of state; the prime minister, as head of government; the legislature; the courts; and the constitutional court, which exercises constitutional review.

Division of Powers

The Executive

President. The president is head of state and is elected for a seven-year term by secret ballot by a two-thirds majority vote of the members of the legislature in joint session, including regional delegates elected to ensure representation of minorities. If there is no winner after the third ballot, the president is chosen by an absolute majority vote of the members. Because of the numerous parties in the Italian political spectrum, electing a president has not always been easy; in 1971, for example, election required twenty-three ballots.

The powers and duties of the president include authorizing the submission of government bills to the legislature, promulgating laws and issuing regulations and decrees with the force of law, appointing certain state officials, accrediting and receiving diplomats, commanding the armed forces, presiding over the supreme law council, granting pardons and commuting sentences, and conferring decorations. The president may dissolve either or both houses of the legislature after consulting the presiding officers, except in the last six months of his or her term.

The president is not responsible for official acts, except in the case of high treason or "offense to the constitution." To be valid the president's acts must be countersigned by a minister, who takes responsibility for the act. If the president is unable to perform his or her duties, the speaker of the legislature's upper house acts for him or her.

Prime Minister and Cabinet. "The government of the republic," notes article 92, "is composed of the prime minister and the ministers. Altogether they make up the council of ministers."

The prime minister is appointed by the president, who appoints the other ministers on the recommendation of the prime minister. The resulting government must receive an initial vote of confidence by both houses of the legislature, and it holds power until the confidence is revoked or the legislature's term expires. The prime minister is responsible for the government's general policy, and the ministers are responsible collectively for their acts as a body and individually for the acts of their respective government departments.

The Legislature

Parliament. The Italian parliament, called the Parlamento, consists of the Senato (senate) and the Camera dei Deputati (chamber of deputies).

Upper House. Most of the members of the senate, whose number is set by the constitution at 315, are elected for five-year terms by direct and universal suffrage from regions based on population. To be eligible to run for the senate one must be more than forty-one years old and eligible to vote. Other members of the senate who serve for life include past presidents and five people of high merit in certain areas of endeavor appointed by the president.

Lower House. The 630 members of the chamber of deputies are elected for five-year terms by direct and universal suffrage to seats distributed among constituencies on the basis of population. Voters who are at least twenty-five years old are eligible to be elected as deputies.

Each house elects a presiding officer or speaker from among its members, and the speaker of the chamber of deputies presides at common sittings or joint sessions. Each house judges the qualifications of its members and determines its own rules. A majority of the members must be present to conduct ordinary business, and a majority vote of those present is required to adopt measures. Members are to represent the nation, and they are granted certain immunities while in office.

Bills may be introduced by the government, any member of parliament, and certain other specified bodies, as well as the people, if proposed by fifty thousand voters. Bills are reviewed by a committee, and then the measures are acted on measure by measure and by final vote, except in the case of bills determined to be urgent. Some bills may be approved by a committee of both houses instead of in open session. Bills on the constitution, elections, legislative delegation, ratification of treaties, and approval of budgets and financial balances must go through the standard procedures.

To become law a bill must be passed by both houses and be promulgated by the president, although the president may require that a bill be reconsidered. If the bill is passed again by both houses, it becomes law. Except in the case of laws regarding taxes, the budget, amnesty and pardons, and ratification of international treaties, fifty thousand voters or five regional councils may require a referendum on the abrogation of a law or act with the force of law. For such a measure to be approved in a referendum, a majority of registered voters must vote and it must receive a majority of the votes cast.

In addition to legislative and investigating powers, the parliament annually passes the state budget and financial balance. Other powers include approving, in exceptional cases, government decrees with the force of law, deciding on a state of war, and authorizing presidential pardons and amnesties. The parliament also oversees the government ministers and has the power to censure the government by a vote of no confidence. Since 1988 political party discipline has been enhanced in the parliament by the elimination of the secret ballot, which allowed some party members to bring down their own government. Even so, since 1968 no Italian parliament has served its full five-year term.

The Judiciary

Title 4, article 101, declares, "Justice is administered in the name of the people. Judges are subject only to the law." The Italian court system is divided into ordinary and administrative courts.

Ordinary courts have jurisdiction over civil, commercial, labor, and criminal matters. The high ordinary court, which hears appeals on questions of law, is the court of cassation; since all courts in Italy are national courts, although organized by regions, conformity of decisions is ensured. The ordinary court system is supervised by a supreme law council presided over by the president.

The judges of the administrative courts are part of the executive branch, as are the administrative law judges in the United States, but they must be graduates of an Italian law school, although not necessarily members of the bar. The highest administrative court authority is the council of state, which hears appeals and gives advisory opinions to the government ministers.

Constitutional Court

Pursuant to title 6, the constitutional court is composed of fifteen judges. One-third of them are appointed by the president, the legislature, and ordinary and administrative judges, respectively. The court has jurisdiction over the constitutionality of national and regional laws and acts having the force of law; conflicts among the branches of government, between the national government and regions, and among regions; and impeachment charges against the president, at which time the court is augmented by sixteen members drawn from a list prepared by the legislature of citizens eligible to be senators.

Amending the Constitution

Except for the republican system of government, the provisions of the Italian constitution may be changed by amendment or enactment of a constitutional law. Proposals must be passed by each house of the legislature in two successive votes with an interval of at least three months; an absolute majority of members is required on the second vote in each house. Three months after publication the proposal is submitted to a referendum if so requested by one-fifth of the members of a house of the legislature, by "fifty hundred thousand" voters, or by five regional councils. A law submitted to a referendum cannot be promulgated unless approved by a two-thirds majority, and a referendum cannot be held if the proposal was approved by a two-thirds majority of the members in each house at the second vote.

JAPAN

With the Meiji constitution of 1889, Japan became the first constitutional state in Asia. An extensive revision of the constitution, including a "no-war" clause, was drafted initially by the staff of the U.S. occupation forces in 1947.

General Information

Approximately 372,000 square kilometers in area, Japan consists of four major islands lying off the east coast of Asia. The country is bounded on the south by the East China Sea, on the east by the Pacific Ocean, on the north by La Pérouse Strait between the northern island of Hokkaido and the Russian island of Sakhalin, and on the west by the Sea of Japan. The capital of this country of 127 million inhabitants is Tokyo, which has a population of approximately ten million persons.

An economically dynamic country with few natural resources, Japan enjoys one of the highest per capita incomes in the world. Major catastrophes aside, there is every reason to believe that the country's economic growth and political stability will continue, even though the increasing average age of the population may be a cause for some concern.

Type of Government: Parliamentary constitutional monarchy, with a monarch, as head of state, a prime minister and cabinet, a bicameral legislature, and a judiciary

Date of Constitution: 1889 (rewritten in 1947)

Constitutional History

Human activity in Japan goes back more than thirty thousand years, when the islands were connected by glaciers to the Asian mainland. People from around the eastern Pacific rim came later, and there remains today a small population of native Caucasians, the Ainu, living on reservations on the northern island of Hokkaido. The ancestors of the Japanese came primarily from the area extending from northeast China through Korea.

The Japanese society that developed after the beginning of the Christian era was influenced by the Korean and Chinese cultures. Because of the abundance of fresh water, no large central authority was needed to implement water control projects, as in China, and local settlements were able to develop independently. Buddhism, introduced from Korea, and Chinese Confucianism had an impact on society and government. In A.D. 603 efforts were made to centralize the government, and in 604 a seventeen-article "constitution" based on these sources was adopted. Chinese writing was imported and modified to represent actual sounds in the Japanese language.

Toward the end of the eighth century the capital was moved from Nara to what is now Kyoto, and the monarchy started reckoning its beginnings from the seventh century B.C. In the twelfth century A.D. the emperor appointed the first shogun, a sort of generalissimo, and the shogunate began running the country. During the following century the shogunate, with the help of typhoons, twice defeated attempted Mongol invasions. A strong central government proved difficult to maintain, and by the sixteenth century warfare had broken out among the *daimyos* (feudal lords).

The first contact with Europeans came in 1543 with Portuguese traders, whose matchlock muskets were soon copied. The added firepower fueled a rapid reunification under the Tokugawa shogunate, named the Edo period after its capital, now Tokyo; it lasted from the beginning of the seventeenth century until the Meiji Restoration in 1868. During the Edo period the shogunate monopolized trade with Holland and China, from which books were imported. Some of the books described the U.S. congress and the British parliament. When a shogunate mission to the United States attended a session of congress in 1860, the head of the mission compared all the activity to that of a Japanese fish market.

Nevertheless, constitutionalism came to Japan. With the apparent restoration of imperial power in 1868, a number of radical reforms were undertaken, including promulgation of the Meiji constitution on February 11, 1889. An imperial diet (parliament) was created with a house of peers, like the house of lords in Britain, and an elected house of representatives. *Kensei* (constitutional or parliamentary politics) did not come naturally to the Japanese, but for a while it worked. At first, the illusion of imperial rule was masked by an oligarchy, which actually ran the government, but its power waned. The void was quickly filled by the military, and in 1940 political parties were abolished. The army refused to accede to the United States's demand for the withdrawal of troops that had occupied parts of China and Indochina. When the army minister, Hideki Tojo, became prime minister in October 1941, war with the United States and its allies was inevitable.

After World War II Japan was placed under the administration of the Allied powers, headed by Gen. Douglas MacArthur. The Potsdam Proclamation of July 26, 1945, set the broad outline for Japan's unconditional surrender, including the requirement that the Japanese people be given the right to decide their future form of government. The American policy was demanding yet flexible enough to allow for a drastic revision or rewriting of the 1889 constitution, keeping the parliamentary form of government the Japanese were accustomed to. The two basic changes required were the transfer of sovereignty from the emperor to the people and the supremacy of the elected lower house of the parliament, as in Britain. The current constitution, which is technically an amendment to the 1889 constitution, was promulgated on November 3, 1946, and went into effect on May 3, 1947. As yet, there have been no amendments to it.

Influences

The Prussian constitution was considered during the initial drafting in 1889, but the British parliamentary system had the greatest impact. The influence of the United States after World War II can be seen particularly in the judicial system.

The Constitution

The preamble to the constitution of Japan specifically states the intent to never again ". . . be visited with the horrors of war through the action of government. . . ." Chapter 2, Renunciation of War, contains only article 9:

Aspiring sincerely to an international peace based on justice and order, the Japanese people forever renounce war as a sovereign right of the nation and the threat or use of force as a means of settling international disputes.

In order to accomplish the aim of the preceding paragraph, land, sea, and air forces, as well as other war potential, will never be maintained. The right of belligerency of the state will not be recognized.

This language, however, has not precluded a "self-defense force" of about a quarter of a million troops.

Article 98 asserts the supremacy of the constitution over any other law or act of government, and article 99 requires the emperor and all other public officials to respect and uphold the constitution.

Fundamental Rights

Chapter 3, Rights and Duties of the People, sets forth the basic rights and freedoms guaranteed "as eternal and inviolate" to the people. They include life, liberty, and the pursuit of happiness; equality under the law; universal suffrage, the secret ballot, and the right to choose public officials; peaceful petition for redress of grievance and redress for illegal acts of public officials; and freedom of thought, conscience, religion, assembly, speech, and the press. Bondage, involuntary servitude, and unwarranted search and seizure are prohibited. All people have the right to maintain a minimum standard of wholesome and cultured living; receive an equal education; work, as well as having the obligation to work; organize and collectively bargain; and own and hold property. The rights of accused persons are enumerated also.

Article 24 requires that a marriage be based on the consent of both sexes and guarantees equal rights for both husband and wife. Laws regarding property rights, choice of domicile, marriage, and the family are to be enacted "from the standpoint of individual dignity and the essential equality of the sexes."

Duties include paying taxes and complying with compulsory educational requirements.

Division of Powers

The law establishing the Meiji government in 1868 divided state power among the legislature, the administration, and the judiciary. The current constitution follows the traditional parliamentary system of the division of power in a unitary state, except that there is a supremacy clause and the courts exercise judicial review.

The Executive

Monarch. Chapter 1 provides that the emperor is the symbol of the state and the unity of the people. Succession is determined by law. The advice and approval of the cabinet are required for all acts of the emperor in matters of state. The emperor's duties, such as promulgating the laws, convoking the legislature, and attesting the appointments and dismissals of ministers, are purely ceremonial.

Prime Minister and Cabinet. According to article 72 the prime minister, representing the cabinet, submits bills, reports to the legislature on general national and foreign affairs, and supervises the administrative departments of government. The prime minister appoints the ministers of state, a majority of whom must be members of the legislature.

Chapter 5, article 65, the Cabinet, vests executive power in the cabinet, which, according to article 66, consists of a prime minister as its head and other ministers of state, who must be civilians. Collectively, the cabinet is responsible to the legislature, which, by resolution, designates the prime minister from among its own members. The cabinet, in addition to performing general administrative duties, administers the laws and conducts affairs of state; manages foreign affairs; concludes treaties approved by the legislature; administers the civil service in accordance with law; prepares and submits the budget; issues orders to implement the constitution and the laws; and decides on matters of amnesty, commutation of sentences, reprieves, and the restoration of rights. The entire cabinet resigns if it loses the confidence of the lower house of the legislature.

The Legislature

Parliament. The Japanese diet, the Kokkai, is the highest organ of state power and the sole law-making body. It consists of two houses: the upper house is the Sangiin (house of councilors), and the lower house is the Shugiin (house of representatives).

Upper House. The house of councilors has 252 members, of which 152 are elected from the prefectures and the rest from the country at large. They must be Japanese and at least thirty years old. They are elected for six-year terms, half of them every three years. The Sangiin's role is overshadowed to a great extent by the lower house.

Lower House. The house of representatives has 511 members from 129 electoral districts. They must be Japanese and at least twenty-five years old, and they are elected for a maximum of four years. From three to five members are elected from each district, so that while each voter has only one vote, minority party candidates have a chance of being elected. Electoral districts and the method of voting and electing members of both houses are determined by law.

A bill generally becomes law when passed by both houses. The budget, which must be introduced in the lower house, may be passed by that house; if the upper house fails to act within thirty days, the bill will, nevertheless, become law. This also applies to approval of treaties. In addition to enacting laws and approving the budget and treaties, the diet is authorized to initiate amendments to the constitution, designate the prime minister, investigate government affairs, require the presence of any minister to give explanations and answer questions, and implement impeachment proceedings for the removal of judges.

Sessions of the diet must be called at least once a year. The cabinet or one-fourth of the members of either house may demand an extraordinary session. One-third of all members of each house constitute a quorum, and matters are passed by a majority vote. Each house selects a president and other officers and establishes its own rules. Members of both houses are "exempt from apprehension" for possible wrongdoing during a session.

Article 76 delineates the role of the judiciary: **The Judiciary**

The whole judicial power is vested in a supreme court and in such inferior courts as are established by law.

No extraordinary tribunal shall be established, nor shall any organ or agency of the executive be given final judicial power.

All judges are to be independent in the exercise of their conscience and bound only by the constitution and the laws.

The 1947 reforms were most extensive with respect to the Japanese judiciary. Under the 1889 constitution, administrative cases were handled by the executive branch, not the judicial branch.

Supreme Court. The supreme court is given authority to make rules for the entire legal system, including the practice of law, internal discipline of the courts, and the administration of judicial affairs.

The judges on the supreme court are appointed by the cabinet, except that the chief judge is designated by the cabinet and appointed by the monarch. Judges of inferior courts are also appointed by the cabinet from nominations made by the supreme court. The appointments, according to the constitution, are to be reviewed by the electorate at the first election after an appointment and every ten years thereafter. As of the early 1990s, no judge had been dismissed in this manner.

The influence of the American legal system is reflected in the focus on judicial independence and guardianship of fundamental rights. Article 81 provides that the supreme court is the final authority on the constitutionality of any law, order, regulation, or official act, and it has ruled that the lower courts may also decide constitutional questions. As in the United States, the Japanese courts have tended to refrain from making decisions with regard to highly political matters, leaving such decisions to the other branches of government and ultimately to the political wisdom of the people. The courts, however, have not shirked from making decisions in administrative cases involving constitutional rights.

Article 96 provides that amendments are to be initiated by a two-thirds vote of the members of each house of the parliament and then submitted to the people for approval by a majority of all votes cast. **Amending the Constitution**

JORDAN

Despite Jordan's inhospitable location and lack of domestic economic resources, its long-time king and its constitution helped maintain the country's stability for more than forty years in an area of the world not known for peaceful coexistence.

General Information

The Hashemite Kingdom of Jordan is approximately 89,200 square kilometers and lies on the eastern side of the Jordan River across from Israel to the west. It is bounded by Syria on the north, Iraq on the east, and Saudi Arabia on the south and has an outlet on the Gulf of Aqaba north of the Red Sea. Amman is the capital of this country of nearly five million persons.

Formerly a land of seminomadic people, Jordan has no significant oil deposits. The country's economy has survived by rescheduling foreign debts, taking austere economic measures, and obtaining aid from richer Arab nations.

Type of Government: Parliamentary constitutional monarchy, with a monarch, a prime minister and council of ministers (cabinet), a bicameral legislature, a judiciary, and a high tribunal

Date of Constitution: 1952

Constitutional History

Some four thousand years ago Semitic Arabs settled in Canaan around the Jordan River. A succession of invasions followed, beginning with the Hittites, Egyptians, and Israelites and ending with the Ottoman Turks, who ruled from the sixteenth century A.D. until the Great Arab Revolt in 1916. Although an Arab government in Damascus claimed sovereignty over the territory, the British divided it into three parts to further their goal of a Jewish homeland in Palestine.

The San Remo Conference in 1920 created a French mandate in Syria and Lebanon and a British mandate in Iraq, Palestine, and Jordan. The British established the semiautonomous Emirate of TransJordan under the rule of Prince Abdullah Ibn Al-Hussein, a descendant of the founder of the Islamic religion and thus a Hashemite. On May 22, 1946, TransJordan became independent, and three days later Abdullah proclaimed himself king.

Abdullah was assassinated in 1951, and after a period of regency his grandson, Hussein Ibn Talal Al-Hashimi, became king in 1953, when he was eighteen years old. Under the constitution promulgated in January 1952, the king retained significant power. A supporter of Arab causes and of Saddam Hussein in Iraq, Jordan lost the West Bank to Israel after the 1967 war and remained under martial law until 1992; during this time the king, who often faced internal political unrest, imposed restrictions on freedoms such as speech and the press.

In 1990, however, political leaders signed a "national charter" that restored multiparty democracy and reaffirmed allegiance to the king. The charter, while reemphasizing the Islamic nature of the state, clearly seeks to promote the rule of law and political pluralism.

Influences

The Jordanian constitution has been influenced by Islamic and European law, particularly English common law.

The Constitution

Chapter 1, the State and System of Government, declares that the people of Jordan form a part of the Arab nation, that Islam is the state religion, and that Arabic is the official language.

Fundamental Rights

Chapter 2, Rights and Duties of Jordanians, provides that Jordanians shall be equal before the law; there shall be no discrimination on the basis of race, language, or religion; to the extent possible, the government shall ensure work and education; personal freedom is guaranteed; no person shall be imprisoned or detained or forced to reside in a specific place, except in accordance with law; dwellings are inviolable; and no loans will be forcibly imposed or property confiscated, except in accordance with the law.

Other freedoms, which may be limited by law, include freedom of worship, opinion, expression, the press, assembly, petition of grievances, and communication. Before martial law was lifted in 1992, freedom of the press was limited; later in 1992 the legislature approved measures again restricting freedom of the press.

The constitution of Jordan, a unitary state, divides power among the monarch, the legislature, the courts, and the high tribunal, which exercises some powers of constitutional review. In fact, however, the monarch and the heir apparent, his younger brother, keep a tight rein on all the powers of government.

Division of Powers

Monarch. Article 26 delineates the monarch's role: "The executive power shall be vested in the king, who shall exercise his powers through his ministers in accordance with the provisions of the present constitution."

The Executive

The Jordanian monarchy is hereditary. If the king is unable to exercise his powers or wishes to leave the country, a viceregent or council of viceregents acts for him. If he is incapacitated by mental illness, the legislature may depose him by resolution.

As head of state, the king is immune from any liability or responsibility. His powers and duties include ratifying and promulgating the laws; declaring war, concluding peace, and ratifying treaties, except that treaties involving financial commitments or the private rights of citizens must be approved by the legislature; calling for elections; convening and closing the legislative sessions; dissolving either of the two chambers of the legislature; appointing and dismissing the prime minister and other ministers on the recommendation of the prime minister; appointing members of the senate and its speaker; creating and conferring civil and military rank, medals, and honors; and granting pardons and remitting sentences. Every decree of the king must be countersigned by the prime minister and other appropriate ministers.

Prime Minister and Cabinet. The cabinet, called the council of ministers, is entrusted with administering the internal and external affairs of state, with some exceptions; its president is the prime minister. The ministers' duties are defined by their own regulations as ratified by the king. Article 49 states that "verbal or written orders of the king shall not relieve the ministers from their responsibilities." The prime minister and ministers are collectively responsible to the elected chamber of the legislature for the public policy of the state, and ministers are individually responsible to that body for the activities of their ministries.

Parliament. According to article 25, "The legislative power is vested in the national assembly [Majlis al-'Umma] and the king. The national assembly shall consist of a senate and a chamber of deputies."

The Legislature

Upper House. Senators are appointed to four-year terms by the monarch, who also appoints one of them to be speaker for a two-year term; the speaker has the power to dissolve the senate. Senators, who must be at least forty years old, are to be appointed from among those who have "the confidence of the people in view of the services rendered by them to the nation and the country"; these include, for example, present and former prime ministers and former ambassadors. The constitution limits the size of the senate to no more than one-half of the members of the elected chamber.

Lower House. Members of the chamber of deputies are elected by secret ballot in direct elections for four-year terms. The monarch may extend the term for between one and two years, or he may dissolve it earlier, as he did in 1974 and 1988. The chamber elects its own speaker every year.

To be a member of the lower house, a person must be thirty years old. As is also the case with senators, he or she must be a Jordanian, must not claim foreign nationality or protection, must have been legally discharged if adjudged bankrupt, must not be insane or an imbecile, and must not be closely related to the monarch, among other requirements.

Each house may make its own rules of procedure, which must be submitted to the monarch for ratification. An initial quorum is two-thirds of the members of either house, but business may continue as long as there is an absolute majority.

Draft laws of the government begin in the chamber of deputies, but to become law a measure must be passed by both houses and ratified by the monarch. A bill rejected twice by one house may be passed by a two-thirds majority vote of both houses in joint session. If the monarch returns a bill unratified, it will still be promulgated if passed a second time by a two-thirds vote in each house. Resolutions are passed by a majority vote, and the speaker may not vote except in the case of a tie.

Members of the legislature have the right of interpellation. Votes of no confidence or on the constitution itself "shall be taken by calling the name of members in a loud voice."

The Judiciary

According to article 27, "The judicial power shall be exercised by the courts of law in their varying types and degrees. All judgments shall be given in accordance with the law and pronounced in the name of the king."

Three categories of courts are created by the constitution: civil, religious, and special. The Jordanian legal system has its roots in both European and Islamic law *(shari'a)*. The civil courts have jurisdiction over both civil and criminal matters, and the religious courts have jurisdiction over matters of personal status where the parties are Muslims and over "cases concerning blood money" where the two parties are Muslims or one is non-Muslim but the parties consent to the religious courts' jurisdiction.

Judges are appointed by the king to the civil and religious courts. "Judges are independent," article 97 states, "and in the exercise of their judicial functions they are subject to no authority other than that of the law."

High Tribunal

A high tribunal established to try impeachments of ministers is also authorized to interpret the constitution at the request of the cabinet or an absolute majority of either house of the legislature. The tribunal consists of the head of the upper house of the legislature as president, three members from that body selected by secret ballot, and five members from the most senior judges of the highest civil court.

Special Tribunal

Article 123 establishes a special tribunal that on the request of the prime minister may interpret any law that has not been interpreted by a court. The tribunal's decisions are published in the official gazette and have the force of law.

Amending the Constitution

Article 126 provides that the same procedure for draft laws applies to draft constitutional amendments, except that an amendment requires approval by a two-thirds majority of the members of either house—or, in the case of a joint session, both houses—as well as the monarch's ratification for approval. During a period of regency, however, no amendment affecting the rights of the monarch may be passed.

For many, Kenya and its capital, Nairobi, conjure up the essence of Africa, but the country is currently struggling to maintain a stable democracy under a constitution amended in 1991 to permit multiparty elections.

The Republic of Kenya in eastern Africa is nearly 583,000 square kilometers and is bounded by Somalia and the Indian Ocean on the east, Tanzania on the south, Lake Victoria and Uganda on the west, and Sudan and Ethiopia on the north. Nairobi is the capital of this country of more than thirty million inhabitants.

Kenya, which has few natural resources, has relied on agricultural products such as coffee and tea for export. A large external debt, high rate of population growth, and a corrupt, repressive regime have dimmed prospects for prosperity.

Type of Government: Presidential-style parliamentary republic, with a president and cabinet, a unicameral legislature, and a judiciary

Dates of Constitutions: 1963 and 1964 (revised in 1969)

In Kenya evidence of probable human ancestors twenty million years old and of the extinct Australopithecine, who lived three million years ago, have been found in the Rift Valley and Lake Turkana, respectively. Cushitic-speaking people arrived during the third millennium B.C., when the climate turned drier, and coexisted with the Negroid and Bushmanoid inhabitants of the Rift Valley. Around A.D. 1000 new Negroid groups introduced agriculture and iron working.

Today people speaking Bantu, Cushitic, and Nilotic languages are found in Kenya. The nation's largest ethnic group is the Kikuyu; other groups include the Gumba and Athi. The coast of Kenya, with its port cities of Mombassa and Malindi, was visited by Greeks, Arabs, Persians, and then Chinese merchants from the first to the fifteenth centuries. Arab families migrated to East Africa, and in 1498 Vasco da Gama initiated two hundred years of Portuguese influence by establishing friendly relations with the sultanate of Malindi. Omani forces drove out the Portuguese at the end of the seventeenth century.

After 1880 German and British interest in East Africa increased. Karl Peters, founder of the German Colonizing Society, began acquiring land through treaties with local rulers, including territory on Kenya's northern coast. A joint British-German commission in 1886 determined the border between the two European countries' spheres of influence at roughly the present boundary between Kenya and Tanzania, except for the coast, which went to the sultan of Zanzibar.

Kenya became a British protectorate in 1895 and beginning in 1907 was administered by a governor with a legislative council that included two appointed representatives of the European settlers. Asians and Indians in Kenya greatly outnumbered the Europeans, but neither they nor the Africans were included on the council. In 1919 the council was expanded to include thirty members, including eleven elected Europeans, one Arab, and two Indians.

Mau Maus, members of a secret society consisting predominantly of Kikuyus, used terrorism between 1952 and 1956 to try to expel European settlers. In 1957 for the first time Africans were nominated for the legislative council and took part in elections, eight of them winning seats. The number increased in the elections of 1961, the year the country gained control of its internal affairs. In 1962 an "independence" constitution was drafted by African Kenyans and British representatives, and, following elections based on this document, self-government was achieved on June 1, 1963. After the constitution became effective, Kenya was accorded dominion status in the British Commonwealth on December 12, 1963. One year later Kenya became an independent republic under a new constitution providing for a central government and a president as head of state.

A 1966 amendment combined the former senate and house of representatives into a unicameral body. In April 1969 the Kenyan legislature revised the constitution. Further amendment in 1991 permitted multiparty balloting.

The Kenyan constitution was originally based on the British parliamentary system, but changes have significantly increased the power of the president.

The Constitution

"The Republic of Kenya," according to section 1A of the document, "shall be a multiparty democratic state." section 3 declares the constitution's supremacy: "This constitution is the constitution of the Republic of Kenya and shall have the force of law throughout Kenya and, subject to [the amendment procedures], if any other law is inconsistent with this constitution, this constitution shall prevail and the other law shall, to the extent of the inconsistency, be void."

Fundamental Rights

Section 70, chapter 5, Protection of Fundamental Rights and Freedoms of the Individual, provides that rights and freedoms are subject to limitations designed to ensure that their enjoyment by any individual does not prejudice the rights and freedoms of others or the public interest.

Rights and freedoms extended by the constitution, regardless of race, tribe, place of origin, residence, or other local connection, political opinions, color, creed, or sex, and subject to the limitations noted earlier, include the right to life and personal liberty; protection from slavery, forced labor, inhumane treatment, deprivation of property, and arbitrary search or entry; protection of law for those charged with a criminal offense; and freedom of conscience, expression, assembly, association, and movement.

Section 84 provides for enforcement of these rights, including application to the high court for redress. In recent years, however, Kenya's human rights record has been criticized.

Division of Powers

In Kenya, a unitary state, power is divided among the president, as head of state and government; the legislature; and the courts, which have judicial review authority.

The Executive

President. According to section 4, the president of Kenya is head of state and commander in chief of the armed forces. He or she is elected for a term of five years after the dissolution of the legislature in a general election; in addition to having a majority of the votes, a candidate must also receive twenty-five percent of the vote in at least five of the eight provinces. To be eligible to be president a person must be a citizen, at least thirty-five years old, and a registered voter in some constituency. Candidates must be nominated by parties participating in the general election.

The constitution provides details on elections of the president and the incumbent's authority to appoint a vice president as his or her principal assistant to act as president when the office is vacant; to appoint, in writing, the vice president to act during the president's absence or in the case of illness or any other cause; removal of the president on the grounds of incapacity; the president's salary and allowances as well as privileges and immunities; and the duties of and restrictions on the vice president.

Section 23 provides that the executive authority is vested in the president but that the legislature may confer functions on other persons and authorities. Section 24 adds other responsibilities: "Subject to this constitution and any other law, the powers of constituting and abolishing offices for the Republic of Kenya, of making appointments to any such office, and terminating any such appointment shall vest in the president." By a controversial amendment in 1988 the president was given the right to dismiss judges summarily. The president is also specifically authorized to grant pardons and commute sentences; and there is an advisory committee on the prerogative of mercy.

Cabinet. Section 16 authorizes the legislature or the president to establish the offices of the government ministers subject to any legislative provisions.

The Legislature

Parliament. According to section 30, "The legislative power of the republic shall vest in the parliament of Kenya, which shall consist of the president and the national assembly." The unicameral parliament is elected by universal suffrage for five-year terms; twelve members are appointed by the president. The attorney general is an ex officio member but cannot vote on any question.

To be a member of the assembly a person must be a citizen, twenty-one years old, registered in a constituency, able to speak and read "the Swahili and English languages" well enough to take an active part in the assembly's proceedings, and nominated by a political party. Disqualifications are detailed in section 35.

A speaker and a deputy are elected from among the members—excluding the president, vice president, ministers, assistant ministers, and the attorney general—or from among those qualified to be elected to the assembly. The speaker is defined as an ex officio member of the assembly, whether chosen from among the elected members or not.

After it is passed by the assembly and presented to the president for assent, a bill becomes law once it is officially published either prospectively or retrospectively, unless otherwise stated in the law. Money bills cannot be acted on except when recommended by the president and a minister.

The Judiciary

High Court. Section 60(1) establishes a "high court, which shall be a superior court of record and which shall have unlimited original jurisdiction in civil and criminal matters and such other jurisdiction and powers as may be conferred on it by this constitution or any other law."

The number of judges, exclusive of the chief justice, is to be prescribed by the legislature. The chief justice is appointed by the president; the other judges are also appointed by the president in accordance with the advice of a judicial service commission, which consists of the chief justice as chairman, the attorney general, and two judges from the high court or a court of appeal.

According to section 67(1), "Where any question as to the interpretation of this constitution arises in any proceeding in any subordinate court and the court is of the opinion that the question involves a substantial question of law, the court may, and shall if any party to the proceeding so requests, refer the question to the high court."

The legislature is authorized to establish courts subordinate to the high court and courts-martial as well as a chief *kadhi* and *kadhis'* courts when all parties profess the Islamic religion; the latter have jurisdiction under Islamic law over such matters as personal status, marriage, divorce, and inheritance.

Amending the Constitution

A bill to amend the constitution must be passed on the second and third readings by a favorable vote of at least sixty-five percent of all members of the legislature, excluding ex officio members. Such a bill may be reconsidered if it was passed by a majority but less than sixty-five percent of the members and it was not opposed by at least thirty-five percent of the members. No alteration may be made to a bill for amendment, unless certified by the speaker to be required technically because of the lapse of time between the bill's introduction and its presentation to the president.

KUWAIT

The 1962 constitution of Kuwait, the victim of aggression by neighboring Iraq in 1990, attempts to bring constitutional democracy to a small, wealthy nation traditionally ruled by a single dominant family.

General Information

The State of Kuwait is approximately 18,000 square kilometers and is located in the northwestern corner of the Arabian Peninsula, south of Iraq and north of eastern Saudi Arabia; the Persian Gulf lies along its eastern shore. Kuwait is a country of approximately two million inhabitants, many of whom are foreigners working there, and its capital is Kuwait City on the Persian Gulf.

By 1953 Kuwait had become the world's second largest oil exporter. For most of the country's preceding two hundred years, Kuwaitis were engaged in harvesting pearls, nomadic herding, and trading by sea.

Type of Government: Parliamentary constitutional monarchy, with a monarch, a prime minister and council of ministers (cabinet), a unicameral legislature, and a judiciary

Date of Constitution: 1962

Constitutional History

The pre-Islamic history of the territory of Kuwait ("little fort") dates from around 5000 B.C., the time of the earliest human civilization in Mesopotamia, just to the north. The interior of the Arabian Peninsula, while fertile enough for some agriculture and herding until about 3000 B.C., remained sparsely populated. Around the Persian Gulf, however, a seafaring trade developed that reached from Mesopotamia and Babylon to East Africa and Asia.

From the first through the third centuries A.D., the mostly tribal nomadic population of Arabia spread throughout the peninsula. Before the establishment of the Islamic religion, a distinction arose that has had a significant impact on politics in the Persian Gulf area. The southern Arabs, the Qahtani, consider themselves "pure," having descended from one line of Shem, a son of the biblical Noah, while the northern Arabs, the Adnani, are said to be descended from another line. Nobility, however, is based on families who can trace their lineage to the seventh century.

The historic tribal social structure involves identification with certain territory and male patrilineal relationships. Each group of descendants goes by the name of the family founder, preceded by *al* ("people of") or *bani* ("sons of"). Political leaders or learned religious leaders are called *shaykhs*, while *emir* (commander) is also used for a ruler or prince.

In the seventh century the Islamic religion spread to the Persian Gulf area by conquest, and soon Baghdad, in Iraq, became a religious and cultural center. The maritime activities in the gulf area increased, although the political organization of the maritime city-states continued to be based on the desert Arab model. The *shaykh* who ruled the dominant tribe was the town leader and often its most affluent merchant.

An unusually severe famine and drought in central Arabia in 1722 led to the migration of the Adnani-Anayzah confederation of tribes, including the Utub (also called Uteiba) tribe. In the mid-eighteenth century the Utub tribe founded Kuwait City on Kuwait Bay in the Persian Gulf. In 1756 the al-Subah family of Kuwait established the present line of rulers, who are selected from senior males in the extended family.

The al-Subah and the al-Khalifa of Qatar captured Bahrain in 1783, ending the Iranian influence in the area and gaining access to the best pearl beds in the gulf. As a small, poor country, Kuwait escaped conquest and direct rule by the Ottoman Empire, but in the latter half of the nineteenth century the Kuwaiti ruler acknowledged the empire's power by paying tribute. His successor, Mubarak, however, feared the Ottoman threat and in 1899 allowed Britain to handle Kuwait's foreign affairs and protect the country.

Mubarek al-Subah's rule was autocratic, but tribal leaders were often consulted in a meeting called a *diwaniyya*. When the second of Mubarak's sons was ruler, he sided with the Ottomans in World War I, and the people demanded that a council of advisers be formed if he were to continue governing. Another call for reform in the late 1930s brought about a fourteen-member legislature composed of "commoners." But when it sought to have more of the country's oil revenues diverted to public needs, it was dissolved and its members were imprisoned. A legislative council was installed in its place, and a number of government departments, run personally by members of the al-Subah, were created. These became the model for a more modern government administration later.

On June 19, 1961, the agreement with the British ended, and Kuwait achieved full independence. Six days later Iraq claimed the territory of Kuwait, which immediately requested British military assistance. To promote national unity, leading merchants were asked to participate in the government, and an assembly was elected to draft a constitution, which was promulgated on November 11, 1962.

Kuwait, unlike most other Persian Gulf states, has a secular legal system. The constitution draws on both Western and Arab models, and Islamic law *(shari'a)* is the main source of legislation.

Influences

The Constitution

The preamble to the 1962 constitution of the State of Kuwait declares that it is "desirous of consummating the means of democratic rule for our dear country," and article 6 states in part that the "system of government in Kuwait shall be democratic, under which sovereignty resides in the people, the source of all powers." However, article 4 provides that Kuwait is a hereditary emirate and that successors to the emir are to be chosen from among the descendants of the late Mubarak al-Subah.

Fundamental Rights

Part 2, articles 7 through 26, Fundamental Constituents of the Kuwaiti Society, and part 3, articles 27 through 49, Public Rights and Duties, define the state's obligations and individual rights and freedoms, respectively.

The state's obligations include ensuring security, tranquillity, and equal opportunities for all citizens; preserving the integrity of the family; caring for and protecting the young; ensuring social services; safeguarding the heritage of Islam and the Arabs; and promoting education, science, the arts, and public health.

Article 16 asserts that "property, capital and work are fundamental constituents of the social structure of the state and of the national wealth. They are all individual rights with a social function as regulated by law." Inheritance is acknowledged as a right governed by Islamic law.

Public rights include freedom of movement; equality before the law without distinction as to race, origin, language, or religion; personal liberty and protections in criminal proceedings; prohibition against torture or degrading treatment; freedom of belief; and freedom of opinion, scientific research, expression, press communication, and association, "in accordance with the conditions and procedures specified by law." Individuals have the right to address grievances to public authorities, but only "duly constituted organizations and bodies corporate" may address them collectively. Women, however, did not yet have full political rights as of early 2001. Duties include serving in the armed forces, paying taxes, observing public order, and respecting public morals.

Division of Powers

Kuwait is a unitary state whose power is divided among the monarch, as head of state; the crown prince, as deputy ruler and prime minister; the legislature; and the courts, which have limited judicial review powers.

Monarch. Article 54 declares, "The emir is the head of state. His person shall be immune and inviolable," and article 55 notes that "the emir shall exercise his powers through his ministers." The monarch takes an oath before the legislature, swearing to respect the constitution. He appoints a deputy to act for him if he is out of the country and the heir apparent is not able to act on his behalf. The deputy must swear to "be loyal to the emir."

The monarch calls the legislature into session, announces the termination of sessions, and may dissolve the legislature by decree, in accordance with the provisions of article 107. He also may initiate, sanction, and promulgate laws and may demand that measures passed by the legislature be reconsidered.

The monarch serves as commander in chief of the armed forces; may declare a defensive war; concludes treaties (those that affect important aspects of the state such as territory, the public or private rights of citizens, or sovereignty must be enacted into law); in emergencies, issues decrees with the force of law when the legislature is not in session or dissolved; issues regulations for the execution of laws and the organization of public services and administration; appoints and dismisses civil and military officials and accepts the credentials of foreign representatives; grants pardons and commutes sentences; confers honors; and has coins minted in his name in accordance with law.

Since the death of Mubarak in 1915, successors as head of state have generally alternated between the descendants of his two sons, Jabir and Salim. One exception was made on the basis of seniority and competence and did not constitute a usurpation.

Prime Minister and Cabinet. The monarch appoints and dismisses the prime minister after "traditional consultation." The other ministers, who form the council of ministers (cabinet), are also appointed by the emir and must meet the same qualifications as members of the legislature; they become ex officio members of the legislature if they are not already members. The number of ministers may not be greater than one-third of the legislature's members.

According to article 123, the council of ministers is to have control over the departments of government, formulate general government policy, and "pursue its execution and supervise the conduct of work in the government departments." The ministers are individually and collectively responsible to the monarch.

Parliament. The Kuwaiti unicameral legislature is called the Majlis al-'Umma (national assembly). It is the first such elected legislative body on the Arabian Peninsula. The fifty members are elected for four-year terms "directly by universal suffrage and secret ballot." To be a member of the assembly a person must be a Kuwaiti as prescribed by law, must qualify as an elector, must be at least thirty years old, and must be able to read and write Arabic well.

According to article 79, "No law may be promulgated unless it has been passed by the national assembly and sanctioned by the emir." Article 87 requires the monarch to summon the assembly to meet within two weeks of the general election, but even if he does not, the constitution provides that the assembly be convened on the first day after the two-week period. At the first session a speaker and deputy speaker are elected from among the members by majority vote. The assembly is required to have an annual session for at least eight months. It may not end until the budget is approved.

Bills may be initiated in either the executive branch or the assembly and are approved by a simple majority, except for retroactive nonpenal laws, which require an absolute majority. Although the monarch's veto may be overridden by a two-thirds vote in the same session, this is unlikely to happen because of the assembly members' strong support for the ruling family. A bill vetoed and then passed again by a majority vote in the following year's session will also become law.

The assembly determines its own procedures. Article 115 directs it to establish standing committees and "a special committee to deal with petitions and complaints" by citizens. This committee seeks information from the proper authorities and informs citizens of the result, as individual members of the U.S. congress do for their constituents.

Other powers of the assembly include seeking the government's clarification on general matters, investigating matters within its competence, requiring ministers and other officials to testify and produce documentation, and inviting ministers to be present whenever a matter under their jurisdiction is to be discussed.

Members enjoy immunity from legal process during sessions, except when caught in flagrante delicto or authorized by the assembly. Article 118 prohibits armed forces from entering or being stationed near the gates of the assembly unless so requested by the presiding officer. Article 181 ensures that neither the assembly's functioning nor the members' immunities may be interfered with even under martial law.

The Judiciary

Chapter 5, article 162, Judicial Power, declares that "the honor of the judiciary and the integrity and impartiality of judges are the bases of rule and a guarantee of rights and liberties." Article 163 reinforces the principle of an independent judiciary.

The constitutional basis for the Kuwaiti judicial system is derived from those in Egypt, Iraq, and Bahrain. French and British influences came from Egypt and Bahrain, respectively. The civil code of the Ottoman Empire and Islamic law, particularly in the areas of civil and personal status law, have also influenced the legal system.

Supreme Council. The supreme council is the highest judicial body to be regulated and given jurisdiction by law. It is to oversee the judiciary and be a guarantor of judicial independence.

Supreme Court of Appeal. Beneath the supreme council is a supreme court of appeal, which hears appeals from a high court of appeal and rules on the constitutionality of laws. Article 173 expressly states that "if the said body decides that a law or regulation is unconstitutional it shall be considered null and void." The monarch, however, is the final source of appeal and pardon and reviews all convictions for capital offenses.

Amending the Constitution

According to article 174, the emir or one-third of the members of the legislature may propose an amendment to the constitution. If the principle of a proposed amendment is approved by the monarch and a majority of the members, the proposal is debated article by article. The revision comes into force after being approved by a two-thirds majority vote by the legislature and sanctioned and promulgated by the emir, regardless of other constitutional provisions concerning ordinary laws. Article 175 prohibits amending the "emiri system in Kuwait," except as to the title of the emirate, or the principles of liberty and equality, except to increase them. "The powers of the emir specified in this constitution," article 176 states, "may not be proposed for revision when a deputy emir is acting for him."

LAOS

After gaining full independence in 1953, Laos became closely associated with Vietnam and the Vietnam War. The communist-dominated government dating from 1975 waited fifteen years before drafting and finally promulgating a constitution in 1991 that endorsed single-party leadership and Marxist-Leninist principles rather than multiparty democracy.

General Information

The Lao People's Democratic Republic on the Indochina Peninsula occupies some 234,800 square kilometers and is bounded on the north by China, on the northeast and east by Vietnam, on the south by Cambodia, and on the west by Thailand and Burma. Vientiane is the capital of this country of approximately 5.5 million inhabitants.

Major industries include wood products, mining, and electrical power; among its chief agricultural products are sweet potatoes, cotton, and coffee. The economy of Laos, one of the poorest nations in the world, suffered from the economic crisis in Thailand in 1997, the same year Laos was admitted into the Association of Southeast Asian Nations (ASEAN).

Type of Government: Communist Party dictatorship, with a presidential-style parliamentary government including a president, a prime minister and cabinet, a unicameral legislature, and a judiciary

Dates of Constitutions: 1945 (provisional), 1947, and 1991

Constitutional History

The first settlers of the region that would become Laos were Austroasiatic peoples. There is evidence of human habitation at least five thousand years ago and of a Bronze Age culture developing in the middle Mekong Valley around the first century B.C. Various political and religious power centers called *mandala* arose in the region, influenced by Indian culture and Buddhism. At the beginning of the eleventh century A.D., immigrants from the southwestern Chinese province of Yunnan—the Lao people—gradually extended their communities southward. The inhabitants of the Louangphrabang region established a large kingdom in the thirteenth century, but by the end of that century Thai rulers, with the support of the Mongols, had seized control in central Laos.

Lao recorded history begins with the reign of Fa Ngum, the ruler of the extensive kingdom of Lan Xang in the fourteenth century. Power struggles continued to embroil Laos for many years. In the eighteenth century the Lao people tried to defend their independence against both the Burmese and the Siamese (now Thai) people, only to succumb to the colonial rule of the French from 1893 to 1953. However, with few resources to exploit, remote Laos went relatively undeveloped by the French during the period of its administration of Indochina.

Territory given to the Thai by the Japanese was returned to Laos after World War II. Anti-French movements, some of which were communist oriented, then arose. The nationalist organization Lao Issara (Free Laos) formed a government under a provisional constitution on October 12, 1945. The following year a constitutional monarchy was proclaimed, and a monarchical constitution promulgated on May 11, 1947, declared Laos to be an independent state within the French union. But it would be October 22, 1953, before true independence would be achieved. Invasions by the Vietnamese in 1953 and 1954 were supported by the communist and procommunist party called the Pathet Lao, which was strongly influenced by the Vietnamese leader Ho Chi Minh. In September 1956 the constitution was amended to permit the formation of coalition governments.

The Vietnam War greatly affected Laos in the 1960s and 1970s. Afterward the Laotian monarchy was abolished and a communist-dominated government—the Lao People's Democratic Republic—was established on December 2, 1975. From then until the 1990s, Laos depended heavily on financial and military support from Vietnam.

It took fifteen years for the draft of a new constitution—not a high priority of the communist leaders—to be approved and circulated for discussion. Although the document was criticized for its failure to provide for multiparty contested elections, the Supreme People's Assembly of the Lao People's Democratic Republic adopted this constitution on August 15, 1991. Despite the constitution's Marxist-Leninist tenor, the country's economic system has evolved since then toward greater capitalism.

Influences

Paying no heed to the movement toward multiparty democracy in the Soviet Union and its Eastern European satellites, the drafters of the 1991 Lao constitution sought to continue the Communist Party's domination by including the Marxist-Leninist principle of "democratic centralism" as a means of determining the country's policies.

The Constitution

The preamble to the constitution harkens back six centuries to the time of the founding of "the unified Lan Xang country" and notes:

Over the past 60 years, under the correct leadership of the former Indochinese Communist Party and the present Lao People's Revolutionary Party, the multi-ethnic Lao people have carried out difficult and arduous struggles full of great sacrifices until they managed to crush the yokes of domination and oppression of the colonialists and feudalist regime, completely liberated the country, and established the Lao People's Democratic Republic on 2 December 1975, thus opening a new era—an era of genuine independence for the country and freedom for the people.

Article 1 proclaims: "The Lao People's Democratic Republic is an independent country with sovereignty and territorial integrity covering both territorial waters and airspace. It is a unified country belonging to all multi-ethnic people and is indivisible." According to article 2, "All powers are of the people, by the people and for the interests of the multi-ethnic people of all strata in society with the workers, farmers and intellectuals as key components." Article 3 provides that "[t]he rights of the multi-ethnic people to be the masters of the country are exercised and ensured through the functioning of the political system with the Lao People's Revolutionary Party as its leading nucleus."

Fundamental Rights

"The state protects the freedom and democratic rights of the people, which cannot be violated by anyone," declares article 6, adding: "All acts of bureaucratism and harassment that can be physically harmful to the people and detrimental to their honor, lives, consciences and property are prohibited." According to article 10, "The state manages the society by the provisions of the Constitution and laws. All party and state organizations, mass organizations, social organizations and all citizens must function within the bounds of the Constitution and laws."

Fundamental rights include equality before the law; the right to vote and be elected, "except insane persons and the persons whose rights to vote have been revoked by a court"; equal political, economic, cultural, social, and family rights of both sexes; and the rights to receive an education, to work, to lodge complaints, and "to believe or not to believe in religions." Citizens are also granted freedom of speech, the press, assembly, and "settlement and movement as prescribed by law," plus "the right to set up associations and to stage demonstrations which are not contrary to the law."

The constitution also notes that Laos "pursues the policy of promoting unity and equality among all ethnic groups," adding that

The state respects and protects all lawful activities of the Buddhists and of other religious followers; mobilizes and encourages the Buddhist monks and novices as well as the priests of other religions to participate in the activities which are beneficial to the country and people. All acts of creating division of religions and classes of people are prohibited.

The constitution further "grants asylum to foreigners who are persecuted for their struggle for freedom, justice, peace and scientific causes."

Social and economic rights outlined in articles 13 through 20 include improvement of "the material and spiritual living conditions of the multi-ethnic people," protection and expansion of "all forms of state, collective and individual ownership, as well as private ownership of domestic capitalists and foreigners who make investments in [Laos]," equality before the law for all economic sectors, state protection of "the right to ownership (rights to governing, rights to using, rights to transferring) and the rights to inherit property of organizations and individuals." The constitution also recognizes education, health care, traditional culture, mothers and children, and "the antiques and shrines of the nation."

Obligations of Laotian citizens include payment of taxes, observation of "labor discipline," defense of the country, and maintenance of "the people's security." Individuals and citizens are also called on in article 17 to "protect the environment and natural resources: land, underground, forests, fauna, water sources and atmosphere."

Division of Powers

According to article 39, the legislature, the national assembly, "has the right to make decisions on the fundamental issues of the country ... [and] supervises and oversees the activities of the administrative and judicial organizations." In fact, the communist Lao People's Revolutionary Party is the highest political authority in Laos.

The Executive

President. "The President of state is the head of state ... and the representative of the multi-ethnic Lao people both at home and abroad," declares article 52. The office holder promulgates "the Constitution and laws already endorsed by the National Assembly," issues "state decrees and state acts on the recommendation of the National Assembly Standing Committee," appoints and removes the prime minister and members of the government based on the assembly's actions, is the head of "the people's armed forces," presides over meetings of the government, grants pardons, declares "ratification or abolition of all treaties," and appoints and recalls "plenipotentiary representatives ... to or from foreign countries."

The president is "elected by the National Assembly with two-thirds of the votes of all members ... attending the session" for a five-year term of office. Article 55 authorizes the position of vice president, who is to "act on behalf of the President during his absence [and who is] elected by ... more than one-half of the total number of the National Assembly members attending the session."

Prime Minister and Cabinet. Pursuant to article 56, "The government is the administrative organization of the state. [It] manages in a unified manner the implementation of duties of state in all fields: political, economic, cultural, social, national defense and security, and foreign affairs." Under article 58, "The government consists of the Prime Minister, Deputy Prime Ministers, ministers and chairmen of the ministry-equivalent committees [whose] term of office ... is five years."

The prime minister is appointed by the president with the approval of the legislature, also for a five-year term. As head of government, the prime minister, among other duties, "supervises the work of the government; represents the government in guiding the work of ministries ... and other organizations ...; and guides the work of the governors of provinces and the mayors of municipalities."

The Legislature

"The National Assembly is the legislative organization," declares article 39. "It has the right to make decisions on the fundamental issues of the country. At the same time it is the organization which supervises and oversees the activities of the administrative and judicial organizations." Earlier in the constitution, article 4 describes the assembly as "the organization of the people's representatives. The election of members ... shall be carried out through the principles of universal, equal and direct suffrage, and secret balloting." Article 5 adds: "The National Assembly and all other state organizations are established and function in accordance with the principle of democratic centralism."

Assembly members are elected by Lao citizens for a term of five years. The legislature must convene at least twice a year and, according to article 47, "The questions related to the destiny of the country and the vital interests of the people must be submitted for approval of the National Assembly or [its] Standing Committee during the two sessions of the National Assembly." Under article 42, the assembly "elects its own Standing Committee which consists of the President, Vice-President and a number of members. The President and Vice-President of the National Assembly are also President and Vice-President of the National Assembly Standing Committee."

The national Assembly under article 40 has the authority to "establish, endorse or amend" the constitution; "consider, endorse, amend, or abrogate laws"; determine taxes and duties; approve "the strategic plans of socio-economic development and the budget of the state"; and elect or remove the president and vice president on the recommendation of the assembly's standing committee. Other powers and duties include "the appointment and removal of the members of the government" on the president's recommendation, the election and removal of the president of the supreme court and the public prosecutor-general on the recommendation of the standing committee, granting general amnesties, and deciding on the ratification and abolition of treaties.

A quorum for doing business in the assembly is more than half the total number of members; resolutions are generally valid only when they are voted for by more than half of the members present. Draft laws may be proposed by the president, the standing committee, the government, the supreme court, the prosecutor-general, and "mass organizations at the central level." Once adopted, laws "must be promulgated by the President of state not later than thirty days after their endorsement, [but] the President of state has the right to request the National Assembly to reconsider such laws. If the National Assembly affirms to adhere to its previous decision in reconsidering such laws, the President of state must promulgate them within fifteen days.

The Judiciary

"The People's Courts," states article 65, "are the judiciary organizations of the state comprising the People's Supreme Court, People's Provincial and Municipal Courts, People's District Courts and Military Courts." Judges are appointed or removed by the national assembly's standing committee. Under article 68, "The People's Courts make judgments and pass sentences collectively. During the trials, the judges are to be independent and subject only to the law." Article 70, however, provides that "[r]epresentatives of social organizations have the right to take part in court proceedings as provided by law."

Supreme Court. "The People's Supreme Court is the highest judiciary organization of the state," declares article 66. The court "scrutinizes the sentences reached by the people's local courts and the military courts." The president of the supreme court is "elected or removed" by the national assembly; the vice president is appointed or removed by the national assembly's standing committee.

Amending the Constitution

Article 80 sets out the procedure for amending the constitution: "Only the National Assembly of the Lao People's Democratic Republic has the right to amend the Constitution." An amendment requires the approval of at least two-thirds of the total number of the national assembly members.

LEBANON

Lebanon's unique, historical division of the national government on the basis of confessionalism—representation of the major religious factions—is reflected in elected as well as administrative positions in the government.

General Information

The Republic of Lebanon is approximately 10,400 square kilometers and is located on the east coast of the Mediterranean Sea, bounded by Syria on the north and east and Israel on the south. Beirut is the capital of this nation of some 3.6 million persons.

The 1975–76 civil war and subsequent destruction and neglect have crippled Lebanon's economy and created runaway inflation. Although steps were taken to reduce drug smuggling, alternative sources of economic production have not been fully realized, and as much as one-third of the rural population is destitute.

Type of Government: Presidential-style parliamentary republic, with a president, a prime minister and council of ministers (cabinet), a unicameral legislature, and a judiciary

Date of Constitution: 1926

Constitutional History

The Phoenicians, who inhabited the area of Lebanon beginning in the third millennium B.C. and whose name comes from the Greek word *phoenix* (purple), traded in purple dye and lumber from their renowned cedar trees. A series of invaders—the Hyksos, Egyptians, Hittites, Assyrians, Babylonians, Persians, Greeks, and Romans—left their mark, but the alphabet devised by the Phoenicians to facilitate trading left an even more indelible legacy.

In the fifth century A.D., a Syrian priest and hermit, Maron, established the Christian religious order of Maronites, whose followers later settled in the northern part of Lebanon. In the seventh century A.D. an Islamic splinter group, the Druze, settled in the southern part of the country. For more than three hundred years Lebanon avoided direct rule by the Ottoman Turks by paying them tribute collected from feudal landlords controlled by the emir, the chief feudal lord. In 1842, however, the country was partitioned into northern Maronite and southern Druze sectors, each administered by a *qaim maqam* (subgovernor) of their respective faiths.

The partitioning of Lebanon, which involved other religious subgroups, was based on the principle of confessionalism—that the relative political power of religious groups, or confessions, must be balanced or held in status quo. After two decades of relative calm, civil strife broke out. In 1861, through the Reglement Organique, an agreement among the major European powers and the Turks, Lebanon became an autonomous province of the Ottoman Empire, administered by a Christian governor and a twelve-member *majlis* (central administrative council).

During World War I Lebanon suffered under the harsh rule of the commander of the Turkish troops in Syria, which along with Lebanon was made a French mandate after the war; a constitution promulgated on May 23, 1926, gave the French high commissioner the ultimate government authority, with extensive constitutional powers. After a period under the Vichy French government, a Free France general declared the country independent in 1941, although independence did not come officially until November 22, 1943. The new government had been amending the constitution even before then, which so angered the French high commissioner that he suspended the constitution and ruled by martial law in the days before November 22.

Lebanon's laws today are derived from the laws of the Ottomans, French, and Muslims, as well as from canon law and laws enacted by the Lebanese legislature. The constitution was amended in 1990 to increase the legislature from ninety-nine to 100 members.

The 1926 constitution was influenced by the 1923 constitution of France, although the president was made relatively stronger and the legislature relatively weaker. It drew on principles from other constitutions, and the concept of confessionalism was grafted onto the system.

The Lebanese constitution, which has been amended often, converted the State of Great Lebanon into the Lebanese Republic, the first republic in the Arab world.

Chapter 2, the Lebanese and the Rights and Obligations of the Lebanese, contains a listing of rights based on France's 1789 Declaration of the Rights of Man and the Citizen and extends to all citizens equality before the law; personal freedom from arrest, except in accordance with the law; complete freedom of conscience and the exercise of all forms of worship; the inviolability of dwellings; and freedom of speech, writing, the press, assembly, and association, within the limits set by law. The rights of ownership of property are also guaranteed.

Lebanon is a unitary state. According to an unwritten 1943 national pact, power is divided on the basis of religion so that the president is a Maronite Christian, the prime minister a Sunni Muslim, and the speaker of the legislature a Shi'a Muslim. The legislature is also divided on the basis of religion. Secular and religious courts have no judicial review.

President. Article 17 delineates the president's role: "The executive power shall be entrusted to the president of the republic, by whom it shall be exercised with the assistance of the ministers, under conditions enumerated in the present constitution."

The president, who is head of state, is elected for a six-year term by secret ballot and by a two-thirds majority of the legislature on the first round of balloting and by a majority in later rounds. A person may be reelected only after an interim of six years. An unusual amendment in 1995 extended the then-president's term for three years; another in 1998 permitted a candidate to run for president who was constitutionally excluded from running because he had held a government position of a certain level within two years before the election. Eligibility for this office is the same as for membership in the legislature.

The duties and powers of the president include promulgating the laws adopted by the legislature and supervising their execution, by regulations if necessary; negotiating and ratifying treaties, informing the legislature only if the interests and safety of the nation permit (treaties involving a charge on the state, commercial treaties, or ones binding the nation for more than a year must be approved by the legislature); appointing and dismissing ministers and selecting the prime minister; and presiding over national ceremonies. The president may adjourn the legislature once a session for up to thirty days and, with the approval of the cabinet, may dissolve the legislature. The president may ask that a law be reconsidered by the legislature but must promulgate it if it is adopted on the second reading by an absolute majority of the members. All instruments signed by the president, except appointments and dismissals of ministers, must be countersigned by the minister or ministers concerned.

Except for treason or a violation of the constitution the president may not be held accountable for official acts but is responsible for ordinary violations of law. A vote of at least two-thirds of the members of the legislature is required to charge the president for official acts, and he or she must be tried by the high court as provided for in the constitution.

Prime Minister and Cabinet. The prime minister is selected by the president from among the ministers. The prime minister and other ministers make up the council of ministers (cabinet), which exercises executive power temporarily if the presidency becomes vacant for any reason. The ministers supervise their respective departments and are jointly and individually responsible to the legislature for the government's general policy.

The Legislature

Parliament. Article 16 provides that legislative power is to be exercised by a unicameral parliament called the Majlis al-'Umma (national assembly). Members of the assembly, formerly called the chamber of deputies, are elected by universal suffrage for four-year terms. Until 1990 the ratio of seats was six Christian seats for every five Muslim seats; now the ratio is one to one. The assembly is authorized to determine its own rules of procedure, and members are granted immunity from prosecution, except when they are caught in the act of committing a crime or if the assembly authorizes prosecution.

The assembly elects the president of the republic, reviews state revenues and expenditures, acts on the national budget, and oversees the government by calling on ministers to justify their actions or approving a vote of no confidence. It may withdraw its confidence from any minister, who must then resign, or may charge ministers with high treason or grave malfeasance.

Under article 19 a law must be adopted by the legislature before it can be promulgated. The assembly makes ordinary laws and urgent laws under its internal regulations. It may also grant authority to the executive branch to issue legislative decrees, as established by custom and tradition; these must, nevertheless, be presented to the legislature for ratification, amendment, or annulment. The president or any member of the assembly may initiate a bill for a law. A majority of all members constitute a quorum, and decisions generally require a majority vote to be approved.

The Judiciary

Article 20 states that judicial power is to be exercised by courts of various classes and degrees within limits established by law and that the limits and conditions of the exercise of that power and the independence of judges shall be fixed by law. There is no provision for review of the constitutionality of laws.

The judicial system of Lebanon is headed by four courts of cassation and includes, at the top, courts of appeal as well as numerous courts of first instance. The cassation courts have civil and criminal divisions composed of three judges each, one of whom is designated as the president. A "first president" presides over the whole court like a chief justice and is the chairman of the supreme judicial council, which is in charge of judicial personnel actions and training.

The court system has ordinary courts and exceptional courts such as religious courts for both Muslims and Christians; administrative courts, with a council of state having general jurisdiction over certain administrative cases; a labor court; and military courts, among others.

Amending the Constitution

The president, through the government, may submit amendment proposals to the legislature, and at least ten members, with the support of two-thirds of the legislature, may submit such proposals to the government. If the government does not agree with a proposal, it may be approved, nevertheless, by a three-fourths majority vote of the lawful legislative members, after which the president's only options are to accede to the proposal or dissolve the legislature and let the newly elected body decide the issue. To be finally approved, a bill embodying the proposed amendment must be passed at a session attended by at least two-thirds of the members of the legislature and receive a majority vote of two-thirds of the lawful members.

The current 1986 constitution of Liberia, Africa's oldest republic, differs little from its 1847 constitution, which was drafted by a Harvard Law School professor. The country's recent history, however, has been marred by civil war.

The Republic of Liberia on the west coast of Africa is 111,370 square kilometers and is bounded by Guinea on the north, Ivory Coast on the east, the Atlantic Ocean on the south, and Sierra Leone on the northwest. Monrovia is the capital of this country of more than three million persons.

Liberia's major resources include iron, diamonds, and gold; among its chief crops are rice and coffee. Civil unrest, support of rebels in Sierra Leone, and an invasion by Guinea in 1999 have created highly unstable conditions for democracy and economic development.

Type of Government: Presidential republic, with a president and cabinet, a bicameral legislature, and a judiciary

Dates of Constitutions: 1820, 1839, 1847, and 1986

The indigenous population before contact with Europeans in 1461 spoke languages derived from the Niger-Congo family of languages, and their largest social and political units were small chiefdoms. The Mandingo, well-organized Muslim traders and warriors whose homeland was farther to the north, nevertheless had a significant impact on the region. The Portuguese arrived on the coast first, to be supplanted later by the British and the French. Beginning in the eighteenth century, a secret society called the Poro brought together tribes in a common religious and judicial bond. Later, the Mandingo-led Kondo confederacy tried to build a state embracing a number of tribes.

Coastal tribes served as middlemen for the slave trade, selling slaves taken from the interior by the Mandingo and others. In 1691 the Virginia colonial legislature required slaveowners who freed slaves to provide transportation for them out of the colony. This, together with plantation owners' fear of rebellious slaves, led many, including Thomas Jefferson, to consider a colonizing plan for the freed and rebellious slaves. Britain prohibited the slave trade in 1807, and the United States did so a year later.

In Britain the courts had emancipated the slaves in 1772, and the government had aided Christian evangelicals and philanthropists in founding a self-governing colony for former slaves in Sierra Leone in 1787. The American Society for Colonizing the Free People of Color was founded in the United States in 1816 by Henry Clay, Daniel Webster, and Francis Scott Key, among others. In 1820, under the auspices of the U.S. government, eighty-eight freed American slaves sailed for Africa. While in transit, they drafted a constitutional document called the Elizabeth Compact, named for the ship, creating a structure of government for the future colony.

The first permanent settlement was at the future site of Monrovia, named for James Monroe, president of the United States. Executive authority was exercised by one of the agents of the society, which had acquired sixty miles of coastal land for goods valued at three hundred dollars. An agent held a court of general sessions monthly. In 1839 a commonwealth was formed, with a new constitution under which Thomas Buchanan, brother of the future president of the United States, James Buchanan, was made governor. He presided over a supreme court. A lieutenant governor and legislative body were elected by the settlers.

The British, however, did not recognize Liberia's sovereignty over the territory, which led to a declaration of independence in 1847 and a new constitution drafted by a Harvard law professor, Simon Greenleaf, president of the Massachusetts Colonizing Society. Similar to many U.S. state constitutions of the day, it was amended in 1907 to increase the president's term from two to four years; the lower house term similarly was increased and the upper house term was increased from four to six years. In 1935 the president's term was increased from four to eight years, and in 1949 the president was allowed to serve two consecutive eight-year terms followed by a four-year term. Finally, in 1974, the president's term was limited to a single eight-year term.

After a military coup in 1980, the constitution was suspended, and legislative and executive functions were exercised by a people's redemption council, which ruled by decree. A new constitution was approved by referendum on July 3, 1984, and went into effect with the inauguration of the president on January 6, 1986. After a four-year civil war a new, unified government took office on March 7, 1994.

Influences

The American presidential model, other national constitutions, and human rights documents such as the African Charter on Human and Peoples' Rights (1981) have influenced Liberia's constitution.

The Constitution

The preamble to the 1986 constitution of the Republic of Liberia declares that the people of Liberia are "solemnly resolved to live in harmony, to practice fraternal love, tolerance, and understanding as a people, fully mindful of our obligation to promote African unity, international peace, and cooperation. . . ."

Article 1 defines the source of sovereignty: "All power is inherent in the people. All free governments are instituted by their authority and for their benefit, and they have the right to alter and reform the same when their safety and happiness so require."

Fundamental Rights

Chapter 3, Fundamental Rights, provides that all persons are equally free and independent and have certain natural, inherent, and inalienable rights to which all persons are entitled regardless of ethnic background, race, sex, creed, place of origin, or political opinion. Rights and freedoms guaranteed include a prohibition against slavery; freedom to move and reside anywhere, as well as the right to enter and leave the country; freedom of thought, conscience, religion, expression, and assembly; and protections against the deprivation of life, liberty, security of the person, property, privilege, or any other right, except in accordance with the constitution and due process of law.

Division of Powers

In Liberia, a unitary state, power is divided among the president, as head of state and government; the legislature; and the courts, which exercise judicial review.

The Executive

President and Cabinet. The president is head of state and government and commander in chief of the armed forces. He or she is elected by universal adult suffrage for a four-year term, with a limit of two consecutive terms. To be eligible for the presidency a person must be a natural-born Liberian citizen, at least thirty-five years old, and the owner of unencumbered property valued at not less than twenty-five thousand dollars.

The president's powers and duties include conducting foreign affairs and concluding treaties with the concurrence of the legislature; appointing and dismissing cabinet ministers, their deputies and assistants, ambassadors, ministers and consuls, and other government officials, both civilian and military; appointing the chief justice and other justices of the supreme court, with the consent of the upper house of the legislature, judges of other courts, magistrates, and justices of the peace from a panel submitted by a judicial service commission; and once a year presenting to the legislature the administration's proposed legislative program and state of the republic report. The cabinet includes both ministers and ministers of state.

Under the constitution the president may not be held legally responsible for his or her actions pursuant to the constitution or the laws. The president may be impeached, however, for treason, bribery, other felonies, violations of the constitution, and gross misconduct. When the office of president becomes vacant, the vice president becomes the president.

The Legislature

Congress. Article 31 provides that "the legislative power of the republic shall be vested in the legislature of Liberia which shall consist of two separate houses: a senate and a house of representatives, both of which must pass on all legislation."

Upper House. The members of the senate are elected for eight-year terms, half every four years by counties. The senate elects a president and vice president every four years.

Lower House. Members of the house of representatives are elected for four-year terms from legislative constituencies in each county. The house elects a speaker and deputy speaker, as well as other officers, every four years.

To be eligible for the legislature a citizen must be at least twenty-five years old and be domiciled in his or her constituency at least one year before seeking election. Members are granted certain privileges and immunities, and each house adopts its own rules of procedure, which, like other actions, must conform to the requirements of constitutional due process of law.

A simple majority constitutes a quorum in each house, and bills and resolutions must be approved by the president to become law. The president's veto may be overridden, however, by a two-thirds majority of the members voting in each house.

The Judiciary

Judicial power is vested in a court system, which is to apply both statutory and customary law in accordance with standards enacted by the legislature. There is a supreme court, and the legislature is authorized to create subordinate courts from time to time.

Supreme Court. The supreme court consists of a chief justice and four associate justices, with a majority of the members required for a quorum. If a quorum is lacking, the most senior circuit court judge sits ad hoc. The justices are appointed by the president with the consent of the upper house of the legislature. They hold office during good behavior and may be removed by the legislature in impeachment proceedings for specified reasons such as misconduct or inability to perform their functions.

Article 69 directs that

the supreme court shall be the final arbiter of constitutional issues and shall exercise final appellate jurisdiction in all cases, both as to law and fact. The legislature shall make no law nor create any exception as would deprive the court of any of the powers granted herein as the final arbiter of disputes. . . .

Amending the Constitution

A proposal to amend the constitution may be made either by two-thirds of the members of both houses of the legislature or by a petition submitted to the legislature that is signed by at least 10,000 citizens and approved by two-thirds of both houses. The proposed amendment becomes effective if it is ratified in a referendum by at least two-thirds of the registered voters no sooner than one year after the legislature's action.

LIBYA

The backdrop for one-man rule in Libya includes a constitutional proclamation issued by a revolutionary council after a military coup in 1969 and a declaration establishing the authority of the people and designating the Qur'an as the country's constitution.

General Information

The Socialist People's Libyan Arab Jamahiriya ("state of the masses") in North Africa is approximately 1.7 million square kilometers and is bounded by Egypt and Sudan on the east, Chad and Niger on the south, Algeria and Tunisia on the west, and the Mediterranean Sea on the north. Tripoli is the capital of this country whose population is approximately five million persons.

Libya's economy before 1959 was rudimentary, but today the country's major export is oil, and its per capita income is consequently the highest in Africa. Limited United Nations sanctions against Libya for seven years for refusing to turn over suspects in the 1988 bombing of a Pan American flight over Lockerbie, Scotland, hurt the country's economy.

Type of Government: Dictatorship supported by the military, with a revolutionary leader, a secretary general (prime minister) and general people's committee (cabinet), a unicameral general people's congress, and a judiciary

Dates of Constitutions: 1951 and 1969 (supplemented by a 1979 declaration)

Constitutional History

A Neolithic culture inhabited the central North African coastal plain ten thousand years ago. Nomads to the south lived on the savanna until about 2000 B.C., when invaders and the desert pushed them out. Mediterranean Caucasians called Berbers, whose political and social life centered around the tribe, clan, and family and who called themselves *imazghan* (free men), had already begun moving in from perhaps southwestern Asia. Phoenicians established a colony that grew into Carthage by the fifth century B.C., and Tripoli was one of its cities.

Besides the Punic civilization of Carthage, the Greeks established the city of Cyrene, and the tribal Garamentes people dominated the southern region of Fezzan. Romans and later Christianity spread to North Africa, but the longest-lasting influence was the establishment of the Islamic religion during the conquest of the area by the Arabs in the seventh century A.D. In the tenth century a Shia'a Islamic sect of Fatimids—named for Fatima, Muhammad's daughter and the wife of Ali, the sect's founder—arose among some of the Berbers. From North Africa Islam spread to the European continent, where it predominated in Spain until around the thirteenth century.

Pirates seized territories along the African coast of the Mediterranean, and in 1460 Tripoli became an independent city-state governed by a merchant class. Spain captured Tripoli in 1510 and turned its defense over to the Knights of Malta, who lost it to the Ottoman Turks in 1551. Tripolitania, the historic northwestern region of Libya administered by the Ottomans as a province under a governor-general, and Cyrenaica, the historic northeastern region that split off in 1879, were both entitled to be represented in the Turkish parliament after 1908. In general, however, Ottoman rule during this period was repressive and corrupt.

Italy's annexation of the two areas in 1912 met with resistance led by an Islamic religious order called Sanusi, whose leader, Muhammad Idris al Sanusi, was recognized as the emir of interior Cyrenaica in 1917. After World War I provincial parliaments and local advisory councils under Italians were set up, and later the fascists tried to create a "fourth shore" in Libya, filling all administrative positions with Italians.

The Libyan Arab Force, also known as the Sanusi Army, fought bravely under British command during World War II. Nonetheless, a four-power commission decided after the war that the country was not ready for self-government, although a majority of Libyans favored independence. In 1950, however, a national constituent assembly drafted a constitution for a federal system of government with Idris as monarch. It was adopted in October 1951, and on December 24 the United Kingdom of Libya became an independent sovereign state. Less than ten years later oil was discovered at Zaltan in Cyrenaica.

On September 1, 1969, seventy young army officers took control of the government and set up a twelve-member revolutionary council. On September 8 Capt. Muammar al Qadhafi was promoted to colonel and made commander in chief of the armed forces. On December 11, 1969, the council issued a constitutional proclamation that replaced the previous constitution and that in turn was to be superseded at an unspecified date by a new constitution. Since then, the country's constitutional development has been guided by various declarations, such as one in 1979 on the establishment of the authority of the people, and Qadhafi's three-volume *Green Book* from 1975, 1977, and 1978 (green being the traditional color of Islam). His theories combine nationalism, the Islamic religion, socialism, and populism, and, according to the ruler's personal ideology, represent an alternative to capitalism and Marxism.

Influences

An admirer of Egypt's Gamal Abdul Nasser, Qadhafi has promoted Arab unity and a form of socialism he finds compatible with the principles of the Islamic religion.

The Constitution

The 1969 constitutional proclamation of Libya confirmed existing laws that were not in conflict with it. Since 1969 a number of measures adopted by the Libyan executive and legislative congress and Qadhafi's utterances have further defined the constitutional aspects of the government.

The preamble to the 1969 proclamation asserts that "the present constitutional proclamation is made to provide a basis for the organization of the state during the phase of the completion of the national and democratic revolution, until a permanent constitution is prepared, defining the objectives of the revolution and outlining the future course."

Fundamental Rights

Libya professes such concepts as the equality of all citizens before the law and freedom of opinion within the limits of the public interest and principles of the revolution, and it has ratified such United Nations agreements as the Universal Declaration of Human Rights (1948) and the International Covenant on Civil and Political Rights (1966). In fact, however, many violations of political and civil rights in Libya have been reported, especially by Amnesty International, a worldwide human rights organization.

Division of Powers

All state power is in the hands of the military-supported dictator, Col. Muammar al Qadhafi, although documents of a constitutional nature vest legislative, executive, and judicial power in the people's congress, the general secretariat, and the courts, which have no powers of review.

The Executive

Head of State. Qadhafi served as secretary general of the general secretariat of the general people's congress from March 1977 to March 1979 and then resigned. He has remained, however, the de facto head of state, supreme commander of the armed forces, and revolutionary leader, as well as chief theoretician of the revolution. In part 1 of his *Green Book,* "The Solution of the Problem of Democracy," he states that "the instrument of governing is the prime political problem which faces human communities," and he concludes that parliaments are elected by undemocratic procedures and that traditional democracy isolates the masses from their representatives. His solution is the establishment of "popular congresses" as the embodiment of direct democracy. Like many other utopian concepts, Qadhafi's theories translate in practice into a brutal and repressive regime, without politically or socially redeeming virtues.

Secretary General and General People's Committee. Under the 1969 proclamation, the revolutionary council was the highest executive and legislative body. The Declaration of the

Establishment of the Authority of the People in 1979 created a general secretariat of the general people's congress as the highest executive body; it was to be composed of members of the defunct revolutionary council, except Qadhafi, who had become the secretary general. The general secretariat consists of a secretary general and other secretaries who supervise the various sectors of state activity.

Article 10 of the 1979 declaration replaced the former council of ministers, which had been appointed by the revolutionary council, with a general secretariat of the people's congress. A resolution in the same year changed the name to the general people's committee.

The Legislature

Congress. The general people's congress is described as a conference of the people's congresses, people's committees, and professional unions. Members of the congress are chosen generally from the leaders of a single party, the Arab Socialist Union, in local congresses and from among other government leaders.

The general people's congress, on paper, has the power to declare war, ratify treaties, and consider general government policy and its implementation. It also chooses a presiding officer, a chairman, who signs laws and accepts the credentials of foreign representatives.

The Judiciary

Article 28 of the 1969 proclamation states that judges shall be independent and free of any authority except the law and their conscience.

A supreme court is located in Tripoli, with separate chambers for civil and commercial cases; criminal, administrative and constitutional cases; and cases involving *shari'a* (Islamic law).

Although religious courts were abolished in 1973, all decisions of secular courts must be in accordance with religious law, emphasizing the fact that Qadhafi and the other revolutionary leaders believe that separation of church and state violates the Qur'an.

People's courts were established to try members of the former royal family and their sympathizers. In 1980 revolutionary courts were set up; these frequently act without regard for judicial norms or safeguards for the accused. In 1988 the courts were replaced by a people's court and a people's prosecution bureau.

Amending the Constitution

Under the 1969 proclamation, the revolutionary council, which has since been abolished, was authorized to make amendments. Today it appears that Qadhafi's approval is the only prerequisite for amending the constitution.

Malaysia's constitution—embodying recommendations by a commission of delegates from the United Kingdom, Australia, India, and Pakistan—accommodates major population groups such as Malays, Chinese, and Indians, as well as Borneo *bumiputras* ("sons of the soil").

The Asian federation known as Malaysia is approximately 330,000 square kilometers and comprises states on the Malay Peninsula south of Thailand and on the northern part of the island of Borneo. To the north of the country lies the South China Sea and to the south of the Malay Peninsula lie the Straits of Malacca and Singapore. The tiny but wealthy nation of Brunei is embedded in the Malaysian state of Sarawak on the northwest coast of Borneo. The federal territory of Kuala Lumpur is the capital of Malaysia, a country with twenty-two million inhabitants; a second federal territory, Lubuan, is on Borneo.

Rich in natural resources, Malaysia exports rubber, tin, and palm oil and has a growing manufacturing sector. The country has a relatively high standard of living for Asia, and a stable government is essential for the success of its aggressive economic policies.

Type of Government: Parliamentary constitutional monarchy, with a monarch and conference of rulers, a prime minister and cabinet, a bicameral legislature, and a judiciary

Date of Constitution: 1957 (revised in 1963)

The Malay Peninsula was inhabited for thousands of years before people from China arrived between 2500 and 1500 B.C. Other peoples who came before the Christian era included the Proto- and Deutero-Malays and the Hindus and Buddhists from India and China. Hindu empires controlled Southeast Asia into the thirteenth century A.D., leaving their mark on the form of government and modifying Malay customary law.

The Islamic religion was established in the fourteenth century, resulting in the Islamic kingdom of Malacca on the peninsula, whose rise to prominence diminished the influence of the earlier religions. Islamic and even Persian culture, together with Chinese culture, had an impact on Malay law and society. In the sixteenth and seventeenth centuries, respectively, the Portuguese and then the Dutch occupied Malacca; the Dutch finally ceded their territory to the British in 1824. By that time the British East India Company had also acquired sovereignty over the islands of Penang and Singapore. English law was introduced in Penang and Malacca, called the Straits Settlements, in 1826.

In 1874 the sultans of various Malay states accepted British protection and court advisers, and in 1888 Sabah, Sarawak, and Brunei in North Borneo became British protectorates. By treaty in 1895 four Malay states formed a loosely bound federation. English law and courts were introduced, a legislature called the federal council was established for the federation in 1909, and more Malay states came under British control.

After the expulsion of the Japanese following World War II, the four federated states of Perak, Selangor, Negri Sembilan, and Pahang and the five unfederated states of Kedah, Perlis, Trengganu, Kelatan, and Jahor joined with Malacca and Penang in 1946 to form a union without a constitution. By a 1948 agreement among the rulers of the Malay states and the British, the Federation of Malaya was formally created. A constitutional conference in London in 1956 led to an independent, multinational commission, headed by Britain's Lord Reid, that developed a constitution for the federation; it went into effect on "Merdeka Day," August 31, 1957. On July 9, 1963, Singapore as well as Sabah, formerly North Borneo, and Sarawak, both located on the island of Borneo, joined the new federation then known as the Federation of Malaysia, although Singapore left in 1965. The present thirteen-state federation, today simply Malaysia, was established on September 16, 1963, and its constitution is the revised 1957 constitution.

In 1969 race riots in the capital before the elections resulted in the declaration of a state of emergency under the constitution, but parliamentary government was restored the following year.

Influences

Modeled on India's constitution, the Malaysian constitution was also influenced by the U.S. constitution and the British parliamentary model.

The Constitution

The federal constitution of Malaysia was officially reprinted by the government in 1988, with amendments through December 31, 1987.

Fundamental Rights

Articles 5 through 13 in part 2, Fundamental Liberties, set forth rights and guarantees for individuals, including protection of life and personal liberty except in accordance with law; protection against slavery; and equality of all persons before the law and equal protection under the law (article 8). However, section 5 of article 8 makes clear that "this article does not invalidate or prohibit—(a) any provision regulating personal law; . . . (c) any provision for the protection, well-being or advancement of the aboriginal peoples of the Malay Peninsula . . . or the reservation to the aborigines of a reasonable proportion of suitable positions in the public service. . . ." Article 153 also reserves public service positions and business and trade permits for the *bumiputras* (Malays and other indigenous peoples).

The constitution's prohibition against banishment and the guarantees of freedom of movement, speech, assembly and association apply to citizens. Property rights and freedom of religion are extended to all persons, whether citizens or not, while certain educational rights apply to citizens, religious groups, and persons.

Part 3, Citizenship, contains twenty chapters dealing extensively with matters relating to citizenship, which is a matter of some concern in Malaysia. In 1962 the basis for acquiring citizenship by birth was switched from *jus soli* (by territorial jurisdiction, as in the United States) to *jus sanguinis* (by citizenship of a parent, as in Japan).

The fundamental rights guaranteed by the Malaysian constitution have been severely limited in the past because of concerns about the security of the federation.

Division of Powers

In Malaysia, a federal state, constitutional power is apportioned between the federal and state governments by means of lists of respective exclusive and concurrent areas of jurisdiction, each having both executive and legislative aspects. Residual power, which is slight, rests with the states. At the national level, power is divided among the monarch, the conference of rulers, the prime minister, the legislature, and the courts, which exercise limited judicial review.

The Executive

Monarch. The position of monarch is ceremonial. The first paragraph of article 32 describes the monarch's position: "There shall be a supreme head of the federation, to be called the Yang di-Perutan Agong [monarch], who shall take precedence over all other persons in the federation and shall not be liable to any proceedings whatsoever in any court, except the special court established under part XV." By amendment in 1993, however, the royal legal immunities were reduced.

During a monarch's term of office, his consort or spouse is accorded the next highest ceremonial rank. The monarch is elected from and by a conference of rulers from the states and may be removed by the conference. A deputy monarch acts when the monarch is unable to function.

Conference of Rulers. The conference of rulers, in addition to selecting the monarch and the deputy, decides on matters involving religious acts, observances, and ceremonies; consents to certain appointments; appoints members of the special court referred to in article 32; and grants pardons and commutes sentences in certain circumstances.

Prime Minister and Cabinet. Article 39 states: "The executive authority of the federation shall be vested in the Yang di-Perutan Agong and exercisable, subject to the provisions of any federal law . . . by him or by the cabinet or any minister authorized by the cabinet, but parliament may by law confer executive functions on other persons."

As in the British parliamentary system, the monarch is expected to act on the advice of the cabinet or a minister. The monarch appoints the prime minister from the lower house of the parliament and other ministers and their deputies from either house. The prime minister appoints parliamentary secretaries from among members of either house. The cabinet is collectively responsible to the parliament; if the prime minister receives a vote of no confidence from the lower house, he or she must tender the resignations of the entire cabinet.

Parliament. Also following the British style of parliamentary democracy, the parliament is the supreme organ of the government. In Malaysia the bicameral parliament consists of the monarch and two houses: an upper house called the Dewan Negara (senate); and a lower house called the Dewan Rakyat (house of representatives). The monarch summons the parliament to meet, and no more than six months may elapse between meetings. Each house regulates its own procedures.

The Legislature

Upper House. The senate is composed of twenty-six members appointed by the state legislatures as well as forty-three members appointed by the monarch. Senators, who must be Malaysian citizens, at least thirty years old, and not otherwise disqualified, hold office for three-year terms, even if the parliament is dissolved sooner. The leaders in the senate are called the president and deputy president.

Lower House. The house of representatives has 193 elected members apportioned among the states and territories. Citizens at least twenty-one years old and not otherwise disqualified are eligible to be elected to the house. The leaders in the house are the speaker and deputy speaker.

Except in the case of a money bill, a bill may originate in either house. After it is passed by both houses, the monarch must assent to it. The monarch has the authority to veto the bill, but the veto may be overridden if the bill is repassed by the two houses or, in the case of a constitutional amendment, by a two-thirds majority. A money bill need not be acted on by the senate to become law.

Reasons for being disqualified from parliament include having been declared of unsound mind or a bankrupt whose legal obligations have not been discharged, having been convicted of certain crimes and not pardoned, and holding an office for profit. A person may not be a member of both houses at the same time.

While the parliament is supreme in the constitutional system, emergency powers have been given to the executive branch because of political instability and fear of subversion.

The Judiciary

The constitution creates a "high court in Malaya," on the peninsula, and "a high court in Borneo" and authorizes such inferior courts as may be established by law. A 1988 amendment to article 121 limited the inferior courts' powers and jurisdiction to that conferred by federal law. These courts have no jurisdiction over Islamic law matters, which are handled by separate *syariah* (Islamic courts).

Supreme Court. A supreme court, called the Mahkamah Agung, is given exclusive jurisdiction over appeals from the high courts; original or consultative jurisdiction over questions of law, other jurisdictional disputes between the federal and state legislatures, and constitutional interpretation, as well as constitutional questions referred by the monarch; and other jurisdiction as conferred by law.

The head of the supreme court is "the lord president," and chief justices head the high courts. A 1989 amendment increased the number of Malay high court members from twenty-seven to thirty-three. The high court in Borneo has eight members. Judges are appointed by the monarch on the advice of the prime minister and after consultation with the conference of rulers. Members of the judiciary enjoy certain constitutional protections that promote independence.

Compared to the United States, judicial review is limited in Malaysia, even though article 4(1) declares that "this constitution is the supreme law of the federation and any law passed after [the effective date] which is inconsistent with this constitution shall, to the extent of the inconsistency, be void." Although a law's constitutionality may be challenged in court, the constitution itself allows restrictions on certain fundamental rights where the security of the federation is at stake.

Amending the Constitution

Article 159 provides that amendments to the Malaysian constitution in the form of bills must pass either house of the legislature on the second and third readings by a vote of at least two-thirds of the total members; amendments that might infringe on the Borneo states of Sarawak and Sabah are treated separately under article 161E. Article 159 exempts certain amendments from the general procedure and specifies areas of amendment that require the consent of the conference of rulers.

Adopted in 1917 during a period of social upheaval and conflict, the Mexican constitution creates a system of government similar to that in the United States. For nearly seven decades the country was dominated by a single political party, but in 2000 the presidential nominee of an opposition party was elected and took office.

The United States of Mexico is nearly 2 million square kilometers and is located on the North American continent south of the United States of America. It is bordered on the east by the Gulf of Mexico, on the southeast by Belize and Guatemala, and on the west by the Pacific Ocean. Mexico has a population of approximately one hundred million persons. Mexico City is its capital.

A 1995 loan from the United States was repaid two years ahead of schedule, and by 2000 Mexico's economy, one of the best in Latin America, received a boost from higher oil prices. The recent inauguration of a true multiparty democracy in Mexico appears to bode well for the country's political and economic future.

Type of Government: Presidential federal republic, with a president and cabinet, a bicameral legislature, and a judiciary

Dates of Constitutions: 1813 (not implemented), 1824 (reinstated in 1847), 1836, 1843 (Organic Bases), 1857, and 1917

For several thousand years Mexico was inhabited by highly skilled and civilized peoples such as the Maya and later, at the time of the arrival of the Spanish explorer Hernán Cortéz in 1519, the Aztecs. On August 30, 1521, Cortéz and his troops killed the ruler of the Aztec Empire, Montezuma, and established Spain's three-hundred-year colonial empire based on the area's mineral wealth and slave labor.

The military theocracy of the Aztec Empire, whose elected monarch headed an elite society of nobles, soldiers, and priests, was soon supplanted by the laws of Spain and Catholic missionaries. Unlike the middle-class European settlers farther north, who sought freedom from political and religious oppression and set up their own local governments, the Spaniards who came to Mexico did so to exploit the resources and convert the indigenous population. The Spanish authorities enacted a body of law—the Derecho Indiano—expressly for application in the New World colonies. While this law purported to protect the native people, the Indians, it was either ignored or perverted to oppressive ends.

The resident head of the colonial government was a viceroy, the king's representative. Together with a high court *(audiencia),* he performed administrative and judicial functions. The system was centralized and hierarchical; the various provinces of the territory were administered by *corregidores* (governors) and the towns by *alcades* (mayors).

The difference in the colonial administrations of Mexico and the British colonies had a profound impact on the constitutional development in these regions, and the difference in the system of land ownership had an effect on their respective political and economic development. In Mexico a feudal-like system called *encomienda* was established. Under it, the Spanish crown gave landholders the right to control and supervise the Indians, leading to a de facto system of Indian slavery. Some Indians who remained outside the *encomienda* system continued to live in their own communities governed by their own leaders *(caciques)* and to hold land in common.

The Mexican movement for independence began in 1810 and was supported by many colonists, Indians, and *mestizos* (people of mixed blood), but independence took eleven years. In 1812, after Napoleon had ousted the king, a liberal Spanish constitution was extended to Spain's American colonies. In 1813 the "constitution of Apatzingan" was drafted, but it never went into effect. Claiming an empire of all the Central American colonies, Augustín de Iturbide, the leader of the successful Mexican rebellion, declared himself emperor. In 1824 Mexico became a federal republic under a constitution that represented a triumph of the liberal federalist faction over the centralist conservatives.

Mexican governments since 1824 can be categorized as follows: a dictatorship from 1824 to 1855; an era of reform under Benito Juárez, an Indian, from 1855 to 1876; a dictatorship from 1876 to 1910; a revolution from 1910 to 1920; and finally the era of modern Mexico, from 1920 to the present.

In 1836, during the first period of dictatorship, a constitution was promulgated that established, at least on paper, a centralist democratic republic. The constitution provided for a "supreme conservative power" to protect the constitution and its guarantees. This document was superseded by the Organic Bases of 1843, which placed less emphasis on separation of powers. Although the 1824 constitution was reinstated in 1847, the concept of the "supreme conservative power" laid the groundwork for the Mexican version of judicial or constitutional review *(amparo)*, a procedure begun with the liberal constitution adopted in 1857 and still available under the current constitution of February 5, 1917.

Article 41 of this constitution, which legitimized the new government of the moderate revolutionary forces in 1917, deals expressly with political parties, but the Institutionalized Revolutionary Party has won every national election since its formation in 1929. The 1917 constitution, which creates a system of government much like that in the United States, has not, in fact, been able to check the federal government's domination over the thirty-one Mexican states. This accretion of power derives from the strong support for a uniform commercial policy, a history of single-party domination of national politics (in elections held on July 2, 2000, the ruling party lost the presidency for the first time in seven decades), and even *amparo*, which allows the federal judiciary to decide issues relating to local administrative, judicial, and legislative matters.

Influences

Spanish law and the U.S. constitution have influenced the Mexican constitution. The general architecture of the 1857 constitution can be recognized in the 1917 document.

The Constitution

The 1917 constitution of the United States of Mexico has no preamble. Article 40, however, declares: "It is the will of the Mexican people to make themselves into a federal, democratic, representative republic composed of free and sovereign states in all that concerns their internal affairs, but united in a federation established according to the principles of this fundamental law."

Fundamental Rights

Article 1 declares: "Every person in the United States of Mexico shall enjoy the guarantees granted by this constitution, which cannot be restricted or suspended except in such cases and under such conditions as herein provided."

The Mexican constitution prohibits slavery and guarantees the right of expression, with some limitations; the right to information, which was added in 1977; freedom of writing and publishing; the right of petition in a peaceful and respectful manner; the right of assembly; and freedom of choice of work and the right to the fruits of one's labor. It confirms the equality of men and women before the law, while providing for the protection of the family; sets out detailed guidelines for education in the nation; grants the right to bear arms, with some exceptions; and prohibits titles, ex post facto laws, and unwarranted searches and seizures. Guarantees relating to fair criminal proceedings are included, as well as requirements for the state to manage national development and organize a system of democratic planning.

Freedom of religion is guaranteed in article 24, and article 130, as amended in 1992, elaborates on the "historical principle of the separation of church and state."

The lengthy article 27 deals with land and water ownership and gives the nation the right to "impose on private property such limitations as the public interest may demand. . . ." The delayed implementation of portions of this article, which before amendment in 1992 guaranteed peasants the rights to certain lands, sparked the 1994 "Zapatista" uprising in the Mexican state of Chiapas.

Injurious monopolies are outlawed in article 28. Article 29 provides that under certain conditions "which may place the society in great danger or conflict" the president, in agreement with other officials and with the approval of the legislature, may suspend guarantees "which may present an obstacle to a rapid and smooth confrontation of the situation. . . ."

Division of Powers

In a manner similar to that of the U.S. constitution, the constitution of Mexico, a federal state, expressly divides power at the national level among the three traditional branches of government, represented by the president, the legislature, and the courts, which exercise judicial review. Most policy making, however, takes place in the executive branch.

The Executive

President. Article 80 provides that "the exercise of the supreme executive power of the union is vested in a single individual who shall be designated 'president of the United States of Mexico.'" According to article 81, the president is directly elected for a six-year term but "can in no case and for no reason again hold that office." To be eligible for the presidency, a person, among other qualifications, must be at least thirty-five years old, "a Mexican citizen by birth . . . and the son of Mexican parents by birth," "in the full enjoyment of his rights," and resident in the country for at least twenty years.

The government is dominated by the president, whose political power is virtually absolute, and the executive branch bureaucracy. The president is viewed as a parental figure on which the structure of the secular government is based. Duties and powers of the president include promulgating and executing the laws; appointing and removing members of the cabinet and other high officials; appointing ministers and diplomats, with the approval of the upper house of the legislature; and appointing military officers. He or she controls the armed forces, conducts foreign policy, and may initiate and veto legislation.

Cabinet. The federal public administration is run according to an organic law, and the cabinet's role is constitutionally limited to participation in reporting to the legislature on the activities of the federal departments.

Inner Council. The inner council consists of close advisers in and out of the government, whom the president also consults.

The Legislature

Congress. "The legislative power of the United States of Mexico," directs article 50 "is vested in a general congress which shall be divided into two chambers, one of deputies and the other of senators."

Upper House. After amendments in 1993 and 1996, the number of senate members has been doubled from 64 to 128; they hold office for six-year terms. Half are elected by a majority vote in each state and the federal district; one-quarter are determined by assignment by the leading minority candidates in each of thirty-two jurisdictions; and one-quarter are chosen on the basis of national proportional representation. Senators must be at least thirty years old and otherwise meet the same qualifications as deputies.

Lower House. The chamber of deputies is composed of 300 members elected by relative majority in single districts and 200 members whose seats are distributed on a proportional basis among parties winning more than 1.5 percent of the vote nationwide. Members and alternates for each seat serve three-year terms. Deputies must be at least twenty-one years old, Mexican citizens by birth, natives or residents for six months of the state in which the election is held, able to exercise their rights, and not subject to the exclusions in article 55.

According to article 59, "Senators and deputies of the congress of the union shall not be re-elected for the immediately following term." But alternates may be elected if they have not actually served in office. Each chamber is headed by a president, who is charged with ensuring that the members respect constitutional authority.

Bills may be introduced by the president of the republic, members of the congress, and members of the state legislatures. The enactment of legislation proceeds in a manner similar to that in the U.S. congress. Each bill must pass both chambers by a majority vote. The president may veto a bill, but that veto may be overridden by a two-thirds vote of each chamber.

The express powers of the congress, collectively and by chamber, are extensive. They include admitting and forming new states; legislating for the federal district; levying taxes and approving loans and payment of the national debt; preventing restrictions on interstate commerce; legislating on industries such as mining, motion pictures, banking, and lotteries; creating public offices and fixing salaries for these offices; raising and maintaining the armed forces; and enacting laws on citizenship, naturalization, and the general health of the country.

The constitution creates a thirty-seven-member permanent committee of the congress to act in enumerated areas during adjournment. It functions essentially as a housekeeping organ but has authority to call either or both houses into extraordinary session.

The Judiciary

According to article 94: "The exercise of the Judicial Power of the Federation is vested in a Supreme Court of Justice, and Electoral Tribunal, Appellate and District . . . Tribunals . . . and a Council of the federal judicature."

Supreme Court. "The Supreme Court . . . is composed of eleven Ministers and shall function in Plenary or in Chambers," states article 94. With the exception of electoral matters, the supreme court has jurisdiction over constitutional controversies involving the federation, states, federal district, and municipalities, as well as "lawsuits of unconstitutionality that have as their object to pose a possible contradiction between a norm of general character and this Constitution."

Electoral Tribunal. The electoral tribunal, as defined by article 99, is "the highest jurisdictional authority on [any subject except for matters of unconstitutionality, which are reserved for the supreme court] and a specialized organ of judicial Power." It is responsible under the constitution and the law for resolving, among other things, "challenges to federal elections for deputies and senators . . . , the election of the President . . . , [and] acts and decisions of the federal electoral authority. . . ."

Amending the Constitution

Amendments may be made by a two-thirds vote of the legislature's members present, with approval by a majority of the state legislatures, whose votes are to be counted by the national legislature or its permanent committee.

The constitution of this tiny European principality protects the privileges of the monarch as much as the rights of the people. Monaco shares its sovereignty with France, the country whose lands surround it.

The Principality of Monaco on the Mediterranean Sea has an area of 1.8 square kilometers and is surrounded on the west, north, and east by the French department of Alpes-Maritimes. Its citizens, called Monegasques, constitute less than twenty percent of the nearly thirty-two thousand residents of this tiny country, whose capital is Monaco-Ville.

The economy of Monaco thrives on tourism, banking, commerce, and light industry. Royalties from gambling casinos constitute less than five percent of the nation's revenues.

Type of Government. Constitutional monarchy, with a monarch, a minister of state and council of government, a unicameral legislature, and a judiciary

Dates of Constitutions: 1848 (not implemented), 1911 (suspended in 1914, restored in 1917, suspended in 1959), and 1962

There is evidence of Stone Age inhabitants in Monaco, which was later settled by the Phoenicians. Under Roman rule it was known as Herculis Moenaci Portus, and it later became a part of the kingdoms of Lombardy and Arles. Following a period of Islamic rule, Genoa took control in 1191 and in 1297 granted dominion over the territory to the Grimaldi family.

For protection Monaco allied itself with France in the sixteenth century, then with Spain, and once again with France in 1641. In 1793, during its revolution, France ousted the Grimaldis, but the Congress of Vienna in 1815 made Monaco a protectorate of Sardinia. It was repossessed by France in 1848, and a constitution was promulgated but never implemented, although a state council was created by decree.

By treaty with France, Monaco gained its independence in 1861, although a customs union was established between the two countries that later served as a basis for the country's membership in the European Economic Community. In 1909 a supreme council of government was created, and in 1911 Prince Albert I granted Monegasques a constitution that made taxation dependent on approval of a legislative advisory council and established a supreme court, although the judiciary was not completely removed from some administrative control. The constitution was suspended in 1914 and restored in 1917, at which time the judiciary was made independent. The constitution underwent a number of changes before being suspended again in 1959 by Prince Rainier, the current monarch.

On December 17, 1962, a new constitution that reduced the power of the monarch and vested legislative power in an elected council was promulgated.

The 1911 constitution was similar to other post-1815 European constitutions based on the legitimacy of the monarch to rule. The 1962 document merely adds some democratic aspects to the government.

The preamble to the Principality of Monaco's constitution has been omitted from official texts because of its dated, "legitimist" nature. Article 2 declares: "The principle of government is that of a hereditary and constitutional monarchy. The principality is the legal state committed to the respect of liberties and fundamental rights."

In title 3, Liberties and Fundamental Rights, Monegasque citizens are guaranteed equality before the law; individual liberty and security; protection in case of criminal arrest and prosecution; inviolability of the home; respect for private and family life and secrecy (privacy) of correspondence; freedom to work and to peaceful, unarmed assembly; and, although article 9 states that the state religion is Catholicism, freedom of religion. The right to property is inviolable, and the right to state assistance, to a free primary and secondary education, to strike, to associate freely with respect for the rules of the constitution, and to petition public authorities are also guaranteed.

In title 4, the Public Domain, the Public Finances, article 34 states that the assets of the crown are inalienable and imprescriptible—that is, they may not be lost or claimed by anyone else—and that their composition and the rules regarding them are determined by statutes of the sovereign family.

Division of Powers

In Monaco, a unitary state, power is divided among the monarch, the legislature, and the judiciary, which exercises limited judicial review. Sovereignty, however, is shared with the French government.

The Executive

Monarch. Article 3 declares: "The executive power is derived from the high authority of the prince. The person of the prince is inviolable." The prince inherits the throne "by order of primogeniture." If he is not twenty-one years old, a regency is provided for by the "statutes of the sovereign family." Article 12 directs: "The prince exercises his sovereign authority in conformity with the provisions of the constitution and the laws."

The prince's powers and duties include representing the state in foreign relations; in consultation with the council of the crown, signing, ratifying, and bringing treaties to the legislative council; and granting amnesty and pardons. He also confers titles and other distinctions, and he retains the right to initiate legislation.

Minister of State. The power of the government, according to article 43, is exercised under the high authority of the prince by the minister of state, assisted by a council of government. The minister of state, representing the prince, directs the activities of the executive branch; supervises the civil police; and presides, with a preponderant vote, over the council of government.

Council of Government. The council of government considers certain "sovereign ordinances," which are signed by the minister of state and then by the prince. It also considers decrees to which the prince does not object and which the minister of state is authorized to issue.

Council of State. The council of state gives advice on bills and ordinances submitted to it by the prince. It may be consulted on other matters also, and its organization and functions are to be determined by "sovereign ordinance."

Council of the Crown. The council of the crown may be consulted by the prince on important matters of state and must be consulted on certain matters such as international treaties.

The Legislature

National Council. The eighteen members of the national council of Monaco are elected for five-year terms by universal direct suffrage and by list vote. Except for those disenfranchised by law, all persons who have been citizens for five years and who are at least twenty-one years of age are eligible to vote. Women were able to vote for the first time in 1963. The courts are entrusted with supervising elections.

The national council prepares an agenda for the minister of state, who, in turn, communicates messages from the monarch. It deliberates and enacts laws. The monarch may introduce bills, and he approves laws, which are countersigned by the minister of state. The national council elects a secretariat including a president and vice president. Members of the national council are granted certain immunities.

Article 88 provides that judicial power belongs to the monarch, who delegates its full exercise to the courts and tribunals, and that the independence of judges is guaranteed by the constitution.

Supreme Tribunal. A supreme tribunal is composed of five members and two alternates nominated in accordance with the provisions of the constitution and appointed by the monarch, who also designates a president of the body. The court rules on the constitutionality of the rules of the legislature and on verdicts that threaten rights and freedoms guaranteed in title 3 of the constitution, as well as enumerated administrative matters, and decides conflicts of jurisdiction.

Court of Appeal. The court of appeal is composed of two Parisian judges, who are a part of the French judicial system.

The constitution may be amended when the monarch and the legislature agree to it. When an amendment proposal is initiated by the legislature, it must be by a two-thirds majority vote of the normal membership.

MONGOLIA

The Mongol leaders Genghis Khan, Kublai Khan, and Tamerlane conquered and ruled over more territory than Alexander the Great or Napoleon. Modern-day Mongolia, now relatively isolated, finally ended seventy-five years of communist rule in 1996.

General Information

Mongolia lies in central Asia, surrounded by Russia on the north and by China on the east, south, and west, and has an area of approximately 1.56 million kilometers. Ulaanbaatar is the capital of this country of some 2.6 million inhabitants.

The major industries of Mongolia include food processing and mining; its chief agricultural products are grain, potatoes, meat products, and wool. Historically a nation of nomads, Mongolia in 1997 became the first country to abolish all tariffs and taxes on trade as part of the process of converting from a socialist to a market economy.

Type of Government: Presidential-style parliamentary republic, with a president, a prime minister and cabinet, a unicameral legislature, a judiciary, and a constitutional court

Dates of Constitutions: 1924, 1940, 1949, 1952, 1960, and 1992

Constitutional History

The Huns settled in this area in the third century A.D., and the Turkic peoples moved in three centuries later. Beginning in 745, peaceful people, the Uigars, established an empire that was conquered by the Kirghiz. By the thirteenth century the Mongols, under Genghis Khan and his successors, had spread out from the region, creating a vast empire in the wake of the destruction and conquest wreaked by fierce warriors on horseback. Kublai Khan, the grandson of Genghis, became the fabled ruler of the Mongol Empire, which stretched as far east as the Pacific Ocean and as far south as Indochina, Malacca, and Java. In the fourteenth century Tamerlane, another Mongol leader, conquered Persia, the Middle East, Transcaucasia, and Iraq. The Mongol Empire disintegrated in the sixteenth century, after which the Mongols were converted to a pacifist sect of Buddhism.

Mongolia's location between Russia and China has had a significant impact. In the nineteenth century Russia focused on Outer (northern) Mongolia, while China's attention was directed more toward Inner Mongolia in the south. After the collapse of the Manchu (Ch'ing) Dynasty in 1911, Mongolia declared its independence with Russia's support. A communist regime was established on July 11, 1921, however, soon making Mongolia Russia's first satellite nation after it was occupied by Russian Bolshevik forces. A constitution adopted on November 26, 1924, was replaced by other Soviet-style constitutions in 1940, 1949, and 1952.

The Soviets entered into a military pact with Mongolia in 1936 and sent troops to help defend the territory against the Japanese in World War II. After the war, the establishment of a communist government in China in 1949 renewed fears of increased Chinese influence in the region. To obtain military protection and economic assistance, the Mongolian government ingratiated itself with the Soviet Union, a relationship resented by many Mongolians. A constitution promulgated on July 6, 1960, based on the Soviet model, provided for elections to the Khural, the highest administrative body, every three years.

The economic and political liberalization policies of the Soviet leader Mikhail Gorbachev and the anticommunist reactions in Europe in 1989 led to the formation of an opposition political party in Mongolia. On February 12, 1992, a new constitution sanctioning multiparty elections went into effect. Communist Party candidates prevailed in the first election, but a democratic alliance won a majority of the seats in parliament in June 1996.

Influences

The 1992 Mongolian constitution is patterned after Western presidential-style parliamentary governments with a unicameral legislature. However, it retains some communal-property aspects of the socialist system, among them public ownership of grazing lands.

The preamble to the constitution invokes the concepts of "human rights and freedoms, justice and national unity," acknowledges respect for "the accomplishments of human civilization," and declares "the supreme objective of building a humane, civil and democratic society in the country."

Articles 1 through 3, respectively, proclaim that "Mongolia is an independent, sovereign republic," that it is "a unitary State," and that "[s]tate power is vested in the People of Mongolia [who exercise] it through direct participation in state affairs and through representative bodies of state power elected by them." According to article 5, "Mongolia's economy is based on different forms of property following both universal trends of world economic development and national specifics. The State recognizes all forms of both public and private property and shall protect the rights of the owner by law."

Fundamental Rights

Under article 14, "persons lawfully residing within Mongolia are equal before the law and the courts. No person may be discriminated against on the basis of ethnic origin, language, race, age, sex, social origin or status, property, occupation or post, religion, opinion or education. Everyone shall have the right to act as a legal person." Other guarantees include the rights to life; a "healthy and safe environment"; "fair acquisition, possession and inheritance of movable and immovable property"; "free choice of employment, favorable conditions of work, remuneration, rest and private enterprise"; "assistance in old age, disability, childbirth and child care"; health and medical care; and education. The constitution also grants the rights "to engage in creative work in cultural, artistic and scientific fields"; "to take part in the conduct of State affairs directly or through representatives bodies"; and "to form a party or other political organization and unite voluntarily in associations according to . . . social and personal interests and opinion."

In addition to equal rights for men and women, the constitution sanctions the rights to enjoy personal liberty and safety, to petition government institutions and officials, and to appeal to the courts. Also protected are freedom of conscience and religion, thought, free expression of opinion, speech, the press, movement, and peaceful demonstrations and meetings, as well as freedom to seek and receive information. According to article 7, "Historical, cultural, scientific and intellectual heritages of the Mongolian people shall be under State protection." Article 9 declares that the nation "shall respect religions and religions shall honor the State. State institutions shall not engage in religious activities and the Church shall not pursue political activities." Church and state relationships are to be regulated by law.

The duties of citizens and others residing in Mongolia as stated in article 17 include "upholding justice and humanism," respecting the constitution and other laws, paying taxes, and defending the "motherland." Citizens also have "a sacred duty . . . to work, protect his/her health, bring up and educate his/her children and to protect nature and the environment."

Division of Powers

The constitution divides power among the legislature, the president, the government (the prime minister and other members), and the judiciary.

The Executive

President. "The President is the Head of State and embodiment of the unity of the people," declares article 30. Citizens who are forty-five years old and have "permanently resided at a minimum for the last five years in Mongolia" are eligible to serve for a term of four years. The chief executive can be reelected only once and is barred from conflicting employmwnt. Candidates may be nominated by political parties that "have obtained seats in the National Parliament"; at "the primary stage of the elections, citizens are eligible to vote [for] President on the basis of universal, free, and direct suffrage by secret ballot," and runoffs are mandated.

The president has the power to "veto, partially or wholly, laws and other decisions adopted by the . . . Parliament," propose to the legislature a candidate for prime minister "in consultation with the majority party or parties in the . . . Parliament," issue decrees countersigned by the prime minister, and "represent the Mongolian State in foreign relations and, in consultation with the . . . Parliament, to conclude international treaties. . . ." Other powers include "to confer state titles . . . , to grant pardons, . . . to head the National Security Council, to declare . . . conscription, [and] to declare a state of emergency or a state of war . . . and to order the deployment of armed forces when extraordinary circumstances . . . arise" but parliament cannot meet. The president is the commander in chief of the armed forces, addresses messages to parliament or the people, and submits to parliament "proposals concerning vital issues of domestic and foreign policies of the country."

Responsible to parliament, the president, according to article 35, may be removed from office for "a violation of the Constitution or abuse of power . . . on the basis of the findings of the Constitutional Court by an overwhelming majority of the members of the National Parliament present and voting." Parliament's chairman takes on the powers of the president during a temporary absence or on his or her resignation, death, or voluntary retirement pending a new president's inauguration after a special election called for by the legislature within four months.

Prime Minister and Cabinet. The government—the "highest executive body of the State," according to article 38—is led by a prime minister who is responsible to parliament. In consultation with the president, the prime minister "submits . . . proposals on the structure and composition of the Government and on the changes in these to . . . Parliament." Stated government powers range from ensuring implementation of the constitution and setting economic and social policy to protecting the environment, strengthening defense capabilities, protecting human rights, and concluding international treaties.

Under article 40, the "mandate of the Government is four years," beginning from the day the prime minister is appointed. The prime minister may resign "if he considers that the Government is unable to exercise its powers," according to article 43, and then the "Government steps down in its entirety" if parliament agrees.

The Legislature

Parliament. Article 20 proclaims that the "National Parliament is the highest organ of state power, and the supreme legislative power is vested only in the National Parliament." Its seventy-six members are elected for four-year terms. To be eligible a person must be a citizen of Mongolia and twenty-five years old. According to article 23, a member of parliament is "an envoy of the people and represents and upholds the interests of all the citizens and the state." Article 29, in part, extends immunity to legislators, except that if a member is found guilty of a crime by a court, he or she will lose membership in the legislature.

Article 24 provides for a parliamentary chairman and vice chairman to be "nominated and elected from among the members by secret ballot" for a term of four years. Regular parliamentary sessions "are to be held once in six months and . . . last not less than 75 working days on each occasion," but "[e]xtraordinary sessions may be convened at the demand of more than one-third of the members of . . . Parliament, or at the initiative of the President and the Chairman of . . . Parliament." A majority of members "is required to consider a session valid."

Under article 25, parliament "may consider at its initiative, any issue pertaining to the domestic and foreign policies of the country" and also has authority "to enact laws and make amendments to them; to determine the basis of the domestic and foreign policies of the State; to set and announce the date of [national] elections . . . ; [and] to determine and change the structure and composition of [its] Standing Committees, the Government, and other bodies directly accountable to it according to law." Parliament is additionally authorized "to pass a law recognizing the full powers of the President after his or her election and to relieve or remove the President; to appoint, replace, or remove the Prime Minister, members of the Government, and other bodies responsible and accountable to the National Parliament . . . ;

[and] to define the State's financial, credit, tax, and monetary policies. . . ." The legislature is also granted authority to define the country's borders, establish a national security council, approve administrative and territorial divisions, issue acts of amnesty, hold national referendums, declare states of emergency or war, and institute titles, orders, and medals. Article 26 grants the president, members of parliament, and the government the right to introduce legislation.

The Judiciary

"The Judicial power is vested exclusively in courts," proclaims article 47. "Courts are instituted solely under the constitution and other laws." The judicial system consists of "the Supreme Court, provincial and capital city courts and region, inter-region, and district courts," as well as specialized courts that may be created. "Judges are independent and subject only to the law," mandates article 49.

Supreme Court. Article 50 provides in part that the supreme court "is the highest judicial organ and exercises the following powers: . . . to try at first instance criminal cases and legal disputes under its jurisdiction; to examine decisions of lower-instance courts through appeal and supervision; [and] to examine and take decision on matters related to the protection of law and human rights and freedoms therein and transferred to it by the Constitutional Court and the Prosecutor General." Supreme court decisions are final "and binding on all courts and other persons." However, if a supreme court decision "is incompatible with law, the Supreme Court itself repeals it."

The court consists of a chief justice and judges who are appointed by the president "upon their presentation to the . . . Parliament by the General Council of Courts." (The chief executive also appoints the judges of other courts on the council's recommendation.) To be a judge of the supreme court a person must be a "Mongolian national of thirty-five years of age with higher education in law and a professional career of not less than 10 years." Removal of judges is restricted to voluntary resignation or the result of a court decision.

Constitutional Court

Article 64 creates a constitutional court as "an organ exercising supreme supervision over the implementation of the Constitution, making judgment on the violation of its provisions, and resolving constitutional disputes. It is the guarantee for the strict observance of the Constitution." Members "are subject to the Constitution only and are independent of any organizations, officials, or anybody else." The nine members of the court "are appointed by the National Parliament for a term of six years upon the nomination of three of them by . . . Parliament, three by the President, and the remaining three by the Supreme Court." A chairman is elected by the other members for a three-year term.

The court is authorized in part by article 66 to examine and settle "constitutional disputes at the request of . . . Parliament, the President, the Prime Minister, the Supreme Court, and the Prosecutor General, or on its own initiative on the basis of petitions and information received from citizens." Decisions "immediately enter into force."

Amending the Constitution

Amendments to the constitution may be initiated by the same organizations and officials empowered to initiate legislation: the president, members of parliament, citizens, and other organizations, as well as the constitutional court. According to article 69, "An amendment to the Constitution is adopted by not less than three-fourths of votes of all members of . . . Parliament." If it fails twice, it cannot be reconsidered until a new parliament convenes. Parliament is barred from undertaking amendments within six months before a general election. Alternatively, two-thirds of the legislators may concur in a call for a national referendum on a constitutional amendment. In that case, a majority of eligible citizens must vote, and the amendment likewise must receive a majority vote, as required by article 25.

MOROCCO

Located closer to Europe than any other African country, Morocco has struggled since independence in 1956 to make its monarchical government work. Mohamed VI, a young monarch who ascended the throne in 1999, has begun promoting reform and human rights.

General Information

The Kingdom of Morocco, together with the part of Western Sahara that it occupies, is some 710,850 square kilometers and is bounded on the north by the Mediterranean Sea, on the east by Algeria, on the south by Western Sahara and Mauritania, and on the west by the Atlantic Ocean. Rabat is the capital of this country of some thirty million persons, although Casablanca is the nation's largest city.

Morocco's major industries include food processing, leather goods, and mining; it is one of the world's largest producers of cannabis, but other key crops include grain, citrus, and grapes. With more than sixty percent of the population illiterate, a large foreign debt, and constant threats to the monarchy from Islamic leaders, the country's future political and economic stability is uncertain.

Type of Government: Parliamentary constitutional monarchy, with a monarch, a prime minister and council of ministers (cabinet), a bicameral legislature, a judiciary, and a constitutional council

Dates of Constitutions: 1962, 1970, 1972, 1992 (revision), and 1996 (revision)

Constitutional History

More than three thousand years ago Berbers inhabited the land now known as Morocco. Around the twelfth century B.C., Phoenicians established outposts along the southwestern coast of the Mediterranean Sea, and by the fifth century B.C. much of the territory was dominated by their colony of Carthage. After Rome defeated Carthage in the three Punic Wars (264–146 B.C.), Morocco became a Roman province until the fifth century A.D.

Conquered by the Arabs in 683, it became a part of the empire of the Moors (Moslems of mixed Arab and Berber descent), who occupied much of the Iberian Peninsula in Europe beginning in 788. By the twelfth century, the Moorish domain encompassed Spain, Morocco, Algeria, Tunisia, and Libya. European Christians subsequently recaptured Spain, and then Spain and Portugal invaded North Africa. The westward expansion of the Ottoman Turks into Moroccan territory was thwarted at the end of the sixteenth century, after which most of the region became unified under Mulay Ishmael, who ruled from 1672 to 1727. In the nineteenth century some parts of Morocco came under Spanish administration. France, after colonizing Algeria, acquired the rest as a protectorate under the Treaty of Fez in 1912 and selected the next Moroccan sultan, Muhammad V, in 1927.

During World War II Moroccans fought willingly for France. The Allies, however, did not support France's presence in Morocco, and an independence movement began in earnest after 1944. In 1952 the titular Moroccan ruler requested that the protectorate status be revised, only to be forced out of the country the following year by the French. When France became absorbed with an uprising in Algeria, Morocco was able to obtain its independence on March 2, 1956. Hassan II succeeded to the throne in 1961, making himself prime minister and drafting a constitution that was approved in a referendum on December 7, 1962. However, after parliamentary elections the government became virtually deadlocked, and the king dissolved parliament and again took personal control of the government as prime minister.

A 1970 constitution, which created a unicameral legislature and increased the king's formal powers, was abandoned a year later in the wake of an attempted military coup. A reform constitution proposed in 1972 and approved by referendum was promulgated on March 10 of that year. While retaining the king's powers, the document defined in greater detail the functions of the government institutions: the monarch, council of ministers, and parliament.

Western Sahara, located south of Morocco on the Atlantic coast, was partitioned in April 1976 under pressure from Morocco, which acquired control of the northern two-thirds of the territory. The constitution was revised in 1992 and again revised in 1996 to create a bicameral legislature. Hassan II died in 1999 and was succeeded by his son Mohamed VI. Since his ascension, efforts have been made to curb government corruption, release thousands of prisoners, and provide redress for violations of human rights.

Elements of the 1958 French constitution and a system of monarchical Islamic rule are combined in the 1972 Moroccan constitution, which leaves political power largely in the hands of a hereditary monarch.

"The Kingdom of Morocco, a Muslim Sovereign State, whose official language is Arabic, constitutes a part of the Great Arab Maghreb [the Islamic world in the West]," states the preamble to Morocco's revised constitution. "As an African State," it adds, "one of its constituted objectives is the realization of African unity." The preamble also "reaffirms its attachment" to human rights and to its "determination to work for the maintenance of peace and security in the world."

Articles 1 and 2 proclaim that "Morocco is a constitutional, democratic and social Monarchy" and that "[s]overeignty belongs to the Nation, which exercises it directly by means of referendum and indirectly through its constitutional institutions." Article 3 provides that "political parties, trade unions, local councils and professional [bodies] participate in the organization of the State and in the representation of the citizens. There can be no single party," it emphasizes.

Article 4 prohibits retroactive laws, while article 5 states that "[a]ll Moroccans are equal before the law." In article 6, the constitution declares that "Islam is the religion of the State, which guarantees to all freedom of worship." According to article 8, "Men and women enjoy equal political rights," including voting. The constitution also guarantees freedom of movement, opinion, expression, assembly, and association. Among other rights extended are freedom from being "arrested, detained or punished except in the cases and forms provided by law"; inviolability of the home; secrecy of correspondence; equal access "to public functions and public employment; equal rights to education and employment; and property ownership, whose "extent and use may be restricted by law if the needs of economic and social planning and development necessitate it."

Duties imposed include contributing "to the common defense of the homeland," to public expenditures "in proportion to [one's] economic capacities," and to "the costs resulting from national calamities."

The constitution is formally divided into chapters on the monarch, parliament, and judiciary, but in actuality political power remains mostly in the hands of the monarch.

Monarch. "The King, Commander of the Faithful, Supreme Representative of the Nation, Symbol of its unity and guarantor of the permanence and continuity of the State," declares article 19, "ensures the observance of Islam and the Constitution." Under article 20, the "Crown ... and its constitutional rights are hereditary" and pass to the oldest male son of the monarch, unless the king during his lifetime designates another son to succeed him; a regency council exercises the throne's powers on behalf of a minor king until he is twenty years of age. According to article 23, "The King's person is inviolable and sacred."

The monarch's executive powers and duties include appointing the prime minister and, on his recommendation, appointing and terminating "the other members of the Government."

The king presides over the council of ministers, promulgates laws within thirty days following their approval, dissolves one or both chambers of parliament under certain conditions prescribed in the constitution, and may "address messages to the Nation and to the Parliament." Among other things, the king is "the Supreme Commander of the Royal Armed Forces," accredits and receives ambassadors and foreign representatives, "signs and ratifies treaties," appoints judges, grants pardons, and may declare a state of emergency after making appropriate consultations and addressing the nation.

Prime Minister and Cabinet. According to articles 59 to 61, "The Government is composed of the Prime Minister and the ministers"; it "is responsible before the law and the Parliament"; and "[u]nder the responsibility of the Prime Minister, the Government assures the execution of the laws and supervises the administration." After the king has nominated the members of the government, the prime minister must present his or her program for a vote in both chambers of parliament.

The prime minister is authorized to introduce laws in parliament but only if a proposal has "been considered in the Council of Ministers."

The Legislature

Parliament. Article 36 states: "The Parliament is composed of two Chambers, the Chamber of Representatives [lower house] and the Chamber of Counselors [upper house]." Each chamber determines its own rules, which must be approved by the constitutional council before becoming effective. Members of parliament are granted immunity for their opinions and votes and from arrest without the authorization of their chamber, "except in the case of a flagrant crime."

Upper House. Article 38 directs that three-fifths of the members of the chamber of counselors are to be elected from regions "by electoral colleges made up of elected members of trade chambers as well as members elected at the national level by an electoral college consisting of wage-earners' representatives." Members serve for nine years, with one-third elected every three years.

Lower House. Members of the chamber of representatives, according to article 37, "are elected for five years through direct universal suffrage." The number of representatives, procedures for election, and qualifications of candidates "are determined by an organic law."

Article 45 requires laws to be "voted on by the Parliament," but under certain conditions measures may be taken "by decree, which are normally in the legislative domain." The legislature is authorized to enact laws "concerning fundamental objectives of the economic, social and cultural action of the State," and other enumerated areas of jurisdiction include "individual and collective rights" set forth in the constitution; "misdemeanors and the penalties which are applicable, penal procedure, civil procedure, and the establishment and the creation of new categories of jurisdiction"; fundamental guarantees accorded to civil and military authorities; and "the nationalization of enterprises and the transfer of enterprises from the public sector to the private sector."

Proposed legislation may be introduced by the prime minister and members of parliament. The government "can express objection to any proposal or amendment which is not within the legislative domain," with disputes being resolved by the constitutional council within eight days. According to article 58, "Every project or legislative proposal is examined successively by the two Chambers of Parliament in order to proceed to the adoption of an identical text." Except when "the Government has declared a state of urgency," a legislative proposal "cannot be adopted until after two readings in each Chamber." Special rules apply to proposals for organic laws, and such laws "cannot be promulgated until after the Constitutional Council has pronounced their conformity with the Constitution."

Pursuant to article 26, the king promulgates laws within thirty days following their transmission to the government. However, he may demand that the chambers "proceed with a new [second] reading of any bill or legislative proposal" and, after the second reading, may refer such a proposal to a referendum, "except in the case [where the proposal] has been adopted or rejected by a two-thirds majority of the members" of each chamber.

The king "may decree the dissolution of the two Houses or of one of them only," according to article 71, after consulting with the chamber presidents and the chairman of the constitutional council and addressing the nation. A new parliament is then elected within three months, during which time the king exercises legislative powers. Once a house is dissolved, its successor cannot be dissolved until a year following the new election.

"The Judiciary shall be independent from the legislative and executive branches," proclaims article 82. Judges or magistrates are recommended "by the Supreme Council of Magistracy [and] . . . appointed by Royal Decrees." The council is presided over by the king and is composed of the minister of justice, the first president and prosecutor-general of the supreme court, the president of the first chamber of the supreme court, two members of the court of appeals, and four "magistrates of first degree jurisdictions elected from among themselves." According to article 83, "Sentences are passed and executed in the King's name."

Supreme Court. As directed in article 91, the supreme court is composed in equal parts of members elected from each chamber of parliament. Pursuant to article 92, "An organic law specifies the number of . . . members, the [method] of their election as well as the applicable procedure." Article 89 gives the supreme court a role in the impeachment of members of the government.

Article 79 establishes a constitutional council, which is composed of six members designated by the king and three designated by each of the presidents of the two parliamentary chambers for nine-year terms. "Each category of the members is renewable by thirds every three years." The president of the council is chosen by the king from his appointees, and no members may be reappointed.

"The Constitutional Council," according to article 81, "exercises the powers vested in it by . . . the Constitution or . . . organic laws." Other responsibilities include providing rulings "on the regularity of the election of the members of the Parliament and the operations of the referendum"; on the conformity of "organic laws, before their promulgation"; and on "the Rules of [the parliamentary chambers], prior to their implementation" to assure "their conformity with the Constitution." Bills may be referred to the council by the king, prime minister, and presidents of each legislative chamber, or a quarter of the members of either chamber. "The decisions of the Constitutional Council are not susceptible to any appeal. They are binding on public powers, and all administrative and jurisdictional authorities."

Article 103 grants the king and the two chambers of parliament the "initiative concerning the revision of the Constitution," although the king "can submit directly to a referendum the . . . revision which he has initiated." Other proposed amendments must be "passed by a majority of two-thirds of the members" of each chamber. Article 106 states: "The monarchic form of the State as well as the provisions relating to the Islamic religion cannot be the object of a constitutional revision."

MOZAMBIQUE

After fifteen years as a single-party socialist state, Mozambique adopted a multiparty democratic constitution in 1990. The new document was followed by peaceful, free elections held in October 1994 under the auspices of the United Nations.

General Information

The Republic of Mozambique, on the east coast of southern Africa, is approximately 800,000 square kilometers. It borders on Tanzania on the north, the Mozambique Channel on the east, Malawi and Zambia on the northwest, Zimbabwe on the west, and South Africa and Swaziland on the southwest and south. Maputo is the capital of this land of more than nineteen million persons.

Agriculture and fishing are the mainstays of the Mozambique economy, but the country has resources such as natural gas and bauxite to be exploited. Fifteen years as a socialist state and ten years of brutal rebel activity have kept Mozambique from reaching its economic and political potential.

Type of Government: Presidential-style parliamentary republic, with a president, a prime minister and council of ministers (cabinet), a unicameral legislature, a judiciary, and a constitutional council

Dates of Constitutions: 1975 and 1990

Constitutional History

Mozambique historically consists of three major regions, which probably have more in common with neighboring countries than with each other: the Zambezi River valley and the regions to the north and south of it. Beginning perhaps as early as the fourth century A.D., Bantu-speaking peoples, who worked iron, migrated into the area, which was inhabited by Bushmanoid hunters and gatherers. Roman coins dating from around the same period have been found off the coast of Mozambique.

By the ninth century Arabs had established fortified towns on the coast and made alliances with African chiefs to facilitate trade of manufactured goods, including weapons, for rhinoceros horns, gold, and slaves. In 1497 Vasco da Gama's small Portuguese fleet rounded the Cape of Good Hope and sailed up the east coast of Africa; after trouble with a *shaykh* (Arab ruler) at the Islamic town of Mozambique, the fleet's guns fired on it. By the time the Portuguese began ousting the Arab traders along the Zambezi River in the mid-1500s, the Maravi (Malawi), an elite warrior people whose paramount chief controlled the ivory trade with the Arabs north of the Zambezi, had established a number of loosely knit kingdoms in the region. Many ancestors of the modern Mozambicans, such as the Shona, were established in the region by the sixteenth century; others, such as the Nguni, arrived in the nineteenth century.

After extracting acceptance of Portuguese sovereignty from African rulers during the sixteenth century, Portugal began parceling out land to settlers *(prazeros)*, who were allowed to use the inhabitants for labor and administer justice on their holdings. During the eighteenth century Portugal neglected its East African territory, but by 1891 France, Germany, and Britain had formally recognized its sovereignty. After World War I German territory was added, and local autonomy was permitted until 1930, when the government was centralized in Lisbon; Mozambique was now considered an overseas province. In 1954 requirements for Africans wishing to acquire Portuguese citizenship were tightened, while a 1955 organic law gave some Africans local councils of their own. The general rise of African nationalism led in 1964 to the start of a guerrilla war for independence, which targeted the colonial government, composed of a governor-general, advisory councils, and an elected, twenty-nine-member legislature.

On June 25, 1975, independence was attained, and Mozambique's first president began implementing his pledge to create the first African communist nation, along the line of Mao

Zedong's China, by nationalizing all land and businesses, outlawing the private practice of law and medicine, and collectivizing the farms. That same day a constitution approved by the ruling party, the Mozambique Liberation Front (Frelimo), went into effect; it proclaimed that power belonged to the workers and peasants and that the Frelimo party was the leading force in the state and society.

After the government abandoned its hard-line communist ideology in 1989, a new constitution instituting multiparty democracy went into effect on November 30, 1990. A rebel group called Renamo objected to it and proposed its own draft extending fundamental rights and giving more power to the legislature rather than to the executive. An accord between Renamo and the government in 1992 provided for new elections under the auspices of the United Nations in October 1994.

Influences

The 1990 constitution is based on the "strong president," presidential-style parliamentary model of government.

The Constitution

The preamble to the 1990 constitution of the Republic of Mozambique acknowledges the role played by Frelimo in the nation's struggle for independence and closes with this declaration: "We, the Mozambican people, determined to strengthen our country's political order, in a spirit of responsibility and pluralism of opinion, have decided to organize society in such a way that the will of the citizens shall be the most important precept of our sovereignty."

Article 6 provides that among the fundamental aims of the nation are defending independence and sovereignty; consolidating national unity; building social justice and achieving material and spiritual well-being for the citizens; strengthening democracy, freedom, and social and individual stability; and defending and promoting human rights and equality of citizens before the law.

Fundamental Rights

According to article 9, Mozambique is a secular state, and the activities of religious denominations are subject to the law. Part 2, Fundamental Rights, Duties, and Freedoms, declares that all citizens are equal before the law; they are entitled to the same rights and subject to the same duties regardless of color, race, sex, ethnic origin, place of birth, religion, education level, social position, the legal status of their parents, or their profession. Men and women are equal before the law in political, economic, social, and cultural affairs, and full rights are extended to the disabled. All citizens are guaranteed the right to life, without fear of the death penalty, and the right to defend a balanced natural environment. Freedom of expression, the press, and information, however, will be regulated by law based on the requirements of foreign policy and national defense, among other things. Economic and social rights and duties and guarantees of rights and freedoms are also covered in part 2.

Division of Powers

In Mozambique, a unitary state, power is shared among the president, as head of state and government; the legislature; the courts, which have judicial review authority; and the constitutional council, which may exercise constitutional review.

The Executive

President. The president is head of state and government and commander in chief of the armed forces and security forces. He or she is elected for a five-year term by universal suffrage and personal and secret ballot on the basis of a majority vote. Any citizen who possesses "original nationality," is the child of parents who held original nationality, is at least thirty-five years old and in full possession of political and civil rights, and is proposed by 10,000 voters, of whom at least 200 must reside in each province of the country, is eligible to run for president. A person is limited to two consecutive terms but may run again after five years.

The duties and powers of the president include addressing the nation; informing the legislature annually on the state of the nation; deciding to hold referendums; calling general elections; dissolving the legislature; dismissing the other members of government if its program is rejected twice by the legislature; appointing the president and deputy president of the supreme court and the presidents of the constitutional and administrative courts; granting pardons and commuting sentences; and conferring awards. Other powers include appointing and dismissing the prime minister and other ministers and provincial governors; establishing ministries; declaring war and its termination; making treaties; and appointing and dismissing heads of the military and the head of the police and other officers, according to law. The president is responsible for guiding foreign policy, appointing and receiving foreign representatives, and promulgating the laws.

The president enjoys full immunity for the discharge of his duties. Article 126 gives the president authority to designate a substitute for a short-term absence; for longer periods the president of the legislature acts as president.

Prime Minister and Cabinet. Article 149 states: "The council of ministers is the government (cabinet) of the Republic of Mozambique." The cabinet is responsible to the president and the legislature and is chaired by the prime minister, to whom such authority is delegated by the president, except when government policy is being formulated.

The Legislature

Parliament. Article 133 establishes the unicameral legislative assembly:

1. The assembly of the republic is the highest body in the Republic of Mozambique.
2. Through laws and resolutions of a general character, the assembly of the republic shall regulate social and economic affairs and the administration of state activity.

Called the Assembleía Popular, the parliament consists of 250 deputies elected by universal suffrage and secret ballot for five-year terms, unless the assembly is dissolved earlier.

The assembly is given the power to legislate on basic questions of the country's domestic and foreign policy and may delimit borders and territorial subdivisions; approve electoral laws and procedures for referendums and propose holding referendums on questions of national interest; ratify the suspension of constitutional guarantees, the declaration of a state of siege or emergency, and certain appointments by the president; approve progress reports from the cabinet and the budget; define defense, security, and tax policy; ratify and terminate international treaties; grant amnesty and pardons; authorize presidential state visits abroad; elect the president and members of the standing commission of the assembly; and adopt rules and set up commissions.

The assembly elects a president from among its members. A quorum is more than one-half of the members, and decisions are made by a majority vote of those present. Bills may be introduced by the president, commissions (committees) of the assembly, deputies, or the cabinet. The president may refuse to promulgate a law, but a veto may be overridden by a two-thirds majority vote.

The Judiciary

Chapter 6, the Courts, provides that the courts are to guarantee and strengthen the rule of law, safeguard the rights and freedoms of citizens, educate citizens in the observance of laws, punish violators of the legal order, and adjudicate disputes. Article 164 calls for judges to be independent and owe obedience only to the law. Article 162 expressly authorizes judicial review. Under the court system there is a supreme court and other courts of justice, an administrative court, courts-martial, and customs, maritime, and labor courts.

Supreme Court. The supreme court is the highest judicial body, with both original and appellate jurisdiction, and in plenary session it is a court of final appeal. Judges of the supreme court may be professionals, appointed by the president after consultation with a supreme judiciary council, or others elected by the legislature.

Administrative Court. The administrative court controls the legality of administrative acts and supervises the legality of public expenditures.

Constitutional Council

Chapter 8 provides for a constitutional council to adjudicate the constitutionality and legality of legislative and regulatory acts of state agencies; settle jurisdictional conflicts between sovereign authorities; and pronounce on the legality of referendums. The court is also charged with responsibilities with respect to the election process.

Amending the Constitution

Amendments may be proposed by the president or at least one-third of the members of the legislature and must be submitted to the legislature ninety days before the opening of debate. If an amendment would fundamentally change the rights of citizens or the organization of public powers, it must be submitted to a referendum. All other amendments must be adopted by a two-thirds majority of the members of the legislature.

NEPAL

In 1990 a modern constitution providing for multiparty elections went into effect in the historic Kingdom of Nepal, which was reunited after nearly three hundred years by a Gurkha warrior in the latter half of the eighteenth century.

General Information

The Kingdom of Nepal, which includes the southern slopes of much of the Himalaya Mountains, is approximately 141,000 square kilometers and is bounded by part of China (formerly Tibet) on the north and by India on the east, south, and west. Katmandu is the capital of this country of approximately twenty-five million persons.

Nepal, which is dependent on an agricultural economy, is one of the poorest countries in the world. Existing between two giants, China and India, the multiparty democracy will undoubtedly face many internal and external challenges in the coming years.

Type of Government: Parliamentary constitutional monarchy, with a monarch, a prime minister and council of ministers (cabinet), a bicameral legislature, and a judiciary

Dates of Constitutions: 1948 (brief), 1951 (interim), 1959 (suspended in 1960), 1962, and 1990

Constitutional History

Nepal has been a kingdom for at least 1,500 years, centering on the fertile Katmandu Valley at the foothills of the Himalayas. In the sixth century B.C. Siddhartha Gautama, the Buddha, was born into a clan of a confederation of the Tarai, a thirty-mile-wide hot marshy strip along Nepal's southern border with India. India and the Hindu and Buddhist religions have greatly influenced the country, as did Tibet to some extent.

The modern nation of Nepal has developed historically from many cultures and civilizations. For a long time peoples speaking Indo-Aryan languages have immigrated into western Nepal. The territory was influenced by the Mauryan Empire of north India in the last centuries before the Christian era and the Gupta Empire in the fourth century A.D. The first Nepalese kingdom founded by the Licchavis lasted until 750. From then until the medieval period, various rulers, many Indian, tried to control the territory. After 1482, as a result of a dispute among six brothers over the throne, the kingdom was divided into three parts, but it was reunited in the eighteenth century by a Gurkha warrior, Prithvi Narayan Shah.

Nepalese law developed from the Hindu principle in which the king is an incarnation of the deity Vishnu; as the "fountain of justice," all power emanates from him. Hindu jurisprudence (the Dharmasastra) was to be applied strictly by the king in every aspect of his rule. In later times, common law principles were borrowed from neighboring India and influenced legislation; but the Hindu legal code—the Muluki Ain (law of the land), which was revised in 1962—is the basic source of Nepalese law.

Around the mid-nineteenth century the Rana family made the prime minister's position hereditary and ruled in the king's stead until a revolution in 1950. A 1948 constitution was effective for a few months in 1950 and 1951, and new constitutions were promulgated in 1951 and 1959. The latter, however, was suspended in 1960 by the king, who then ruled under emergency powers until 1962. That year a new *panchayat* (a village public assembly of the five important castes) constitution that limited democratic participation in the government went into force. In 1980 the constitution was revised to provide for direct, rather than indirect, election of members to the legislature; and on November 9, 1990, another constitution that did away with the last vestiges of the *panchayat* system was promulgated.

Influences

The 1962 constitution was influenced by the constitutions of Pakistan and Indonesia, as well as some other Islamic countries. The new constitution is based on models of a limited parliamentary monarchy, although the monarch's role is not merely ceremonial.

The preamble to the 1990 constitution declares that its purpose is to guarantee basic human rights to every citizen; consolidate the adult franchise, parliamentary system of government, constitutional monarchy, and multiparty democracy; and establish a system of justice that will transform the concept of the rule of law into a living reality.

Article 3 specifically states that "the sovereignty of Nepal is vested in the Nepali people and shall be exercised in accordance with the provisions of this constitution."

Fundamental Rights

According to article 2, the people of Nepal, "united by a bond of common aspirations and faith in the independence and integrity of the nation, irrespective of religion, race, caste, or tribe, collectively constitute this nation." Specific guarantees include equality before the law; freedom of thought, expression, and peaceful assembly; the right to form unions and associations; the right to reside anywhere in Nepal; and the right to choose a profession, occupation, or trade or start an industry. Freedom of the press is guaranteed, as is freedom of religion, the right to privacy, and rights for accused persons.

Division of Powers

In Nepal, a unitary state, power is divided among the monarch, as head of state; the prime minister, as head of government; the legislature; and the courts, which exercise judicial review.

The Executive

Monarch. Executive authority, according to the constitution, is vested in the monarch, as head of state, and the cabinet, called the council of ministers. The monarch's powers generally must be exercised with the advice and consent of the cabinet, which is given the responsibility of controlling and regulating the administration of the kingdom. Article 41 notes that "(1) the allocation and transaction of the business of his majesty's government shall be carried out in accordance with the rules approved by his majesty" and that "(2) no question shall be raised in any court about compliance or otherwise of rules under clause (1)."

The monarch is nominally commander in chief, but the military is actually commanded by a three-member defense council headed by the prime minister. The monarch also summons and dissolves the legislature, grants pardons and commutes sentences, confers titles and honors, and appoints ambassadors.

Prime Minister and Cabinet. The monarch appoints the prime minister as head of government from the majority party in the lower house of the legislature; he also selects other ministers from members of the legislature on the recommendation of the prime minister. If there is no clear majority, a coalition or relative party majority may be formed.

The constitution requires the prime minister to inform the monarch of decisions in the council of ministers regarding administration of the kingdom, bills introduced and additional information about these bills required by the monarch, and the general state of affairs, both internal and external.

The Legislature

Parliament. Article 44 provides that a legislature, consisting of the monarch and two houses, the Rashtriya Sabha (national council) and the Pratinidhi Sabha (house of representatives), is to be called the parliament.

Upper House. The national council has sixty members; ten are nominated by the monarch from among citizens who have distinguished themselves in national life; thirty-five, including at least three women, are to be elected by the lower house; and fifteen are to be elected by an electoral college of officials at the village, town, and district levels. The national council may not be dissolved. Its members serve for six-year terms, one-third retiring every two years, and it elects a chairman and a vice chairman.

Lower House. The house of representatives has 205 members elected from population-based constituencies for five-year terms, unless dissolved earlier or extended for one year during a state of emergency. It elects a speaker and deputy speaker.

Any citizen eighteen years old may vote. If not otherwise disqualified by law or the constitution, any person twenty-five years old may be elected to the house or if thirty-five years old to the national council. Questions regarding qualifications are to be referred to the chief justice of the supreme court or another justice of that court designated by the chief justice. Members are afforded immunities and privileges while in office.

Each house makes its own rules of procedure. The constitution, however, provides that bills may be introduced in either house, except finance bills, which must be introduced in the house of representatives, and that all bills except finance bills must pass both houses and be approved by the monarch to become law. Articles 64, 65, and 66 direct the lower house to establish committees for such areas as finance, human rights, and protection of the environment; create a joint committee with members from both houses; and set up a general secretariat of the parliament, with secretaries appointed by the monarch on the recommendation of the speaker of the house and the chairman of the national council. One-fourth of the members of each house are necessary for a quorum.

The Judiciary

Pursuant to article 85, the Nepalese court system consists of a supreme court, appellate courts, district courts, and other courts and tribunals created to hear special types of cases. Historically under the control of the rulers, the courts have undergone reforms that have increased their independence and fairness in applying the law to all citizens.

Supreme Court. All courts, except military courts, and all other judicial institutions are supervised by the supreme court. It consists of a chief justice appointed by the monarch on the recommendation of a constitutional council that includes the prime minister and other government officials. Additional members are appointed by the monarch on the recommendation of the judicial council, made up of the chief justice, the minister of justice, two judges, and a distinguished jurist. This council also oversees appointments, promotions, transfers, and disciplinary actions involving judges on the other courts.

The jurisdiction of the supreme court includes declaring laws unconstitutional. According to article 88, the court has extraordinary power to enforce constitutional rights, in addition to appellate and original jurisdiction defined by law.

Ombudsman

Article 97 establishes an abuse of authority investigation commission, appointed by the monarch to investigate complaints of any person of "misuse of authority by improper or corrupt deeds of any person holding public office." However, the commission, which functions like an ombudsman, may not initiate proceedings against officials otherwise covered by the constitution or liable under military law.

Amending the Constitution

Article 115 provides that a proposal to amend any part of the constitution, except article 115 and anything contrary to the preamble, may be introduced as a bill in either house. If passed by a two-thirds vote of the members present, it is to be sent to the monarch for assent. If the monarch returns the proposal and it is again passed in its original form or with amendments by the previously required majority, the monarch must assent.

In 1581 the Dutch parliament declared that rulers are responsible to the people and may be overthrown if they violate the people's established rights. Today Netherlanders are continuing to explore reforms to their 1814 constitution.

THE NETHERLANDS

General Information

The Kingdom of the Netherlands, also called Holland, in northern Europe is approximately 42,000 square kilometers and is bounded by the North Sea on the west and north, Germany on the east, and Belgium on the south. It includes the Netherlands Antilles islands in the Caribbean, which in 1954, pursuant to the Charter for the Kingdom, acquired associated statehood, becoming responsible for their own internal affairs; Holland continues to handle foreign affairs and provide for their defense. Although Amsterdam is the capital of this country of nearly sixteen million persons, the seat of government and the parliament is The Hague.

The Netherlands has been an industrial country since World War II. It joined with Belgium and Luxembourg to form the Benelux countries, a free-trade area that later became a part of the European Economic Community.

Type of Government: Parliamentary constitutional monarchy, with a monarch, a council of state, a prime minister and council of ministers (cabinet), a bicameral legislature, a judiciary, and a general chamber of audit

Date of Constitution: 1814 (revised in 1815, 1848, 1917, and 1983)

Constitutional History

Before A.D. 1000 the present-day territory of the Netherlands was barely habitable. After 1400 the land was protected from the North Sea by specially built defenses and the water drained by windmill power. Holland, whose inhabitants speak Dutch, a Germanic language, soon grew to encompass Belgium and Luxembourg. The duchies and principalities that constituted the northern provinces joined to form the United Provinces in 1579. The Netherlands declared independence from Spain in 1581, driving out the Spanish by 1595. It was extended formal international recognition under the Treaty of Westphalia in 1648.

A commercial people, the Dutch sent ships around the world to seek new trade routes to the East; in 1625 they established a colony in North America called New Amsterdam, now New York, and others, including one in Indonesia. In 1806 the Dutch took the British Cape Colony. Holland itself had been occupied by the French in 1795. The Dutch legal system developed from the French model during the time of Napoleon as well as German and Roman law. After the French left in 1813, a constitutional monarchy was installed for the first time since 1581, with King William I, prince of Orange-Nassau, assuming the throne in 1815 under a constitution adopted in 1814 and revised a year later to create a second house of parliament.

Following Belgium's independence in 1830, the Dutch constitution was revised in 1848 to provide for the direct election of members of the lower house of the legislature by certain taxpayers and the election of members of the upper house by members of the provincial councils. Constitutional reform in 1917 brought full suffrage for men and women and introduced a system of proportional representation.

During the spring of 1940 Holland was defeated by the Nazis in five days and was not liberated until the end of the war in Europe. After the war the Netherlands lost its possession of Indonesia but retained Surinam in South America and the Netherlands Antilles, six islands in the Caribbean governed under a 1954 Charter for the Kingdom. Surinam became an independent republic in 1975, and one of the Antilles, Aruba, is seeking to obtain its independence by 1996. In 1982, following a period of economic recession, a new coalition government agreement was reached and led to a nonstructural revision of the constitution on February 17, 1983.

Influences	Somewhat uniquely, the constitution of the Netherlands has developed along its own lines, without outside influence.

The Constitution

Unlike those of Belgium, France, and Germany, this constitution contains no unequivocal foundation for government power, such as the sovereignty of the nation or the people. Article 54 of the 1972 constitutional text, which remains in force under later revision, requires the members of the national legislature to take an oath of homage to a new monarch.

Fundamental Rights

Chapter I, Fundamental Rights, provides that the rights of the citizens, with some restrictions, include association, assembly, and demonstration; inviolability of the person; privacy, including privacy in correspondence and telephone; full compensation for public taking of private property, as well as freedom from illegal entry into a home; protection against illegal loss of liberty; freedom from discrimination; freedom of the press; freedom of religion; freedom to speak in court; protection against ex post facto laws; and the right to legal representation. The constitution also states that the government will promote sufficient employment, the rights of working people, their means of subsistence, and the distribution of wealth.

Division of Powers

The Netherlands is a unitary state in which power is divided among the monarch, as head of state; the prime minister, as head of government; the legislature; the courts, which have no power of judicial review; and a general chamber of audit.

The Executive

Monarch. Historically, if not expressly, the monarch is head of state. The position is hereditary and vests in the legitimate descendants of King William I, prince of Orange-Nassau, in order of seniority, although a person may be excluded by a two-thirds vote of the legislature. If there is no legal successor, the legislature may appoint one. The monarch may not exercise the royal prerogative—that is, act officially—before the age of eighteen, and, if unable to carry out his or her duties, a regent may be appointed. The council of state exercises the royal prerogative until a regent or successor can act.

Article 42 delineates roles and responsibilities:

1. The Government shall comprise the King and the Ministers.
2. The Ministers, and not the King, shall be responsible for the acts of government.

The power and duties of the monarch include opening the annual session of the legislature with a "speech from the throne"; establishing ministries; appointing and dismissing ministers, including the prime minister; and appointing and dismissing the state secretaries. Before the 1848 constitution the ministers advised the monarch and carried out his or her royal commands. However, because of the difficulty in not being able to criticize the government without criticizing the monarch, the absolute power of the royal prerogative was replaced with the concept of ministerial responsibility. The monarch still signs all acts of parliament and royal decrees, but these documents must be countersigned by at least one minister or state secretary. State secretaries are political appointees under the ministers, who are also responsible to the legislature.

Council of State. The monarch also appoints the ministers of state and presides over meetings of the council of state, an advisory body. "Minister of state" is an honorary title bestowed on exceptional politicians or statesmen who have generally retired from full-time political activity.

By request of the monarch, the council of state is consulted on bills and drafts of general administrative orders. A section of the council investigates administrative disputes and may actually decide such disputes pursuant to an act of parliament. A 1976 law allows members of the public who are directly affected by a decision of a government authority to appeal such a decision in the judicial section of the council.

Prime Minister and Cabinet. The Dutch prime minister, by law, has no hierarchical powers over the other ministers. But by virtue of his or her role in forming the cabinet and presiding over it, as well as the fact that in international affairs the officeholder represents the nation, the prime minister has become the central focus of government authority.

All the government ministers form the council of ministers (cabinet), whose meetings are chaired by the prime minister. The council generally meets once a week and discusses all matters relating to government policy, including all bills, international agreements and treaties, and the appointment of senior officials such as members of the council of state, commissioners, and burgomasters (mayors) of large municipalities. The agenda may include current social and economic policy and European Economic Community policy, as well as questions posed by the legislature. The council makes decisions by majority vote; when there is no clear majority and the matter is considered urgent, the prime minister casts the deciding vote.

Parliament. Before 1815 the Staten Generaal (states general) was a unicameral body representing the various independent provinces of the Netherlands. In 1815, however, a bicameral parliament was introduced.

Upper House. The upper house, the Eerste Kamer, has seventy-five members chosen by members of provincial councils.

Lower House. The lower house, the Tweede Kamer, corresponds generally to the British house of commons. It has 150 members elected by Dutch nationals over seventeen years of age. In 1848 a constitutional revision provided for the election of the members of the lower house by the direct vote of those citizens who paid a certain minimum amount of tax. In 1917 full suffrage for men was introduced, and in 1919 suffrage was extended to women.

Members of both houses represent all the people of the Netherlands and serve for four years. Each house appoints one of its members president. It is not possible to be a member of both houses at the same time, nor for a minister or state secretary to be a member of either house.

The parliament cannot make laws without the concurrence of the monarch. Both the government and the lower house may introduce legislation. Once submitted in the lower house by the government—the common practice—a bill goes to a committee for preliminary review. The committee prepares an initial report on the proposed measure, the appropriate minister responds, and a final report is issued. The bill is then debated, acted on by the lower house, and sent to the upper house, which has no authority to amend it. On passage by the upper house, the legislation goes to the monarch for ratification and then to the minister or ministers for countersignature. Measures introduced by members of the lower house are sent to the council of ministers and the council of state only after passage by both houses. Such bills are then forwarded to the monarch and finally to the appropriate minister or ministers for countersignature.

In addition to acting on legislative matters, an equally important function of the parliament is supervising the government's actions. The constitution provides for parliamentary control over the government in four major ways: the requirement that the national budget be implemented by an act of parliament and that all expenditures be included in the budget; the right of either house, as a whole, to ask for information from the ministers, called the right of interpellation; the right of individual members to put questions to ministers; and the power to establish an independent body to investigate complaints relating to actions of government authorities. Pursuant to the seldom-used right of inquiry *(enquête)* under article 70, the lower house has initiated several investigations into the government's activities in the past few years.

The Judiciary

According to chapter 6, on the Administration of Justice, the judiciary is given authority to judge offenses as well as disputes under civil law and over debts. Courts that form a part of the judiciary are specified by law, and the organization, composition, and powers of the judiciary are to be regulated by law.

Supreme Court. The constitution establishes a supreme court, whose members are to be appointed from a list of three people proposed by the upper house of the legislature. In fact, the names proposed are the three highest on a list submitted by the supreme court itself. According to article 119, "present and former members of the states general, ministers and state secretaries shall be tried by the supreme court for offenses committed while in office." Such proceedings are to be instituted by royal decree or by resolution of the upper house of the legislature.

Other courts include courts of appeal, regional courts, and district courts. The prosecutor general and the prosecution service are referred to as a part of the judiciary, but in practice they are a part of the executive branch.

Article 120 expressly prohibits the courts from reviewing the constitutionality of acts of parliament and treaties. Although there was some discussion about this provision when the 1983 constitutional revision was drafted, it was retained for the following reason: the legislature makes not only the laws but also the constitution, so it can change the constitution if it wishes. However, under Netherlands law, treaty provisions supersede all national law, even the constitution, and the Netherlands is a party to international conventions that guarantee to its citizens the protection of a number of fundamental rights.

General Chamber of Audit

The general chamber of audit is independent of the government and parliament and is responsible for examining the state's revenues and expenditures.

Water Control Boards

The unique character of the Dutch geography and reliance on land recovered from the sea have given rise to constitutionally defined institutions called water control boards, which date back in some cases to the twelfth century. The boards are established by the provinces and are responsible for water management within specified areas.

Amending the Constitution

According to article 137, an amendment requires an act of the legislature. Such a bill may be divided into two or more bills by the lower house, which is dissolved after the proposed act has been published. After a newly elected lower house has met, both houses then consider the proposed amendment on second reading, and it must be passed by "at least two-thirds of the votes cast." Article 139 provides that amendments "passed by the legislature and ratified by the King shall enter into force immediately after they have been published." Section 140, however, provides that current laws in conflict with constitutional reform remain in effect until changed to conform with the revisions.

In 1840 Maori leaders signed the Treaty of Waitangi, relinquishing their claim to New Zealand, and the following year it became a British colony. Today Elizabeth II of England is New Zealand's sovereign, and its inhabitants are often characterized as being more British than the British.

New Zealand, with its two main islands, is approximately 268,000 square kilometers and lies in the south Pacific Ocean approximately 2,000 kilometers east of Australia across the Tasman Sea. Wellington is the capital of this country whose population is nearly four million persons.

New Zealand's economy is basically agricultural; wool, meat, and dairy products, as well as timber and iron ore, contribute to the support of its social welfare state, modeled on that of the Scandinavian countries. The first nation to grant women's suffrage in 1893 installed its first woman prime minister in 1997.

Type of Government: Parliamentary constitutional monarchy, with a monarch, a governor-general and executive council, a prime minister and cabinet, a unicameral legislature, and a judiciary

Date of Constitution: Unwritten; 1840 (Treaty of Waitangi, earliest constitutional document)

The indigenous people of New Zealand are the Maoris, Polynesians whose ancestors arrived between the tenth and the thirteenth centuries A.D. They settled mostly on North Island, where even today about two-thirds of all New Zealanders live.

The first European contact was made by a Dutch ship captained by Abel Janszoon Tasman in 1642, and the Dutch named the land Nieu Zealande. In 1769 Capt. James Cook landed and made detailed maps of the islands for Britain. Whalers and missionaries followed, and soon Bay of Islands at the northeast end of North Island, particularly the town of Kororareka, had become a notorious and lawless "red light" district. To quell the lawlessness, in 1833 Australia sent to New Zealand an agent who had no apparent legal authority.

Originally the British government believed that it had no power in New Zealand. As their settlements grew and commercial land development schemes attracted attention, however, the British agent from Australia was replaced by a consul, who recommended acquiring sovereignty over the territory. On February 6, 1840, a number of Maori chiefs, who had been invited to the first agent's residence on a stream called the Waitangi, signed a treaty giving the British sovereignty in exchange for certain guarantees. More than five hundred people—both Maoris and British, including six women—signed the document, and on May 3, 1841, New Zealand became a separate crown colony.

A bicameral national legislature and six provincial legislatures were created by the British New Zealand Constitution Act of 1852, but the monarch could disallow laws, even if the British governor had assented to them. In 1857 New Zealand's legislature was given authority to amend or repeal the 1852 act, although an 1865 United Kingdom act codified the basis for voiding laws of the colonies repugnant to British laws. During this time gold was discovered on South Island, and conflicts with the Maoris over land broke out, leaving a bitter memory that has not yet completely faded. Maori affairs were placed in the hands of the New Zealand government in 1870, and the provincial governments were abolished in 1875. In the same year suffrage was extended to all adult males, and in 1893 women were enfranchised.

New Zealanders loyally supported the British in the Boer War and World War I, and in 1917 the position of governor was promoted to governor-general, although the legal status of the position has long been questioned. In 1947 the nation's legislature adopted the United Kingdom's 1931 Statute of Westminster, which in effect offered the dominions—including Canada, Australia, South Africa, Newfoundland, and the Irish Free State—legislative autonomy.

A 1956 act established new rules for electing members of the legislature, the former upper house or legislative council having been abolished a few years earlier. In 1962 the office of ombudsman was created, a first for any English-speaking country, and a number of amendments to the constitution followed.

The 1986 constitution act, which encompasses most of the constitutional law of New Zealand but not the many constitutional conventions under which power is actually wielded, went into effect on January 1, 1987. The 1852 act, the 1947 adoption of the Statute of Westminster, and other related acts were repealed. Since then, a bill of rights and electoral reforms have been enacted. Although there is no strong movement for New Zealand's becoming a republic, since 1995 the country's court of appeal, rather than the privy council in London, has functioned as its highest judicial body.

Influences

The British parliamentary system has had the greatest influence. Historic constitutional documents and acts of the British parliament, such as Magna Carta and the Habeas Corpus Act of 1679, respectively, have been incorporated into New Zealand law.

The Constitution

The 1986 constitution act is the most comprehensive law relating to New Zealand's current constitution. It is supplemented, however, by the 1840 Treaty of Waitangi, as amended; a 1956 electoral act, as amended; and the 1990 Bill of Rights Act. The Imperial Laws' Application Act of 1988 lists and defines traditional constitutional materials related to the United Kingdom's constitution that have been incorporated into New Zealand law.

The Treaty of Waitangi begins:

Her majesty, therefore, being desirous to establish a settled form of civil government with a view to avert the evil consequences which must result from the absence of the necessary laws and institutions alike to the native population and to her subjects, has been graciously pleased to empower and authorize me . . . [to be] consul, and Lieutenant Governor of such parts of New Zealand as may be, or hereafter shall be, ceded to her majesty. . . .

The first article of the treaty declares the transfer of sovereignty:

The chiefs of the confederation of the united tribes of New Zealand, and the separate and independent chiefs who have not become members of the confederation, cede to her majesty the queen of England, absolutely and without reservation, all rights and powers of sovereignty which the said confederation or individual chiefs respectively exercise or possess, or may be supposed to exercise or to possess, over their respective territories as sole sovereigns thereof.

The Constitution Act of 1986 describes its purpose: ". . . to reform the constitutional law of New Zealand, to bring together into one enactment certain provisions of constitutional significance, and to provide that the New Zealand Constitution Act 1852 of the parliament of the United Kingdom shall cease to have effect as part of the law of New Zealand."

Fundamental Rights

The 1990 Bill of Rights Act expressly secures, subject to some limitations, rights including freedom of religion, speech, and assembly; protects against discrimination; and extends to persons accused of crimes fundamental rights of due process, including access to legal counsel and a fair trial. The act does not empower the courts to nullify legislation inconsistent with its provisions; however, if a law is ambiguous, the courts must interpret it in a manner consistent with the act, which is subject to change by a simple majority vote in the legislature.

Division of Powers

In New Zealand, a unitary state, there is no strict separation of powers. Power is divided among the monarch (the queen of England), who is the titular head of state and is represented by a governor-general, now a New Zealander; the prime minister, who is head of government; the legislature; and the courts, which do not have judicial review authority.

Monarch. The 1986 act provides that "the sovereign in right of New Zealand" is the head of state but acts through an appointed representative, the governor-general. Elizabeth II, queen of England, is also the queen of New Zealand.

Governor-General. By convention, only the nominee of the ministers of New Zealand is appointed, generally for a five-year term. The governor-general is commander in chief of the armed forces but in title only. He or she appoints ministers nominated by the prime minister.

Executive Council. The executive council is a formal enacting body composed of ministers. The prime minister and other ministers, in fact, exercise their powers through the cabinet.

Prime Minister and Cabinet. As in other British-style governments, the leader of the elected legislature's controlling party or of a coalition of parties is designated the prime minister. The prime minister forms a government after a general election by nominating ministers to be appointed by the governor-general. He or she sets the agenda and presides over cabinet meetings and has the power to make decisions despite objections from other cabinet members. The prime minister's ability to run the government was enhanced in the late 1970s by the creation of a small, well-staffed office directly responsible to him or her. Another key position is that of minister of finance, who often serves as deputy prime minister. The roles of the prime minister and cabinet are examples of constitutional practices that have developed by convention, rather than by law.

Part 2 of the 1986 act, on the Executive, requires, with a variance, that ministers and members of the executive council be members of the legislature. Typically, the executive includes the cabinet, the executive council, and the departments of government; but vital decisions are made by the cabinet, which exists by convention, and real executive power rests in the hands of a small group of ministers together with a small group of key civil servants.

As in other parliamentary-style governments, the ministers are responsible to the legislature collectively for cabinet decisions and individually for the acts of their respective departments.

Parliament. New Zealand's general assembly was created by the 1852 act. Bicameral until 1950, today the parliament consists of the governor-general, as representative of the monarch, and a house of representatives.

Representatives are elected by secret ballot for three-year terms from electoral districts based on population, although Maoris and persons of Maori descent may register in either a Maori or a general electorate. Citizens who are eighteen years old and have been a resident of their district continuously for one month are eligible to vote or be elected a representative, unless otherwise disqualified.

After elections, a speaker is elected from among the members and confirmed by the governor-general. Even after the house is dissolved the speaker remains in office until the close of the polling day of the following general election. In 1975 the position of house leader was created to help the legislative process run smoothly; a chairman of the house takes charge when the legislature sits in committee.

The day-to-day running of the parliament is outlined in the Parliamentary Service Act of 1985. The legislative process begins with the introduction of a bill in the house. Public bills, as opposed to local and private bills, are generally submitted by the government. Since 1980 every bill, except a money bill and those certified by the speaker as urgent, is sent to a committee after being passed on a formal first reading. The committee, after hearing from interested parties, reports the bill out with any amendments for the second reading, after which it must be considered clause by clause by the house in committee. After passage on the third reading, a bill goes to the governor-general for approval.

Ombudsman. Since 1962 there has been a parliamentary commissioner (ombudsman) to investigate citizen complaints relating to acts of officials.

The Judiciary

Supreme Court. Except for some special courts with limited jurisdiction created by acts of parliament, the only court of general jurisdiction in New Zealand is the high court, formally known as the supreme court, which was established in 1841.

Court of Appeal. A court of appeal, which reviews criminal and civil, including administrative, decisions, is New Zealand's highest judicial body.

The 1986 constitution act provides certain protections in the case of removal and against salary reduction of judges, who are appointed by convention from the ranks of the most experienced practitioners in the courts of law. The chief justice, by convention, is also appointed from the members of the practicing bar and not from among sitting judges.

Under its British-style government, New Zealand's parliament is supreme in its authority to make laws, even constitutional ones, so no true judicial or constitutional review by the courts is possible. A provision of the 1956 electoral act, however, requires a seventy-five percent majority vote by the house to amend certain parts of the act. The question therefore arises whether a parliament has the power to bind a future parliament to a minimum vote higher than a simple majority and how the courts would deal with such a question.

Amending the Constitution

Constitutional legislation may be enacted in New Zealand, as in the United Kingdom, by a simple majority vote of the legislature. Because much of the constitution is rooted in convention as well as in law, however, hasty, drastic, or unpopular changes to the constitution are not likely.

The conflict between the Sandinistas and the Contras in Nicaragua polarized the United States in the 1980s, but the Central American country has enjoyed a period of relative stability since the election of Violeta Barrios de Chamorro in 1990.

General Information

The Republic of Nicaragua in Central America is approximately 130,000 square kilometers and is bounded by Honduras on the north, the Caribbean Sea on the east, Costa Rica on the south, and the Pacific Ocean on the west. Managua is the capital of this country of approximately five million persons.

Nicaragua's natural resources remain mostly unexploited; bananas, cotton, coffee, and sugar are its major crops. A decade of rule by the Castro-like Sandinist National Liberation Front (Sandinistas), Hurricane Joan in 1988, and a mud slide that killed some two thousand persons in 1998 have impeded economic progress.

Type of Government: Presidential republic, with a president and cabinet, a unicameral legislature, a judiciary, and a supreme electoral council

Dates of Key Constitutions: 1826, 1838, 1937, 1948, 1950, 1974 (abrogated in 1980), and 1987 (significantly amended in 1996)

Constitutional History

Shortly after Vasco Núñez de Balboa first glimpsed the Pacific Ocean from the Isthmus of Panama in 1513, Spaniards fought each other for control of the region around Lake Nicaragua, named for a powerful native chieftain, and established the settlements of Granada and Leon in 1524. A rivalry between conservative, wealthier Granada and liberal, anticlerical Leon developed and continues today. Placed under the captaincy-general of Guatemala, Leon became the administrative center because of its proximity to the Pacific.

Pedrarias de Avila, who had been removed in Panama for excessive cruelty, took control of the Nicaragua area along with Hernando de Soto and later ruled as governor. The eastern coast, ignored by the Spanish, was settled by the English, who cut timber there commercially. Nicaragua's independence from Spain on September 15, 1821, resulted from the general independence movements in Latin America. Nicaragua joined a confederacy of states, the Central American Federation, which included Mexico, and then the new republic of the United Provinces of Central America, which included neither Mexico nor Panama.

The last of the Central American Federation states to do so, Nicaragua wrote its first constitution in 1826. Like many other Latin American countries whose liberal and conservative factions vied for political expression, Nicaragua wrote many constitutions—in fact, a total of seventeen. Nicaragua's first chief of state was executed in 1828, and the third was murdered in office in 1837. A new constitution in 1838, after Nicaragua left the federation, created the position of supreme director.

Americans such as Cornelius Vanderbilt and the soldier of fortune William Walker played key roles in the development of the country in the latter half of the nineteenth century. Between 1909 and the 1933 elections, supervised by the United States, the U.S. marines intervened in Nicaragua's affairs almost continuously. An opponent of U.S. intervention was Augusto Cesar Sandino, who dressed like an American cowboy and was assassinated in 1934 by the American-trained national guard.

In 1937, after U.S. troops had been withdrawn and he had eliminated all of his opponents, Gen. Anastasio Samoza Garcia ("Tacho"), commander of the national guard, was "elected" president. By this time the country had been through nine constitutions, and after taking office Samoza arranged for a new one to extend his term for ten years. A new constitution in 1948 granted "Tacho" an additional six years as president, and one in 1950 allowed him to run for a four-year term but not succeed himself. Samoza ruled until his assassination in 1956.

A son succeeded him in 1957, a close family friend became president in 1963, and then another son, "Tachito," became president in 1967. Unable constitutionally to succeed himself, the last Samoza formed a three-man junta to rule the country in 1971. "Tachito" was reelected president in 1974 under a new constitution. The Sandinist National Liberation Front was founded in 1962 in opposition to the Samozas. Misuse of aid to earthquake victims in 1972 and the murder in 1978 of the newspaper publisher Pedro Joaquin Chamorro, a government critic, led to a successful revolution by the Sandinistas in 1979.

In 1980 the Sandinista junta abrogated the 1974 constitution, which provided for a presidential-style government, but promulgated a law restoring citizens' rights. A counterrevolutionary army, the Contras, supported by the United States, fought a guerrilla war against the Sandinistas for several years. A cease-fire was negotiated in 1987, but it took an economic crisis and the Soviet Union's withdrawal of its support of the Sandinistas to bring about free elections in 1990. Violeta Barrios de Chamorro, widow of the slain publisher, was elected president under a new constitution promulgated on January 9, 1987, and extensively amended in 1996.

Influences

Government sources indicate that the drafters of the 1987 constitution studied nineteen countries, including recent Latin American constitutions and the constitutions of the United Kingdom, France, Spain, Sweden, the United States, Bulgaria, and the Soviet Union.

The Constitution

The preamble to the 1987 constitution of the Republic of Nicaragua invokes a mixture of Christian and Marxist elements, as evident in the following passage:

The Nicaraguan people, all the democratic, patriotic, and revolutionary parties and organizations of Nicaragua, its men and women, its workers and peasants, its glorious youth, its heroic mothers, its Christians who from their faith in God have committed themselves to the struggle for the liberation of the oppressed, its patriotic intellectuals, and all those who, through their productive work, contribute to the defense of the homeland. . . .

Article 2, as amended in 1996, states:

National sovereignty resides in the people, who exercise it by means of democratic instruments, deciding and participating freely in the building and improvement of the nation's economic, political, and social system. The people exercise political power through their representatives freely elected by universal, equal, free, direct, and secret suffrage, barring any [others] . . . from arrogating upon themselves such power. . . .

Article 129 declares that "the legislative, executive, judicial, and electoral branches are independent of one another and coordinate harmoniously, subordinated only to the supreme interests of the nation and to what is established in the constitution."

Article 182 sets forth the constitution as the supreme law of the land, and article 184 states that the electoral and emergency laws and the law of *amparo* are "constitutional laws."

Fundamental Rights

Title 4, Rights, Duties, and Guarantees of the Nicaraguan People, provides for all people the right to life, with no fear of the death penalty; personal freedom, security, and access to legal redress; a private individual and family life; the inviolability of their homes, correspondence, and communication, except as provided for by law; and respect for honor and reputation. Other guarantees include equality before the law and equal protection under the law; freedom of conscience, thought, and religion; freedom of expression; the right to travel; and recourse in accordance with the law of *amparo* for violations of rights.

Separate chapters in title 4 discuss political, social, family, and labor rights, as well as the rights of communities of the Atlantic, or Caribbean, coast to express and preserve their languages, art, and culture.

In Nicaragua, a unitary state, power is divided among the president, as head of state and government; the legislature; the courts, which exercise some judicial review; and the supreme electoral council.

President. The president, who is authorized to exercise executive power, is head of state and government and commander in chief of the army. A vice president is to act for the president if she or he is temporarily or permanently absent. Both are elected by universal, equal, direct, free, and secret vote and by a "relative majority." To be eligible for either office, among other qualifications, a person must be a Nicaraguan national, enjoy full civil and political rights, and be at least twenty-five years old.

The duties and powers of the president include complying with and enforcing the constitution and the laws; representing the nation; initiating and vetoing bills; issuing executive decrees in administrative matters; preparing the budget; appointing and removing ministers, vice ministers, and other officials; negotiating and formalizing treaties; declaring a state of emergency, which must be ratified by the legislature; adopting regulations to implement the laws; organizing and directing the government; administering the economy and determining the country's socioeconomic policy; and nominating judges, the comptroller general, and other officials for election by the legislature.

Cabinet. The number, organization, and jurisdiction of the ministers of the state and autonomous and government institutions are to be determined by law. According to article 151, the cabinet consists of the vice president and ministers of state and is "headed by the President."

Congress. The unicameral national assembly consists of ninety representatives and alternates elected for five-year terms on the basis of proportional representation. Article 133 provides that unsuccessful candidates for president and vice president who receive a certain percentage of votes also become members and alternates, respectively. Eligibility requirements include possessing Nicaraguan nationality and "complete civil and political rights" and being more than twenty-one years of age. Once elected, members enjoy certain legal immunities.

Members of the assembly and the president may introduce bills, as may the supreme court and supreme electoral council for bills relating to matters within their jurisdiction. A quorum is half the members plus one, and generally a simple majority vote of those present is required to approve measures. Once passed, a bill must be sanctioned by the president to become law. A presidential veto may be overridden by a vote of one-half plus one of the total lawmakers.

The powers and duties of the legislature include officially interpreting the law; ratifying international treaties; electing judges to the supreme court and supreme electoral council from nominees submitted by the president; authorizing presidential trips abroad of longer than fifteen days; decreeing amnesty and pardons; and granting and canceling the legal status of civil associations.

Article 158 declares: "Justice emanates from the people and shall be carried out in their name and proxy by the judicial branch, composed of the courts of justice that the law establishes." In exercising their jurisdiction, the courts are responsible to the judicial branch.

Supreme Court. The highest court is the "Supreme Court of Justice." Judges serve for seven-year terms, may be dismissed only for causes determined by the Constitution and the law, and "enjoy immunity." The court consists of twelve magistrates, or judges, each of whom is elected by the legislature from persons nominated by the president. The court elects its own president.

The powers and duties of the supreme court include organizing and directing the administration of justice; deciding ordinary and extraordinary appeals from lower court decisions; deciding cases in *amparo* for the violation of constitutional rights; ruling on remedies regarding the unconstitutionality of the law; and appointing judges to other courts, including appeals courts.

According to article 166, "The administration of justice shall be organized and shall function with popular participation as determined by the laws. The members of the courts of justice, be they lawyers or not, have equal authority in the exercise of their legal functions."

Supreme Electoral Council

Article 169 states: "The electoral branch is composed of the supreme electoral council and other subordinate electoral bodies." The supreme electoral council consists of five judges elected by the legislature for five-year terms, and the legislature selects its president. The council's functions include organizing and conducting elections, plebiscites, and referendums; appointing members of other electoral bodies in accordance with the electoral law; establishing the calendar for elections; applying the constitution and the law to the election process; serving as final arbiter in disputes; and developing "full guarantees within the electoral processes."

Amending the Constitution

The president or one-third of the members of the legislature may initiate partial reform of the constitution. A special commission is to render an opinion on a proposed amendment in sixty days. The proposal then is handled as a bill, except that it must be discussed in two legislative sessions, must be approved by at least sixty percent of the representatives, and may not be vetoed by the president.

A total revision of the constitution requires the election of a constituent assembly and approval of at least two-thirds of its members at a single session.

Since obtaining its independence in 1960, Nigeria—Africa's most populous nation—has been searching for economic and political stability under a succession of constitutions and military governments.

The Federal Republic of Nigeria in central West Africa is approximately 924,000 square kilometers and is bounded by Benin on the west, Niger and Chad on the north, Cameroon on the east, and the Gulf of Guinea in the south Atlantic Ocean on the south. Nigeria has approximately 123 million persons, and its capital has been moved recently from Lagos, on the south coast, to the centrally located Abuja, in a federal capital territory.

Nigeria is rich in natural resources; the United States buys a large percentage of its oil exports. In a move to diversify its economy, it intends to place future emhasis on recovering natural gas associated with oil production. However, ethnic and religious conflicts, as well as corruption, contribute to the nation's instability.

Type of Government: Presidential federal republic, with a president and cabinet, a bicameral legislature, and a judiciary

Dates of Constitutions: 1922, 1946, 1951, 1954, 1960, 1963, 1979, 1989 (never implemented), and 1999

The Nok people, skilled artisans and ironworkers, were the first distinctive culture to inhabit the area of Nigeria between the fourth century B.C. and the second century A.D. By the beginning of the eleventh century, trade routes through the region between northern and southern Africa were important to the local economy.

The Yoruba kingdoms in the southwest and the Hausa cities to the north, as well as many smaller states, were well established before the middle of the second millennium. Beginning in the thirteenth century the Fulani, herders from the Senegal Valley, migrated into the area. The Igbo, about whom there is almost no precolonial history, also lived in the territory of what is today Nigeria, apparently without centralized government or even tribal chiefs.

Soon after discovery by the Portuguese in the fifteenth century, the area of Nigeria became prominent in the developing slave trade, a practice not outlawed internally until 1901. After the defeat of Napoleon at Waterloo, British colonization efforts in Nigeria increased, and Lagos was founded in 1862. By 1900 administration of the territory had been placed in the hands of the British colonial office, but control of the people was difficult. In the north the Hausa and Fulani had adopted the Islamic faith and were governed by feudal monarchs called emirs. With protectorates set up in both northern and southern Nigeria, the British began subduing the Muslim region. British control was complete by 1903, after protracted battles against the Kano and Sokoto sultanates, but in many cases British rule was indirect, allowing local rulers to remain in power even when the two protectorates were consolidated in 1914.

Nigeria was treated as a unitary state and administered by a governor and executive council. The 1922 "Clifford" constitution, named after the governor, provided for a legislative council of forty-six members, four of whom were to be elected. Opposition to this system of government grew, as did the spirit of nationalism. By 1946, when the "Richards" constitution was approved by the British parliament, political parties were actively maneuvering in anticipation of independence. The new constitution moved the country toward a federal system by creating a legislative assembly with only consultative powers in each of the three major regions of the country—east, west, and south—but it preserved the powers of the governor while expanding the existing legislative council. Constitutions were promulgated again in 1951 and 1954. The constitution adopted in 1960, the year of Nigeria's independence, created a parliamentary form of government and contained an elaborate section on fundamental rights.

On leaving the British Commonwealth in 1963, Nigeria became a republic. A new constitution replaced the British monarch's representative, the governor-general, with a president and created a fourth geographical region, the midwest, from the western region. Civil disorder grew after the defeat of Biafran rebel forces in 1970, and officials including the prime minister were assassinated. Instability continued following the installation of a military government. A new constitution was promulgated in 1979, but in 1983 a military coup toppled the civilian government.

In 1989, with the military still in power, a constitution was promulgated by decree and was scheduled to take effect on October 1, 1992. The military, however, refused to reinstate civilian rule, and the constitution never went into effect. On May 5, 1999, by decree of the military government, a new constitution was promulgated; although it basically reinstates the 1979 constitution, it contains some provisions from the unexecuted 1989 document. Within a month the former military ruler, Olesgun Obansanjo, became the first elected civilian head of the Nigerian government to take office in fifteen years.

Influences

Nigerian constitutions were originally influenced by the British parliamentary system.

The Constitution

The preamble states that "we the people ... [have] firmly and solemnly resolved: To live in unity and harmony as one indivisible and indissoluble Sovereign Nation under God dedicated to the promotion of inter-African solidarity, world peace, international co-operation and understanding." It adds that the constitution is designed to promote "the good government and welfare of all persons in our country on the principles of Freedom, Equality and Justice, and for the purpose of consolidating the Unity of our people."

Sections 1 and 2, respectively, provide that the constitution "is supreme and its provisions shall have binding force on all authorities and persons ..." and that "Nigeria shall be a Federation consisting of States and a Federal Capital Territory." Thirty-six states and 768 local government areas are provided for. A chapter entitled "Fundamental Objectives and Directive Principles of State Policy," which is similar to a statement in the Ugandan constitution of 1995, includes sections on political, economic, education, foreign policy, and environmental objectives, as well as directives on Nigerian cultures, obligations of the mass media, national ethics, and duties of citizens.

Fundamental Rights

Among the fundamental rights guaranteed in articles 33 through 44 are the right to life, although the death penalty is permitted; personal dignity; liberty, except when a criminal sentence is imposed; the rights of those accused of crimes, including the right to a fair hearing and the presumption of innocence; privacy; family life; freedom of thought, conscience, religion, expression, and the press, provided that "[n]othing shall invalidate any law that is reasonably justifiable in a democratic society ... for the purpose of ... regulating ... television or ... films." Other guarantees include the rights to peaceful assembly and association; the right to "acquire and own immovable property anywhere in Nigeria"; freedom of movement; a prohibition against discrimination on the basis of ethnic group, place of origin, sex, religion, political opinion, or "circumstances of ... birth."

Article 45 addresses restrictions and derogations from fundamental rights "in the interest of defense, public safety, public order, public morality or public health," as well as "for the purpose of protecting the rights and freedom of other persons." Article 46 grants access to the high court for violations of the constitution's provisions on fundamental rights.

Division of Powers

The constitution divides power among the national, state, and local governments. At the national level, it is allocated among the executive, legislative, and judicial branches of government.

President. Article 130 declares: "The President shall be the Head of State, the Chief Executive of the Federation and Commander-in-Chief of the Armed Forces." No other responsibilities are expressly enumerated. To be president a person must be a Nigerian citizen by birth, forty years old, a member of and sponsored by a political party, and have a school certificate or its equivalent; disqualifications include allegiance to another country and having been elected president twice before. Different criteria are used for electing the president, who runs with a vice presidential candidate for a four-year term, depending on whether there are one, two, or more candidates. The winner generally must receive a majority of the votes cast at large and "not less than one-quarter of the votes cast at the election in each of at least two-thirds of all the States . . . and the Federal Capital Territory." Before taking office, the chief executive must declare "his assets and liabilities."

The president or vice president may be removed from office based on allegations by "not less than one-third of the members of the [legislature], . . . presented to the President of the Senate, . . . of gross misconduct in the performance of the functions of his office," after an investigation authorized by a vote "of not less than two-thirds" of both houses of the legislature, followed by a final vote of two-thirds of all the members of each house on a report confirming the allegations. Either official may also be removed for permanent incapacity. The vice president succeeds to the office of president in the event of the incumbent's death, resignation, impeachment, permanent incapacity, or removal.

Cabinet. Article 147 mandates: "There shall be such offices of Ministers of the Government . . . as may be established by the President." Ministers are appointed by the president and confirmed by the legislature's upper house. Members of the national legislature or a state legislature must resign if appointed to the cabinet.

Congress. According to article 47, "There shall be a National Assembly for the Federation which shall consist of a Senate [upper house] and a House of Representatives [lower house]." Resident Nigerian citizens at least eighteen years old may vote in elections for each chamber, both of which are "dissolved at the expiration of . . . four years."

Upper House. The constitution divides each state into three senatorial districts for elections. Senators must be citizens of Nigeria, thirty-five years old, "educated up to at least School Certificate level," and members of and sponsored by a political party. The senate elects its president and deputy president from among its members.

Lower House. For elections to the house of representatives, the country is divided "into three hundred and sixty Federal constituencies." One representative is elected from each constituency, each subject to the same qualifications as senators, except that the age requirement is thirty years. The house elects a speaker and a deputy speaker.

Bills may originate in either house. A quorum is one-third of all the members, and decisions generally "shall be determined by the required majority of the members present and voting." After passage, bills "shall be sent to the other House, and . . . [are then] presented to the President for assent." If the president withholds assent, a bill may nevertheless become law if it is "again passed by each House by [a] two-thirds majority." Separate provisions are specified for money bills and constitutional amendments.

"The judicial powers of the Federation," states article 6, "shall be vested in the courts," which include a supreme court, a court of appeal, a federal high court, a high court of the federal capital territory, high courts of the states, and other courts including *shari'a* (Islamic) courts.

Supreme Court. As specified in articles 230 and 231, respectively, the supreme court consists of a chief justice and a number of members determined by law, "not exceeding twenty-one," who are appointed "by the President on the recommendation of the National Judicial Council subject to confirmation ... by the Senate."

The court has "original jurisdiction in any dispute between the Federation and a State or between States" and such other original jurisdiction, except in criminal matters, as provided for by the legislature. It also hears appeals from the court of appeal in certain cases including "questions of law ... in any civil or criminal proceedings," "decisions in any civil or criminal proceedings on questions as to the interpretation or application" of the constitution, and questions regarding the validity of the election of the president or vice president.

Amending the Constitution

Under article 9, the legislature "may, subject to the provisions of this section, alter any or all of the provisions of this Constitution." An amending act must be proposed by at least two-thirds of all the members of the house in which it originates and "approved by resolution of the [legislatures] of not less than two-thirds of all the States." However, amendments to section 8, regarding new states and boundary adjustments; section 9, on amending the constitution; and the chapter on fundamental rights additionally require passage in the national legislature by "not less than four-fifths of all the members of each House."

On Christmas Day, 1945, the Allied powers agreed to establish a national government for Korea under a five-year trusteeship administered jointly by U.S. and U.S.S.R. occupation authorities. In 1948, however, Kim Il Sung, a communist, assumed dictatorial power, which passed to his son, Kim Jong Il, after his death in 1994.

NORTH KOREA

The Democratic People's Republic of Korea, or North Korea, is approximately 121,000 square kilometers and is located on the northern part of the Asian peninsula of Korea, extending into the continent of Asia just south of China and Russia. It is bounded by the Korea Bay and the Yellow Sea on the west, the Sea of Japan on the east, and South Korea on the south. North Korea has a population of some 21.7 million persons, and its capital is Pyongyang.

North Korea's economy has gradually deteriorated to the point of near-collapse. The country remained isolated and hostile to South Korea during Kim Il Sung's regime, even threatening to produce a primitive nuclear weapon in defiance of the Nuclear Non-Proliferation Treaty (1968). His successor, Kim Jong Il, unexpectedly attended the first summit meeting between the leaders of North and South Korea in 2000.

Type of Government: Communist Party dictatorship, with a parliamentary government including a chairman (premier) and cabinet, a unicameral legislature, and a judiciary

Dates of Constitutions: 1948 and 1972 (revised in 1998)

The long history shared by North and South Koreans (see South Korea) ceased at the close of World War II, when Japanese colonial rule in Korea ended and the country was occupied by the Allies. After the war the area of Korea below the thirty-eighth parallel (degrees north latitude) was placed under U.S. administration, while the area above it came under U.S.S.R. administration. In February 1947 the general congress of the North Korean provisional people's committee met and established the North Korean people's assembly and the people's committee; its chairman was Kim Il Sung, a Korean communist in the Soviet army then occupying Korea above the thirty-eighth parallel.

In April 1948 South Korean leaders met with their counterparts in Pyongyang about forming a postwar government for Korea; at this meeting Kim pledged not to form a separate government in the north. When the meeting was not reconvened in July, North Korea, whose population was approximately eight million, or about a third of the total Korean population, held elections for a 572-member supreme people's assembly; it claimed that nearly nine million voters in the south had participated by secret ballot, electing 360 members to the assembly.

A Stalinist-style constitution was adopted on September 8, 1948, and the Democratic People's Republic was established the next day. The 1948 constitution, ostensibly for all of Korea, was instigated by Kim, in spite of his earlier pledge. Under the constitution the supreme people's assembly, created in August 1948, was to be the highest organ of state power. In fact, it merely heard reports and approved the national budget, appointments, and proposals of its supervisory and policy-making central committee. Until 1957 the assembly had 572 seats, but only 212 members actually met because 360 seats were reserved for the South Korean members.

On December 27, 1972, a new constitution was introduced to reflect the considerable changes in North Korean society and state policy and to end debate over whether the transition to socialism was complete and whether the proletarian dictatorship and the class struggle were still necessary. Compared to the constitutions of most Marxist socialist states, North Korea's new constitution is unique in its integration of nationalism and socialism and its introduction of the concept of *chuch'e* (self-reliance) as the driving force behind the move toward economic independence; other unique concepts also arise from the socialist revolution in North Korea.

Influences

The 1948 constitution was influenced by the 1936 Soviet constitution, whereas the 1972 document incorporates a number of purely North Korean concepts.

The Constitution

Kim Il Sung's 1972 North Korean constitution had no preamble. The preamble to the document as revised in 1998, like that of other communist constitutions, provides insight into the direction in which the Communist Party leadership would like to move. References to the deceased "Comrade Kim Il Sung" in each of the preamble's eleven paragraphs indicate a direction focused on the past.

"The Democratic People's Republic of Korea," proclaims article 1, "is an independent socialist state representing the interests of all the Korean people." Article 2 declares the nation's history as "a revolutionary state which has inherited brilliant traditions formed during the glorious revolutionary struggle against the imperialist aggressors ... to achieve the liberation of the homeland and the freedom and well-being of the people." Article 11 mandates that the republic "shall conduct all activities under the leadership of the Workers' Party of Korea."

Fundamental Rights

"[T]he rights and duties of citizens," states article 63, "are based on the collectivist principle, 'One for all and all for one.'" Rights set forth include equal rights and the right of all citizens at least seventeen years of age to vote and be elected, "irrespective of sex, race, occupation, length of residence, property status, education, party affiliation, political views or religion." Also enumerated are freedom of speech, the press, assembly, demonstration, and association, as well as the rights to submit complaints and petitions and to work. The "right to relaxation" is "ensured by the establishment of the working hours, the provision of holidays, paid leave, accommodation at health resorts and holiday homes at State expense and by a growing network of cultural facilities."

While article 8 indicates that the "social system ... is a people-centered system under which the working people are masters of everything, and everything in society serves the working people," other provisions note that "the means of production are owned only by the State and social cooperative organizations" and that North Korea's economy "is a planned economy." The right to private property, under article 24, is expressly limited to "property meeting the simple and individual aims of the citizen." Article 30 specifies that the "daily working hours of the working masses are eight hours." Child labor is prohibited, and compulsory eleven-year education beginning with preschool is made a goal, but the "State shall draw up a proper plan for scientific research [and] develop ... revolutionary literature and art, national in form and socialist in content."

Division of Powers

According to article 87, "The Supreme People's Assembly is the highest organ of State power." In fact, North Korea is a communist dictatorship in which all political power is in the hands of the Workers' Party and its leader, Kim Jong Il, the son of the deceased dictator Kim Il Sung.

The Executive

Premier and Cabinet. "The Cabinet," according to article 117, "is the administrative and executive body of the highest organ of State power [the legislature] and a general state management organ." It "consists of the Premier, vice premiers, chairmen of commissions, ministers and some other necessary members" and "is accountable" to the legislature.

The cabinet's specified powers and duties include adopting "measures to execute state policy," directing "state management based on the Constitution and departmental laws," and guiding "the work of the Cabinet commissions, ministries, direct organs of the Cabinet, [and] local people's committees." The cabinet also drafts "the State plan for the development of the national economy"; compiles the national budget; has responsibilities "in the fields of industry, agriculture, construction, transportation, communications, commerce, trade, land management, city management, education, science, culture, health, physical training, labor administration, environmental protection, tourism and others"; conducts "inspection and control work to establish a state management order"; adopts "measures to maintain social order"; and concludes and abrogates treaties.

Parliament. Article 88 vests legislative power in the Supreme People's Assembly. When it is not in session, its "Presidium also can exercise legislative power." The legislature is composed of deputies "elected on the principle of universal, equal and direct suffrage by secret ballot" for five-year terms "unless extended . . . due to unavoidable circumstances." It elects a chairman and a vice chairmen and adopts laws and decisions by a majority "of the deputies attending [by] a show of hands." A quorum is two-thirds of the deputies.

The Legislature

The assembly has authority to "amend and supplement the Constitution"; "adopt, amend and supplement departmental laws"; set basic principles of domestic and foreign policy; and elect officials, including the president, premier, and national defense commission chairperson. It also appoints and removes or transfers the prosecutor-general, chief justice, and the chairmen, vice chairmen, and members of the legislative committees; approves the state budget; and approves the ratification or abrogation of treaties.

According to article 153, "Justice is administered by the Central Court, Provincial . . . Court, People's Court or by the Special Court. Verdicts are delivered in the name of the [republic]." The courts are charged with protecting "through judicial procedure the State power and the socialist system . . . , the property of the State and social, cooperative organizations, personal rights as guaranteed by the Constitution, and the lives and property of citizens." Other duties include to "ensure that all institutions, enterprises, organizations and citizens abide strictly by State laws and staunchly combat class enemies and all law-breakers," as well as to give "judgments and findings with regard to property and conduct notarial work."

The Judiciary

Supreme Court. "The Central Court is the supreme court of the [republic]," states article 161. It supervises the "trial activities of all courts" and "is accountable to the [legislature and] the . . . Presidium when the [legislature] is in recess." The court's president serves for a term of five years unless it is extended.

Article 97 states in part: "The Constitution is amended and supplemented with the approval of more than two-thirds of the total number of deputies to the [legislature]." In actuality, amendments are approved by the head of the Korean Workers' Party, with the legislature's role being merely a formality.

Amending the Constitution

NORWAY

Norway's 1814 constitution, influenced by the French constitution of 1791, is the second oldest written constitution still in effect. Today the country seems content to maintain its independence from the European community.

General Information

The Kingdom of Norway, the fifth largest country in Europe, is approximately 324,000 square kilometers, not including its island territories. Half of the country lies above the Arctic Circle. Continental Norway is bounded by Sweden on the east, Finland and Russia on the northeast, and the Skagerrak, North Sea, Norwegian Sea, Atlantic Ocean, Arctic Ocean, and Barents Sea on the west and south. Oslo is the capital of this country of more than four million persons.

Norway's economy has traditionally relied on the abundant fish off its extensive coastline, but today, because of the country's large supplies of oil and hydroelectric power for industrialization, the majority of its work force is in manufacturing-related activities and service industries. Norwegians voted in 1994 not to join the European Union, although the vote was close.

Type of Government: Parliamentary constitutional monarchy, with a monarch, a prime minister and council of state (cabinet), a semibicameral legislature, and a judiciary

Date of Constitution: 1814

Constitutional History

By the end of the ninth century Norway was a unified kingdom. Previously, only petty kingdoms has existed; each one had an *allting* (local assembly), where men of some status in the community met to discuss matters of common interest and settle disputes under customary law. Some of these assemblies evolved into a *lagting* (law-making body), and eventually four large assemblies developed for the four regions of the country.

During the reign of Magnus the Lawmender, which began in 1263, Norway's national laws were codified in the Landslov. During that century Norway acquired Iceland and Greenland. But on the death of Haakon VI in 1380, Norway merged with Denmark and in 1397, along with Sweden, the country became a part of the Danish-dominated Union of Kalmar.

In 1665 the Danish king promulgated a royal instrument called the Konglov. The king was an absolute monarch, but by his authority Norwegians were protected from foreign nobility in their country. The code of King Magnus was revised and translated into Danish, and in 1687 the law was again completely codified and called Christian V's Norwegian Law, influenced, not surprisingly, by Danish law.

After the defeat of Napoleon at Leipzig, with whom the Danes had sided, Denmark was forced to cede Norway to Sweden under the terms of the Treaty of Kiel on January 14, 1814, although Iceland and Greenland remained Danish possessions. On May 17 the Norwegian national assembly at Eidsvoll adopted an extremely liberal constitution that, with some major changes, still governs the country. The people at that time wanted complete independence, but Sweden's might and its leniency persuaded the government to accept an arrangement whereby the Swedish monarch would become the king of Norway and a viceroy would be appointed to carry out the functions of the Norwegian prime minister. Norway was free to conduct its own national affairs, while Sweden handled its foreign affairs. The union with Sweden was peacefully dissolved in 1905, after which a monarch was elected from the royal house of Denmark.

The 1814 constitution made the right to vote conditional on property ownership, but the requirement was set low enough that half of the adult male population was eligible to vote. Public employees and farmers received protective guarantees under the constitution, the latter becoming the cornerstone of a free peasant society in Norway. Unfortunately, the provision on religious freedom was literally lost or misplaced during the deliberations, while an exception to the provision, which discriminated against certain religious groups, was included.

The framers of the 1814 Norwegian constitution considered a number of foreign constitutions, but the most influential model was the 1791 French constitution.

Influences

The Constitution

"The Kingdom of Norway is a free, independent, indivisible and inalienable realm," states article 1 of the constitution. "Its form of government is a limited and hereditary monarchy." The document's 112 concise articles are the supreme source of law in Norway, but common practice under customary constitutional law *(konstitusjonell sedvanerett)* has evolved away from the original provisions. The constitution is considered a framework and has not required extensive revision, in part because of a liberal interpretation by the courts.

The Norwegian constitution guarantees due process of law; the right of freedom, equality, and justice under the law; freedom of the press, with some limitations; freedom of expression; prohibition against the search of private homes except in criminal cases; compensation for private property taken for public use; and the right to a healthy environment. The constitution also requires that every citizen is equally bound to serve in the defense of the country and provides that the state is responsible for creating conditions that will allow every person capable of working to earn a living. Article 110a requires the state to help the Sami people (Laplanders)—a reindeer-herding, nomadic people living in the northern part of the country—preserve and develop their language, culture, and way of life.

Fundamental Rights

A unitary state, power in Norway is divided among the monarch, as head of state; the prime minister, as head of government; and the courts, which exercise restrained judicial review.

Division of Powers

Monarch. The executive power, according to article 3, is vested in the king or queen. The monarch's role today is mostly ceremonial. Article 17 authorizes the monarch to issue and repeal orders provisionally until the next meeting of the parliament, a power applicable only in extraordinary circumstances when the legislature is not in session. The Norwegian government relied on this power while in exile during World War II, and the supreme court subsequently held its use to be constitutional.

The Executive

Prime Minister and Cabinet. The prime minister is the chief executive of the government. He or she is officially appointed by the monarch but in fact is always someone in whom the majority party or parties in the legislature have confidence.

The government, which includes the prime minister and other ministers who are members of the council of state (cabinet), runs the national administration and has authority to make promises and agreements binding the state. Although the constitution does not refer to ministries as such, this institution has been established, and there are a number of ministries, each headed by a cabinet minister. Cabinet meetings are held at least once a week.

Parliament. The Norwegian parliament, the Storting, has been called a modified unicameral or semibicameral legislature. After each election, every four years, the parliament divides into two parts. One-fourth of the members form the Lagting, and the rest the Odelsting. The bicameral feature is used for most legislative matters, but items such as the budget and appropriations, taxation, international treaties, and constitutional amendments are considered in

The Legislature

joint session. Unlike most parliaments, the Storting may not be dissolved before its four-year term expires.

One hundred sixty-five representatives are elected by constituencies or counties under a system of proportional representation and distribution of seats among the political parties. The purpose of this system is to help the political parties function when a number of them are fielding and electing candidates.

To be eligible for election to parliament a person must have resided in the realm for at least ten years and be eligible to vote. Article 50 states: "Those entitled to vote are Norwegian citizens, men and women, who at the latest in the year when the election is held, have completed their 18th year." Others, residing outside the realm or who are incapacitated, may vote as determined by law. Reasons for being disqualified from voting include criminal conviction, entering the service of a foreign government without permission, and being guilty of voting fraud.

The parliament, jointly and in each of the two chambers, elects a speaker and lieutenant speaker. These six persons make up the presidency of the national parliament. According to article 76: "Every bill shall first be proposed in the Odelsting, either by one of its own members, or by the government through a member of the council of state."

After a bill is introduced it goes to a committee; after debate, the identical wording of the bill must be approved by both chambers by a simple majority vote. If a bill is referred to a plenary session of the Storting after being twice rejected by the Lagting, it may be passed by a two-thirds majority vote. Once passed, a bill is sent to the monarch for the royal assent. A three-fourths majority of at least two-thirds of the members is required to allow any international organization to exercise powers under the constitution.

Other responsibilities of the parliament include supervising the monetary affairs of the realm and appropriating funds for the government. Its role in micromanaging the government's activities has increased over the years, creating a check on the broad powers of the executive branch. The parliament has the traditional powers of interpellation, or questioning ministers, and the no-confidence vote. It also may obtain opinions from the supreme court on points of law.

Ombudsman. An ombudsman has been appointed by the Storting since 1963; in 1995 the office was incorporated into the constitution "to assure that no injustice is done against the individual citizen."

The Judiciary

Articles 86 through 91 (article 89 has been repealed) establish a court system that is divided into four levels, with a supreme court at the top. By customary constitutional law, as in the United States, the courts practice judicial review and may declare a law unconstitutional. In Norway, however, the courts generally defer to parliament, so that such rulings are rare. Norway's system includes a court of impeachment, although today impeachment is a remote possibility.

Supreme Court. Under the constitution, the highest court consists of a president and at least four other members. "The supreme court pronounces judgment in the final instance," provides article 88. "Nevertheless, limitations on the right to bring a case before the supreme court may be prescribed by law."

Amending the Constitution

A proposal to amend the constitution must be submitted during the first three years of the legislature's four-year term. After a general election, it may be considered in the new parliament, which may either approve or reject the unaltered proposal by a two-thirds majority vote with a quorum of at least two-thirds of the members in attendance.

After eight years of martial law in Pakistan ended on December 30, 1985, the country's 1973 constitution was reinstated. Shortly thereafter, in 1988, Pakistan became the first Islamic nation to select a woman as its prime minister. In 1999 its constitution was again suspended.

The Islamic Republic of Pakistan is approximately 800,000 square kilometers and is bounded by the Arabian Sea on the south, Iran and Afghanistan on the west, China on the north, and India on the east. Since 1947 Pakistan and India have contended over the former British-Indian states of Jammu and Kashmir, with Pakistan now controlling a little more than one-third of the disputed territory. Islamabad is the capital of this country of approximately 142 million persons.

Agriculture accounts for about eighty percent of Pakistan's national income; natural resources, except for natural gas, are scarce. After an attempt at a government-run industrial base, the recent policy has been toward privatization and encouragement of the private-sector economy. The Pakistani propensity for political instability, violence, and corruption, however, could cause setbacks in planned economic development.

Type of Government: Military government since 1999; the constitution, which was suspended, creates a presidential-style parliamentary federal republic, with a president, a prime minister and cabinet, a bicameral legislature, and a judiciary

Dates of Constitutions: 1956 (abrogated in 1958), 1962, and 1973 (suspended 1977–85 and 1999)

By the third millennium B.C. the Indus River valley and the surrounding area had become a center of early civilization, along with Egypt and Mesopotamia to the west. The Persian Empire extended its control over the region in the sixth century B.C., followed by the Greeks under Alexander the Great, whose troops reached the rivers of the Punjab in the fourth century B.C.

Subsequently, the Parthians of the Iranian plateau extended their control east to the Indus River, which lasted until around A.D. 225, when the Sasanians moved in, bringing a higher level of civilization, the development of cities, and Zoroastrianism as the government religion. With the decline of the Roman Empire to the west, the Sasanian Empire became the most powerful in the world.

After the fall of the Sasanian Empire, Islam came to the region of present-day Pakistan in 711, and in the thirteenth century the Sultanate of Delhi was established across the northern part of the Indian subcontinent. At the end of the fourteenth century Tamerlane of Samarkand destroyed the sultanate in a military raid. In the sixteenth century the Moghul Empire controlled the area until its defeat by British East India Company forces under Robert Clive in 1757.

The Muslim and Hindu rulers did little to establish a legal system or government institutions, although Akbar, grandson of the founder of the Moghul Empire, set up a stable government with Hindus as governors and military commanders. The British, galvanized by their war with France and the desire to eliminate France's influence in India, as well as by reports of the great wealth of local rulers, continued to expand their domain through the East India Company. But ill treatment of the local population resulted in passage of the India Act of 1784 by the British parliament, which placed its territory under the rule of a government-appointed governor-general; the first of these was Lord Cornwallis, whose surrender at Yorktown in 1781 had ended the American Revolution. After the defeat of Napoleon in 1815, the regions of Punjab, Kashmir, and Baluchistan, which borders on Iran, were added to the British Raj (dominion).

Following a mutiny in 1857 by Muslim and Hindu soldiers over the rumored use of animal fats in the ammunition, India—including what is now Pakistan and Bangladesh—became a part of the British Empire under the terms of the India Act of 1858. One legacy of British rule is its bureaucracy, which still serves as a model for government administration in Pakistan.

The nationalistic movement for an independent Islamic state separate from Hindu India was rooted in the centuries when a minority of Muslims ruled large Hindu populations. Under the British the Muslims saw themselves reduced to the level of the Hindus. In 1906 they formed the All India Muslim League to protect their interests, and the league's Lahore Resolution of March 23, 1940, concluded that an independent state was necessary. After World War II Britain granted India its independence, and on August 14, 1947, with territory on both the east and the west sides of northern India, Pakistan became a self-governing member of the British Commonwealth.

In 1950 a bicameral legislature for Pakistan was proposed with one house having equal representation for all provinces and a second house having equal powers but with representation based on popular election. A later proposal based on parity for both East and West Pakistan was vigorously opposed by the somewhat more populous eastern half of the country. In 1954 a unicameral legislature was agreed on, but the governor-general dissolved the constituent assembly after seven years, ordering new elections.

A second assembly draft was adopted in 1956, providing for a unicameral parliament with 155 representatives each from the western and eastern sections and a government with a prime minister and cabinet. It remained in effect only until October 27, 1958. As the democratic government disintegrated, martial law was imposed under the prime minister, Gen. Ayub Khan, who abrogated the constitution and assumed the presidency. Later he was indirectly elected president for a five-year term.

On March 1, 1962, Khan promulgated a new constitution establishing a legislature whose role was simply to legitimize the central government's decisions. Reelected in 1965, he was forced to resign in 1969. East Pakistan declared its independence in 1971, taking the name Bangladesh. Ali Bhutto became president of the demoralized State of Pakistan and began nationalizing major industries and banks. A new constitution went into effect on August 14, 1973; with many amendments, it remains the constitution in force today, although it was suspended during a period of martial law between 1977 and 1985 and again in 1999.

Influences

Pakistan's constitution is based on the British parliamentary system of government, although the head of state has more real power; some Islamic principles have also influenced the document.

The Constitution

The constitution of the Islamic Republic of Pakistan is a long, detailed document consisting of more than two hundred fifty articles, with an annex and schedules attached. The preamble sets forth the Islamic character of the document.

Fundamental Rights

Under the constitution all citizens are equal before the law, no person shall be deprived of life or liberty except in accordance with law, and every citizen has the right of peaceful assembly and to form associations or unions; these rights may be suspended under certain circumstances, however. Although Benazir Bhutto was the first female prime minister in the Islamic world, women in fact are so far removed from importance in society that many have not even been counted in Pakistan's national census. Violations of the civil rights of both women and men have been reported.

Division of Powers

Pakistan is a federal state, with power divided between the national government and the governments of the provinces. At the national level power is shared among the president, as head of state; the prime minister, as head of government; the legislature; and the courts, which have some powers of judicial review.

President. Article 41 provides that the president is head of state and "shall represent the unity of the republic." He or she is also the chief executive officer of the government and has extensive powers that, however, have been somewhat reduced by amendments in 1997.

To be eligible to be elected president one must be forty-five years old, a Muslim, and otherwise qualified to be elected to the lower house of the legislature. The term is five years, with reelection for one term permitted. The president is selected by an electoral college consisting of members of both houses of the legislature and provincial assemblies.

The duties and powers of the president include granting pardons and commuting sentences; appointing ministers, the provincial governors on the advice of the prime minister, the chiefs of the branches of the armed forces, and the chairman of the joint chiefs of staff; dissolving the lower house on the advice of the prime minister having the confidence of that house, and calling for elections; and vetoing legislation, although a veto may be overridden if repassed by a majority vote of both houses. Article 232 gives the president the power to proclaim an emergency, which may lead to the suspension of certain rights under the constitution.

Prime Minister and Cabinet. In making decisions the president is required to act in accordance with the advice of the prime minister and cabinet members, whom the president appoints from among the members of the lower house. The president may ask that they reconsider their advice, although the recommendation must be followed if the advice does not change. But subsection 48(2) states that notwithstanding the foregoing, "the president shall act in his discretion in respect of any matter in respect of which he is empowered by the constitution to do so and the validity of anything done by the president in his discretion shall not be called in question on any ground whatsoever."

Parliament. Article 50 provides that "there shall be a Majlis-e-Shoora (parliament) of Pakistan consisting of the president and two houses to be known respectively as the national assembly and the senate."

Upper House. The senate consists of eighty-seven members, fourteen each elected to staggered six-year terms by the provincial assemblies, eight elected by members from the tribal areas in the national assembly, three from the federal capital, and five more elected by each of the provincial assemblies from religious scholars and professionals. A senator must be a citizen and thirty years old. The senate elects a chairman and deputy chairman for two-year terms and, unlike the assembly, is not subject to dissolution.

Lower House. The national assembly has more than two hundred "Muslim members elected for a maximum of five years by direct and free vote." Seats are allocated to each province, tribal area, and the federal capital on the basis of population. Ten additional seats are set aside proportionally for religious minorities; and for a ten-year period twenty seats were to be set aside for women and allocated to the provinces. To be a member of the assembly a person must be a citizen and twenty-five years old. After elections the assembly elects both a speaker, who stays on until replaced even after dissolution of the assembly, and a deputy speaker. The assembly must meet for at least three sessions a year for a total of at least 130 days, with no more than 120 days between sessions.

Except for money bills, which must originate and be passed in the assembly, bills concerning matters within the competence of the national legislature as set forth in the constitution

The Executive

The Legislature

may originate in either house. If passed by both houses, a bill is sent to the president for his or her assent. A bill that is passed but amended in the second house may be passed in a joint session by a majority of the total membership of both houses; it then goes to the president. Presidential vetoes may also be reconsidered in a joint session.

The president may from time to time summon either house or both houses to meet and may terminate such sessions. Decisions are made by a majority of those present and voting; the presiding officer votes only in the case of a tie vote. One-fourth of the members constitute a quorum. A number of qualifications and disqualifications for service are set forth in the constitution, some with fairly subjective standards, and the parliament is permitted to prescribe even more.

The Judiciary

Part 7, article 175, the Judicature, provides that

(1) There shall be a supreme court of Pakistan, a high court for each province and such other courts as may be established by law.

(2) No court shall have jurisdiction save as it is or may be conferred on it by the constitution or by or under any law.

(3) The judiciary shall be separated progressively from the executive within fourteen years from the commencing day.

Supreme Court. The supreme court is made up of a chief justice and other judges determined by law "or, until so determined, as may be fixed by the president." It has exclusive and original jurisdiction in disputes between the federal and provincial governments but may make only declaratory judgments in such cases. It is also authorized to enforce fundamental rights and hear appeals from the high courts. The president may refer questions of law to the supreme court.

The chief justice and the other judges are appointed by the president, after consulting with the chief justice, from among citizens with at least five years of experience as a judge on a high court or fifteen years of experience as an advocate of a high court. The supreme court has undertaken some judicial review, and the constitution makes its decisions binding on all courts; however, article 239(6) provides that there is no limit to the power of the legislature to amend any provision of the constitution.

The constitution also creates a federal Shariat court, which decides whether a law is repugnant to the injunctions of Islam, and a supreme judicial council, which may inquire into the capacity or conduct of a judge and report to the president, who then may remove the judge from office.

Other Government Bodies

Pakistan's constitution also creates a council of common interests that is responsible to the federal parliament and that formulates policy with respect to natural resources, transportation, and industry; a national security council to advise when a state of emergency should be declared or to make recommendations on other matters referred to it; and a council for Islamic ideology, which may be consulted by the executive and legislative branches about the conformity of proposals to Islamic principles.

Amending the Constitution

Since 1985 amendment proposals may originate in either house of the legislature, must be approved by at least two-thirds of the membership of each house, and then must go to the president for approval. Amendments to a proposal passed by the second house may be passed by a two-thirds vote in the originating house.

Geography and the engineering technology that built the Panama Canal have made Panama a strategic country, but its history of political and economic instability has hindered the development of constitutional government.

The Republic of Panama is approximately 77,000 square kilometers and is bounded by Costa Rica on the northwest, Colombia on the east, the Caribbean Sea on the north, and the Pacific Ocean on the south. Panama's population is roughly 2.8 million persons, and its capital is Panama City.

Some twenty percent of Panama's gross national product is derived from the Panama Canal, which contributes to the country's relatively high per capita wealth. Banking, particularly the laundering of illegal drug money, also contributes to its economic activity. A constitutional amendment to permit the incumbent president to run for an additional term was rejected by the voters in 1998, making way for the election of Panama's first woman president in 1999.

Type of Government: Presidential republic, with a president and cabinet, a unicameral legislature, and a judiciary

Dates of Constitutions: 1904 (revised in 1928 and 1941), 1946, and 1972

Various native peoples populated the Isthmus of Panama before the arrival in 1501 of Christopher Columbus, who named it Verguas, and Vasco Núñez de Balboa, the first European in the New World to view the Pacific Ocean in 1513. At first a base of exploration for Peru and Central America, Panama later became a major part of the commercial route to Spain; a road linked the shipping terminal of Portobello on the Atlantic, or Caribbean, coast with the city of Panama on the Pacific coast. Like other Spanish colonies in the Western Hemisphere, Panama was subject to laws enacted and enforced by the Council of the Indies, and its legal system developed from Roman-based Spanish civil law.

For two centuries English and other European privateers reduced Panama's economic potential, and in 1739 a British naval force destroyed Portobello. In 1717 Spain created the viceroyalty of New Granada out of Panama, Colombia, Venezuela, and Ecuador and in 1774 permitted unrestricted trade among several of its colonies, including New Granada.

Panama declared its independence from Spain in 1821 and formed Gran Colombia with the members of the former New Granada, remaining a part of Colombia when the union was dissolved. It again declared its independence on November 6, 1903, with support from the United States, which wanted to build a canal in Panama. In 1904 a constitution authorizing intervention by the United States in the event of disorder was adopted; it was amended in 1917 to provide for the popular election of the president and other executive leaders; revisions were made in 1928 and 1941. A new constitution was adopted in 1946.

The years following World War II were politically and economically unstable. In 1964 Panamanians fought against American troops in the U.S.-controlled Canal Zone. Four years later Lt. Col. Omar Torrijos led a successful coup. Free elections were not held again until 1980. The October 11, 1972, constitution created a six-year term for the president, which was changed to five years in 1983; special powers were granted to Torrijos, who held office until 1980. He remained the power behind a new government elected that year but died in a plane crash the following year. Gen. Manuel Noriega quickly took his place, but by the middle of 1987 his involvement in drug trafficking became a concern to the United States.

In 1977 treaties between the United States and Panama provided for the transfer of the canal to Panama and guaranteed its neutrality and use by all nations; in 1978 the constitution was amended to reflect this change. U.S. troops invaded Panama in 1989, after which Noriega was sentenced in the United States in 1992 to forty years in prison for his drug-related activities.

The Constitution

The 1972 constitution was modeled on previous documents, particularly Panama's 1946 constitution.

Although the constitution has no preamble, article 2 defines the source of the nation's sovereignty: "Public power emanates solely from the people. It is exercised by the state, in conformity with this constitution, through legislative, executive, and judicial branches of the government which act within limits and separately, but in harmonious cooperation."

Fundamental Rights

Article 17 outlines the bases of fundamental rights granted by Panama:

The authorities of the Republic of Panama are established for the purpose of protecting the lives, honor, and property of all nationals, wherever they may be, and aliens who may be under the Republic's jurisdiction, of insuring the effectiveness of the individual and social rights and duties, and of observing and enforcing the constitution and the law.

Chapter 1, Fundamental Guarantees, of title 3, Individual and Social Rights and Duties, provides that discrimination based on race, birth, social class, sex, religion, and political ideology is prohibited; Panamanians and aliens are equal before the law; no one may be deprived of liberty except in accordance with law, including access to habeas corpus procedures; and the home is inviolable, except with the consent of the owner, by order of a competent authority, or to assist victims of crimes or disasters. By amendment in 1983 persons arrested for crimes must be notified of the charges and given an opportunity to present a defense. Other rights, with some limitations, include freedom of religion, expression, assembly, and association.

Title 4 deals with political rights and describes suffrage as a right and duty of all citizens and the vote as free, equal, universal, secret, and direct. Article 136 establishes an electoral tribunal to guarantee the freedom, honesty, and effectiveness of popular elections. Other constitutional sections address issues such as the family, work, national culture, education, health, social security and welfare, ecology, and the agrarian system.

The position of general ombudsman was retained after the termination of the U.S. administration of the Panama Canal Zone.

Division of Powers

In Panama, a unitary state, power is divided among the president, the legislature, and the courts, which have, at least de jure, the power of judicial review.

The Executive

Article 170 provides that "the executive branch of government is composed of the president of the republic and the ministers of state, according to the provisions of this constitution."

President. The president is elected to a five-year term by a majority of direct votes, along with a first and second vice president, each of whom must be Panamanian by birth and thirty-five years old. Once elected president, a citizen is banned from running for the same office "in the two presidential terms immediately following."

The president appoints and removes "freely" the ministers of state; coordinates the work of the administration and public authorities; calls the legislature into ordinary or extraordinary session and submits a message on the affairs of the administration; vetoes bills; and invalidates actions of ministers, as provided for in the constitution. Together with the participation and countersignature of the respective ministers, the president approves and promulgates laws; appoints officers "of the public force" and directs them; appoints and dismisses "freely" the governors of the provinces; supervises the collection and administration of the national revenues; appoints certain public officials; directs foreign relations; issues pardons, grants parole, and commutes sentences; and confers military rank.

The president may be absent from the national territory for ten days without authorization, for up to thirty days with authorization by the cabinet, and more than thirty days only with authorization by the legislature.

Cabinet. The cabinet council is composed of the president, who presides; the vice presidents; and the ministers of state. It advises the president, approves his or her appointments, issues decrees declaring a state of emergency and suspension of certain constitutional guarantees, and, among other responsibilities, issues regulations for its internal government.

The general council of state is composed of the general directors of autonomous and semi-autonomous government entities, the commander in chief of the national guard, and other officials of the national and provincial governments. It is strictly an advisory body for the president of the republic and the president of the legislature.

General Council of State

Congress. According to article 140, "The legislative branch of government shall be composed of a body named the legislative assembly, whose members shall be elected by means of party nominations, and direct popular vote, in accordance with this constitution."

The Legislature

Legislators are elected at the same time as the president and vice presidents but from electoral circuits based on population. Only political parties may nominate candidates, and two alternates are elected on the same day and in the same manner for each legislator, whose term of office is five years. Candidates must be Panamanian citizens and, if naturalized, must have resided in the country for fifteen years, must be twenty-one years old and residents of the circuit for one year before their nomination, and must not otherwise have been disqualified.

The assembly's express legislative functions include issuing or changing national codes; issuing general law on salary proposals by the executive branch; ratifying treaties; participating in the approval of the national budget; declaring war and authorizing the executive branch to negotiate peace; issuing standards to the executive branch and other public entities regarding financial matters; approving the structure of the national government proposed by the executive branch; granting, on request, precise extraordinary powers to the executive branch to issue legal decrees during recess of the assembly; and determining its own rules of procedure. The assembly is forbidden to issue laws contrary to the letter or the spirit of the constitution.

Article 154 authorizes the assembly to judge the president and supreme court justices for acts performed or violations of the constitution or laws, as well as charges brought against its own members.

The judicial branch of the government of Panama includes a supreme court of justice and lesser courts established by law.

The Judiciary

Supreme Court. Justices of the supreme court and alternates are appointed by the president with the approval of the cabinet and the legislature for ten-year terms. They must be Panamanian by birth and thirty-five years old, have a university law degree and ten years of legal experience, and must not otherwise be disqualified. Article 207 directs that justices and judges are to be independent and subject only to the constitution and the law.

The supreme court is charged with guarding the integrity of the constitution and has jurisdiction over administrative litigation. While in theory this gives the court broad powers, concern expressed about the court's lack of political independence makes rulings against the government unlikely.

Amending the Constitution Article 308 provides that an amendment may be proposed by the legislature, the cabinet, or the supreme court. A proposal may be approved in two ways: first, by an absolute majority vote in the legislature in three readings and a similar vote after elections in one reading without modification; and second, by an absolute majority vote at three readings each in two successive legislative periods, during which modifications may be made, although the final form of the amendment must be approved by a direct and popular referendum.

One of the first countries in South America to achieve independence from Spain, two centuries later Paraguay struggles to maintain its civilian constitutional government under a constitution adopted in 1992.

The Republic of Paraguay occupies some 406,750 square kilometers in the interior of South America and is bounded on the north by Bolivia, on the east by Brazil, and on the south and west by Argentina. Asuncíon is the capital of this country whose population is approximately 5.6 million persons.

Paraguay's major industries include food processing, textiles, and cement; among its chief crops are cotton, soybeans, and coffee. A feudal system of land tenure and a lack of mechanization hamper agricultural production. The Paraguayan economy also relies heavily on illicit activities such as smuggling, drug trafficking, and money laundering.

Type of Government: Presidential republic, with a president and council of ministers (cabinet), a bicameral legislature, and a judiciary

Dates of Constitutions: 1813, 1844, 1870, 1940, 1967, and 1992

The part of South America that would become Paraguay was home to the Guarani people before the first Europeans arrived in 1527. Colonized by the Spanish together with Argentina, Uruguay, part of Chile, and large portions of Brazil and Bolivia, Paraguay became a province under the Spanish viceroyalty of Peru in 1542. Jesuit missionaries sent to convert and teach the native peoples in 1588 were expelled in 1767. In 1810, after Napoleon's conquest of Spain, the Spanish viceroy in Buenos Aires was ousted, but an attempt by Buenos Aires to enforce its authority over Paraguay was defeated. On May 14, 1811, Spanish rule in Paraguay was overthrown and independence was declared.

In 1813 Paraguay's first supreme laws, called the Constitutional Government Regulations, created two consuls (executives), each of whom was a brigadier general and controlled half the armed forces, and a thousand-member legislature. One of the consuls, José Gaspar Rodríguez de Francia, began ruling alone in 1814 and was given the title of El Supremo Dictador by the country's congress in 1816. Intolerant of human rights, he diminished the power of the Paraguayan elite and the church while creating a strong and prosperous independent nation.

El Supremo was succeeded by Carlos Antonio López, known as "the Most Excellent One," who became president under a new constitution promulgated in 1844. Solano López succeeded his father in 1862 and embarked on a disastrous war with Argentina, Brazil, and Uruguay—more than half the country's population of approximately 500,000 was slaughtered and much territory was lost. Solano died in 1870, and that same year a new liberal constitution, based on popular sovereignty and separation of powers but leaving much power still in the hands in a chief executive, was adopted.

Between 1870 and 1954 Paraguay had thirty-nine presidents, most of whom left office under less than constitutional procedures. In 1940 a new constitution was promulgated by President José Félix Estigarribia after he declared himself absolute dictator. Alfredo Stroessner came to power in Paraguay in a military coup in 1954 and soon became the model of the modern South American dictator. In part to extend his eligibility for reelection as president for two more five-year terms, Stroessner had the 1940 constitution rewritten in 1967. In 1989 he was ousted and exiled by the military, under the leadership of Gen. Andrés Rodríguez.

After 1989 a split in the ruling party created a "democratic" faction and led to democratic reform. A new constitution that attempted to create a true constitutional democracy was promulgated on June 20, 1992, and the "democratic" opposition captured the presidency in

1993. In March 1999, however, the vice president was assassinated, forcing President Raúl Cubas to resign his office and calling into question the stability of constitutional government in Paraguay.

Influences

Paraguay's 1992 constitution consists of 291 articles exhibiting elements of the *dirigiste* type of constitution (one that proposes economic and social goals) like that of Brazil. Lifetime senate membership for past presidents is similar to provisions in the Chilean constitution.

The Constitution

"The Republic of Paraguay is and will always be independent," proclaims article 1. "It is constituted as a social state of law, which is unitary, indivisible, and decentralized ... [and it] adopts as its system of government a representative, participatory, and pluralistic democracy, which is founded on the recognition of human dignity." Article 3 states: " The people exercise public powers through their right to vote ... ," adding: "Dictatorship is against the law." Article 137 declares that the "Constitution is the supreme law of the Republic."

Fundamental Rights

Articles 4 through 8, respectively, address the "right to live," prohibitions against torture and other human rights violations such as genocide, the state's obligation to promote "the quality of life," citizens' right to "a healthy, ecologically balanced environment," and protection of the environment. Other rights include protections for those accused of crimes, freedom of religion and ideology, expression of one's personality, freedom of the press and of information, the right to assemble and demonstrate peaceably, privacy, conscientious objection, and the right, "either individually or within a group, to demand that public officials adopt measures" to defend common interests such as environmental protection, public health, consumer interests, and preservation of the national cultural heritage. Freedom of movement, association, and the right to "territorial and diplomatic asylum" are also guaranteed.

Equal rights for women and men, family rights, and the rights of indigenous peoples are set forth in articles 46 through 130, along with provisions relating to health, education, cultural identity and heritage, the "role played by the Catholic Church," labor, "public functions" (including the rights of public officials and employees), economic rights, agrarian reform, and political rights and duties. The use of the popular initiative to generate laws is expressly granted in article 123, and enforcement of constitutional guarantees, including habeas corpus and *amparo* procedures, is provided for in articles 131 through 136.

Division of Powers

"The government is exercised by the legislative, executive, and judicial powers," provides article 3. However, article 291 declares that where reform and amendment of the constitution are concerned, a "National Constituent Assembly is independent from the branches of government."

The Executive

President. "The powers of the executive branch are exercised by the president of the Republic," declares article 226. In case of the president's absence or disability, the "vice president ... will immediately assume all presidential powers." To be eligible for the presidency a person must be "a natural Paraguayan national," at least thirty-five years old, and capable of exercising "one's civil and political rights." Disqualifications for president and vice president include being a cabinet minister, a judge, a minister or clergy of any religion, and persons on active duty in the armed forces or the national police. The term of the president and vice president is five years, and they cannot be reelected. The vice president may run for the presidency if he or she resigns from office "six months prior to the general election," but presidents in office "for more than 12 months are ineligible to run for vice president."

The duties and powers of the president under article 238 include representing the state and generally administering the country; enforcing the constitution and the law; developing and promulgating laws; vetoing laws approved by Congress; appointing and removing cabinet ministers and certain other officials; and overseeing the foreign relations of the nation, including, when authorized by Congress, declaring "a State of National Defense." The president also informs Congress of the executive branch's activities and the state of the nation at the beginning of the legislative session, serves as commander in chief of the armed forces, pardons or commutes sentences, and calls special sessions of Congress and proposes draft laws.

The president, vice president, and other officials may be impeached "for malfeasance in office, for crimes committed in office, or for common crimes . . . by a two-thirds majority" of the lower house of Congress. Conviction on impeachment requires a two-thirds absolute majority of the upper house. And, according to article 236,

Military or civilian leaders of a coup d'etat, armed revolution, or similar movement aimed at disrupting the order established by this Constitution, who may eventually become president or vice president of the Republic, cabinet minister, or hold a military post requiring a senior rank, will be ineligible for any public office for two consecutive constitutional terms, in addition to their respective civil liability or criminal responsibility.

Cabinet. "Ministers are the chief administrators of their respective ministries in which, under the leadership of the president of the Republic, they promote and implement policies relating to matters falling within their jurisdiction," according to article 242. Article 243 provides that "[w]hen summoned by the president of the Republic, the ministers gather in a council in order to coordinate the executive tasks, to set . . . the policy of the government and to adopt collective decisions."

Congress. "The legislative branch will be exercised by Congress, which consists of the Senate [upper house] and of the Chamber of Deputies [lower house]," proclaims article 182.

The Legislature

Upper House. The senate numbers forty-five members and at least thirty alternates. To be eligible, a senator must be "a natural Paraguayan citizen" who is thirty-five years or older. Article 189 makes former elected presidents "national senators for life. . . . They will have the right to speak, but not to vote."

Lower House. Deputies in the lower house, of which there are eighty plus eighty alternates, must be at least twenty-five years of age.

Legislators are elected for five-year terms and may be reelected, but persons participating "in companies exploiting services or holding concessions of the State . . . , [t]hose sentenced to a prison term by a final court decision until their prison term ends," judges, ministers and clergy, and police and military personnel on active duty are disqualified from office. "Members and alternate members [who replace members in case of death, resignation, or disability] of both chambers will be directly elected by the people in accordance with the law." Legislators are granted certain immunities under article 191, including protection from arrest "unless [one] is caught in *flagrante delicto* in relation to a crime meriting a prison sentence."

Joint congressional sessions are the subject of articles 183 and 185. In joint session congress has the power to administer the oath of office to the president, vice president, and supreme court justices; grant or deny "the appropriate authorization to the president . . . in those cases established in this Constitution"; "authorize the entry of foreign armed forces into the national territory and . . . the departure abroad of national forces"; and receive chiefs of state of other governments.

Among the powers and duties of congress as set forth in article 202 are ensuring "observance of this Constitution and the laws," enacting "codes and other laws," establishing "a division of the territory of the Republic into political units," legislating "on tax matters," approving "the national general budget law," enacting "the electoral law," and approving "treaties or other international agreements signed by the executive branch." Each chamber may request reports from "other branches of government … on matters of public interest … ," and each, "by an absolute majority, may individually summon and interpellate [question] ministers and senior administration officials … pertaining to their respective activities."

Noting constitutionally established exceptions, article 203 provides that a "law may be originated by a proposal from a member of either of the chambers of Congress, from the executive branch, by popular initiative, or by the Supreme Court of Justice. …" A draft law must be approved by both chambers, and if it is not vetoed by the president or returned to the originating chamber "within six working days if it has less than 10 articles, within 12 days if it has 11 to 20 articles, or within 20 days if it has more than 20 articles, will be considered … approved … [and] automatically promulgated. …" If a bill approved by one chamber "is completely rejected by the other … [and] the originating chamber passes [it] again by an absolute majority," it will become law unless the reviewing chamber "reject[s] it again through a two-thirds absolute majority." The executive branch may totally or partially veto proposed laws. Vetoed legislation generally may be overridden by an absolute majority vote of both chambers. According to article 213, "A law is not enforceable until it is promulgated and published."

The Judiciary

"The judicial branch is the guardian of the Constitution," notes article 247. "It interprets the Constitution, complies with it, and orders its enforcement. The judicial branch is in charge of administering justice. It is exercised by the Supreme Court of Justice, and by appellate and lower courts as established by this Constitution and the laws." The independence of the judicial branch is guaranteed in article 248 and is supported by provisions mandating the "irremovability" of judges, a separate judicial branch budget, and certain immunities for judges.

Supreme Court. Pursuant to article 258, the supreme court numbers nine members. "It is organized in chambers, one of which will hear constitutional matters. Every year, the members … will elect one of the justices as their president." A justice "must have natural Paraguayan nationality, be 35 years old, hold a doctorate in law, and enjoy an honorable reputation … , [as well as] have practiced law, held a court office, or held a teaching job at a law school for at least 10 years. …"

When supreme court positions become vacant, a council of magistrates—consisting of a designated member of the supreme court, a representative of the executive branch, members of the upper and lower houses of Congress, two practicing attorneys elected by their colleagues, and two law professors—submits the names of three candidates to the senate, which then appoints a justice with the concurrence of the executive branch. "Justices of the Supreme Court of Justice," article 261 declares, "may be removed only through impeachment. Their mandatory retirement age is 75."

Some of the duties and powers of the supreme court included under article 259 are to "supervise every judicial branch organization," "issue its own bylaws" and "submit an annual report to [the other branches]," "hear and decide the appeals established by law," receive "habeas corpus petitions," decide "cases of unconstitutionality," and hear cases "on final sentences. …"

Constitutional Chamber. Article 260 prescribes the duties and powers of the constitutional chamber of Paraguay's supreme court, which include hearing and resolving "the unconstitutionality of the laws and of other related instruments … and … final or interlocutory decisions, nullifying those that contradict this Constitution."

Under article 289, "25 percent of the members of any of the two chambers of Congress, ...
the president, ... or ... 30,000 voters through a signed petition" may request reform of the
constitution, and then a "two-thirds absolute majority vote of [the] members [of] the two
chambers ... may declare the need for constitutional reform." A national constituent assembly, not exceeding the total number of members of congress, is elected thereafter, and a
new constitution would be automatically promulgated after approval by the assembly.

Amendments are initiated by one-fourth of the members of either of the two chambers
of Congress, the president, or 30,000 voters signing petitions. Changes must then "be approved by an absolute majority [of] the originating chamber" and "the reviewing chamber" and subsequently approved by a referendum. However, the "procedures established for
the reform of the Constitution, rather than those established for its amendment, will be followed with regard to those provisions affecting the election, composition, term in office, or
powers of any of the three branches of government or the provisions of Chapters I, II, III
and IV of Title II [About Rights, Duties, and Guarantees] of Part I."

PERU

After the president of Peru seized power extraconstitutionally in 1992, Peruvians in 1993 narrowly approved a new constitution that retreats from decentralization and restricts free education and labor rights but expands the power of the president.

General Information

The Republic of Peru in South America is almost 1.3 million square kilometers and is bounded by Ecuador and Colombia on the north, Brazil and Bolivia on the east, Chile on the south, and the Pacific Ocean on the west. Lima is the capital of this country of approximately twenty-seven million persons.

Peru is rich in minerals and oil, although forty percent of the country's work force is engaged in farming and fishing. Alberto Fujimori, three-time president, was deposed in 2000 and fled to Japan, allowing for the possibility of a return to constitutional democracy.

Type of Government: Presidential republic, with a president, a prime minister and cabinet, a unicameral legislature, a judiciary, and a constitutional court

Dates of Constitutions: 1823, 1826, 1828, 1834, 1839, 1855 (temporary), 1856, 1860, 1920, 1933, 1980, and 1993

Constitutional History

Twenty thousand years ago descendants of Asians who entered America via the land bridge that is now the Bering Strait made their way into South America, and by 2500 B.C. the north coast of Peru was well settled by farmers and fishermen. Around the thirteenth century B.C., with the development of irrigation and maize (corn) as an annual crop, the basis for the great civilizations of the Andes Mountains—the Chavin, Mochica, Chimu, Tiwanaku, and Wari—was created. Larger civilizations declined between A.D. 1000 and 1450, when a relatively minor ethnic group, the Quechuas, rose to prominence. Some members of the Quechuas, the Incas of Cuzco, eventually controlled more than one-third of South America and a population ranging from nine to sixteen million.

The basic social unit under the Incas was the *ayllu,* a grouping of people who generally intermarried, were self-governing and landowning, and were ruled by *curacas* (local lords) in the name of the Incas, who were believed to be representatives of the god of the sun. Everyone worked for the Incas and the royal family, and during famine, war, and natural disasters the Incas redistributed the tribute paid to them. The people farmed on the principle of vertical complementarity, whereby different crops were cultivated at different elevations, allowing them to cultivate four times as much arable land as Peruvians do today.

When Francisco Pizarro arrived in 1532 with 180 men and thirty horses, the Inca Empire had been split between two sons of the former ruler, Atahualpa and his half brother, and fell easy prey to the Spaniards' perfidy and superior weapons, as well as foreign diseases. Lima, founded by Pizarro near the coast, became the headquarters for Spanish authority. Under Francisco Toledo y Figueroa, the viceroy from 1568 to 1582, the native communities were forced into *reducciones* (ghettos) to make administration easier, and the Inca system of *mita* (involuntary servitude) shifted from public works to mining and other economic needs of the state. As in the rest of Spain's colonial empire in the New World, the government consisted of the viceroy as the representative of the king; the *audiencia* (a council with executive, legislative, and judicial functions); the *cabildos* (town councils); and the *encomienda* system of native slave labor under the control of landowners who were to protect them and see to their conversion to Christianity.

Although there were rebels within, independence came from without, with the armies of José de San Martín beginning the rebellion and those of Simón Bolívar Palacios and Antonio José de Sucre defeating the Spanish royalist forces decisively on December 9, 1824.

Bolívar became president under an 1823 constitution influenced by France and Spain. When he left in 1826, instability set in. Between the 1826 constitution and 1845, the presidency changed twelve times and three more constitutions were promulgated—in 1828, 1834, and 1839; all of them provided for a centralized government and executive, legislative, and judicial branches, with indirect elections for president and the legislature. The 1839 document increased the president's term from four to six years and did not allow reelection.

After a temporary constitution in 1855, a more liberal and democratic constitution was promulgated in 1856 amid relative peace and prosperity. In 1860 a more conservative constitution went into effect and lasted, with only minor interruptions, until 1920, when a somewhat more liberal supreme law was adopted that enhanced the powers of the president, increased civil rights, and changed the president's term again, from four to five years. In 1933 a mixed presidential-style parliamentary system was attempted. Government gridlock, however, led to a military coup in 1968 and a new constitution on July 28, 1980.

A weak economy, violence, and "disappearances" of citizens marked the 1980s, as well as Maoist-style, guerrilla warfare by the Shining Path, an organization that claimed more than twenty-five thousand lives and nearly destroyed the nation. But elections were held in 1990, and Alberto Keinya Fujimori became Peru's president. In 1992, however, he seized extraconstitutional power in an *autogolpe* (self-coup); later in the year a democratic constituent congress was elected to draft a new constitution, which was approved by referendum on October 31, 1993. Fifty-three percent of the voters approved it, but the narrow margin of the vote—the Lima voters, who historically represent an elite class, voted sixty to forty percent for the new constitution while fourteen of the nation's twenty-four provinces opposed it— casts doubts on any real consensus for the new plan of government.

Earlier constitutions were influenced by French and Spanish models, while the current "Fujimori" constitution enhances the authority of the president.

Influences

The Constitution

The preamble to the 1993 constitution of the Republic of Peru states: "The democratic constituent congress, calling upon almighty God, obeying the will of the Peruvian people, and commemorating the sacrifice of all of our nation's preceding generations, has resolved to enact the following constitution. . . ."

Fundamental Rights

Article 1, chapter 1, Fundamental Rights of the Individual, section 1, Concerning the Individual and Society, declares that "the protection of the individual and respect for his dignity are the supreme goal of society and the government."

Article 2 enumerates twenty-four basic individual rights, including the right to life, identity, "free fulfillment" and well-being, and physical, psychological, and moral integrity; equality before the law; freedom of conscience and religion, as long as the expression thereof does not constitute an offense against morals or a disturbance of the peace; freedom of information, opinion, expression, and dissemination of thought through various media, in accordance with the law; the right to request information, with exceptions; the right to personal and family privacy and to correction of information without charge; inviolability of the home and secrecy of private documents and communications; and the right to assemble peacefully without arms, form associations, own and inherit property, petition authorities, and retain ethnic and cultural identity.

According to article 3, "The enumeration of rights established in this chapter does not exclude any others guaranteed by the constitution, those of an analogous nature or based on the dignity of man, the principles of the sovereignty of the people, the democratic state of law, and the republican form of government." Early in 1994, however, the prime minister resigned over a law enacted to send a sensitive human rights case to a military court.

Peru is a unitary state in which power is divided among the president; the legislature; the courts, which may exercise judicial review; and the constitutional court, which has specified powers of constitutional review.

The Executive

President. The president, who is head of state and government, is elected along with two vice presidents by direct suffrage and an absolute majority of the vote for a five-year term. He or she may be reelected but must sit out a term before running again. To be president a person must be a native-born Peruvian, more than thirty-five years old, and eligible to vote.

The powers and duties of the president include obeying and ensuring obedience to the constitution, treaties, laws, and other legal provisions; representing the government at home and abroad; directing the government's general policy; guaranteeing domestic order and external security; calling elections; convening the legislature in special session; sending messages to the legislature at any time; issuing regulations; complying and ensuring compliance with rulings and resolutions of jurisdictional organs; directing foreign policy and concluding and ratifying treaties; appointing ambassadors with the approval of the cabinet and reporting as required to the legislature; receiving foreign diplomats; presiding over the national defense system, commanding the armed forces and the national police; declaring war and concluding peace, with the authorization of the legislature; administering the public treasury; granting pardons and commuting sentences; conferring decorations; and exercising other functions entrusted to him or her under the constitution or the law.

During his or her term, the president may be accused only of treason, preventing elections or interfering with the national election board or the election process, or unconstitutionally dissolving the legislature.

Prime Minister and Cabinet. Under article 120 the cabinet, which is charged with directing and managing public services, as in a parliamentary system, must approve acts of the president. The prime minister is appointed or removed by the president, and other ministers are appointed or removed by the president on the recommendation of the prime minister and with his or her approval. Article 128 provides that ministers are individually responsible for their acts and presidential acts that they approve and are collectively responsible for violations of the constitution or laws by the president that were approved by the cabinet, unless they took exception and immediately resigned.

The Legislature

Congress. The unicameral Peruvian legislature, despite the fact that it may be dissolved before its term expires and that there is a prime minister, is more like a congress than a parliament. It consists of 120 members elected in accordance with law for five-year terms unless the legislature is dissolved earlier.

To be elected a person must be a native-born Peruvian, at least twenty-five years old, and eligible to vote. Article 91 sets forth certain positions—including ministers and deputy ministers, certain members of the judicial branch, and members of the armed forces or the national police on active duty—that must be vacated six months before an election in order for the incumbent to be eligible for the congress. The candidate for president may not also run for the congress, but the vice presidents may.

Once elected, members are accorded certain immunities, and the body as a whole is authorized to adopt bylaws, which have the force of law; elect members to serve on a standing committee or other committees; and appoint its own officers and employees. Any member may request in writing information from the government and certain institutions and by law must receive a response. The congress may initiate investigations and request that the president provide members of the armed forces or the national police for its use.

Express powers of the congress, in addition to enacting legislation, include ensuring respect for the constitution and the law, ratifying treaties, passing the budget, consenting to foreign troops entering the country, and authorizing the president to leave the country. Article 103, chapter 2, Concerning the Legislative Function, provides that there may be no retroactive criminal law, except if it favors the defendant, and that an unconstitutional law may be declared invalid. Article 104 authorizes the congress to delegate the power to legislate by means of legislative orders to the executive branch for a specific subject and under terms established by law.

The standing committee may bring charges against the president and other high officials, and the congress decides on which measures to take against them, if any. If the charges are criminal in nature, the prosecutor general files them with the supreme court. The standing committee, in addition to other powers, may exercise delegated legislative powers.

According to article 138, "The power to administer justice emanates from the people and is exercised by the judicial branch through its hierarchical organs based on the constitution and the law." The supremacy of the constitution over other laws is also set forth.

Article 149 provides that "authorities of the peasant and native communities, with the support of the peasant patrols, may exercise jurisdictional functions within their territory in accordance with common law, provided they do not violate the fundamental rights of the individual."

Supreme Court. The constitution creates a supreme court as a court of appeal and last resort, but the decisions of the national election board concerning elections and those of the council of magistracy on evaluation and confirmation of judges may not be reviewed. Article 144 provides that the chief justice of the supreme court is head of the judicial branch and that the supreme court is the highest organ of deliberation.

Section 5, On Constitutional Guarantees, sets forth a number of specific rights, including the right of habeas corpus and of unconstitutionality, and article 201 in that section establishes a constitutional court "that watches over the constitution."

The court consists of seven members elected by a two-thirds vote of the legislature for five-year terms. It hears cases, without appeal, involving the "right of unconstitutionality," decisions denying habeas corpus and other rights, and conflicts over powers assigned by the constitution. Article 203 provides that the president, prosecutor general, public defender, twenty-five percent of the legislature, five thousand citizens, regional presidents, and professional associations in their sphere of activity are entitled to "file for the right to unconstitutionality."

Amendments may be initiated by the president with cabinet approval, by members of the legislature, or by at least 0.3 percent of the voting population. They must be approved by an absolute majority of the legislature's members and be ratified either by referendum or the vote of at least two-thirds of the members of the legislature in two successive regular sessions.

The Judiciary

Constitutional Court

Amending the Constitution

THE PHILIPPINES

Although President Corazon Aquino's assumption of power in 1986 was technically unconstitutional, she nevertheless kept her promise to restore constitutional democracy to the Philippines.

General Information

Located on an archipelago southeast of Asia, the Republic of the Philippines consists of more than seven thousand islands of approximately 300,000 square kilometers and is surrounded by seas—the South China Sea on the west, the Philippine Sea on the east, and the Sulu and Celebes Seas on the south. The population of the Philippine Islands is more than eighty-one million persons. Its official capital of Quezon City is in metropolitan Manila.

The major sectors of the economy are services and industry, with agriculture, forestry, and fishing contributing approximately one-fourth of the country's gross national product. The country has numerous dormant and active volcanoes and is often visited by typhoons, but potential for hydroelectric and geothermal energy production is excellent. A popular revolt, fanned by allegations of corruption, led to the ouster of President Joseph Estrada in early 2001.

Type of Government: Presidential republic, with a president and cabinet, a bicameral legislature, and a judiciary

Dates of Constitutions: 1899, 1935, 1973 (significantly amended in 1981), 1986 (provisional), and 1987

Constitutional History

Although peoples from the East had migrated to the Philippine Islands for thousands of years, around 2000 B.C. a fairly advanced Asian people settled in the larger islands, and their descendants are still there. The Malay and Polynesian peoples arrived from the eighth to the fifteenth centuries A.D. They were followed by Muslim seafarers and some Chinese who came before 1512, when Spain's Ferdinand Magellan landed in the islands, where he met his death.

Spain at first used the islands as a transshipment point between its colony in Mexico and the Orient and, as in the New World, gave large tracts of land to prominent Spaniards to exploit and rule. The Roman Catholic Church converted the native inhabitants and provided some education and social services. Under the colonial administration the local government was based on the traditional village *(barangay)* structure: a chief *(datu)*, nobles, freemen, and dependents, which included all others, even slaves taken as war captives. This system of indirect rule by the Spanish led to the development of a rural elite *(principalia)*, who received titles and the private ownership of land formerly owned communally.

Nationalism developed among the intelligentsia called *ilustrados* (enlightened ones), particularly in Manila and other major towns. Filipino émigrés who lived in Europe, such as José Rizal, contributed to the movement, and the outbreak of the Spanish-American War in 1898 presented the opportunity to establish an independent government. A constitution modeled on the constitutions of France, Belgium, and some South American republics was drafted in the town of Malolos, north of Manila, and promulgated on January 21, 1899. Under the Treaty of Paris of December 10, 1898, Spain ceded the islands to the United States.

After quelling attempts by Filipino insurgents who fought for total independence, the United States immediately set about developing democratic principles and a basis of self-government for the Philippines. In 1902 it enacted an organic law that created a bicameral legislature with shared legislative powers, and in 1916 it passed another organic law, the Jones Act, which predicated independence on government stability. U.S. legislation in 1934 provided for a ten-year transition period as a commonwealth before independence, and the Filipinos approved an "independence" constitution in a plebiscite in 1935.

Although the islands were devastated by World War II and the Japanese occupation, after the war the transition to full independence proceeded. Manuel Roxas became the first president of the republic on July 4, 1946. His administration and that of his successor, however, were marked by corruption and scandal. Ramon Magsaysay, president from 1953 to 1957, espoused a pro–United States policy and brought the country into the Southeast Asia Treaty Organization (SEATO), a collective defense organization, but after his death in an air crash his successors struggled to move the nation forward.

In 1969 Ferdinand Marcos became the first president of the Philippines to be reelected. Serious flooding and communist insurgency in 1972 gave him an excuse to declare a state of martial law. Although martial law was not lifted until January 17, 1981, a new constitution went into effect in 1973. However, Marcos ruled by decree until 1978, when a parliamentary system replaced the presidential one. Amendments in 1981 restored executive powers to the president. Still, Marcos and his wife, Imelda, virtually ruled the country, living in lavish style, until the election fraud of 1986. His opponent, Corazon Aquino, widow of a slain political adversary, won the election, but Marcos was declared the winner constitutionally. The Catholic Church and outraged citizens combined to drive Marcos into exile.

Once in office, Aquino repealed her predecessor's repressive regulations. Solely on her own authority, she issued a proclamation on March 25, 1986, establishing a provisional constitution with sweeping powers, which she promised to use to restore democratic government under a new constitution. The new constitution was approved by a large majority and went into effect on February 11, 1987.

The Philippine legal system began as an amalgam of Roman, Spanish, and Anglo-American law. The U.S. constitution influenced the 1935 Philippine constitution, and the drafters of the 1987 constitution favored the 1935 form of government. However, the 1987 constitution, except in the traditional bill of rights provisions, is a truly Filipino document.

The Constitution

The short preamble to the constitution of the Republic of the Philippines states:

We, the sovereign Filipino people, imploring the aid of the almighty God, in order to build a just and humane society and establish a government that shall embody our ideals and aspirations, promote the common good, conserve and develop our patrimony, and secure to ourselves and our posterity the blessings of independence and democracy under the rule of law and a regime of truth, justice, love, equality, and peace, do ordain and promulgate this constitution.

Article 2, Declaration of Principles and State Policies, among other things, renounces war as an instrument of national policy, proclaims civilian authority to be supreme over the military, and makes serving and protecting the people the government's prime duty.

Article 3, Bill of Rights, contains language that, as in previous constitutions, can be traced directly to the U.S. constitution, although the Malolos constitution of 1899 had provisions on civil and political rights.

Rights enumerated include equal protection of the law and due process for deprivation of life, liberty, and property; protection from unreasonable search and seizure; privacy of communication, including the inadmissibility of evidence improperly obtained; and freedom of speech, expression, the press, assembly, and petition. Other rights include freedom of religion, residence, and information, including access to government records and information, and the right to form unions and other lawful associations. Just compensation for the taking of private property, the inviolability of contractual obligations, free access to the courts, and generally accepted legal rights for accused persons are also established.

A provision prohibiting substantive tests for suffrage and one for enabling the disabled to vote without assistance are found in article 5.

Article 13, Social Justice and Human Rights, commits the state to enhancing human dignity and reducing social, economic, and political inequalities by regulating "the acquisition, ownership, use, and disposition of property and its increments." Other areas of state policy covered include labor, agrarian and natural resources reform, urban land reform and housing, health, women, the role and rights of people's organizations, and human rights.

Division of Powers

In the Philippines, a unitary state, power is divided among the president, the legislature, the courts, which exercise judicial review, and three independent regulatory commissions.

The Executive

President and Cabinet. The president is head of state and chief executive of the national government. The powers of the president, especially in times of emergency, are now subject to significant checks by the other branches. The cabinet includes the vice president, secretaries, and others.

To be elected president or vice president, a person must be at least forty years old, able to read and write, a registered voter, a natural-born citizen, and a resident for ten years. The president and vice president are elected by direct vote for six-year terms. The president may not be reelected, and the vice president may not serve more than two consecutive terms, but the vice president may be appointed to a cabinet post without confirmation.

The president nominates the heads of executive departments, ambassadors, and other high officials and military officers, all of whom must be confirmed by a commission on appointments made up of twelve members of each house of the legislature. He or she also is given "control of" the executive departments and is required to ensure that the laws are faithfully executed. The president is commander in chief of the armed forces and may declare a state of martial law or suspend the writ of habeas corpus, although for no more than sixty days. Article 7, section 20, permits the president to contract or guarantee foreign loans with the concurrence of the monetary board.

If a permanent vacancy occurs in the office of the president, the vice president becomes president for the remainder of the term. The vice president also assumes office whenever a majority of the cabinet communicates to the heads of the houses of the legislature that the president is unable to discharge the powers and duties of the office.

The Legislature

Congress. Article 6 states, in part, that "the legislative power shall be vested in the congress of the Philippines which shall consist of a senate and a house of representatives, except to the extent reserved to the people by the provision on initiative and referendum."

Upper House. Each of the twenty-four senators, who must be at least thirty-five years old, a resident for two years, and meet other qualifications similar to those for the president, is elected at large for a six-year term.

Lower House. The lower house, the house of representatives, is limited to 250 members who must be twenty-five years old and otherwise eligible to be elected. They are elected for three-year terms from districts. Twenty percent of the total membership in the house of representatives is chosen "through a party-list system."

After general elections, the senate elects a president and the house a speaker; other officers may be chosen as necessary. Each house determines its own rules of procedure, and a majority of members of each house constitute a quorum for doing business. Members of both houses are free from arrest for certain crimes during sessions of the congress.

The congress has the sole power to declare war and does so by a two-thirds vote of both houses. Section 22 grants it the power of interpellation, or to question heads of government offices. According to section 25, all money bills must originate in the lower house, but the senate may "propose or concur with amendments." A bill passed by both houses may be vetoed by the president, but the veto may be overridden by a two-thirds vote of all the members of each house.

The Judiciary

Judicial power is vested by the Philippine constitution in one supreme court and lower courts established by law.

Supreme Court. The supreme court is composed of a chief justice and fourteen other justices appointed by the president without confirmation, from lists of three nominees provided by the judicial and bar council. Several provisions in the constitution protect the independence of the judiciary.

In addition to having administrative supervision over all courts, as provided under section 5 of article 8, Judicial Department, the supreme court has original jurisdiction in cases involving ambassadors and other public ministers and such petitions as those for certiorari and habeas corpus. It also has review authority in cases involving the constitutionality or validity of any treaty, international or executive agreement, law, presidential decree, proclamation, order, instruction, ordinance or regulation, taxes, and criminal cases in which the penalty imposed is "reclusion perpetua [life imprisonment] or higher."

Court guidelines for reviewing constitutional questions, which underscore a policy of judicial restraint, require an appropriate case, a personal and substantial interest by the party raising the question, a request for a determination at the earliest opportunity, and the necessity of passing on the constitutional question to decide the matter.

Independent Commissions

Article 9, Constitutional Commissions, provides for a civil service commission to act as a central personnel agency for the government, a commission on elections to enforce and administer all election laws and regulations, and a commission on audit to examine audits and settle fund and property accounts of the government and certain nongovernment entities.

Ombudsman

Article 11 provides for an independent office of ombudsman, who may, among other responsibilities, investigate citizen complaints against the government.

Amending the Constitution

Amendments may be proposed by a three-fourths vote of all members of the congress, by a constitutional convention, or by the people through an initiative once every five years. To become valid, the amendment or revision must be ratified by a majority of the votes in a plebiscite.

POLAND

Since its inception in A.D. 966, Poland has seldom enjoyed unchallenged territorial integrity. Steadfast allegiance to the idea of a Polish state and to the Roman Catholic Church, however, has finally resulted in an independent republic under a multiparty constitution.

General Information

The Republic of Poland in central Europe is approximately 313,000 square kilometers and is bounded by the Baltic Sea, Russia, and Lithuania on the north; Ukraine and Belarus on the east; the Czech and Slovak Republics on the south; and Germany on the west. Warsaw is the capital of this nation of more than thirty-nine million persons.

Until recently Poland was a communist country. Except for high unemployment, its overall economy is improving, particularly in the private sector, which now employs more than half of the work force. About ninety percent of Poles are Roman Catholic, and the fact that in 1978 a Pole was elected pope has had a strong influence on the nation and its people.

Type of Government: Presidential-style parliamentary republic, with a president, a prime minister and cabinet, a bicameral legislature, a judiciary, a constitutional tribunal, and a tribunal of state

Dates of Constitutions: 1791 (never implemented), 1815, 1921, 1952, 1992, and 1997

Constitutional History

Poland's unreserved adoption of Roman Catholicism in the tenth century and assimilation of the Latin cultural tradition have kept it linked with western, rather than eastern, Europe. The major pre-Christian characteristic of Polish society, however, was a strong clan system, which mitigated against the traditional European feudal structure. Legal equality of all clan members resulted in an insistence on unanimity in decision making, known as the *liberum veto;* anyone with political rights could veto the will of the majority by simply saying *"nie pozwalam"* ("I do not allow"). The concept of primogeniture (leaving one's title and all lands to the eldest son) never took root in Poland, creating a larger class of nobles.

Following a period of fragmentation and loss of territory to the Germans, Prussians, and Teutonic knights, Poland was reunified in the fourteenth century under Kazimierz the Great, who also founded the University of Krakow in 1364. Later in the century the marriage between the Polish monarch Jadwiga and Grand Duke Jagiello of Lithuania forged an alliance between the two countries that lasted until the end of the eighteenth century. Constitutional developments included limiting the monarch's power to tax by requiring the consent of the nobles in 1374; guaranteeing the nobility freedom from arbitrary arrest and confiscation of property under the terms of the 1430 Privilege of Jedlna, more than 250 years before the Habeas Corpus Act in England; creating a parliamentary system of government in 1496; and prohibiting the king from enacting any new law without the parliament's consent in 1509.

Throughout much of the eighteenth century foreign troops occupied Polish territory, and it was partitioned in three phases in 1772, 1793, and 1795 by Russia, Prussia, and Austria. On May 3, 1791, with the support of the last king of Poland, a new constitution was proposed to abolish the *liberum veto* and establish a hereditary monarchy in place of an elected one. The world's second written constitution, like the U.S. constitution, was the product of the Age of Enlightenment, and the similarity is even more evident in the preamble, which states, in part: ". . . desirous, moreover, to deserve the blessing and gratitude, not only of our contemporaries, but also of future generations . . . for the sake of the public good . . . for securing our liberty . . . we do solemnly establish this present constitution. . . ." Unlike the U.S. constitution, however, the Polish constitution of 1791 never went into effect.

The Congress of Vienna in 1815 restored the Kingdom of Poland under a new constitution but as a separate possession of the Russian Empire. After an 1830 rebellion, however, Czar Nicholas I abolished it. On November 11, 1918, the Polish nation was reborn and a new democratic constitution adopted in 1921, only to be dismembered by Germany, Russia, and the events of World War II. Poland was later reconstituted as a Soviet satellite with a new constitution adopted on July 22, 1952, that vested authority in the working people.

Not until the strikes and demands for reforms fomented by the unofficial union called Solidarity, under the unyielding leadership of Lech Walesa in the 1980s, was Poland finally able to extricate itself from communism and begin anew the process of self-government under a democratic constitution. After major amendments in 1989 and 1990 eliminated Marxist-Leninist principles and terminology in the earlier 1952 Soviet-style constitution, a "small" constitution entered into force on December 8, 1992. On May 25, 1997, a referendum confirmed a new constitution that prohibits political parties based on "nazism, fascism and communism." Poland's new constitution became effective on October 17, 1997.

Influences

The basic structure of government is similar to that created by the 1992 constitution adopted after the fall of the communist regime. The 1997 constitution, however, was influenced by Poland's desire to join the North Atlantic Treaty Organization (NATO), which required, among other things, guaranteeing civilian control over the military.

The Constitution

The preamble to the 1997 constitution of Poland states in part: "Having regard for the existence and future of our Homeland, which recovered, in 1989, the possibility of a sovereign and democratic determination of its fate, We, the Polish Nation ... call upon all those who would apply this Constitution ... to do so paying respect to the inherent dignity of the person, his or her right to freedom, the obligation of solidarity with others, and respect for these principles as the unshakable foundation of the Republic of Poland."

Articles 1, 2, and 3 proclaim that the "Republic of Poland shall be the common good of all its citizens[,] ... a democratic State ruled by law and implementing the principles of social justice[, and] ... a unitary State." Article 8 declares: "The Constitution shall be the supreme law of the Republic of Poland."

Fundamental Rights

Article 5 affirms that "Poland shall ... ensure the freedoms and rights of persons and citizens...." Article 11 guarantees "the creation and functioning of political parties," with a stipulation in article 13 adding that "[p]olitical parties and other organizations ... based upon totalitarian methods [such as] nazism, fascism and communism, [or that] sanction racial or national hatred, the application of violence for the purpose of obtaining power or to influence the State policy, or provide for the secrecy of their own structure or membership, shall be forbidden." The constitution also states that churches and other religious organizations "shall have equal rights," noting that "relations between ... Poland and the Roman Catholic Church shall be determined by international treaty concluded with the Holy See, and by statute."

Citizens' rights and freedoms, as well as their obligations, are further set forth in articles 30 to 86. These guarantees include "legal protection of the life of every human being," the right to one's faith and religion, freedom of movement, prohibitions against torture or "medical experimentation, without ... voluntary consent," privacy, "personal inviolability and security," as well as defense in criminal matters and "a fair and public hearing." Among political rights enumerated are freedom of communication, opinion, the press, peaceful assembly, and association and the right to information. "There shall be no statute of limitation," adds article 43, "regarding war crimes and crimes against humanity." Also protected are marriage and parental rights "to rear their children in accordance with their own convictions."

Economic, social, and cultural rights separately enumerated include the right to property ownership, choice of occupation, "safe and hygienic conditions of work," health, education, housing, and social security, as well as family, maternal, and children's rights. The constitution states that the nation's economic system is a "social market economy, based on the freedom of economic activity, private ownership, and solidarity, dialogue and cooperation between social partners." Also addressed are consumer rights, the "right to compensation for any harm done . . . by any action of an organ of public authority contrary to law," artistic creation, and scientific research. Citizens' obligations range from observation of the law and defense of the homeland to paying taxes and caring for the environment.

Division of Powers

Article 10 decrees that the government "shall be based on the separation of and balance between the legislative, executive and judicial powers." In support of this division, rulings by the constitutional tribunal are no longer "subject to examination" by the legislature's lower house, as was provided for under the 1992 constitution.

The Executive

President. "The President of the Republic," states article 126, is "the supreme representative of . . . Poland and the guarantor of the continuity of State authority." The chief executive ensures "observance of the Constitution" and acts "in accordance with [its] principles . . . and statutes." Elected directly for a five-year term, the president may be reelected only once. To be president, a person must be a Polish citizen, thirty-five years old, entitled to vote for members of the legislature's lower house, and supported by the signatures of at least 100,000 voters. A majority vote is necessary to win, with a runoff being held between the two candidates who receive the most votes if an absolute majority is not achieved on the first vote.

The president's powers and duties include representing the country in foreign affairs; ratifying and renouncing international agreements; appointing, recalling, and receiving diplomatic representatives; and cooperating with the government on foreign policy. The president is also the supreme commander of the armed forces, grants citizenship, confers orders and decorations, grants pardons (except to persons "convicted by the Tribunal of State"), convenes the cabinet "regarding particular matters," and issues regulations, executive orders, and "Official Acts," which "require, for their validity, the signature of the Prime Minister who . . . accepts responsibility therefor to the House of Representatives."

According to article 145, "The President . . . may be held accountable before the Tribunal of State for an infringement of the Constitution or statute, or for commission of an offense." An indictment requires a majority of at least two-thirds of the statutory number of members of the legislature, "on the motion of at least 140 members." The marshal of the legislature's lower house acts as president in the case of the incumbent's removal or incapacity.

Prime Minister and Cabinet. As article 147 provides, the council of ministers is composed of the prime minister and the ministers. "The Prime Minister shall represent the [cabinet and] manage [its] work." The cabinet conducts "the internal affairs and foreign policy of . . . Poland" and "shall manage the government administration." The president nominates the prime minister, who then proposes the composition of the council of ministers and submits "a program . . . to the [lower house], together with a motion requiring a vote of confidence," which requires a majority "in the presence of at least half the statutory number of Deputies."

The Legislature

Parliament. "Legislative power," declares article 95, "shall be exercised by the House of Representatives (*Sejm*) [lower house] and the Senate [upper house]." When the two sit in constitutionally required joint sessions, they act as the national assembly. Candidates are nominated by political parties or voters, according to procedures specified by statute. The four-year terms of both chambers may be shortened by a majority of at least two-thirds of the members of the lower house, which triggers a reduction in the senate's term as well.

Upper House. One hundred senators, each at least thirty years of age, are elected by universal, direct, and secret elections.

Lower House. Article 95 gives the house of representatives control over the activities of the council of ministers. It is composed of 460 deputies who are at least twenty-one years old and are chosen by "universal, equal, direct and proportional" elections. Certain immunities are extended to deputies, who elect a marshal and vice marshals; the marshal presides over debates and represents the chamber in external matters.

Bills may be introduced by deputies and senators, the president, the cabinet, and "100,000 citizens having the right to vote." Bills are considered in three readings and passed by a "simple majority vote" in the lower house. The senate then has thirty days to act or a bill is "considered adopted." The president must then sign the proposed legislation within twenty-one days, refer to the constitutional tribunal any question about its constitutionality, or veto it and return it to the lower house with objections. Such a veto may be overridden by "a three-fifths majority vote in the presence of at least half of the statutory number of Deputies," after which it must be signed and promulgated by the president.

The Judiciary

"The courts and tribunals shall constitute a separate power and shall be independent of other branches of power," declares article 173. According to article 175, "The administration of justice . . . shall be implemented by the Supreme Court, the common courts, administrative courts and military courts." Judges are to be independent, subject only to the constitution and laws, and they are "appointed for an indefinite period by the President . . . on the motion of the National Council of the Judiciary."

Supreme Court. In addition to exercising "supervision over common and military courts regarding judgments," the supreme court, as indicated in article 183, performs "other activities specified in the Constitution and statutes," such as adjudicating the validity of national elections. A first president of the supreme court is appointed by the president for a six-year term from candidates proposed by the general assembly of the judges of the supreme court.

Constitutional Tribunal

The tribunal, according to article 188, adjudicates the constitutionality of "statutes and international agreements," "legal provisions issued by central State organs," "the purposes and activities of political parties," and individual complaints regarding infringement of constitutional rights. Its fifteen judges are chosen by the lower house for nine-year terms.

Tribunal of State

Composed of a chairperson, two deputy chairpersons, and sixteen members chosen by the legislature's lower house for the term of the legislature, the tribunal of state, details article 198, holds the president, the prime minister, and members of the council of ministers, the president of the National Bank of Poland, and other high officials accountable for "violations of the Constitution or of a statute committed by them within their office or within its scope."

Ombudsman

According to articles 208 and 209, a commissioner for citizens' rights is appointed by the lower house of the legislature to "safeguard the freedoms and rights of persons and citizens specified in the Constitution and other normative acts."

Amending the Constitution

Under article 235, a proposed constitutional amendment may be initiated by one-fifth of the members of the lower house of the legislature, by the upper house, or by the president. It must be adopted by the lower house "by a majority of at least two-thirds . . . in the presence of a least half" of the members and, within sixty days, by the upper house "by an absolute majority . . . in the presence of at least half" of the members. Amendments dealing with the nature of the republic, rights and obligations of citizens, and amendments to the constitution have additional requirements, which may include "a confirmatory referendum."

PORTUGAL

After Portugal's rebellion against Spain in 1640, it established and lost worldwide empires. A revolution in April 1974 led to the development of a democratic government under a new constitution adopted in 1976.

General Information

The Portuguese Republic, which shares the Iberian Peninsula with Spain, is approximately 92,100 square kilometers and is bounded on the west and south by the Atlantic Ocean. Portugal ("land of the port") also includes the Azores and Madeira as well as Macau, which is near Hong Kong and is scheduled to revert to China in 1999. Lisbon is the capital of this country of approximately ten million persons.

Historically, Portugal's economy has depended on the production of wine, trade ties with Britain, and exploitation of its colonies in Africa, Asia, and South America. In 1986 the country was admitted to the European Economic Community, and its neighbor and traditional enemy, Spain, soon became a major commercial partner.

Type of Government: Presidential-style parliamentary republic, with a president and council of state, a prime minister and council of ministers (cabinet), a unicameral legislature, a judiciary, and a constitutional court

Dates of Key Constitutions: 1822, 1826 (proposed charter), 1911, 1933, and 1976

Constitutional History

The Portuguese culture has roots reaching back to the Stone Age, with successive influxes of Celts, Phoenicians, Greeks, Carthaginians, Romans, Visigoths, Muslims, and the French, all of whom left some mark on the Lusitanians, as the early Portuguese people were called. As a result of the four centuries of Roman colonization, the language became Latinized, and Roman legal and administrative principles were adopted, at least in the cities. Outside the urban areas Roman villas and landed estates (*latifunda*) proliferated. The Moors, consisting of North African Arabs and Berbers, conquered the Iberian Peninsula in the early eighth century A.D.

Henry of Burgundy laid claim to the Atlantic plains in northern Portugal between the Minho and Mondego Rivers as a Christian state on April 9, 1097. After many devastating wars the Muslims were finally driven out of the southern half of Portugal, and the territory was united by 1250. In 1256 a monarchy based on the French model, with a parliament, was established. Portugal's expansion collided with the territorial pursuits of Castile in central Spain, and the ensuing conflicts dominated Portuguese foreign policy for the next seven hundred years.

From the thirteenth century on, Portuguese society can be divided into three types by regions: a feudal agrarian economy in the north, towns in the central region dominated by middle-class burghers, and a society in the south dominated by knights of religious orders. For centuries foreign relations centered around trade and alliances with England. The Portuguese economy was also fueled by trade with Asia and India, partly the result of explorations by Prince Henry ("the Navigator") and by the lure of Africa, first for gold and then for slaves; after 1500 came the exploitation of Brazil. Toward the end of the sixteenth century the throne devolved on a Spanish Hapsburg who guaranteed Portugal's legal and constitutional autonomy; nevertheless, the two countries were united.

After a revolt in 1640 and a long war of independence from Spain, the aristocracy required Portuguese monarchs to be appointed by the parliament and dependent on it for revenues, even for defense. By 1656, however, Portugal had regained Angola in Africa and significant gold deposits were soon to be discovered in Brazil. The new supply of funds allowed the Portuguese monarchs to defer convening the parliament again until 1822. By that time revolution had broken out in the wake of the French Revolution, Lisbon had been devastated by the earthquake of 1755, and the gold in Brazil had been mined out.

In 1822 a radically liberal constitution was adopted, but an army coup in 1823 ended the constitutional experiment. In 1826 a constitutional charter, which was modeled on the Brazilian constitution and which represented a compromise between the liberals and the absolutists, was proposed; instead, civil war ensued. A bloodless revolution resulted in a parliamentary republic under a constitution adopted in 1911. The 1933 Portuguese constitution was drafted in 1932 by the dictator Antonio Salazar, who was finally driven from power in 1974.

Portuguese law by the fifteenth century consisted mostly of the ordinances of Alfonso V; by the seventeenth century local and canon law had been supplanted to a large extent. Influenced by French law, the commercial law in Portugal was codified in 1833, then replaced in 1888, taking into account the codes of Italy and Spain. A civil code, significantly different in style from that of the French, went into effect in 1867, to be replaced in 1967 by a new code, influenced by German, Swiss, and Italian law.

On April 25, 1976, a new constitution was adopted; important amendments were made in 1982, 1989, 1992, and 1997. The Portuguese parliament in 1978 approved the International Covenant on Civil and Political Rights (1966) of the United Nations, to which Portugal had been admitted in 1955, despite its poor record on democracy. A number of amendments were adopted in accordance with the covenant, and under article 40 of the covenant reports on its effect on the domestic legal system are made regularly to the United Nations.

Influences

Other European presidential-style parliamentary systems influenced the 1976 document, along with principles of socialism, which have since been diluted. A *dirigiste* type of constitution like Brazil's, the Portuguese document goes beyond simply organizing the government and guaranteeing rights to include programs for shaping society.

The Constitution

The preamble to the constitution of the Portuguese Republic, which contains 299 articles, harkens back to the revolution of April 25, 1974, and the liberation from the Salazar dictatorship. The language of at least one stated goal—to "open the way to socialist society"—appears to be out of date in light of the general declarations of democratic principles in the main text, although the Egyptian and Turkish constitutions likewise still contain references to historic socialist goals.

Fundamental Rights

Article 10 guarantees universal, equal, direct, secret, and periodic suffrage and lays down broad guidelines for political parties. Fundamental rights and duties include equality before the law; freedom from discrimination on the basis of ancestry, sex, race, language, territory of origin, religion, political or ideological convictions, education, economic situation, or social condition; protection for citizens abroad; the standard of the United Nations International Declaration of Human Rights for the interpretation of fundamental rights; access to law and the courts; the right to resist orders that infringe rights, freedoms, or safeguards; and the right to repel aggression by force if recourse to public authority is impossible.

Other rights specifically guaranteed include access to the law and the courts, legal advice and information, and legal aid, as well as the right to be accompanied by a lawyer when appearing before any public authority.

Division of Powers

The president is head of the unitary state of Portugal, the prime minister is head of government but is responsible to both the president and the legislature, and the constitution provides for both judicial and constitutional review.

The Executive

President. "The President of the Republic," states article 120, "represents the Portuguese Republic, guarantees national independence, the unity of the state and the regular functioning of the democratic institutions, and is *ex officio* commander in chief of the armed forces."

Any citizen of Portuguese origin and thirty-five years of age is eligible to be president. He or she must be nominated by no less than 7,500 and no more than 15,000 citizens who are eligible to vote. The president is directly elected for a five-year term and may not be reelected for a third term until five years have elapsed. The president may forfeit the office by leaving the national territory without the consent of the legislature.

The president's powers and duties include presiding over the council of state; fixing the dates of national elections in accordance with law; convening extraordinary sessions of the legislature; addressing the legislature; dissolving the legislature in accordance with constitutional provisions; appointing the prime minister after consulting the parties in the legislature and taking into consideration election results; dismissing or relieving the prime minister of his or her post as provided for in the constitution; appointing and dismissing members of the government on the recommendation of the prime minister; presiding over the council of ministers when asked by the prime minister; appointing and dismissing national ministers for the autonomous regions at the proposal of the government; appointing five members to the council of state and two to the higher council of the bench; presiding over the higher council of national defense; and appointing the chief of the general staff of the armed forces and other top military officers.

Other powers and duties of the president include requesting review by the constitutional court of provisions of laws, treaties, and decrees; granting pardons and commuting sentences; submitting relevant matters for national referendum; performing acts concerning the territory of Macao; and promulgating laws and decrees. Article 140 provides that certain acts of the president are null and void unless countersigned by the government.

The president of the legislature becomes acting president if the president is temporarily incapacitated.

Council of State. The council of state is a political advisory body to the president of the republic, who presides over it. Members of the council include the president of the legislature, the prime minister, the president of the constitutional court, the ombudsman, the chairman of the regional governments, former presidents elected under the constitution if not removed from office, and ten citizens, half appointed by the president and half elected by the legislature.

Prime Minister and Cabinet. In the Portuguese constitution the government is described as the organ for implementing the general policy of the nation and the highest organ of public administration. According to article 190, it is responsible for its actions to the president and the legislature. The government includes the prime minister, other ministers, state secretaries, and undersecretaries and possibly one or more deputy prime ministers. Within the government is the council of ministers (cabinet), consisting of the prime minister, deputies, and other ministers. A member of the government may not also be a member of the legislature.

The Legislature

Parliament. The unicameral Portuguese parliament is called the assembly of the republic. It consists of between 180 and 230 members elected from electoral districts as provided by law. Any citizen eligible to vote may stand for election, and nominations are to be made by political parties. Terms of office begin and end with the first meeting of the assembly after an election. Once elected, members are entitled to certain privileges and immunities.

Powers of the assembly include enacting legislation, except on subjects reserved by the constitution to the government; granting amnesties and general pardons; adopting laws concerning the major options for the plans and budget of the state; authorizing loans; approving international treaties; recommending to the president questions for national referendum; authorizing declarations of a state of siege or emergency, as well as authorizing the president to declare war or make peace; and carrying out other duties entrusted by the constitution and the law.

Article 164 contains a list of twenty-one areas of exclusive legislative power. These broad areas include making rules for referendums and determining the organization, functions, procedures of the constitutional court.

According to article 156, members may present proposals for constitutional amendments; present bills and draft resolutions; put questions to the government concerning any of its acts or any act of the public administration and receive an answer within a reasonable time, without prejudice to what the law states on the subject of state secrecy; request and obtain from the government or from the organs of any public body such data, information, and publications as they may consider useful; request the setting up of parliamentary committees of inquiry; and exercise other prerogatives as are written in the assembly's rules of procedure.

Ombudsman. Article 23 establishes the position of ombudsman, who is to be independent and appointed by the legislature to receive citizen complaints against public authorities and to recommend remedies.

The Judiciary

Article 202 provides that the courts are the supreme authorities to administer justice in the name of the people. They are to be independent, and they are not to apply unconstitutional provisions or principles to matters that come before them.

Influenced early on by Roman civil law and later by the law of other western European countries such as France, the Portuguese judicial and legal systems developed into two separate court systems: one having original and appellate jurisdiction in criminal and civil cases and the other having jurisdiction over military, administrative, fiscal, and labor disputes. Article 207, paragraph 2, provides that "lay magistrates may be called to court for hearings on labor disputes, offenses against public health, minor offenses . . . and other matters which call for special consideration of social values." Portugal was apparently satisfied with the judicial system before the 1974 revolution, and the basic structure was maintained in its 1976 constitution.

Supreme Court. The supreme court of justice is the highest judicial court. It functions as a court of first or second instance where the law so provides, but in general the law courts of first instance are district courts and the law courts of second instance are courts of appeal. Appointment to the supreme court is to be in accordance with law; its president is elected by the other members.

Additional courts established by the constitution include a supreme administrative court, a court of accounts, and military courts.

Constitutional Court

The constitutional court consists of thirteen judges, ten appointed by the legislature and three others chosen by the members of the court for nine-year, nonrenewable terms. Six of the members must be judges of other courts, and the remaining members must be jurists.

The court is authorized to exercise preventive review of constitutionality as well as review of laws in effect and acts committed. Under article 281, the president of the republic, president of the legislature, prime minister, ministers, one-tenth of the deputies of the legislature, and others "may request the . . .Court to make generally binding rulings on questions of unconstitutionality and illegality." For example, the president may ask for "anticipatory review" of treaties, laws, or law-decrees, and a minister may similarly request such review of the constitutionality of "a regional legislative decree or a regulative decree." If the court finds that a decree or treaty is unconstitutional, "the instrument must be vetoed by the President . . . or the Minister."

On appeal, according to article 280, the court has jurisidiction with respect to decisions involving questions of the constitutionality of laws and acts; however, such appeals are "restricted to questions of unconstitutionality or illegality, as the case requires." The constitution also gives the court the authority of general review of constitutionality and legality in such matters as the "[u]nconstitutionality of any legal norm," the "[i]llegality of any provisions of legislation, on the ground that it contravenes superior law," as well as in the case of the illegality of regional legislative instruments or national instruments that allegedly contravene the rights of a region.

Amending the Constitution

Amendments may be initiated by members of the legislature and must be approved by a two-thirds vote of those entitled to vote; the president may not refuse to promulgate any revised law.

The legislature may revise the constitution if five years have elapsed since publication of the latest law of ordinary revision; however, at any time after such revision and by a four-fifths majority vote, the legislature may assume powers of extraordinary revision. According to article 288, any laws revising the constitution must, among other requirements, safeguard national independence and the unity of the state, the republican form of government, separation of church and state, and other rights and guarantees.

Despite a history of anticommunism and distrust of Russia, Romania was one of the first countries to be subverted by the Soviet Union following World War II. Two years after the overthrow of a brutish communist dictator in 1989, Romania adopted a constitution that provides for a multiparty democracy.

A Balkan state in eastern Europe, Romania is 237,500 square kilometers. It is bounded by Ukraine on the north and east, the Black Sea and Moldova on the east, Bulgaria on the south, and Hungary and the former Yugoslav territory on the west. Bucharest is the capital of this country of approximately twenty-two million persons.

Romania is an extremely poor country, with three-fourths of the work force engaged in agriculture. Many of the nation's economic problems are the result of policies of the former communist regime. Romania signed an association agreement with the European Union in 1993, but in a recent poll more than half of the citizens said life had been better under communism.

Type of Government: Presidential-style parliamentary republic, with a president, a prime minister and cabinet, a bicameral legislature, a judiciary, and a constitutional court

Dates of Constitutions: 1861, 1866, 1923, 1948, 1952, 1965, and 1991

From the earliest times Romania has been a site of human habitation. Around 5500 B.C. Indo-Europeans settled in the area, followed by the Gatae and other Thracian tribes. Greek culture also made an impact. The Emperor Trajan established the Roman province of Dacia around the beginning of the second century A.D. When the Romans left Dacia in the face of invaders from the east, there was an influx of Slavic peoples, and in 676 much of Dacia was annexed by the Bulgar Empire.

In the thirteenth century people from Transylvania founded the principalities of Walachia and Moldavia, which prospered under the absolute rule of princes elected for life by assemblies of nobles (boyars) and church leaders. Walachia gained independence from Hungary in 1380. In the fifteenth century the Ottoman Turks invaded; the Walachian prince Vlad the Impaler acquired his epithet when, after thwarting an assassination attempt by the Turks, he impaled the heads of the would-be assassins on stakes. Moldavia also fought the Turks but ended up a vassal state of the Ottoman Empire.

Russia's interest in the territory was formally recognized by the Turkish sultan in 1829, and a Russian sent to be governor helped draft organic laws for the people. After electing the same governor in 1859, Moldavia and Walachia united officially in 1861 as Romania under a constitution giving the ruler, now a prince, broad powers. The prince, Alexandru Cuza, who had begun initiating reforms, was forced to abdicate by army officers loyal to the boyars, and a German prince, Charles Hohenzollern-Sigmaringen, was brought in under a new constitution in 1866 that gave him veto power over a bicameral legislature and paid lip service to certain fundamental rights.

The 1923 constitution of Greater Romania, now with a king as monarch, centralized the state administration. In 1948 it was replaced by a socialist constitution that did not provide for separation of powers and did not mention the Romanian Communist Party, which, in fact, ruled the country. The 1952 constitution stressed the close ties with the Soviet Union, while the 1965 constitution renamed the country the Socialist Republic of Romania and acknowledged the role of the Communist Party, the only party allowed by law. A 1974 amendment created the office of president of the republic.

In 1989, following the overthrow and expedited execution of both President Nicolae Ceauşescu, a communist dictator, and his wife, the nation began the process of establishing a multiparty democratic system of government under a constitution approved by national referendum on December 8, 1991. It remains to be seen, however, if the old order has truly been reformed.

In many ways similar to the French constitution, Romania's 1991 constitution also clearly reflects rejection of the previous communist system and the "cult of the personality."

The Constitution

According to article 2:

(1) National sovereignty resides with the Romanian people, who shall exercise it through its representative bodies and by referendum.
(2) No group or person may exercise sovereignty in one's own name.

Fundamental Rights

Article 1 provides that Romania is a democratic and social state governed by the rule of law in which human dignity, the citizen's rights and freedoms, the free development of human personality, justice, and political pluralism represent supreme values and shall be guaranteed.

Title 2, Fundamental Rights, Freedoms, and Duties, contains a number of articles guaranteeing equality of rights; legal protection in the cases of extradition or expulsion; right to life and to physical and mental integrity; freedom of movement; personal and family privacy; inviolability of the home; secrecy (privacy) of correspondence; freedom of expression, religion, and assembly; and other rights and freedoms.

Division of Powers

In Romania, a unitary state, power is divided among the president, the prime minister, the legislature, the courts, and the constitutional court, which has limited powers of constitutional review.

The Executive

President. The head of state is the president, who is elected for a four-year term by universal, equal, direct, secret, and free suffrage. He or she may hold office for only two terms, but a term may be prolonged by an organic law in the event of war or a catastrophe.

Duties and powers of the president include designating a prime minister and appointing the ministers of the government, which must receive a vote of confidence from the legislature; consulting with the government on urgent and extremely important matters; presiding over meetings of the government, which he or she attends; dissolving both houses of the legislature, after consulting with their top officials and with party leaders; calling for a referendum on matters of national interest after consulting with the legislature; concluding treaties that must be ratified by the legislature; commanding the armed forces and presiding over the supreme council of national defense; and, in accordance with law, instituting a state of siege or emergency to be approved by the legislature. Other powers include conferring decorations, making promotions to high military rank and appointments to public office as provided for by law, and granting individual pardons.

Article 84 prohibits the president, while in office, from being a member of a political party or holding any other public or private office. It extends immunity to the president and provides for his or her impeachment for high treason by a two-thirds vote of the members of the legislature in joint session, with the trial to be conducted by the supreme court.

The order of succession in the event of a vacancy in the presidency or the incapacity of the president, pending new elections, is, first, the president of the upper house and then the president of the lower house of the legislature.

Prime Minister and Cabinet. The government consists of the prime minister, ministers of state, and ministers, who make up the cabinet, as well as other positions established by organic law. In accordance with its program as approved by the legislature, the government implements domestic and foreign policy and generally manages the public administration.

Parliament. Romania's bicameral parliament includes an upper house, the Senat (senate), and a lower house, the Camera Deputaților (chamber of deputies). According to article 58, the parliament "is the supreme representative body of the Romanian people and the sole legislative authority of the state." Articles 58 through 71 address both houses together.

The number of senators and deputies is determined by electoral law based on population; in 1992 there were 143 senators and 328 deputies. Article 59 provides that national minorities, in accordance with electoral law, have a right to at least one seat in the chamber of deputies. Members of both houses are elected by universal, equal, direct, secret, and free suffrage for four-year terms, which, like the president's, may be extended by organic law. According to article 60, the term of the lower house is prolonged until a newly elected parliament meets, but no constitutional or organic acts may be passed during the extension.

The government, members of the parliament, and a sufficient number of citizens may introduce bills. In addition to ordinary laws, certain areas of legislation—such as the electoral system, organization of political parties, and referendums—require an organic law; unlike ordinary laws that may be passed by a majority vote of the members present, these must be approved by a majority vote of the members of each chamber. After passage a bill is sent to the president, who may return it or request the constitutional court to review its constitutionality. If repassed or determined to be constitutional by the court, the bill becomes law.

Senators and deputies have parliamentary immunity, but article 68 provides that they may not hold other public office. Each chamber establishes its own procedures, elects a president and other members of a standing bureau, and forms standing committees "so as to reflect the political spectrum of each chamber." A majority of the members is required to pass laws and carry resolutions and motions.

The constitution also provides for a legislative council "that initials draft normative acts for the purpose of a systematic unification and coordination of the whole body of laws."

Ombudsman. An advocate of the people is authorized by the constitution to report at least annually to the legislature on citizens' grievances related to fundamental rights.

Supreme Court. The judges of the supreme court of justice are appointed by the president of the republic and, like all Romanian judges, are to be independent and subject only to the law. The president of the court and other members hold office for six-year terms and may be reappointed.

Superior Council of the Magistracy. The competence and procedure of the courts is to be regulated by law, and the promotion, transfer, and sanctions against judges are handled by a superior council of the magistracy, which consists of magistrates elected for four-year terms by the parliament in joint session.

Public Prosecutors. The constitution also creates a public ministry, acting through public prosecutors, to represent the general interests of society and defend legal order and citizens' rights and freedoms.

A constitutional court in Romania consists of nine judges appointed for nine-year terms. Three are appointed by each of the two houses of the legislature and three by the president; one-third are to be renewed every three years.

The court's duties include determining the constitutionality of a proposed law when requested by the president, the legislature, the government, or the supreme court; determining the constitutionality of standing orders of the parliament; and deciding on exceptions brought to the courts of law regarding the constitutionality of laws and orders. The court's decisions in the first two instances are prospective only and may be overridden by a two-thirds majority vote in each chamber.

Amending the Constitution

An amendment may be introduced by the president on behalf of the government, one-fourth of the deputies or senators, or five hundred thousand voters meeting certain demographic requirements. It must be approved by a two-thirds vote of the members of each house of the legislature or by three-fourths of the members in a joint session, and then must be approved by referendum. Certain specified aspects of the constitution, however, may not be revised.

It is said that Czarist soldiers in 1825 mistook the "Constitution" the revolutionaries were demanding for the name of the wife of an heir to the throne. The demand for a genuine democracy, however, led the Russian people to adopt a new, multiparty constitution in 1993 after nearly seventy-five years of communist rule.

RUSSIA

General Information

The largest country in the world, the Russian Federation, or simply Russia, has an area of more than 17 million square kilometers spanning north-central Europe eastward to the farthest reaches of northeast Asia. Moscow, with a population of nearly nine million persons, is the capital of this country of approximately 146 million inhabitants.

Rich in natural resources, including sources of energy that are often costly to extract and transport to markets, Russia is undergoing a wrenching change from a planned economy, in which the government favored heavy industry over consumer goods and set production quotas, to a freely fluctuating market economy that Karl Marx, the founder of communism, called anarchy. International assistance and political stability while the changes occur are Russia's best hope for future prosperity.

Type of Government: Presidential-style parliamentary federal republic, with a president, a chairman (prime minister) and council of ministers (cabinet), a bicameral legislature, and a judiciary, including a constitutional court

Dates of Constitutions: 1905, 1918, 1924, 1936, 1977 (significantly amended 1988–90), and 1993

Constitutional History

While there is evidence of Stone Age settlements, the history of Russia begins with Iranians and Scythians, who inhabited the territory of Ukraine from 600 to 200 B.C. This area north of the Black Sea then became home to the eastern branch of Slavic-speaking peoples; the western branch became Poles and Czechs; and the southern branch became groups in the Balkans, such as Bulgarians and ethnic units in what was Yugoslavia.

In the ninth century A.D. Rurik, one of the Scandinavians called Varangians who had moved into the area, became the first ruler of the Kievan Rus' in Novgorod and Kiev. The Rurikid dynasty lasted until the end of the sixteenth century. During the Middle Ages the Russians (east Slavs) split into three language groups: Great Russians, Ukraines, and White Russians (Belorussians). By now the government was based on an autocratic ruler, a council of aristocrats, and a more democratic city assembly *(veche)*.

After Mongol hordes overran the area in the thirteenth century, Moscow grew in power, becoming the state of Moscovy, in which land was held collectively. The semi-independent princedoms that arose were all subordinated by Ivan III of Moscovy, who married the niece of the last Byzantine emperor and took the title "czar and autocrat." In the sixteenth century Ivan IV ("the Terrible)" developed his autocratic powers to their fullest while introducing military reforms, reorganizing local government, and conducting an *oprichina* (purge) of the *boyars* (nobles). His feeble-minded son brought about the independence of the Russian Orthodox Church, and after his death in 1598 a *zemskii sobor* (national assembly) proclaimed Boris Godunov, a *boyar,* as the new czar. In 1613 the assembly choose Mikhail Romanov for the job.

In 1649 a legal code that put the state's interests above those of individuals went into effect, and the bureaucracy grew dramatically. Russia's subsequent Westernization and transformation into an empire was due largely to the efforts of Peter the Great, who lived from 1682 to 1725. Catherine the Great, a German princess who came to power after her husband, Czar Peter III, was killed in a coup in 1762, added much new territory, including an outlet to the Black Sea. During the nineteenth century Russia opposed the liberalizing trends in Europe, but young military officers who had followed Napoleon's retreat returned with the seeds of revolutionary ideas, such as representative government and mass democracy.

In December 1825 a group called the Decembrists began the process of revolution. In 1905 an attempted revolution wrested from Nicholas II, who was to be the last Romanov czar, a limited constitution creating a legislative body called the Duma. Such a legislative council had been used by Russian rulers for centuries, but Nicholas circumvented it at first and then ignored it during World War I. With the war and the autocracy going badly, the legislature began preparing for a provisional government. Elsewhere, a soviet (council) of workers' deputies was set up. By October 25, 1917 (under the old calendar), the Bolsheviks—a radical faction of the Social Democratic Labor Party led by Vladimir Lenin (born Ulianov)—had gained control of key military units. So began the history of communist rule in Russia.

For Karl Marx constitutions described existing class and political relationships. Joseph Stalin (born Djugashvili), like Lenin, held Marx's view; he said about his 1936 Soviet constitution that it should show the gains of socialism, not the aims. The 1918 constitution, however, formally recognized the Bolshevik Party as wielding all political power through the dictatorship of the proletariat and noted that the party was an alliance between the workers and the peasants, who were granted broad equal rights. A 1924 constitution recognized the Soviet Union as a federation of socialist republics, including Ukraine, Belorussia, and Transcaucasia. In place of an assembly called the congress of soviets, it created a central executive committee as the supreme state authority, with a bicameral body consisting of a soviet of the union representing the republics and a soviet of nationalities. A presidium of the committee was to act as a collegial president.

The "Stalin" constitution of 1936 permitted direct elections for government bodies by universal suffrage and renamed the highest governing body the supreme soviet of the Soviet Socialist Republics; the presidium of this body exercised power between sessions. On October 7, 1977, the "Brezhnev" constitution, named for Leonid I. Brezhnev, was approved. It confirmed that the dictatorship of the proletariat was complete and now expressed the will of all working people. The Communist Party still had the leading role, and society and the economy would continue to be managed by the state. In 1988, 1989, and 1990 significant amendments were made that allowed multiparty candidates, created a constitutional oversight committee to review laws and suggest changes, and gave formal expression to the power of Mikhail S. Gorbachev, who was named to the new post of president of the Soviet Union on March 15, 1990. Gorbachev had succeeded Brezhnev in 1977 as head of the Communist Party and the government.

A failed coup attempt by conservative communists in August 1991 discredited the party, the union collapsed, and eleven of the Soviet republics formed the Commonwealth of Independent States. Boris N. Yeltsin had already been elected president of the Russian Republic in June, pursuant to amendments to its constitution in May. After a number of early drafts, a new constitution was finally approved by referendum on December 12, 1993.

Influences

The constitution of the Fifth Republic of France has influenced particularly the relationship between the Russian president and the legislature, but elements of the U.S. constitution can also be seen.

The Constitution

One reason for adopting the 1993 constitution of the Russian Federation, says its preamble, was the desire for "renewing the sovereign statehood of Russia and acknowledging the immortality of its democratic foundations." Article 1(1) states: "The Russian Federation—Russia—shall be a democratic, federative, law-based state with a republican form of government."

Article 2 states: "Human beings and human rights and freedoms shall be of the highest value. Recognition of, and respect for, and protection of human and civil rights and freedoms shall be the duty of the state."

Chapter 2, Human and Civil Rights and Freedoms, provides that basic rights and freedoms will be guaranteed under universally acknowledged principles of international law, that they are inalienable and belong to each person from birth, but that their exercise may not infringe on the rights and freedoms of others.

The rights and freedoms guaranteed include equality before the law; no discrimination on the basis of sex, race, nationality, language, origin, property, or official status, place of residence, attitude toward religion, persuasions, affiliation with social associations, or other circumstances. Other guarantees include the right to life (although the death penalty is not abolished); protection against torture; and the right to freedom and personal inviolability. A limit of forty-eight hours is set on nonjudicial detention. Each person is also guaranteed social security in old age, in the event of sickness, disability, or loss of family provider.

In Russia, a federal state, power is divided between the national government and the members of the federation; at the national level it is divided among the president, the prime minister, the legislature, and the courts, which exercise certain powers of constitutional review through the constitutional court.

President. Pursuant to article 80, the president is head of state, guarantor of the constitution, and protector of sovereignty, independence, and state integrity. He or she is the dominant constitutional power and sets domestic and foreign policy guidelines, represents the state domestically and internationally, and is commander in chief of the armed forces.

The president is elected as head of state to a four-year term by universal, direct, and equal suffrage and by secret ballot but may not be elected to more than two consecutive terms. Any citizen and resident for ten years who is at least thirty-five years old is eligible for the office.

The duties and powers of the president include appointing, with approval of the lower house of the legislature, the chairman (prime minister) of the government; presiding over sessions of the government; accepting the resignation of the government; nominating and removing the head of the central bank, with the approval of the lower house of the legislature; appointing deputy chairmen of the government and federal ministers nominated by the chairman and removing them; nominating judges to the highest courts and the prosecutor general for appointment by the upper house of the legislature; supervising the security council and the executive office; approving military policy and appointing and dismissing top military commanders; and appointing and dismissing foreign representatives and plenipotentiary representatives of the president of the Russian Federation. The president is also in charge of foreign policy, conducts negotiations, accepts credentials of foreign representatives, decides questions of citizenship and asylum, confers awards, grants pardons, and is authorized to issue decrees and directives as long as they do not contravene the constitution or laws.

Under article 85 the president is given authority to reconcile differences between state authorities or send such matters to court. He or she is entitled to suspend acts of the executive bodies if they contradict the constitution, laws, international obligations, or breach civil or human rights, until such matters are decided by the appropriate court.

The president may be removed from office by the upper house of the legislature on accusations by the lower house of high treason or other grave crimes, if the supreme court finds that the president's actions are criminal and that the procedures for accusation have been observed.

Prime Minister and Cabinet. Chapter 6 of the constitution declares that executive power is vested in the government, which is composed of a chairman (prime minister), deputy chairmen, and ministers. The government is responsible for implementing national policy and laws.

The Legislature

Parliament. According to article 94, the bicameral Russian parliament, called the Federalnoe Sobranie (federal assembly), is the supreme representative and legislative body. It consists of an upper house, the federation council, and a lower house, the state Duma.

Upper House. The powers of the federation council, made up of a representative from the executive and legislative branches of each member of the federation, include approving internal border changes, the president's decree of martial law or emergency, and the external use of the military; calling presidential elections; removing the president if impeached; and appointing judges to the highest courts.

Lower House. The powers of the state Duma, composed of 450 deputies elected for four-year terms, include approving the president's nominee for chairman of the government; deciding on votes of no confidence for the government; appointing the head of the central bank and the head of the accounting chamber as well as half of its auditors; declaring amnesty; and impeaching the president. Deputies must be citizens, twenty-one years old, and qualified to vote.

Once in office, a member of the parliament enjoys certain immunities, and each house elects a chairman and deputy chairman from among its members. Each house adopts its own rules of procedure, and to supervise the execution of the federal budget each forms an accounting chamber, whose makeup and rules are determined by law.

The parliament enacts legislation, which may be introduced by the president, the federation council or its members, deputies of the Duma, the government, and legislatures of the federation members. Bills, however, must be introduced in the Duma, and money bills must first have the consent of the government.

Generally federal laws are adopted by a majority vote of the total members of the Duma and then by the federal council if "more than half of the general number of deputies have voted for it." A bill is also considered passed if the council does not act on it within fourteen days of receipt. If the council rejects a bill a joint commission may settle the disagreement, and the matter again goes to the Duma, which may override the council by a vote of two-thirds of all members. The president must either sign a bill or reject it; a veto may be overridden by a two-thirds vote of the total members of each house.

Federal constitutional laws are adopted on matters specified in the constitution by a vote of at least three-fourths of the members of the federation council and by at least two-thirds of the deputies in the state Duma and then must be signed by the president.

Ombudsman. Under article 103(e) the lower house of the legislature may appoint a human rights officer to act in accordance with federal constitutional law.

The Judiciary

Article 118 provides that the judicial system is to be established by the constitution and federal constitutional law. Article 120 requires judges to be independent and subject only to the constitution and federal law. According to article 124, the courts are to be financed in such a way that they can "administer justice fully and independently in accordance with federal law."

The constitution creates three courts in the judicial system: a supreme court, a supreme arbitration court, and a constitutional court. Their judges are nominated by the president and appointed by the federation council; other judges of federal courts are appointed by the president in accordance with law.

Supreme Court. The supreme court is the highest court with respect to civil, criminal, administrative, and other cases. It oversees the judiciary in accordance with procedures established by law and advises on legal practice.

Supreme Arbitration Court. The supreme arbitration court is charged with settling economic and other disputes of the courts of arbitration.

Constitutional Court. The constitutional court's jurisdiction includes constitutional compliance in cases of federal laws and presidential enactments, constitutions of the republics as well as statutes and other laws and enactments of federation members, treaties between federal and member authorities, and international treaties not yet in force. It also settles disputes between specified government entities, verifies the constitutionality of laws where citizens' rights and freedoms are involved, and interprets the constitution at the request of the president and certain government bodies. Requests for review may be made by the president and other government entities and one-fifth of the members of the federation council or the state Duma.

Chapter 9, Constitutional Amendments and Revision of the Constitution, provides that proposals for amendments are introduced like bills, except that one-fifth of the members of both houses of the legislature may introduce an amendment in addition to the president, the federation council, the Duma, the government, and the legislatures of the federation members.

Amending the Constitution

If changes in chapters regarding the constitutional system, rights and freedoms, or the amendment process are proposed by three-fifths of the total members of the legislature, a constituent assembly must be convened and a new constitution written and submitted for approval by referendum; otherwise those sections may not be amended. Other amendments may be adopted by a three-fourths vote of all the federation council and a two-thirds vote of all the Duma members, if then approved by two-thirds of the legislatures of the federation members. Changes to article 65, the Organization of the Federation, must be treated in accordance with specific federal constitutional law.

SAUDI ARABIA

The Saudi people and their system of government were able to adapt to enormous changes in the twentieth century while retaining their traditional character. The nation's constitution, in essence, is the Qur'an.

General Information

The Kingdom of Saudi Arabia on the Arabian Peninsula is approximately 2 million square kilometers and is bounded by Jordan, Iraq, and Kuwait on the north; Bahrain, Qatar, the United Arab Emirates, and the Persian Gulf on the east; Oman on the southeast; Yemen on the south; and the Red Sea on the west. Riyadh is the capital of this country of more than twenty-two million persons.

Saudi Arabia is one of the world's richest nations, with its wealth derived from the production of oil. A reduction in oil prices and massive aid to Iraq in its war with Iran brought on a recession in the early 1980s. Recent reductions in oil production have raised prices and revenues, but long-term sustainable economic growth will require unpopular measures.

Type of Government: Traditional monarchy, with a monarch who is also the prime minister, a council of ministers (cabinet), a consultative council, and a judiciary

Date of Constitution: None

Constitutional History

People living along the coast of the Arabian Peninsula profited from trade with inhabitants of the Nile, Tigris, and Euphrates river valleys, and by 1000 B.C. their civilization had developed a number of small kingdoms and city-states. The Romans later called this prosperous area Arabia Felix ("happy Arabia"). Camels made desert crossings practical, giving rise to caravan cities such as Mecca. The Roman and Persian Empires paid Arab tribes to protect their southern borders.

The current ruling Saud family (al-Saud) and other Arabs and Muslims trace their lineage to the time of Muhammad's birth in Mecca in 570. At his death in 632 the Prophet commanded the loyalty of most of Arabia, and his successors (caliphs) ruled until the last one and his family were slain by the Mongols in 1258.

Around 1500 the al-Saud clan began its rise to prominence by taking over date groves near Riyadh. In the eighteenth century Muhammad ibn Saud and the leader of an Islamic reform movement opposed to the Shi'a Muslim sect swore a traditional oath to establish a state governed by Islamic principles. In 1816 the overextended Ottoman Empire commissioned one of its officers in Egypt, Muhammad Ali, to capture the Arabian region of Hijaz on the peninsula's west coast, but a few years later a member of the Saudi family recaptured the central region of Najd and Riyadh, its capital.

The Saudi family remained in control by playing off the Ottomans against the British during much of the nineteenth century. Fierce internal rivalries had to be quelled before Abdul Aziz Bin Abdul Rahman Al-Saud laid the foundation of the modern Saudi state in 1924. In 1926 a constitution was promulgated for the kingdom of Hijaz, and in 1927 it was declared an Islamic constitutional monarchy and united with Najd under Aziz as king. In 1932 he named the new country Saudi Arabia, after the family name, and issued a royal order to his advisers to "embark immediately on drafting a basic law for the kingdom."

By his death in 1953 the king had established only a council of ministers to assist him in governing. He left more than thirty sons, and although the eldest was named the crown prince, there was no orderly mechanism for succession. The new king also had more than thirty sons, as well as ambitious brothers, which made for political instability in the kingdom. In 1958, however, the council of ministers was transformed into a policy-making body with apparent executive and legislative functions.

In 1962 the Saudi government adopted a ten-point reform program considered revolutionary at the time. After a family coup in 1964, the new king decided to act as head of both state and government; he was assassinated in 1975. On March 1, 1992, King Fahd Bin Abdul Aziz, by decree, announced the establishment of a *majlis* (consultative council). A speaker was named the following September, members were appointed in 1993, and additional decrees affecting the form of the government were also issued that year.

Influences

Traditional Arab institutions and the Islamic religion have had the greatest influences on Saudi Arabia's system of government.

The Constitution

Saudi Arabia has no true constitutional document, only a series of royal decrees, most recently in 1992 and 1993. Through them, the monarch has formulated rules for the various institutions that act on matters of state on his behalf or with whom he may consult. It is often said that the Qur'an, the holy book of the Islamic faith, is the constitution of Saudi Arabia.

Fundamental Rights

Article 26 of the Basic Law of Government, a 1992 royal decree, provides that "the state shall protect human rights according to the *shari'a* [Islamic law]." Basic rights extended include a prohibition against restricting anyone's actions or detaining or imprisoning anyone, except according to law, as well as a prohibition against ex post facto laws and protections for the privacy of communication and the sanctity of the home against entry and search, except according to law. Economic and social rights granted in the document include a guarantee to all citizens and their families of protection in the case of illness, disability, and old age, and support for the social welfare system. The state also undertakes to facilitate employment, provide education, and fight illiteracy.

Division of Powers

In Saudi Arabia, a unitary state, all power resides in the monarch and those to whom he delegates it.

The Executive

Monarch. The monarch, who holds the title Custodian of the Two Holy Mosques and king of Saudi Arabia, is a member of the Saud family and rules by tradition as an absolute monarch and head of the Islamic faith, with the acceptance of the ranking members of the royal family.

In an interview in 1992, after issuing three major laws—the Basic Law of Government, the Consultative Council Law, and the Law of Provinces—King Fahd remarked:

The democratic system that is predominant in the world is not a suitable system for the people of our region. Our peoples' make-up and unique qualities are different from those of the rest of the world. We cannot import the methods used by people in other countries and apply them to our people. We have our Islamic beliefs that constitute a complete and fully integrated system. Free elections are not within this Islamic system, which is based on consultation *(shura)* and the openness between the ruler and his subjects before whom he is fully responsible. . . .

The royal Diwan is the king's primary executive office. It contains his office and the offices of his principal advisers for domestic politics, religious affairs, and international relations. The king holds a regular meeting *(majlis)* or court with his subjects in the Diwan.

Prime Minister and Cabinet. Since 1964 the king has also been the prime minister and head of government, with a council of ministers (cabinet). He is, therefore, the final arbiter of all government decisions; no laws restrain the cabinet, which was created on May 11, 1958, by a royal decree entitled the Law of the Council of Ministers.

In 1993 the king promulgated general rules for the council of ministers, over which he presides, but many key government posts are held by members of the royal family. Under the rules meetings are "held under the chairmanship of the kingdom, the prime minister, or any of the deputy premiers," and resolutions become final after approval by the king. In article 9 of a 1993 royal decree, the Council of Ministers System General Rules, the monarch provided for "reshuffling" the council before the end of or sometime after the four-year term. This body may initiate laws, review domestic and foreign policy, and review the budget.

The Legislature

Consultative Council. Saudi Arabia has no true legislature or elected representatives. Legislation *(tashri'a)* is considered unnecessary because God is the supreme and only legislator. On March 1, 1992, the monarch replaced the old consultative council created in 1926. The reorganized council is called the Majlis al-Shura and is composed of sixty members and a speaker appointed by the monarch for four-year terms.

The council meets at least twice a week and is supervised by a chairman, who represents the council in relations with other bodies and speaks for it. Decisions are based on a majority vote. The council also has a vice chairman, a secretary general, and a general board, which prepares a general plan for the council and its committee as well as the agenda for the council's sessions.

The Judiciary

Article 48 of the Basic Law of Government directs that "courts shall apply the provisions of *shari'a* according to the Holy Book and the tradition and to the laws issued by the king that do not conflict with [them]." The Saudi Arabian judicial system, therefore, is based on Islamic law, which includes a number of approved "schools" of Islamic jurisprudence and ancient commentaries that often have no relevance to modern legal problems. Article 49 provides that "courts adjudicate all conflicts and crimes."

The ministry of justice since 1970 has administered the legal system through the courts. At the trial level are the general courts, or courts of first instance; above these are an appellate court and a high Islamic law court. The next level includes the court of appeals. In addition, there is a board of grievances, which handles disputes involving codified regulations, and special courts for labor and commercial disputes. The courts' decisions may be appealed to the office of the monarch or the crown prince and are handled by the cabinet's legal office. A decision by the cabinet, signed by the monarch, is final.

Although article 46 declares that the judiciary is an independent authority, jurists on occasion bow to the influence of the royal family, and the government occasionally bypasses the courts altogether and disposes of legal problems administratively in summary proceedings closed to the public.

Amending the Constitution

Because all rights of citizens and the form of government are contingent on the will of the monarch, the minimal constitutional procedures that exist in Saudi Arabia are subject to change at any time by royal fiat, although presumably after some degree of consultation with key members of the royal family and advisers.

A tightly controlled society dominated by a single political party for a quarter of a century, Singapore recently broadened the powers of its president, who was directly elected for the first time in 1993.

The Republic of Singapore, an island just south of Johor Province in western Malaysia, is some 600 square kilometers and is bounded on the north by the Johor Strait, on the west by the Strait of Malacca, on the south by the Singapore Strait, and on the east by the South China Sea. Singapore is the capital of this country of approximately four million persons.

With a growing economy based historically on transshipping and processing such regional products as rubber and tin, as well as on banking and insurance services, densely populated Singapore has one of the highest standards of living in Asia and the highest savings rate in the world. One of the globe's busiest ports and home to the global operations of thousands of multinational corporations, the country has been ruled by a single party since 1959.

Type of Government: Presidential-style parliamentary republic, with a president, a prime minister and cabinet, a unicameral legislature, and a judiciary

Dates of Constitutions: 1959, 1963 (significantly amended in 1965)

By the seventh century A.D. the island of Singapore was most likely one of many ports in the Srivijaya Empire, a maritime state whose capital was in eastern Sumatra. Chinese and Javanese chroniclers in the fourteenth century referred to it as a settlement of Malay and Chinese peoples—and a haven for pirates. Singapura ("lion city") was given its name by the founder of a settlement at the end of the thirteenth century, who thought he saw a lionlike beast there.

Javanese and Thai kingdoms claimed sovereignty over the island, but in the sixteenth century Singapura became a part of the Johore sultanate in the southern Malay Peninsula, only to be virtually abandoned for two hundred years. The Dutch also ignored the island, but Sir Thomas Raffles of the British East India Company occupied it in 1819, and by 1867 it was a crown colony of Britain. It soon burgeoned into a transshipping point and processing facility for rubber and tin, attracting workers from China.

In a stinging military defeat, Britain was ousted temporarily by the Japanese in 1942. After World War II the British in 1959 granted Singapore self-government and a constitution, although they retained control of military and foreign affairs. On September 16, 1963, the island became an autonomous state in the Federation of Malaysia, with its own constitution. Tensions between Singaporean Buddhists and Malay Muslims led to Singapore's separation from the federation on August 9, 1965, and a constitutional amendment created a presidential-style parliamentary government.

Singapore's constitution reflects the British parliamentary system, although a significant change in 1991 gave wide-ranging powers to the formerly mostly ceremonial president.

Article 4 declares: "The constitution is the supreme law of the Republic of Singapore and any law enacted by the legislature after commencement of this constitution which is inconsistent [therewith] shall, to the extent of the inconsistency, be void."

Part 4, Fundamental Liberties, provides that no person may be deprived of life or liberty except by law and that certain rights are extended to those accused of crimes; however, article 9(6) exempts arrests and detention in the interests of public safety, peace, and good order as well as in the case of misuse of drugs and, by amendment in 1984, the misuse of intoxicating substances.

All persons are considered equal before the law, and, unless authorized by the constitution, there is to be no discrimination solely on the basis of religion, race, descent, or place of birth. Other guarantees, with some limitations, include freedom of movement, speech, expression, assembly, and association.

Division of Powers

Singapore is a unitary city-state, and power is divided among the president, as head of state; the prime minister, as head of government; the legislature; and the courts, which exercise judicial review.

The Executive

Article 23 declares: "The executive authority . . . shall be vested in the President and exercisable . . . by him or by the Cabinet or any minister authorized by the Cabinet." But the legislature may confer executive functions on other persons.

President. In 1991, the same year in which Bangladesh reverted to a ceremonial presidency, Singapore amended its constitution to give the president, now directly elected by the people, new fiscal and appointive powers. The president is head of state and is elected for a six-year term. To be eligible for the presidency a person must be a citizen, at least forty-five years old, and not a member of a political party when nominated and must meet stated criteria for experience and ability.

The constitution now gives the president certain discretionary powers in financial matters, appointments, and authority to withhold consent on certain bills. Section 22F entitles the president to request information concerning the government that is available to the cabinet, and under section 22H he or she may withhold assent if a bill "provides directly or indirectly, for the circumvention or curtailment" of the president's discretionary powers under the constitution. The court may be called on to determine if a bill would, in fact, affect the president's discretion. The president also —unlike other ceremonial heads of state—may withhold consent to act on the prime minister's recommendation to dissolve the parliament.

The president may be removed from office for intentional violation of the constitution, treason, misconduct, corruption, or any offense involving fraud, dishonesty, or moral turpitude, as well as for mental or physical infirmity. The chairman of a five-person advisory council appointed by the president or the speaker of the legislature acts as president until a vacancy can be filled by election.

Prime Minister and Cabinet. According to article 25, the prime minister is to be one who, in the judgment of the president, is likely to command the confidence of a majority of the members of the parliament. Article 24 directs that the cabinet is to consist of the prime minister and other ministers; subject to the constitution, they are to have general direction and control of the government and be collectively responsible to the parliament.

The Legislature

Parliament. Singapore's unicameral parliament is elected by direct universal suffrage for five-year terms, unless dissolved earlier. By amendment in 1984, three new nonconstituency seats in the legislature were created to provide opposition representation, although these representatives may not vote on important matters. Later, thirty-nine of the eighty-one single-member constituencies were merged into thirteen three-member constituencies, with one member of the three-member group required to be non-Chinese. By amendment up to six nonconstituency and up to nine presidentially appointed members are authorized.

To be elected or appointed to the legislature a person must be a citizen, at least twenty-one years old, a registered voter, and a resident of Singapore. Members must also have a degree of proficiency in the English, Malay, Mandarin, or Tamil languages, among other qualifications.

After elections members choose a speaker, who presides at each sitting of the parliament, and a deputy speaker from among themselves or elsewhere. Article 58(1) provides that the legislature's power to make laws is exercised by means of bills passed by the parliament and assented to by the president. With the exception of money bills, which must be introduced on the recommendation of the president and a minister, any member may introduce a bill. A quorum constitutes one-fourth of the total members, and decisions are made, except as otherwise provided in the constitution, by a majority vote of those present and voting.

The Judiciary

"The judicial power of Singapore," according to article 93, "shall be vested in a supreme court and in such subordinate courts as may be provided by any written law for the time being in force."

Supreme Court. Pusuant to article 94: "The Supreme Court shall consist of the Court of Appeal and the High Court. . . ." "The Chief Justice, Judges of Appeal, and . . . of the High Court [are] appointed by the President . . . with the advice of the Prime Minister." Judges hold office until the age of sixty-five, and their conduct may not be discussed in parliament unless "substantive notice has been given by not less than one quarter of the total . . . Members." A judge of the supreme court may not be removed except on the recommendation of the prime minister or chief justice and after a hearing by a tribunal appointed by the president. Pay for judges may not be reduced after appointment.

In addition to authorizing judicial review of the constitutionality of laws, the constitution provides that all proceedings relating to the election of the president are to be heard and determined by the chief justice or a judge of the supreme court designated by the chief justice for such purpose and called the election judge.

Amending the Constitution

In general, under article 5, amendments may be passed by the legislature if "supported on Second and Third Readings by the votes of not less than two-thirds of the total . . . Members." However, proposals to amend certain provisions also require approval by "not less than two-thirds of the total . . . votes cast" in a national referendum. These provisions include the guaranteed fundamental liberties, the nature of the presidency and the procedure for determining the validity of the election of the president, the prorogation and dissolution of parliament, certain general election procedures, and articles 5 and 5A. Article 5A, added in 1996, relates to the president's veto power over bills to amend the constitution by providing "directly or indirectly, for the circumvention or curtailment of the discretionary powers conferred upon the President by [the] Constitution."

SLOVAKIA

A separate region inhabited by Slavic people under Hungarian rule for a millennium, Slovakia agreed in 1918 to become a part of Czechoslovakia. On January 1, 1993, however, the independent Slovak Republic came into existence peacefully under a democratic constitution.

General Information

The Slovak Republic in central Europe is approximately 49,000 square kilometers and is bounded by Poland on the north, Ukraine on the east, Hungary on the south, and Austria and the Czech Republic on the west. Bratislava is the capital of this country of more than five million persons.

Slovakia is heir to much of the Czechoslovakian weapons industry, for which there is now little demand, and much of its farmland. Privatization is not moving rapidly. With a culture more akin to that of its eastern neighbors, Slovakia has faced some difficulties in changing from a controlled economy under communist rule to a market economy.

Type of Government: Presidential-style parliamentary republic, with a president, a prime minister and cabinet, a unicameral legislature, and a judiciary, including a constitutional court

Dates of Constitutions: 1920, 1939, 1948, 1960, 1969, and 1993

Constitutional History

Slovaks from the southern branch of Slavic-speaking peoples inhabited the eastern part of the Moravian Empire by the ninth century A.D. The Roman Catholic Church sent missionaries from Rome, but Cyril and Methodius, who were sent by the Eastern Church, introduced the Cyrillic alphabet, allowing the local language to be converted to writing. At the end of the ninth century Magyars, the ancestors of modern Hungarians, claimed Slovakia, then the eastern end of the Moravian Empire, and ruled over it for a millennium.

Catholicism prevailed in Slovakia, and Latin was the official language until 1792. Czech and Slovak intellectuals had close contacts during the nineteenth century, but many Slovaks promoted independence, particularly from Hungarian control, while being divided on the question of unity with the Czechs. In 1907 a Slovak League of America was founded with strong support especially in Cleveland and Pittsburgh, and in 1918 an agreement was reached in Pittsburgh between Czechs and Slovaks to form the nation of "Czecho-Slovakia."

The 1920 constitution of Czechoslovakia created a unitary state, but the Slovaks wanted a federal system. Following an agreement with Hitler for "protection," a 1939 constitution mostly for show was adopted for a separate Slovak state; the Soviet Union quickly recognized the Nazi puppet government. For three years after World War II a reunited Czechoslovakia was governed by the National Front, a coalition of four Czech and two Slovak parties, which maintained close ties with the Soviet Union. A communist coup in February 1948 and the promulgation of a communist constitution on May 9 drew the country even closer to the leadership in Moscow.

Eduard Beneš, the president of the government of Czechoslovakia in exile since 1940, refused to sign the 1948 constitution and resigned on principle a month later. Although the document proclaimed the people to be the source of all power in the state, the Communist Party was firmly in control. And although decentralization was a stated aim, the hierarchy of the government structure placed power in the hands of the central authorities and the ministry of interior in particular.

In 1960 a new communist constitution created Czech and Slovak nations within Czechoslovakia, with the Slovak national council the highest executive and legislative organ in the Slovak territory. The Slovaks, however, still wanted the autonomy of a federal system of government. In January 1968 Alexander Dubček became the first Slovak to be elected first secretary of the Czechoslovakian Communist Party, and in March the Slovak national council again sought to change the country into a federation. A new constitution implementing this concept in theory was to take effect on October 28. However, East Germany's fears of Dubček's liberalizing reforms, called the "Prague Spring," caused the Soviet Union and its satellites to invade in August, thus postponing the change until January 1, 1969. Under the new constitution both republics agreed to mutually respect each other's sovereignty and the sovereignty of Czechoslovakia. Only hard-line communists, however, liked the new arrangement.

The "velvet revolution" of November 1989 dislodged the communists from power. On December 29 Václav Havel, a playwright and founder of Charter 77, a 1977 declaration of human rights violations, was elected president of Czechoslovakia by acclamation. He was reelected in free elections in June 1990, and in 1991 and 1992 Slovak nationalism became the major issue on the national agenda. After attempts at holding together the nation failed, Slovak representatives blocked Havel's reelection by the legislature in June 1992; on September 3 the Slovak national council adopted a constitution for an independent Slovak Republic, which went into effect on January 1, 1993.

The new constitution of the Slovak Republic incorporates elements of other European presidential-style parliamentary constitutions as well as concern for the rights of the nation's ethnic minorities.

Influences

The Constitution

The preamble to the 1993 constitution invokes "the spiritual heritage of Cyril and Methodius and the historical bequest of Great Moravia."

Article 2 states:

(1) The power of the state derives from the citizens, who exercise this power through their elected representatives or directly.

(2) State bodies may act only on the basis of the constitution, within its limits, and to the extent and in a manner set down by law.

(3) Everyone may do whatever is not prohibited by law, and no one may be forced to do what the law does not command.

Certain property rights are to remain under public ownership. "Raw materials, underground waters, natural springs, and water streams," states article 4, "are the property of the Slovak Republic."

Chapter 2, Fundamental Rights and Freedoms, begins by declaring that ratified international agreements extending greater rights and freedoms than the constitution take precedence over Slovak laws, that all people are free and equal in their dignity and rights, and that their fundamental rights and freedoms are inherent, inalienable, imprescriptible, and indissoluble.

Fundamental Rights

Various rights and freedoms are carried over from the Czechoslovakian document and guaranteed to everyone within the republic's territory regardless of sex, race, skin color, language, faith, religion, political or other convictions, ethnic or social origin, nationality or ethnic group, property, birth, or other status. These include choice of nationality; freedom to exercise rights; the right to life without a death penalty; inviolability of the person, his or her privacy, and the home; a prohibition on torture, cruel and unusual punishment, and forced labor; protections for those accused of a crime; the right to own and inherit property; and freedom of thought, conscience, and religious conviction and belief. Also included are sections on political rights; the rights of national minorities and ethnic groups; economic, social, and cultural rights; protection of the environment and cultural heritage; and judicial and other legal protections.

In Slovakia, a unitary state, power is divided among the president, as head of state; the prime minister, as head of government; the legislature; and the courts, which exercise limited constitutional review through a constitutional court.

Division of Powers

| The Executive | **President.** The president, who is head of state and supreme commander of the armed forces, is elected to a five-year term by the valid votes of qualified voters, otherwise a runoff election is held between the two candidates with the most votes. To be a candidate, a person must be "proposed by at least 15 Deputies of the [legislature] . . . on the basis of a petition signed by at least 15,000 citizens." Before amendment in 1999, the president was elected by a majority of at least three-fifths of all members of the legislature by secret ballot. Every citizen is eligible to be elected to the legislature and is at least forty years old is eligible for the presidency, but the same person may not be elected for more than two consecutive terms. |

The powers and duties of the president include representing the nation and negotiating and ratifying treaties, although some treaties require the approval of the legislature; receiving and accrediting foreign representatives; dissolving the legislature under certain conditions; signing laws; appointing and dismissing the prime minister and other members of the government and charging them with their duties; conferring distinctions; and granting amnesty, if countersigned by a cabinet minister, and pardons and commuting sentences. The president may also declare a state of war on the basis of a decision by the legislature and may declare a state of emergency on the basis of a constitutional act. The president may be prosecuted for "intentional violations of the Constitution or for treason" only on indictment by the vote of three-fifths of all the members of the legislature; the verdict is rendered by the constitutional court. There are also provisions for recalling the president by a resolution of at least three-fifths of the members of the legislature.

Prime Minister and Cabinet. According to article 108, "The government (cabinet) is the supreme body of executive power" and consists of the prime minister, deputy prime ministers, and other ministers. "The prime minister is appointed and dismissed by the president . . . [and at] the proposal of the prime minister, the president appoints and dismisses the other members of the government, [which] is accountable for the exercise of its functions to the [legislature]."

| The Legislature | **Parliament.** The unicameral legislature, the Národná Rada Slovensky Repubiky (national council), has 150 members called deputies who are elected for four-year terms by universal, equal, direct, and secret ballot. Election details are determined by law. To be eligible to be elected a deputy, a person must be a citizen, have the right to vote, be at least twenty-one years old, and live in the territory of the republic. Deputies may not hold certain positions such as president, judge, prosecutor, or professional soldier; if appointed to the government, they may not exercise their legislative mandate. Once elected, deputies enjoy certain immunities. |

The national council is declared to be in session continuously and may not be suspended for more than four months a year. The presiding chairman, together with vice chairmen, is elected or dismissed by a majority of the deputies by secret ballot. A quorum is an absolute majority of the members, and generally measures are approved by a majority vote of those present. Adopting or amending the constitution, passing constitutional laws, declaring war, and dismissing the president require approval by three-fifths of the members. Article 89(f) authorizes the legislature to call a popular vote for the purpose of recalling the president.

In addition to enacting laws, any deputy may interpellate, or ask questions of, a member of the government; the national council "shall debate the response" and may link it with a vote of no confidence. Article 88 provides that a vote of no confidence in the government or one of its members must be requested by at least one-fifth and approved by an absolute majority of the deputies.

Other powers of the national council include approving treaties by constitutional act when they involve union with other states and consenting to certain treaties before ratification; deciding on proposals for holding referendums; establishing by law ministries and other state bodies; approving the state budget; electing judges and the president and vice president of the supreme court and the constitutional court; and declaring war and consenting to send armed forces outside the country.

Slovakian courts include a supreme court and a constitutional court.

Supreme Court. The supreme court and other courts whose jurisdiction and organization are determined by law decide civil and criminal matters; lay assessors are authorized to participate in panel decisions. The judges are proposed by the government and elected by the legislature initially for four-year terms and indefinitely thereafter. The legislature elects the president and vice president of the court from among the judges for a period of five years and at most for two consecutive terms.

The judges are declared to be independent and bound only by the law and specified international treaties. Article 144 directs judges to institute proceedings in the constitutional court if a government regulation may be contrary to the law.

Constitutional Court. The constitutional court consists of ten judges appointed for seven-year terms by the president from among twenty nominees of the legislature. Any citizen at least forty years old who has a university law degree and fifteen years of experience in the legal profession may be appointed to the court. The president of the republic selects the president and vice president of the court from among the judges.

The constitutional court is charged with deciding on the conformity of laws with the constitution and constitutional acts and of government decrees with the laws. The court may also review generally binding regulations vis-a-vis the constitution, laws, and international treaties and may give interpretation of constitutional acts in controversial cases. Proceedings may be instituted by specified government entities, including the legislature (at least one-fifth of the members), by the president, and by private parties, if they assert an infringement of their rights. The court also rules on an indictment of the president for an intentional breach of the constitution and for treason, as well as on the constitutionality of elections and the recall of the president.

The legislature may amend the constitution or enact a constitutional law with the approval of at least three-fifths of its members. A constitutional act uniting with or withdrawing from a union with another state requires a referendum.

SOUTH AFRICA

After the collapse of the segregation policy known as apartheid, an interim constitution guaranteeing equality to all citizens was adopted in 1994. Three years later this was replaced with a permanent constitution confirming universal suffrage and a commitment to human rights.

General Information

The Republic of South Africa, which lies at the southern end of the African continent, is some 1.2 million square kilometers. It surrounds the country of Lesotho and is bounded by Namibia, Botswana, and Zimbabwe on the north; Mozambique and Swaziland on the east; the Indian Ocean on the southeast; and the Atlantic Ocean on the southwest. Pretoria is the administrative capital, Cape Town the legislative capital, and Bloemfontein the judicial capital of this nation of approximately forty-three million persons.

The most industrially developed of the African countries, South Africa is rich in natural resources. However, the nation faces a number of problems, including drugs, the HIV/AIDS virus, high unemployment, and a slowing economy.

Type of Government: Presidential republic, with a president and cabinet, a bicameral legislature, and a judiciary, including a constitutional court

Dates of Constitutions: 1909, 1961 (significantly revised in 1984), 1994 (interim), and 1997

Constitutional History

Phoenicians first circumnavigated the continent of Africa in the seventh century B.C. Portuguese sailors also rounded the Cape of Good Hope in the late fifteenth century A.D., seeking a sea route to India and the Orient. European settlements began in earnest in the 1600s, but not until Henry M. Stanley reported his meeting with David Livingstone in 1871 was the interest of European developers in central and southern Africa truly piqued.

The first English settlement at the cape was abandoned to the Dutch in 1651, retaken in 1795, and given to the Batavian Republic, by treaty, in 1802. The British captured the territory again in 1806, and in 1820 some five thousand English settlers arrived. To escape the oppression of the British colonial regime, which had emancipated the slaves in 1834, descendants of the early Dutch settlers and French Huguenots known as the Boers (Dutch for "farmers") made their Great Trek north in 1835–37. Roman-Dutch law in effect in 1806, influenced by the law of England, continues to be the common law of South Africa.

The migrating Boers *(Voortrekkers)* went on to establish a number of small republics, as well as the South Africa Republic, later called the Transvaal, and the Orange Free State, which was annexed by the British in 1848 and relinquished in 1852. The Transvaal Republic was annexed by Britain again in 1877 and subsequently given back, with the agreement that its foreign relations, except with the Orange Free State, would be handled by Britain. After the Boer Wars of 1881 and 1899–1902, the two Boer colonies were returned to British rule.

In 1908 Britain agreed to let the whole area become self-governing, and the South Africa Act of 1909 became the constitutional basis for the Union of South Africa, combining the Cape of Good Hope colony, Natal, Transvaal, and the Orange River colonies. Each subdivision had its own legislative council, although all were under the central authority of the national parliament and any provincial enactments had to be approved by the British monarch or his or her representative, the governor-general. The provincial executive function was in the hands of a committee with an administrator appointed by the governor-general on the advice of the cabinet and four members elected by the council.

By a simple majority vote in 1961, the union's bicameral parliament enacted the Republic of South Africa Act 32, ending its membership in the British Commonwealth. The new constitutional provisions merely replaced the monarch and governor-general with a president as the symbolic head of state, retained the legislative supremacy of the parliament, and limited separation of powers; two entrenched sections guaranteed the equality of the English and Afrikaans languages. A 1984 act, while not repealing the 1961 constitution outright, made sweeping structural changes: the president was made not only head of state but also head of government, and a tricameral parliament was established, with houses for whites, coloreds of mixed race, and Indians.

Apartheid, the South African policy of segregation and denial of political rights on the basis of race, oppressed a majority of the nation's citizens for more than a century. The system was challenged by South African leaders, including Nelson Mandela of the African National Congress and Anglican Bishop Desmond Tutu, as well as the international community. Apartheid laws were finally dismantled early in the 1990s, launching a transition to equality. In 1991 a peace accord was signed between the government and antiapartheid leaders, and an interim constitution based on equal rights for all went into effect on April 27, 1994.

Two years later the draft of a permanent constitution was submitted by a constitutional assembly to the constitutional court for certification that it complied with the constitutional principles set forth in the 1994 interim constitution. The court found compliance "with the overwhelming majority of the requirements of the ... Principles." Redrafted to meet the court's remaining concerns, the constitution entered into force on February 4, 1997.

South Africa's constitution was originally based on the British parliamentary model. The 1997 constitution conforms more to the system in other African nations in that it provides for a strong president as head of state and government.

Influences

The Constitution

Recognizing "the injustices of our past," the preamble notes that the new constitution was adopted, among other things, to "[h]eal the divisions of the past and establish a society based on democratic values, social justice and fundamental human rights."

Section 1 proclaims that the Republic of South Africa "is one sovereign democratic state founded on ... [h]uman dignity, the achievement of equality and the advancement of human rights and freedoms," "[n]on-racialism and non-sexism," "[s]upremacy of the constitution and the rule of law," [and] "[u]niversal adult suffrage, ... regular elections, and a multi-party system of democratic government, to ensure accountability, responsiveness and openness." According to section 2, "This Constitution is the supreme law of the Republic; law or conduct inconsistent with it is invalid, and the obligations imposed by it must be fulfilled." Section 6 designates nine African languages in addition to Afrikaans and English as "official languages of the Republic."

A "bill of rights," presented in sections 7 through 39, is described as "a cornerstone of democracy in South Africa." It encompasses equality and "equal protection and benefit of the law" without discrimination on the basis of "race, gender, sex, pregnancy, marital status, ethnic or social origin, color, sexual orientation, age, disability, religion, conscience, belief, culture, language and birth." Everyone is also entitled to "inherent dignity"; "freedom and security of the person"; freedom from "slavery, servitude or forced labor"; freedom of religion, belief, opinion, expression, assembly, demonstration, assembly, and association.

Fundamental Rights

Political rights include the ability to form a political party and to vote and stand for public office; "[n]o citizen may be deprived of citizenship," adds section 20. Also guaranteed are freedom of movement and residence; the right to a "trade, occupation and profession"; the right "to form and join a trade union"; a healthful environment; property ownership; and "access to adequate housing," health care, food, water, and social security. Children's rights, education, language and cultural rights, as well as access to information and the courts and to protection for those accused of crimes are included in the bill of rights as well.

Limitations on rights and the effect of a state of emergency are addressed in sections 36 and 37. The latter contains a "Table of Non-Derogable Rights," among them "human dignity" and "life," which "[n]o Act of Parliament [authorizing] . . . a state of emergency, and no legislation . . . or other action" based thereon may limit.

Division of Powers

Section 40 proclaims that the government has "national, provincial and local spheres . . . , which are distinctive, interdependent and interrelated." The "spheres . . . must conduct their activities within the parameters" of the chapter of the constitution entitled "Co-operative Government."

The Executive

President. Section 85 vests the republic's executive authority in the president, who, according to section 83, "is the Head of State and head of the national executive; [and] must uphold, defend and respect the Constitution as the supreme law of the Republic." The president is elected from among the members of the legislature "[a]t its first sitting after its election, and whenever necessary to fill a vacancy," and serves until "the person next elected President assumes office." No one may serve for more than two terms.

The chief executive is responsible, among other duties, for assenting to and signing bills; referring a bill back to the legislature or to the constitutional court over constitutional issues; making certain appointments, including a deputy president and cabinet ministers; calling a national referendum pursuant to an act of parliament; appointing diplomatic representatives; and granting pardons and reprieves, as well as "conferring honors."

The deputy president acts when the president is absent or unable to fulfill the duties of office. The president may be removed from office by "a supporting vote of at least two-thirds" of the members of the legislature "on the grounds of a serious violation of the Constitution or the law; serious misconduct; or inability to perform the functions of office."

Cabinet. The cabinet consists of the president, who heads it, as well as the deputy president and ministers. The president appoints cabinet members, all of whom, except for two, must be members of the legislature; deputy ministers come from the legislature. The president assigns powers and functions to cabinet members, but under section 92 they "are accountable collectively and individually to Parliament. . . ." Members may attend and speak at sessions of each house, but only those who are also members of the lower house may vote there. Members of both the cabinet and the legislature have specified privileges and immunities, including freedom of speech and immunity from certain civil and criminal proceedings.

The Legislature

Parliament. Legislative authority is vested by section 43 in a parliament made up of a national assembly (lower house) and a national council of provinces (upper house).

Upper House. According to section 60, "The National Council of Provinces is composed of a single delegation from each province consisting of ten delegates," which includes the "Premier of the province . . . and three other special delegates; and six permanent delegates" based on political "[p]arties represented in a provincial legislature."

Lower House. "The National Assembly," states section 46, "consists of no fewer than 350 and no more than 400 women and men." The system is "prescribed by national legislation; . . . based on the national common voters roll; provides for a minimum voting age of 18 years; and results, in general, in proportional representation." With certain exceptions, any citizen "qualified to vote for the [lower house] is eligible to be a member." Members are elected for five years or until the body is dissolved earlier for new elections. The chamber elects a speaker and a deputy speaker from among its members.

A majority of the members constitute a quorum to act on bills, but only one-third is necessary for a vote on any other question. "[A]ll questions before the Assembly are decided by a majority of the votes cast." The lower house's powers include initiating and passing legislation, except money bills, as well as ensuring the accountability of the executive agencies and maintaining oversight of the "national executive authority . . . and any organ of state."

Bills may be introduced by a cabinet member or a member or committee of the lower house, except that only the appropriate cabinet member may introduce financial measures. Both houses must act on bills, but if an ordinary bill does not affect the provinces, each member of the upper house has a vote, one-third must be present, and a majority vote is required; otherwise, each province in the upper house has one vote, and all questions require the approval of at least five provinces. In general, bills passed by the legislature are submitted to the president for his assent.

Section 165 vests judicial authority in the courts, which "are independent and subject only to the Constitution and the law. . . . No person or organ of state," it adds, "may interfere with the functioning of the courts." According to section 166, the judicial system consists of a constitutional court, a supreme court of appeal, high courts, magistrates' courts, and other courts established by an act of parliament.

The Judiciary

Supreme Court of Appeal. According to section 168, the court "may decide appeals in any matter. It is the highest court of appeal except in constitutional matters. . . ." The court consists of a chief justice, a deputy chief justice, and additional judges as determined by law.

Constitutional Court. The highest court on constitutional matters, the court decides, among other matters, "disputes between organs of state in the national or provincial sphere," "the constitutionality of any parliamentary or provincial Bill," and "the constitutionality of any amendment to the Constitution." In the interests of justice, an individual may bring a matter directly to the court or appeal directly to it from any other court. On this court a president and a deputy president are joined by nine other judges; eight judges constitute a quorum.

The constitution provides for a public protector, similar to an ombudsman, who is authorized under section 182 "to investigate any conduct in state affairs, or in the public administration . . . ; to report on that conduct; and to take appropriate remedial action." A South African Human Rights Commission and other institutions also support constitutional democracy.

Ombudsman

Section 211 recognizes the "institution, status and role of traditional leadership, according to customary law" and requires the courts to "apply customary law when [it] is applicable." Section 212 authorizes national legislation to "provide for a role for traditional leadership as an institution at the local level on matters affecting local communities."

Traditional Leaders

Amendments are introduced in the same manner as any other bill; however, according to section 74(1), a bill to amend section 1 and this subsection requires approval of at least seventy-five percent of the members of the lower house and of at least six provinces. To amend the bill of rights requires a vote of two-thirds in the lower house and at least six provinces in the upper house. Other amendments require a vote of two-thirds in the lower house and at least six provinces if they would affect the the upper house; alter provincial boundaries, powers, functions, or institutions; or specifically deal with a provincial matter.

Amending the Constitution

At least thirty days before being introduced, a proposed amendment must be published "in the national Government Gazette . . . for public comment," submitted "to the provincial legislatures for their views," and submitted to the upper house "for a public debate, if [it] is not an amendment that is required to be passed by the Council." Once passed by the applicable houses, an amending bill "must be referred to the President for assent."

SOUTH KOREA

Since the division between northern and southern Korea after World War II, South Koreans have sought the right combination of a constitutional form of government and political leadership to create a stable democracy.

General Information

The Republic of Korea (South Korea) is approximately 99,000 square kilometers, including adjacent islands. It is bounded on the north by the Democratic People's Republic of Korea (North Korea), on the west by the Yellow Sea, on the south by the East China Sea and the Korea Strait, and on the east by the Sea of Japan. The population of South Korea is approximately forty-seven million persons, and its capital is Seoul.

The foreign policy of South Korea, a major worldwide trading nation, has been dominated by the separation from North Korea, which has been governed by a rigid communist regime since after World War II. In 1945 U.S. military forces liberated Korea from Japanese rule and from 1950 to 1953 helped defend the southern half of Korea against aggression from the north. The U.S. presence in the country has led to a strong U.S.–South Korean alliance, with U.S. troops still stationed there under a status of forces agreement.

Type of Government: Presidential-style parliamentary republic, with a president, a prime minister and state council (cabinet), a unicameral legislature, a judiciary, and a constitutional court

Date of Constitution: 1948 (revised most recently in 1988)

Constitutional History

The Korean people can trace their beginnings as far back as 2333 B.C. During the Yi or Choson Dynasty, which lasted from A.D. 1392 until 1910, the Taoist and Buddhist religions in Korea were supplanted by Confucianism, which does not acknowledge the concepts of privacy, self-determination, or rights of the individual but rather teaches paternalism by those in authority toward their inferiors. This, combined with the traditional Korean reliance on royal law made by the monarch "in council" with high officials of the bureaucracy, has influenced the development of constitutional values and government in South Korea.

The rule of law and the advantages of a constitutional form of democracy with traditional checks and balances were discussed by Korean intellectuals as early as the last decade of the nineteenth century, and associations such as the Self-Strengthening Society studied European constitutions and legal systems before Korea's annexation by Japan in 1910. But the primary inspiration for the first South Korean constitution, which took effect on July 12, 1948, was undoubtedly the U.S. military government in Korea, known as USAMGIK, during the time that southern Korea was administered by the United States and northern Korea was administered by the Soviet Union.

When the Soviets refused to allow free elections in the north, the United States and a number of Korean political leaders decided that a constitution should be drafted for the south. The Republic of Korea came into existence on August 15, 1948, and Syngman Rhee was elected by the parliament as its first president under the new constitution. Like the U.S. constitution, the 1948 South Korean constitution did not provide for the direct election of the president. Rhee had it amended in 1952 to allow a direct popular presidential election when he became unpopular with the parliament. To be able to run for a third term, Rhee in 1954 engineered another amendment to the constitution.

After a series of constitutional revisions, five republics, and several military regimes, the disclosure of a student's death by police torture in Seoul in 1987—referred to in South Korea as the Miracle Year—broke a stalemate between the ruling party and the opposition over constitutional reform. In the wake of the incident, the head of the ruling Democratic Justice Party agreed to constitutional reform, which included a return to direct election of the president. The current revised constitution of the sixth republic was approved by ninety-three percent of the valid votes on October 28, 1987, and became effective on February 25, 1988.

Influences

The U.S. military government in South Korea originally influenced the constitution, but a number of major changes have since been made.

The Constitution

The preamble to the constitution of the Republic of Korea looks back, to its "resplendent history and traditions dating from time immemorial," as well as forward, expressing hope for "democratic reform and peaceful unification of our homeland."
Article 1 states:

(1) The Republic of Korea shall be a democratic republic.
(2) The sovereignty of the Republic of Korea shall reside in the people, and all state authority shall emanate from the people.

Article 3 asserts that the territory of the republic consists of the Korean Peninsula and adjacent islands. Article 4 proclaims the goal of peaceful unification with North Korea. The constitution also provides that international treaties have the force of law and that aliens will be treated in accordance with international law and treaties.

Fundamental Rights

Article 10, chapter 2, Rights and Duties of Citizens, provides: "All citizens shall be assured of human worth and dignity and have the right to pursue happiness. It shall be the duty of the state to confirm and guarantee the fundamental and inviolable human rights of individuals."
The rights of citizens include equality before the law; freedom from discrimination in political, societal, and cultural life on account of sex, religion, or social status; a prohibition against privileged castes and against extending the benefits of decorations or honors to anyone other than the recipient; the right to personal liberty; prohibitions against torture and self-incrimination in criminal cases; the requirement of a judicial warrant in cases of arrest, detention, or search and seizure, with some exceptions; the right to counsel; prohibitions against ex post facto criminal laws, restrictions on political rights by means of retroactive laws and against unfavorable treatment as a result of an act by a relative. Other express freedoms include freedom of residence, movement, occupation, and intrusion into the home; freedom of conscience, religion, speech, assembly, press, and association; and the right to vote and hold office as prescribed by law. Article 20 expressly prohibits the recognition of a state religion and requires the separation of church and state.

Division of Powers

In South Korea, a unitary state, power is shared among the president, as head of state; the prime minister, as head of government; the legislature; the courts; and the constitutional court, which exercises constitutional review.

The Executive

President. The executive power of the South Korean government is vested in the president as head of state. The president represents the nation in foreign affairs; safeguards the independence, integrity, and continuity of the state and the constitution; and has the duty to sincerely pursue the unification of the homeland.
The president now may be elected to only a single five-year term by universal, equal, direct, and secret ballot. Before the 1988 constitutional reform the president was elected by more than five thousand electors. The direct election of the president was a major reform sought by the opposition party in South Korea.
The president is commander in chief of the armed forces, ratifies treaties, and may submit

important policy questions to a national referendum. The president's powers and duties also include accrediting and receiving diplomats and issuing decrees relating to matters delegated to him or her by law. In emergency situations the president is given broad authority to act to preserve the interests of the nation. Other responsibilities include appointing certain public officials; granting amnesty, commuting sentences, and restoring rights as authorized by law and the legislature; awarding decorations and honors; and executing written documents, which are countersigned by the prime minister and members of the state council (cabinet). The president may attend and address the legislature and is granted legal immunity, except in cases of insurrection and treason.

The executive offices in South Korea are headed by ministers appointed by the president from among the members of the state council on the recommendation of the prime minister.

Prime Minister and Cabinet. If the president becomes unable to perform his or her duties, the prime minister or the members of the state council (cabinet) will act, in an order determined by law. The prime minister is to assist the president and directs the executive ministries under the president's order.

The state council is composed of the president, as its chairman; the prime minister, who is appointed by the president with the consent of the legislature, as its vice chairman; and fifteen to thirty other members appointed by the president on the recommendation of the prime minister.

The council deliberates on important executive policies and assists the president in the conduct of state affairs. Matters falling under the jurisdiction of the council include general plans and policies; declarations of war and peace, as well as other foreign policy issues; draft amendments to the constitution, national referendum proposals, bills, treaties, and presidential decrees; the budget; emergency orders; important military affairs; dissolution of a political party; appointments of high officials in the government; and other matters presented by members of the council.

The Legislature

Parliament. Article 40 of the constitution vests the legislative power of the nation in a unicameral parliamentary-type body called the Kuk Hoe (national assembly). It is composed of two hundred or more members, as determined by law, who are elected for four-year terms by universal, equal, direct, and secret ballot. The constituencies of the members and the manner of election are determined by law. By amendment in 1988 the single or small constituency system was restored and the number of seats increased to 299, with sixty-five seats distributed among the parties on the basis of their performance in the election. An election management commission ensures fair elections.

Members of the assembly may not concurrently hold other offices as prescribed by law, be arrested or detained unless apprehended in flagrante delicto, or be held responsible outside the assembly for opinions officially expressed or votes cast.

The assembly convenes in regular session once every year; extraordinary sessions may be convened by the president or by at least one-fourth of the members. The assembly elects a speaker and two vice speakers. Generally, a quorum for conducting business consists of a majority of the members, and measures are passed by a majority vote of those present. Tie votes result in rejection of a measure.

Bills may be introduced by members of the assembly or the executive branch. All bills passed are sent to the president to be promulgated. The president may object to a bill and return it to the assembly, which may repass it by a vote of two-thirds of the members present, if a quorum has been established.

In addition to regular legislative measures, the assembly deliberates and decides on the national budget bill, treaties, declarations of war, dispatch of armed forces to foreign states, and stationing of foreign troops on South Korean territory. The assembly may inspect and investigate affairs of state; request that the prime minister, members of the state council, and government delegates answer questions; remove the prime minister or members of the state council on a recommendation of at least one-third of the members of the assembly and a concurrent vote of a majority of the total members; and impeach the president, prime minister, and other members of the state council and other high officials.

The judicial power of the nation is vested in courts whose organization and qualifications for judges are determined by law. According to article 103, "Judges shall rule independently according to their conscience and in conformity with the constitution and law."

The Judiciary

Supreme Court. The supreme court is the highest court in the nation. The chief justice is appointed by the president with the consent of the legislature, and the other members are similarly appointed on the recommendation of the chief justice. Supreme court justices serve for six years, and all but the chief justice may be reappointed as prescribed by law.

Lower court judges serve for ten years and may be reappointed. Trials are required to be open to the public, except in cases that might undermine national security, disturb public safety and order, or be harmful to public morals.

Article 111 establishes a constitutional court that adjudicates issues including the constitutionality of a law, on request of the courts; impeachment; dissolution of a political party; disputes about the jurisdiction between state agencies, between state agencies and local governments, and between local governments; and petitions relating to the constitution as prescribed by law.

Constitutional Court

The constitutional court is composed of nine members, qualified to be judges, who are appointed by the president. Three members must be appointed from persons recommended by the legislature and three members from persons nominated by the chief justice. The members serve for six-year terms and may be reappointed. Decisions involving the unconstitutionality of a law, impeachment, the dissolution of a political party, or a petition relating to the constitution require the concurrence of at least six court members.

Either a majority of the members of the legislature or the president may introduce a proposal to amend the constitution. Amendments extending the term of or allowing reelection of the president, however, will not apply to the incumbent. After a proposal has been put before the public by the president for at least twenty days, the legislature may pass it by a concurrent vote of two-thirds of its total members, and then the proposal must be approved in a referendum by at least one-half of the voters eligible to vote for members of the legislature. If approved, the amendment is to be promulgated by the president without delay.

Amending the Constitution

SPAIN

After centuries of rule by absolute monarchs and military leaders, interspersed with brief attempts at liberal republican governments, Spain in 1978 adopted a constitution that establishes a parliamentary monarchy based on the sovereignty of the Spanish people.

General Information

The Kingdom of Spain on the Iberian Peninsula is 492,503 square kilometers; including the Balearic Islands in the Mediterranean Sea, the Canary Islands in the Atlantic Ocean, and the enclaves of Cueta and Melilla on the coast of Morocco in Africa, it has an area of approximately 504,750 square kilometers. Iberian Spain is bounded on the north by France, Andorra, and the Bay of Biscay; on the east and south by the Mediterranean Sea and Gibraltar; and on the west by Portugal and the Atlantic Ocean. The nation includes a number of ethnic and linguistic regions such as Castille, Catalonia, Galicia, and the Basque country. Spain's population is approximately forty million persons, and its capital is Madrid.

During the late twentieth century Spain's economy changed from primarily agricultural to industrial; it now produces automobiles, steel, shoes, leather goods, clothing, and rubber products. Spain has made rapid economic progress and joined the European Economic Community in 1986.

Type of Government: Parliamentary constitutional monarchy, with a monarch, a president (prime minister) and council of ministers (cabinet), a council of state, a bicameral legislature, a judiciary, and a constitutional court

Dates of Key Constitutions: 1812 (abrogated in 1814 and reinstated 1820–23 and 1836–37), 1873, 1876, 1931, and 1978

Constitutional History

Since the dawn of history, the Iberian Peninsula has been host to wave after wave of diverse immigrants. When the Iberians, as they were called by the early Greeks, arrived around the third millennium, the area was already inhabited by the ancestors of the present-day Basques. Celts, Phoenicians, Greeks, Romans, Vandals, Suevi, and Visigoths, as well as Arabs and Berbers from North Africa (Moors), followed. The Spanish throne has been held by Austrian Hapsburgs and Frenchmen; the present king, Juan Carlos de Borbón, is descended from a French royal family.

The legal and constitutional history of Spain has not evolved smoothly. For four hundred years the ancestors of the present-day Spanish people were exposed to the legal code of the Romans and then for three hundred years to the laws of the Visigoths. The laws were formally merged at the end of the seventh century into the Liber Judicorum. From the eighth century to the end of the fifteenth century, the Islamic Qur'an was the supreme guide for the territory, but with the return of Christianity new concepts, such as the divine right of kings, replaced the old Islamic civil and religious controls.

Napoleon's brother Joseph became king of Spain in 1808 following the forced abdication of Charles IV, a Bourbon, whose family's right to succeed to the Spanish throne had been recognized by the Treaty of Utrecht in 1713. The *afrancesados*, a small but influential group of Spaniards who favored restructuring the country's government along the lines of the French model, welcomed the Bonapartist regime. But a "war of independence" ensued, during which the first representative body, the Cadiz Cortes, grew out of a meeting of representatives of local military juntas in 1810. Liberals, who were in the majority, transformed the meeting into a constitutional convention, and the Cadiz Cortes culminated in the proclamation on March 19, 1812, of the first Spanish constitution, which became a model for liberal constitutions of Latin nations during the nineteenth century. When a Bourbon king regained the throne in 1814, however, he refused to recognize the new constitution.

The absolute monarchy lasted until 1820, when the military demanded that the 1812 constitution be observed. For a period of three years, called the Constitution Triennium, Ferdinand VII acquiesced until he obtained support from the French king, Louis XVIII, after which he abrogated the supreme law. Following Ferdinand's death in 1833, there was a period of weak monarchy, backed by liberal elements. A revolt by the army led to another constitution and the founding of the first republic, which lasted one year, from 1873 to 1874. Under an 1876 constitution the monarchy was again restored along the lines of the British parliamentary model and lasted for forty-seven years. It was followed by the dictatorship of Primo De Rivera from 1923 to 1930. A second republic, which described itself as a democratic republic of workers of all classes, was established in 1931, and a new constitution was promulgated.

During the civil war that swept Spain between 1936 and 1939, the military leader Francisco Franco y Bahamonde seized power, assuming the position of head of state. After the outbreak of World War II in 1939, Generalissimo Franco, as he styled himself, promulgated fundamental laws under which Spain was governed. After his death on November 22, 1975, Juan Carlos was crowned king. Under his general guidance a new constitution was written; predicated on the consent of the governed, it allows the king a purely ceremonial role. The new Spanish constitution became effective on December 29, 1978, after the final text was approved by a national referendum in which the negative vote amounted to only 7.8 percent.

Influences

Modeled generally after European constitutions, Spain's constitution is to some extent influenced by the German constitution and to a lesser extent by the Italian, Portuguese, and Greek constitutions. Modern European concepts, the Roman Catholic Church, and the terrorist activities of the nationalistic movements in Spain also influenced the drafters.

The Constitution

The preamble to the Spanish constitution pledges to guarantee democratic coexistence; ensure the rule of law; protect human rights, cultures, and languages; ensure a worthy quality of life for all; establish a democratic and advanced society; and strengthen peaceful relations and cooperation among all the peoples of the world.

Fundamental Rights

In addition to the rights set forth in chapter 2, title 1, Concerning Fundamental Rights and Duties, article 10 requires that rights be interpreted in conformity with the United Nations Universal Declaration of Human Rights (1948) and other international agreements ratified by Spain. This reference to external, international standards helps ensure that these rights and liberties will be treated fairly and objectively by the national government.

Under the constitution all Spanish citizens are equal before the law, not subject to discrimination by reason of birth, race, sex, religion, opinion, or any other personal or social condition or circumstance. Basic rights include prohibitions against torture, inhumane treatment, and the death penalty, except in time of war under military criminal law; freedom of ideology and religion; the right to due process of law, including the presumption of innocence, the right to legal assistance and a public trial; prohibitions against self-incrimination and ex post facto criminal laws; the right to privacy; the right to travel freely; and freedom of expression, the press, assembly, and association. While it expressly disavows a state religion, the constitution does acknowledge the fact that ninety-nine percent of the Spanish population is Roman Catholic by directing public authorities to take religious belief into account and to cooperate with the Catholic Church. Other rights include the right to education and to unionize and strike.

Title 1, chapter 5, strictly limits the rights and liberties that may be suspended during a state of emergency or siege and provides that unjustified or abusive use of power under an organic act limiting rights and liberties will constitute a criminally actionable offense.

Division of Powers

In Spain, a unitary state except for the autonomous communities, power is shared among the monarch, as head of state; the president (prime minister); the legislature; the courts; and the constitutional court, which exercises specific powers of constitutional review.

The Executive

Monarch. Article 56 establishes the monarch's role: "The king is the head of state, the symbol of its unity." The monarch's role is purely symbolic; he is personally inviolate and not subject to liability. His official acts must always be countersigned by the president of the government (prime minister) and, where appropriate, by the proper minister. The crown of Spain is hereditary and follows the regular order of primogeniture and representation. The crown prince is given the title of prince of Asturias.

The king's responsibilities include representing the nation in international relations; sanctioning and promulgating laws; summoning and dissolving the legislature; calling for elections and referendums; and nominating, appointing, and removing the president. The king appoints and dismisses members of the government on the recommendation of the president, issues decrees agreed on by the council of ministers (cabinet), presides over meetings of the council of ministers at the request of the president, commends the armed forces, grants specific (not general) pardons, and exercises the "high patronage of the royal academies." The king accredits and receives diplomats, assents to treaties, declares war and makes peace as authorized by the legislature, and freely appoints and dismisses the civil and military members of the royal household.

Prime Minister and Cabinet. The president of the government (prime minister) and the ministers together constitute the council of ministers (cabinet). The government consists of the president, who generally is the leader of the majority party in the lower house of the legislature; any vice presidents; cabinet members, which the president may select only after being confirmed by an absolute majority of the lower house; and other members as may be provided for by law.

The government directs the domestic and foreign policy of the state, as well as the civil and military administration and the national defense, and prepares the annual budget. The government is supervised by the lower house of the legislature, and members of the government are subject to criminal prosecution for abuse of power. After a general election or a vote of no confidence, the government must resign.

Council of State. The supreme consultative body under the Spanish constitution is the council of state, which consists of a president and twenty-two high political or administrative officials appointed by the king. The council renders advice to the government on questions submitted to it or on its own initiative.

The Legislature

Parliament. Article 66 provides for a bicameral parliament, called the Cortes Generales:

1. The Cortes Generales represent the Spanish people and consist of the congress of deputies and the senate.
2. The Cortes Generales exercise the legislative power of the state, approve its budget, control government action, and hold all powers vested in them by the constitution.
3. The Cortes Generales are inviolable.

The parliament wields the most power in the government structure by making laws and overseeing the execution of the laws.

Upper House. Territorial representation is the basis of the senate, with each mainland province electing four senators, the larger islands three senators each, two each from the cities of Cueta and Melilla, and one each from smaller islands and island groups.

Lower House. The congress of deputies consists of a minimum of 300 to a maximum of 400 deputies elected by universal, free, equal, direct, and secret suffrage from districts or provinces based on proportional representation, except that Cueta and Melilla each elect one deputy.

The head of each house of the parliament is called the president. The constitution prohibits deputies or senators from being high administrative officers or members of the constitutional court, public defenders, active judges, soldiers or police, or members of the election commission, but they may be members of the government itself.

Article 81 defines organic laws as those concerning fundamental rights, public liberties, self-government, general elections, and other laws specified in the constitution. Final votes on organic laws as a whole require an absolute majority of the lower house. Article 82 grants the parliament authority to expressly delegate to the government the power to issue rules with the status of law on specific matters. International treaties that would invest an international organization or institution with powers encompassed in the constitution require an organic law. Treaties of a political, military, or territorial nature or those that involve a debt obligation of the government or a change in existing laws or that require implementing legislation require prior authorization by the parliament.

Bills may be introduced by the government or either house of the parliament. Government bills must first be approved by the council of ministers and then referred to the congress of deputies along with supporting justification. A bill for organic or ordinary legislation must first be passed by the lower house; the senate then has two months in which to veto the measure or propose amendments. A veto may be overridden by an absolute majority of the lower house. Once finally passed, measures go to the king for promulgation within fifteen days of passage. If the senate fails to act on a measure in the two months, it may be passed again by a simple majority in the lower house. Amendments by the senate are handled similarly. The constitution also provides for the introduction of bills by popular initiative and for referendums on political decisions of special importance.

The Judiciary

Article 117, section 1, of the constitution states: "Justice emanates from the people and is administered on behalf of the king by judges and magistrates who shall be independent, irremovable, liable and subject only to the rule of law." Under the constitution judges and magistrates are prohibited from holding public office or belonging to a union or a political party.

General Council of the Judiciary. Except for the supreme court and the public prosecutor's office, which are provided for in the constitution, the judicial system is established by law and governed by a general council of the judiciary; this is made up of the president of the supreme court, who presides over the council, and twenty members appointed by the king for five-year terms. Twelve members of the council must be judges or magistrates, four are appointed by the congress, and four are nominated by the senate from among qualified lawyers and jurists.

Supreme Court. The supreme court, with jurisdiction over all of Spain, is the highest court, except with respect to upholding constitutional guarantees. The president of the supreme court is appointed by the monarch on the proposal of the general council of the judiciary.

Constitutional Court

The monarch appoints the twelve members of the constitutional court, which rules on the constitutionality of laws and regulations, violations of basic constitutional rights and liberties, conflicts among autonomous communities and between autonomous communities and the state, the constitutionality of actions by state agencies, organic laws, statutes of autonomy, and unratified treaties.

Autonomous Communities   Autonomous or self-governing communities, such as Catalonia and the Basque provinces, have a special status under the Spanish constitution. It extends the right to initiate the process of self-government to provincial councils, inter-island bodies, and municipalities. These communities may legislate locally on matters not proscribed in the constitution, and the legislature may confer on the self-governing communities the power to enact legislation in matters of state jurisdiction within the framework of principles, bases, and guidelines established by state law.

Amending the Constitution   Title 10, Concerning Constitutional Amendment, provides that the government, either house of the legislature, or the assemblies of self-governing communities may propose constitutional amendments. Proposals must be approved by a three-fifths majority of the members of each house. If there is no agreement between the houses, a joint commission may reintroduce a new text. If that fails but an absolute majority of the upper house has passed the proposal, the lower house may do so by a two-thirds vote. Amendments approved by the legislature must be submitted to a referendum. Other procedures apply for a complete revision of the constitution.

Violence between the majority Buddhist Sinhalese and the minority Hindu Tamils continues to plague Sri Lanka. A new constitution has been proposed to replace the nation's 1978 constitution as a means of easing tension and restoring stability.

Some 65,600 kilometers in area, the Democratic Socialist Republic of Sri Lanka (formerly Ceylon) is an independent island nation in the Indian Ocean off the southeastern coast of India. Colombo is the capital of this country of more than nineteen million persons.

Sri Lanka's major industries include clothing, oil refining, and textiles; among its chief agricultural products are tea, coconuts, and rice. A world-famous provider of tea since it was a British colony, Sri Lanka is still the largest exporter of tea in the world. Its bitter ethnic conflicts, however, overshadow prospects for economic improvement.

Type of Government: Presidential-style parliamentary republic, with a president, a prime minister and cabinet, a unicameral legislature, and a judiciary

Dates of Constitutions: 1833, 1910, 1920, 1924, 1931, 1946, 1972, and 1978

The island called Lanka ("resplendent land") was first settled by Indo-Aryans and Dravidians, whose physical differences have been blurred by centuries of intermarriage. The division of the island into Sinhalese Buddhists and Tamil Hindus, however, remains a source of ethnic friction in Sri Lanka. The Sinhalese date their arrival in the north-central region around 500 B.C., after which they created a kingdom centered around Anuradhapura that lasted from approximately 200 B.C. to the end of the tenth century A.D. Whether the Tamil people arrived earlier is unclear, but there is no evidence that they did not coexist amicably during the first few centuries the two groups shared the island.

The Tamils became rulers for the first time in 237 B.C., but Sinhalese hegemony was restored twenty-two years later. Alternating conflicts and alliances between the two peoples subsequently came to determine who ruled the island. Contact with both the Roman and the Chinese empires began around the beginning of the first millennium A.D.; until the sixteenth century, Indian invasions and internal conflicts plagued the island.

Portugal made contact in 1505, but in 1638 the Dutch agreed to help oust the Portuguese in exchange for exclusive trade rights—especially with respect to the lucrative cinnamon spice trade. The Napoleonic wars in the eighteenth century pitted France and Holland against Great Britain, resulting in the British conquest of Ceylon and formal transfer under the terms of the Treaty of Amiens (1801). The British slowly developed representative government, promulgating a constitution in 1833 that created a legislative council; the council, however, censured the colonial government in 1864 and resigned when the censure was ignored.

A second constitution that became effective on November 24, 1910, provided for the election of a territorial council member to represent those Ceylonese "educated on European lines." A new constitution in 1920 brought criticism from the Tamils over their lack of representation on the council. A fourth constitution in 1924 allotted twenty-three council seats to represent territorial constituencies. The "Donoughmore" constitution of 1931 (named after Britain's Lord Donoughmore, whose special commission made recommendations for constitutional changes) gave more authority over internal matters to elected representatives.

The "Soulbury" constitution (named after Lord Soulbury, chairman of the new constitutional commission) was promulgated by Britain in 1946. Among other provisions it prohibited discrimination based on religion, but its primary aim was to move the colony of Ceylon toward dominion status within the British Empire. Ceylon declared its independence from Britain on February 4, 1948, but remained in the British Commonwealth. A new constitution adopted by a constitutional assembly on May 16, 1972, declared the island nation of Sri ("holy") Lanka an independent republic. To effect radical changes and counteract the Maoist communist opposition, the government promoted socialist policies. Another constitution dated August 31, 1978, attempted to meet some of the concerns of the Hindu-minority Tamil population by granting greater local autonomy and making Tamil and Sinhala both national languages, although Sinhala remains the official language.

In 1995 Prime Minister Chandrika Kumaratunga, the former president, offered greater autonomy for the Tamil regime. In 2000 the legislature proposed a new constitution that would create a federal system or "Union of Regions" to address Tamil demands for a separate state.

Influences

The government structure of Sri Lanka is based generally on the British parliamentary model, with a president instead of a monarch.

The Constitution

The preamble to the 1978 constitution of Sri Lanka states that the document was drafted after

The People of Sri Lanka . . . , by their Mandate freely expressed and granted on the sixth day of the waxing moon in the month of Adhi Nikini in the year two thousand five hundred and twenty-one of the Buddhist Era . . . , entrusted to and empowered their Representatives elected on that day to draft, adopt and operate a new Republican Constitution in order to achieve the goals of a Democratic Socialist Republic.

The preamble also notes that the people are hereby "ratifying the immutable republican principles of Representative Democracy, and assuring to all peoples Freedom, Equality, Justice, Fundamental Human Rights and the Independence of the Judiciary as the intangible heritage that guarantees the dignity and well-being of succeeding generations. . . ."

Articles 1 and 2 proclaim: "Sri Lanka (Ceylon) is a Free, Sovereign, Independent and Democratic Socialist Republic [and] . . . a Unitary State." Article 3 underscores that "sovereignty is in the People and is inalienable . . . [and] includes the powers of government, fundamental rights and the franchise." Article 27 declares: "The Directive Principles of State Policy herein contained shall guide Parliament, the President and the Cabinet of Ministers in the enactment of laws and the governance of Sri Lanka for the establishment of a just and free society." Following are guiding principles such as the "full realization of the fundamental rights and freedoms of all persons," "promotion of the welfare of the People," and "realization by all citizens of an adequate standard of living for themselves and their families." The directives also promote an equitable distribution of material resources and "establishment of a just social order in which the means of production, distribution and exchange are not concentrated or centralized in the State . . . or in the hands of a privileged few but are dispersed among, and owned by, all the People of Sri Lanka." The article further calls for raising moral standards, eradicating illiteracy, eliminating "the exploitation of man by man or by the State," ensuring social security, assisting cultural development, promoting international peace, and protecting the family, children, and the environment.

Fundamental Rights

Articles 10 through 14 extend certain fundamental rights such as freedom of thought, conscience, and religion, "including the freedom to have or to adopt a religion or belief of [one's] choice." However, article 9 states:

The Republic of Sri Lanka shall give to Buddhism the foremost place and accordingly it shall be the duty of the State to protect and foster the Buddha *Sasana*, while assuring to all religions the rights granted [elsewhere in the constitution].

Other rights and freedoms guaranteed include equality before the law; a prohibition of discrimination "on the grounds of race, religion, language, caste, sex, political opinion, [or] place of birth . . ."; the rights of those accused of crimes, including the presumption of innocence and the right to "a fair trial by a competent court"; "freedom of speech and expression including publication"; peaceful assembly; and freedom of association and movement.

Article 15 sets forth a number of restrictions that may apply to various rights and freedoms. For example, freedom of movement is subject to restrictions "as may be prescribed by law in the interests of national economy." Other restrictions are authorized to secure "racial and religious harmony" or "national security, public order and the protection of public health or morality." However, according to article 17, "Every person shall be entitled to apply to the Supreme Court ... in respect of the infringement or imminent infringement ... of a fundamental right to which such person is entitled under the provisions of this Chapter."

"The Sovereignty of the People," states article 4, "shall be exercised [through] the legislative power ... , the executive power ... , [and] the judicial power...."

Division of Powers

President. "There shall be a President ... , who is the Head of the State, the Head of the Executive and of the Government, and the Commander-in-Chief of the Armed Forces," directs article 30. The president is elected by the people, according to procedures prescribed by parliament, for a term of six years and may be elected for only two terms. According to article 31, "Any citizen who is qualified ... may be nominated ... by a recognized political party, or if he is or has been an elected member of the legislature, by any other political party or by an elector whose name has been entered in any register of electors."

The Executive

"The President shall be responsible to Parliament," states article 42, "for the due exercise, performance, and discharge of his powers, duties and functions under the Constitution and any written law...." Powers and duties of the president include appointing the prime minister and cabinet ministers, the chief justice, and other judges of the supreme court; attending, addressing, and sending messages to parliament; presiding "at ceremonial sittings of Parliament"; and receiving, recognizing, appointing, and accrediting "Ambassadors ... and other diplomatic agents." The president also declares war and peace, grants pardons and stays of execution, and commutes sentences.

Article 35 provides that "no proceedings shall be instituted or continued against [the president] in any court or tribunal in respect to anything done or omitted ... by him either in his official or private capacity." However, two-thirds of the members of parliament may impeach the president for, among other transgressions, "intentional violation of the Constitution." The speaker of parliament then refers the matter to the supreme court "for inquiry and report." If the supreme court's report warrants it, two-thirds of the total number of legislators may remove the president from office. In this case, the prime minister acts as president until a new chief executive is elected.

If temporarily unable to perform his or her duties, the president is authorized by article 37 to "appoint the Prime Minister to exercise ... [such] ... duties ... during such period, and [he or she] may also appoint [a minister] to act in the office of Prime Minister...."

Cabinet. Article 43 mandates a cabinet of ministers "charged with the direction and control of the Government of the Republic, which shall be collectively responsible and answerable to Parliament." The president, in consultation with the prime minister, is to "determine the number of Ministers of the Cabinet of Ministers and the Ministries and the assignment of subjects and functions to such Ministers." The president is a member and head of the cabinet but continues in office if the cabinet is dissolved, after which the chief executive appoints as prime minister "the Member of Parliament who in his opinion is most likely to command the confidence of Parliament."

The Legislature

Parliament. Pursuant to article 62, "There shall be a Parliament which shall consist of one hundred and ninety-six Members elected by the electors of . . . electoral districts . . . for six years . . . [u]nless Parliament is sooner dissolved." According to article 67, the "privileges, immunities, and powers of Parliament and of its Members may be determined and regulated by Parliament by law. . . ." Parliament must elect from its members three officers: a speaker, deputy speaker–chairman of committees, and deputy chairman of committees.

Article 70 authorizes the president to "from time to time, by Proclamation summon, prorogue and dissolve Parliament." A quorum of twenty members is necessary to conduct business, and article 72 requires that, except "as otherwise provided in the Constitution, any question proposed for decision by Parliament shall be decided by the majority of votes of the Members present and voting." According to article 76, "Parliament shall not abdicate or in any manner alienate its legislative power, and shall not set up any authority with any legislative power."

"The passing of a Bill or a resolution by Parliament," states article 78, "shall be in accordance with the Constitution and the Standing Orders of Parliament," after which the legislation becomes law upon the speaker's endorsement. In the case of "any Bill or any provision thereof" that is certified by the cabinet to require approval by referendum, the president endorses it, and it "shall be final and conclusive, and shall not be called into question in any court."

The Judiciary

Article 105 enumerates "the institutions for the administration of justice which protect, vindicate and enforce the rights of the People" as the supreme court, court of appeal, high court, "and such other Courts . . . as Parliament may from time to time ordain and establish." Unlike other courts, however, the supreme court may not be abolished or changed by parliament.

Supreme Court. The chief justice and other judges of the supreme court are appointed by the president and "hold office during good behavior" or until reaching the age of retirement, sixty-five years. "The Supreme Court," according to article 119, "shall consist of the Chief Justice and of not less than six and not more than ten other Judges. . . ."

The "highest and final superior Court of record," the supreme court has "sole and exclusive jurisdiction to determine any question as to whether any Bill or any provision thereof is inconsistent with the Constitution." In addition to such "constitutional matters," the court's jurisdiction extends to "protection of fundamental rights," final appeals, "election petitions" (including "any legal proceeding relating to the election of the President"), "any breach of the privileges of Parliament," and "other matters which Parliament may by law vest or ordain." The court also has "consultative jurisdiction."

Amending the Constitution

Pursuant to article 82, a bill in parliament to amend the constitution must meet certain formal requirements, including express language to the effect that it is "an Act for the amendment of the Constitution." Such a bill becomes law if "not less than two-thirds of the whole number of Members (including those not present)" vote for it and it is certified by the president, in the case of a referendum on the proposed amendment, or by the speaker of parliament. The amendment of certain provisions, including articles 1, 2, 3, 6, 7, 8, 9, 10, 11, and 82, must be approved by referendum.

Article 84 permits the enactment of bills not intended to amend the constitution but that are inconsistent with it. In this instance the need for a special parliamentary majority must be certified by the cabinet or the supreme court and parliament must pass the legislation by "not less than two-thirds of the whole number of Members"; either the speaker or the president as appropriate must then endorse the bill.

The largest country in Africa, Sudan shares with Egypt the longest river in the world—the Nile. Since obtaining independence in 1956, the country has been marked by political instability and civil strife that its 1998 constitution is unlikely to change in the near future.

Approximately 2.5 million kilometers in area, the Republic of the Sudan is bounded on the north by Egypt; on the east by the Red Sea, Eritrea, and Ethiopia; on the south by Kenya, Uganda, and Congo (formerly Zaire); and on the west by the Central African Republic, Chad, and Libya. Khartoum is the capital of this nation of some thirty-five million persons.

Sudan's major industries include cotton, textiles, and cement; sesame, gum arabic, and raw cotton are among its chief agricultural products. In 1999 the country began exporting oil, which should have a positive effect on the economy, although it may also fuel the nation's continuing internal conflicts.

Type of Government: Presidential federal republic, with a president and council of ministers (cabinet), a unicameral legislature, a judiciary, and a constitutional court

Dates of Constitutions: 1952, 1956 (transitional), 1964 (suspended in 1969), 1971 (provisional), 1973, 1985 (transitional), and 1998 (partially suspended in 1999)

The land now known as Sudan was inhabited by gatherers and hunters more than twenty thousand years ago. Nubia, or northern Sudan, was settled by Egyptians and came under Egyptian rule around the end of the fourth millennium B.C. In the eighth century B.C. rulers of Nubia conquered Egypt, but their capital fell to the Egyptians several centuries later.

Converted by Christian missionaries during the sixth century A.D., the three major kingdoms of black Coptic Christians in the region remained basically unaffected by the wave of Muslim Arab conquests that swept many nations in that part of the world, including their neighbor Egypt to the north, until the thirteenth century. The southernmost Christian kingdom finally came under the rule of an Arab confederation around 1500. Central Sudan was ruled by the Funj, a strange non-Arab, non-Muslim people, from the sixteenth to the nineteenth centuries.

Sudan came under Ottoman-Egyptian rule from 1821 to 1885, which was followed by a period of administration by Great Britain. After World War I the Sudanese were divided between independence and union with Egypt. A self-determination agreement was reached with the British in 1952, and the Sudanese legislative assembly enacted a constitution in the same year. Following a three-year transition period, Sudan declared its independence on January 1, 1956, and put in place a transitional constitution.

A military government ruled Sudan from 1958 to 1964, but civilian rule was restored and a new constitution promulgated on November 5, 1964. The constitution was suspended, however, after a military coup in 1969 led by Jaafar an Nimeiri. A civilian premier and cabinet were appointed, and Sudan was declared a socialist state under Islamic guidance with a provisional constitution published on August 13, 1971. In 1973 Nimeiri promulgated his own undemocratic constitution.

Rebellion by the southern Christian Sudanese in the mid-1980s led to a military takeover of the central government dominated by northern Moslems. A transitional constitution invoked in 1985 after Nimeiri's ouster was abolished after another coup in 1989. With the approval in a referendum of a reported 96.7 percent of voters, a new constitution was promulgated on June 30, 1998, but parts of it were suspended in December 1999 after a state of emergency was declared.

Like the constitutions of some other developing nations—Ireland's 1937 constitution, for example—the 1998 Sudanese constitution contains "directive principles" to guide the conduct of government and public life in addition to presenting a government structure and a catalogue of individual rights.

The Constitution

"The State of Sudan is an embracing homeland, wherein races and cultures coalesce and religions conciliate," proclaims article 1. "Islam is the religion of the majority of the population. Christianity and customary creeds have considerable followers." Sudan, according to article 2, "is a federal republic [and] the supreme authority thereof is based on the federal system drawn by the Constitution ... and administered ... in accordance with the law, to ensure popular participation, consultation and mobilization, and to provide justice in the distribution of power and wealth."

Articles 6 through 18 contain policy statements regarding the state's role in such areas as national unity, defense, national economy, natural resources, financial obligations, social justice and mutual aid, science, art and culture, public health, sports, the environment, children and youth, family and women, morals and social unity, foreign policy, and religion. Article 19 defines "directive principles" as "general objectives which State organs and employees seek and ... are guided by." However, it adds, "They are not defined rules controlled by constitutional adjudication...."

Fundamental Rights

"Every human being shall have the right to life, freedom, safety of person and dignity of honor ... [and shall be] free of subjection to slavery, forced labor, humiliation or torture," states article 20. Articles 21 through 26 guarantee equality before the law; the inalienable right to Sudanese nationality for anyone born of a Sudanese mother or father; freedom of movement, which shall not be restricted "save under safeguards of the law"; freedom of conscience and religious creed; freedom of opinion and expression, subject to restrictions necessary for "security, order, safety and public morals, all as regulated by law"; and freedom of association and organization "as regulated by law."

Article 27 guarantees the right to preserve one's cultural heritage, and articles 28 through 30 address the right to "property and knowledge" and privacy of communication and residence, "not to be infringed save upon permission or by law." The rights of persons accused of crimes are provided, and the death penalty is limited to "extremely serious offenses."

Duties of citizens listed in article 35 include "allegiance to the Republic of the Sudan not to an enemy thereof," defense of the country, respect for the constitution and the law, and caring for "the sanctities of society and its public interests ... [including] a pure environment [and] good morals and justice." It also notes:

The duties of a citizen shall be a general obligation observed by conscience and by the vigilant society. They are the source of policies and legislation upon which a legal obligation secured by sanction may be imposed.

Division of Powers

The structure of the constitution divides power superficially—for example, under article 100 the judiciary is responsible to the president—among executive, legislative, and judicial branches of government. Power is also divided federally between the national and state governments.

The Executive

President. The president of Sudan is elected by the people for a term of five years and may be reelected only once. A candidate must be a Sudanese national, of sound mind, at least forty years of age, and not have been convicted in the last seven years of a crime involving honor or honesty. Any voter may nominate a candidate for president, "provided that the candidate shall be seconded in accordance with the law." At least fifty percent of the vote is required for a candidate to become president; otherwise a runoff election is held between the two candidates receiving the highest number of votes.

Article 43 provides that the president represents "the government and the supreme sovereignty of the land." The office holder is "the supreme commander of the people's armed forces" and supervises "the process of justice and public morals...." Other powers include appointing constitutional federal officers, presiding over the council of ministers, declaring war and states of emergency in accordance with the constitution and law, initiating and signing amendments to the constitution and laws, approving death sentences, granting pardons, representing the nation in foreign relations, and appointing and accrediting ambassadors.

The president is authorized to appoint two vice presidents with the same qualifications as the president, together with "assistants and advisers." In the president's absence or during a vacancy in the office, "his First Vice-President shall temporarily assume the functions of the Presidency" until the president's return or a new president is chosen in an election to be held within sixty days. Article 45 extends the president immunity from criminal proceedings without the written permission of the legislature.

Cabinet. According to article 47, "The Council of Ministers shall have the supreme federal executive authority in the State...." Ministers are appointed by the president and take the following oath of office (a similar one is required of legislators):

I swear by Almighty God, to assume my office as a minister in the worship and obedience of God, performing my duties diligently and honestly and striving for the order and progress of the country, detached from any fanaticism or personal fancy; and swear by Almighty God, to respect the Constitution and the law and accept consultancy and advice, and God to what I say is witness.

The powers of the council, as set forth in article 49, include general planning for the nation, approving important policies of the federal ministries, initiating draft international agreements and legislation, and setting general budgets. An individual minister is "the highest responsible authority in his ministry ... [but the] Council of Ministers may amend or cancel" a minister's decisions.

Congress. Article 65 proclaims the nation's legislative authority:

Islamic Law and the consensus of the nation, by referendum, Constitution and custom ... shall be the sources of legislation; ... however, the legislation shall be guided by the nation's public opinion, the learned opinion of scholars and thinkers, and then by the decision of those in charge of public affairs.

The national legislature of Sudan, the national assembly, is established under article 67 "to assume the legislative authority and any other powers by virtue of the Constitution." Seventy-five percent of the assembly members are directly elected "from the geographical constituencies which are divided by fair representation of the population in the country." Twenty-five percent are elected by special or indirect elections to include women, scientists, and professionals "representing States or national electoral colleges, as may be prescribed by law." If an election cannot be held in any constituency "for compelling security reasons," the president may appoint a member to occupy the seat pending a formal election. Members serve for four years, the constitutionally set length of the assembly's session.

Qualification for assembly membership is the same as for president, except that members must be at least twenty-one years of age; state legislators, governors, and state ministers are not eligible. According article 74, members are granted certain immunities from criminal proceedings, unless caught "in the very act of crime." Article 82 grants legislators freedom of expression for their opinions in the assembly. A speaker, elected from among the members at the assembly's first sitting, presides at legislative sittings and is authorized to appoint a nonmember to serve as general secretary with responsibility for the legislature's administrative affairs.

The functions of the assembly, detailed in article 73, include passing "plans, programs and policies relating to the State and the society"; constitutional amendments, bills, and provisional decrees"; and "the general budget of revenues and expenditure," as well as "ratifying international conventions and agreements." The assembly is also responsible for monitoring the performance of the executive, initiating or participating in "political and social mobilization," and issuing "resolutions on public affairs." Article 84 authorizes any member to question a federal minister on any subject relating to his or her functions.

Legislation may be initiated by the president, the council of ministers or a federal minister, or a committee of the assembly or any of its members. Bills must be presented and passed four times and become law on the president's signature "or upon lapse of thirty days after submitting it to him, and he neither signs nor decides to have it revised." The president may veto legislation, but the veto may be overridden by a two-thirds majority vote.

Article 95 empowers the legislature to delegate the authority to issue rules, regulations, orders, or other measures having the effect of law "to the President, the Council of Ministers or any public body." However, such legislation "shall be tabled before the Assembly, and [is] subject to annulment or amendment by [the Assembly]." Article 66 authorizes the president or fifty percent of the legislators to refer to a referendum any matter concerning "higher values, the national will or public interests."

The Judiciary

"Judicial competence in the Republic of the Sudan," states article 99, "shall vest into an independent authority to be known as the 'Judiciary' to assume the judicial power in adjudication of disputes and judgments on the same in accordance with the Constitution and the law." Article 100, however, provides that the judiciary "shall be responsible for the performance of its work before the President of the Republic."

The judiciary includes a "supreme court, appeals courts, and courts of first instance," as well as a president known as the chief justice and a supreme council of the judiciary, whose "composition and functions shall be prescribed by law." According to article 104, "The President of the Republic shall appoint the Chief Justice and his deputies according to law" along with "all other judges upon the recommendation of the Supreme Council of the Judiciary." It adds that the law "shall determine the terms of service, discipline and immunities of judges. No judge shall be removed save under disciplinary measures and upon a recommendation from the Supreme Council of the Judiciary."

Constitutional Court

A constitutional court is created by article 105. Its president and other members are appointed by the president and approved by the legislature "from persons of high experience in matters of justice." The court's jurisdiction extends to "interpreting constitutional and legal provisions submitted by the President of the Republic, the National Assembly, half the number of Governors or half the States' Assemblies." It also decides claims by the aggrieved based on constitutional rights, claims concerning conflicts between state and federal authorities over their powers, and other matters under the constitution and the law.

Amending the Constitution

Pursuant to article 139, the president, one-third of the members of the national assembly, or one-third of the state assemblies may propose "amendment of the Constitution." Such proposals must be approved by a two-thirds majority of the members of the national assembly.

A popular referendum is necessary to amend certain basic principles of the constitution, such as "Islamic law and the legislative consensus of the people . . . , the Constitution or custom," "freedom of creed and worship," governance "in accordance with a federal system," and a presidential system of leadership. The article also notes that "Southern Sudan has a transitional system for a term, . . . which . . . shall expire by the exercise of the right of self-determination." Amendments approved by referendum require the president's signature.

Until its current constitution was enacted on January 1, 1975, Sweden had the oldest written constitution in Europe still in effect. The new constitution continues the tradition of a constitutional monarchy but provides for a strong parliamentary government more indicative of the modern age.

The Kingdom of Sweden, the largest and most populous of the five Nordic countries, is approximately 450,000 square kilometers and is bounded by Finland on the north and east, the Gulf of Bothnia on the east, the Baltic Sea on the east and south, outlets to the North Sea on the southwest, and Norway on the west. Stockholm is the capital of this country of nearly nine million persons.

Long a dominant Nordic power, Sweden has recently fallen on hard times economically, while Norway and Denmark are now exploiting oil-rich deposits. Sweden's economic woes and the end of the cold war have forced reconsideration of its policy of neutrality, as evidenced by its application for full membership in the European Union.

Type of Government: Parliamentary constitutional monarchy, with a monarch, a prime minister and cabinet, a unicameral legislature, and a judiciary

Dates of Constitutions: 1809 and 1975 (supplemented by other documents)

The Romans paid little attention to Scandinavia, although they were aware of the existence of the Svear tribe, from which the Swedish word *Sverige*, hence Sweden, is derived. The Vikings, also known as Norsemen or Normans, made themselves known in the ninth century, when they began sailing around Europe, sometimes trading but more often pillaging where they landed. European feudalism—the exchange of allegiance for protection—was to some extent a response to the Norse marauders.

By the twelfth century Christianized Swedes were conducting crusades in Finland and annexing the territory. Together with Norway, Sweden became a member of the Union of Kalmar, with Denmark at its head, in an alliance against Germany in the late fourteenth century, by which time Sweden had its own national laws. A peasant uprising against Danish domination resulted in the formation of the first Swedish parliament in 1435. After the Danes again asserted their rule in the sixteenth century, another successful uprising culminated in the crowning of the first Swedish king, Gustav I, in 1523 to rule at least in the north. He supported the Christian reformation and built a strong centralized government. In 1634 the first Instrument of Government, the forerunner of the basic Swedish constitutional document, was issued to deal with the regency after the death of Gustav II.

When the Treaty of Westphalia was concluded in 1648, Sweden recovered its southern territory from Denmark and was recognized as a force in Europe; during the seventeenth century it briefly held a colony in America. The eighteenth century is known in Sweden as the Age of Liberty. During this period Sweden's constitutional development was noted by Voltaire and Jean-Jacques Rousseau and gave rise to a new Instrument of Government in 1719. In 1766 the first freedom of the press act was promulgated, and a new Instrument of Government was adopted in 1772. Falling prey to Russian aggression, Sweden in 1809 lost Finland, which it had held for a century, only to gain Norway in 1814 from the Danes, who had supported Napoleon.

In the nineteenth century the aristocracy gradually relinquished its power to the growing middle and working classes, and representative assemblies became a regular fixture of government. Defeat by Russia and the ensuing revolution forced the last of the absolute monarchs to abdicate and initiated the creation of a constitutional monarchy under the Instrument of Government of 1809 and a new parliament act in 1810.

Sweden obtained full parliamentary government in 1917 and achieved universal suffrage in 1921. The country escaped destruction and occupation by the Nazis during World War II, although its sovereignty was severely compromised. After the war Sweden continued its policy of nonalignment; its postwar economy grew even though it had to produce most of its own weapons for its armed forces. In 1959 Sweden joined the Economic Free Trade Association with Denmark and Norway; Finland and Iceland joined later.

Like the other Nordic countries, Sweden is highly socialized, and despite its current economic problems there appears to be a consensus for maintaining the traditional welfare state as much as possible. To update its constitution, a new Instrument of Government went into effect on January 1, 1975.

Influences

The Swedish institution of the ombudsman, an independent officer of the government who is responsible for the protection of the constitutional process and individual rights and freedoms, has been adopted by many other countries, including Finland and Austria.

The Constitution

The Swedish constitution consists of four documents: the Act of Succession, amended in 1980 to extend the right of inheritance of the crown equally to female as well as male heirs; the Freedom of the Press Act, as amended in 1992; the Freedom of Expression Act of 1992; and the most significant document, the Instrument of Government of 1975, which replaced the 1809 law. The Riksdag Act of 1974, although not a fundamental law, is of constitutional importance as evidenced by the special procedures required for its amendment.

Chapter 1 of the 1975 Instrument of Government, on the Basic Principles of the Constitution, defines the source of governmental authority:

All public power in Sweden proceeds from the people.

Swedish democracy is founded on freedom of opinion and on universal and equal suffrage. It shall be realized through a representative and parliamentary polity and through local self-government.

Public power shall be exercised under law.

Fundamental Rights

Chapter 2 of the 1975 Instrument of Government sets forth both absolute freedoms and freedoms that may be restricted by laws passed by the legislature. In the first group are freedom of worship, protection of personal views, prohibition against being identified in a public register solely on the basis of political views, the right to travel, prohibition against retroactive penal laws, and others. In the second category are freedom of speech, freedom of information and assembly, and protection from assault, house search, and similar intrusions.

In addition to these basic explicit rights, Sweden has acceded to various international conventions that extend rights to citizens. Among them are the United Nations Universal Declaration of Human Rights (1948), the European Convention for the Protection of Human Rights and Fundamental Freedoms (1950), the European Social Charter (1961), the International Covenant on Civil and Political Rights (1966), and the International Covenant on Economic, Social, and Cultural Rights (1966).

The Freedom of Press Act, which recognizes the general conviction in Sweden that freedom of the press is of fundamental importance in a free society, provides that every Swedish citizen is free to "publish his thoughts and opinions in print, to publish official documents and to make statements and communicate information on any subject whatsoever." In principle, aliens are treated equally with citizens under the act.

The Freedom of Expression Act protects expression on radio, television, film, videos, sound recordings, and the like. It provides the same protections as does the Freedom of the Press Act, except that by its nature the radio frequency spectrum, unlike the print medium, may be regulated, and materials to be publicly exhibited are subject to prior review. An amendment in 1995 recognized the rights of the Sami people "to conduct their lifestyle."

In Sweden, a unitary state, power is divided among the monarch, as head of state; the prime minister, as head of government; the legislature; and the courts, which exercise limited judicial review.

Division of Powers

Monarch. The executive branch consists of the monarch and the government, but the monarch takes no part, even formally, in the decision-making process of the government. As head of state, however, the monarch must be kept informed by the prime minister of the affairs of the realm and must consult with the prime minister before traveling abroad. The monarch may not be prosecuted for acts or omissions but otherwise is subject to the law in civil matters.

The Executive

Prime Minister and Cabinet. The head of government, the prime minister, is proposed for the office by the speaker of the legislature after consulting with representatives of the parties and the deputy speakers. If approved by at least half the members, he or she begins forming a government by appointing ministers. The new government takes office in the presence of the monarch if possible but always in the presence of the speaker. The prime minister may dismiss any minister, and when the prime minister resigns, even for reasons not related to a vote of no confidence, the cabinet must resign also.

The constitution gives the government wide latitude in running the country, requiring only that there be a chancery made up of the various ministries and that the government's business be distributed among the ministries. The government is permitted to enter into treaties on its own, except if the treaties require legislation or affect the legislature's sphere of authority, in which case they must be approved by the legislature.

Parliament. Article 6, chapter 1, of the 1975 Instrument of Government declares: "The government rules the country. It is responsible to the Riksdag."

The Legislature

The major check on the government's power is its ultimate responsibility to Sweden's unicameral parliament, the Riksdag, which alone has the authority to legislate, levy taxes, decide budget matters, and oversee the administration of the country. Government based on the parliamentary principle set forth in the 1975 Instrument of Government is a natural extension of the Swedish constitutional traditions embodied in previous constitutional documents.

Membership in the Swedish parliament is determined by free, secret, and direct election of 349 members, each of whom has an alternate. Ordinarily elections are held every four years, and resident citizens eighteen years of age or older may vote and be elected. Once elected, a member or alternate may not resign without the permission of the parliament. The Riksdag meets in session every year in Stockholm. It selects a speaker and three deputies for the parliamentary term, which is usually three years, barring a special election.

Generally, bills may be introduced by the government or a member of the parliament. Committees must consider nearly all matters before final action may be taken. The Instrument of Government specifies a committee on the constitution as well as other committees. Ordinary legislation requires a majority vote of those present and voting to be approved, although most decisions are made by acclamation rather than a formal vote. In the voting process the vote of a member who serves as speaker or who is also a member of the government must be exercised by an alternate. Acts adopted are to be promulgated without delay by the government; however, acts dealing with the parliament or its agencies passed in the ordinary course of business may be promulgated by the Riksdag itself. The opinion of a law council made up of members of the supreme court and the supreme administrative court must be sought before proposals involving certain significant laws may be enacted. Like most other parliaments, the Riksdag has the power of interpellation, the right to formally question ministers.

Ombudsman. A gift of the Swedes to parliamentary democracy is the ombudsman, a term derived from the Germanic tribes' word for a person chosen to collect *Wergild* (blood money) on behalf of an offended party. The position of ombudsman, which was modeled on an agent of an exiled Swedish king in the early eighteenth century, is not strictly a fourth branch of government; since 1809 it has been filled by the parliament but is independent of both the executive and legislative branches. An institution to improve the effectiveness and fairness of government for the Swedish people while protecting basic rights, the ombudsman supervises the application of laws by public servants and may initiate legal proceedings when required. In addition to four parliamentary ombudsmen, as of 2000 Sweden had seven other ombudsmen, one each for consumer affairs, equal opportunity, ethnic discrimination, sexual orientation discrimination, disability, children, and the press.

The Judiciary

Chapter 11 of the 1975 Instrument of Government, entitled Judicial and General Administration, establishes the supreme court as the highest court of general jurisdiction and the supreme administrative court as the highest administrative court. Under the constitution other courts and the particulars of the administration of justice in Sweden are to be established by law. There are six appeals courts and 100 district courts in the Swedish judicial system.

Article 2, chapter 11, states: "Neither a public authority nor the Riksdag may determine how a court shall adjudicate a particular case or how a court shall in other respects apply a rule of law in a particular case." Judges are permanent and may be removed only for a criminal act or gross neglect of duty or on reaching retirement age. A judge is given the right of court review for any removal action by an authority other than a court.

Article 14, chapter 11, expressly authorizes the courts and other bodies to reject the application of any provision that conflicts with a provision of a fundamental law or superior statute; however, if the provision in question has been approved by the legislature or the government, "it may be set aside only if the fault is manifest."

Amending the Constitution

A proposal to amend constitutional laws may be passed only if the legislature approves it twice in identical form. The second action must be taken by a newly elected parliament. If the parliament puts off action on such a proposal, a referendum may be called by a vote of a minority of the members.

The Riksdag Act may be amended in the same manner as a fundamental law or by a vote in the parliament of at least three-fourths of the members present if they represent a total of at least one-half of the members.

Switzerland, a land of linguistic, religious, and cultural diversity, can trace its roots to the Ever-lasting Alliance of three cantons in 1291. Since 1815 its proclaimed neutrality has become a principle of international law.

The Swiss Confederation in central Europe is some 42,300 square kilometers and is bounded by Germany on the north, Liechtenstein and Austria on the east, Italy on the south, and France on the west. The population of Switzerland is approximately seven million persons. The capital is Bern, although the federal supreme court and some other federal government offices are located elsewhere.

Switzerland, whose name is derived from the central canton of Schwyz, has evolved into a modern industrial nation from a basically agrarian country whose main export was mercenary troops. The country's policy of neutrality, however, will undoubtedly have to be reassessed in light of the political changes taking place in Europe.

Type of Constitution: Collegial executive confederation, with a federal council whose president is chosen annually, a bicameral legislature, and a judiciary

Dates of Constitutions: 1803, 1848 (totally revised in 1874), and 2000

The Helvetians, one of the Celtic tribes that settled in the region between the Jura mountain range and the more southern Alps nearly six thousand years ago, are the ancestors of the modern-day Swiss. Ambitious, literate warriors able to write their own language using the Greek alphabet, they moved south toward Rome in the first century B.C., only to be badly beaten by Caesar's legions. Soon Romanized, they prospered from the trade routes through their territory.

When the Romans withdrew in the early fifth century A.D., two Germanic tribes—the Burgundians in the west and the Alemanni in the central plains and the Alps—moved in, displacing the Latin language and Roman culture. The territory was absorbed into Charlemagne's empire around the year 800 and partitioned by Burgundy and Swabia in the tenth and eleventh centuries. In 1230 the St. Gotthard Pass through the Alps was opened, making the area more strategically important to its neighbors. Two small cantons at the northern end of the pass, Schwyz and Uri, populated by rugged mountain people who already met in assemblies to elect leaders and administer common land, rebelled and were granted semi-independent status in the Holy Roman Empire in the thirteenth century.

Schwyz, Uri, and an adjacent canton, Unterwalden, formed a peace alliance in August 1291 for their mutual protection against the Hapsburgs; the Schwyz banner, a white cross on a red field, became the Swiss flag. The cantons retained their own local governments but pledged mutual assistance against outsiders. In 1315 the alliance was put to the test against a much larger Hapsburg force and won. In time the alliance grew, adding more independent cantons. When it tried to conquer more territory in 1515, it was defeated by the French; however, a treaty with France in 1521 secured its territorial integrity for the next three centuries.

In 1648 Switzerland's full independence was recognized, and prosperity ensued. The Reformation brought skilled immigrants and radical democratic ideas. In the eighteenth century Geneva attracted Voltaire and Jean-Jacques Rousseau, among others. After its revolution in 1789, France began to intervene in Swiss affairs, and battles with Austrian and Russian troops in 1799 devastated large parts of the country. Napoleon prevailed, setting up a centralized state in Switzerland under an 1803 constitution called the Act of Mediation, which introduced individual rights based on the French Declaration of the Rights of Man and of the Citizen (1789). After Napoleon's defeat, the Congress of Vienna in 1815 added three new cantons and proclaimed Switzerland's neutrality and inviolability, which became a principle of international law.

By referendum on April 18, 1999, a revised Swiss constitution was approved and went into effect on January 1, 2000. It codifies the 1874 constitution and its amendments without radically changing the federal nature of the Swiss confederation or the structure of the government, basically putting the old constitutional provisions into more modern form. For example, it organizes citizen rights under a separate title like most other national constitutions and clarifies the jurisdictions of the federal government and the governments of the cantons. It does extend some new rights, however, such as protecting persons "against the abuse of medically assisted procreation and gene technology" including cloning.

Influences

U.S. and French constitutional principles informed the 1848 constitution. The 2000 document continues the country's limited system of federal government.

The Constitution

"In the Name of God Almighty!" begins the preamble, which goes on to assert that the nation will "live its diversity in unity" and to note that "only those are free who use their freedom, and the strength of the people is measured by the well-being of the weakest of its members. . . ."

Article 1 defines the Swiss confederation as "[t]he Swiss people and the Cantons," which are named. Article 2 sets forth certain goals, including protecting "the freedom and the rights of the people," fostering their "general welfare," and ensuring "the greatest possible equality of opportunities between female and male citizens." But, pursuant to article 6, "All persons are responsible for themselves and contribute according to their capacities to the accomplishment of the tasks of State and Society."

Fundamental Rights

Fundamental and civil rights, as well as social goals, are enumerated in articles 7 through 41. Among the rights guaranteed are human dignity, equality before the law, protection against arbitrary treatment by state authorities, the right to life and personal freedom, protection of children and youth, aid for those in need, privacy, marriage and family, as well as freedom of conscience and belief, opinion, information, the media, language, a basic education, science, art, assembly, and association. Other rights, in addition to economic freedom and political and civil rights, include the right to settle any place in Switzerland, to leave the country and return, to own property, and to address petitions to government authorities. Rights of persons accused of crimes, such as publicly rendered judgments, habeas corpus, and the presumption of innocence, are also extended. An amendment in 2000, however, allows the federal and canton governments in exceptional cases to exclude legal disputes from being judged by a judicial authority.

Social goals, according to article 41, seek to ensure that "every person benefits from social security . . . [and] necessary health care," "families . . . are protected and encouraged," "people capable of working can sustain themselves through working under fair and adequate conditions," appropriate and affordable housing is available, and children and young people benefit from education and are encouraged and supported "in their social, cultural, and political integration."

Division of Powers

Articles 43 and 47, respectively, provide that between the federal government and the government of the individual cantons, the cantons "determine the tasks which they accomplish within the framework of their competencies. . . . The Confederation respects the autonomy of the Cantons." Federal law, however, "takes precedence over conflicting cantonal law," and the constitution details specific subject areas of federal and cantonal law. Article 148 declares with respect to the federal government: "Subject to the rights of the People and the Cantons, the Federal Assembly [legislature] is the highest authority of the Confederation."

Federal Council. "The Federal Council is the highest directing and executive authority of the Confederation," states article 174. It consists of seven members elected by the legislature after each full renewal of the lower house, but only one member may be elected from a canton.

"The Federal Administration," according to article 178, "is divided into Departments; each Department is directed by one member of the Federal Council." Article 180 adds that the council "determines the goals and the means of government policy"; in this regard, it is similar to the council of ministers (cabinet) in a parliamentary system of government. The council may also legislate "in the form of ordinances, insofar as the Constitution or the law empower it to do so." In addition, it "submits to the [legislature] drafts of its legislation," "ensures the implementation of laws [or] decrees of the [legislature]," "conducts foreign relations," "signs treaties and ratifies them," and "takes measures to secure the external [and internal] security, the independence, and the neutrality of Switzerland."

President. The legislature "elects for a term of one year, one of the members of the Federal Council as President of the Confederation, and another as Vice-President of the Federal Council." He or she may not be reelected president or elected vice president the following year. The president chairs meetings of the federal council, but the council "decides as a collegial body."

Parliament. As provided in article 148, Switzerland's parliament is called the federal assembly and "has two Chambers, the National Council [lower house] and the Council of the States [upper house]," but "both have equal powers." The two houses "deliberate together ... to hold elections; to resolve conflicts of competence between the highest federal authorities; [and] rule on petitions for pardon." Otherwise they meet separately, with decisions of the legislature requiring agreement of both houses.

Upper House. The council of the states consists of forty-six senators, two elected from each canton, except for six that elect one each.

Lower House. The national council numbers 200 deputies "elected directly by the People according to the system of proportional representation ... every four years." Each canton forms an electoral district, with seats "distributed among the Cantons in proportion to their population," except that each canton has at least one seat.

Members of the legislature, like those of the federal council, are granted certain immunities, including freedom from responsibility "for their statements in the Chambers and before parliamentary organs." Each house elects a president and two vice presidents who serve for one year but may not be immediately reelected.

A majority of the members of each house constitute a quorum, and, except for certain actions including "the declaration of urgency of federal laws" and certain monetary measures, "decisions are taken by the majority of those voting." Proposed legislation may be submitted by any member of the legislature, "every parliamentary group [and] commission, and every Canton." Article 164 requires that measures dealing with "the exercise of political rights," "restrictions of constitutional rights," and "the rights and duties of persons," among others, "must be enacted in the form of federal laws."

In addition to enacting laws, the legislature "participates in shaping foreign policy and supervises foreign relations," "decides on federal spending, adopts the budget, and approves the federal accounts," "exercises the high supervision over the Federal Council, the Federal Administration, the Federal Courts and other organs entrusted with tasks of the Confederation," and "ensures that the efficacy of measures taken by the Confederation is evaluated."

The Judiciary

In addition to a federal court, article 191a, added in 2000, authorizes the establishment of a criminal court and other judicial authorities. Under 191b, also added in 2000, "The Cantons establish judicial authorities for the adjudication of civil law and public law disputes, as well as criminal cases."

Federal Court. Pursuant to article 188, as amended in 2000: "The Federal Court is the jurisdiction of the Confederation. The law regulates [its] organization and procedure. The Court administers itself." The court's jurisdiction extends to violations of federal, international, and "intercantonal" law, "cantonal constitutional rights," and political rights. "It decides disputes between the Confederation and the Cantons or between Cantons," but "[a]cts of the Federal Assembly and the Federal Council may not be contested before the Federal Court," unless otherwise authorized by law. Article 191, as amended in 2000, states: "The law provides access to the Federal Court."

Amending the Constitution

In general, article 192 directs that "revision [of the constitution] shall follow the legislative process." Under article 193, "A total revision . . . may be proposed by the People or by one of the [houses of the legislature], or may be decreed by the Federal Assembly." A referendum must be held if the proposed revision comes from the people or if the two houses disagree on it. If the proposal is approved by referendum, an election is held for a new legislature; however, "imperative provisions of international law may not be violated" by the proposed revision.

A partial revision, according to article 194, "may be requested by the People, or be decreed by the Federal Assembly." A proposed amendment must possess "unity of subject matter" and "not violate the imperative provisions of international law." It adds that a "popular initiative . . . must . . . respect the principle of the unity of form." Either type of constitutional revision "enters into force as soon as it is accepted by the People and the Cantons."

The Phoenicians, founders of seafaring city-states thousands of years ago, once occupied pre-sent-day Syria. Since 1970, when Hafiz al-Assad assumed control of the government, Syria has had a period of uncommon stability that contrasts with its own history and that of the region.

The Syrian Arab Republic is approximately 185,200 square kilometers. Situated at the eastern end of the Mediterranean Sea, it is bounded on the southwest by Lebanon and Israel, on the south by Jordan, on the east by Iraq, and on the north by Turkey. Damascus is the capital of this country of more than sixteen million persons.

Syria's economy depends on oil exports, agriculture, and textile manufacture. Frequent wars and a strict authoritarian regime do not augur well for dramatic economic and political progress in the near future.

Type of Government: Presidential-style parliamentary republic, with a president, a prime minister and council of ministers (cabinet), a unicameral legislature, and a judiciary, including a constitutional court

Dates of Constitutions: 1920 (short lived), 1930 (suspended after two months and restored in 1943; suspended again in 1949), 1950 (suspended in 1951 and restored in 1954 and 1961), 1953, 1958 (provisional), 1961 (provisional), 1964 (provisional; suspended in 1966), 1969 (provisional), and 1973

Greater Syria, the area at the eastern end of the Mediterranean Sea that links three continents, has a history extending back some six thousand years. More than four thousand years ago it was inhabited by Phoenicians, who became great seafaring merchants and founded a network of city-states, including Carthage on the north coast of Africa. Israelites and Aramaeans migrated to Greater Syria around the end of the thirteenth century B.C., and the Aramaic language, based on a simplified Phoenician alphabet, became the language of commerce in the Middle East and the official language of the Persian Empire.

A series of empires invaded the territory: Assyrians, Babylonians, and Persians. Alexander the Great conquered the area in 333 B.C., and after his death the descendants of his general Seleucus ruled for three centuries, making Damascus the capital. The Romans followed, and from A.D. 324 the Byzantines reigned. In 637 Damascus fell to the Muslims, and a member of the Quraysh, Muhammad's tribe, set up the Umayyad caliphate, again with Damascus as its capital. The disintegration of the Muslim regime led to more invasions. In 1516 the Ottoman Turks took control and remained in power until the end of World War I.

Islamic law *(shari'a)* was introduced during the military government of the Umayyad, but it applied only to Muslims. Under the Ottoman constitution of 1876, Syria had an administrative council consisting of elected and appointed members, and municipalities had councils whose members were chosen by religious leaders. The Ottoman rulers' cruelty and repressive measures encouraged Arab nationalism in Syria; when World War I broke out, government controls had to be tightened for fear of rebellion.

After the war the whole area was partitioned by the British and the French, although a Syrian national congress in 1920 proclaimed sovereignty over historical Greater Syria and named Sherif Hussein of Mecca monarch of the independent Kingdom of Syria. On July 3, 1920, the congress approved a constitution, but when the Syrians ignored a French ultimatum of July 14 to accept partitioning along with the French mandate to administer Syria and Lebanon, approved by the League of Nations, the French occupied Damascus by force on July 25.

On May 14, 1930, the French promulgated their own version of a Syrian draft constitution, based on the one for France's Third Republic, with a president and a unicameral legislature called the *majlis.* On July 8 the French high commissioner suspended the constitution and dissolved the parliament. During World War II the Vichy government administration was ousted by the Free French with the help of the British, and the Syrians were promised independence.

The 1930 constitution was restored in 1943 but suspended in 1949; pending a new document promulgated in 1950, temporary constitutional provisions were issued. A new document became effective in 1953, after a coup in 1951 brought about the suspension of the 1950 constitution, which was restored in 1954. A provisional constitution resulted in 1958 from a merger with Egypt to form the United Arab Republic (UAR). In 1961, after a Syrian army revolt ended participation in the UAR, the 1950 constitution was briefly reinstated, followed by a provisional constitution that was subsequently approved by referendum.

In 1964 a new provisional constitution vested power in a revolutionary council, but in 1966, after the ninth successful coup in seventeen years, the military leaders, who were members of the Ba'ath (Renaissance) Arab Socialist Party, suspended the 1964 constitution and established a sixteen-member regional command with executive and legislative powers. Another provisional constitution was then promulgated in 1969.

In 1970 another group of army officers, also members of the Ba'ath Party, led by Gen. Hafiz al-Assad, seized power. Assad was elected president in 1971 and held the office until his death in 2000. Syria's current constitution became effective by presidential decree on March 14, 1973.

Influences

The committee members drafting the 1973 constitution were guided by the mandate of Hafiz al-Assad, who wanted a document that would build "one Arab state for one Arab nation." Under the leadership of the Ba'ath Party, it was the first Arab constitution to make socialist nationalist thought its guiding principle.

The Constitution

The preamble to the 1973 constitution of the Syrian Arab Republic begins:

When united, the Arab nation played a great role in the development of human civilization; but when its national solidarity weakened, its civilization role receded and waves of colonial invasion were able to shatter its unity, occupy its lands, and plunder its resources.

The preamble sets forth five main principles: the Syrian Arab revolution is part of the total Arab revolution; dangers that threaten one Arab country threaten the entire Arab nation; the drive to create a socialist regime includes combating Zionism and imperialism; freedom is a sacred right and a people's democracy is the ideal form of government to guarantee the citizen's exercise of freedom; and the Arab revolution is a part of the world liberation movement.

Article 1 declares that the Syrian Arab Republic is part of the Arab homeland. Article 2 states that sovereignty resides in the people and is to be exercised in the manner defined by the constitution. Article 3 establishes that Islam is the religion of the president of the republic and that Islamic jurisprudence is a principal source of legislation (in contrast, see the amended language in the current Egyptian constitution).

Fundamental Rights

Chapter 4, Freedom, Public Rights and Obligations, asserts that freedom is a sacred right, that the state shall guarantee the personal freedom of citizens and safeguard their dignity and security, and that supremacy of the law is a basic principle of the state and society.

The rights and freedoms guaranteed by the constitution include equality before the law; equal opportunity; participation in political, economic, social, and cultural life; and legal protections for those accused of crimes. Other guarantees, with some limitations, include the inviolability of houses, privacy of communication, freedom of movement, performance of all religious rituals, and freedom of speech, the press, and assembly.

Among the duties of citizens are defending the homeland, respecting the constitution and the unionist and socialist regime, serving in the military, paying taxes, and safeguarding national unity and state secrets.

In Syria, a unitary state, power is divided among the president, who as head of state has some legislative powers; the prime minister, as head of government; the legislature; and the courts, including a constitutional court with specified limited powers of constitutional review. In fact, the president, as leader of the ruling Ba'ath Party and the military, controls the Syrian government.

President. The president is elected by universal suffrage for a seven-year term. A candidate must be a Syrian Arab, enjoy civil and political rights, and be at least forty years old. Article 84(1) states: "Candidature for the post of president of the republic shall be made by the people's council at the suggestion of the regional leadership of the Ba'ath Arab Socialist Party. It shall be submitted to the citizens in a referendum." Assad, the sole nominee for president in 1991, was elected for a fourth term by a majority of 99.98 percent of the vote.

Vice presidents, including a first vice president, may be nominated by the president. One of them may act when the president is unable to function or the office becomes vacant.

In addition to being commander in chief of the armed forces, the president's powers and duties include overseeing adherence to the constitution, guaranteeing the regular functioning of public authorities, and "upholding the state"; exercising executive power on behalf of the people; developing the general policy of the state and supervising its implementation with the council of ministers; and nominating ministers and deputy ministers, including the prime minister as president of the council of ministers. The president may call meetings of the council and preside over them. The president also issues laws passed by the legislature, as well as decrees, decisions, and orders in accordance with legislation; declares war and concludes peace, with the assent of the legislature; accredits representatives to foreign countries and receives the credentials of foreign representatives; concludes international treaties; grants pardons and confers decorations; and appoints civil and military officials and dismisses them in accordance with law.

When the legislature is not in session, the president is authorized to assume legislative powers, although legislative acts must be submitted to the legislature at the next session. The president may also submit important matters for a referendum.

Article 91 exempts the president from responsibility for official acts, except in the case of high treason.

Prime Minister and Cabinet. Article 115 provides that the council of ministers (cabinet) is the highest executive and administrative body of the state and that it consists of the president of the council (prime minister) and deputies and ministers. The cabinet supervises enforcement of laws and regulations and controls the machinery of state. The prime minister supervises the work of the ministers.

Parliament. The unicameral Syrian legislature is called the Majlis al-Sha'ab (people's council). Members are elected by universal and equal suffrage in secret and direct elections for four-year terms, which may be extended in case of war. Article 58 provides that after a ninety-day lapse, if no elections are held, the previous council continues until a new council is elected. The number of members, 250 in 1993, and constituencies are to be determined by law; however, at least one-half must be "peasants and workers," as defined by law.

To be elected to the council a person must be a citizen and at least eighteen years old, must be listed in the "civil status register," and must fulfill other conditions prescribed in the electoral law.

After elections the council elects a speaker and members of a bureau and is authorized to adopt its own rules of procedure. Members are granted immunity from criminal and civil proceedings unless "caught in the act" or if the council or the speaker (if the council is not in session) consents. Members may not take part in certain activities defined by law as incompatible with membership in the council.

The council is authorized by article 70 to suggest laws and direct questions or interpellations to the council of ministers or any minister. Its functions include nominating the president on the suggestion of the Ba'ath Party, passing laws, discussing cabinet policy, approving the general budget and development plans, ratifying international treaties, granting a general amnesty, accepting or rejecting members' resignations, and passing a vote of no confidence with respect to the cabinet or one of its members.

The Judiciary

Article 131 declares that "the judicial power is independent. The president of the republic, assisted by the supreme judiciary council, shall guarantee this independence." The supreme judicial council, over which the president of the republic presides, appoints judges who may not be removed or transferred without the council's approval. The organization of the courts is entrusted to law.

Syrian law establishes secular and religious courts as well as many specialized courts. At the lower levels the secular courts have jurisdiction over both civil and criminal matters. The court of assizes has jurisdiction over major crimes, and there are criminal and civil divisions of the court of appeals. The highest court is the court of cassation for appeals on matters of law and procedure, which is divided into sections such as criminal, civil, military, lease, commercial, admiralty, religious, and real estate. In addition to canonical or Islamic religious courts, there are spiritual courts for Christians, Jews, and other non-Muslims with jurisdiction over personal status laws. Article 138 provides that a council of state has jurisdiction over administrative matters.

Constitutional Court. The constitution creates a five-member high constitutional court appointed by the president to investigate and decide on the constitutionality of laws before promulgation, if requested by the president or by one-fourth of the members of the legislature, or of a legislative decree, if requested by one-fourth of the members. The high constitutional court may not challenge laws approved by popular referendum but may give opinions on bills and decrees if requested by the president.

Amending the Constitution

Amendments may be proposed by the president or one-third of the members of the legislature. After being studied by a special committee of the legislature, they become effective if approved by three-fourths of the members of the legislature and ratified by the president.

After the defeat of the Nationalist Party on the mainland of China in 1949, party members took refuge on the island of Formosa, now called Taiwan, and brought their 1947 constitution with them.

The Republic of China, which encompasses the island of Taiwan (formerly Formosa) and certain offshore islands including Quemoy and Matsu, is approximately 36,000 square kilometers. It is located off the southeast coast of the Chinese mainland and is bounded on the west by the Taiwan (Formosa) Strait, on the north by the East China Sea, on the east by the Pacific Ocean, and on the south by the South China Sea. The Republic of China, whose capital is Taipei, is inhabited by more than twenty-two million persons.

At the beginning of the 1990s the growth of Taiwan's economy surpassed the average growth of all Asian nations. One of the world's strongest economies, Taiwan faces constant pressure from the People's Republic of China (mainland China) for reunification.

Type of Government: Presidential-style parliamentary republic, with a president; a premier and executive branch council (cabinet); a bicameral legislature; a judiciary, including a constitutional tribunal; and separate audit and civil service authorities

Dates of Constitutions: 1905, 1912 (provisional), and 1947

From around 8000 B.C. until 1949, the Chinese people—those who emigrated to Taiwan and those who remained on the Asian mainland—shared a common history. In the third century B.C. the Qin (Chin) dynasty replaced the existing feudal order with a centralized administrative system of thirty-six prefectures and a number of counties. In the third century A.D. Confucianism became the official ideology of the government; its teachings make humble obedience to authority and the family, rather than the value of the individual, a basic political principle.

The Han dynasty, which ended in A.D. 221, had inherited the political institutions of the Qin, but it did away with some of the totalitarian features and had a legal code drawn up that became the model for later codes. Dynasties rose and fell. In 1644 the last dynasty of the northern nomadic Manzhous (Manchus), also called the Qing (Ch'ing), came to power. Initially their policy was isolationism, but the lure of selling tea and silk and the prospect of buying opium from the British led to international trade and the opium wars of 1839 to 1842. By means of "most favored nation" clauses in commercial agreements, other major powers, including the United States, emulated the British, exacting concessions from the Manzhou leaders and gaining access to China for Christian missionaries. A number of unequal treaties soon eroded the country's sovereignty, so that Britain, France, Russia, Japan, and Germany obtained influential commercial and territorial rights. The Qing dynasty, however, was able to survive a major revolt in the mid-nineteenth century, in part because of officials still loyal to Confucian traditions.

In 1861, to regain their sovereignty and improve their expertise in the areas of science and technology, the Chinese initiated a thirty-year "self-strengthening" program. It was a case of too little too late, however, and in 1894 Japan easily defeated China's navy, exacting a large indemnity, including the surrender of Taiwan to Japan. The defeat spurred a reform movement in 1898; and in 1900, in what is known as the Boxer Rebellion, Chinese peasants in Beijing, hoping to drive out the foreign interests, besieged the Japanese, British, French, and Russian diplomatic offices. This led to a constitution in 1905, but the Chinese government had to pay large indemnities for the damage.

Defeats and administrative corruption under the Manzhous led Sun Yat-sen to start a revolutionary resistance movement through secret societies, including one in Japanese-controlled Taiwan. A revolutionary alliance organized in exile instigated an uprising on the mainland and succeeded in establishing a provisional parliament on January 1, 1912. A provisional constitution was promulgated on March 11. Sun became the president of the new Republic of China but soon resigned in favor of a former Manzhou (Manchu) official. He then organized the Kuomintang (Nationalist People's Party), which broke with the new government, whose leader wanted to found a new dynasty as emperor.

The Kuomintang's goal was to set up a democratic government in China. After Sun's death in 1925 his successor, Chiang Kai-shek, defeated a number of the warlords and nominally unified the country by 1928. Japanese aggression escalated in 1931, thus strengthening the military's hand and postponing implementation of a constitutional government. A constitution was drafted in 1936, but war with Japan in 1937 thwarted further development.

After the war a new constitution, incorporating some concessions by the Nationalists, went into effect on December 25, 1947. It is still the fundamental law in Taiwan, where the Nationalist government took refuge after being defeated by the communist Chinese forces on the mainland in 1949. The relationship between the People's Republic of China and Taiwan is still evolving. In recognition of the need to deal with these changes, Additional Articles of the Constitution of the Republic of China, promulgated in 1994 and revised in 1997, provide: "Rights and obligations between the people of the Chinese mainland area and those of the free area [Taiwan] . . . may be specified by law."

Influences

In accordance with Sun Yat-sen's ideas that China must adopt the Western form of democracy, the constitution of the Republic of China draws on Western political philosophies for its design. The final version, however, created a more authoritarian form than the model Western-style government.

The Constitution

The short preamble to the constitution of the Republic of China states that it is based on the mandate of "the whole body of citizens" and that it is in accordance with the teachings of Sun Yat-sen. Article 1 declares: "The Republic of China, founded on the three principles of the people, shall be a democratic republic of the people, to be governed by the people and for the people." Article 2 defines the source of sovereignty: "The sovereignty of the Republic of China shall reside in the whole body of citizens."

Fundamental Rights

Purportedly modeled on American constitutional concepts, the general guarantees of rights and freedoms enumerated in chapter 2, Rights and Duties of the People, include equality before the law regardless of sex, religion, race, class, or party affiliation; rights of the subjects of criminal arrest and detention; freedom to change residence; freedom of speech, teaching, writing, and publication, as well as privacy of correspondence; freedom of religious belief, assembly, and association; the right to work and own property; the right to present petitions, lodge complaints, and institute legal proceedings; the right of election, recall, initiative, and referendum; and the right to hold public office. Duties of citizens include paying taxes, performing military service, and receiving education.

"All other freedoms and the rights of the people that are not detrimental to social order or public welfare," asserts article 22, "shall be guaranteed under the constitution." Article 23 states that the enumerated freedoms and rights may not be restricted by law except to prevent "infringement upon the freedom of other persons, to avert an imminent crisis, to maintain social order, or to advance public welfare."

Division of Powers

In Taiwan, a unitary state, power is divided among the president, as head of state; the premier, called the president of the executive branch council (cabinet); the legislature; the courts, which exercise constitutional review; and two additional independent bodies responsible for auditing or checking the government and managing the civil service.

President. The president is the head of state. Until recently, the legislature elected the president, but now the president and vice president run as a ticket and are "directly elected by the entire populace" for four-year terms, with reelection limited to one consecutive term.

The Executive

Any citizen of the republic who is at least forty years of age may be elected president or vice president. Chiang Kai-shek was elected for five consecutive terms, and after his death his son, who died in 1988, was elected in 1978 and 1984.

The president represents the nation in foreign relations and is commander in chief of the armed forces; promulgates laws passed by the legislative branch of the parliament; concludes treaties, declares war, and makes peace in accordance with the constitution; and declares martial law subject to the approval of the legislature. The president also appoints and removes civil and military officials, confers honors and decorations, and grants pardons and restores civil rights. The vice president succeeds to the office if it becomes vacant.

Executive Branch. Article 53 creates an administrative body called the executive branch (*yuan*) headed by a president (premier) who is similar to a prime minister. He or she is appointed by the president of the republic and serves with a vice president, ministers, chairs of commissions, and ministers without portfolio, all of whom are recommended by the premier and appointed by the president of the republic. The executive branch is required to present to the legislative branch "a statement on its administrative policies and a report on its administration," and the legislature may "interpellate" or ask questions of the members of the executive branch.

Parliament. The bicameral parliament in Taiwan consists of the Kuo-min Ta-hui (national assembly) and the legislative *yuan*. These bodies differ functionally from the upper and lower houses of a traditional parliament.

The Legislature

Upper House. The first national assembly was elected in 1947, and another election was not held until December 1991. Originally the term was for six years, but now it is four. The basis for electing members to the national assembly, which is complex, and to other elective bodies was amended in 1991 to "meet the requisites of national unification.. . ." The powers of the assembly include electing and recalling the country's president and vice president, amending the constitution, altering the territorial boundaries, and confirming certain appointments of specified government officials.

Lower House. The 225 members of the legislative *yuan* are elected for three years. According to article 4 of the 1997 Additional Articles of Amendment, 168 members are "elected from the Special Municipalities, counties, and cities in the free area [Taiwan], . . . [f]our from among the lowland and highland aborigines . . . , [e]ight . . . from among the Chinese citizens who reside abroad, [and] [f]orty-one . . . from the nationwide constituency." The members in the last two categories are "elected according to a formula for proportional representation among political parties," and some seats are reserved for women candidates.

The legislative *yuan*, whose organization is determined by law, has the power to enact laws, confirm emergency orders, review the budget and audit reports, initiate proposals for the impeachment of the president and vice president, and initiate constitutional amendments.

The judicial *yuan* is the highest judicial body of the nation. It has jurisdiction over civil, criminal, and administrative cases and cases involving disciplinary measures against public

The Judiciary

officials. Article 78 confers on it the powers to interpret the constitution and unify the interpretation of laws and orders, and article 171 declares that laws in conflict with the constitution will be null and void. The chief judge, called the president, together with a vice president, is nominated by the president of the republic with the consent of the national assembly.

Judges are independent and nonpolitical and are to hold office for life. They may be removed, however, if "found guilty of a criminal offense or subject to disciplinary measure, or declared to be under interdiction." Judges may not be suspended, transferred, or have their salary reduced, except in accordance with law. The organization of the judiciary is to be prescribed by law.

Grand Justices. The constitution also creates the positions of grand justices, appointed by the same procedure as other judges, who handle article 78 matters. The grand justices also form a constitutional tribunal to adjudicate "the dissolution of unconstitutional political parties."

Control Branch

The control *yuan* is required to exercise the powers of impeachment, censure, and audit. The twenty-nine members, who are appointed by the president of the republic with the consent of the national assembly, serve six-year terms.

Examination Branch

The examination *yuan* is responsible for public employment actions, including screening, employment, promotion, discharge, and benefits. A president and vice president and members are appointed by the national president with the consent of the national assembly.

Amending the Constitution

Article 174 provides two methods for amendment. First, one-fifth of the members of the national assembly may propose an amendment, and three-fourths of the delegates present, a quorum being two-thirds of the members, may approve it. Second, one-fourth of the members of the legislative *yuan* may propose an amendment, and three-fourths of the members present, a quorum being three-fourths of the members, may approve it and submit it to the national assembly "by way of referendum."

As indicated, significant amendments to the constitution were passed by the first national assembly in 1991 and by an extraordinary session of the second national assembly in 1992. Ten additional articles to the constitution were promulgated on July 28, 1994. These were amended on July 21, 1997, bringing the total number of additional articles to eleven.

Tanzania is a union of the East African country of Tanganyika and the nearby island republic of Zanzibar that took place in 1964. The country's constitution was amended in 1992 to permit a transition from a single-party to a multiparty system.

Approximately 940,000 square kilometers in size, the United Republic of Tanzania in East Africa is bounded on the north by Burundi, Rwanda, Uganda, and Kenya; on the east by the Indian Ocean; on the south by Mozambique, Malawi, and Zambia; and on the west by Congo (formerly Zaire). Dar es Salaam is the capital of this nation of some 35.3 million persons, although there are plans to move the capital to Dodoma.

Agriculture, mining, and textiles are the major industries of Tanzania; its chief crops include sisal, coffee, cotton, and tobacco. Some international debt relief was granted by the International Monetary Fund and the World Bank in 2000, but the nation's economy is still weighed down by a heavy debt burden.

Type of Government: Presidential-style parliamentary republic, with a president, a prime minister and cabinet, a unicameral legislature, and a judiciary, including a constitutional court

Dates of Constitutions: 1965 (interim), 1977, and 1985

Home to Khoisan-speaking peoples as early as five thousand years ago, the mainland of what is today Tanzania, along with Kenya and Ethiopia, may have been the cradle of humankind. Occupied by cattle herders around 1000 B.C., the region later attracted Bantu-speaking and other diverse peoples. For many centuries traders from Persia, Arabia, India, and Portugal interacted with the native population at ports of call on the mainland and on Zanzibar.

The Portuguese left the area at the end of the seventeenth century, after which the Omani Arabs moved in. By 1840 the sultan of Oman had relocated his capital from Muscat to Zanzibar. Following his death, an international arbitration settlement declared Zanzibar to be independent from Oman. Great Britain led efforts to stop the island's involvement in slave trading, although slavery was not formally abolished in Zanzibar until 1887. Britain's competition with Germany for colonial domination of the region ended in the latter part of the nineteenth century with formal recognition by the other European powers of British interests in Zanzibar and German interests in mainland Tanzania (Tanganyika), Rwanda, and Burundi.

During World War I the British seized control of Tanganyika, and on July 22, 1922, it was named a British territory under a League of Nations mandate. After World War II it became a British trusteeship under the United Nations. Julius K. Nyerere's rise as the leader of the Tanganyika African National Union in 1954 accelerated the nation's drive toward independence.

On December 9, 1961, Tanganyika became an independent dominion of Great Britain, with Elizabeth II as head of state. A 1961 constitution, however, was replaced in 1962 when the country opted to become a republic rather than a monarchy. Zanzibar became an independent constitutional monarchy, with a sultan as its ruler, on December 10, 1963. After the ruling sultan of Zanzibar was deposed and a republic declared on January 12, 1964, Tanganyika—fearing destabilization of its island neighbor—sent in a contingent of police. The countries united on April 26, 1964, adopting the name Tanzania six months later.

On July 11, 1965, Tanzania adopted an interim constitution, which was superceded by a permanent document on April 26, 1977. In 1979 the local government of Zanzibar adopted its own constitution with respect to its internal administration. A new constitution mandating a single political-party system was approved by President Nyerere and took effect in January 1985. An amendment in 1992, however, provides for multiparty elections. While mainland Tanzania remains a model of political stability, Zanzibaris rioted during the 2000 elections, fueling speculation that the union may not be stable.

The 1985 constitution of Tanzania (particularly as amended in 1992, 1994, and 1995) is generally based on the British parliamentary system of government, although the country's president has real executive powers.

The Constitution

The preamble to the constitution of Tanzania notes that the people wish to build "a society founded on . . . freedom, justice, fraternity and concord," principles that can be realized only in a democratic environment including an executive accountable to an elected representative legislature, aided by a judiciary "which is independent and dispenses justice without fear or favor, thereby ensuring that all human rights are preserved. . . ."

"Tanzania is one State and is a sovereign United Republic," declares article 1, while article 3 provides: "The United Republic is a democratic and socialist state which adheres to multi-party democracy." (Before 1992 the constitution had proclaimed: "The Revolutionary party . . . is the only political party in the United Republic.") According to article 9, "The object of this Constitution is to facilitate the building of the United Republic as a nation of equal and free individuals enjoying freedom, justice, fraternity and concord, through the pursuit of the policy of Socialism and Self Reliance. . . ."

Fundamental Rights

"[H]uman dignity and other human rights are respected and cherished," declares article 9, which cites "the spirit of the Universal Declaration of Human Rights" (1948). "All human beings are born free, and are all equal," adds article 12. Rights guaranteed include equality before the law and freedom from discrimination; the right to life; freedom of movement, expression, religion, and association; the right to privacy and personal security; the rights to work and own property; and the right to participate in governing the nation. Article 5 extends voting rights to Tanzanian citizens eighteen years and older, but this right may be abrogated by parliament in the case of dual citizenship, mental sickness, conviction for certain crimes, and failure to prove age, citizenship, or registration.

"The human rights and freedoms . . . set out in this Constitution," states article 30, "shall not be exercised by a person in a manner that causes interference or curtailment of the rights and freedom of other persons or of the public interest." Other limitations—for example, laws and legal actions taken in accordance with the law to ensure the security and safety of the public—are also enumerated.

The constitution also sets forth citizen obligations, including the obligation to work, which, states article 25, "creates the material wealth in society and is the source of the well-being of the people and the measure of human dignity." Other duties include to obey the country's laws, to safeguard public property including natural resources, and to defend the nation. Article 25 specifies that "there shall be no forced labor in the United Republic," with certain exceptions such as "compulsory national service provided for by law."

Division of Powers

"All state authority," indicates article 4, "shall be exercised and controlled by two organs [one for Tanzania and one for Zanzibar] vested with executive powers, two organs vested with judicial powers and two organs vested with legislative and supervisory powers over the conduct of public affairs." However, the president, who heads the executive branch, is expressly made a part of parliament, as is the monarch in Great Britain. The island of Zanzibar has its own president, legislature (called the house of representatives), and judiciary.

The Executive

President. Article 33 proclaims: "There shall be a President of the United Republic [who] shall be the Head of State, the Head of Government and the Commander-in-Chief of the Armed Forces." To be qualified, a candidate must be a citizen by birth, forty years of age, nominated by a political party, and otherwise "qualified to be a Member of Parliament or a Member of the House of Representatives."

The executive "shall be elected by the people in accordance with the . . . Constitution and . . . the law" and "shall be declared duly elected President only if he has obtained more than half of all the valid votes cast"; in a runoff election, the president is elected by "more votes than any of the other candidates." The president serves essentially until parliament is dissolved, although the incumbent remains in office even following a no-confidence vote against the prime minister. "No person," however, "shall be elected more than twice." A vice president, "who shall be the principal assistant to the president in . . . all matters," is nominated and elected together with the president.

According to article 34, government authority "shall be exercised by either the President himself directly or by delegation . . . to other persons holding office in the service of the United Republic." Under article 35, "All Executive functions . . . shall be discharged by officers of the Government on behalf of the President." The president's powers include creating and abolishing offices of government; appointing, promoting, and removing persons in the civil service; declaring war; and granting pardons and commuting sentences. In the case of absence or illness, the president is empowered to "direct in writing, any Minister to discharge such functions of the office of President as the President may specify. . . ."

Although criminal proceedings against the president are barred during his or her term of office, parliament is authorized under article 46A to impeach the incumbent for the commission of "acts which generally violate the Constitution or the law concerning the ethics of public leaders; . . . [and] acts which contravene the conditions concerning the registration of political parties," as well as if the office holder "has conducted himself in a manner which lowers the esteem of the office. . . ." After a report by a special committee of inquiry, parliament may force the president to resign "by the votes of not less than [a] two-thirds majority of all the Members of Parliament."

Prime Minister and Cabinet. Appointed by the president within fourteen days of assuming office, the prime minister must be a "Member of Parliament elected from a constituency from a political party having a majority of Members in [parliament] or, if no political party has a majority, who appears to have the support of the majority. . . ." The nominee must first be "confirmed by a resolution . . . by a majority vote." The prime minister then controls, supervises, and executes "the day-to-day functions and affairs of the Government of the United Republic," serving as "the Leader of Government Business in [parliament and being] accountable to the President for the exercise of his authority."

The cabinet consists of the vice president, the president of Zanzibar, the prime minister, and all the ministers. Tanzania's president presides at meetings of the cabinet, which "shall be the principal organ for advising the President regarding the exercise of his powers. . . ." The prime minister and cabinet must resign if "a majority of the members of Parliament" vote no confidence in them.

Parliament. "There shall be a Parliament . . . which shall consist of two parts, . . . the President and the National Assembly," states article 62. The assembly comprises "members elected to represent constituencies," "women members being not less than fifteen percentum," as well as "five members elected by the [Zanzibar] House of Representatives from among its members" and the attorney general; the president and vice president are not members of parliament, with the president's role specified as being to "exercise all the authority vested in him by this Constitution for that purpose." Qualifications for members include citizenship, having reached twenty-one years of age, being able to read and write in Kiswahili or English, and nomination by a political party. Article 100 extends certain privileges and immunities to members of parliament, including freedom of opinion and debate and immunity from prosecution for "anything . . . said or done in . . . or . . . submitted to the National Assembly."

The assembly elects a speaker and a deputy from among its members and adopts "Standing Orders ... prescribing procedure for the conduct of its business." Half the members constitute a quorum, and bills passed must receive the president's assent to become law. However, if a bill is returned by the president, it generally may be sent back to the president if "supported by the votes of not less than two-thirds of all the Members of Parliament." In some cases, if the president still refuses to assent to the bill, he or she is required to dissolve the assembly.

In addition to passing bills for laws, debating the performance of ministries, and ratifying treaties, "Parliament may enact legislation for altering any provision of this Constitution ...," states article 98. The assembly is also charged with overseeing and advising "the Government ... and all its organs in the discharge of their respective responsibilities," and legislators "may ... put any question to any Minister concerning ... his responsibility." Matters not relating to the union or to mainland Tanzania are "vested in the [Zanzibar] House of Representatives."

The Judiciary

According to article 116, "'the Judiciary' means the Court of Appeal of the United Republic ..., the High Court ..., together with any other court subordinate to the High Court."

Court of Appeal. The Court of Appeal determines appeals "arising from ... [a] decision of the High Court or [other legal authority]." "The Chief Justice of the Court of Appeal [is] appointed by the President," and together with four other justices constitutes a full bench. The constitution specifically excludes jurisidiction of the court and the chief justice over disputes between "the Government of the United Republic and the Revolutionary Government of Zanzibar" or "any matter concerning the structure and administration of the day-to-day business of the courts ... of Zanzibar."

High Court. Article 108 provides for "a High Court ... the jurisdiction of which shall be as specified in this Constitution or in any other law." The court consists of a "principal judge" and at least fifteen additional judges "appointed by the President after consultation with the Judicial Service Commission." The principal judge "shall be the special assistant to the Chief Justice in the administration of the High Court and of all the other courts subordinate to it."

The court has original jurisdiction in matters "which, according to legal traditions obtaining in Tanzania, [are] ordinarily dealt with by a High Court," as well as issues that should "first be heard by a court specified for that purpose."

Constitutional Court. Article 125 creates "the Special Constitutional Court ... [whose] sole function ... is to hear and give a conciliatory decision over a matter referred to it concerning the interpretation of this Constitution ... in [a] dispute between the Government of the United Republic and the ... Government of Zanzibar." Each government appoints half the court's members. Qualifications include being or having been a member of the court of appeals or the high court of Tanzania or Zanzibar or being qualified to be appointed a judge or an acting judge. The court sits only when there is a dispute to be heard, and determinations are based on "the opinion of two-thirds of the members appointed" by each government.

Ombudsman

Article 129 creates a permanent commission of enquiry, "which shall have jurisdiction to enquire into the conduct of any person" regarding performance or abuse of authority.

Amending the Constitution

With the exception of provisions such as the republic itself, a bill to amend the constitution and basic laws, including the "whole Act of Union between Tanganyika and Zanzibar," requires a two-thirds vote of all legislators, according to article 98. Changes to the republic's existence and the number of representatives from Zanzibar require a two-thirds vote of all legislators from mainland Tanzania and two-thirds of those from Zanzibar.

The only country in Southeast Asia to remain independent throughout its history, Thailand ("land of the free") continues to be a relatively stable, prosperous nation. Nonetheless, it has had sixteen constitutions since 1932.

The Kingdom of Thailand, whose territory is approximately 514,000 square kilometers, is bounded on the west by Myanmar (formerly Burma), on the south by Malaysia and the Gulf of Thailand, and on the east by Laos and Cambodia. Bangkok, with approximately six million inhabitants, is the capital of this country of more than sixty-one million persons.

An agricultural exporter, Thailand has made great industrial progress that has led, however, to environmental and technological problems, particularly in its capital city. Thailand is a charter member of the Association of Southeast Asian Nations (ASEAN), along with Indonesia, Malaysia, the Philippines, and Singapore. Communist control in China, Laos, Cambodia, and Vietnam has had an important effect on its foreign policy, leading to strong ties with the United States.

Type of Government: Parliamentary constitutional monarchy, with a monarch, a prime minister and cabinet, a bicameral legislature, and a judiciary, including a constitutional court

Dates of Key Constitutions: 1932, 1949, 1960 (interim), 1968, 1974, 1978, 1991 (revised in 1992), and 1997

People from southern China migrated to Southeast Asia very early, and there is evidence of a twenty-thousand-year-old Paleolithic culture. Kingdoms in the area before the first millennium B.C. were recorded by the Chinese, and by the second century B.C. the Funan state had developed. The Srivijaya Empire, a confederation of maritime states, dominated Southeast Asia between the seventh and the thirteenth centuries A.D.; during this time Buddhism was adopted in the north and Islam in the south. The Thais, ancestors of Tai-speaking people from south of the Yangtze River, controlled much of the western part of the peninsula from the fifteenth century to the modern era.

Thailand's early legal system was strongly influenced by the ancient Hindu jurisprudence found in the Code of Manu, which was later harmonized with the principles of the state religion of Buddhism and called the Dhammasattham. Beginning in the fourteenth century this body of law, based on the concepts of individual freedom and private rights in both criminal and civil matters, developed alongside the jurisprudence based on decisions made by Thai rulers in disputes.

In the fifteenth century King Baroma Trailokanat is believed to have begun defining an individual's status under the law based on the amount of land he or she possessed; the higher the status, the more severe would be the penalty for wrongdoing. In 1805 Thai law was codified into the Law of the Three Great Seals. Later, concepts from English law were adopted in the areas of commercial activities, bankruptcy, and bills of exchange, while a general law reform adopted the idea of codified laws based on the Roman model.

A series of enlightened absolute monarchs and a bloodless revolution in 1932 led to the introduction of a democratic constitutional form of government. After a coup in 1947 the country's name was changed from Siam back to Thailand, and a new constitution was promulgated in 1949. In 1960 an interim constitution was decreed by those who had taken control of the government. A new constitution was adopted in 1968, but martial law, imposed in 1958, remained in effect. A 1972 interim constitution provided for an appointed legislative assembly, but a new document in 1974 called for an elected lower house of the legislature. In 1978 a constitution provided for a parliamentary form of government with the king as the titular head. The current constitution was approved on December 7 and published on December 9, 1991, or year 2534 of the Buddhist era, and was revised on June 10, 1992, to reduce the powers of a military-dominated upper house of the legislature and ensure that the prime minister would be selected from the elected lower house.

After another revision to the 1991 constitution in 1995, a constitutional assembly drafted a new document that went into effect on October 11, 1997. Its adoption helped the new administration stabilize Thailand's failing economy and start the country on the road to recovery.

Influences

Thai constitutions have generally been influenced by the British parliamentary model. The 1997 constitution contains a number of departures, however, including the requirement that the prime minister and cabinet members must resign from the lower house of the legislature after their appointment and the creation of an independent administrative judicial system similar to the French model.

The Constitution

The preamble to the 1997 constitution of Thailand ends by calling on the Thai people to "unite in observing, protecting and upholding the Constitution ... in order to maintain the democratic regime of government ... and to bring about happiness, prosperity, and dignity to His Majesty's subjects ... according to the will of His Majesty in every respect."

Sections 1 and 2 declare that "Thailand is a unified and indivisible Kingdom [that] adopts a democratic regime of government with the King as Head of the State." Adds section 3: "The sovereign power belongs to the Thai people." Section 6 makes the constitution "the supreme law of the State."

Fundamental Rights

Section 4 mandates that the "human dignity, right and liberty of the people shall be protected," while section 5 states that the "Thai people, irrespective of their origins, sexes or religions, shall enjoy equal protection under this Constitution." Rights and liberties are detailed in sections 30 through 65. They encompass equality before the law; equal protection under the law for both men and women; a prohibition against discrimination on the basis of "origin, race, language, sex, age, physical or health condition, personal status, economic or social standing, religious belief, education, or ... political view"; a ban on "torture ... or punishment by a cruel or inhumane means"; family rights; privacy; and "liberty of dwelling," travel, and communication. Also specified are "full liberty to profess a religion"; "to express [an] opinion, make speeches, write, [and] print"; "academic freedom"; free, fundamental education for twelve years; peaceful assembly without arms; association; the rights to access and receive information; and private property rights. Children, persons over sixty and in need, and the disabled are extended special protection, as are consumers. In addition to the presumption of innocence guaranteed in section 33, a number of rights of those accused of crimes—including the requirement of a court order or a warrant for an arrest and the right to consult with legal counsel—are set forth in sections 237 to 247.

Division of Powers

According to section 3, "The King as Head of the State shall exercise [the sovereign power of the Thai people] through the National Assembly [legislature], the Council of Ministers and the Courts in accordance with the provisions of this Constitution."

The Executive

Monarch. "The King shall be enthroned in a position of revered worship and shall not be violated," proclaims section 8, adding: "No person shall expose the King to any sort of accusation or action." The monarch "is a Buddhist and upholder of religions," as well as "Head of the Thai Armed Forces." Succession to the throne is governed by the Palace Law on Succession, which may be amended by the king. He appoints the president and not more than eighteen members of the privy council that advises him. Among the king's other powers are appointing the prime minister and a cabinet of up to thirty-five ministers, appointing and removing a minister on the advice of the prime minister, issuing emergency decrees with the force of law, declaring and lifting martial law with the legislature's approval, appointing and removing high military and civil service officials, and granting pardons. The king may also "create titles and confer decorations," as well as remove and recall them.

Prime Minister and Cabinet. Under section 201, the prime minister and the council of ministers (cabinet) "carry out the administration of the State affairs." The prime minister must be or have been a member of the lower house of the legislature and must be endorsed by at least one-fifth of its total membership and approved by more than one-half of them. Section 204 mandates: "No Prime Minister and Ministers shall be members of the [upper or lower houses] simultaneously," and they must resign from the lower house after their appointment by the king.

Ministers are individually responsible to the lower house for the performance of their duties and collectively to the legislature for the cabinet's general policies. They must vacate their office on the termination of the prime minister, the expiration of the term or the dissolution of the lower house, the cabinet's resignation, or the demand of the king.

Parliament. "The National Assembly consists of the House of Representatives [lower house] and the Senate [upper house]," and they may hold joint and separate sittings "in accordance with the provisions of this Constitution," states section 90.

The Legislature

Upper House. The senate consists of 200 members elected for six years "by direct suffrage and secret ballot" from *Changwats* (constituencies). The number of senators from each constituency is determined by a formula similar to one set forth in section 102 for the lower house. Qualifications are also similar to those for the lower house, except that the age requirement is forty years and a candidate may not be a member of a political party and "a Senator … during the term … preceding the application for the candidacy."

Lower House. Of the 500 members of the house of representatives, 100 are elected on a party-list basis and 400 are elected on a constituency basis. In the first case, "a voter [may vote for] the lists of candidates prepared by political parties." In the second case, voters "shall cast a ballot for one candidate in each constituency." A candidate must be Thai by birth, be at least twenty-five years of age, have a bachelor's degree or its equivalent (except for former legislators), be a member of a political party, and, if running from a constituency, meet other criteria for election from that area.

The upper and lower houses, as section 151 instructs, each have a president and one or two vice presidents, who are appointed by the king from their membership in accordance with legislative resolutions. A resolution requires a majority of votes, while a quorum for conducting business is generally "not less than one-half of the total existing members of each House." Certain privileges and immunities are extended to legislators, including immunity from arrest and detention, except in the case of arrest "in *flagrante delicto*," and even in such cases the president of the house of the member involved "may order the release of the person so arrested."

Bills involving revenues require endorsement by the prime minister, but other legislative proposals may be introduced by members of the lower house or the cabinet. After approval by the lower house, bills must be approved by the senate, signed or deemed signed by the king, and countersigned by the prime minister. As part of their government oversight responsibilities, members of both houses may "interpellate [question] a Minister on any matter within the scope of his or her authority."

Ombudsman	Section 196 authorizes up to three ombudsmen—appointed by the king on the advice of the senate for one six-year term—who investigate complaints regarding the actions of government officials and agencies and report back to the legislature.
The Judiciary	"All Courts," according to section 234, "may be established only by Acts [law]." Judges, who are appointed and removed by the king, "are independent," and "trial and adjudication [by] the Courts ... must proceed in accordance with the Constitution and the law and in the name of the King." In addition to courts of justice, administrative and military courts and a constitutional court are provided for.

Supreme Court. Although the constitution provides little detail on the supreme court itself, article 272 calls for courts of first instance, a court of appeals, and a supreme court, which includes a criminal division for persons holding political positions. Other courts of justice are administratively responsible to the president of the supreme court.

Constitutional Court. The constitutional court, states section 255, "consists of the President and fourteen judges ... to be appointed [for a single nine-year term] by the King upon advice of the Senate." Its basic function is to rule on the constitutionality of proposed laws. Seven members are named from judges sitting on the major courts and eight from nominees with special qualifications recommended by a selection committee and elected by the senate.

Amending the Constitution	Under section 313, a motion for a constitutional amendment may be proposed by the cabinet or, with the concurrence of the members' political parties, by at least one-fifth of the members of the lower house or both houses of the legislature. The measure is considered in three readings, with the first vote requiring not less than one-half of the members of both houses, the second a simple majority, and the third one-half of the members of both houses. Once approved, an amendment is presented to the king, who may sign it or return it as with any other bill. The proposed amendment may be passed again by the legislature by a vote of not less than two-thirds of the members of both houses and promulgated by the king or, if he refuses, by the prime minister.

Tibetans, who live in what is often called the "Roof of the World," have been seeking independence from China since 1951. The Tibetan government in exile—led by the Dalai Lama—has drafted several proposed constitutions to promote the movement to achieve the right of self-determination.

General Information

Tibet, or the Autonomous Region of Xizang (Tibet) in the People's Republic of China, occupies some 1.22 million square kilometers in central Asia and is bounded on the north and east by China and on the south and west by Myanmar (formerly Burma), India, Bhutan, and Nepal. Lhasa is the capital of this land of approximately 2.5 million persons.

Tibetans live in some of the world's highest terrain, including the northern side of Mount Everest, and generally practice relatively primitive agriculture. The region's industries include forestry, hydroelectric power, and handicrafts; among its key agricultural products are barley, wheat, rice, and yak butter. Its economy remains relatively undeveloped, although rich mineral resources—including gold, borax, radium, iron, titanium, and lead—have been discovered.

Type of Government (proposed): Theocratic Buddhist federal republic, with a religious leader, a prime minister and council of ministers (cabinet), a unicameral legislature, and a judiciary

Dates of Constitutions: Under China: 1954, 1975, 1978, and 1982. Government in exile: 1961, 1963, and 1991

Constitutional History

There is evidence of a civilization in the region that is now called Tibet at least four thousand years ago. Chinese records mention the Ch'iang tribe living in the region in 200 B.C., and a Tibetan kingdom flourished there between the seventh and ninth centuries A.D. Buddhism began playing an important role in Tibet's development in the seventh century. Between 1207 and 1368 Tibet was ruled by the Mongols, and in 1642 the Buddhist religious leader called the Dalai Lama became both a spiritual and a political authority. Chinese influence increased after the Manzhou (Manchu) dynasty helped Tibet repulse another Mongol invasion in 1720.

China effectively dominated Tibet from the eighteenth century until the collapse of the Qing dynasty in 1911. Tibet was also influenced by India and Great Britain from the nineteenth century until India's independence in 1947. China regained control by military force in 1951, and a rebellion crushed by Chinese troops in 1959 led the Dali Lama and about 100,000 other Buddhists to flee to India. Since then Tibetans both inside, through demonstrations, and outside, through constant appeals for international support by the Dalai Lama in exile, have worked for the region's independence.

An autonomous region in the People's Republic of China since 1965, Tibet is subject to the constitution of China. However, the current Dalai Lama sponsored draft constitutions in 1961 and 1963 for a future independent Tibet. In 1991 the Tibetan government in exile drafted another proposed constitution that reflects aspirations for a government instituted by Tibetans based on the universally accepted right of self-determination. The Dalai Lama has expressed the hope that Tibetan democracy one day "will derive its inspiration from the Buddhist principles of compassion, justice, and equality" and that Tibet will become a "zone of peace where environmental protection becomes the official policy."

Influences

The 1991 draft constitution of the Tibetan government in exile generally follows the form of a parliamentary government; however, unlike constitutions such as those of Nepal and Thailand that recognize the divine nature of the monarchical head of state, the Tibetan document elevates its spiritual leader, the Dalai Lama, to the position of head of state.

The Constitution

In its proposed constitution, officially named the Charter of the Tibetans in Exile, the Eleventh Assembly of Tibetan People's Deputies observes that

His Holiness the Dalai Lama has offered a democratic system to Tibetans, in order that the Tibetan People in Exile be able to preserve their ancient traditions of spiritual and temporal life, unique to the Tibetans, based on the principles of peace and non-violence, aimed at providing political, social and economic rights as well as the attainment of justice and equality for all Tibetan people.

[E]fforts shall be made to transform a future Tibet into a Federal Democratic Self-Governing Republic and a zone of peace throughout her three regions.

[E]fforts shall be made in promoting the achievement of Tibet's common goal as well as to strengthen the solidarity of Tibetans, both within and out of Tibet, and to firmly establish a democratic system, suitable to the temporary ideals of the Tibetan people. . . .

Article 1 indicates that after having been passed by the Assembly of Tibetan People's Deputies (the government in exile), the charter "shall come into force on the day appointed by His Holiness the Dalai Lama." According to article 2, it is "binding and enforceable" for all Tibetans "under the jurisdiction of the Tibetan Administration in Exile."

Article 3 declares: "The future Tibetan polity shall uphold the principle of non-violence and shall endeavor to be a Free Social Welfare State with its politics guided by the Dharma [the "ultimate law of all things" in the Hindu and Buddhist religions], a Federal Democratic Republic; and the polity of the Tibetan Administration in Exile shall conform to the provisions hereinafter specified."

Fundamental Rights

"It shall be the duty of the Tibetan administration," mandates article 4, "to adhere to the principles of the Universal Declaration of Human Rights [1948] as specified by the United Nations, and to also urge and encourage all other countries of the world to respect and comply with such Declarations. . . ." The policy of nonviolence is underscored in article 7, which states:

Future Tibet shall remain a zone of peace and shall strive to disengage itself in the production of all destructive weapons, including Nuclear and Chemical; and, currently refrain from the use of all offensive methods as a means to achieve the common goal of Tibet, or for any other purpose.

Rights extended in articles 9 through 12 include equality before the law, the right to vote and be a candidate for office, and freedom of thought, conscience, and religion, including that "[a]ll religious denominations are equal before the law." Among other rights guaranteed are the right "to life, liberty and property"; freedom of speech and expression; freedom of movement; freedom of the press; peaceful assembly "without arms"; freedom of association; and the right to practice a profession or trade, "including acquisition of land and property." Children below the age of fourteen years would be barred from manual labor. Under article 12, persons "charged and required to appear before a court of law [are entitled] to obtain financial assistance, and acquire an interpreter." Tibetans are expressly granted the "right to approach the Tibetan Supreme Justice Commission and all Tibetan Local Justice Commissions in the event of violations of rights and duties."

The obligations of citizens set forth in article 13 include to "bear true allegiance to Tibet" and to "faithfully comply [with] and observe the Charter and the laws enshrined therein"; they are also called on to "perform such obligations as may be imposed by law in the event of a threat to the interest of Tibet, or other public catastrophe."

Articles 15 through 18 set out "directive principles" for social welfare. "The primary aim of the Tibetan Administration in Exile," states article 15, "shall be to endeavor to maintain a just policy for the achievement of the common goal of Tibet, and in addition, at the present moment, protect Tibetans in Tibet from present hardships and danger." Succeeding articles address means of achieving social welfare (including cottage and home industries "to prevent Tibetan settlements and communities from disintegration"), providing education (including "games and athletic sports"), protecting Tibetan culture (including "those aspects of Tibetan arts and sciences which are on the verge of extinction"), promoting health (including "ancient astro-medical sciences"), and supporting "equal opportunity for the economic development of Tibetans in exile."

The charter divides powers among executive, legislative, and judicial branches.

Division of Powers

Dalai Lama. "The executive power," declares article 19, "shall be vested in His Holiness the Dalai Lama, and shall be exercised by Him, either directly or through officers subordinate to Him, in accordance with the provisions of this Charter." Article 20 directs the creation of "a Kashag [council of ministers] and a Chief Kalon [minister] primarily responsible for exercising executive powers ... subordinate to His Holiness the Dalai Lama."

The Executive

The executive powers of the Dalai Lama include approving and promulgating bills and regulations passed by the legislature; promulgating acts and ordinances with the effect of law; conferring honors; summoning, adjourning, and dissolving the legislature; dissolving the Kashag and removing any minister; and authorizing "referendums in cases involving major issues in accordance with this Charter."

Prime Minister and Cabinet. According to article 21, the Kashag (cabinet) "shall consist of seven Kalons [ministers] ... elected by the [legislature] ... by ... secret ballot." Qualifications much like those for legislators are set out, including a minimum age of thirty-five years. A chief minister is elected from among the council's members, also by secret ballot. The Kashag's tenure is five years.

Meetings are presided over by the Dalai Lama or, in his absence, by the chief minister. The Kashag is "exclusively responsible for the expeditious execution of resolutions passed" and is "collectively ... and in general ... accountable and answerable" to the legislature, where ministers "have the right to take part in debate, discussion and submit any explanation...." In the event that "the elected Kalons are so few that they are unable to discharge their responsibilities properly, then the Kashag may approach the Tibetan Assembly, whereupon the matter may be submitted to His Holiness the Dalai Lama, and following His assent, the vacancies for the remaining positions of Kalons within the Kashag may be elected by the Tibetan Assembly."

Council of Regency. "The Council of Regency," states article 31, "shall exercise executive powers and authority ... at such time [among others] as His Holiness the Dalai Lama has not assumed or retained the powers of the head of the Tibetan Administration ...; [or] when the Tibetan Assembly, by more than two-thirds of its total members in consultation with the Tibetan Supreme Justice Commission, decides that ... it is imperative that the executive functions ... be exercised by the Council of Regency." This three-member body is elected jointly by the Kashag and the Tibetan Assembly by secret ballot and is headed by a chief regent.

Parliament. Under article 36, "All legislative power and authority shall rest in the Tibetan Assembly, and such legislation shall require the assent of His Holiness the Dalai Lama to become law." The legislature consists of ten members elected for five-year terms from each of the three regions of Tibet, including at least two women from each region. Also specified are two members "from each religious denomination: Nyingma, Kagyud, Sakya, Geluk and Yungdrung Bon; 1 to 3 members directly nominated by His Holiness the Dalai Lama; 1 member elected by Tibetans residing in Canada and the United States of America; [and]

The Legislature

2 members elected by Tibetans residing in European countries." Members, among other qualifications, must be citizens of Tibet, at least twenty-five years of age, not declared mentally unsound or bankrupt, free of criminal conviction, and not a member or beneficiary of the Tibetan civil service.

Assembly members elect a speaker and a deputy speaker and are granted certain immunities "for any statements made or voting procedures." A permanent secretary-general and staff provide administrative support. Regular sessions are called by the Dalai Lama and must be held no less than six months apart. Two-thirds of the total number of members constitute a quorum, and in general "all business of the . . . Assembly shall be determined by a majority vote," with the speaker casting tie-breaking votes.

According to article 51, the legislature or any of its members "is entitled to introduce any bill or legislation," except for certain tax measures that require a recommendation from the council of ministers. The assembly is also permitted under article 52 to discuss the annual budget, which is submitted by the council of ministers, but it may not vote to approve or reject it except for certain subsidiary expenditures. Article 54 bars discussion in the assembly "with respect to the conduct of the Chief Tibetan Justice Commissioner" unless a recommendation has been made to remove the incumbent. Bills passed become law once they are assented to within fourteen working days by the Dalai Lama, who is further empowered to promulgate laws in consultation with the assembly's standing committee if the legislature is not in session.

The Judiciary

The charter provides for a "supreme justice commission" to serve as Tibet's supreme court, and it may "from time to time" authorize a Tibetan person to act as a "Circuit Tibetan Local Justice Commissioner," aided by a panel of judges. A judicial administrative office is designated to serve as the judiciary's secretariat.

Supreme Court. "There shall be a Tibetan Supreme Justice Commission vested with judicial powers suitable to the temporary and special needs of the Tibetan administration and citizens in exile," states article 62. "It shall consist of a Chief Tibetan Justice Commissioner until such time as the Tibetan Assembly passes a resolution demanding the appointment of additional Justice Commissioners of law." The commission "shall be the supreme appellate court regarding legal issues involving individuals and public institutions of the Tibetans in exile. It shall be the highest judicial authority of the Tibetan Administration."

The chief justice commissioner is named by the Dalai Lama and must be approved by more than two-thirds of the legislators. Nominees are required to have five years of legal experience or to have been licensed for ten years. Article 64 allows for a permanent jury of three citizens (at least two of them having law degrees) to assist with judicial proceedings. They are appointed by the chief justice commissioner in consultation with the council of ministers and serve for three years.

Article 5 empowers the justice commission to decide the legality of laws and other measures vis-a-vis the constitution, while article 66 sets forth other responsibilities, including inquiring into "cases involving the conduct of business of the executive department" and "disputes involving land and property of the Tibetan settlements."

Amending the Constitution

According to articles 111 and 112, amendments to the charter may generally be made by an act passed by more than two-thirds of the total members of the Tibetan Assembly and assented to by the Dalai Lama, who "may, if He thinks fit, direct that . . . the [proposed] amendment . . . be submitted for a referendum." In this case the amendment requires approval "by more than two-thirds of the total number of Tibetan citizens qualified to vote.

By an overwhelming vote, the people of Turkey in 1982 adopted a new constitution that strengthens presidential authority and confirms the ideals of Mustafa Kemal Atatürk, the father of modern Turkey.

The Republic of Turkey is approximately 780,000 square kilometers and is bounded on the north by the Black Sea; on the south by the Mediterranean Sea, Syria, and Iraq; on the west by the Aegean Sea, Greece, and Bulgaria; and on the east by Georgia, Armenia, and Iran. About three percent of the country's territory and approximately eight percent of its 65.7 million persons are located across the Sea of Marmara in European Turkey, and a significant minority population lives on the partitioned island of Cyprus. Ankara is the capital.

Although not without its problems, the Turkish economy has generally been strong. Turkey is a predominantly Sunni Muslim, Turkish-speaking land, but other religious and ethnic groups, such as the Alevis and Kurds, make up about ten percent of the population. To date Turkey has been able to maintain a secular government and political system in the midst of a strongly Islamic society.

Type of Government: Presidential-style parliamentary republic, with a president, a prime minister and council of ministers (cabinet), a unicameral legislature, and a judiciary, including a constitutional court

Dates of Constitutions: 1876 (abrogated in 1878 and restored in 1908), 1921, 1924, 1961, and 1982

Anatolia, as the Greeks called that portion of the Byzantine Empire taken by the Turks in the eleventh century A.D., may have been the site of the world's first urban settlement. In the eighth century B.C., however, the Huns became the first Turkish tribe to settle in the land of Troy. In the sixth century A.D. the Gokturks moved in, followed shortly by the Uygurs.

The Seljuk Empire, established in the eleventh century, was influenced by Persian intellectuals and administrators. After the fall of the Byzantine capital of Constantinople (now Istanbul) in 1453, the Ottoman Empire held the territory until after World War I. During this period, government administration was completely integrated with the Islamic religion; the codified Islamic system of justice *(shari'a)*, together with the sultan as absolute monarch and God's representative on earth, constituted the source of all law. In addition to the Qur'an, other guidelines based on custom and derived from the sayings and behavior of Muhammad and his companions (Sunna) came to be used as sources of *shari'a*. (After 1923 the legal system was reformed along European lines to conform to the ideals and goals of Mustafa Kemal Atatürk ("Father Turk"), Turkey's president from 1923 to 1938.)

Toward the end of the eighteenth century an advisory assembly of the sultan's, the Meclis-i-Meshveret, was created. In 1808 the sultan's power was limited by a charter of alliance, which also delegated some authority to a body called the Ayan. Unilateral declarations by the sultan such as the rescripts of Tanzimat in 1839 and of Islahat in 1856 established other reforms, including an extension of basic human rights. Further reforms culminated in a 1876 constitution, which included basic rights for the people, independence for the judiciary, and a parliamentary system of government. Absolute rule was reestablished in 1878, but the constitution was restored in 1908. After its defeat in World War I the Ottoman Empire collapsed and the country was occupied by troops of the victors.

On January 20, 1921, an elected assembly adopted a radically different constitution that vested legislative power in a parliament and executive power in an executive council elected from the members of the parliament, similar to the present Swiss model. This system of government, which had no head of state, was modified a year after the parliament established the Republic of Turkey on October 29, 1923, but a 1924 constitution retained the main features of the previous document. A new constitution adopted in 1961 proved ineffective, and political instability and civil violence led to intervention by the Turkish military in 1971 and 1980.

The present constitution, approved by 91.4 percent of the voters and promulgated on November 9, 1982, attempts to prevent a recurrence of the previous government instability and civil unrest by expanding the role of the president and to some extent limiting the rights of individuals and associations that could undermine unity and security. While retaining the basic structure of government of its predecessor, the 1982 constitution also abolished the upper house of the legislature. An amendment in 1995 lowered the voting age from twenty to eighteen years of age.

Influences

The 1924 constitution was influenced by French democratic principles. Atatürk's reforms have had an impact on Turkey's constitutional development since the 1920s.

The Constitution

The preamble to the constitution of the Republic of Turkey, as amended in 1995, contains a recital of its history and the ideals it embraces, including specific reference to Atatürk as the founder of the republic, his concepts of nationalism, and the admonition that "no thought or consideration contrary to the Turkish national interests, the principle of indivisible integrity of the Turkish existence with its state and territory, Turkish historical and moral values, and the nationalism, principles and reforms and modernization of Atatürk can be protected. . . ."

Article 2 declares that "the Republic of Turkey is a democratic, secular and social state governed by the rule of law; bearing in mind the concepts of public peace, national solidarity and justice; respecting human rights; loyal to the nationalism of Atatürk, and based on the fundamental tenets set forth in the preamble."

Fundamental Rights

Fundamental rights and freedoms apply to Turkish citizens. The rights and freedoms applicable to foreigners are to be determined by reference to international law.

Article 12 states: "Everyone possesses inherent fundamental rights and freedoms which are inviolable and inalienable. The fundamental rights and freedoms also include duties and responsibilities of the individual toward society, his family and other individuals." Following this article are restrictions, prohibitions of abuse, and conditions for suspension of fundamental rights and freedoms.

Citizens are granted the right to life; the right to protect and develop the material and spiritual entity of the individual; the right to personal liberty, security, and privacy of individual and family life and of domicile; and freedom of communication, residence, movement, religion, conscience, thought, opinion, expression, science, the arts, the press, assembly, and association. The right of property ownership and procedural rights in court are also guaranteed. The constitution establishes and defines social and economic rights and duties, such as protection of the family and the right and duty of training and education, and political rights and duties, such as the right to vote, to be elected, to engage in political activity independently or in a political party, and to take part in a referendum.

Division of Powers

Turkey is a unitary state, in which power is divided among the president, as head of state; the prime minister, as head of government; the legislature; the courts, which include a constitutional court that exercises limited constitutional review.

The Executive

President. The president of the republic is elected for a seven-year term by a two-thirds majority vote of the total members of the legislature and by secret ballot. Candidates may be selected from those members of the legislature who are at least forty years old and have completed their higher education, or from among other Turkish citizens who fulfill these requirements and are otherwise eligible to be members of the legislature. The nomination of a candidate who is not a legislator requires a written proposal by at least one-fifth of the members. A president may not be reelected. If he or she is a member of a political party, relations with the party, as well as membership in the legislature, must cease.

As head of state, the president represents the country and the unity of the nation and ensures the implementation of the constitution and the regular and harmonious functioning of the government. The president's duties include delivering the opening address each year to the legislature, if he or she deems it necessary; summoning the legislature to meet, when necessary; promulgating laws; returning laws to the legislature for reconsideration; submitting proposed amendments for referendum, if he or she deems it necessary; submitting appeals to the constitutional court on questions of the constitutionality of laws, decrees, and procedures of the parliament; and calling new parliamentary elections.

The president also appoints the prime minister and accepts his or her resignation; appoints and dismisses ministers as proposed by the prime minister; presides over the council of ministers and calls it to meet whenever he or she deems it necessary; accredits and receives diplomats; ratifies and promulgates international treaties; represents the office of commander in chief on behalf of the legislature and appoints the chief of the general staff; presides over the national security council and calls it to meet; proclaims a state of martial law or emergency and issues decrees having the force of law in accordance with decisions of the council of ministers; signs decrees; remits sentences; appoints the chairman and members of the state supervisory council and instructs it to carry out inquiries, investigations, and inspections; and appoints members of the higher education council and rectors of universities.

The president's powers and duties also include appointing high officials of the government, including members of the constitutional court, one-fourth of the members of the council of state, and the chief and the deputy chief public prosecutor of the high court of appeals.

Decrees of the president, with some exceptions, must be countersigned by the prime minister and the appropriate minister, who will be accountable for the decrees. Decrees signed only by the president may not be questioned by any court.

The president may be impeached for high treason on the proposal of at least one-third of the members of the legislature and a decision of at least three-fourths of the total number of members.

Prime Minister and Cabinet. The council of ministers (cabinet) is composed of the prime minister, who is appointed by the president from among the members of the legislature, and other ministers, who are nominated by the prime minister from among the members of the legislature or those eligible to be elected to that body and who are appointed by the president. A majority of the members of the legislature present must give the new government program as presented to them and the council a vote of confidence after it is formed, and votes of confidence may be requested later by the prime minister.

The prime minister, as chairman of the council of ministers, ensures the ministers' cooperation and the exercise of their functions in accordance with the constitution and the laws and supervises implementation of the government's general policy.

Members of the council of ministers are jointly responsible for the implementation of this policy. Each minister is individually responsible to the prime minister and also responsible for the conduct of affairs under his or her jurisdiction and for the acts and activities of subordinates.

Parliament. By amendment in 1987, the unicameral parliament called the Türkiye Büyük Millet Meclisi (grand national assembly) is composed of 550 deputies elected by universal suffrage for five-year terms, unless the assembly or the president, in accordance with provisions of the constitution, decides to hold elections sooner.

The Legislature

Article 76 states that every Turk over the age of thirty is eligible to be elected a deputy; however, a number of limitations and disqualifications are enumerated. Article 79 requires elections to be held under the general supervision of judicial bodies, and a supreme election council, whose decisions are unreviewable, is established to ensure orderly and fair elections.

Deputies must represent the entire nation, not just their own constituencies, and they are prohibited from holding positions that might pose a conflict of interest. As in Thailand, political parties are expressly referred to in the constitution, and switching parties, as well as other activities, may result in expulsion after an absolute majority vote.

The basic functions and powers of the assembly are set forth in article 87:

The functions and powers of the Turkish Grand National Assembly comprise the enactment, amendment, and the repeal of laws; the supervision of the council of ministers and the ministers; authorization of the council of ministers to issue governmental decrees having force of law on certain matters; debating and approval of the budget draft and the draft law of the final accounts; making decisions regarding printing of currency and declaration of war; ratifying international agreements; deciding on the proclamation of amnesties and pardons excluding those who have been convicted for activities set out in article 14 [Prohibition of Abuse of Fundamental Rights and Freedoms] of the constitution; confirming death sentences passed by the courts; and exercising the powers and executing the functions envisaged in the other articles of the constitution.

Bills may be introduced by the council of ministers and members of the assembly. The rules for drafting bills and debating measures are to be established by the assembly. The assembly may authorize the council of ministers to issue decrees having the force of law, but these decrees may not infringe certain fundamental or individual rights or duties established by the constitution.

The constitution requires that international treaties and other agreements of more than one year in duration be adopted by the assembly. According to article 90, "International agreements duly put into effect carry the force of law. No appeal to the constitutional court can be made with regard to these agreements on the ground that they are unconstitutional."

The constitution gives the assembly the authority to supervise the government through interpellation, or questioning the prime minister and other ministers; and it may also act on the request of one-tenth of the members to formally investigate matters concerning the prime minister or other ministers. Under article 100 political parties are forbidden to discuss or make decisions relating to an investigation.

The Judiciary

With a few major exceptions the organization and procedures of the courts are to be regulated by law, and generally court hearings must be open to the public.

According to article 154, the high court of appeals has final review of decisions by the courts of justice that are not referred by law to another judicial authority. In addition to judicial or criminal courts, there are courts of the security of the state, which handle crimes against the state; courts of military justice, including the military high court of appeals; a high military administrative court of appeals, which is a court of first and last instance for the judicial supervision of disputes arising from administrative acts and actions relating to military personnel or service, even if carried out by civilians; the council of state, which both advises the government and rules on administrative and tax cases; an audit court, which acts as the watchdog for the parliament with respect to the budget, revenue, expenditures, and government property; and the constitutional court.

The judiciary is declared to be independent, and all government authorities are directed to comply with court decisions. Judges and prosecutors serve until the retirement age of sixty-five and are supervised by a supreme judicial council of judges and prosecutors, chaired by the minister of justice.

Constitutional Court. A constitutional court was established in 1961 to ensure that laws conform to the constitution. It decides on certain specific questions regarding the unconstitutionality of laws. The court consists of eleven members and four substitutes. The constitutional court also tries the president of the republic or other high officials for offenses relating to their functions.

One-third of the members of the legislature may propose, in writing, a constitutional amendment, which must be debated twice in plenary session and adopted by secret ballot by a three-fifths majority of all the members. If the president returns the amendment for reconsideration and the assembly adopts it by a two-thirds majority, the president may call for a referendum. If it "is adopted by a three-fifths vote or less than a two-thirds majority of the total votes" of the legislature and is not referred by the president for further consideration, then it must be submitted to a referendum.

Amending the Constitution

UGANDA

Recognizing the country's history of unconstitutional military dictatorships, Uganda's 1995 constitution expressly prohibits anyone from taking control of the government by other than constitutional transitions of power. Multiparty politics, however, have been put "on probation" until sometime in the future.

General Information

The Republic of Uganda in central East Africa is approximately 236,000 square kilometers and is bounded on the east by Kenya, on the southeast by Lake Victoria, on the south by Tanzania and Rwanda, on the west by Zaire, and on the north by Sudan. Kampala is the capital of this country of twenty-three million persons.

Although Uganda is relatively rich in natural resources, nearly all its export revenue comes from agriculture, including coffee, cotton, tea, and tobacco. Since gaining independence in 1962, the country has endured almost continuous tribal strife and a sharply declining economy. Its future depends partly on reducing the size of its army without creating civil unrest.

Type of Government: Presidential parliamentary republic, with a president and cabinet, a unicameral legislature, and a judiciary, including a constitutional court

Dates of Constitutions: 1955, 1962 (suspended in 1966), 1967, 1992 (draft), and 1995

Constitutional History

Shortly after the fourth century B.C. Bantu-speaking people who could smelt iron inhabited the Great Rift Valley and the Lake Victoria Basin in central Africa. In small groups they were content to be governed by clan chiefs, but by around A.D. 1000 larger statelike arrangements were formed, some having more than one million people. Herders from the north, seeking better pasture land, soon formed an elite, allowing local farmers to tend their herds in exchange for manure for the overfarmed fields. The first of these pastoral ruling groups, which appeared around the fifteenth century, was the Chwezi, who were probably the ancestors of the Watusi in Rwanda and Burundi. They were followed by the Bito.

Three distinct political systems evolved: the Hima caste system; the Bunyoro royal clan system, which claimed a political monopoly; and the Buganda kingship system, in which all clans were eligible for the kingship, because all the clans provided the king with wives, one of whose sons would then be selected by the clan elders to replace the king *(kabaka)* when he died.

With the rise of the ivory trade in the mid-nineteenth century, the area's isolation ended. The British contended with the Germans for control, and missionaries contended with one another for souls. In 1894 a British protectorate was established, and the Baganda (the people of Buganda) were made administrators to collect taxes throughout the jurisdiction. In 1902 a special commissioner was invested with executive, legislative, and judicial powers, although a British-style high court of Uganda and an appeals court for all eastern African protectorates were also set up. An attempt was made to rule indirectly through the *kabakas*, with succession being determined by an assembly of chiefs (*Lukiiko*). In 1955, pursuant to a British law, a constitutional monarchy was created with a ministerial government. Political parties were formed, and direct elections were held in 1957.

Uganda became an independent British Commonwealth nation on October 9, 1962, with Kabaka Mutesa II its first elected president under a constitution that gave the Buganda kingdom supremacy over the three other kingdoms—Ankole, Toro, and Bunyoro—which were called federal states. The prime minister, Milton Obote, suspended the constitution in 1966 and directed the parliament to approve an interim document. A new constitution on September 8, 1967, created a more centralized system, with the president to be elected by the parliament. Later, one-party rule was installed, and a state of emergency was declared.

In 1971 Maj. Gen. Idi Amin Dada seized power and began issuing constitutional decrees, such as one in 1972 authorizing the military police to shoot people who held political meetings at night. After being attacked by Amin's army, Tanzanian forces took Kampala in April 1979, but the dictator escaped into exile. Obote was declared the winner of an election for president but was ousted by the military in 1985. A national resistance council began ruling in consultation with a national resistance army council, as portions of the 1967 constitution had been suspended.

Although the military rulers have continually postponed action on a new constitution and a return to multiparty elections and civilian government, a draft constitution was prepared by a constitutional commission and presented to the government in December 1992. In 1993 a presidential commission recommended postponing multiparty democracy until the year 2000. Elections for a constituent assembly that could draft a new constitution, however, took place in March 1994. The constitutional assembly promulgated a new constitution on September 27, 1995.

The 1995 constitution extends and expands on the 1967 document and the 1992 constitutional commission's draft constitution. The constitutions of Bangladesh, India, and Sri Lanka provided examples for the inclusion of an even more extensive list of national objectives and principles of state policy, making Uganda's new constitution similar in this regard to the constitution of Nigeria, for example.

The preamble to the 1995 constitution of Uganda begins by "[r]ecalling our history [of] ... political and constitutional instability [and] [r]ecognizing our struggles against the forces of tyranny, oppression and exploitation." It adds that the new constitution is "based on the principles of unity, peace, equality, democracy, social justice and progress...."

Following is a long introduction presenting goals and guidelines entitled "National Objectives and Directive Principles of State Policy." Outlined under the heading "Political Objectives" are subsections on democratic principles, national unity and stability, and national sovereignty, independence, and territorial integrity. Other major topics covered are protection and promotion of human rights, social and economic objectives, cultural objectives, accountability, the environment, foreign policy objectives, and citizen duties.

Article 1 proclaims: "All power belongs to the people ... [and they] shall express their will and consent on who shall govern them and how they should be governed, through regular, free and fair elections of their representatives or through referenda." As stated in article 5, "Uganda is one Sovereign State and a Republic." Article 7 prohibits the adoption of a state religion.

"Fundamental rights and freedoms of the individual are inherent and not granted by the State," asserts article 20. Specific rights and freedoms set forth include equality "before and under the law," without discrimination on the basis of "sex, race, color, ethnic origin, tribe, birth, creed or religion, or social or economic standing, political opinion or disability"; the right to life and personal liberty, with certain exceptions such as "in execution of the sentence or order of a court"; the rights of persons accused of crimes, including the right of habeas corpus; and a prohibition against "any form of torture, cruel, inhuman or degrading treatment or punishment." Among other rights guaranteed are freedom from slavery and servitude; property ownership; privacy; education; family rights; and freedom of conscience, expression, movement, religion, assembly, and association. Express reference is made to rights of women, children, the disabled, and minorities. Article 51 establishes a human rights commission authorized, among other responsibilities, "to investigate, at its own initiative or on a complaint made by any person or group of persons against the violation of any human right."

With respect to political rights, article 69 provides that the "people of Uganda shall have the right to choose and adopt a political system [of their choice through free and fair elections or referenda" from among "the movement political system; the multi-party political system; and any other democratic and representative political system."

Division of Powers

Uganda is a unitary state with a quasi-parliamentary system of government. Cabinet ministers are appointed by the president with the approval of parliament, but according to article 117 they "shall individually be accountable to the President," although they may be censured by a vote of "more than half of all members of Parliament"; there is no prime minister.

The Executive

President. Article 98 directs that the president is "the Head of State, Head of Government and Commander-in Chief." This chief executive "shall take precedence over all persons in Uganda" and is to "execute and maintain this Constitution and all laws ... and ... safeguard this Constitution...." With the legislature's approval, the president appoints a vice president, who acts in his or her place if "for any reason" the president is "unable to perform the functions of the office."

A presidential candidate must be a citizen by birth, between thirty-five and seventy-five years of age, and qualified to be a member of parliament. Article 103 requires that the nomination be "supported by one hundred voters in each of at least two-thirds of all the districts in Uganda" and that the "election ... be by universal adult suffrage through a secret ballot" for a term of five years. To be elected, a candidate must receive more half the votes cast, otherwise a runoff election is held between the two candidates with the most votes.

The president may be removed from office for such offenses as "abuse of office" or certain "misconduct or misbehavior ... which brings or is likely to bring the office of President into hatred, ridicule, contempt or disrepute." Such an action may be brought by one-third of all the members of parliament, investigated by a special tribunal made up of three justices of the supreme court, and confirmed by "not less than two-thirds of all the members of Parliament."

Cabinet. According to article 111, the cabinet consists of the president, the vice president, "and such number of Ministers as may appear to the president to be reasonably necessary for the efficient running of the State." Its main function is "to determine, formulate and implement the policy of the Government." Ministers are "individually ... accountable to the President for the administration of their Ministries."

The Legislature

Parliament. Articles 77 and 78 establish a parliament composed of "members directly elected to represent constituencies," including "one woman representative for every district," as well as "representatives of the army, youth, workers, persons with disabilities, and other groups as Parliament may determine," all elected for five years. Citizens who are registered voters and have "completed a minimum formal education of Advanced Level standard or its equivalent" are eligible to be members of parliament. Exclusions include being of unsound mind, holding an office with election responsibilities, or being "a traditional or cultural leader." The vice president and the cabinet ministers, who if not already members of parliament, are made ex officio members without the right to vote.

Members elect a speaker and a deputy speaker "from among their number," and, along with others involved in legislative activities, are "entitled to such immunities and privileges as Parliament shall by law prescribe." One-third of all the members constitute a quorum, whereas generally "any question ... shall be determined by a majority of [those] present and voting."

Article 91 requires that a "bill passed by Parliament shall, as soon as possible, be presented to the President for assent." However, the president may return a bill for reconsideration or refuse assent in writing. In either case, if the bill is passed a second time it is again presented to the president. If returned once more, it must be passed by at least two-thirds of all members to become law. If the president does not act on a bill within thirty days, his or her assent is presumed.

The Judiciary

"Judicial power is derived from the people," states article 126. Among other directives, the constitution indicates that "substantive justice shall be administered without undue regard to technicalities." Laws "providing for participation of the people in the administration of justice by the courts" are authorized, and the courts are to be independent. "Courts of judicature" include the supreme court, court of appeal, high court, and "such subordinate courts as Parliament may by law establish, including *Qadhis'* courts for marriage, divorce, inheritance of property and guardianship."

Supreme Court. The supreme court consists of the chief justice and "not . . . less than six" other justices, as determined by law. A quorum is any "uneven number not being less than five members of the Court." Adds article 132: "The Supreme Court shall be the final court of appeal."

Constitutional Court. Although this court is not expressly included as one of the "courts of judicature," article 137 provides that "[a]ny question as to the interpretation of this Constitution shall be determined by the Court of Appeal sitting as the Constitutional Court." Its jurisdiction includes allegations by individuals that "an Act of Parliament or any other law . . . or any act of omission by any person or authority, is inconsistent with or in contravention of a provision of this Constitution. . . ."

Ombudsman

The office of "Inspectorate of Government," begun in 1986, is continued under article 223. Similar to that of an ombudsman in other countries, the office is charged with promoting and fostering "strict adherence to the rule of law and principles of natural justice in administration; [and] . . . the elimination of corruption [and] abuse of authority and of public office."

Traditional Leaders

Article 246 notes that "the institution of traditional leader or cultural leader may exist in any area of Uganda in accordance with the culture, customs and tradition or wishes and aspirations of the people to whom it applies." The South African constitution also provides for traditional leaders.

Amending the Constitution

According to articles 258 and 259, amendments to specified articles—including articles 259, 1, 2 (supremacy of the constitution), and 44 (barring derogation from certain human rights)—require an "Act of Parliament . . . supported at the second and third readings . . . by not less than two-thirds of all members of Parliament," followed by approval in a popular referendum.

Amendments affecting Uganda's districts, in addition to being passed on second and third readings by at least two-thirds of the legislators, must also be "ratified by at least two-thirds of the members of the district council in each of at least two-thirds of all the districts of Uganda." Other amendments simply require the two-thirds vote of all the members of parliament on the second and third readings. If certain requirements are certified as met, the president must assent to the amendments or "the President shall be taken to have assented to the bill. . . ."

UKRAINE

The second largest country in Europe after Russia, Ukraine throughout much of its history has been divided and dominated by its neighbors, most recently by Russia. Having attained independence in 1991, Ukraine now has a strong legislature empowered under its 1996 constitution.

General Information

The Republic of Ukraine is approximately 603,700 kilometers in area and is bounded on the north by Belarus, on the east by Russia, on the southwest by Moldova and Romania, and on the west by Hungary, Slovakia, and Poland. Kiev is the capital of this nation of more than forty-nine million persons.

Among Ukraine's major industries are mineral and gas production and chemical and food processing; its chief agricultural products include grain, potatoes, sugar beets, and fruit. Historically known as the "breadbasket" of Russia, Ukraine has the resources for a productive economy.

Type of Government: Presidential-style parliamentary republic, with a president, a prime minister and cabinet, a unicameral legislature, a judiciary, and a constitutional court

Dates of Constitutions: 1919, 1937, and 1996

Constitutional History

The Ukraine region was inhabited by Trypilian people along the Dnieper River as early as the seventh millennium B.C. By the twelfth century B.C., farmers and nomadic overlords had taken over the area. Later invasions by various tribes—the Cimmerians and then the Scythians and the Sarmatians—led to new cultures and forms of political organization. Greek colonies and influence developed beginning in the seventh century B.C., and by the first century B.C. the Roman Empire had extended its legions into parts of the territory.

Immigration and invasions of various peoples including the Goths, Huns, Bulgars, Avars, Magyars, Pechenegs, Polovtsians, and East Slavs affected Ukraine. The Kievan state, however, began its development in the mid-ninth century A.D., and Kiev remained the capital of the first Russian state until 1169. Kiev continued to be an important trading center until it was devastated by the Mongols, who added the southern part of the Kievan Rus' state to their empire in the thirteenth century. Slavic peoples eventually immigrated there from Lithuania and Moscow, creating Cossack enclaves.

After 1569 Catholic Lithuanian and Polish influence increased but was resisted by the Russian Orthodox Cossacks, a conflict that eventually led Ukrainians to seek protection from the duchy of Moscovy. Until the territory's complete absorption into the Russian empire in the second half of the eighteenth century, the autonomous form of Cossack self-government in Ukraine was called Hetmanate. By the end of the eighteenth century, parts of Ukraine were occupied by both Russia and Austria-Hungary.

Ukrainian nationalism began increasing during the nineteenth century, and after the Russian Revolution in 1917 a free and independent Ukraine Republic was proclaimed on January 22, 1918. A Soviet Ukrainian constitution was adopted in March 1919 by the All-Ukrainian Congress of Soviets, and then in 1922 the Ukrainian Soviet Socialist Republic was made a constituent member of the Soviet Union. The 1924 constitution of the U.S.S.R. made Ukraine virtually an administrative subdivision of Moscow. A new constitution, closely modeled on the U.S.S.R.'s 1936 Stalinist constitution, was adopted in 1937.

Faced with the imminent breakup of the Soviet Union, Ukraine on August 24, 1991, reasserted its independence, which was confirmed by referendum on December 1. The new republic included the Crimean Autonomous Republic, which before 1954 had been part of the Russian Soviet Republic (a 1997 treaty between Ukraine and Russia, however, recognizes its incorporation within Ukraine's borders). In July 1990 Ukraine had adopted a Declaration of State Sovereignty that set forth the basic principles of government, including separation of the legislative, executive, and judicial branches and guarantees of citizens' rights. After independence the government functioned under "a muddle of laws, decrees and [the] heavily amended Soviet charter." After a long political struggle, led by President Leonid Kuchma, a formal constitution was finally adopted by the Ukrainian parliament on June 28, 1996.

Ukraine's 1996 constitution reflects a compromise between a typical presidential-style government like the French and Russian versions and the desire to continue the major role of the Ukrainian legislature, which had its own executive organ called the presidium.

Influences

The Constitution

The introduction to the 1996 Ukrainian constitution states in part: "The Supreme Rada [parliament] of Ukraine, on behalf of the Ukrainian people . . . , based on the centuries-old history of Ukrainian state-building and on the right to self-determination . . . , [and] providing for the guarantee of human rights and freedoms . . . , adopts this Constitution—the Fundamental Law of Ukraine."

"Ukraine is a sovereign and independent, democratic, social, law-based state," proclaims article 1. According to articles 2 and 5, "Ukraine is a unitary state . . . [and] a republic. The people are the bearers of sovereignty and the only source of power in Ukraine."

Fundamental Rights

Article 92 provides in part that "[t]he following [are] to be determined solely by the laws of Ukraine: the rights and freedoms of individuals and citizens, guarantees of these rights and freedoms, the main duties of a citizen; . . . the rights of indigenous peoples and national minorities; . . . [and] the bases of social protection. . . ."

Fundamental rights and freedoms are set forth in articles 21 to 68. Although article 21 declares that "[h]uman rights and freedoms are inalienable and inviolable," article 22 asserts that "[h]uman and citizens' rights and freedoms affirmed by this Constitution are not exhaustive." Among the rights guaranteed are development of one's personality, equality before the law regardless of "race, color of skin, political, religious and other beliefs, sex, ethnic and social origin, property status, place of residence, linguistic or other characteristics"; "the inalienable right to life"; respect for a person's dignity; "freedom and personal inviolability"; inviolability of one's "dwelling place"; a "personal and family life"; and freedom of movement. Other rights include "freedom of thought and speech," "free expression," "freedom of personal philosophy and religion," and freedom of association.

Rights regarding peaceful assembly, petitions or appeals to the government, ownership and disposal of property, entrepreneurial activity, work, and rest are also guaranteed. However, according to article 37, political parties and public associations whose aims are incompatible with such concerns as Ukrainian independence, sovereignty, and security are prohibited.

Division of Powers

"State power in Ukraine," states article 6, "is exercised on the principles of its division into legislative, executive and judicial power. Bodies of legislative, executive and judicial power exercise their authority within the limits established by this Constitution and in accordance with the laws of Ukraine."

The Executive

President. Article 102 designates Ukraine's president as head of state and "guarantor of state sovereignty, the territorial integrity of Ukraine, compliance with the Constitution of Ukraine, and the rights and freedoms of individuals and citizens." Under article 103, the president is elected directly by secret ballot for a five-year term; any "citizen of Ukraine who has attained the age of thirty-five years, has the right to vote, has lived in Ukraine for the previous ten years . . . , and is fluent in the state language" may stand for election. The president may not serve more than two consecutive terms and, according to article 105, "enjoys the right of immunity during the term of his authority."

Article 106 states that the president "safeguards independence, national security, and legal succession of the State"; "represents the State in foreign relations, manages [its] foreign political activity ... , ... conducts negotiations and concludes international treaties"; and "appoints and dismisses" diplomatic officials and "accepts and withdraws the credentials of diplomatic representatives of foreign states." Other powers and responsibilities include calling referendums on constitutional amendments and special parliamentary elections, appointing as well as dismissing the prime minister with the consent of parliament, appointing cabinet members on the prime minister's recommendation, and making various other appointments. The president is the commander in chief of the armed forces; heads the national security council; decides on military mobilization and introduction of martial law; "appoints one-third of the membership of the Constitutional Court"; and grants pardons.

According to article 111, the president "may be removed from office by the Supreme Rada [parliament] by impeachment in the event of ... state treason or another crime," when "initiated by a majority of the constitutional composition of [parliament]." After an investigation and a recommendation by a temporary commission, the president may be indicted by a two-thirds majority and removed by not less than three-fourths of all the members of parliament after opinions by both the constitutional and supreme courts. If the president's authority is terminated, the prime minister "executes the duties of the President," except with respect to certain enumerated paragraphs of article 106, which include addressing the people and parliament, calling referendums on constitutional amendments, and revoking acts of the cabinet or the council of ministers of the Autonomous Republic of Crimea.

Prime Minister and Cabinet. "The Cabinet of Ministers ... is the highest organ ... of executive authority," declares article 113. It is "responsible before the President ... and accountable to [parliament]." The cabinet "guarantees ... implementation of the domestic and foreign policy of the State, ... of the Constitution and laws ... , and acts of the President ...";ensures "the rights and freedoms of individuals and citizens [and] the implementation of financial, price, investment, and revenue policies ... ," as well as other policies and programs regarding "the environment, ecological safety, and the utilization of natural resources" and the "economic, scholarly, technological, social, and cultural development of Ukraine."

According to article 114, the cabinet consists of the prime minister, a first vice prime minister, three vice prime ministers, and other ministers. The prime minister is appointed by the president "upon the consent of more than one-half" of parliament's members, while the other members are named by the president on the prime minister's recommendation. "The Prime Minister ... submits proposals to the President ... on the creation, reorganization, and liquidation of ministries and other central bodies of executive authority."

The Legislature

Parliament. "The sole organ of legislative authority in Ukraine shall be the parliament—the Supreme Rada of Ukraine," declares article 75. The Rada consists of "450 National Deputies ... elected for a four-year term on the basis of universal, equal, and direct suffrage through secret ballot." To be eligible a citizen must be at least twenty-one years of age, be able to vote, have resided in Ukraine for at least five years, and not have been convicted of "a premeditated criminal offense." Article 76 adds that "[t]he authorities of the [deputies] are prescribed by the Constitution and laws of Ukraine."

Deputies are guaranteed certain immunities with respect to their votes or statements made in parliament, "with the exception of liability for insult or defamation," and they may not be arrested "without the consent of [parliament]." Article 84 mandates open meetings of parliament, unless a majority vote of all the members chooses otherwise. All decisions are made by voting, which must be done in person. The Rada elects a chairman, a first deputy, and a deputy chairman from among its members and may remove them.

In addition to passing laws, parliament's authority pursuant to article 85 includes introducing "amendments to the Constitution"; "calling all-Ukrainian referenda on [altering Ukraine's territory]"; "adopting the State Budget . . . , determining the principles of domestic and foreign policy, . . . designating elections to the Presidency . . . , receiving the annual and special reports of the President . . . , [and] declaring war and concluding peace upon the recommendation of the President. . . ." Parliament also consents to the appointment of the prime minister, monitors the cabinet's work, and appoints and dismisses the "Authorized Representative of the Supreme Rada . . . on Human Rights." Parliament may also question cabinet members and other officials and pass votes of no confidence in the cabinet.

Legislation may be initiated by the president, deputies, cabinet ministers, and the National Bank of Ukraine. Laws passed are signed by the president or returned within fifteen days. A veto may be overridden by "no less than two-thirds of its constitutional composition." Article 94 directs that a law enters "into legal force within ten days of its official promulgation unless otherwise foreseen by the law itself, but no earlier than its publication."

"Justice in Ukraine," declares article 124, "is administered solely by courts. The delegation of court functions, as well as their usurpation by other organs and officials is not allowed." However, it adds, "People directly participate in the administration of justice through people's adjudicators and juries."

The Judiciary

The independence and immunity of judges are guaranteed under article 126, which specifies that "[i]t is prohibited to influence judges in any manner." A judge must be at least twenty-five years old, have a "higher legal education and at least three years' work experience in the field of law, [have] resided in Ukraine for at least ten years, and speak the state language [and] may be recommended by the Qualifications Commission of Judges" but may not be active in politics. A judge must first be appointed by the president for a five-year term, after which all judges, except those on the constitutional court, are elected by parliament. Most judges "hold their position permanently" but are terminated at age sixty-five.

Supreme Court. The supreme court, under article 125, "is the highest judiciary organ of general jurisdiction." The constitution is silent about further working of the court, except to indicate in article 128 that its chairman "shall be elected and dismissed by the Plenum of the Supreme Court of Ukraine via secret ballot according to the procedure prescribed by law."

Constitutional Court

According to article 147, the constitutional court resolves issues regarding the constitutionality of laws and legal acts of the executive and legislative branches and issues "official interpretations" of the constitution and laws. Its authority may be invoked by the president, "no fewer than forty-five National Deputies . . . , the Supreme Court . . . , the Authorized Representative of [parliament] on Human Rights [and] the Supreme Rada of . . . Crimea." Eighteen justices serve on the court, six appointed each by the president, parliament, and "the assembly of judges of Ukraine" for a one-time appointment of nine years.

Amending the Constitution

Pursuant to article 154, an amendment may be introduced in parliament by the president or at least one-third of its members. Except for changes to certain provisions, an amendment becomes effective if first approved by a parliamentary majority and then at the next regular session by at least two-thirds of all members. Amendments to the chapters on general principles, elections and referendums, and amending the constitution require a two-thirds majority for introduction, followed by a referendum. Article 157 prohibits amendments that "nullify or restrict the rights and freedoms of individuals or citizens" or that would affect Ukraine's independence or territorial integrity. And, it adds, "The Constitution . . . may not be amended under conditions of a state of emergency or martial law."

UNITED KINGDOM

Magna Carta, the house of commons, and the parliamentary-cabinet system of government are constitutional ideas that have greatly influenced many countries. The constitutional system of the United Kingdom, the birthplace of these developments, however, is still evolving.

General Information

The United Kingdom of Great Britain and Northern Ireland includes England, Scotland, and Wales, as well as Northern Ireland, but not the Channel Islands and the Isle of Man. Great Britain, or simply Britain, refers to England, Scotland, and Wales, although before the 1967 Welsh Language Act England included Wales. With an area of some 240,000 kilometers, not including dependent territories, the United Kingdom lies across the English Channel, north and west of continental Europe. London, which has an urban population of around seven million, is the capital of this country of approximately fifty-nine million persons.

The United Kingdom ushered in the industrial revolution, and its economy today is based on services and manufacturing. A tunnel under the English Channel directly linking Britain with continental Europe was opened in 1994. Constitutional reforms at the end of the decade led to the devolution of local authority to Scotland and Wales and to elections for their new local parliaments in 1999.

Type of Government: Parliamentary constitutional monarchy, with a monarch, a prime minister and cabinet, a bicameral legislature, and a judiciary

Date of Constitution: Unwritten; 1215 (Magna Carta, earliest constitutional document)

Constitutional History

Julius Caesar led two expeditions to the British Isles in the first century B.C., subduing at least in the south the native Celts, who had settled there during the Iron Age. Roman settlements in England lasted for about four hundred years. The Romans were followed by Germanic invaders—including the Angles, from whom England derives its name, and the Saxons—who drove the natives to the west and north.

Because the newcomers did not integrate with the inhabitants and because Latin had not become entrenched in England, the Anglo-Saxon language took root and flourished. Alfred the Great, who ruled from A.D. 871 to 899, translated Latin works into Anglo-Saxon when he was not busy efficiently administering his kingdom, which included meeting with regional leaders in a council called the Witenagemot.

The true Kingdom of England, however, dates from 927, when the king of Wessex and Mercia incorporated territory recently occupied by the Danes and the English portions of Northumbria, creating an east-west demarcation line between England and Scotland. By this time the English king was the keeper of the laws, and his writ conveyed his authority throughout the realm. By the eleventh century the continued policy of taxing freeholders of land for protection against the Danes had made the English crown wealthy, even by continental European standards.

A descendant of Alfred's failed to produce an heir, however, thus setting the stage for Duke William of Normandy in France to dispute the title of the Anglo-Saxon Harold. In 1066 Harold's forces, weary from fighting off a Norwegian attack, were beaten by William's invading army. The previous two hundred years of Anglo-Saxon rule, however, were not dramatically affected by the twelve thousand foreigners who followed William to England, except that the English feudal system acquired a stronger European flavor and the administration of the government was reformed.

The thirteenth century was pivotal: in 1204 King John lost Normandy to the French king, and in 1215 English barons in the north refused to support the recapture of Normandy and forced concessions on John—specifically, Magna Carta. Although he later canceled the document, it was restored by Henry III and confirmed by Edward I in 1297. Magna Carta was the first document of constitutional stature in what is now the United Kingdom, whose constitution remains unwritten.

The first use of the term *parliament* was recorded in 1236, but it was not until the fourteenth century that the institution took shape. In 1340 what had started out as a way for the king to give instructions and receive information from the far reaches of the kingdom had broadened to include representatives of the counties (shires), called the commons. By 1350 the parliament was chiefly engaged in authorizing funds and making laws requested by the monarch, judges, or the commons, and the king's council had become the house of lords.

Although the parliament could raise concerns about the government—for example, the need to reform the king's council—it was dependent on the monarch to call it to meet. By 1500, after civil strife, England emerged a whole nation now including Wales, and by mid-century Henry VIII and the "Reformation Parliament" had severed official ties with the Catholic Church of Rome.

In 1628 Edward Coke and others in the house of commons pushed through a bill, the Petition of Right—not sent to the house of lords—that limited the king's powers. Later, civil war again broke out over the very nature of English society, and the rebel Oliver Cromwell, leader of the parliamentary forces, was able to purge the parliament of all opposition, abolish the house of lords, and behead the king. Yet, in 1660, after Cromwell's death, the monarchy was restored, and parliament resumed its prerevolutionary role. In 1680 parties called the Whigs and the Tories arose from those who were "for" and "against" the king's meeting with the parliament.

England expanded overseas and built an empire between 1688–89—the years of the Glorious Revolution, when William of Orange ascended the throne and the English bill of rights was enacted—and the Reform Act of 1832. Scotland and Ireland were added to England in 1707 and 1800, respectively. At home, however, the monarchy became isolated from the realities of government, permitting the realization of a liberal, democratic constitution. With the first Hanoverian monarch, George I, who spoke only German, the leader of the majority party in the house of commons began speaking for the cabinet, whose members were selected from that body. While Thomas Paine fulminated against the monarchy in the wake of the American and French Revolutions—calling the English bill of rights the "bill of wrongs"—the United Kingdom of Great Britain and Ireland moved incrementally forward toward a stable political system without major internal disruptions.

Influences

To a unique extent the British constitution developed without outside influence. Today, however, as a member of the European Union and a ratifier of the European Convention for the Protection of Human Rights and Fundamental Freedoms (1950), its government actions are increasingly subject to outside influence. The British constitution has had a tremendous influence on many countries, such as Australia, India, and Malaysia, to name only a few.

The Constitution

The British constitution is a tapestry, deftly woven and embellished over time. The warp is the monarchy, and the woof is the indomitable self-esteem of the descendants of the first Anglo-Saxon invaders.

The United Kingdom has fostered and even exported the notion of the rule of law—that a government's actions are limited by law and are not merely the whims of some human authority. However, the concept of the supremacy of constitutional laws, which is found either expressly or implicitly in the constitutions of most other countries, such as the United States, France, and Germany, does not apply in the United Kingdom. The British constitution is an agglomeration of statutes, judicial interpretations, conventions, laws and customs of the parliament, common law principles, and selective jurisprudence, such that even scholars may disagree on what is and what is not a part of the constitution. The one indisputable fact is the supremacy of the British parliament, which in theory precludes judicial review. As Sir William Blackstone quoted in his famous legal commentaries: "The power and jurisdiction of parliament, says Sir Edward Coke [chief justice of the King Bench court in the seventeenth century], is so transcendent and absolute, that it cannot be confined, either for causes or persons, within any bounds" (*Commentaries on the Laws of England*, 1771. 1:160).

Fundamental Rights

The first generally recognized individual rights in England were those under common law: the rights inherent in access to the monarch's courts for remedies even against feudal lords. But the form of pleading at common law soon became rigid, and for justice to be done, equity courts emerged and even became supreme in matters of conflict with the common law. The parliament passed laws that laid a foundation for individual rights—for example, the Petition of Right of 1628, the Habeas Corpus Act of 1679, and the Bill of Rights of 1689, basically declaring rights of the parliament. However, the United Kingdom, like Australia, has no enacted individual bill of rights as is found in the U.S. constitution. Constitutional traditions inherent in the United Kingdom's system of government are its only real constitutional protections.

In 1951, however, the nation ratified the European Convention for the Protection of Human Rights and Fundamental Freedoms (1950); grievances for alleged violations of human rights in the United Kingdom have been filed with the convention court. And in 2000 the Human Rights Act, incorporating the convention into British law, went into effect.

Division of Powers

The United Kingdom is a unitary state like France, although special provisions apply to Northern Ireland, Scotland, and Wales, and "the British Islands"—the Channel Islands and the Isle of Man, which are part of Britain only for defense and foreign relations purposes. A strict separation of powers does not exist in the United Kingdom: the monarch, who is head of state, and the parliament formally constitute the legislature; the prime minister, who is head of government, is an elected member of the legislature and chosen by and responsible to the lower house of the legislature; and the highest appeals court consists of the lords of appeal, or "law lords," who sit in the upper house of the legislature. Technically, the courts have no power of judicial review.

The Executive

Monarch. In the United Kingdom the monarch, also known as the sovereign, is the hereditary head of state. But Elizabeth II, the queen, is as much a subject of the British constitution as any of her subjects. She is granted the "royal prerogative," or preeminence over and above all other persons, but she may claim no prerogatives except those the law allows. Theoretically, she appoints the prime minister, assembles and dissolves the legislature, approves all laws, makes foreign policy, and commands the armed forces.

Prime Minister and Cabinet. Since the Glorious Revolution in 1688–89, the supremacy of the parliamentary legislature has in fact reduced the monarch to a figurehead, albeit a wealthy and pampered one. Today in the United Kingdom, the prime minister and the sixteen to twenty-three cabinet members he or she presides over rule on behalf of the people.

The prime minister, about whom there are almost no statutory provisions, is the government's chief executive and chief legislator. The paramount constitutional convention is that the sovereign must act on the advice of the ministers and, in particular, the prime minister. The ministers, in turn, are individually and collectively responsible to the lower house of the legislature and therefore ultimately to the electorate, as the upper house is not elected. Civil servants are not political but are responsible to the political government administration.

As leader of the controlling party in the lower house, which is not always the absolute majority party, the prime minister is someone who has come up through the party ranks. As head of the cabinet and the controlling party, the prime minister has enormous power,

among its members. Recently, a woman was elected speaker for t'
constitution the prime minister may ask the monarch to disso'
for elections, usually about a year and a half before the five yc
appears to favor the party in office.

Except for money bills, which must originate in the lower house, .
in either house by members or the government, and they are debatea
has to pass three readings, although the first reading is a formality. The .
the important one, with serious debate held. If not rejected, it goes to a stan
tee, then to the committee of the whole lower house, and then to a fairly formal
ing. After action by the lower house, a bill is sent to the upper house, which in mc
may not withhold its consent. Finally, to become effective, a bill must have the royal as.
which today is merely a formality.

The Judiciary

Lord Chancellor. At the apex of the British judicial system is the lord chancellor, who is a
member of the government and generally a member of the cabinet as well as a barrister holding political office and a member of the house of lords. The lord chancellor's position and
duties, which defy any notion of a true separation of powers, are those of senior law officer
of the government, head of the judiciary, and law lord entitled to sit in the house of lords
in both a legislative and a judicial capacity.

The highest court of appeal is the house of lords. The Appellate Jurisdiction Act of 1876 requires that appeals be heard by the lord chancellor, lords of appeal in ordinary (senior members of the judiciary), and peers who have held high judicial office. There is also a court of
appeals, whose ex officio members include the high officials of the judiciary, former lord
chancellors, and the lords of appeal in ordinary. Other courts include the high court of justice, the crown court, and county courts.

High court officials such as the lord chief justice, the master of the rolls, and the lords and
lords justices of appeal, like the lord chancellor, are appointed by the monarch on the recommendation of the prime minister. Inferior court judges are appointed by the monarch
on the advice of the lord chancellor. Membership in the British judicial system has tended
to be narrowly limited to the upper and upper-middle classes, and the judiciary as a whole
tends to be conservative. The parliament has enacted laws to enhance the independence of
judges by restricting the power to remove them, although the lord chancellor under certain
conditions can remove inferior court judges for misconduct or proven incapacity, and there
is a mandatory retirement age.

The government rarely interferes with the courts, but it may in appropriate cases file as
amicus curiae ("a friend of the court"); the court may attempt to resolve such cases in light
of the government's concerns. In a constitutional system in which the legislature is acknowledged as supreme by the courts, as in fact occurred in the *Sheriff of Middlesex* case in
1840, true constitutional review is not possible because the legislature is free to change the
constitution by passing ordinary legislation.

the Constitution

The constitution of the United Kingdom may be amended by a simple majority vote of the
legislature, by legal decisions unchallenged by the legislature, by international agreements,
and by custom and traditional usage that become accepted as having constitutional status.

however, to a large extent by convention and the not-so-easily cowed "loyal oppo-
... minority party in the lower house. Nevertheless, the prime minister decides the
... or cabinet meetings, makes key policy decisions, deals with urgent matters of state,
... velops foreign and domestic policy and legislative programs. No votes are taken in the
... et meetings, so the prime minister must sense support or the lack of it.
... ther limits on the prime minister's power are the narrow range of people, all politicians
... h their own constituencies, available for selection to key posts; the need to appease his
... her own party and factions within the party; and the fact that he or she must work
... hrough a powerful civil service bureaucracy known as Whitehall. The United Kingdom,
unlike the United States, has no political spoils system. As in most parliamentary-cabinet
type governments, ministers are put in charge of government departments, but they must
deal with the entrenched bureaucracy to get things done.

Parliament. The British parliament, a bicameral legislature, consists of an upper and a lower
house: the house of lords and the house of commons. Compared to the United States, the
two houses are extremely unequal in power. As the nineteenth-century English philosopher
John Stuart Mill described it, the function of representative bodies such as the house of commons is to control the business of government, but not actually do it, because such a body
is best suited to deliberating rather than administering. The proper duty of a representative
body, according to Mill, is to ensure that the proper persons decide matters of administration and control the government by compelling a full justification for all its acts.

Upper House. The house of lords consists of about eight hundred members known as peers,
who have inherited their seats; more than three hundred life peers, who have acquired their
seats by appointment pursuant to a 1958 law; twenty-six Church of England bishops; and
twenty-one law lords, who constitute the highest appellate court in the nation. Only several
hundred, however, attend sessions with any degree of regularity.

During the first half of the twentieth century, the upper house's veto power was taken
away, except in the case of an act to extend parliament beyond five years. Although there is
a movement to abolish the house of lords altogether, a royal commission proposal in 2000
called for most members of the upper house to be appointed and some to be elected.

Lower House. The house of commons has 651 members elected at least every five years. All
men and women at least eighteen years old may vote, including citizens of the Republic of
Ireland residing in the United Kingdom. Unlike most other western European democracies,
which have some form of proportional representation, candidates for the lower house with
a relative majority of the votes in their constituencies are elected, a process that tends to
maintain the basically two-party system. The United Kingdom's system of government
differs from the two-party system in the United States, where the size and diversity of the
country have created a plethora of interest groups that only come together as two parties to
compete for the presidency every four years, not necessarily to form a unified party government. While the lower house in the United Kingdom is supposed to act as a check on the
prime minister and his or her government, it is not sufficiently staffed to perform this function well, and the committee system is not as developed as in the United States.

The house of commons physically reflects the concept of a party in power and a party
out of power: the members of the two groups sit facing each other across a wide aisle, t¹
majority party on the right of the speaker's throne and the opposition party on the left, v
a "shadow cabinet," ready and waiting to take office, on the front row. The speaker doe
have to be a member of the majority party.

Being supreme, the parliament determines its own rules, and it elects a speak

Amending

372

The constitution of the United States, the oldest written constitution still in effect, was a novelty when it took effect in 1789. It created a set of rules for governing a nation—out of reach of change by ordinary legislation—and a unique division of power among the federal government, state governments, and the people. Today, with only twenty-seven amendments, the U.S. constitution remains a source of inspiration for people throughout the world.

UNITED STATES

General Information

The United States of America occupies approximately 9.8 million square kilometers. Its forty-eight contiguous states on the North American continent are bounded by Canada on the north, the Atlantic Ocean on the east, Mexico on the south, and the Pacific Ocean on the west. The state of Alaska lies on the West Coast, north of Canada, and the state of Hawaii consists of a group of islands in the north Pacific Ocean. The United States also has island territories and possessions, including the Virgin Islands and Puerto Rico in the Caribbean Sea and American Samoa and Guam in the Pacific Ocean. Washington, District of Columbia, is the federal capital of this country of approximately 281 million persons.

The United States is the most economically productive country in the world and has generally experienced long-term economic growth since its inception. It is a nation of ethnic and religious diversity resulting from waves of worldwide immigration. Since the fall of the Soviet Union, the United States may be considered the world's only true superpower both militarily and economically.

Type of Government: Presidential federal republic, with a president and cabinet, a bicameral legislature, and a judiciary

Dates of Constitutions: 1781 (Articles of Confederation) and 1789

Constitutional History

The first Americans apparently came to the continent of North America from Asia via a land bridge to the Alaska Peninsula tens of thousands of years ago. While there is some evidence that Europeans and Africans made contact with North America earlier, the discovery of land on the western shores of the Atlantic Ocean by Christopher Columbus in 1492 had the most profound effect on both the New and the Old Worlds.

The wave of European immigration five hundred years ago found Native American civilizations living in harmony with the ecology, if not always with each other. The indigenous peoples spoke approximately 1,200 languages or dialects, but in the eastern half of North America there were three major language groups: the Algonquians in the north, the Muskogeans farther south and west, and the Iroquois both around the eastern Great Lakes and in Georgia, where a dialect was spoken by the Cherokee. Although the European concept of individual land ownership was foreign to the Native Americans, some—for example, the Iroquois—were particularly skilled in creating sophisticated and long-lasting political alliances in which decisions were made by a central council made up of a specified number of representatives from each tribe.

Spurred on by the merchant class's accumulation of capital and the eviction of people when Henry VIII seized church property, England's colonizing efforts began in earnest with the settlement on Roanoke Island, promoted by Sir Walter Raleigh in the 1580s. The colony disappeared, but by 1700 England had acquired an overseas empire in North America.

In 1620 separatists (today known as Puritans) who wished to break away from the Church of England arrived at Cape Cod on a ship named the *Mayflower*. Before settling in nearby Plymouth, forty-one adult males signed a written agreement "for our better ordering and preservation," called the Mayflower Compact, which dealt with the form of their future government.

In contrast to the Spanish, whose method of colonization was uniform, the English settlements and later colonies were diverse in their organizational structures. Virginia held the first legislative assembly in America in 1619, called by its governor. Massachusetts, initially administered by a governor under a charter from the king, set up a bicameral legislature in the 1640s along with the position of governor, elected by adult male members of the church. Similarly, Roger Williams obtained a charter for Rhode Island, but suffrage was not limited to church members, and all Christian religions were protected from government interference. New Hampshire became a separate colony in 1670, with a governor appointed by the king.

Maryland, Carolina, and New Jersey, on the other hand, were proprietorships that the king gave in outright ownership to individuals. Maryland was conveyed to George Calvert, a Roman Catholic, but its charter provided for a representative assembly. William Penn acquired Pennsylvania and set up a liberal government, extending the right to vote to all adult landowners and taxpayers. Besides English colonists, the original thirteen colonies were settled by Dutch, Scotch-Irish, German, Swiss, French Huguenot, Jewish, Swedish, and Welsh settlers.

After the Glorious Revolution of 1688–89 in England, a new committee to govern the colonies and protect trade and navigation there was created. Customs offices with the power to search private premises were established. The 1763 Treaty of Paris, which ended the Seven Years' War, required both France and Spain to cede territory in America to Britain, whose parliament began levying direct taxes on the colonists and imposing other onerous measures. With the Stamp Act in 1765, which levied a duty on a range of items from legal documents to playing cards, the seeds of revolt were sown. The colonial assemblies agreed on a joint protest, which led to a congress held in New York City and the assertion of colonists' rights in a Declaration of Rights and Grievances. The Stamp Act was repealed, but British soldiers' massacre of a rioting mob in Boston and the British parliament's attempt to allow the East India Company to monopolize the tea trade fanned the flames of revolution.

At the First Continental Congress, which met in Philadelphia in 1774, a majority of the members agreed that the British parliament had no right to pass any laws for the colonies, and in 1775 war broke out between British troops and colonial minutemen (militia members). The following year the tone for the conflict and its aftermath was set by the Declaration of Independence, written by Thomas Jefferson, and a pamphlet entitled "Common Sense," by Thomas Paine, a recent British immigrant. Well before the British surrender in 1781, each of the thirteen colonies had adopted written documents of fundamental law. Some were merely amended royal charters, but all except one provided for a bicameral legislature, and most contained a version of a bill of rights and expanded suffrage. The prototypes for these fundamental laws were the constitution and declaration of rights drafted in Williamsburg, Virginia, in 1776, largely the work of George Mason.

The Articles of Confederation, drafted by the Second Continental Congress and ratified in 1781, broke new ground in terms of a formal separation of powers between the national and state governments but did little to promote economic development or political cohesion. It provided for a unicameral legislature in which each state had one vote regardless of the size of its population or its delegation to the congress; important legislation had to be approved by a two-thirds vote, or nine out of thirteen states; the executive consisted of a committee of one delegate from each state; and any amendments had to be by unanimous consent.

In 1785 the congress recommended revisions to the articles, and the process began in earnest in early 1786, when a resolution by the Virginia legislature called for a meeting in Annapolis, Maryland, of "commissioners" from the states to improve trade and create uniform commercial regulations. A second meeting, endorsed by the congress, was held in Philadelphia to make the constitution of the federal government adequate for the union.

On May 25, 1787, the convention, made up of delegates from all the states except for Rhode Island, met and elected George Washington its president. The draft constitution was signed by all but three delegates and transmitted to the congress, which in turn directed that it be submitted to the state legislatures for approval. Ignoring the unanimity requirement of the

Articles of Confederation, the new constitution after ratification by nine states would be valid by its own terms for those states that had ratified it. Ratification occurred in 1788, and on April 30, 1789, George Washington was inaugurated as the first president under the new constitution. In 1790 Rhode Island became the thirteenth state to ratify it.

Most issues at the convention were resolved with little debate. The concept of the separation of powers, particularly between the legislature and the judiciary, for example, was well known and already incorporated in a majority of the individual constitutions of the colonies or states. Even the extensive grant of power to the legislature by the "commerce clause"—clause 3, section 8, of article 1—caused little concern because it was part of the proposals submitted by the two major factions at the conventions, the large states and the small states.

The major issue of proportional or equal representation for the states in the national legislature was framed by two proposals—one by the large states, known as the Virginia Plan, and one by the small states, known as the New Jersey Plan. The small states proposed a unicameral legislature, with each state having one vote, as under the Articles of Confederation. The large states' proposal called for a bicameral legislature with membership in both houses based on population, the lower house to be elected by the people and the upper house by the lower house. The entire legislature would elect the judiciary. The Great Compromise that came about created an upper house (senate) in which each state would have two members, who were to be elected by their state legislatures. Direct elections for members of the senate were instituted by the seventeenth amendment in 1913.

The first ten amendments, called the bill of rights, were ratified on December 15, 1791, and provide guarantees against the national government's infringement on fundamental rights and freedoms of the people and the states.

Influences

Contemporaneous writings on the constitution in *The Federalist* by Alexander Hamilton, James Madison, and John Jay indicate that, in addition to the early Greek democracies and the Roman republic, the framers of the constitution were influenced, both positively and negatively, by the constitutions of many existing and past nations and confederations of Europe, including, of course, the British constitution. Perhaps the most profound influence, particularly with respect to the bill of rights, was English common law. The U.S., British, and French constitutions together have had a profound effect on the modern constitutions of the world in the last two hundred years.

The Constitution

William Gladstone, who served as the British prime minister four times in the late nineteenth century, called the U.S. constitution "the most wonderful work ever struck off at a given time by the brain and purpose of man" (letter to the committee in charge of the celebration of the centennial of the American constitution, July 20, 1887).

The constitution of the United States of America, as do other constitutions, contains both substantive as well as procedural aspects: while the document describes in broad outline and some specifics how the government should operate, the framers also incorporated underlying beliefs and goals. Such substantive concepts as "the consent of the governed" or the idea "that an individual is an end, not a means" may not be expressly stated, but they inform the document and provide a touchstone for understanding and interpreting both the constitution and the Declaration of Independence.

The preamble is short (as is the entire document, which, including the twenty-seven amendments, contains only approximately three thousand five hundred words):

We the people of the United States, in order to form a more perfect union, establish justice, insure the domestic tranquillity, provide for the common defense, promote the general welfare, and secure the blessings of liberty to ourselves and our posterity, do ordain and establish this constitution for the United States of America.

Fundamental Rights

In addition to the bill of rights, article 1, section 9, of the constitution prohibits, among other things, suspension of the writ of habeas corpus, except in time of rebellion or invasion; any bill of attainder or ex post facto law; direct taxation not based proportionally on the latest census; and taxation on goods exported from a state.

The first ten amendments that constitute the bill of rights were originally intended to protect individual rights against actions by the national government, but by the terms of the fourteenth amendment, ratified after the Civil War, individual rights are now protected against actions by the states. The rights and freedoms include freedom of religion, speech, the press, assembly, and petition of the government for a redress of grievances; because of the necessity for a well-regulated militia, the right to bear arms; protection against unreasonable searches and seizures, double jeopardy, and self-incrimination in criminal cases; the right to a speedy and public trial, an impartial jury, and legal counsel; and guarantees against excessive bail and cruel and unusual punishment.

Article 9 states that the enumeration of rights does not preclude other rights retained by the people, and article 10 provides that powers not granted to the national government nor prohibited to the states are reserved to the states and the people, respectively. Other rights such as protection against involuntary servitude and discrimination in voting on the basis of race or sex have been added by amendment. A right of privacy, although not expressly stated in the constitution, has also been identified by the courts in certain cases.

Division of Powers

The United States is a federal state, with a national government and governments in each of the fifty constituent states. According to the fourteenth amendment, persons born in the country or naturalized are citizens of the United States and the state in which they reside. The national government handles defense and foreign policy exclusively, while the states have individual militia and police power. At the national level power is divided among three coequal branches: the executive branch headed by a president, who is head of state and government; the bicameral legislative branch with houses of basically coequal power; and the independent judiciary, which exercises judicial review.

The Executive

President. One of the more original aspects of the U.S. constitution is the nature of the presidency. While the actual power of the president swells and ebbs with the incumbent's personality and the times, the president's role as both head of state and government, the almost exclusive authority over the armed forces and foreign affairs, his or her position as head of one of the two major political parties, and security in office for at least four years make the position potentially powerful.

The president is elected indirectly by the people through electors (the electoral college) from the states equal to the number of members of the national legislature to which they are entitled, and, by amendment in 1961, electors from the federal capital district, limited, however, to no more than the number from the least populous state. A close presidential election in 2000, which was settled by the Supreme Court, has raised questions about election procedures and the electoral college itself.

Only natural-born citizens who are at least thirty-five years old and have been a resident for fourteen years are eligible to be president or vice president. By amendment in 1804, the electors vote for the vice president on a separate ballot, although the president and vice president run for office together on a party ticket. Until the mid-twentieth century it was traditional for a president to serve only two terms; after Franklin D. Roosevelt was elected for a fourth term, an amendment in 1951 provided that no person may be elected to the office of the president more than twice.

According to article 2, section 2, the president is commander in chief of the armed forces and the militia of the states when called to national service; has oversight of the executive departments; grants reprieves and pardons, except in cases of impeachment; makes treaties with the advice and consent of two-thirds of the upper house of the legislature; and, subject to the confirmation, that is, "with the advice and consent," of the upper house, appoints ambassadors, public ministers, federal judges, and other high officials of the national government, including cabinet secretaries, who are heads of departments, and many subcabinet-level officials. The authority to change policy-making officials on the inauguration of a new president, especially one from a different party, is called patronage or the spoils system.

The president also is required to advise the legislature from time to time, generally once a year, on the state of the nation; may convene and adjourn the legislature on extraordinary occasions; receives ambassadors; commissions all the officers of the United States; and "shall take care that the laws be faithfully executed. . . ."

The president, vice president (whose only official duty is to serve as the president of the upper house and cast tie-breaking votes), and all civil officers of the United States may be removed from office by impeachment on being convicted of "treason, bribery, or other high crimes and misdemeanors." There have been three attempts to impeach a president: Andrew Johnson escaped conviction in 1868 when the upper house fell one vote shy of the two-thirds vote necessary to convict him. Richard Nixon resigned in 1974 after the judiciary committee of the lower house recommended impeachment, which would have had to be approved by the lower house and then tried in the upper house with the chief justice of the supreme court presiding. And William Jefferson Clinton's impeachment by the lower house in 1999 was not confirmed by the upper house.

Cabinet. Clause 1 of section 2, article 2, refers to the principal officer in each executive department, and clause 2 charges the president with the power to appoint all other officers of the United States not otherwise provided for in the constitution, with the advice and consent of the upper house of the legislature. The heads of executive departments such as state, justice, defense, the treasury, and others are called secretaries; collectively, with certain other officials accorded cabinet rank, they make up the cabinet.

Members of the U.S. cabinet, in contrast to the traditional parliamentary system of government, have no role in the legislature nor generally any individual constituency, although in most cases they are members of the incumbent president's party. They are responsible to the president, who may reassign or dismiss them. Also in contrast to the parliamentary system, cabinet secretaries are the sole administrative heads of their departments, and a number of their top-level subordinates are also political appointees rather than career civil servants.

Congress. Article 1, section 1, provides that "all legislative powers shall be vested in a congress of the United States, which shall consist of a senate and a house of representatives."

The Legislature

Upper House. The members of the senate, two from each state, are elected directly and at large from their states, one-third every two years for six-year terms. Senators must be thirty years old and a citizen for nine years in addition to being inhabitants of the state from which they are elected. The vice president of the United States is the official presiding officer of the senate.

Lower House. The house of representatives consists of 435 members elected every two years on the basis of population and by districts in the states. To be eligible for the house, a person must have been a citizen for at least seven years and be at least twenty-five years old and an inhabitant of the state from which he or she is elected.

After every general election the majority and minority parties in both houses organize and elect party leaders, and the majority party elects the chairman of committees and selects the majority of the members on each committee. The house elects a speaker from the majority party along with other officers.

Among the powers given to the congress are regulating commerce, levying taxes, declaring war, establishing inferior courts, regulating the currency, and establishing the post office. Bills for raising revenue must originate in the house of representatives, where by tradition appropriations bills also originate. Exclusive powers of the senate include confirming major appointments by the president and ratifying major treaties.

Bills may be introduced only by members of congress. A majority of the members in each house constitutes a quorum. Bills passed by a majority in both houses must be approved by the president, who may veto a bill, but that veto may be overridden by a two-thirds vote in both houses. Some matters, such as proposing constitutional amendments, ratifying treaties, and convicting on impeachment (in the senate) require a two-thirds vote for passage.

Unlike the British parliament, the U.S. congress is not "supreme" but is expressly subject to the checks and balances of the executive and judicial branches. It also does not have the parliamentary right of controlling the executive branch through interpellation, or questioning the heads of executive departments with a view to withdrawing its vote of confidence in the government; the congress does have investigative authority, however. The president, unlike the British prime minister, is elected independently of the congress every four years and, therefore, as is often the case, may not be a member of the majority party in either or both houses of congress.

Three major factors not dealt with in the constitution have significantly affected the way the U.S. congress works today: the rise of the two-party system, the development of a large lobbying industry on behalf of special-interest groups, and the power of the congressional committees, particularly the chairmen and their staffs.

The Judiciary

Article 3, section 1, establishes the judicial branch:

The judicial power of the United States, shall be vested in one supreme court, and such inferior courts as the congress may from time to time ordain and establish. The judges, both of the supreme and inferior courts, shall hold their offices during good behavior, and shall, at stated times, receive for their services, a compensation, which shall not be diminished during their continuance in office.

The power of the federal judiciary extends to all cases arising under the constitution, the national laws, and treaties; cases affecting foreign representatives; cases of admiralty and maritime jurisdiction; cases in which the United States is a party; cases between states; cases between a state and a citizen of another state; cases between citizens of different states; and cases between a state or its citizens and foreign countries, citizens, and subjects. The federal court system in the United States is three-tiered, with district courts throughout the nation, circuit courts of appeal in many regional centers, and the supreme court in the nation's capital. There is a separate state court system in each of the fifty states.

Supreme Court. The court currently has nine justices, including a chief justice, who are appointed by the president with the advice and consent of the upper house of the legislature. The supreme court has original jurisdiction in cases involving foreign representatives and cases in which a state is a party. In all other cases its jurisdiction is on appeal.

While it is not expressly stated in the constitution, the framers were aware of the concept of judicial review, in which independent courts determine whether legislation or government action is unconstitutional and therefore void. In 1776 Thomas Paine declared that in America the law, rather than a monarch, should be king. The foundation for judicial review was laid even earlier by the English jurist Edward Coke when he described Magna Carta as "being the fountain of all the *fundamental* laws of the realm [emphasis added]" (Edward Coke, *Institutes,* 1628, 1:81). But it was not until the case of *Marbury v. Madison,* at the beginning of the nineteenth century, that the U.S. supreme court declared invalid an act of the congress extending to the court authority that had not been granted by the constitution. Speaking for a unanimous court, Chief Justice John Marshall ruled: "Thus the particular phraseology of the constitution of the United States confirms and strengthens the principle, supposed to be essential to all written constitutions, that law repugnant to the constitution is void; and that courts, as well as other departments, are bound by that instrument."

The U.S. constitution became effective extraconstitutionally, because under the Articles of Confederation amendments required the unanimous consent of the thirteen states. But by its own terms the constitution was to become effective for those states that ratified it once only nine states had ratified it—thus confirming that the people always retain a fundamental right to change their form of government even under an existing constitution.

Amending the Constitution

The U.S. constitution, according to article 5, may be amended when two-thirds of both houses of the congress propose amendments or when the congress is requested by two-thirds of the state legislatures to call a constitutional convention. All amendments must then be ratified by three-fourths of the state legislatures or conventions, based on the mode of ratification proposed by the congress. No amendment, however, may deprive any state of equal suffrage in the senate without its consent. To date no constitutional convention to propose amendments has been called.

VENEZUELA

Venezuela—"Little Venice," as Amerigo Vespucci named it—was Christopher Columbus's first landfall on the South American continent. The birthplace of the "Liberator," Simón Bolívar Palacios, Venezuela has had twenty-six constitutions since becoming independent in 1811.

General Information

The Bolivaran (added in 1999) Republic of Venezuela in northern South America is approximately 912,000 square kilometers and is bounded on the east by Guyana, on the south by Brazil, on the west by Colombia, and on the north by the Caribbean Sea. Caracas is the capital of this country of approximately twenty-three million persons.

One of the world's leading oil producers, Venezuela has the highest per capita income in Latin America. But mismanagement, corruption, and the transfer of profits earned from oil exports to foreign countries, as well as chronic political unrest, especially among the military (there were two coup attempts in 1992), make its future difficult to predict.

Type of Government: Presidential federal republic, with a president, an executive vice president, and a council of ministers (cabinet); a unicameral legislature; and a judiciary

Dates of Key Constitutions: 1811, 1821, 1830, 1857, 1864, 1936, 1947, 1953, 1961, and 1999

Constitutional History

Lying outside the ambit of the great pre-Columbian civilizations, Venezuela lacked precious stones and minerals but attracted the Spanish first as a source of pearls, until the 1520s, and then as a source of Indian slaves. Germans administered and exploited the western portion under a Spanish grant from 1528 to 1556; what would become Caracas was not established until 1567. Oil was first noticed in 1500, but the value of the "devil's excrement," as it was then called, was not known, and the area's only importance for Spain was in securing the Caribbean coastline against pirates.

Partly because it lacked economic importance, Venezuela did not develop political unity until 1777, when Caracas was given political and military control over the territory as the captaincy-general of Venezuela under the Spanish crown. The society consisted of the *peninsulares* (persons born in Spain) at the top and, in descending order, the *criollos* (persons born of Spanish parents); the white Canary Islanders, who performed paid labor; the *pardos* (racially mixed); the African slaves; and, finally, the Indians.

After Napoleon's troops invaded Spain in 1808, the Caracas *cabildo* (city council) refused to accept French sovereignty and in 1810 ousted the governor. A junta took control in the name of the deposed Spanish king, Ferdinand VII, and on July 5, 1811, Venezuela declared its independence and under the first constitution in South America established the first republic, later called the "Silly Republic" because of its many difficulties.

Spain retook Venezuela in 1812, but Simón Bolívar Palacios, born of a *criollo* family in Caracas, established the second republic, only to be driven out in 1814. A third republic was established in 1819, with Bolívar as president. After more military successes a constitution for Gran Colombia was signed by both Venezuela and Colombia in 1821, with Bolívar again as president. Rising nationalism led to Venezuela's leaving the union in 1829, and a century of the *caudillo* (dictator) ensued. An 1830 constitution survived until 1857, when a new centralizing constitution was promulgated, but it was quickly replaced by a more federalist one in 1858. In 1864 a constitution modeled on the U.S. constitution was adopted for the United States of Venezuela.

In 1936 a new document, building on the traditions of the past, included for the first time a declaration of rights and reduced the president's term from seven to five years. The incumbent president voluntarily relinquished his term after five years, although legally it would have lasted for two more years. The rule of law *(estado de derecho)* seemed to have been accepted, because the next president continued respect for the constitution; the government was overthrown by a military coup in 1945, however. A new constitution, which included habeas corpus protection, social rights, and expanded suffrage, was promulgated in 1947, and political parties developed. A bloodless coup took place in 1948. In 1953 a constitution reminiscent of the 1936 one was promulgated.

During the 1958 election campaign the three major parties, including the Communist Party, agreed to govern through a coalition government, regardless of the outcome of the election. Out of this unity the constitution of January 23, 1961, was developed by a constitutional reform commission set up by the newly elected legislature. The concerns of the three parties—including the rights and duties of citizens, division of power, the organization of the municipalities, national economy, and the problem of federalism—were considered by the commission.

After suspension of some constitutional rights in 1994 and 1995 and an economic recession in the mid-1990s, President Hugo Chávez used the referendum on a new constitution to confirm his tight control of political power in Venezuela. The new constitution, which garnered strong support from the electorate, was promulgated on December 20, 1999.

Influences

Without changing the basic nature of the Venezuelan government, the 1999 constitution is an attempt to reduce the conflict between the executive and legislative branches and to broaden the scope of participation in the governing process at all levels.

The Constitution

In the preamble to the 1999 constitution, the people of Venezuela invoke "protection from God, the historical example of our Liberator Simón Bolívar and the heroism and sacrifice of our aboriginal predecessors." They also identify "the supreme goal of reestablishing the Republic [as] a democratic, participative and leading, multiethnic and multicultural society in a State of justice...."

Article 1 proclaims: "The Bolivaran Republic of Venezuela is irrevocably free and independent and bases its moral patrimony and its values of freedom, equality, justice and international peace on the doctrine of Simón Bolívar, the Liberator." Article 2 indicates that "Venezuela constitutes itself as a democratic and social State of Law and Justice, which advocates as superior values ... life, freedom, justice, equality, solidarity, democracy, social responsibility and, in general, the prominence of human rights, ethics and political pluralism." According to articles 4, 5, and 7, respectively: "Venezuela is a federal decentralized State.... Sovereignty resides un-transferably in the people, who exercise it directly.... The Constitution is the supreme norm and the foundation of the juridical order."

Fundamental Rights

Article 26 guarantees "[e]very person ... a right of access to the organs of ... justice in order to assert his rights and interests ... ," while article 29 declares that the nation "will be obligated to investigate and legally sanction [punish] the crimes against human rights committed by its authorities." Rights, guarantees, and citizens' duties are expressly set forth among articles 19 through 135 and include freedom to develop one's personality, equality before the law, "right to life," a prohibition against the death penalty, the right to address international bodies for redress under international human rights treaties ratified by Venezuela, the rights of detainees, privacy of the home and communication, due process in "judicial and administrative actions," and respect for each person's "physical, psychological and moral integrity."

Political rights, including the right to vote at eighteen years of age and the rights of assembly and association, are guaranteed. Separate chapters are devoted to social, family, cultural, educational, economic, environmental, and indigenous peoples' rights. Among the duties of citizens set forth in articles 130 to 135 are to "honor and defend the homeland, its symbols, [and] cultural values ... ," "comply with and ... observe this Constitution," "participate jointly in the political, civil and community life of the country," and pay taxes.

Division of Powers

Article 136 mandates that public power "is distributed among the Municipal Power, the State Power and the National Power. The National Public Power is divided into Legislative, Executive, Judicial, Civic and Electoral [Powers]." Subject areas of national power, such as international policy and the national police, are set forth in article 156; those of the states, such as administration and use of state highways and the organization of state public services, are covered in article 168. Article 159 declares that the states "are autonomous and equal entities in political [matters]" but "are obligated ... to comply with the Constitution and the laws of the Republic."

The Executive

President. Executive power, according to article 225, "is exercised by the President of the Republic, the Executive Vice President, the Ministers and other functionaries that this Constitution and the law determine." The president is "the Head of the State and of the National Executive, under which capacity he leads the action of the Government." The president is elected for a six-year term "by universal, direct and secret ballot" by a "majority of the valid votes" and "may be reelected, immediately and for one time only, for an additional term." Candidates are required to be Venezuelan by birth and not to have another nationality, be older than thirty years of age, and have "secular status."

The president "is obligated to secure the guarantee of the rights and freedoms of Venezuelans," as well as to "promulgate the law," comply with and secure compliance with the constitution and the law, appoint and remove the executive vice president and ministers, direct foreign relations, exercise supreme command of the armed forces as commander in chief, "declare ... states of exception and decree the restriction of guarantees in the cases specified in this Constitution," administer the treasury, and "formulate the National Plan of Development and ... manage its execution with prior approval from the [legislature]."

If the president is permanently disabled or absent—for example, dismissed "by sentence of the Supreme Tribunal of Justice"—or temporarily absent, the executive vice president generally takes charge. However, if the office is vacant and a new president has not yet taken office, the president of the legislature acts as president until elections can be held within thirty days.

Executive Vice President and Cabinet. According to article 239, the powers and duties of the executive vice president include collaborating "with the President of the Republic in the management of the ... Government," coordinating the government under the president's instructions, proposing to the president the nomination and removal of ministers, presiding over the federal council of government and, "with the prior authorization of the President," over the council of ministers. He or she also substitutes during the president's temporary absences.

The council of ministers (cabinet) consists of the president, executive vice president, and ministers. "The Ministers are direct organs of the President," states article 242, and they and the executive vice president are jointly responsible for the cabinet's decisions in which they have concurred.

Also part of the executive branch are a consultative body called the council of state and a federal council charged with planning and coordinating "the process of decentralization."

The Legislature

Congress. As specified in article 186, a national assembly is "composed of deputies elected [together with a substitute] in each federal entity by universal, direct, personalized and secret vote with proportional representation, according to ... population.... Each federal entity will elect, as well, three deputies ... [and the] indigenous peoples ... will elect three deputies...." Qualifications to be a legislator include having Venezuelan nationality and residing in the country for fifteen years, being older than twenty-one years of age, and being a resident of the electoral entity for four consecutive years. Among the disqualifications are holding certain offices, including those of president, executive vice president, and state governor. Deputies enjoy certain immunities, although the "Supreme Tribunal of Justice ... will be able to order, with prior authorization from the [legislature], their detention and continue their judgment."

In addition to passing legislation, the assembly is authorized to propose "amendments and reforms to the Constitution," exercise control over the government, decree amnesties, approve the national budget, and censure and dismiss the executive vice president and ministers by a three-fifths vote. The legislature also authorizes the deployment of troops abroad or of foreign troops in Venezuela and approves international treaties.

Laws may be initiated by, among others, the "National Executive Power," at least three members of the legislature, the supreme tribunal of justice and the Civic Power (see below) with respect to laws related to their functions, no less than one-tenth of one percent of registered voters, and state legislatures. Organic laws, as defined in article 203, may be introduced in the legislature by a vote of two-thirds of the members present and must be submitted to the constitutional chamber of the supreme tribunal to determine their constitutionality. Other enabling laws require a three-fifths vote of the legislature. To enact a law, two debates, a committee report, and a majority vote are generally required. After approval, laws are promulgated by the president within ten days.

The Judiciary

According to article 253, "The system of justice is constituted by the Supreme Tribunal of Justice [and] other tribunals that the law determines," as well as other institutions.

Supreme Tribunal. "The Supreme Tribunal," states article 262, "will function in Plenary Chambers and in Constitutional, Politico-Administrative, Electoral, Civil Cassation, Penal Cassation and Social Cassation Chambers, the composition and competences of which will be determined by its organic law." In addition to the constitutional review function of its constitutional chamber, the tribunal confirms judgments of the legislature against the president and other high officials, settles "administrative controversies," nullifies "regulations and other general or individual administrative acts of the National Executive," adjudicates conflicts between tribunals, and hears appeals from lower courts. A member must be a citizen by birth and of "recognized honor," as well as a "jurist of recognized competence."

Civic Power

"The organs that exercise the Civic Power," declares article 274, "are charged with ... preventing, investigating and sanctioning the acts that threaten public ethics and administrative morals." They are also empowered "to see to ... the fulfillment and application of ... legality in the entire administrative activity of the State."

Amending the Constitution

Pursuant to article 340, amendments may be proposed by fifteen percent of citizens eligible to vote, thirty percent of the members of the legislature, or the president "in the Council of Ministers." Proposals by the legislature require an absolute majority of all members. Amendments are additionally submitted to a referendum within thirty days of approval.

A proposal for a complete revision of the constitution comes from the legislature "by means of an agreement approved by the vote of the majority of its members, by the President of the Republic in the Council of Ministers or by request of a number no less than fifteen percent" of registered voters. Three debates on the proposal are required in the legislature, after which it must be adopted within two years by a vote of two-thirds of its members; a referendum is then held within thirty days. If the revision is voted affirmatively by more than half of those voting, the president is "obligated to promulgate the Amendments and Reforms within the ten days following their approval."

VIETNAM

After centuries of foreign domination and decades of war, Vietnam remains under the rule of the Communist Party. However, its 1992 constitution and increased interaction with Western democracies, particularly the United States, may provide a basis for democratic reforms.

General Information

The Socialist Republic of Vietnam in Southeast Asia is approximately 332,000 square kilometers and is bounded by mainland China on the north, Laos and Cambodia on the west, the Gulf of Tonkin on the northeast, and the South China Sea on the east and south. Hanoi is the capital of this nation of approximately seventy-seven million persons.

Vietnam exports rice and oil, and since the beginning of the 1990s the economy has improved, attracting foreign investment. Normalization of relations with the United States and further political reforms moving away from Communist Party controls and state management could improve the country's prospects for the future.

Type of Government: Communist Party dictatorship, with a presidential-style parliamentary government including a president, a prime minister and cabinet, a unicameral legislature, and a judiciary with people's organs of control

Dates of Constitutions: 1946, 1959, 1980, and 1992

Constitutional History

Vietnamese civilization, which dates from the late Stone Age and early Bronze Age, is said to have been founded by Hung Vuong, son of the mythological Lac Dragon Lord. The people cultivated rice with extensive irrigation systems called Lac fields (*Lac* was the early name for the Vietnamese people). The culture developed from a complex mixture of Austronesian, Mon-Khmer, and Tai language groups whose family and social relationships tended to be more open than in India and China. Women were accorded individual legal status, as reflected in a later compilation of laws called Le Code, begun in A.D. 1449.

In 111 B.C. Vietnam was incorporated into the Chinese Han dynasty and remained part of it until A.D. 939. In the fifteenth century Confucianism, which grounds the rulers' authority and the subjects' total allegiance in a "mandate from heaven," became the official state ideology, but the Vietnamese continued to believe in an amalgam of animism and Buddhism. Contact with Europeans introduced Catholicism; to avenge the death of Catholic missionaries, the French seized the port city of Da Nang in 1858.

In 1867 Cochine-China, the southern third of Vietnam, became a French colony, and in 1883 the middle and northern portions—Annam and Tonkin, respectively—became French protectorates. By 1893 Vietnam, Cambodia, and Laos formed the French-controlled Indochina Union. During the colonial period nationalist and revolutionary groups, including communists, emerged; in 1941 Nguyen Ai Quoc (later known as Ho Chi Minh) formed from some of these groups a league for independence called the Viet Minh.

The Japanese, who had ousted the French in March 1945, surrendered in August 1945. Viet Minh forces took Hanoi and established the Democratic Republic of Vietnam as a communist regime. The constitution promulgated in 1946, with its guarantees of freedom of speech, the press, and assembly, may have seemed democratic but was just a facade. In 1954 the country was partitioned into northern and southern sections, and in 1959 a new, more overtly communistic constitution was adopted. It described North Vietnam as a people's democratic state led by the working class. With the reunification of the country in 1979, the constitution was amended to emphasize the development of a new culture and the socialist person.

Seriously threatened by its neighbor China, Vietnam became heavily dependent on the Soviet Union, and its 1980 constitution resembled the 1977 U.S.S.R. constitution—concentrating power in the hands of a council of state, like the presidium of the supreme soviet, and giving it both legislative and executive functions while reducing the power of the legislature to some degree. The new constitution emphasized such concepts as "collective mastery" of society and "social legality," which means that laws must conform to Communist Party directives.

On April 15, 1992, the Vietnamese legislature adopted a new constitution. Internally it is considered only a revision because in communist-controlled countries a new constitution generally signals a significant change in the leadership, which is not the message the Communist Party wanted to convey with this document.

The 1992 constitution has replaced the former document with a more Western, democratic model, but the general state policy is still in the hands of the Communist Party.

The preamble to the 1992 constitution of the Socialist Republic of Vietnam states, in part:

This constitution stipulates the political, economic, cultural, social, national defense, and security systems; the basic rights and duties of citizens; and the structure and the organizational and operational principles of various state agencies. It institutionalizes the system of relations by which the party is the leader, the people the master, and the state the manager.

Article 4 declares the country's true allegiance:

The Communist Party of Vietnam, the vanguard unit of the Vietnamese working class and the faithful representative of the interests of the working class, of the laboring people, and of the entire nation, pursues Marxism-Leninism and Ho Chi Minh thought and is the leading force of the state and society. All party organizations operate within the framework of the constitution and the law.

Chapter 5, Citizens' Fundamental Rights and Duties, declares that in the Socialist Republic of Vietnam all human rights—political, economic, cultural, and social—are respected and established as citizens' rights in the constitution but that citizens' rights are not separate from their duties.

Rights expressly mentioned include equality before the law; the right to participate in running the state, petition state agencies, and vote in referendums; the right to vote if at least eighteen years old and the right to stand for election to the national legislature and people's councils if at least twenty-five years old, regardless of ethnicity, sex, social status, faith, religion, education, occupation, or length of residence; state protection for the legal right to ownership and inheritance; and equal rights in political, economic, cultural, social, and familial aspects for citizens of both sexes. Moreover, article 69 notes, "Citizens have the right to enjoy the freedom of speech and the press, to inform and hold meetings, establish associations, and demonstrate as stipulated by law." According to article 64, families are declared to be the "cells of society" and the state and society will not accept discriminatory treatment of children. True fundamental rights, however, are problematic at best in Vietnam.

The constitution of Vietnam, a unitary state, assigns the role of the highest organ of the state to the legislature; the government and the judicial branch are responsible to it. In fact, the Communist Party leadership exercises the power of the state indirectly through the government apparatus.

President. The president is head of state and represents Vietnam in domestic and foreign affairs. He or she and the vice president are elected by the legislature from among its members for the term of the legislature, five years, and remains in office until a new president is elected.

The powers and duties of the president include promulgating the constitution, laws, and regulations; commanding the armed forces and chairing the national defense and security council; requesting the legislature to appoint or dismiss the vice president, prime minister, chief justice of the supreme people's court, and chief procurator of the supreme people's organ of control; on resolution of the legislature, appointing or dismissing a deputy prime minister, cabinet ministers, and other members of the government; declaring war, granting amnesty, and ordering mobilization of troops and declaring a state of emergency; and appointing or dismissing the deputy chief justice or other judges of the supreme people's court and certain officials of the people's organs of control. The president also confers high military rank and decorations; appoints or recalls foreign representatives and receives ambassadors; and grants or revokes citizenship. He or she is authorized to attend meetings of the legislature and, when necessary, cabinet meetings and to issue orders and decrees.

Prime Minister and Cabinet. The government (cabinet) consists of a prime minister, deputy prime ministers, and others. According to article 109, it is an executive organ of the legislature that manages the affairs of state and ensures the effectiveness of state activities from the top down and compliance with the constitution and the laws, promoting the people's right to mastery over national construction and defense.

The Legislature

Parliament. According to article 83, the unicameral legislature, the Quoc Hoi (national assembly), is the highest organ of state power. It exercises the supreme right of supervision over all operations of the state. The election of the nearly four hundred members or councilors to five-year terms is based on universal, equal, direct, and secret balloting. Members may be impeached by the voters or the assembly itself "if they no longer prove worthy of the people's confidence." The term of the assembly may be shortened or extended "under special circumstances" by a vote of at least two-thirds of all the members.

As in other communist-controlled countries, winning candidates are determined in advance of scheduled elections, the elections may not even take place, and a person chosen by the party is simply declared the winner. In recent years, however, there has been a slight trend toward a wider range of candidates and more open political debate.

The powers and duties of the assembly include drafting and amending the constitution, making and amending laws, and deciding on "law-building" programs; supervising the observance of the constitution, laws, and resolutions of the assembly and scrutinizing reports on government activities; determining the country's socioeconomic development plans, financial and monetary policies, and policy toward nationalities; defining the activities of the president of the state, the organization and operation of the assembly, the government, the people's courts, people's organs of control, and local administrations; electing, dismissing, and impeaching the president of the state and other officials such as the chairman, vice chairmen, and members of the standing committee of the assembly, as well as the prime minister and chief justice of the supreme people's court; establishing and dissolving ministries and other agencies; abrogating government documents that are unconstitutional; defining ranks and positions in the military; deciding on matters of war and peace and fundamental foreign policy; and holding referendums.

Standing Committee. A standing committee composed of the chairman, vice chairmen, and other members of the assembly has broad powers to act, including the power to declare war when the country is faced with foreign aggression and the assembly is not in session.

The Judiciary

Article 126, chapter 10, People's Courts and People's Organs of Control, decribes the role of the judiciary:

The people's courts and the people's organs of control in the Socialist Republic of Vietnam are, within the sphere of their function, obliged to protect the socialist system, the people's right to mastery, the assets of the state and collectives, and the lives, property, freedom, honor, and dignity of the citizens.

These bodies have far-reaching powers to oversee the operations of the government, including the courts and law enforcement activities at every level. A penal code adopted in 1986 defines crime broadly, encompassing economic crimes such as hoarding and currency speculation.

People's Courts. The judiciary includes a supreme people's court, the highest tribunal, local people's courts, military tribunals, and other courts and special tribunals set up by law. According to article 130, "During trials, judges and people's jurors are independent and subject only to law."

The supreme people's court generally supervises the other courts, and the presiding judge is accountable to the legislature, when in session, or to the standing committee. Presiding judges of local courts are accountable to the local people's councils. The term of office of the presiding judge or chief justice of the supreme court is the same as that of the legislature. The system of appointing and removing judges from office, election procedures, and the term of office of people's jurors or assessors, who may also act as judges, are defined by law.

People's Organs of Control. The constitution also creates a supreme people's organ of control and local organs of control to ensure observance of the law by the ministries and other government activities, including economic and social organizations, the armed forces, and all citizens. They have the power of public prosecution and are led by a chief procurator at the national and local levels.

Article 147 provides that constitutional amendments require a majority vote of no fewer than two-thirds of the total members of the legislature.

Amending the Constitution

YUGOSLAVIA

Yugoslavia—originally a federation of Bosnia and Herzegovina, Croatia, Macedonia, Montenegro, Serbia, and Slovenia—now consists of only two constituent states, Serbia and Montenegro, governed by a federal constitution adopted in 1992.

General Information

The Federal Republic of Yugoslavia on the Balkan Peninsula in southeastern Europe occupies some 102,260 square kilometers and is bounded on the north by Hungary and Romania, on the east by Bulgaria, on the south by Macedonia and Albania, and on the west by Bosnia and Herzegovina and Croatia. Belgrade, located in Serbia, is the capital of this country whose population numbers nearly eleven million persons.

Chemicals, machinery, and mining are among Yugoslavia's main industries; its chief crops include cereal, fruits, and vegetables. Yugoslavia's economy was devastated in the 1990s by wars and attempts at ethnic cleansing instigated by the Serbian dictator Slobodan Milošević, which in the province of Kosovo resulted in massive retaliatory bombing by the North Atlantic Treaty Organization (NATO).

Type of Government: Presidential-style parliamentary federal republic, with a president, a prime minister and cabinet, a bicameral legislature, a judiciary, and a constitutional court

Dates of Constitutions: 1838, 1921, 1931, 1946, 1953, 1963, 1974, and 1992

Constitutional History

People lived in the territory that would become Yugoslavia as long ago as 200,000 B.C. By around 700 B.C. Illyrian tribes were trading with the city-states on the Greek and Italian peninsulas. In the fourth century B.C. the conquests of Alexander the Great, who was born in Macedonia, included territory as far north as Serbia. A century later the Romans exacted tribute from the Illyrians, and by the first century A.D. they brought the Celtic Serbs under their control.

An important influence on the Yugoslav region was the division of the Roman Empire into eastern and western spheres in 395, which began the cultural and religious divide between the inhabitants of the Balkan Peninsula. South Slavs (*Yugoslavia* means "land of the south Slavs") began migrating into the territory in the sixth century, after which the Serbs and Croats arrived. The Slovenes were converted to Roman Catholicism in the eighth century, and during the ninth century the Serbs fell under the control of the Byzantine Empire.

The territory of Yugoslavia was also greatly influenced by the Turks, who in 1389 defeated the Serbs in the Battle of Kosovo. During the eighteenth century Russia and Austria vied for control of areas in the Balkans as the Ottoman Empire waned. In 1815 the Ottomans accorded the Serbs some autonomy under their overall control but imposed a constitution in 1838 that forced the ruling prince to abdicate. A constitutional monarchy was installed in Serbia in 1903, while Montenegro had extended its borders in the early nineteenth century.

The Balkan wars in 1912 and 1913 and World War I in 1914–18 created conditions promoting the formation of a federation of south Slavs. The Kingdom of Yugoslavia, comprising Bosnia and Herzegovina, Croatia, Macedonia, Montenegro, Serbia, and Slovenia, was proclaimed on December 4, 1918, and recognized by the Paris Peace Conference in 1919. On June 28, 1921, a constitution was adopted based on the Serbian constitution of 1903, the kingdom's interim constitution, French principles, and the Belgium constitution. This document was abrogated in 1929, and a royal dictatorship held power until 1931, when a new constitution created a limited democracy.

Under the communist regime established after World War II by Josip Broz, known as Marshall Tito, Yugoslavia had four constitutions. The 1946 constitution was based on the 1936 "Stalin" constitution of the Soviet Union. A 1953 constitution, however, departed from the Soviet model, separating the Communist Party somewhat from the government and extending some civil rights and authority to the six republics. Because the economic decentralization fostered by the new constitution caused friction among the six separate republics, in 1963 a new constitution was put into place. Tito continued as president of the Socialist Federal Republic of Yugoslavia and in 1974 oversaw the drafting of another constitution that gave him increased powers and reconfirmed the Yugoslav regime's Marxist-Leninist character.

After the collapse of the Soviet Union in 1991 and the fall of communist governments in Eastern Europe, internecine conflict in Yugoslavia—resulting largely from Serbia's attempt to impose its hegemony over the other former Yugoslav republics—reduced the nation's constituent member states to only Serbia and Montenegro. A new constitution embodying their federal relationship was adopted on April 27, 1992, ten days after the proclamation by Serbia and Montenegro of the new Federal Republic of Yugoslavia. A constitutional amendment in 2000 required direct election of the president. There continue to be significant movements in Kosovo and Montenegro for achieving independence from Serbia-dominated Yugoslavia.

The 1992 Yugoslav constitution is based on the prior 1974 document and reflects Serbia's desire to maintain its position of dominance in the federation vis-a-vis Montenegro through its overwhelmingly majority population.

The preamble to the constitution notes Yugoslavia's "freedom-loving, democratic and nation-building traditions, historical ties and shared interests of ... Serbia and ... Montenegro," adding that the document arose "from the unbroken continuity of Yugoslavia and voluntary association between Serbia and Montenegro."

Article 1 proclaims: "The Federal Republic of Yugoslavia shall be a sovereign federal state, founded on the equality of citizens and the equality of its member republics." Article 6 provides that each member republic "shall be a state in which power is vested in its citizens ... [and] shall autonomously organize its government under its own constitution." According to article 115, "The constitutions of the members republics, federal statutes, the legislation of member republics and all other laws and general enactments must be in conformity with [this] Constitution."

Articles 19 through 68 set forth rights and duties of citizens. Rights guaranteed include equality regardless of "nationality, race, sex, language, faith, political or other beliefs, education, social origin, property, or other personal status"; personal freedom; privacy; and the physical and psychological integrity of the individual. The inviolability of human life is proclaimed, and the death penalty is prohibited. Also guaranteed are freedom of movement, the inviolability of the home, privacy of mail, the right to vote and be elected to office for all persons over eighteen years of age, freedom of the press, and the right to correct false published information. "Freedom of confession, conscience, thought and public expression of opinion" are protected under article 35, while article 18 states: "Church and state shall be separate ... [and c]hurches shall be free and equal in conducting religious affairs and in the performance of religious rites."

Freedom of speech, assembly, and association are extended, except that organizations that are "aimed at the violent overthrow of the constitutional order" and "secret societies and paramilitary groups" are banned; members of the armed forces and police may not unionize; and justices and certain others may not belong to political parties. Under article 123, compensation is authorized for "damages sustained as a result of unlawful or improper [public] actions." Rights are also extended to persons accused of crimes, including the right of appeal and freedom from torture.

Article 77 authorizes government agencies, among other activities, to "enact and enforce federal legislation ... and ensure judicial protection in matters concerning ... the freedoms, rights and duties of man and the citizen, enshrined in the present Constitution. . . ." Among citizen duties, as specified in article 137, is compulsory military service, although conscientious objectors are permitted to serve in the Yugoslav army "without bearing arms or in civilian service."

Division of Powers

The republic, states article 12, "shall be organized on the principle of the separation of powers between the legislature, executive, and judiciary."

The Executive

President. Before the 2000 amendment requiring direct election of the president, article 97 provided that parliament elect the chief executive by secret ballot for a four-year term. However, the president may not be reelected for a second term, and "[a]s a rule, the President . . . and the federal prime minister may not be from the same member republic." The president "may not hold other public office or engage in professional activities," enjoys the same immunity as members of parliament and as determined by parliament, and "may only be dismissed if [parliament] ascertains that he has violated the Constitution."

According to article 96, the president "shall represent the . . . Republic . . . at home and abroad; promulgate federal laws by decree; issue instruments of ratification of international treaties; nominate a candidate for prime minister . . . ; recommend to [parliament] candidates for . . . the Federal Constitutional Court, justices of the Federal Court, and the governor of the National Bank of Yugoslavia . . . ; call elections for [parliament]; appoint and recall . . . ambassadors . . . ; [and] receive the letters of credence of foreign diplomatic envoys." Under article 135, the president also commands the army and presides over a supreme defense council, which includes the presidents of the two republics. Other powers and duties include conferring decorations and honors and granting "pardons for federal statutory criminal offenses."

If the presidency is vacant or the incumbent is temporarily unable to perform designated duties, they "shall be performed by the President of the Chamber of Republics," the upper house of parliament.

Prime Minister and Cabinet. "The federal government shall be made up of a prime minister, deputy prime minister, and federal ministers," states article 100. Among other responsibilities, the federal government formulates and conducts domestic and foreign policy, introduces bills for legislation and gives opinions on bills introduced by others, adopts decrees and resolutions to enforce federal statutes, creates and abolishes federal ministries, and directs and coordinates their work as well as the work of other federal agencies, which, states article 122, "shall be open to the public."

According to article 102, the prime minister "shall direct the work of the federal government." He or she is nominated by the federal president "after having heard the opinions of . . . the parliamentary groups" and is confirmed by parliament. The office holder is responsible to parliament, which "may vote no confidence" in the government on the initiative of "no fewer than 20 [members] of one chamber . . . [and a] majority of votes of the total number of [members] in each of the two chambers." Under article 106, "A federal government whose mandate has been terminated shall continue performing its duties until the formation of a new federal government."

The Legislature

Parliament. According to article 80, "The Federal Assembly shall be composed of the Chamber of Citizens [lower house] and the Chamber of Republics [upper house]."

Upper House. Each republic is allowed to send twenty deputies to serve in the chamber of republics for four-year terms, for a total of forty. The election and termination of these members, who "represent the member republic from which they were elected," are "regulated by the laws of each member republic."

Lower House. The chamber of citizens includes one deputy elected directly for every 65,000 voters for four-year terms, unless their mandate is terminated earlier, but each member republic can have "no fewer than 30 deputies." Federal law controls the election and termination of these deputies, who represent the federal republic.

Deputies in both houses are granted certain immunities, including immunity "for expressing an opinion or for . . . voting in the . . . Assembly," and they "may not be detained without the consent of the . . . chamber of which [they] are a member, unless caught in the act of committing a criminal offense carrying a prison sentence of more than five years." Article 88 authorizes the deputies of both chambers to elect a president and vice president from their own ranks and to "adopt rules of procedure regulating their work and organization."

The federal assembly's duties, as set out in article 78, include deciding on the constitution, determining the admission of other states, adopting federal statutes, overseeing the work of the federal government, confirming and dismissing the prime minister, granting amnesty, and appointing and dismissing justices of the federal constitutional court and federal court, the governor of the national bank, and other federal officials.

Bills may be introduced by the government, a deputy, or "not less than 30,000 voters"; the national bank may also introduce legislation "concerning the monetary, foreign exchange and credit systems." Action on certain subjects—for example, decisions concerning the flag, coat of arms, or national anthem—require a supermajority in both chambers. If an identical bill is not passed by each house and cannot be "harmonized" by a joint commission of deputies, "the text approved in the Chamber of Citizens shall be temporarily adopted." If after a year the legislation still has not been adopted identically in both chambers, "the mandate of the Federal Assembly shall be terminated," says article 93.

Judicial authorization is provided under articles 108 to 110, which are devoted solely to creation of a federal court.

The Judiciary

Federal Court. According to article 108, the federal court is to "act as a court of the highest instance [and] decide on appeals against rulings by courts of the member republics in cases concerning enforcement of federal statutes; . . . property suits between member republics, as well as between . . . Yugoslavia and member republics; determine the legality of [federal] administrative regulations . . . ; decide on [certain] conflicts of jurisdiction . . . ; [and] lay down principles governing the uniform enforcement of federal statutes. . . ." The court is to be regulated by federal statute.

Justices are appointed by parliament for nine-year terms, and they select a president from among their members. A justice, states article 110, may be dismissed for certain reasons including being convicted of a crime that "renders him unfit to carry out judicial functions," being found to be "incompetent or unconscientious," or becoming "permanently incapacitated."

Constitutional Court

A federal constitutional court is composed of seven justices who are appointed by parliament on the president's recommendation for nine-year terms; they elect their own president by secret ballot to serve for three years. According to article 127, proceedings before the court may be initiated by anyone, including specifically "government authorities or artificial persons if they believe that a right or interest has been violated," as well as by the court itself.

The court's jurisdiction includes ruling on the conformity with the federal constitution of the constitutions of the member republics as well as statutes, other laws, general enactments, and treaties; the conformity of laws of member republics with federal law; and the conformity of regulations of federal agencies with federal law. It may also rule on complaints by citizens involving the violations of "the rights and freedoms of man and the citizen enshrined in the present Constitution"; on conflicts "of jurisdiction between federal and republican authorities" and "between the authorities of member republics"; on "prohibition of activities of political parties and other associations of citizens"; and on federal election violations.

Amending the Constitution

Article 139 authorizes the federal government, at least thirty members of the lower house, twenty members of the upper house, or 100,000 voters to propose constitutional amendments. Proposals to amend the constitution "shall be decided upon by the chambers of the Federal Assembly by a two-thirds majority . . . in each of the two chambers." Approved proposed amendments must then be adopted by the same majorities. If an amendment fails, it cannot be resubmitted for one year.

Under article 140, a proposal to amend articles 1, 2, 3, 6, 7, 77, 140, and 141 may be submitted by no fewer than 100,000 voters, thirty members of the lower house, the federal government, or the assembly of a member republic. Approval requires a two-thirds majority of the members of the lower house, which "may decide to amend the Constitution . . . after the assemblies of the member republics have approved the proposal." Or, pursuant to article 141, approval of "[t]he draft to amend" the excepted articles may be approved by a two-thirds majority in the lower house, and such amendment "shall be deemed to be accepted when the assemblies of the member republics have approved the text adopted by the [lower house]."

Article 142 provides that any amendments "shall be promulgated by the Federal Assembly."

On October 31, 1991, Zambia held its first multiparty election in twenty-three years. The presidential election of 1996, however, was criticized by international observers for harassment of opposition parties.

The Republic of Zambia in south-central Africa is approximately 752,000 square kilometers and is bounded by Zaire and Tanzania on the north; Malawi and Mozambique on the east; Zimbabwe, Botswana, and a sliver of Namibia on the south; and Angola on the west. Lusaka is the capital of this nation of approximately ten million persons.

Although Zambia owns one-fourth of the world's known copper reserves, at the current rate of production this important resource may be exhausted in ten years. Falling copper prices and a large external debt have strained Zambia's economy, and a coup attempt in 1997 reinforced the fragility of the country's democracy.

Type of Government: Presidential parliamentary republic, with a president and cabinet, a unicameral legislature, a judiciary, and an ad hoc constitutional tribunal

Dates of Constitutions: 1964, 1973, and 1991

Human development began in Zambia around two hundred thousand years ago, during the Stone Age; the remains of an early human ancestor, *Homo Rhodesiensis,* dating back one hundred twenty-five thousand years, have been found at Kabwe. Between the fourth and the sixth centuries A.D., Negroid peoples who spoke Bantu-related languages immigrated from the north, west, and south, carrying Iron Age technology with them. During the second millennium another wave of immigration brought the ancestors of the present-day inhabitants of Zambia.

After A.D. 1500 political organization, which had previously been based on lineage and clans and frequently extended beyond commonality of language and leaders, was changed to a system based on chieftains and kings. The earliest kingdom in Zambia was the Malawi kingdom of Kalonga, dating from around the fourteenth century. The concept of tribe tends to be subjective and of little value in analyzing stable political relationships in Zambia.

During the eighteenth century the Portuguese established a series of forts and trading posts along the Zambezi River and exported copper, ivory, and gold. Following missionaries and explorers such as David Livingstone in the second half of the nineteenth century, the industrialist and imperialist Cecil Rhodes instigated treaties with local chiefs in 1889 and 1890; he secured much of Zambia for British interests and blocked German expansion in the area. This land-grab tactic accounts for the awkward shape of Zambia's borders today.

Zambia was at first run by the British South Africa Company, founded by Rhodes in 1889. Beginning in 1911 it was administered as Northern Rhodesia jointly with Southern Rhodesia, and an advisory council was created in 1918 to assuage the demands of the European settlers. In 1924 Northern Rhodesia became a separate British protectorate, with a legislative council that included five members elected by the settlers. From 1924 to 1953 major copper deposits were discovered in the country's north-central part, luring more settlers. Political awareness among the Africans propelled the rise of nationalism, creating insecurity among the immigrants. As a result, European settlers in Northern Rhodesia joined with those in Southern Rhodesia and Nyasaland (Malawi) in 1953 to form the Central African Federation of Rhodesia and Nyasaland. In 1962 elections resulted in an African majority in the legislative council, and the next year the federation was dissolved. The independent Republic of Zambia was established on October 24, 1964, under a constitution effective the same day.

Also in 1964, Kenneth D. Kaunda, head of the United National Independence Party, was selected the first president of the country. In 1972 he banned all other parties, including the rival National Congress Party; the only legal party then adopted a new constitution for the second republic in 1973, confirming the principle of one-party participatory democracy introduced the year before.

On August 2, 1991, the Zambian legislature adopted a new constitution reinstating the multiparty system, restoring the position of vice president, eliminating the position of prime minister, authorizing the president to select the cabinet from among members of the legislature, and prohibiting the president from declaring martial law. After a new party won the elections in October 1991, the new president, Fredrick Chiluba, permitted the twenty-seven-year-long state of emergency to lapse.

Influences

The constitution of the Republic of Zambia reflects the influence of the British parliamentary system but contains modifications similar to some other central and southern African nations.

The Constitution

By Act No. 1, assented to on August 24, 1991, the Republic of Zambia repealed the 1973 constitution and enacted a new constitution. Among other things, the preamble declares the country's "determination to uphold our inherent and inviolable right to decide, appoint, and proclaim the means and style whereby we shall govern ourselves . . . [as] a unitary, indivisible, multi-party, and democratic sovereign state." It also declares the republic "a Christian nation while upholding the right of every person to . . . freedom of conscience or religion."

Fundamental Rights

Part 3, Protection of Fundamental Rights and Freedoms of the Individual, provides that every person in Zambia is entitled to the fundamental rights and freedoms regardless of race, place of origin, political opinions, color, creed, sex, or marital status but subject to certain limitations. These rights include life, liberty, security of the person and the protection of the law; freedom of conscience, expression, assembly, movement, and association; protection of young persons from exploitation; and protection for the privacy of the home and other property and from deprivation of property without compensation. The rights are elaborated on individually, and enforcement procedures, such as application to the high court for redress, are provided for in article 28. Article 125, as amended in 1996, establishes a human rights commission whose "function, powers, composition, funding and administrative procedures . . . shall be prescribed by . . . an Act of Parliament," according to article 126.

Division of Powers

In Zambia, a unitary state, power is divided among the president, the legislature, and the courts, which exercise little, if any, judicial review, but some preenactment constitutional review is provided by an ad hoc tribunal.

The Executive

President. Article 33(2) describes the president's role: "The executive power shall be vested in the president and, subject to the other provisions of this constitution, shall be exercised by him either directly or through officers subordinate to him." The president is head of state and head of government and commander in chief of the defense forces.

To be eligible to be president a person must be a citizen of Zambia and his or her parents must be Zambian, at least thirty-five years old, a member of or sponsored by a political party, otherwise qualified to be a member of the legislature, and domiciled in Zambia for at least twenty years. He or she must also pay an election fee, declare his or her assets and liabilities, and be supported in the nomination by no fewer than two hundred registered voters. Candidates are elected by direct, universal, adult suffrage by secret ballot and must receive "the highest number of the total votes cast." The term is five years unless the legislature is dissolved sooner. No person who has held the office for two five-year terms is eligible for reelection. The president is granted immunity from legal proceedings for any acts or omissions while in office.

Article 44 provides that the president is to discharge the functions of government in accordance with the constitution and the laws of Zambia. The powers and duties of the president include negotiating international agreements, signing and promulgating laws and initiating laws for adoption by the legislature, dissolving the legislature, establishing and dissolving government ministries and departments as approved by the legislature, receiving and appointing foreign representatives, granting pardons and reprieves, conferring honors, and making appointments as required by the constitution. In consultation with the cabinet, the president is authorized to declare a state of emergency or war.

The president may in writing authorize the vice president to discharge the functions of the office when he or she is absent or ill; if the president is physically or mentally incapable of performing these functions, the vice president or, in his or her absence, a member of the cabinet elected by that body performs these functions. The president may be removed, in accordance with constitutional procedures, on charges brought by one-third of all the members of the legislature, followed by a supporting vote of two-thirds of all the members and then a vote of no less than three-fourths of all the members, after a report is made substantiating the charges by a tribunal appointed by the chief justice.

Cabinet. The president appoints the cabinet ministers, selected from among the members of the legislature, as well as deputy ministers. The president may assign cabinet ministers the administration of any province, ministry, or department of government.

Parliament. According to article 62, "The legislative power of the Republic of Zambia shall vest in parliament which shall consist of the president and the national assembly."

The assembly includes 150 elected members, no more than eight members appointed by the president, and the speaker, who is to be elected from among persons qualified to be members of the assembly but are not. The speaker alone remains in office after the dissolution of the assembly. A deputy speaker is elected from among the members. To be qualified to be a member a person must be a citizen, at least twenty-one years old, and literate and conversant in the official language, which is English. A number of disqualifications are listed in article 65.

The legislative power is to be exercised by bills passed by the assembly and assented to by the president. No fewer than thirty members may submit a bill or statutory instrument to an ad hoc tribunal, which is to report to the president and the speaker whether the measure is inconsistent with the constitution, except in the case of appropriations or constitutional amendment bills. When the president withholds assent, his or her veto may be overridden by a vote of two-thirds of all the members, except when the ad hoc tribunal finds the bill inconsistent with part 3 on fundamental rights; the bill is then returned to the assembly. To be effective, laws must be officially published, but laws may be prospective or retrospective in nature. Money bills must have the recommendation of the president and the concurrence of either the vice president or a minister. A quorum is one-third of all the members, and generally measures are passed by a majority of the members present and voting, with the speaker or acting speaker voting only in the case of a tie vote.

Ombudsman. Article 90, part 5, on the Legislature, provides for an investigator-general to be appointed by the president in consultation with a judicial service commission.

The judiciary of Zambia consists of a supreme court, a high court, and other courts created by the legislature. Article 91 provides that the judges of these courts are to be independent, impartial, and subject only to the constitution and the law and that the judicature shall be autonomous and administered in accordance with an act of the legislature.

Supreme Court. The supreme court is a superior court of record and the final court of appeal. The chief justice of the supreme court, who, like the other judges of that court, is appointed by the president and confirmed by the legislature, is authorized to make rules and regulations for court practice and procedure.

High Court. The high court, except with respect to proceedings in the industrial relations court, has unlimited or original jurisdiction to hear and determine any civil or criminal proceedings and such other jurisdiction conferred by the constitution or any other law. It is given jurisdiction to supervise any civil or criminal proceedings before any court or court-martial. The chief justice is also an ex officio judge of the high court.

Ad Hoc Tribunal

Historically, the courts in Zambia have had no real power of judicial review, although they are given a role by the constitution in the enforcement of fundamental rights. Constitutional review consists of an ad hoc tribunal that may report on the constitutionality of certain laws before enactment.

Traditional Leaders

Article 127 establishes the institution of "chief," defined in article 128 as "a traditional leader or cultural leader [who] shall enjoy such privileges and benefits as may be conferred by the Government and the local government or as that leader may be entitled to under culture, custom and tradition." Article 130 creates an advisory body to the government called the "House of Chiefs," which, according to article 131, may discuss and consider bills relating to custom and tradition and customary law and practice.

Amending the Constitution

A bill for a constitutional amendment must be officially published thirty days before the first reading in the legislature and must be supported on the second and third readings by a vote of no less than two-thirds of all the members. Proposed amendments to part 3 on fundamental rights must be approved by a referendum vote of no less than fifty percent of the people entitled to be registered as voters in general elections.

In 1979 the white electorate in Southern Rhodesia approved majority rule and a new constitution. By order of the British government the independent Republic of Zimbabwe came into existence on April 18, 1980.

The Republic of Zimbabwe in southern Africa is approximately 391,000 square kilometers and is bounded by Zambia on the northwest, Mozambique on the northeast and east, South Africa on the south, and Botswana on the southwest. Harare is the capital of this country of more than eleven million persons.

Zimbabwe has an abundance of natural resources, including chrome and copper, but production of corn, the main crop, has decreased significantly since independence. A 1992 land acquisition law permitted commercial farm land to be taken for resettlement of poor farmers, but government corruption, despotic rule, and one of the world's worst AIDS epedemics have virtually bankrupted the nation.

Type of Government: Presidential parliamentary republic, with a president and cabinet, a unicameral legislature, and a judiciary

Dates of Constitutions: 1923, 1961, 1965, 1969, 1979, and 1980

Zimbabwe lies in the region of southwest Africa where evidence of hominids more than four million years old has been found. Much later, Bantu-speaking people moved into the area. Shona-speaking people, who arrived around the third century A.D., built a kingdom associated with the Great Zimbabwe, a large stone enclosure probably built between 1100 and 1300. The Shona word *Dzimbahwe* gives the country its name.

Social organization developed, creating kingships based on divine sanction, and in the second half of the fifteenth century the central part of southern Africa was ruled by Mwanamutapa ("lord of the plunderers"). Changamire, a noble who rebelled against Mwanamutapa with the help of soldiers he referred to as *rozvi* (destroyers), established a separate kingdom in what is today the southern part of Zimbabwe. Changamire Dombo, his successor as *mambo* (king), drove out the few Portuguese who tried to settle in the area in 1690, and by 1696 his empire was firmly established south of the Zambezi River.

By the end of the nineteenth century the territory of Zimbabwe and Zambia had come under the control of the British South Africa Company, founded by Cecil Rhodes of the Cape Colony in 1889. Rhodes fraudulently entered into a treaty with the Ndebele people, hoping to exploit rumored gold in the Great Zimbabwe. In 1896, after a raid by the company's police into the Transvaal, Rhodes was implicated and lost control of the company, but Southern Rhodesia, as it was named in 1898, remained under the company's control, with an administrator, advisory council, and legislative council with some appointed and some elected members.

The company was replaced by a formal British-style government in 1923 under a constitution, with a governor representing the British monarch, a thirty-member legislative assembly, and six ministers chosen from the assembly. The country was classified as a self-governing colony rather than a dominion, such as Canada. A land apportionment act in 1931 instituted racial segregation. In 1953 Northern and Southern Rhodesia joined with other territory to form the Central African Federation of Rhodesia and Nyasaland, which lasted until 1963. African nationalism had become a force in 1957, and a 1961 constitution moved the country closer to independence.

In 1965 the government of Southern Rhodesia unilaterally declared its independence under a new constitution, but the United Kingdom reaffirmed its authority and imposed sanctions, as did the United Nations. In 1969 Rhodesians voted to become a republic under a new constitution, replacing the British monarch with a nonexecutive president as head of state. Political leaders in Southern Rhodesia agreed to a transitional government, the land apportionment act was repealed, and racial discrimination in public places was banned. After a short-lived 1979 Zimbabwean constitution, the British, who had not recognized the country's earlier unilateral declaration of independence, enacted a new constitution for Zimbabwe in 1979. It took effect on April 18, 1980, when the country became independent.

Influences

Zimbabwe's constitution was initially based on the British parliamentary system, but major revisions since independence have greatly increased the power of the president.

The Constitution

The constitution of Zimbabwe, amended in 1990 to change the name of the country to the Republic of Zimbabwe, was enacted in the United Kingdom and approved by referendum in 1979.

Fundamental Rights

Chapter 3, Declaration of Rights, sets forth a number of fundamental rights and freedoms to which every person in Zimbabwe is entitled, whatever "his race, tribe, place of origin, political opinions, color, creed, or sex, but subject to respect for the rights and freedoms of others. . . ." These include the right to life, liberty, security of the person, and the protection of the law; freedom of conscience, expression, and assembly and association; protection for the privacy of the home and other property; and, according to article 16, freedom from the compulsory acquisition of property without compensation. The latter article, however, was amended in 1993 to provide, among other things, for application to the courts for the return of improperly taken property.

An amendment in 2000 provided that where "the former colonial power fail[ed] to pay compensation" for agricultural land "compulsorily acquired for resettlement," the government of Zimbabwe "has no obligation to pay compensation" for such land.

Division of Powers

Zimbabwe is a unitary state, in which power is divided among the president, as head of state and government; the legislature; and the courts, which have limited judicial review.

The Executive

President. The president, who is elected by registered voters for a six-year term, is head of state and government and commander in chief of the armed forces. Under the constitution he or she takes precedence over all other people in Zimbabwe. To be eligible to be president, a person must be a citizen by birth or descent, at least forty years old, and ordinarily a resident of the country.

The duties and powers of the president include entering into international agreements (the treaties must be ratified by the legislature), declaring war and making peace, appointing and receiving foreign dignitaries, appointing ministers and deputy ministers and assigning them functions, appointing some members of the legislature, and granting pardons.

According to a 1990 amendment, the president may appoint two vice presidents and designate one of them to act as president should he or she become unable to perform the required functions.

Cabinet. The cabinet consists of the president, vice presidents, and "such ministers as the President may from time to time appoint."

Ombudsman. The president also appoints an ombudsman to investigate complaints against government authorities. Unlike in Nigeria and some other countries, however, this official lacks the authority to initiate investigations and seems to have little effect on correcting abuses of power.

Parliament. By amendment in 1989, the bicameral parliament of Zimbabwe became unicameral. Article 32 now declares that the legislature, called the house of assembly, "consists of the president and parliament." Under another amendment in 1993 the legislature was authorized to confer "legislative functions on any person or authority."

Of the 150 members of parliament, 120 are elected, eight are provincial governors appointed by the president as ex officio members, ten are elected chiefs, and twelve are appointed by the president. The attorney general is an ex officio member of the parliament and the cabinet but does not have the right to vote. The term of the legislature is six years. Article 49, as amended, provides that privileges, immunities, and powers of the members and the parliament may be regulated by law.

Bills are passed by a majority vote of those present and voting, with a quorum being at least twenty-five members plus the presiding officer, who may not vote. After passage, bills are presented to the president for assent; if it is withheld, such a veto may be overridden by a vote of two-thirds of all the members. Unless the president first dissolves the parliament, he or she must then assent to the measure.

Article 31F, as amended in 1989, authorizes the parliament to pass a vote of no confidence in the government by a majority of at least two-thirds of all the members.

As of 1990 article 79 of the constitution provides that the judicial authority of Zimbabwe vests in the supreme court, the high court, and such other courts subordinate to them as may be established by the legislature. Article 24 gives the courts authority to hear appeals arising out of alleged contravention of the constitution's section on the declaration of rights.

Article 79A provides that the judiciary is to consist of the chief justice as its head, the judges of the supreme court, the "judge president" and other judges of the high court, and people presiding over other courts subordinate to the two courts that are established by the legislature. To be qualified to be appointed to either court a person must be a judge or a legal practitioner in a country whose common law is Roman-Dutch or English and where English is the official language. By amendment in 1987, the appointment of the chief justice is made by the president, after consulting the judicial service commission, rather than by the president "acting on the advice of the prime minister," as before.

According to article 79B, members of the judiciary are not controlled by any person or authority in the exercises of their judicial functions, except where the law places them under another member of the judiciary.

Article 111 provides for "chiefs to preside over the tribespeople," who are appointed by the president, giving "due consideration to the customary principles of succession of the tribespeople. . . ."

Following several revisions of the amendment process, amendments are now made by bills passed by an affirmative vote of two-thirds of the total membership of the legislature with the assent of the president.

Amparo. Protection against unlawful imprisonment, a concept first developed in Mexico and now incorporated into many constitutions of Latin American countries; similar to the *writ* of *habeas corpus* in *common law* countries.

Assessors. Lay persons who assist judges in making decisions; often used in countries dominated by the Communist Party.

Autogolpe. A self-*coup d'etat*, whereby a head of state or *government* who is in power constitutionally seizes control of the government extraconstitutionally, generally to thwart a loss of power by constitutional means.

Bill of attainder. A pronouncement of guilt by legislative act for a crime such as treason, resulting in an extinction of civil rights, a forfeiture of property, and a "corruption of criminals' blood" such that title to property could not be traced through them nor could they bring suit in court.

Checks and balances. The principle of *government* organization that, along with *separation of powers*, gives the branches of government responsibilities for overseeing—checking—each other's actions; it also requires that the powers of each branch be relatively equal—balanced—to prevent one branch from becoming dominant.

Common law. Legal precedents derived from the decisions of courts of law as opposed to equity courts or statutes. Common law countries are generally those that have derived their legal systems from England.

Confederation. A league or group of states united for a common purpose, similar to an alliance.

Constitutional. In accordance with or authorized by a constitution, thus legal; also, authority limited by a constitution, such as a constitutional monarchy.

Constitutionalism. Adherence to constitutional principles, not necessarily to a particular constitution. A law that is not in conflict with the express provisions of a particular constitution may nevertheless be unconstitutional in a broader sense because it is in conflict with accepted constitutional norms.

Coup d'etat. A change in *government* by unconstitutional means, usually by force. *See also* Autogolpe.

Cour de cassation. The highest court of appeal in France and other countries.

Crown. Originally, the sovereign; also now refers to the *government* under a constitutional monarchy, including the prime minister and other members of the cabinet who are said to carry out their official duties on behalf of the crown.

Decree-law. An order by an officer of the executive branch of *government* that has the force of an enacted law and that in many cases must be authorized in advance or subsequently approved by the legislature; identical to a law-decree.

Dominion. Derived from the British North America Act of 1867, which created "one Dominion under the name of Canada." In the early 1900s the term also came to denote other countries in the British Empire that had a measure of self-government and that were not colonies, such as Australia, New Zealand, and South Africa.

Entrenched provision. A section in a constitution that is protected from deletion or change by the ordinary process of amendment.

Ex post facto law. Latin: made after the occurrence. Legislation that would have a retroactive effect, especially a criminal law.

Federal state. A *nation-state* that distributes power vertically between a national *government* and state or provincial government units; the opposite of a *unitary* or completely centralized nation-state.

Government. Generally, the combination of political institutions, laws, and customs through which the function of governing is carried out. Also refers to (1) the executive branch of a presidential constitutional system, as opposed to the administration alone, which consists of the political officeholders from the president on down; and (2) the cabinet, which in a constitutional parliamentary monarchy includes political officeholders.

Habeas corpus. Latin: that you have the body. A *writ* or legal instrument developed in England to enforce obedience to the courts. It commands anyone, particularly a *government* official, to bring an imprisoned person before the court and explain the legal basis for detaining that person. Like the Latin American concept of *amparo,* it is a protection against illegal detention that is often incorporated into written constitutions.

Imprescriptible. Inalienable, such as a right that is not subject to being taken away or lost.

Interpellation. A procedure by which members of a parliament may formally question a member of the *government* or cabinet about an official action, policy, or personal conduct. If the inquiry is not answered to the satisfaction of the parliamentary majority, it may lead to a vote of no confidence in the official or the government as a whole and to a consequent resignation.

Junta. A self-appointed body, generally of military officers, that often takes over after a *coup d'etat.*

Law-decree. *See* Decree-law.

Legitimist. One who bases the right to rule on the hereditary or "legitimate" right of the sovereign.

List vote, party list system. A method of *proportional representation* using slates of political party candidates, or lists, in each electoral district. Winners of seats in the legislature are determined from the top of the list down based on the percentage of the vote the party receives in that district.

Mandate. Authorization given by the League of Nations to a member country to administer a territory.

Martial law. The suspension of ordinary constitutional *government*, in which enforcement of the law is carried out by the military rather than by civilian police.

Ministry in waiting. The shadow cabinet or leaders of the minority party who would presumably hold cabinet positions were their party to become the majority party in a parliamentary system of *government*.

Money bill. Appropriations legislation that authorizes the expenditure of *government* funds or revenue legislation that seeks to raise funds for the government, generally by taxation; often treated specially by legislatures in accordance with provisions of the constitution.

Nation-state. The basic unit of territorial sovereignty in the modern world and the primary unit of international relations.

Ombudsman. A position with authority to receive citizens' complaints and to investigate wrongdoing or inefficiency on the part of *government* officials; the position was first established in Sweden and is generally filled by the legislature.

Organic law. Legislation affecting the organization of *government* or another entity. It may or may not have constitutional status, but it usually requires more than a simple majority vote in the legislature. It may also be enacted to apply to possessions or territories of a *nation-state*.

Party list system. *See* List vote.

Plebiscite. A popular vote on a proposal or an expression of opinion by voters, especially on the choice of a *government* or a ruler; often used in English-language constitutions and English-language translations of constitutions in place of *referendum.*

Plenary session. A meeting that all qualified members of a body attend.

Prerogative. Discretionary power that is an attribute of sovereignty, such as the authority historically inherent in the British *crown*.

Presidium. A permanent executive committee of a larger body, generally a legislature; often used in countries dominated by the Communist Party.

Privy council. Originally, an advisory body to the *crown*; in the United Kingdom, now refers to the Judicial Committee of the Privy Council, which consists of lords of appeal (law lords), who sit in the house of lords and hear final legal appeals.

Proportional representation. Preference voting, in which voters in electoral districts may rank candidates so that second- and third-place votes count toward determining a winner if no single candidate receives more than fifty percent of the vote.

Reading(s). Consideration of proposed legislation before passage. Parliamentary rules generally require that bills be read completely to the legislature before members are called on to vote. This literal procedure is frequently dispensed with, but constitutions or legislative procedures often provide that bills be debated during at least three readings, or votes, before a law may be considered to be passed.

Referendum. The practice of submitting a proposed law, including a constitutional law, revision, or amendment, to a popular vote. *See also* Plebiscite.

Rescript. A form of official order, decree, or announcement.

Res judicata. A matter that has already been judicially decided and therefore conclusive unless the determination is reversed.

Ridings. An administrative or electoral district, especially in Canada.

Rule of law. A standard for holding *government* officials to the same substantive law to which all citizens are subject; generally, government by laws rather than by people. The term is mentioned in the Universal Declaration of Human Rights (1948).

Separation of powers. A constitutional principle that divides the power of *government* into three functions or branches: making the laws (legislative), interpreting the laws (judicial), and enforcing the laws (executive). This formal division is designed to prevent tyranny or a monopoly of government power in the hands of a single person or group. It was first described by the Greek scientist and philosopher Aristotle and restated by the French lawyer and philosopher Montesquieu in his *Spirit of the Laws* (1748). *See also* Checks and balances.

Shadow cabinet. *See* Ministry in waiting.

Single transferable vote. A method of *proportional representation*, similar to a *list vote,* but in which voters using a multiparty ballot rank various candidates first, second, third, and so on, without confining choices to one party.

Soviet. Russian: council. A legislature-like body in the former Union of Soviet Socialist Republics; also, a U.S.S.R. resident or the *government*.

Unitary state. A *nation-state* in which sovereignty is not shared vertically with other units such as states or provinces; not a *federal state*.

Veto. The refusal of an executive officer, generally the president of a country, to assent to the passage of a law where his or her assent is required for the law to become effective.

Writ. A legal instrument to enforce obedience to an authority, generally a court of law.

Materials used in researching *Constitutions of the World* were obtained for the most part from the governments of the countries and from original sources available at the Law Library of the Library of Congress, Law Library of the George Washington University National Law Center, and International Law Institute, all in Washington, D.C., as well as the United Nations Library in New York.

Basic reference works for general information and historical background on each country were the Area Handbook series (Washington, D.C.: Library of Congress, 1979–94); the World Today series (Washington, D.C., and Harpers Ferry, W.Va.: Stryker-Post Publications, 2000); and CSA Publications, *Political Handbook of the World: 1999* (Binghamton, N.Y.: State University of New York, 1999). Reference works on constitutional materials, in addition to constitutional documents and materials provided by the governments of the countries, were Albert P. Blaustein and Gisbert H. Flanz, *Constitutions of the Countries of the World* looseleaf service (Dobbs Ferry, N.Y.: Oceania Publications, various dates); Kenneth Robert Redden, ed., *Modern Legal Systems Cyclopedia* looseleaf service (Buffalo, N.Y.: William S. Hein, various dates); Amos J. Peaslee, *Constitutions of Nations* (Concord, N.H.: Runford Press, 1950, 3 vols.; The Hague, the Netherlands: Martinus Nijhoff, 1965, rev. 3d ed., 4 vols.); and Michal Rozbicki, ed., *European and American Constitutionalism in the Eighteenth Century* (Warsaw, Poland: American Studies Center, Warsaw University, 1990).

In addition to the above sources, major materials consulted for individual countries include the following:

Vickers, Miranda, and James Pettifer. *Albania: From Anarchy to Balkan Identity*. New York: New York University Press, 1997. **Albania**

Ageron, Charles-Robert. *Modern Algeria: A History from 1830 to the Present*. Trenton, N.J.: Africa World Press, 1990. **Algeria**

Hanks, Peter. *Constitutional Law in Australia*. Adelaide: Butterworths, 1991. **Australia**

Lane, Patrick H. *Manual of Australian Constitutional Law*. Sydney: Law Book Company, 1991.

Landfried, Christine, ed. *Constitutional Review and Legislation: An International Comparison*. Baden-Baden, Germany: Nomos Verlagsgesellschaft, 1988. **Austria**

Alen, André, ed. *Treatise on Belgian Constitutional Law*. Deventer, the Netherlands: Kluwer Law and Taxation Publishers, 1992. **Belgium**

Donia, Robert J. *Bosnia and Hercegovina: A Tradition Betrayed*. New York: Columbia University Press, 1994. **Bosnia and Herzegovina**

Dolinger, Jacob, and Keith S. Rosenn, eds. *A Panorama of Brazilian Law*. Miami: North-South Center, University of Miami, 1992. **Brazil**

Bumsted, J. M. *The Peoples of Canada: A Pre-Confederation History*. Toronto: Oxford University Press, 1992. **Canada**

Laskin, John B., Edward L. Greenspan, Marc Rosenberg, Michael A. Penny, and Marie Henein, eds. *The Canadian Charter of Rights, Annotated*. Aurora, Ontario: Canada Law Book, 1993.

Strayer, Barry L. "Canada, the Canadian Constitution and Diversity." In *Forging Unity Out of Diversity: The Approach of Eight Nations,* edited by Robert A. Goldwin, Art Kaufman, and William A. Schambra. Washington, D.C.: American Enterprise Institute for Public Policy Research, 1989.

Chile   Codevilla, Angelo. "Is Pinochet the Model?" *Foreign Affairs,* November–December 1993, 127–40.

China   Black, George, and Robin Munro. *Black Hands of Beijing: Lives of Defiance in China's Democracy Movement.* New York: John Wiley and Sons, 1993.

Chiu, Thomas C. W., Ian R. Dobinson, and Mark Findlay. *Legal Systems of the PRC.* Hong Kong: Longman Group (Far East), 1991.

Jones, William C. "The Constitution of the People's Republic of China." In *Constitutional Systems in Late Twentieth-Century Asia,* edited by Lawrence W. Beer. Seattle: University of Washington Press, 1992.

Cuba   Oppenheimer, Andres. *Castro's Final Hour: The Secret Story Behind the Coming Downfall of Communist Cuba.* New York: Simon and Schuster, 1992.

Denmark   Gammeltoft-Hansen, Hans, Bernhard Gomaed, and Allan Philip. *Danish Law: A General Survey.* Copenhagen: g-e-c Gads, 1982.

Egypt   Saleh, Ibrahim. "The Writing of the Egyptian Constitution." In *Constitution Makers on Constitution Making: The Experience of Eight Nations,* edited by Robert A. Goldwin and Art Kaufman. Washington, D.C.: American Enterprise Institute for Public Policy Research, 1988.

Finland   Häikiö, Martti. *A Brief History of Modern Finland.* Helsinki: University of Finland, 1992.

Uotila, Jaakko, ed. *The Finnish Legal System.* Helsinki: Finnish Lawyers Publishing, 1985.

France   Bell, John. *French Constitutional Law.* New York: Oxford University Press, 1992.

Foyer, Jean. "The Drafting of the French Constitution of 1958." In *Constitution Makers on Constitution Making: The Experience of Eight Nations,* edited by Robert A. Goldwin and Art Kaufman. Washington, D.C.: American Enterprise Institute for Public Policy Research, 1988.

Price, Roger. *A Concise History of France.* Cambridge, England: Cambridge University Press, 1993.

Germany   Fulbrook, Mary. *A Concise History of Germany.* Cambridge, England: Cambridge University Press, 1990.

Hucko, Elmar M. *The Democratic Tradition: Four German Constitutions.* Providence, R.I.: Berg Publishers, 1987.

Wellenreuther, Hermann, ed. *German and American Constitutional Thought: Contexts, Interaction, and Historical Realities.* Providence, R.I.: Berg Publishers, 1990.

Elias, Taslim Olamale. *Ghana and Sierra Leone: The Development of Their Laws and Constitutions.* London: Stevens and Sons, 1962.

Ghana

Clogg, Richard. *A Concise History of Greece.* Cambridge, England: Cambridge University Press, 1992.

Greece

Kerameus, Konstantinos D., and Phaedon J. Kozyris, eds. *Introduction to Greek Law.* Deventer, the Netherlands: Kluwer Law and Taxation Publishers, 1988.

Tsatsos, Constantine D. "Making the Constitution of Greece." In *Constitution Makers on Constitution Making: The Experience of Eight Nations,* edited by Robert A. Goldwin and Art Kaufman. Washington, D.C.: American Enterprise Institute for Public Policy Research, 1988.

Nariman, Fali Sam. "The Indian Constitution: An Experiment in Unity amid Diversity." In *Forging Unity Out of Diversity: The Approach of Eight Nations,* edited by Robert A. Goldwin, Art Kaufman, and William A. Schambra. Washington, D.C.: American Enterprise Institute for Public Policy Research, 1989.

India

Hunter, Shireen T. *Iran After Khomeini.* New York: Praeger, 1992.

Iran

Amin, S. H. *The Legal System of Iraq.* Glasgow: Royston Publishers, 1989.

Iraq

Casey, James. *Constitutional Law in Ireland.* London: Sweet and Maxwell, 1992.

Ireland

Foster, Robert Fitzroy. *Modern Ireland: 1600–1972.* London: Penguin Books, 1988.

Ginsborg, Paul. *A History of Contemporary Italy: Society and Politics, 1943–1988.* New York: Penguin Books, 1990.

Italy

Rubino-Sammartano, Mauro, and Girolamo Abbatescianni. "Italy." In *World Litigation Law and Practice.* Vol. b2, edited by Ronald E. Myrick. New York: Matthew Bender, 1986.

El-Gemayel, Antoine. *The Lebanese Legal System.* Washington, D.C.: International Law Institute, 1985.

Lebanon

Reischauer, Edwin O. *Japan: The Story of a Nation.* New York: Knopf, 1989.

Japan

Ibrahim, Ahmad, and M. P. Jain. "The Constitution of Malaysia and the American Constitutional Influence." In *Constitutional Systems in Late Twentieth-Century Asia,* edited by Lawrence W. Beer. Seattle: University of Washington Press, 1992.

Malaysia

SuYan, Tun Mohamed, H. P. Lee, and F. A. Trindade, eds. *The Constitution of Malaysia, 1957–1977.* Kuala Lumpur: Oxford University Press, 1978.

Petrov, Victor P. *Mongolia: A Profile.* New York: Praeger, 1970.

Mongolia

Kortmann, Constantijn A.J.M., and Paul P. T. Bovend'Eert. *The Kingdom of the Netherlands: An Introduction to Dutch Constitutional Law.* Deventer, the Netherlands: Kluwer Law and Taxation Publishers, 1993.

The Netherlands

New Zealand	Mulholland, Raymond Douglas. *Introduction to the New Zealand Legal System*. Wellington: Butterworths, 1990.
North Korea	Cho, Sung Yoon. *Law and Legal Literature of North Korea: A Guide*. Washington, D.C.: Library of Congress, 1988.
Norway	Victorin, Anders, ed. *Scandinavian Studies in Law*. Vol. 35. Stockholm: Almqvist and Wiksell International, 1991.
Pakistan	Duncan, Emma. *Breaking the Curfew: A Political Journey through Pakistan*. London: Michael Joseph, 1989.
Panama	Krauss, Clifford. "Inside Central America: Its People, Politics, and History." In *Panama: A Nation Without Heroes*. New York: Summit Books, 1991.
The Philippines	Ferando, Enrique M., and Emma Quisumbing-Ferando. "The 1987 Constitution of the Philippines: The Impact of American Constitutionalism Revisited." In *Constitutional Systems in Late Twentieth-Century Asia,* edited by Lawrence W. Beer. Seattle: University of Washington Press, 1992.
Poland	Wagner, Wenceslas J., ed. *Polish Law throughout the Ages*. Stanford, Calif.: Hoover Institution Press, Stanford University, 1970.
Portugal	Birmingham, David. *A Concise History of Portugal*. Cambridge, England: Cambridge University Press, 1993.
Russia	Daniels, Robert V. *End of the Communist Revolution*. London: Routledge, 1993.
Saudi Arabia	Amin, S. H. *Middle East Legal Systems*. Glasgow: Royston Publishers, 1985.
South Africa	Carpenter, Gretchen. *Introduction to South African Constitutional Law*. Durban: Butterworths, 1987.
South Korea	Kim, Tscholsu, and Sang Don Lee. "Influences of U.S. Constitutional Law Doctrines in Korea." In *Constitutional Systems in Late Twentieth-Century Asia,* edited by Lawrence W. Beer. Seattle: University of Washington Press, 1992.
Spain	Bonime-Blanc, Andrea. S*pain's Transition to Democracy: The Politics of Constitution-Making*. Boulder, Colo.: Westview Press, 1987.
	Llorente, Francisco Rubio. "The Writing of the Constitution of Spain." In *Constitution Makers on Constitution Making: The Experience of Eight Nations,* edited by Robert A. Goldwin and Art Kaufman. Washington, D.C.: American Enterprise Institute for Public Policy Research, 1988.
Sweden	Al-Wahab, Ibrahim. *The Swedish Institution of Ombudsman*. Stockholm: LiberFörlag, 1979.
	Strömholm, Stig, ed. *An Introduction to Swedish Law*. Stockholm: P. A. Norstedt and Söners Förlag, 1981.

Dessemontet, F., and T. Ansay, eds. *Introduction to Swiss Law.* Deventer, the Netherlands: Kluwer Law and Taxation Publishers, 1983.

Kaufmann, Otto. "Swiss Federalism." In *Forging Unity Out of Diversity: The Approach of Eight Nations,* edited by Robert A. Goldwin, Art Kaufman, and William A. Schambra. Washington, D.C.: American Enterprise Institute for Public Policy Research, 1989.

Shakya, Tsering. *The Dragon in the Land of Snows: A History of Modern Tibet.* New York: Columbia University Press, 1999.

Magocsi, Paul R. *A History of Ukraine.* Seattle: University of Washington Press, 1996.

Elton, Geoffrey. *The English.* Oxford: Blackwell Publishers, 1992.

Halsbury's Laws of England. Vol. 8. London: Butterworths, 1974.

Halsbury's Statutes of England and Wales. Vol. 10. London: Butterworths, 1985.

Abrahamson, Shirley S. "The State and Federal Courts of the United States as Guardians of Individual Rights." In *Law, Justice, and the Judiciary: Transnational Trends,* edited by Tun M. S. Abas and Visu Sinnadurai. Kuala Lumpur: Professional (Law) Book Publishers, 1988.

Glazer, Nathan. "The Constitution and American Diversity." In *Constitution Makers on Constitution Making: The Experience of Eight Nations,* edited by Robert A. Goldwin and Art Kaufman. Washington, D.C.: American Enterprise Institute for Public Policy Research, 1988.

Loss, Richard, ed. *Corwin on the Constitution.* Vol. 1. Ithaca, N.Y.: Cornell University Press, 1981.

Mitchell, Ralph. *CQ's Guide to the Constitution of the United States.* Washington, D.C.: Congressional Quarterly, 1998.

Rakove, Jack N. Commentary on "Writing the Constitution of the United States," by Walter Berns. In *Forging Unity Out of Diversity: The Approach of Eight Nations,* edited by Robert A. Goldwin, Art Kaufman, and William A. Schambra. Washington, D.C.: American Enterprise Institute for Public Policy Research, 1989.

Manrique, Gustavo Planchart. "The Making of the Venezuelan Constitution." In *Constitution Makers on Constitution Making: The Experience of Eight Nations,* edited by Robert A. Goldwin and Art Kaufman. Washington, D.C.: American Enterprise Institute for Public Policy Research, 1988.

Switzerland

Tibet

Ukraine

United Kingdom

United States

Venezuela

Index